T0215565

Jakarta EE Recipes

A Problem-Solution Approach

Josh Juneau

Apress®

Jakarta EE Recipes: A Problem-Solution Approach

Josh Juneau
Hinckley, IL, USA

ISBN-13 (pbk): 978-1-4842-5586-5   ISBN-13 (electronic): 978-1-4842-5587-2
https://doi.org/10.1007/978-1-4842-5587-2

Managing Director, Apress Media LLC: Welmoed Spahr
Acquisitions Editor: Jonathan Gennick
Development Editor: Laura Berendson
Coordinating Editor: Jill Balzano

Cover image designed by Freepik (www.freepik.com)

Distributed to the book trade worldwide by Springer Science+Business Media New York, 233 Spring Street, 6th Floor, New York, NY 10013. Phone 1-800-SPRINGER, fax (201) 348-4505, e-mail orders-ny@springer-sbm.com, or visit www.springeronline.com. Apress Media, LLC is a California LLC and the sole member (owner) is Springer Science + Business Media Finance Inc (SSBM Finance Inc). SSBM Finance Inc is a **Delaware** corporation.

For information on translations, please e-mail rights@apress.com, or visit http://www.apress.com/rights-permissions.

Apress titles may be purchased in bulk for academic, corporate, or promotional use. eBook versions and licenses are also available for most titles. For more information, reference our Print and eBook Bulk Sales web page at http://www.apress.com/bulk-sales.

Any source code or other supplementary material referenced by the author in this book is available to readers on GitHub via the book's product page, located at www.apress.com/9781484255865. For more detailed information, please visit http://www.apress.com/source-code.

Printed on acid-free paper

This book is dedicated to my wife, Angela, and my five children, Kaitlyn, Jacob, Matthew, Zachary, and Lucas. You are my joy and inspiration. It is also dedicated to the many Java and Jakarta EE developers worldwide. I hope that these recipes can lead you to developing the sophisticated solutions of tomorrow.

—Josh Juneau

Table of Contents

About the Author

Josh Juneau has been developing software and database systems for several years. Database application development and sophisticated web apps have been the focus of his career since the beginning. Early in his career, he became an Oracle database administrator and adopted the PL/SQL language for performing administrative tasks and developing applications for the Oracle database. In an effort to build more complex solutions, he began to incorporate Java into his PL/SQL applications and later developed stand-alone and web applications with Java. Josh wrote his early Java web applications utilizing Java Database Connectivity (JDBC) to work with backend databases. Later, he incorporated frameworks into his enterprise solutions, including Java EE, Spring, and JBoss Seam. Today, he primarily develops enterprise web solutions utilizing Java EE.

He extended his knowledge of the JVM by developing applications with other JVM languages such as Jython and Groovy. In 2006, Josh became the editor and publisher for the *Jython Monthly* newsletter. In late 2008, he began a podcast dedicated to the Jython programming language. Josh was the lead author for *The Definitive Guide to Jython*, *Oracle PL/SQL Recipes*, and *Java 7 Recipes*, which were published by Apress. Since then, he has continued to author Java-related books for Apress. He is an avid contributor to Oracle's *Java Magazine*, and he speaks at Java User Groups and conferences when he has the opportunity.

He works as an application developer and systems analyst, and he is a contributor to Apache NetBeans, Jakarta Server Faces, and Jakarta EE Ambassadors. Josh is a Java Champion, participates in the JCP, and is a co-host for the following podcasts: Java Offheap, Stackd, and Breaking Into Open Source. Josh has a wonderful wife and five children with whom he loves to spend time. To hear more from Josh, follow his blog, which can be found at `http://jj-blogger.blogspot.com`. You can also follow him on Twitter via @javajuneau.

About the Technical Reviewer

Alexandru Jecan is a software engineer, author, trainer, and speaker residing in Munich, Germany. He earned a degree in computer science from the Technical University of Cluj-Napoca, Romania. Alexandru provides professional in-house training on various software technologies across Germany. He also speaks at tech conferences and user groups, both in Europe and the United States, on different topics related to software development. He was awarded the title of "Author of the Month" by the German *Java Magazine*. Alexandru likes to read during his free time and to spend time with his family.

Acknowledgments

To my wife Angela: I am still amazed by you and always will be. Thanks again for helping to inspire me and keep me moving forward in my endeavors. You continue to be my rock, and I am so grateful for all you do.

To my children, Kaitlyn, Jacob, Matthew, Zachary, and Lucas: I love you all so much, and I cherish every moment we have together. I hope that you'll find your passion in life and enjoy each day as much as I enjoy each day spending time with you. Wish I could slow time down...you are growing up too fast!

I want to thank my family for their continued support in my career. I also want to thank my coworkers for allowing me to guide the organization's application development efforts and build successful solutions to keep us moving forward.

To the folks at Apress, I thank you for providing me with the chance to share my knowledge with others, once again. I especially thank Jonathan Gennick for the continued support of my work and for providing the continued guidance to produce useful content for our readers. I also thank Jill Balzano for doing a great job coordinating this project and many of my others before it. To my technical reviewer, Alex Jecan, you have become a great friend. It was great to meet at Code One, and I look forward to future discussions on Java and Jakarta EE. You have done an excellent job of solidifying the book content. Thanks again for your hard work and technical expertise. Lastly, I'd like to thank everyone else at Apress who had a hand in this book.

To the Java community: Thanks again for helping to make the Java platform such an innovative and effective realm for application development. I especially want to thank those in the Jakarta EE community who have a hand in helping to move things forward via Eclipse Enterprise for Java (EE4J), the Eclipse Working Group, Jakarta EE Ambassadors, and other speakers, writers, and evangelists of Java EE and Jakarta EE. To the members of the Chicago Java Users Group, I want to thank you for helping Chicago to be one of the best locations for Java expertise. I also want to thank my close friends of the Java Offheap podcast: Freddy Guime, Bob Paulin, and Michael Minella—you help me to remain engaged in all of Java technologies, and it is a privilege to have the opportunity to meet and discuss Java each month. I'm also grateful to my fellow hosts of the Stackd podcast with Java experts Kito Mann, Daniel Hinojosa, and Ian Hlavats—it is always great recording with you.

Introduction

The Java platform is one of the most widely used platforms for application development in the world. The platform is so popular that there are several different flavors of Java that can be used for developing applications that run on different mediums. From development of desktop, mobile, or web applications and hardware operating systems, Java can be utilized for development of just about any solution. As such, Java has become a very popular platform for development of web and enterprise applications, offering web services, reliability, security, and much more.

Java Enterprise Edition was originally released in 1999 as Java 2 Platform, Enterprise Edition (J2EE). Although several enterprise frameworks were available for development of reliable and secure applications on the Java platform, it made sense to standardize some solutions in order to minimize customization and help provide standards around Java Enterprise development to make it more prevalent in the industry. The platform originally included a terse number of specifications for standardization, including Java Servlet, JavaServer Pages (JSP), RMI, Java Database Connectivity (JDBC), Java Message Service (JMS) API, Java Transaction API (JTA), and Enterprise JavaBeans (EJBs). Early development of J2EE applications had a large learning curve, and it was cumbersome because it required lots of XML configuration. Even with these setbacks, it became popular among larger organizations and companies due to the prevalence of Java and its well-known security benefits. In 2001, J2EE 1.3 was released, adding more specifications to the platform, including the JavaServer Pages Standard Tag Library (JSTL) and Java Authentication and Authorization Service (JAAS). Other specifications, such as Java Servlet, also gained enhancements under the J2EE 1.3 release, making evolutionary enhancements to the platform. The release of J2EE 1.4 in 2003 marked a major milestone for Java Enterprise, as many new specifications were added to the platform, providing standards for even more Java technologies. The release of J2EE 1.4 marked the first iteration of web services for J2EE 1.1, JavaServer Faces (JSF), and Java APIs for XML solutions such as JAXP, JAXR, and more. Although the release of J2EE 1.4 included many specifications, it was still deemed as "difficult to learn," "cumbersome," and "not productive."

Over the next few years, J2EE was reworked in an attempt to make it easier to learn and utilize for the construction of modern web applications. Although XML is an excellent means for configuration, it can be cumbersome and difficult to manage, so configuration was a big item that was being addressed for the next release. Technologies such as Enterprise JavaBeans (EJBs) included some redundant characteristics, making EJB coding time consuming and difficult to manage, so an overhaul of EJB was also in order. In May of 2006, Java EE 5 was released, leaving the J2EE acronym behind and changing to simply Java EE instead. The Java EE 5 platform was significantly easier to use and maintain because features such as annotations were introduced, cutting down the amount of XML configuration significantly, as configuration could now be injected via annotations. EJBs were made easier to develop, and Java Persistence API (JPA) became a marketable technology for object-relational mapping (ORM). Java Enterprise Edition has since become a widely adopted and mature platform for enterprise development. Java EE 6 was released in 2009, making configuration and APIs even easier and adding more specifications to the platform. Specifications such as Contexts and Dependency Injection (CDI) and Bean Validation were introduced, vastly changing the landscape of the platform and streamlining development. Java EE 7 (released in 2013) continued to strengthen and modernize the platform, adding the WebSockets and JavaScript Object Notation (JSON)-P specifications. In the Java EE 7 release, specifications such as JSF and EJB were also enhanced, adding even more features to increase productivity and functionality and allowing them to work better for more modern web solutions.

What occurred next in the timeline was a definitive game changer for the Java EE platform. The Java EE 8 initiative had begun in 2015, and many of the specifications that make up the platform had begun to work. The focus of Java EE 8 was to continue to work toward Java SE 8 compatibility throughout the APIs and also to continue making the APIs easier to use. There was also a focus on creating new specifications around making microservices easier to develop with Java EE. In late 2015, many of the specifications stopped moving forward, and there was a halt in progress across the board. A few specifications, such as JSF, CDI, and JSON-B, continued to progress, while many of the others stalled. During this stall, the community became concerned about the future of Java EE, and there was a perception that it was going to be dropped. Oracle was silent on the progress of Java EE 8, and uncertainty was in the air. It was during this same time frame that the Java EE Guardians group was formed, with the focus on trying to make Oracle produce a statement about the future direction of the platform, and to make open source the platform rather than dropping it. Around that same time, the MicroProfile project was started as a collaborative effort by a number of the Java EE container vendors, with the focus on providing a true microservices profile for the Java EE platform.

In late 2016, Oracle changed the direction of Java EE 8 by removing some of the previously planned specification updates and adding others. There became a renewed effort to keep Java EE 8 moving forward in the hopes to produce a final release in 2017, working toward a better platform for producing microservices-based applications. The Java EE 8 release was final in the fall of 2017, and it included updates to many of the specifications. However, even some of the specifications that were planned for enhancing microservices development were dropped in an effort to produce a timely release, including MVC and the Health Checking API.

In early fall 2017, just before the release of Java EE 8, Oracle announced that they were going to open source Java EE. After a short while, it was announced that Oracle was going to contribute all of the Java EE sources (for each of the underlying specifications), along with all documentation and TCKs (Technology Compatibility Kits), to the Eclipse Foundation. In late 2017, the EE4J (Eclipse Enterprise for Java) project was formed, and the transfer of each specification began. In early 2018, it was voted that the new name for the platform under the open source EE4J project would become Jakarta EE. Once all of the specification sources, documentation, and TCKs were transferred, Jakarta EE 8 was released, which was in parity with Java EE 8.

This book focuses on the Jakarta EE 8 release, as well as some portions of the platform that are expected to be introduced in future Jakarta EE releases. The platform is covered as a whole, touching upon each of the widely used specifications that make up Jakarta EE. You will learn how to make use of each of the major specifications, making use of real-world examples and solutions. This book will cover APIs that have not been updated for Jakarta EE 8, as well as those that have been enhanced, providing complete coverage for those who are newer to the platform. It also features recipes that cover the newest features of the platform, so that seasoned Jakarta EE developers can skip those introductory concepts and delve into newer material.

I work with Java EE/Jakarta EE on a daily basis, and I have a deep passion for the technologies involved in the platform. I hope that this book increases your passion and productivity using the platform in its entirety.

Who This Book Is For

This book is intended for all those who are interested in learning Jakarta EE development and/or already know Java EE but would like some information regarding the new features included in Jakarta EE. Those who are new to Jakarta EE development can read this book, and it will allow them to start from scratch to get up and running quickly. Intermediate and advanced Java developers who are looking to update their arsenal with the latest features that Jakarta EE 8 has to offer can also read the book to quickly update and refresh their skill set.

How This Book Is Structured

This book is structured so that it does not have to be read from cover to cover. In fact, it is structured so that developers can choose which topics they'd like to read about and jump right to them. Each recipe contains a problem to solve, one or more solutions to solve that problem, and a detailed explanation of how the solution works. Although some recipes may build upon concepts that have been discussed in other recipes, they will contain the appropriate references so that the developer can find other related recipes that are beneficial to the solution. The book is designed to allow developers to get up and running quickly with a solution so that they can be home in time for dinner.

Conventions

Throughout the book, I've kept a consistent style for presenting Java code, Structured Query Language (SQL), command-line text, and results. Where pieces of code, SQL, reserved words, or code fragments are presented in the text, they are presented in a fixed-width font, such as in the following example:

```java
public class MyExample {
    public static void main(String[] args){
        System.out.println("Jakarta EE is excellent!");
    }
}
```

Downloading the Code

The code for the examples shown in this book is available on the Apress web site, www.apress.com. A link can be found on the book's information page under the Source Code/Downloads tab. This tab is located underneath the Related Titles section of the page.

Note The sources for this book may change over time, to provide new implementations that incorporate the most up-to-date features in Jakarta EE. That said, if any issues are found within the sources, please submit them via the Apress web site "Errata" form, and code will be adjusted accordingly.

Configuring Database for the Book Sources

This book's sources have been developed using the Apache Derby database, which ships with NetBeans IDE and GlassFish. Please install and configure the database for use with the book sources using either of those database choices prior to working with the sources. The database configuration involves creation of a database schema or user, as well as execution of the create_database.sql script (contained within the book sources) that goes along with the database of your choice. You must also place the appropriate database JDBC driver into the GlassFish CLASSPATH. You can do this by copying the ojdbcx.jar (Oracle) or derbyclient.jar (Apache Derby) JAR file into your integrated development environment (IDE) project for the book sources or into the <GlassFish-Home>\glassfish5\domains\domain1\lib\ext directory. If copying into the GlassFish lib directory, then once the JAR file has been copied into place, the GlassFish server will need to be restarted, if it is already running. If using Payara, the JAR file can be placed into the respective location.

Once the database has been installed/configured, and the SQL scripts contained within the book sources have been executed, please log into the GlassFish administrative console and set up a database connection pool to work with the database of your choice.

After a connection pool has been configured, please update the persistence.xml file that is contained within the book sources accordingly, so that the data source name aligns with the one you've assigned to the GlassFish JDBC resource.

Setting Up the Apache NetBeans Project

∗∗ Before setting up an Apache NetBeans project for the book sources, please install and configure GlassFish or Payara accordingly.

∗∗∗ Before setting up an Apache NetBeans project for the book sources, please install and/or configure Apache Derby or another database accordingly.

Note regarding dependencies   This project depends upon the use of the third-party PrimeFaces library. At the time of this book publication, the PrimeFaces API was used and available for free download.

Please perform the following steps to set up the Apache NetBeans Maven web project:

1) Open NetBeans IDE 11 or greater.

2) Choose the File ➤ New Project ➤ Maven ➤ Web Application menu option.

3) Title the project "JakartaEERecipes", and choose a desired project location.

4) Server and Settings:

– If you have not yet registered your GlassFish server with NetBeans, please click the "Add" button in this dialog and add the server. To do so, you will need to know the location of the GlassFish server on your file system.

– Java EE Version: As of NetBeans 11, you only have the option to choose "Java EE 8 Web." However, with Apache NetBeans 11.2, Java EE 8 is an available option.

5) Frameworks:

– Select JavaServer Faces, and then accept all defaults.

6) Click "Finish."

7) Go to your file system and copy the contents from within the JakartaEERecipes-BookSources\NBProject\src directory into your new NetBeans project "src" directory.

8) Add the required library dependencies to your project by right-clicking the project and choosing the "Properties" option. Once the "Properties" dialog is open, select "Libraries," and add the following dependencies:

– PrimeFaces

– Database JDBC JAR file, if not already placed within the GlassFish "lib" directory

CHAPTER 1

Servlets and JavaServer Pages

Java servlets were the first technology for producing dynamic Java web applications. Sun Microsystems released the first Java Servlet specification in 1997. Since then it has undergone tremendous change, making it more powerful and easing development more with each release. Servlets are at the base of web content for many Java EE applications. Servlets are Java classes that conform to the Java Servlet API, which allows a Java class to respond to requests. Although servlets can respond to any type of request, they are most commonly written to respond to web-based requests. A servlet must be deployed to a Java servlet container, be it a full stack application server or a micro container, in order to become usable. The Servlet API provides a number of objects that are used to enable the functionality of a servlet within a web container. Such objects include the request and response objects, `pageContext`, and a great deal of others, and when these objects are used properly, they enable a Java servlet to perform just about any task a web-based application needs to do.

As mentioned, servlets can produce not only static content but also dynamic content. Since a servlet is written in Java, any valid Java code can be used within the body of the servlet class. This empowers Java servlets and allows them to interact with other Java classes, the web container, the underlying file server, and much more. Although many developers use servlet frameworks such as JavaServer Pages (JSP) and JavaServer Faces (JSF), both of these technologies compile pages into Java servlets behind the scenes via the servlet container. That said, a fundamental knowledge of Java servlet technology could be very useful for any Java web developer.

1

© Josh Juneau 2020
J. Juneau, *Jakarta EE Recipes*, https://doi.org/10.1007/978-1-4842-5587-2_1

This chapter will get you started developing and deploying servlets. You will be taught the basics of developing servlets, how to use them with client web sessions, and how to link a servlet to another application. All the while, you will learn to use standards from the latest release of the Java Servlet API under the Jakarta EE platform, which modernizes servlet development and makes it much easier and more productive than in years past.

The JavaServer Pages (JSP) web framework introduced a great productivity boost for Java web developers over the Java Servlet API. Built as a façade on top of the Servlet API, when the JSP technology was introduced in 1999, it was Sun's answer to PHP and ASP, which provided web developers with a quick way to create dynamic web content. JSP contains a mix of XML and HTML but can also contain embedded Java code within scripting elements known as *scriptlets*. Indeed, JSP is easy to learn and allows developers to quickly create dynamic content and use their favorite HTML editor to lay out nice-looking pages. JSP was introduced several years ago, and although JSP technology has changed over the years, there are still many applications using older JSP variations in the world today.

Over the years, the creation of dynamic web content has solidified, and the techniques used to develop web applications have become easier to maintain down the road. Whereas early JSP applications included a mix of Java and XML markup within the pages, today the separation of markup from business logic is increasingly important. Newer releases of the JSP technology have accounted for these changes in the web space, and the most recent releases allow developers the flexibility to develop highly dynamic content without utilizing any embedded Java code but, instead, making use of markup and custom tags within pages.

This chapter contains a number of recipes that will show you the ins and outs of JSP development. You will learn how to develop applications using JSP technology from the ground up and harness the productivity and power that the technology has to offer. The chapter also brushes upon advanced techniques such as the development of custom JSP tags and the invocation of Java functions utilizing conditional tags. Although entire books have been written on JSP, the recipes within this chapter will lay a solid foundation on which you can begin to develop applications utilizing JSP.

1-1. Developing a Servlet

Problem

You wish to develop a web page that enables the use of dynamic content.

Solution

Develop a Java Servlet class, compile it, and deploy it within a compliant Java Servlet container, such as Eclipse GlassFish or Apache Tomcat. In this example, a simple servlet is created, which will be used to display dynamic content onto a web page. The following example demonstrates how to code a servlet which will display HTML content. In this particular example, the content is hard-coded, but it could be easily modified to pull in dynamic content from a database or external properties file:

```
package org.jakartaeerecipes.chapter01.recipe01_01;

import java.io.IOException;
import java.io.PrintWriter;
import javax.servlet.ServletException;
import javax.servlet.http.HttpServlet;
import javax.servlet.http.HttpServletRequest;
import javax.servlet.http.HttpServletResponse;

public class SimpleServlet extends HttpServlet {

    protected void processRequest(HttpServletRequest request,
    HttpServletResponse response)
            throws ServletException, IOException {
        response.setContentType("text/html;charset=UTF-8");
        PrintWriter out = response.getWriter();
        try {
            // Place page output here
            out.println("<html>");
            out.println("<head>");
            out.println("<title>Servlet SimpleServlet</title>");
            out.println("</head>");
            out.println("<body>");
```

```
            out.println("<h2>Servlet SimpleServlet at " + request.
            getContextPath() + "</h2>");
            out.println("<br/>Welcome to Java EE Recipes!");
            out.println("</body>");
            out.println("</html>");
        } finally {
            out.close();
        }
    }

    @Override
    protected void doGet(HttpServletRequest request, HttpServletResponse
    response)
            throws ServletException, IOException {
        processRequest(request, response);
    }

    @Override
    protected void doPost(HttpServletRequest request, HttpServletResponse
    response)
            throws ServletException, IOException {
        processRequest(request, response);
    }

    @Override
    public String getServletInfo() {
        return "Short description";
    }// </editor-fold>
}
```

To compile the servlet, use the `javac` command-line utility or a Java integrated development environment (IDE) such as Apache NetBeans. The following line was excerpted from the command line, and it compiles the `SimpleServlet.java` file into a class file. First, traverse into the directory containing the `SimpleServlet.java` file. Next, execute the following command:

```
javac -cp /JAVA_DEV/Glassfish/glassfish/modules/javax.servlet-api.jar
SimpleServlet.java
```

Note that the path in the preceding example utilizes the `javax.servlet-api.jar` file which is part of GlassFish 5.1. Once the servlet code has been compiled into a Java class file, then it is ready to package for deployment to a servlet container.

Note   You may want to consider installing a Java integrated development environment (IDE) to increase your development productivity. There are several very good IDEs available to developers, so be sure to choose one that contains the features you find most important and useful for development. As the author of this book on Jakarta EE, I recommend installing Apache NetBeans 11 or newer for development. Apache NetBeans is an open source IDE that is maintained by Apache, and it includes support for all the cutting-edge features that the Java industry has to offer, including development with Jakarta EE, OpenJFX support, and more. To learn more about working with Apache NetBeans and Jakarta EE, please see the appendix of this book.

How It Works

Java servlets provide developers with the flexibility to design applications using a request-response programming model. Servlets play a key role in the development of service-oriented and web applications on the Java platform. There are different types of servlets that can be created, and each of them is geared toward providing a different functionality. The first type is known as a `GenericServlet`, which provides services and functionality to other resources. The second type, `HttpServlet`, is a subclass of `GenericServlet` and provides functionality and a response utilizing HTTP. The solution to this recipe demonstrates the latter type of servlet because it displays a result for the user to see within a web browser.

Servlets conform to a life cycle for processing requests and posting results. First, the Java Servlet container calls the servlet's constructor. The constructor of every servlet must accept no arguments. Next, the container calls the servlet `init` method, which is responsible for initializing the servlet. Once the servlet has been initialized, it is ready for use. At that point, the servlet can begin processing. Each servlet contains a `service()` method, which handles the requests being made and dispatches them to the appropriate methods for request handling. Implementing the `service()` method is optional. Finally, the container calls upon the servlet `destroy()` method, which takes care of finalizing the servlet and taking it out of service.

Every servlet class must implement the `javax.servlet.Servlet` interface or extend another class that does. In the solution to this recipe, the servlet named `SimpleServlet` extends the `HttpServlet` class, which provides methods for handling HTTP processes. In this scenario, a browser client request is sent from the container to the servlet; then the servlet `service()` method dispatches the `HttpServletRequest` object to the appropriate method provided by `HttpServlet`. Namely, the `HttpServlet` class provides the `doGet()`, `doPut()`, `doPost()`, and `doDelete()` methods for working with an HTTP request. The most often used methods are the `doGet()` and `doPost()`. The `HttpServlet` class is abstract, so it must be subclassed, and then an implementation can be provided for its methods. Table 1-1 describes each of the methods available to an `HttpServlet`.

Table 1-1. *HttpServlet Methods*

Method Name	Description
doGet	Used to process HTTP GET requests. Input sent to the servlet must be included in the URL address. For example: `?myName=Josh&myBook=Jakar taEERecipes`.
doPost	Used to process HTTP POST requests. Input can be sent to the servlet within HTML form fields.
doPut	Used to process HTTP PUT requests.
doDelete	Used to process HTTP DELETE requests.
doHead	Used to process HTTP HEAD requests.
doOptions	Called by the container to allow OPTIONS request handling.
doTrace	Called by the container to handle TRACE requests.
getLastModified	Returns the time that the `HttpServletRequest` object was last modified.
init	Initializes the servlet.
destroy	Finalizes the servlet.
getServletInfo	Provides information regarding the servlet.

A servlet generally performs some processing within the implementation of its methods and then returns a response to the client. The HttpServletRequest object can be used to process arguments that are sent via the request. For instance, if an HTML form contains some input fields that are sent to the server, those fields would be contained within the HttpServletRequest object. The HttpServletResponse object is used to send responses to the client browser. Both the doGet() and doPost() methods within a servlet accept the same arguments, namely, the HttpServletRequest and HttpServletResponse objects.

Note   The doGet() method is used to intercept HTTP GET requests, and doPost() is used to intercept HTTP POST requests. Generally, the doGet() method is used to prepare a request before displaying for a client, and the doPost() method is used to process a request and gather information from an HTML form.

In the solution to this recipe, both the doGet() and doPost() methods pass the HttpServletRequest and HttpServletResponse objects to the processRequest() method for further processing. The HttpServletResponse object is used to set the content type of the response and to obtain a handle on the PrintWriter object in the processRequest() method. The following lines of code show how this is done, assuming that the identifier referencing the HttpServletResponse object is response:

```
response.setContentType("text/html;charset=UTF-8");
PrintWriter out = response.getWriter();
```

A GenericServlet can be used for providing services to web applications. This type of servlet is oftentimes used for logging events because it implements the log() method. A GenericServlet implements both the Servlet and ServletConfig interfaces, and to write a generic servlet, only the service() method must be overridden.

1-2. Packaging, Compiling, and Deploying a Servlet

Problem

You have written a Java servlet and now want to package it and deploy it for use.

Solution

Compile the sources, set up a deployable application, and copy the contents into the GlassFish deployment directory. From the command line, use the `javac` command to compile the sources:

```
javac -cp /PATH_TO_GLASSFISH/Glassfish/glassfish/modules/javax.servlet-api.
jar SimpleServlet.java
```

After the class has been compiled, deploy it along with the `web.xml` deployment descriptor, conforming to the appropriate directory structure.

Quick Start

To quickly get started with packaging, compiling, and deploying the example application for the servlet recipes in this chapter on GlassFish or other servlet containers such as Apache Tomcat, follow these steps:

1. Create a single application named `SimpleServlet` by making a directory named `SimpleServlet`.

2. Create the `WEB-INF`, `WEB-INF/classes`, and `WEB-INF/lib` directories inside `SimpleServlet`.

3. Drag the Chapter 1 sources (beginning with the `org` directory) in the `WEB-INF/classes` directory you created, as well as the contents of the web folder, into the root of your `SimpleServlet` directory.

4. Copy the `web.xml` file that is in the source's `recipe01_01` directory into the `WEB-INF` directory you created.

5. Download the JavaMail API code from Oracle, and copy the `mail.jar` file from the download into the `WEB-INF/lib` directory you created. This API will be used to send mail in future recipes.

6. Set your CLASSPATH to include the `mail.jar` file you downloaded in step 5.

7. At the command prompt, change directories so that you are in the classes directory you created in step 2. Compile each recipe with the command `javac org\jakartaeerecipes\chapter01\recipe1_x\*.java`, where x is equal to the recipe number.

8. Copy your `SimpleServlet` application directory to the `/JAVA_DEV/Glassfish/glassfish/domains/domain1/autodeploy` directory for Glassfish or the `/Tomcat/webapps` directory for Tomcat.

Test the application by launching a browser and going to http://localhost:8080/SimpleServlet/servlet_name, where `servlet_name` corresponds to the servlet name in each recipe. If using Tomcat, you may need to restart the server in order for the application to deploy.

How It Works

To compile the sources, you can use your favorite Java development environment such as Apache NetBeans or Eclipse IDE, or you can use the command line. For the purposes of this recipe, I will use the latter. If you're using the command line, you must ensure you are using the `javac` command that is associated with the same Java release that you will be using to run your servlet container. In this example, we will say that the location of the Java SE 11 installation is at the following path:

`/Library/Java/JavaVirtualMachines/jdk-11.jdk/Contents/Home`

Note   The Java JDK that is used to compile is dependent upon the application server container that is being used for deployment. At the time of this writing, most containers were either compatible with JDK 8 or JDK 11.

This path may differ in your environment if you are using a different operating system and/or installation location. To ensure you are using the Java runtime that is located at this path, set the `JAVA_HOME` environment variable equal to this path.

On OS X and *nix operating systems, you can set the environment variable by opening the terminal and typing the following:

```
export JAVA_HOME=/Library/Java/JavaVirtualMachines/jdk-11.jdk/Contents/Home
```

If you are using Windows, use the SET command within the command line to set up the JAVA_HOME environment variable:

```
set JAVA_HOME=C:\your-java-se-path\
```

Next, compile your Java servlet sources, and be sure to include the javax.servlet-api.jar file that is packaged with your servlet container (use servlet-api.jar for Tomcat) in your CLASSPATH. You can set the CLASSPATH by using the -cp flag of the javac command. The following command should be executed at the command line from within the same directory that contains the sources. In this case, the source file is named SimpleServlet.java:

```
javac -cp /path_to_jar/javax.servlet-api.jar SimpleServlet.java
```

Next, package your application by creating a directory and naming it after your application. In this case, create a directory and name it SimpleServlet. Within that directory, create another directory named WEB-INF. Traverse into the WEB-INF directory, and create another directory named classes. Lastly, create directories within the classes directory in order to replicate your Java servlet package structure. For this recipe, the SimpleServlet.java class resides within the Java package org.jakartaeerecipes. chapter01.recipe01_01, so create a directory for each of those packages within the classes directory. Create a final directory within WEB-INF and name it lib; any JAR files containing external libraries should be placed within the lib directory. In the end, your directory structure should resemble the following:

```
SimpleServlet
|_WEB-INF
     |_classes
       |_org
          |_jakartaeerecipes
     |_chapter01
                 |_recipe01_01
            |_lib
```

Place your web.xml deployment descriptor within the WEB-INF directory, and place the compiled SimpleServlet.class file within the recipe01_01 directory. The entire contents of the SimpleServlet directory can now be copied within the deployment directory for your application server container to deploy the application. Restart the application server if using Tomcat, and visit the URL http://localhost:8080/SimpleServlet/SimpleServlet to see the servlet in action.

Note   If using an integrated development environment or a build tool such as Maven, all of the manual work of generating directories and placing files into the correct locations is done automatically. In general, the use of an IDE is greatly recommended, as it can increase productivity and reduce the chance for errors.

1-3. Registering a Servlet Without Web.xml

Problem

Registering servlets in the web.xml file is cumbersome, and you want to deploy servlets without modifying web.xml at all.

Solution

Use the @WebServlet annotation to register the servlet, and omit the web.xml registration. This will alleviate the need to modify the web.xml file each time a servlet is added to your application. The following adaptation of the SimpleServlet class that was used in Recipe 1-2 includes the @WebServlet annotation and demonstrates its use:

```
import java.io.IOException;
import java.io.PrintWriter;
import javax.servlet.ServletException;
import javax.servlet.annotation.WebServlet;
import javax.servlet.http.HttpServlet;
import javax.servlet.http.HttpServletRequest;
import javax.servlet.http.HttpServletResponse;
```

```java
/**
 * Recipe 1-3 - Registering Servlets without WEB-XML
 * @author juneau
 */
@WebServlet(name = "SimpleServletNoDescriptor", urlPatterns =
{"/SimpleServletNoDescriptor"})
public class SimpleServletNoDescriptor extends HttpServlet {

    protected void processRequest(HttpServletRequest request,
    HttpServletResponse response)
            throws ServletException, IOException {
        response.setContentType("text/html;charset=UTF-8");
        PrintWriter out = response.getWriter();
        try {
            /*
             * TODO output your page here. You may use following sample code.
             */
            out.println("<html>");
            out.println("<head>");
            out.println("<title>Servlet SimpleServlet</title>");
            out.println("</head>");
            out.println("<body>");
            out.println("<h2>Servlet SimpleServlet at " + request.
            getContextPath() + "</h2>");
            out.println("<br/>Look ma, no WEB-XML!");
            out.println("</body>");
            out.println("</html>");
        } finally {
            out.close();
        }
    }
```

```
@Override
protected void doGet(HttpServletRequest request, HttpServletResponse
response)
        throws ServletException, IOException {
    processRequest(request, response);
}

@Override
protected void doPost(HttpServletRequest request, HttpServletResponse
response)
        throws ServletException, IOException {
    processRequest(request, response);
}
}
```

In the end, the servlet will be accessible via a URL in the same way that it would if the servlet were registered within web.xml.

Note   Remove any existing servlet mapping within the web.xml file in order to make use of the @WebServlet annotation.

How It Works

There are a number of ways to register servlets with a web container. The first way is to register them using the web.xml deployment descriptor, as demonstrated in Recipe 1-1. The second way to register them is to use the @WebServlet annotation, which provides an easier technique to use for mapping a servlet to a URL. The @WebServlet annotation is placed before the declaration of a class, and it accepts the elements listed in Table 1-2.

Table 1-2. *@WebServlet Annotation Elements*

Element	Description
description	Description of the servlet
displayName	The display name of the servlet
initParams	Accepts list of @WebInitParam annotations
largeIcon	The large icon of the servlet
loadOnStartup	Load on startup order of the servlet
name	Servlet name
smallIcon	The small icon of the servlet
urlPatterns	URL patterns that invoke the servlet

In the solution to this recipe, the @WebServlet annotation maps the servlet class named SimpleServletNoDescriptor to the URL pattern of /SimpleServletNoDescriptor, and it also names the servlet SimpleServletNoDescriptor:

```
@WebServlet(name="SimpleServletNoDescriptor", urlPatterns=
{"/SimpleServletNoDescriptor"})
```

1-4. Displaying Dynamic Content with a Servlet

Problem

You want to display some content to a web page that may change depending upon server-side activity or user input.

Solution

Define a field within your servlet to contain the dynamic content that is to be displayed. Post the dynamic content on the page by appending the field containing it using the PrintWriter println() method. The following example servlet declares a Date field and updates it with the current date each time the page is loaded:

```java
import java.io.IOException;
import java.io.PrintWriter;
import java.util.Date;
import javax.servlet.ServletException;
import javax.servlet.annotation.WebServlet;
import javax.servlet.http.HttpServlet;
import javax.servlet.http.HttpServletRequest;
import javax.servlet.http.HttpServletResponse;

/**
 * Recipe 1-4: Displaying Dynamic Content with a Servlet
 *
 * @author juneau
 */
@WebServlet(name = "CurrentDateAndTime", urlPatterns =
{"/CurrentDateAndTime"})
public class CurrentDateAndTime extends HttpServlet {

    Date currDateAndTime;

    protected void processRequest(HttpServletRequest request,
    HttpServletResponse response)
            throws ServletException, IOException {
        response.setContentType("text/html;charset=UTF-8");
        PrintWriter out = response.getWriter();
        try {
            out.println("<html>");
            out.println("<head>");
            out.println("<title>Servlet CurrentDateAndTime</title>");
            out.println("</head>");
            out.println("<body>");
            out.println("<h1>Servlet CurrentDateAndTime at " + request.
            getContextPath() + "</h1>");
            out.println("<br/>");
            synchronized(currDateAndTime){
              currDateAndTime = new Date();
              out.println("The current date and time is: " + currDateAndTime);
```

```
            }
            out.println("</body>");
            out.println("</html>");
        } finally {
            out.close();
        }
    }

    @Override
    protected void doGet(HttpServletRequest request, HttpServletResponse
    response)
            throws ServletException, IOException {
        processRequest(request, response);
    }

    @Override
    protected void doPost(HttpServletRequest request, HttpServletResponse
    response)
            throws ServletException, IOException {
        processRequest(request, response);
    }
}
```

Note   Servlets are multithreaded, and many client requests may be using a servlet concurrently. When a field is declared as a servlet class member (not within a method) as you have done with `currDateAndTime`, you have to assure that only one client request can manipulate the field at any instance. You do this by synchronizing around the use of the field, as shown in the `processRequest()` method. You synchronize around the smallest block of code you can manage in order to minimize latency. The resulting output from this servlet will be the current date and time.

```
synchronized( currDateAndTime ) {
    currDateAndTime = new Date();
    out.println("The current date and time is: " + currDateAndTime);
}
```

How It Works

One of the reasons why Java servlets are so useful is because they allow dynamic content to be displayed on a web page. The content can be taken from the server itself, a database, another web site, or any other web-accessible resource. Servlets are not static web pages; they are dynamic, and that is arguably their biggest strength.

In the solution to this recipe, a servlet is used to display the current time and date on the server. When the servlet is processed, the `doGet()` method is called, which subsequently makes a call to the `processRequest()` method, passing the request and response objects. Therefore, the `processRequest()` method is where the bulk of the work occurs. The `processRequest()` method creates a `PrintWriter` by calling the `response.getWriter()` method, and the `PrintWriter` is used to display content on the resulting web page. Next, the current date and time are obtained from the server by creating a new `Date` and assigning it to the `currDateAndTime` field. Lastly, the `processRequest()` method sends the web content through the `out.println()` method, and the contents of the `currDateAndTime` field are concatenated to a String and sent to `out.println()` as well. Each time the servlet is processed, it will display the current date and time at the time in which the servlet is invoked because a new `Date` is created with each request.

This example just scratches the surface of what is possible with a Java servlet. Although displaying the current date and time is trivial, you could alter that logic to display the contents of any field contained within the servlet. Whether it be an `int` field that displays a calculation that was performed by the servlet container or a `String` field containing some information, the possibilities are endless.

1-5. Handling Requests and Responses

Problem

You want to create a web form that accepts user input and supplies a response based upon the input that has been received.

Solution

Create a standard HTML-based web form, and when the submit button is clicked, invoke a servlet to process the end user input and post a response. To examine this technique, you will see two different pieces of code. The following code is HTML that is used to generate the input form. This code exists within the file recipe01_05.html. Please browse to /SimpleServlet/recipe01_05.html to execute the example. Pay particular attention to the <form> and <input> tags. You will see that the form's action parameter lists a servlet name, MathServlet:

```html
<html>
    <head>
    <title>Simple Math Servlet</title>
    </head>
    <body>
        <h1>This is a simple Math Servlet</h1>
        <form method="POST" action="MathServlet">
            <label for="numa">Enter Number A: </label>
            <input type="text" id="numa" name="numa"/><br><br>
                            <label for="numb">Enter Number B: </label>
                            <input type="text" id="numb"
                            name="numb"/><br/><br/>
            <input type="submit" value="Submit Form"/>
            <input type="reset" value="Reset Form"/>
        </form>
    </body>
</html>
```

Next, take a look at the following code for a servlet named MathServlet. This is the Java code that receives the input from the HTML code listed earlier, processes it accordingly, and posts a response:

```java
import java.io.IOException;
import java.io.PrintWriter;
import java.util.Date;

import javax.servlet.*;
import javax.servlet.annotation.WebServlet;
import javax.servlet.http.*;

/**
 * Recipe 1-5: Handling Requests and Responses
 */
```

```java
// Uncomment the following line to run example stand-alone
//@WebServlet(name="SessionServlet", urlPatterns={"/MathServlet"})

// The following will allow the example to run within the context of the
JakartaEERecipes example
// enterprise application (JakartaEERecipes.war distro or Netbeans Project
@WebServlet(name = "MathServlet", urlPatterns = {"/chapter01/MathServlet"})
public class MathServlet extends HttpServlet {

    public void doPost(HttpServletRequest req, HttpServletResponse res)
            throws IOException, ServletException {

        res.setContentType("text/html");

        // Store the input parameter values into Strings
        String numA = req.getParameter("numa");
        String numB = req.getParameter("numb");

        PrintWriter out = res.getWriter();
        out.println("<html><head>");
        out.println("<title>Test Math Servlet</title>");
        out.println("\t<style>body { font-family: 'Lucida Grande', "
                + "'Lucida Sans Unicode';font-size: 13px; }</style>");
        out.println("</head>");
        out.println("<body>");

        try {
            int solution = Integer.valueOf(numA) + Integer.valueOf(numB);

            /*
             * Display some response to the user
             */
            out.println("<p>Solution: "
                    + numA + " + " + numB + " = " + solution + "</p>");

        } catch (java.lang.NumberFormatException ex) {
            // Display error if an exception is raised
            out.println("<p>Please use numbers only...try again.</p>");
        }
```

```
        out.println("<br/><br/>");
        out.println("<a href='recipe1_6.html'>Add Two More Numbers</a>");
        out.println("</body></html>");

        out.close();
    }
}
```

Note   To run the example, copy the previous HTML code into an HTML file within the web root of your `JakartaEERecipes` application named `recipe01_05. html`, and then enter the following address into your browser: http:// localhost:8080/JakartaEERecipes/recipe01_05.html. This assumes you are using default port numbers for your application server installation. If using the Apache NetBeans project that was packaged with the sources, you do not need to worry about copying the code as everything should be preconfigured.

How It Works

Servlets make it easy to create web applications that adhere to a request and response life cycle. They have the ability to provide HTTP responses and also process business logic within the same body of code. The ability to process business logic makes servlets much more powerful than standard HTML code. The solution to this recipe demonstrates a standard servlet structure for processing requests and sending responses. An HTML web form contains parameters that are sent to a servlet. The servlet then processes those parameters in some manner and publishes a response that can be seen by the client. In the case of an `HttpServlet` object, the client is a web browser, and the response is a web page.

Values can be obtained from an HTML form by using HTML `<input>` tags embedded within an HTML `<form>`. In the solution to this recipe, two values are accepted as input, and they are referenced by their `id` attributes as `numa` and `numb`. There are two more `<input>` tags within the form; one of them is used to submit the values to the form action, and the other is used to reset the form fields to blank. The form action is the name of the servlet that the form values will be passed to as parameters. In this case, the action is set to MathServlet. The <form> tag also accepts a form-processing method, either GET or POST. In the example, the POST method is used because form data is being sent to the action; in this case, data is being sent to MathServlet. You could, of course, create an HTML form as detailed as you would like and then have that data sent to any servlet in the same manner. This example is relatively basic; it serves to give you an understanding of how the processing is performed.

The <form> action attribute states that the MathServlet should be used to process the values that are contained within the form. The MathServlet name can be mapped back to the MathServlet class via the web.xml deployment descriptor or the @WebServlet annotation. Looking at the MathServlet code, you can see that a doPost() method is implemented to handle the processing of the POST form values. The doPost() method accepts HttpServletRequest and HttpServletResponse objects as arguments. The values contained within the HTML form are embedded within the HttpServletRequest object. To obtain those values, call upon the request object's getParameter() method, passing the id of the input parameter you want to obtain. In the solution to this recipe, those values are obtained and stored within local String fields:

```
String numA = req.getParameter("numa");
String numB = req.getParameter("numb");
```

Once the values are obtained, they can be processed as needed. In this case, those String values are converted into int values, and then they are added together to generate a sum and stored into an int field. That field is then presented as a response on a resulting web page:

```
int solution = Integer.valueOf(numA) + Integer.valueOf(numB);
```

As mentioned, the HTML form could be much more complex, containing any number of <input> fields. Likewise, the servlet could perform more complex processing of those field values. This example is merely the tip of the iceberg, and the possibilities are without bounds. Servlet-based web frameworks such as JavaServer Pages and JavaServer Faces hide many of the complexities of passing form values to a servlet and processing a response. However, the same basic framework is used behind the scenes.

1-6. Listening for Servlet Container Events

Problem

You want to have the ability to listen for application startup and shutdown events.

Solution

Create a servlet context event listener to alert when the application has started up or when it has been shut down. The following solution demonstrates the code for a context listener, which will log application startup and shutdown events and send email alerting of such events:

```
package org.jakartaeerecipes.chapter01.recipe01_06;

import java.util.Properties;
import javax.mail.Message;
import javax.mail.Session;
import javax.mail.Transport;
import javax.mail.internet.InternetAddress;
import javax.mail.internet.MimeMessage;
import javax.servlet.ServletContextListener;
import javax.servlet.ServletContextEvent;
import javax.servlet.annotation.WebListener;

@WebListener
public class StartupShutdownListener implements ServletContextListener {

    public void contextInitialized(ServletContextEvent event) {
        System.out.println("Servlet startup...");
        System.out.println(event.getServletContext().getServerInfo());
        System.out.println(System.currentTimeMillis());
        // See error in server.log if mail is unsuccessful
        sendEmail("Servlet context has initialized");
    }
```

```java
public void contextDestroyed(ServletContextEvent event) {
    System.out.println("Servlet shutdown...");
    System.out.println(event.getServletContext().getServerInfo());
    System.out.println(System.currentTimeMillis());
    // See error in server.log if mail is unsuccessful
    sendEmail("Servlet context has been destroyed...");
}

/**
 * This implementation uses the GMail smtp server
 * @param message
 * @return
 */
private boolean sendEmail(String message) {
    boolean result = false;
    String smtpHost = "smtp.someserver.com";
    String smtpUsername = "username";
    String smtpPassword = "password";
    String from = "fromaddress";
    String to = "toaddress";
    int smtpPort = 587;
    System.out.println("sending email...");
     try {
        // Send email here

        //Set the host smtp address
        Properties props = new Properties();
        props.put("mail.smtp.host", smtpHost);
        props.put("mail.smtp.auth", "true");
        props.put("mail.smtp.starttls.enable", "true");

        // create some properties and get the default Session
        Session session = Session.getInstance(props);

        // create a message
        Message msg = new MimeMessage(session);
```

```
            // set the from and to address
            InternetAddress addressFrom = new InternetAddress(from);
            msg.setFrom(addressFrom);
            InternetAddress[] address = new InternetAddress[1];
            address[0] = new InternetAddress(to);
            msg.setRecipients(Message.RecipientType.TO, address);
            msg.setSubject("Servlet container shutting down");
            // Append Footer
            msg.setContent(message, "text/plain");
            Transport transport = session.getTransport("smtp");
//          transport.connect(smtpHost, smtpPort, smtpUsername,
            smtpPassword);

//          Transport.send(msg);

            result = true;
        } catch (javax.mail.MessagingException ex) {
            ex.printStackTrace();
            result = false;
        }
        return result;
    }
}
```

Note   To run this example, you may need additional external JARs in your CLASSPATH. Specifically, make sure you have `mail.jar` and `javaee.jar`.

How It Works

Sometimes it is useful to know when certain events occur within the application server container. This concept can be useful under many different circumstances, but most often it would be used for initializing an application upon startup or cleaning up after an application upon shutdown. A servlet listener can be registered with an application to indicate when it has been started up or shut down. Therefore, by listening for such events, the servlet has the opportunity to perform some actions when they occur.

To create a listener that performs actions based on a container event, you must develop a class that implements the ServletContextListener interface. The methods that need to be implemented are contextInitialized() and contextDestroyed(). Both of the methods accept a ServletContextEvent as an argument, and they are automatically called each time the servlet container is initialized or shut down, respectively. To register the listener with the container, you can use one of the following techniques:

- Utilize the @WebListener annotation, as demonstrated by the solution to this recipe.

- Register the listener within the web.xml application deployment descriptor.

- Use the addListener() method defined on ServletContext.

For example, to register this listener within web.xml, you need to add the following lines of XML:

```
<listener>
    <listener-class> org.jakartaeerecipes.chapter01.recipe01_06.
    StartupShutdownListener</listener-class>
</listener>
```

Neither way is better than the other. The only time that listener registration within the application deployment descriptor (web.xml) would be more helpful is if you had the need to disable the listener in some cases. On the other hand, to disable a listener when it is registered using @WebListener, you must remove the annotation and recompile the code. Altering the web deployment descriptor does not require any code to be recompiled.

There are many different listener types, and the interface that the class implements is what determines the listener type. For instance, in the solution to this recipe, the class implements the ServletContextListener interface. Doing so creates a listener for servlet context events. If, however, the class implements HttpSessionListener, it would be a listener for HTTP session events. The following is a complete listing of listener interfaces:

```
javax.servlet.ServletRequestListener
javax.servlet.ServletRequestAttrbuteListener
```

```
javax.servlet.ServletContextListener
javax.servlet.ServletContextAttributeListener
javax.servlet.http.HttpSessionListener
javax.servlet.http.HttpSessionAttributeListener
javax.servlet.http.HttpSessionIdListener
```

It is also possible to create a listener that implements multiple listener interfaces.

1-7. Reading and Writing with Nonblocking I/O

Problem

You want to read and write I/O in an asynchronous, nonblocking manner.

Solution

Use the Non-Blocking I/O API that was part of the Servlet 3.1 release. To use the technology, implement the `ReadListener` interface when performing nonblocking reads, and implement the `WriteListener` interface for performing nonblocking writes. The implementation class can then be registered to a `ServletInputStream` or `ServletOutputStream` so that reads or writes can be performed when the listener finds that servlet content can be read or written without blocking.

The following sources are those of a `ReadListener` implementation that reside in the source file `org.jakartaeerecipes.chapter01.recipe01_07.AcmeReadListenerImpl.java`, and they demonstrate how to implement the `ReadListener`:

```
package org.jakartaeerecipes.chapter01.recipe01_07;

import java.io.IOException;
import java.util.logging.Level;
import java.util.logging.Logger;
import javax.servlet.AsyncContext;
import javax.servlet.ReadListener;
import javax.servlet.ServletInputStream;

public class AcmeReadListenerImpl implements ReadListener {

    private ServletInputStream is = null;
    private AsyncContext async = null;
```

```java
public AcmeReadListenerImpl(ServletInputStream in, AsyncContext ac) {
    this.is = in;
    this.async = ac;
    System.out.println("read listener initialized");
}

@Override
public void onDataAvailable() {
    System.out.println("onDataAvailable");
    try {
        StringBuilder sb = new StringBuilder();
        int len = -1;
        byte b[] = new byte[1024];
        while (is.isReady()
                && (len = is.read(b)) != -1) {

            String data = new String(b, 0, len);
            System.out.println(data);
        }
    } catch (IOException ex) {
        Logger.getLogger(AcmeReadListenerImpl.class.getName()).
        log(Level.SEVERE, null, ex);
    }
}

@Override
    public void onAllDataRead() {
    System.out.println("onAllDataRead");
    async.complete();

}

@Override
    public void onError(Throwable thrwbl) {
    System.out.println("Error: " + thrwbl);
    async.complete();
}
}
```

Next, use the listener by registering it to a ServletInputStream (in the case of the ReadListener) or a ServletOutputStream (in the case of a WriteListener). For this example, I show a servlet that utilizes the AcmeReadListenerImpl class. The sources for the following class reside in the org.jakartaeerecipes.chapter01.recipe01_07. AcmeReaderExample.java file:

```java
package org.jakartaeerecipes.chapter01.recipe01_07;

import java.io.IOException;
import java.io.PrintWriter;
import javax.servlet.AsyncContext;
import javax.servlet.ServletException;
import javax.servlet.ServletInputStream;
import javax.servlet.annotation.WebServlet;
import javax.servlet.http.HttpServlet;
import javax.servlet.http.HttpServletRequest;
import javax.servlet.http.HttpServletResponse;
@WebServlet(urlPatterns = {"/AcmeReaderServlet"}, asyncSupported = true)
public class AcmeReaderServlet extends HttpServlet {

    protected void processRequest(HttpServletRequest request,
    HttpServletResponse response)
            throws ServletException, IOException {
        response.setContentType("text/html;charset=UTF-8");
        try (PrintWriter output = response.getWriter()) {

            AsyncContext asyncCtx = request.startAsync();
            ServletInputStream input = request.getInputStream();
            input.setReadListener(new AcmeReadListenerImpl(input, asyncCtx));

        } catch (Exception ex) {
            System.out.println("Exception Occurred: " + ex);
        }
    }

  // Http Servlet Methods ...

...

}
```

The last piece of code that we need is the servlet that invokes the `AcmeReaderServlet`, passing the message that needs to be processed. In this example, a file from the server is passed to the `AcmeReaderServlet` as input, which then is asynchronously processed via the `AcmeReadListenerImpl` class. The following code is taken from `org.jakartaeerecipes.chapter01.recipe01_07.ReaderExample.java`:

```java
package org.jakartaeerecipes.chapter01.recipe01_07;

import java.io.BufferedReader;
import java.io.BufferedWriter;
import java.io.IOException;
import java.io.InputStream;
import java.io.InputStreamReader;
import java.io.OutputStreamWriter;
import java.io.PrintWriter;
import java.net.HttpURLConnection;
import java.net.URL;
import java.util.logging.Level;
import java.util.logging.Logger;
import javax.servlet.ServletContext;
import javax.servlet.ServletException;
import javax.servlet.annotation.WebServlet;
import javax.servlet.http.HttpServlet;
import javax.servlet.http.HttpServletRequest;
import javax.servlet.http.HttpServletResponse;

@WebServlet(name = "ReaderExample", urlPatterns = {"/ReaderExample"})
public class ReaderExample extends HttpServlet {

    protected void processRequest(HttpServletRequest request,
    HttpServletResponse response)
            throws ServletException, IOException {
        response.setContentType("text/html;charset=UTF-8");
        String filename = "/WEB-INF/test.txt";
        ServletContext context = getServletContext();
```

```
InputStream in = context.getResourceAsStream(filename);
try (PrintWriter out = response.getWriter()) {
    String path = "http://"
            + request.getServerName()
            + ":"
            + request.getServerPort()
            + request.getContextPath()
            + "/AcmeReaderServlet";
    out.println("<html>");
    out.println("<head>");
    out.println("<title>Intro to Java EE 7 - Servlet Reader
    Example</title>");
    out.println("</head>");
    out.println("<body>");
    out.println("<h1>Servlet ReaderExample at " + request.
    getContextPath() + "</h1>");
    out.println("Invoking the endpoint: " + path + "<br>");
    out.flush();
    URL url = new URL(path);
    HttpURLConnection conn = (HttpURLConnection) url.openConnection();
    conn.setChunkedStreamingMode(2);
    conn.setDoOutput(true);
    conn.connect();
    if (in != null) {
        InputStreamReader inreader = new InputStreamReader(in);
        BufferedReader reader = new BufferedReader(inreader);
        String text = "";
        out.println("Beginning Read");
        try (BufferedWriter output = new BufferedWriter(new
        OutputStreamWriter(conn.getOutputStream()))) {
            out.println("got the output...beginning loop");
            while ((text = reader.readLine()) != null) {
                out.println("reading text: " + text);
                out.flush();
                output.write(text);
```

```
                    Thread.sleep(1000);
                    output.write("Ending example now..");
                    out.flush();
                }
                output.flush();
                output.close();
            }
        }
        out.println("Review the Glassfish server log for messages...");
        out.println("</body>");
        out.println("</html>");
    } catch (InterruptedException | IOException ex) {
        Logger.getLogger(ReaderExample.class.getName()).log(Level.
        SEVERE, null, ex);
    }
}
// Http Servlet Methods ...
...
}
```

When the servlet is visited, the asynchronous, nonblocking read of the test.txt file will occur, and its text will be displayed in the server log.

How It Works

Servlet technology has allowed only traditional (blocking) input/output during request processing since its inception. In the Servlet 3.1 release, the Non-Blocking I/O API was introduced to make it possible for servlets to read or write without any blocking. This means other tasks can be performed at the same time that a read or write is occurring, without any wait.

To implement a nonblocking I/O solution, programming interfaces were added to ServletInputStream and ServletOutputStream with the release of Servlet 3.1, as well as two event listeners: ReadListener and WriteListener. ReadListener and WriteListener interfaces make the servlet I/O processing occur in a nonblocking manner via callback methods that are invoked when servlet content can be read or written without blocking. Use the ServletInputStream.setReadListener

(ServletInputStream, AsyncContext) method to register a ReadListener with a ServletInputStream, and use the ServletInputStream.setWriteListener (ServletOutputStream, AsyncContext) method for registering a WriteListener. The following lines of code demonstrate how to register a ReadListener implementation with a ServletInputStream:

```
AsyncContext context = request.startAsync();

ServletInputStream input = request.getInputStream();

input.setReadListener(new ReadListenerImpl(input, context));
```

Note   In Servlet 3.0, AsyncContext was introduced to represent an execution context for an asynchronous operation that is initiated on a servlet request. To use the asynchronous context, a servlet should be annotated as a @WebServlet, and the asyncSupported attribute of the annotation must be set to true. The @WebFilter annotation also contains the asyncSupported() attribute.

After a listener has been registered with a ServletInputStream, the status on a nonblocking read can be checked by calling the methods ServletInputStream. isReady() and ServletInputStream.isFinished(). For instance, a read can begin once the ServletInputStream.isReady() method returns a true, as shown here:

```
while (is.isReady() && (b = input.read()) != -1)) {

    len = is.read(b);

    String data = new String(b, 0, len);

}
```

To create a ReadListener or WriteListener, three methods must be overridden: onDataAvailable(), onAllDataRead(), and onError(). The onDataAvailable() method is invoked when data is available to be read or written, onAllDataRead() is invoked once all the data has been read or written, and onError() is invoked if an error is encountered. The code for AcmeReadListenerImpl in the solution to this recipe demonstrates how to override these methods.

The AsyncContext.complete() method is called in the onAllDataRead() method to indicate that the read has been completed and to commit the response. This method is also called in the onError() implementation so that the read will complete, so it is important to perform any cleanup within the body of the onError() method to ensure that no resources are leaked, and so on.

To implement a WriteListener, use the ServletOutputStream.canWrite method, which determines whether data can be written in a nonblocking fashion. A WriteListener implementation class must override the following methods: onWritePossible() and onError(). The onWritePossible() method is invoked when a nonblocking write can occur. The write implementation should take place within the body of this method. The onError() method is much the same as its ReadListener implementation counterpart, because it is invoked when an error occurs.

The following lines of code demonstrate how to register a WriteListener with a ServletOutputStream:

```
AsyncContext context = request.startAsync();
ServletOutputStream os = response.getOutputStream();
os.setWriteListener(new WriteListenerImpl(os, context));
```

The WriteListener implementation class must include overriding methods for onWritePossible() and onError(). The following is an example for a WriteListener implementation class:

```
import javax.servlet.AsyncContext;
import javax.servlet.ServletOutputStream;
import javax.servlet.WriteListener;

public class WriteListenerImpl implements WriteListener {

    ServletOutputStream os;
    AsyncContext context;

    public WriteListenerImpl(ServletOutputStream out, AsyncContext ctx){
        this.os = out;
        this.context = ctx;
        System.out.println("Write Listener Initialized");
    }
```

```java
    @Override
    public void onWritePossible() {
        System.out.println("Now possible to write...");
        // Write implementation goes here...
    }

    @Override
    public void onError(Throwable thrwbl) {
        System.out.println("Error occurred");
        context.complete();
    }
}
```

Note   In most cases, the ReadListener and WriteListener implementation classes can be embedded within the calling servlet. They have been broken out into separate classes for the examples in this book for demonstration purposes.

The Non-Blocking I/O API helps bring the Servlet API into compliance with current web standards while making it possible to create web-based applications that perform well in an asynchronous fashion.

1-8. Pushing Resources from a Server to a Client

Problem

You want to push resources to your clients automatically when they visit a particular page within your web application, rather than sending multiple requests.

Solution

Use the Servlet HTTP/2 Push API to push the resources before the page is loaded. This will cause all of the resources to be included with the single response, rather than multiple responses that used to be needed for HTTP 1.1 implementations. In the following example, a PushBuilder is created, and then a number of statically typed resources are pushed to the client prior to loading the page:

```java
@WebServlet(name = "PushServlet", urlPatterns = {"/PushServlet"})
public class PushServlet extends HttpServlet {

    protected void processRequest(HttpServletRequest request,
HttpServletResponse response)
            throws ServletException, IOException {
        response.setContentType("text/html;charset=UTF-8");
        try (PrintWriter out = response.getWriter()) {
            /* TODO output your page here. You may use following sample code. */
            out.println("<!DOCTYPE html>");
            out.println("<html>");
            out.println("<head>");
            out.println("<title>Servlet PushServlet</title>");
            out.println("</head>");
            out.println("<body>");
            out.println("<h1>Servlet PushServlet at " + request.
            getContextPath() + "!</h1>");
            out.println("</body>");
            out.println("</html>");
        }
    }

    @Override
    protected void doGet(HttpServletRequest request, HttpServletResponse
    response)
            throws ServletException, IOException {
        System.out.println("In the servlet");
        if(request.getRequestURI().equals("/Jakartaeerecipes/PushServlet")
        && request.getPushBuilder() != null) {
            System.out.println("Pushing resources");
            PushBuilder builder =
            request.getPushBuilder().path("/resources/images/
            javaee9recipes.png");
            builder.path("/resources/images/javaee7recipes.png");
            builder.push();
```

```
        }
        processRequest(request, response);
    }
. . .
}
```

How It Works

A significant problem with serving content from the Web has always been the request and response life cycle. HTTP 1.1 requires multiple TCP connections issuing parallel requests in order to load page content containing various resources such as JavaScript files and images. This can not only lead to significant performance issues but also starves network resources. HTTP/2 is fundamentally different in that it is fully multiplexed, rather than being ordered and blocking. It also allows a single connection to be used for issuing requests in parallel, making performance much better and using much less network resource. Other differences for HTTP/2 include using header compression to help reduce overhead and allowing servers to have the ability to push resources proactively to active clients. This latter feature of HTTP/2 is covered by the example in this recipe, pushing resources from the server, rather than making the client fetch each required resource.

The PushBuilder interface was introduced with Servlet 4.0, which is part of the Java EE 8 and Jakarta EE platforms. The PushBuilder is used to build a push request based on the HttpServletRequest. Once the PushBuilder is obtained, it can be used to add resources via the path() method, which are subsequently pushed to the client while the target page is being processed. In the example, a couple PNG image resources are added using the path method. However, an application can be coded such that any resource that is required by a specified page can be pushed preemptively to the client and loaded into the browser cache. Once obtained, the PushBuilder can be used as many times as required. After all resources have been loaded, initiate the PushBuilder.push() method to perform the push action.

After the resources have been pushed, the invoked page will be loaded in an effort to process resources, determining which resources have already been cached and which need to be loaded from the server push. If a client browser already has the resource in the cache, it returns an RST_STREAM to indicate that the server does not need to end it.

1-9. Creating a Simple JSP Page

Problem

You want to develop a web page using HTML markup that enables you to include dynamic content.

Solution

Use JavaServer Pages to create a web page that combines standard markup with blocks of Java code that are embedded within the markup. The following JSP markup demonstrates how to include dynamic code into a page:

```
<%--
    Document   : recipe01_09
    Author     : juneau
--%>

<%@page contentType="text/html" pageEncoding="UTF-8"%>
<!DOCTYPE html>
<html>
    <head>
        <meta http-equiv="Content-Type" content="text/html; charset=UTF-8">
        <title>JSP Page Example</title>
    </head>
    <body>
        <jsp:useBean id="dateBean" scope="application" class="org.
         jakartaeerecipes.chapter02.recipe02_01.DateBean"/>
        <h1>Hello World!</h1>
        <br/>
        <p>
            The current date is: ${dateBean.currentDate}!
        </p>
    </body>
</html>
```

The previous JSP code uses a JavaBean to pull the current date into the page. The following Java code is the JavaBean that is used by the JSP code:

```
package org.jakartaeerecipes.chapter01.recipe01_09;

import java.util.Date;
public class DateBean {

    private Date currentDate = new Date();

    /**
     * @return the currentDate
     */
    public Date getCurrentDate() {
        return currentDate;
    }

    /**
     * @param currentDate the currentDate to set
     */
    public void setCurrentDate(Date currentDate) {
        this.currentDate = currentDate;
    }
}
```

The following output would result. Of course, the page will display the current date when you run the code:

```
Hello World!
The current date is: Fri Dec 23 10:41:07 CST 2011!
```

How It Works

The JavaServer Pages technology makes it easy to develop web pages that can utilize both static and dynamic web content by providing a set of tags and value expressions to expose dynamic Java fields to a web page. Using the JSP technology, a page developer can access the underlying JavaBean classes to pass content between the client and the server. In the example within this recipe, a JSP page is used to display the current date and time, which is obtained from a JavaBean class on the server. Therefore, when a user visits the JSP page in a browser, the current time and date on the server will be displayed.

A JSP page should use a document extension of `.jsp` if it is a standard HTML-based JSP page. Other types of JSP pages contain different extensions; one of those is the JSP document type. A JSP document is an XML-based well-formed JSP page. This example contains the `<jsp:useBean>` tag, as well as a value expression to display the content of a field that is contained within the JavaBean. The `<jsp:useBean>` tag is used to include a reference to a Java class that will be referenced in the JSP page. In this case, the class that is referenced is named `org.jakartaeerecipes.chapter01.recipe01_09.DateBean`, and it will be referenced as dateBean within the page:

```
<jsp:useBean id="dateBean" scope="application" class="org.jakartaeerecipes.
chapter01.recipe01_09.DateBean"/>
```

Since the `<jsp:useBean>` tag contains a reference to the `DateBean` Java class, the JSP page that includes the tag can make use of any public fields or methods that are contained within the class or private fields through public "getter" methods. This is demonstrated by the use of the Expression Language (EL) value expression, which is enclosed within the ${} characters. To learn more about JSP EL expressions, please see Recipe 1-10. In the example, the value of the JavaBean field named `currentDate` is displayed on the page. The value of the private field is retrieved automatically via the public "getter" method `getCurrentDate`:

```
The current date is: ${dateBean.currentDate}!
```

Life Cycle of a JSP Page

The life cycle of a JSP page is very much the same as that of a Java servlet. This is because a JSP page is translated to a servlet (the `HttpJspBase` JSP servlet class) behind the scenes by a special servlet. When a request is sent to a JSP page, the special servlet checks to ensure that the JSP page's servlet is not older than the page itself. If it is, the JSP is retranslated into a servlet class and compiled. The JSP-to-servlet translation is automatic, which is one of the most productive reasons to use JSP.

When a JSP page is translated, a servlet with a name such as `0002fjspname_jsp.java` is created, where `jspname` is the name of the JSP page. If errors result during the translation, they will be displayed when the JSP page response is displayed.

Different portions of the JSP page are treated differently during the translation to a Java servlet. Template data is translated into code. JSP scripting elements are inserted into the JSP page's servlet class. `<jsp:XXX ...>` elements are converted into method calls.

After translation, the life cycle works similarly to the servlet life cycle.

If the JSP page's servlet does not already exist, then the container does the following:

1. Loads the servlet class

2. Instantiates the servlet class

3. Initializes the servlet instance with a call to the `jspInit` method

This recipe contains only beginning knowledge of what is possible with the JSP technology. To learn more regarding the technology and best practices when using JSP, please continue reading the recipes in this chapter.

1-10. Embedding Java into a JSP Page
Problem

You want to embed some Java code into a standard JSP web page.

Solution

Use JSP scripting elements to embed Java code into the page and then display Java fields. The following JSP code demonstrates how to import the Java Date class and then use it to obtain the current date without using a server-side JavaBean class:

```
<%@page import="java.util.Date"%>
<%@page contentType="text/html" pageEncoding="UTF-8"%>
<!DOCTYPE html>
<%! Date currDate = null; %>
<% currDate = new Date(); %>
<html>
    <head>
        <meta http-equiv="Content-Type" content="text/html; charset=UTF-8">
        <title>Recipe 2-2: Embedding Java in a JSP</title>
    </head>
    <body>
        <h1>Hello World!</h1>
        <br/>
        <br/>
```

```
    The current date and time is: <%= currDate %>

  </body>
</html>
```

This page will display the current system date from the server that hosts the JSP application.

How It Works

Using scripting elements (<% %>) within a JSP page allows you to embed Java code directly in a web page. However, it should be noted that this is not the best approach to web development. Scripting element programming used to be one of the best ways to code web applications using JSP technology. However, when it came time to perform maintenance activities on a JSP page or to introduce new developers to a code base that used scripting elements in JSP, nightmares ensued because in order to debug a problem, the developer had to search through scripts embedded within HTML, as well as Java classes themselves. Sometimes it is still nice to have the ability to embed Java code directly into a page, even if for nothing more than testing, so that is why I show how it is done in this recipe. A better approach would be to separate the business logic from the view code, which you will see in Recipe 1-11.

In the example, the current date is pulled into the JSP page via the use of the Java Date class. A new Date instance is assigned to a field that is named currDate. An import page directive is used to import the java.util.Date class into the JSP page using the following line:

```
<%@page import="java.util.Date"%>
```

The declaration of currDate is done within a declaration scripting element. Declaration scripting elements begin with the character sequence <%! and end with the character sequence %>. Excerpted from the example, the currDate field is declared in the following line of code:

```
<%! Date currDate = null; %>
```

Anything that is contained inside declarations goes directly to the jspService() method of the generated JSP servlet class, creating a global declaration for the entire servlet to make use of. Any variable or method can be declared within declarations' character sequences.

> **Note**   Declarations are executed only once for the JSP page, when it is initially converted into a servlet. If any code on the JSP page changes, it will be translated to a servlet again, and the declaration will be evaluated again at that time. If you want for code to be executed each time the JSP page is loaded by the browser, do not place it in a declaration.

In the example for this recipe, you can see that there are no JSP tags used to reference a server-side JavaBean class to create a new instance of the Date class, and that is because the instantiation is done directly within the JSP code in between character sequences known as scriptlets, <% %>.

Scriptlets basically have the same syntax as declarations, except that they do not include the exclamation point in the first character sequence. Scriptlets are used to embed any Java code that you want to have run each time the JSP is loaded, at request-processing time. At translation time, anything contained within a scriptlet is placed into a method named _jspService within the translated JSP servlet, and that method is executed with each request on the JSP page. Scriptlets are the most common place to use embedded Java in a JSP page. Since in this example you want the current date to be displayed each time the page is loaded, the new Date class is instantiated and assigned to the currDate variable within a scriptlet:

```
<% currDate = new Date(); %>
```

Later in the JSP page, the currDate field is displayed using an expression, which is enclosed using the <%= and %> character sequences. Expressions are used to display content, and anything that is contained within an expression is automatically converted to a String when a request is processed. After the String conversion, it is displayed as output on the page:

```
The current date and time is: <%= currDate %>
```

> **Note**   If the code within an expression is unable to be converted into a String, an exception will occur, and it will be displayed on the page.

While embedding Java code in a JSP page is possible to do, it is frowned upon within the Java community since the Model-View-Controller (MVC) paradigm makes coding much cleaner. To learn more about coding JSP applications without using scripting elements, please see the next recipe, Recipe 1-11.

1-11. Separating Business Logic from View Code

Problem

You want to separate the business logic from the code that is used to create a view within your web application.

Solution

Separate the business logic into a JavaBean class, and use JSP tags to incorporate the logic into the view. In the following example, a JavaBean is referenced from within a JSP page, and one of the JavaBean fields is displayed on the page. Each time the page is refreshed, the field value is updated because the page calls the underlying JavaBean field's getter method, where the field is initialized.

The following JSP markup contains a reference to a JavaBean named RandomBean and displays a field from the bean on the page:

```
<%@page contentType="text/html" pageEncoding="UTF-8"%>
<!DOCTYPE html>
<html>
    <head>
        <meta http-equiv="Content-Type" content="text/html; charset=UTF-8">
        <title>Recipe 1-11: Separating Business Logic from View Code</title>
    </head>
    <body>
        <jsp:useBean id="randomBean" scope="session" class="org.
         jakartaeerecipes.chapter01.recipe01_11.RandomBean"  />
        <h1>Display a Random Number</h1>
        <br/>
        <br/>
        <p>
            Your random number is ${randomBean.randomNumber}.  Refresh page
            to see another!
        </p>
    </body>
</html>
```

The next code is that of the JavaBean class referenced in the JSP code, known as RandomBean:

```
package org.jakartaeerecipes.chapter01.recipe01_11;

import java.util.Random;

public class RandomBean implements java.io.Serializable {
    Random randomGenerator = new Random();
    private int randomNumber = 0;

    /**
     * @return the randomNumber
     */
    public int getRandomNumber() {
        randomNumber = randomGenerator.nextInt();
        return randomNumber;
    }

}
```

The resulting output for the page resembles the following, although the random number will be different every time the page is loaded:

```
Your random number is -1200578984. Refresh page to see another!
```

How It Works

Sometimes embedding Java code directly into a JSP page can be helpful, and it can satisfy the requirement. However, in most cases, it is a good idea to separate any Java code from markup code that is used to create the web view. Doing so makes maintenance easier, and it allows a page developer to focus on creating nice-looking web pages rather than wading through Java code. In some organizations, a Java developer can then write the server-side business logic code, and a web developer can focus on the view. In many organizations today, the same person is performing both tasks, and using the MVC methodology can help separate the logic and increase productivity.

In the early days of JSP, embedding Java directly into a JSP page was the only way to go, but as time went on, the MVC paradigm caught on, and JSP has been updated to follow suit. As a best practice, it is good to use JSP tags to separate Java code from page markup.

In the example, the `<jsp:useBean>` element is used to reference a server-side JavaBean class so that the public fields and methods from that class, as well as private fields via public "getter" methods, can be incorporated into the JSP page. The `jsp:useBean` element requires that you provide an ID and a scope, along with a class name or a beanName. In the example, the id attribute is set to `randomBean`, and this id is used to reference the bean within the JSP page. The scope attribute is set to application, which means that the bean can be used from any JSP page within the application. Table 1-3 displays all the possible scopes and what they mean. The class attribute is set to the fully qualified name of the Java class that will be referenced via the name that is set with the id attribute, in this case `randomBean`.

Table 1-3. *jsp:useBean Element Scopes*

Scope	Description
page (default)	The bean can be used within the same JSP page that contains the `jsp:useBean` element.
request	The bean can be used from any JSP page processing the same request.
session	The bean can be used from any JSP page within the same session as the JSP page that contains the `jsp:useBean` element that created the bean. The page that creates the bean must have a page directive with `session="true"`.
application	The bean can be used from any JSP within the same application as the JSP page that created it.

After the `jsp:useBean` element has been added to a page, JavaBean properties can be used in the JSP page, and public methods from the bean can also be called upon from the page. The example demonstrates how to display the value of a JavaBean property using the ${ } notation. Any variable that contains a "getter" and a "setter" method in the JavaBean can be accessed from a JSP page by referencing the class member field in between the ${ and } character sequences, better known as an Expression Language expression. The following excerpt from the example demonstrates how to display the `randomNumber` field from the JavaBean:

```
Your random number is ${randomBean.randomNumber}. Refresh page to see another!
```

The key to separating business logic from view logic in the JSP technology is the `jsp:useBean` element. This will allow you to use JavaBean classes from within the JSP page, without embedding the code directly in the page. Separating business logic from view code can help make it easier to maintain and reuse code in the future, as well as make the code easier to follow.

1-12. Yielding or Setting Values
Problem

You want to display values from a JavaBean in a JSP page. Furthermore, you want to have the ability to set values in a JSP page.

Solution

Expose the values from a JavaBean in a JSP page using EL expressions with the `${bean.value}` syntax. In the following JSP code, a Java class by the name of `EasyBean` will be used to hold the value that is entered into a text field by a user. The value will then be read from the bean and displayed on the page using EL expressions.

The following code shows a JSP page that contains an input form and displays the value that is entered into the text box:

```
<%@page contentType="text/html" pageEncoding="UTF-8"%>
<!DOCTYPE html>
<html>
    <head>
        <meta http-equiv="Content-Type" content="text/html; charset=UTF-8">
        <title>Recipe 1-12: Yielding and Setting Values</title>
    </head>
    <body>
        <jsp:useBean id="easyBean" scope="page" class="org.
          jakartaeerecipes.chapter01.recipe01_12.EasyBean"/>
        <jsp:setProperty name="easyBean" property="*"/>
        <form method="post">
        Use the input text box below to set the value, and then hit submit.
        <br/><br/>
```

```
    Set the field value:
    <input id="fieldValue" name="fieldValue" type="text" size="30"/>
    <br/>
    The value contained within the field is currently: ${easyBean.
    fieldValue}

    <input type="submit">
    </form>
  </body>
</html>
```

Next, the JavaBean class, which is used to hold the value that is used by the page, looks like the following:

```
package org.jakartaeerecipes.chapter01.recipe01_12;

public class EasyBean implements java.io.Serializable {
    private String fieldValue;

    public EasyBean(){
        fieldValue = null;
    }

    /**
     * @return the fieldValue
     */
    public String getFieldValue() {
        return fieldValue;
    }

    /**
     * @param fieldValue the fieldValue to set
     */
    public void setFieldValue(String fieldValue) {
        this.fieldValue = fieldValue;
    }

}
```

This simple example demonstrates how to enter a value, "set" it into the JavaBean variable, and then display it on the page.

How It Works

Perhaps one of the most useful web constructs is the input form, which allows a user to enter information into text boxes on the page and submit them to a server for processing. JSP makes it easy to submit values from an HTML form, and it is equally easy to display them back on a page. To do so, a field is declared in a Java class, and accessor methods (aka getters and setters) are provided so that other classes can save values to the field and obtain values that are currently stored in it. Sometimes Java classes that contain fields with accessor methods are referred to as JavaBean classes. The classes can also contain other methods that can be used to perform tasks, but it is a best practice to keep JavaBeans as simple as possible. JavaBean classes should also implement `java.io.Serializable` so that they can be easily serialized and deserialized.

In the example for this recipe, a Java class named `EasyBean` contains a private field named `fieldValue`. The accessor methods `getFieldValue()` and `setFieldValue()` can be used to obtain and store the value in `fieldValue`, respectively. Those accessor methods are declared as public, and thus they can be used from another Java class or JSP page. The JSP page uses the `jsp:useBean` element to obtain a reference to the `EasyBean` class. The scope is set to page so that the class can be used only within the JSP page that contains the `jsp:useBean` element. Table 1-2, which can be found in the previous recipe, lists the different scopes available for use with the `jsp:useBean` element:

```
<jsp:useBean id="easyBean" scope="page" class="org.jakartaeerecipes.
chapter01.recipe01_12.EasyBean"/>
```

Next, an HTML form is defined in the JSP page with the POST method, and it contains an input field named `fieldValue`, which allows a user to enter a String of text that will be submitted as a request parameter when the form is submitted. Note that the form in the example does not have an action specified; this means that the same URL will be used for form submission, and the same JSP will be used for form submission and will be displayed again once the form is submitted. Since the JSP has a `jsp:useBean` element specified on the page, all request parameters will be sent to that bean when the page is submitted.

The key to ensuring that the value entered into the `fieldValue` input text field is stored into the `fieldValue` variable within the Java class is using the `jsp:setProperty` element within the form. The `jsp:setProperty` element allows one or more properties to be set in a JavaBean class using the corresponding setter methods. In the example, `<jsp:useBean>` is used to instantiate the `EasyBean` Java class, and `<jsp:setProperty>` is used to set the value that is entered within the `fieldValue` input text box to the fieldValue variable within the EasyBean class. The jsp:setProperty name attribute must equal the value of the jsp:useBean id attribute. The jsp:setProperty property attribute can equal the name of the field within the Java class that you want to set in the bean, or it can be a wildcard * character to submit all input fields to the bean. The value attribute of jsp:setProperty can be used to specify a static value for the property. The following excerpt from the example shows how the jsp:setProperty tag is used:

```
<jsp:setProperty name="easyBean" property="*"/>
```

Note: The ordering of the JSP elements is very important. <jsp:useBean> must come before <jsp:setProperty> because the jsp:useBean element is responsible for instantiating its corresponding Java class. Since the JSP page is executed from the top of the page downward, the bean would be unavailable for use to any elements prior to when jsp:useBean is specified.

When the user enters a value into the input field and submits the request, it is submitted as a request parameter to the Java class that corresponds to the jsp:useBean element for that page. There are a couple of different ways to display the data that has been populated in the JavaBean field. The example demonstrates how to use the jsp:getProperty element to display the value of the fieldValue variable. The <jsp:getProperty> element must specify a name attribute, which corresponds to the id of the Java class that was specified within the jsp:useBean element. It must also specify a property attribute, which corresponds to the name of the JavaBean property that you want to display. The following excerpt from the example demonstrates the use of the jsp:getProperty tag:

```
<jsp:getProperty name="easyBean" property="fieldValue"/>
```

It is also possible to display the value of a JavaBean property using EL expressions, using the id of the bean specified in the jsp:useBean element, along with the property name you wish to display. To try this, you can replace the jsp:getProperty element with the following EL expression:

```
${easyBean.fieldValue}
```

The JSP framework makes the development of web applications using Java technology much easier than using servlets. Input forms such as the one demonstrated in this example show how much more productive JSP is compared to standard servlet coding. As with anything, both servlets and JSP technology have their place in your toolbox. For creating simple data entry forms, JSP definitely takes the cake.

1-13. Invoking a Function in a Conditional Expression

Problem

You want to use a Java function to perform a conditional evaluation within your JSP. However, you do not want to embed Java code into your JSP page.

Solution

Code the function in a JavaBean class and then register the bean with the JSP via the `<jsp:useBean>` tag. You will then need to register the function within a tag library descriptor (TLD) so that it can be made usable on the JSP page via a tag. A TLD is a document that contains information about an XML document and its associated tags. Finally, set up a page directive for the TLD in which the function is registered, and use the function tag within the page. In the example that follows, a JSP page will use a function to tell the user whether a given Java type is a primitive type. The user will enter a String value into a text box, and that value will be submitted to a JavaBean field. The contents of the field will then be compared against a list of Java primitive types to determine whether it is a match. If the value entered into the field is a primitive, a message will be displayed to the user.

The following code is the Java class that contains the implementation of the function which is going to be used from within the JSP. The bean also contains a field that will be used from the JSP page for setting and getting the value that is entered by the user:

```
package org.jakartaeerecipes.chapter01.recipe01_13;

public class ConditionalClass implements java.io.Serializable {
    private String typename = null;
    public static String[] javaTypes = new String[8];

    public ConditionalClass(){
        javaTypes[0] = "byte";
        javaTypes[1] = "short";
        javaTypes[2] = "int";
        javaTypes[3] = "long";
        javaTypes[4] = "float";
```

```
        javaTypes[5] = "double";
        javaTypes[6] = "boolean";
        javaTypes[7] = "char";
    }

    public static boolean isPrimitive(String value){
        boolean returnValue = false;
        for(int x=0; x<=javaTypes.length-1; x++){
            if(javaTypes[x].equalsIgnoreCase(value)){
                returnValue = true;
            }
        }
        return returnValue;
    }

    // Getter and Setter for typename
}
```

The field typename will be used from the JSP page to set the value that is entered by the user and to retrieve it for passing to the function named isPrimitive();, which is used to compare the given value to a list of Java primitives. Next is a listing of the TLD that is used to register the function so that it can be used as a tag within the JSP. For simplicity, the TLD file is named functions.tld:

```
<?xml version="1.0" encoding="UTF-8"?>
<taglib version="2.1" xmlns="http://xmlns.jcp.org/xml/ns/
javaee" xmlns:xsi="http://www.w3.org/2001/XMLSchema-instance"
xsi:schemaLocation="http://xmlns.jcp.org/xml/ns/javaee http://java.sun.com/
xml/ns/javaee/web-jsptaglibrary_2_1.xsd">
    <tlib-version>1.0</tlib-version>
    <short-name>fct</short-name>
    <uri>functions</uri>
    <function>
      <name>isPrimitive</name>
      <function-class>org.jakartaeerecipes.chapter01.recipe01_13.
      ConditionalClass</function-class>
```

```
<function-signature>boolean isPrimitive(java.lang.String)</function-
    signature>
  </function>
</taglib>
```

Last is the JSP code that contains the page directive for using the TLD and the conditional call to the function isPrimitive() via a tag:

```
<%@page contentType="text/html" pageEncoding="UTF-8"%>
<!DOCTYPE html>
<%@ taglib uri="http://java.sun.com/jsp/jstl/core"
    prefix="c" %>
<%@ taglib uri="/WEB-INF/tlds/functions.tld" prefix="fct" %>
<html>
    <head>
        <meta http-equiv="Content-Type" content="text/html; charset=UTF-8">
        <title>Recipe 1-13: Invoking a Function in an Expression</title>
    </head>
    <body>

        <form method="get">
            <p>Name one of the primitive Java types:
                <input type="text" id="typename" name="typename" size="40"/>
            </p>
            <br/>
            <input type="submit">
        </form>
        <jsp:useBean id="conditionalBean" scope="page" class="org.
         jakartaeerecipes.chapter01.recipe01_13.ConditionalClass"/>
        <jsp:setProperty name="conditionalBean" property="typename"/>
        <c:if test="${fct:isPrimitive(conditionalBean.typename)}" >
            ${ conditionalBean.typename } is a primitive type.
        </c:if>

        <c:if test="${conditionalBean.typename ne null and !fct:isPrimitive
         (conditionalBean.typename)}" >
```

```
        ${ conditionalBean.typename } is not a primitive type.
    </c:if>
  </body>
</html>
```

Following the strategy used in this solution, you can create a conditional test that is usable via a JSP tag for your pages.

How It Works

You need to take a few different steps before a Java function can become accessible from a JSP page. One of the most commonly overlooked conditions is that the function must be declared with a static modifier in the Java class. In the example for this recipe, the function isPrimitive() is declared as static, and it returns a boolean value indicating whether the web page user types the name of a Java primitive type.

The next step toward making a function accessible via a JSP page is to register it with a TLD. In the example, a TLD named functions.tld is created, although if there is already a custom TLD in your application, then you could register the function with it rather than creating an additional one if you want. The TLD in this example has a short-name attribute of fct, which will be used from within JSP tags. To actually register the function, you must create a function element within the TLD, provide a function name, indicate the class that the function resides within, and, finally, specify the function signature:

```
<function>
    <name>isPrimitive</name>
    <function-class>org.jakartaeerecipes.chapter01.recipe01_13.
    ConditionalClass</function-class>
    <function-signature>boolean isPrimitive(java.lang.String)</function-
    signature>
    </function>
```

The function is now ready for use within the JSP. To make the function accessible via the JSP, register the TLD that contains the function element by including a taglib directive specifying the uri and prefix for the TLD. The uri is the path to the TLD, and the prefix should match the name given in the short-name element of the TLD. The following excerpt from the JSP in this example shows the taglib directive:

```
<%@ taglib uri="/WEB-INF/tlds/functions.tld" prefix="fct" %>
```

The function will now be accessible via an EL expression within the JSP by specifying the `taglib` prefix along with the name of the function as it is registered in the TLD. The EL expression in the example calls the function, passing the `typename` parameter. The `isPrimitive()` function is used to determine whether the text contained within the `typename` bean field is equal to one of the Java primitive types:

```
<c:if test="${fct:isPrimitive(conditionalBean.typename)}" >
```

The solution in this recipe also uses the Java Standard Tag Library (JSTL) core. Depending upon the server environment being used, this may be a separate download. The JSTL provides an extension to the standard set of tags provided with the JSP API. For more information regarding JSTL, please refer to the online documentation, which can be found at `www.oracle.com/technetwork/java/index-jsp-135995.html`.

The JSTL `<c:if>` tag can be used to test conditions, executing the directives between its opening and closing tags if the condition test returns a true value. Not surprisingly, the `<c:if>` tag includes a test attribute that specifies an EL expression that indicates the test that needs to be performed. In the example, the isPrimitive function is called within the EL expression, passing the bean value. If the test returns a `true`, then a message is printed indicating that the given value is equal to a Java primitive type. Another `<c:if>` test follows the first in the example, and this time it tests to ensure that the property value is not equal to `null` and also that it is not a Java primitive type. Expression Language is used to determine whether the property value is equal to `null` via the ne expression. The and expression ties both the first and second conditional expressions together within the EL expression, meaning that both of the expressions must evaluate to a value of `true` in order for the condition to be met. If both conditions are met, then the value specified by the user is not a Java primitive type, and a corresponding message is printed:

```
<c:if test="${conditionalBean.typename ne null and !fct:isPrimitive
(conditionalBean.typename)}" >
            ${ conditionalBean.typename } is not a primitive type.
</c:if>
```

It takes only a few easy steps to create a conditional function for use within JSPs. First, in the JavaBean class, you must create a public static function, which returns a Boolean value. Second, create a TLD, which will make the function available via a JSP tag. Lastly, use the custom tag from within the JSP page along with JSTL conditional test tags to display the content conditionally.

1-14. Creating a JSP Document

Problem

Rather than using standard HTML format, you want to ensure that your JSP code follows the XML standard and contains only valid HTML and JSP tags.

Solution

Create a JSP document rather than a standard JSP. A JSP document is an XML-based representation of a standard JSP document that conforms to the XML standard. The following JSP document contains the same code that is used in the JSP code for Recipe 1-13, but it uses the JSP document format instead. As you can see, not much is different because well-formed tags were already used to create the standard JSP document. The page is also saved with an extension of jspx rather than jsp:

```
<html xmlns:jsp="http://xmlns.jcp.org/JSP/Page" version="2.0"
     xmlns:c="http://xmlns.jcp.org/jsp/jstl/core"
     xmlns:fct="/WEB-INF/tlds/functions.tld">

   <jsp:directive.page contentType="text/html" pageEncoding="UTF-8"/>

   <body>
      <form method="get">
         <p>Name one of the primitive Java types:
            <input type="text" id="typename" name="typename" size="40"/>
         </p>
         <br/>
         <input type="submit"/>
      </form>
      <jsp:useBean id="conditionalBean" scope="request" class="org.
       jakartaeerecipes.chapter01.recipe01_13.ConditionalClass"/>
      <jsp:setProperty name="conditionalBean" property="typename"
                       value="${param.typename}" />
      <c:if test="${fct:isPrimitive(conditionalBean.typename)}" >
         ${ conditionalBean.typename } is a primitive type.
      </c:if>
```

```
    <c:if test="${fn.length(conditionalBean.typename) > 0 and !fct:
    isPrimitive(conditionalBean.typename)}" >
        ${ conditionalBean.typename } is not a primitive type.
    </c:if>

  </body>
</html>
```

This JSP document will yield the same output as the one in Recipe 1-13. However, a well-formed document will be enforced, and this will exclude the use of scripting elements within the page.

How It Works

As foreshadowed in previous recipes, separating business logic from markup code can be important for many reasons. Standard JSP pages can adhere to the MVC paradigm, but they are not forced into doing so. Sometimes it makes sense to enforce the separation of business logic, by strictly adhering to a well-formed XML document using only JSP tags to work with server-side Java classes. Well-formed means that there should be only one root element and each starting tag must have a corresponding ending tag. Creating a JSP document is one answer because such documents enforce well-formed XML and do not allow scripting elements to be used within the JSP page.

Several JSP tags can be used to communicate with Java classes, perform JSP-specific functionality, and make markup easy to follow. As such, modern JSP-based applications should make use of well-formed JSP documents utilizing such JSP tags, rather than embedding scripting elements throughout markup. Table 1-4 describes what the different JSP tags do.

Table 1-4. *JSP Tags*

Tag	Description
`<jsp:attribute>`	Defines attributes for a JSP page.
`<jsp:body>`	Defines an element body.
`<jsp:declaration>`	Defines page declarations.
`<jsp:directive>`	Defines page includes and page directives.
`<jsp:doBody>`	Executes the body of the JSP tag that is used by the calling JSP page to invoke the tag.
`<jsp:element>`	Generates an XML element dynamically.
`<jsp:expression>`	Inserts the value of a scripting language expression, converted into a string.
`<jsp:forward>`	Forwards a request to another page. The new page can be HTML, JSP, or servlet.
`<jsp:getProperty>`	Obtains the value of a bean property and places it in the page.
`<jsp:include>`	Includes another JSP or web resource in the page.
`<jsp:invoke>`	Invokes a specified JSP fragment.
`<jsp:output>`	Specifies the document type declaration.
`<jsp:plugin>`	Executes an applet or bean with the specified plug-in.
`<jsp:root>`	Defines standard elements and tag library namespaces.
`<jsp:scriptlet>`	Embeds code fragment into a page if necessary.
`<jsp:setProperty>`	Sets specified value(s) into a bean property.
`<jsp:text>`	Encloses template data.
`<jsp:useBean>`	References and instantiates (if needed) a JavaBean class using a name and providing a scope.

Creating a well-formed JSP can lead to easier development, ease of maintenance, and better overall design. Since it is so important, the remaining recipes in this chapter will use the JSP document format.

1-15. Embedding Expressions in EL

Problem

You want to use some conditional and/or arithmetic expressions within your JSP without embedding Java code using scripting elements.

Solution

Use EL expressions within JSP tags to perform conditional and/or arithmetic expressions. This solution will look at two examples of EL expressions. The first example demonstrates how to perform conditional logic using EL expressions. Note that the JSTL is also used in this case, to conditionally display a message on the page if the expression results to true.

Note   The JSP pages in this example and all remaining examples in this chapter make use of JSP documents (`.jspx` extension). A JSP document is an XML-based representation of a standard JSP document that conforms to the XML standard.

```
<html xmlns:jsp="http://xmlns.jcp.org/JSP/Page"
    xmlns:c="http://xmlns.jcp.org/jsp/jstl/core"
    version="2.0">

    <jsp:directive.page contentType="text/html" pageEncoding="UTF-8"/>
    <head>
        <title>Recipe 1-15: Embedding Expressions in EL</title>
    </head>
    <body>
        <h1>Conditional Expressions</h1>
        <p>
            The following portion of the page will only display conditional
            expressions which result in a true value.
        </p>
```

```
<c:if test="${1 + 1 == 2}">
    The conditional expression (1 + 1 == 2) results in TRUE.
    <br/>
</c:if>

<c:if test="${'x' == 'y'}">
    The conditional expression (x == y) results in TRUE.
    <br/>
</c:if>

<c:if test="${(100/10) gt 5}">
    The conditional expression ((100/10) > 5) results in TRUE.
    <br/>
</c:if>

<c:if test="${20 mod 3 eq 2}">
    The conditional expression (20 mod 3 eq 2) results in TRUE.
    <br/>
</c:if>

</body>

</html>
```

This JSP page will result in the following output being displayed:

```
...
The conditional expression (1 + 1 == 2) results in TRUE.
The conditional expression ((100/10) > 5) results in TRUE.
The conditional expression (20 mod 3 eq 2) results in TRUE.
...
```

Arithmetic expressions can also be evaluated using EL. The following JSP code demonstrates some examples of using arithmetic within EL:

```
<html xmlns:jsp="http://xmlns.jcp.org/JSP/Page"
    xmlns:c="http://xmlns.jcp.org/jsp/jstl/core"
    version="2.0">

  <jsp:directive.page contentType="text/html" pageEncoding="UTF-8"/>
```

```
    <head>
        <title>Recipe 1-15: Embedding Expressions in EL</title>
    </head>
    <body>
        <jsp:useBean id="expBean" class="org.jakartaeerecipes.chapter01.
         recipe01_15.Expressions"/>
        <h1>Arithmetic Expressions</h1>
        <p>
            The following expressions demonstrate how to perform arithmetic using EL.
        </p>
        10 - 4 = ${10 - 4}
        <br/>
        85 / 15 = ${85 / 15}
        <br/>
        847 divided by 6 = ${847 div 6}
        <br/>
        ${expBean.num1} * ${expBean.num2} = ${expBean.num1 * expBean.num2}

    </body>

</html>
```

The code contained within the Expressions class is as follows:

```
public class Expressions implements java.io.Serializable {
    private int num1 = 5;
    private double num2 = 634.324;
    private float num3 = 98.4f;
// Getters and Setters
}
```

The preceding JSP will result in the following output being displayed:

```
...
10 - 4 = 6
85 / 15 = 5.666666666666667
847 divided by 6 = 141.16666666666666
5 * 634.324 = 3171.62
...
```

How It Works

The JSP technology makes it easy to work with expressions. Conditional page rendering can be performed using a combination of EL value expressions, which are enclosed within the ${ } character sequences, and JSTL tags. Arithmetic expressions can also be performed using EL expressions. To make things easier, the Expression Language contains keywords or characters that can be used to help form expressions. The example for this recipe contains various expressions and conditional page rendering using the JSTL `<c:if>` tag.

In the first JSP page displayed in the example, there are some examples of conditional page rendering. To use the `<c:if>` tag to perform the conditional tests, you must be sure to import the JSTL with the JSP page. To do so, add an import for the JSTL and assign it to a character or string of characters. In the following excerpt from the recipe, the JSTL is assigned to the character `c`:

```
<html xmlns:jsp="http://xmlns.jcp.org/JSP/Page"
      xmlns:c="http://xmlns.jcp.org/jsp/jstl/core"
      version="2.0">
```

An EL value expression is contained within the ${ and } character sequences. Anything within these characters will be treated as EL, and as such, the syntax must be correct, or the JSP page will not be able to compile into a servlet, and it will throw an error. All expressions using the ${ } syntax are evaluated immediately, and they are **read-only** expressions. That is, no expressions using this syntax can be used to set values into a JavaBean property. The JSP engine first evaluates the expression, and then it converts into a String and lastly returns the value to the tag handler. Four types of objects can be referenced within a value expression. Those are JavaBean components, collections, enumerated types, and implicit objects. If using a JavaBean component, the JavaBean must be registered with the JSP page using the `jsp:useBean` element (see previous recipe for details). Collections or enumerated types can also be referenced from a JavaBean that has been registered with the page. Implicit objects are those that allow access to page context, scoped variables, and other such objects. Table 1-5 lists different implicit objects that can be referenced from within EL expressions.

Table 1-5. *Implicit JSP Objects*

Object	Type	Description
pageContext	Context	Provides access to the context of the page and various subobjects
servletContext	Page context	Context for JSP page servlet and web components
session	Page context	Session object for the client
request	Page context	Request that invoked the execution of the page
response	Page context	Response that is returned by the JSP
param	N/A	Responsible for mapping parameter names to values
paramValues	N/A	Maps request parameter to an array of values
header	N/A	Responsible for mapping a header name to a value
headerValues	N/A	Maps header name to an array of values
cookie	N/A	Maps a cookie name to a single cookie
initParam	N/A	Maps a context initialization parameter to a value
pageScope	Scope	Maps page scope variables
requestScope	Scope	Maps request scope variables
sessionScope	Scope	Maps session scope variables
applicationScope	Scope	Maps application scope variables

The following are some examples of expressions that make use of JavaBean components, collections, enumerated types, and implicit objects:

```
// Displays the value of a variable named myVar within a JavaBean
referenced as elTester
${ elTester.myVar }
// Does the same thing as the line above
${ elTester["myVar"] }

// Evaluates an Enumerated Type in which myEnum is an instance of MyEnum
${ myEnum == "myValue" }
// Reference a getter method of the Enum named getTestVal()
${ myEnum.testVal}
```

```
// References a collection named myCollection within the JavaBean
referenced as elTester
${ elTester.myCollection }

// Obtain the parameter named "testParam"
${ param.testParam }  // Same as: request.getParameter("testParam")
// Obtain session attribute named "testAttr"
${ sessionScope.testAttr } // Same as: session.getAttribute("testAttr")
```

In the recipe example, the `<c:if>` tag is used to test a series of value expressions and conditionally display the page content. The test attribute of `<c:if>` is used to register a test condition, and if the test condition returns a `true` result, then the content contained between the `<c:if>` starting and ending tags is displayed. The following excerpt from the example demonstrates how a test is performed:

```
<c:if test="${'x' == 'y'}">
        The conditional expression (x == y) results in TRUE.
        <br/>
    </c:if>
```

EL expressions can contain a series of reserved words that can be used to help evaluate the expression. For instance, the following expression utilizes the `gt` reserved word to return a value indicating whether the value returned from the calculation of 100/10 is greater than 5:

```
<c:if test="${(100/10) gt 5}">
        The conditional expression ((100/10) > 5) results in TRUE.
        <br/>
</c:if>
```

Table 1-6 lists all the JSP EL expression reserved words and their meanings.

Table 1-6. *EL Expression Reserved Words*

Reserved Word	Description
and	Combines expressions and returns true if all of them evaluate to true
or	Combines expressions and returns true if one of them evaluates to true
not	Negates an expression
eq	Equal
ne	Not equal
lt	Less than
gt	Greater than
le	Less than or equal
ge	Greater than or equal
true	True value
false	False value
null	Null value
instanceof	Used to test whether an object is an instance of another object
empty	Determines whether a list or collection is empty
div	Divided by
mod	Modulus

Arithmetic expressions are demonstrated by the second example in this recipe. The following arithmetic operators can be utilized within expressions:

+ (addition), - (binary and unary), * (multiplication), / and div (division), %, and mod (modulus)

and, &&, or, ||, not, !

==, !=, <, >, <=, >=

X ? Y : Z (ternary conditional)

Entire chapters of books have been written on the use of EL expressions within JSPs. This recipe only touches upon the possibilities of using value expressions. The best way to get used to expressions is to create a test JSP page and experiment with the different options that are available.

1-16. Accessing Parameters in Multiple Pages

Problem

You want to access a parameter from within multiple pages of your web application.

Solution

Create an input form to submit parameters to the request object, and then utilize the request object to retrieve the values in another page. In the example that follows, a JSP page that contains an input form is used to pass values to another JSP page by setting the HTML form action attribute to the value of the JSP page that will utilize the parameters. In the case of this example, the receiving JSP page merely displays the parameter values, but other work could be performed as well.

The following JSP code demonstrates the use of an input form to save parameters into the request object and pass them to a page named recipe01_16b.jspx:

```
<html xmlns:jsp="http://xmlns.jcp.org/JSP/Page"
    xmlns:c="http://xmlns.jcp.org/jsp/jstl/core"
    version="2.0">

    <jsp:directive.page contentType="text/html" pageEncoding="UTF-8"/>
    <head>
        <title>Recipe 1-16: Passing Parameters</title>
    </head>
    <body>

        <h1>Passing Parameters</h1>
        <p>
            The following parameters will be passed to the next JSP.
        </p>
        <form method="get" action="recipe01_16b.jspx">
        Param 1: <input id="param1" name="param1" type="text" value="1"/>
        <br/>
        Param 2: <input name="param2" type="text" value="2 + 0"/>
        <br/>
        Param 3: <input id="param3" name="param3" type="text" value="three"/>
```

```
        <br/>
        <input type="submit" value="Go to next page"/>
        </form>
    </body>

</html>
```

The next JSP code receives the parameters and displays their values:

```
<html xmlns:jsp="http://xmlns.jcp.org/JSP/Page"
    xmlns:c="http://xmlns.jcp.org/jsp/jstl/core"
    version="2.0">

    <jsp:directive.page contentType="text/html" pageEncoding="UTF-8"/>
    <head>
        <title>Recipe 1-16: Passing Parameters</title>
    </head>
    <body>

        <h1>Passing Parameters</h1>
        <p>
            The following parameters were passed from the original JSP.
        </p>
        <form method="post" action="recipe01_16a.jspx">
        Param 1: <jsp:expression>request.getParameter("param1") </jsp:expression>
        <br/>
        Param 2: <jsp:expression> request.getParameter("param2") </jsp:expression>
        <br/>
        Param 3: <jsp:expression> request.getParameter("param3") </jsp:expression>
        <br/>
        OR using value expressions
        <br/>
        Param 1: ${ param.param1 }
        <br/>
        Param 2: ${ param.param2 }
        <br/>
        Param 3: ${ param.param3 }
        <br/>
```

```
        <input type="submit" value="Back to Page 1"/>
        </form>
    </body>
</html>
```

As you can see, a couple of variations can be used to display the parameter values. Both of the variations will display the same result.

How It Works

Request parameters are one of the most useful features of web applications. When a user enters some data into a web form and submits the form, the request contains the parameters that were entered into the form. Parameters can also be statically embedded within a web page or concatenated onto a URL and sent to a receiving servlet or JSP page. The data contained in request parameters can then be inserted into a database, redisplayed on another JSP page, and used to perform a calculation or a myriad of other possibilities. The JSP technology provides an easy mechanism for using request parameters within other JSP pages, and the example in this recipe demonstrates how to do just that.

Note   Request parameters are always translated into String values.

Note that in the example, the first JSP page uses a simple HTML form to obtain values from a user and submit them to the request. Another JSP page named `recipe01_16b.jspx` is set as the form action attribute, so when the form is submitted, it will send the request to `recipe01_16b.jspx`. The input fields on the first JSP page specify both an `id` attribute and a `name` attribute, although only the name attribute is required. The name that is given to the input field is the name that will be used to reference the value entered into it as a request parameter.

Note   It is a good programming practice to always include an id attribute. The ID is useful for performing work with the Document Object Model (DOM) and for referencing elements via a scripting language such as JavaScript.

The receiving action, `recipe01_16b.jspx` in this example, can make a call to `response.getParameter()`, passing the name of a parameter (input field name) to obtain the value that was entered into its corresponding text field. To adhere to JSP document standards, the scriptlet containing the call to `response.getParameter()` must be enclosed within `<jsp:expression>` tags. The following excerpt demonstrates how this is done:

```
Param 1: <jsp:expression>request.getParameter("param1") </jsp:expression>
```

Optionally, an EL expression can contain a reference to the implicit param object and obtain the request parameter in the same way. When the expression `${param.param1}` is called, it is evaluated by the JSP engine, and it is translated into `response.getParameter("param1")`. The following excerpt demonstrates this use of EL expressions:

```
Param 1: ${param.param1}
```

Either technique will perform the same task; the named request parameter will be obtained and displayed on the page.

1-17. Creating a Custom JSP Tag

Problem

You want to create a JSP tag that provides custom functionality for your application.

Solution

Create a custom JSP tag using JSP 2.0 simple tag support. Suppose you want to create a custom tag that will insert a signature into the JSP where the tag is placed. The custom tag will print out a default signature, but it will also accept an authorName attribute, which will include a given author's name to the signature if provided. To get started, you'll first need to define a Java class that extends the SimpleTagSupport class. This class will provide the implementation for your tag. The following code is the implementation for a class named Signature, which provides the implementation for the custom tag.

Note   To compile the following code, you will need to add `javax.servlet.jsp-api.jar` to classpath:

```
cd recipe01_17
javac -cp...\glassfish5\glassfish\modules\javax.servlet.jsp-api.jar *.java
```

```java
package org.jakartaeerecipes.chapter01.recipe01_17;

import javax.servlet.jsp.JspException;
import javax.servlet.jsp.JspWriter;
import javax.servlet.jsp.PageContext;
import javax.servlet.jsp.tagext.SimpleTagSupport;

public class Signature extends SimpleTagSupport {

    private String authorName = null;

    /**
     * @param authorName the authorName to set
     */
    public void setAuthorName(String authorName) {
        this.authorName = authorName;
    }

    @Override
    public void doTag() throws JspException {
        PageContext pageContext = (PageContext) getJspContext();
        JspWriter out = pageContext.getOut();

        try {
            if(authorName != null){
                out.println("Written by " + authorName);
                out.println("<br/>");
            }
```

```
        out.println("Published by Apress");

    } catch (Exception e) {
        System.out.println(e);
    }

  }

}
```

Next, a TLD is created to map the Signature class tag implementation to a tag. The TLD that includes the custom tag mapping is listed here:

```
<?xml version="1.0" encoding="UTF-8"?>
<taglib version="2.1" xmlns="http://xmlns.jcp.org/xml/ns/
javaee" xmlns:xsi="http://www.w3.org/2001/XMLSchema-instance"
xsi:schemaLocation="http://xmlns.jcp.org/xml/ns/javaee http://xmlns.jcp.
org/xml/ns/javaee/web-jsptaglibrary_2_1.xsd">
  <tlib-version>1.0</tlib-version>
  <short-name>cust</short-name>
  <uri>custom</uri>
  <tag>
   <name>signature</name>
   <tag-class>org.jakartaeerecipes.chapter01.recipe01_17.Signature</tag-
   class>
   <body-content>empty</body-content>
   <attribute>
       <name>authorName</name>
       <rtexprvalue>true</rtexprvalue>
       <required>false</required>
    </attribute>
  </tag>
</taglib>
```

Once the class implementation and the TLD are in place, the tag can be used from within a JSP page. The following JSP code is an example of using the custom tag on a page:

```
<html xmlns:jsp="http://xmlns.jcp.org/JSP/Page"
      xmlns:c="http://xmlns.jcp.org/jsp/jstl/core"
      xmlns:cust="custom"
      version="2.0">

    <jsp:directive.page contentType="text/html" pageEncoding="UTF-8"/>
    <head>
        <title>Recipe 1-17: Creating a Custom JSP Tag</title>
    </head>
    <body>

        <h1>Custom JSP Tag</h1>
        <p>
            The custom JSP tag is used as the footer for this page.
            <br/>
        </p>
        <cust:signature/>

    </body>

</html>
```

The custom tag output will now be displayed in place of the cust:signature element within the JSP page.

How It Works

One of the most useful new features of JSP 2.0 was the inclusion of the SimpleTagSupport class, which provides an easier way for developers to create custom tags. Prior to the 2.0 release, custom tag creation took a good deal of more work, because the developer had to provide much more code to implement the tag within the tag's implementation class. The SimpleTagSupport class takes care of much implementation for the developer so that the only thing left to do is implement the doTag method in order to provide an implementation for the custom tag.

In the example for this recipe, a custom tag is created that will print out a signature on the JSP page in the position where the tag is located. To create a custom tag implementation, create a Java class that will extend the `SimpleTagSupport` class, and provide an implementation for the `doTag()` method. The example class also contains a field named `authorName`, which will be mapped within the TLD as an attribute for the custom tag. In the `doTag()` method, a handle on the JSP page context is obtained by calling the `getJspContext()` method. `getJspContext()` is a custom method that is implemented for you within `SimpleTagSupport` and makes it easy to get ahold of the JSP page context. Next, to provide the ability to write to the JSP output, a handle is obtained on the `JspWriter` by calling `PageContext`'s `getOut()` method:

```
PageContext pageContext = (PageContext) getJspContext();
JspWriter out = pageContext.getOut();
```

The next lines within `doTag()` provide the implementation for writing to the JSP output via a series of calls to `out.println()`. Any content that is passed to `out.println()` will be displayed on the page. Note that in the example, the `authorName` field is checked to see whether it contains a `null` value. If it does not contain a `null` value, then it is displayed on the page; otherwise, it is omitted. Therefore, if the tag within the JSP page contains a value for the `authorName` attribute, then it will be printed on the page. The `out.println()` code is contained within a `try-catch` block in case any exceptions occur.

Note   To allow your tag to accept scriptlets, you will need to use the Classic Tag Handlers. The Classic Tag Handlers existed before the JSP 2.0 era and can still be used today alongside the Simple Tag Handlers. The Simple Tag Handlers revolve around the `doTag()` method, whereas the Classic Tag Handlers deal with a `doStartTag()` method and a `doEndTag()` method, as well as others. Since the Simple Tag Handlers can be used alongside the Classic Tag Handlers, it is possible to use some of the more complex Classic Tag methods while utilizing Simple Tag methods in the same application. This eases the transition from the Classic Tag Handlers to the Simple Tag Handlers. For more information regarding the differences between the two APIs, please see some online documentation by searching for the keywords "Simple vs. Classic Tag Handlers."

That's it; the implementation for the tag is complete. To map the implementation class to the Document Object Model (DOM) via a tag name, a TLD must contain a mapping to the class. In the example, a TLD named `custom.tld` is created, and it contains the mapping for the class. The short-name element specifies the name that must be used within the JSP page to reference the tag. The `uri` element specifies the name of the TLD, and it is used from within the JSP page to reference the TLD file itself. The meat of the TLD is contained within the `tag` element. The `name` element is used to specify the name for the tag, and it will be used within a JSP page in combination with the `short-name` element to provide the complete tag name. The `tag-class` element provides the name of the class that implements the tag, and `body-content` specifies a value to indicate whether the body content for the JSP page will be made available for the tag implementation class. It is set to empty for this example. To specify an attribute for the tag, the attribute element must be added to the TLD, including the `name`, `rtexprvalue`, and `required` elements. The `name` element of the attribute specifies the name of the attribute, `rtexprvalue` indicates whether the attribute can contain an EL expression, and `required` indicates whether the attribute is required.

To use the tag within a JSP page, the `custom.tld` TLD must be mapped to the page within the `<html>` element in a JSP document or a `taglib` directive within a standard JSP. The following lines show the difference between these two:

```
<!—JSP Document syntax -->
xmlns:cust="custom"

<!—JSP syntax -->
<%@taglib prefix="cust" uri="custom" %>
```

To use the tag within the page, simply specify the TLD short-name along with the mapping name for the tag implementation and any attributes you want to provide:

```
<cust:signature authorName="Josh Juneau"/>
```

Creating custom tags within JSP is easier than it was in the past. Custom tags provide developers with the ability to define custom actions and/or content that can be made accessible from within a JSP page via a tag rather than scriptlets. Custom tags help developers follow the MVC architecture, separating code from business logic.

1-18. Including Other JSPs into a Page

Problem

Rather than coding the same header or footer into each JSP, you want to place the content for those page sections into a separate JSP page and then pull them into JSP pages by reference.

Solution

Use the `<jsp:include>` tag to embed other static or dynamic pages in your JSP page. The following example demonstrates the inclusion of two JSP pages within another. One of the JSP pages is used to formulate the header of the page, and another is used for the footer. The following page demonstrates the main JSP page, which includes two others using the `<jsp:include>` tag. The JSPX files named `recipe01_18-header.jspx` and `recipe01_18-footer.jspx` are included within the body of the main JSP page in order to provide the header and footer sections of the page:

```
<html xmlns:jsp="http://xmlns.jcp.orgm/JSP/Page"
    xmlns:c="http://xmlns.jcp.org/jsp/jstl/core"
    version="2.0">

    <jsp:directive.page contentType="text/html" pageEncoding="UTF-8"/>
    <head>
        <title>Recipe 1-18: Including Other JSPs into a Page</title>
    </head>
    <body>
        <jsp:include page="recipe01-18-header.jspx" />
        <h1>This is the body of the main JSP.</h1>
        <p>
            Both the header and footer for this page were created as
            separate JSPs.
        </p>
        <jsp:include page="recipe01_18-footer.jspx"/>

    </body>

</html>
```

Next is the JSP code that comprises the page header. It's nothing fancy but is a separate JSP page nonetheless:

```
<html xmlns:jsp="http://xmlns.jcp.org/JSP/Page" version="2.0">

    <jsp:directive.page contentType="text/html" pageEncoding="UTF-8"/>

    <p>This is the page header</p>
</html>
```

The next JSP code makes up the page footer:

```
<html xmlns:jsp="http://xmlns.jcp.org/JSP/Page" version="2.0">

    <jsp:directive.page contentType="text/html" pageEncoding="UTF-8"/>

    <p>This is the page footer</p>
</html>
```

In the end, these three pages create a single page that contains a header, a body, and a footer.

How It Works

Including other JSP pages helps increase developer productivity and reduces maintenance time. Using this technique, a developer can extract any JSP features that appear in multiple pages and place them into a separate JSP page. Doing so will allow a single point of maintenance when one of these features needs to be updated.

To include another page within a JSP page, use the `<jsp:include>` tag. The `<jsp:include>` tag allows embedding a static file or another web component. The tag includes a page attribute, which is used to specify the relative URL or an expression that results in another file or web component to include in the page.

Note: The tag also has an optional flush attribute, which can be set to either true or false to indicate whether the output buffer should be flushed prior to the page inclusion. The default value for the flush attribute is false.

Optionally, `<jsp:param>` clauses can be placed between the opening and closing `<jsp:include>` tags to pass one or more name-value pairs to the included resource if the resource is dynamic. An example of performing this technique would resemble something like the following lines of code. In the following lines, a parameter with a name of bookAuthor and a value of Juneau is passed to the header JSP page:

```
<jsp:include page="header.jspx">
    <jsp:param name="bookAuthor" value="Juneau"/>
</jsp:include>
```

The ability to include other content within a JSP page provides a means to encapsulate resources and static content. This allows developers to create content once and include it in many pages.

1-19. Creating an Input Form for a Database Record
Problem

You want to create a JSP page that will be used to input information that will be inserted as a database record.

Solution

Create an input form and use a Java servlet action method to insert the values into the database. This solution requires a JSP document and a Java servlet in order to complete the database input form. In the following example, an input form is created within a JSP document to populate records within a database table named RECIPES. When the user enters the information into the text fields on the form and clicks the submit button, a servlet is called that performs the database insert transaction.

The following code is the JSP document that is used to create the input form for the database application:

```
<html xmlns:jsp="http://xmlns.jcp.org/JSP/Page"
      xmlns:c="http://xmlns.jcp.org/jsp/jstl/core"
      version="2.0">

    <jsp:directive.page contentType="text/html" pageEncoding="UTF-8"/>
    <head>
        <title>Recipe 1-19: Creating an Input Form</title>
    </head>
    <body>
        <h1>Recipe Input Form</h1>
```

```
<p>
    Please insert recipe details using the text fields below.
</p>
${ recipeBean.message }
<form method="POST" action="/JakartaEERecipes/RecipeServlet">
    Recipe Number: <input id="recipeNumber" name="recipeNumber"
    size="30"/>
    <br/>
    Recipe Name: <input id="name" name="name" size="30"/>
    <br/>

    <br/>
    <input type="submit"/>
</form>
</body>
```

```
</html>
```

Next is the code for a servlet named RecipeServlet. It is responsible for reading the request parameters from the JSP document input form and inserting the fields into the database:

```java
package org.jakartaeerecipes.chapter01.recipe01_19;

import org.jakartaeerecipes.common.CreateConnection;
import java.io.IOException;
import java.io.PrintWriter;
import java.sql.Connection;
import java.sql.PreparedStatement;
import java.sql.SQLException;
import javax.servlet.ServletException;
import javax.servlet.annotation.WebServlet;
import javax.servlet.http.HttpServlet;
import javax.servlet.http.HttpServletRequest;
import javax.servlet.http.HttpServletResponse;

@WebServlet(name = "RecipeServlet", urlPatterns = {"/RecipeServlet"})
public class RecipeServlet extends HttpServlet {
```

```java
/**
 * Processes requests for both HTTP
 * <code>GET</code> and
 * <code>POST</code> methods.
 *
 * @param request servlet request
 * @param response servlet response
 * @throws ServletException if a servlet-specific error occurs
 * @throws IOException if an I/O error occurs
 */
protected void processRequest(HttpServletRequest request,
HttpServletResponse response)
        throws ServletException, IOException {
    response.setContentType("text/html;charset=UTF-8");

    int result = -1;
    try(PrintWriter out = response.getWriter()) {
        /*
         * TODO Perform validation on the request parameters here
         */
        result = insertRow (request.getParameter("recipeNumber"),
                    request.getParameter("name"),
                    request.getParameter("description"),
                    request.getParameter("text"));
        out.println("<html>");
        out.println("<head>");
        out.println("<title>Servlet RecipeServlet</title>");
        out.println("</head>");
        out.println("<body>");
        out.println("<h1>Servlet RecipeServlet at " + request.
        getContextPath() + "</h1>");
        out.println("<br/><br/>");

        if(result > 0){
            out.println("<font color='green'>Record successfully
            inserted!</font>");
```

```
            out.println("<br/><br/><a href='/JakartaEERecipes/
            chapter01recipe01_19.jspx'>Insert another record</a>");
        } else {
            out.println("<font color='red'>Record NOT inserted!</font>");
            out.println("<br/><br/><a href='/JakartaEERecipes/
            chapter01recipe01_19.jspx'>Try Again</a>");
        }

        out.println("</body>");
        out.println("</html>");
    }
}

public int insertRow(String recipeNumber,
                     String name,
                     String description,
                     String text) {

    String sql = "INSERT INTO RECIPES VALUES(" +
                 "RECIPES_SEQ.NEXTVAL,?,?,?,?)";

    int result = -1;
    CreateConnection createConn = new CreateConnection();
    try(Connection conn = createConn.getConnection();
        PreparedStatement stmt = (PreparedStatement) conn.
        prepareStatement(sql)) {

        stmt.setString(1, recipeNumber);
        stmt.setString(2, name);
        stmt.setString(3, description);
        stmt.setString(4, text);
        // Returns row-count or 0 if not successful
        result = stmt.executeUpdate();
        if (result > 0){
            System.out.println("-- Record created --");
        } else {
```

```java
                System.out.println("!! Record NOT Created !!");
            }
        } catch (SQLException e) {
            e.printStackTrace();
        }
        return result;
    }

    @Override
    protected void doGet(HttpServletRequest request, HttpServletResponse
    response)
            throws ServletException, IOException {
        processRequest(request, response);
    }

    @Override
    protected void doPost(HttpServletRequest request, HttpServletResponse
    response)
            throws ServletException, IOException {
        processRequest(request, response);
    }

}
```

If the request is successful, the record will be inserted into the database, and the user will be able to click a link to add another record. Of course, in a real-life application, you would want to code some validation using JavaScript either within the input form or within the server-side Java code to help ensure database integrity.

How It Works

A fundamental task to almost every enterprise application is the use of a database input form. Database input forms make it easy for end users to populate database tables with data. When using JSP technology along with servlets, this operation can become fairly simple. As you have seen in the example for this recipe, writing a JSP input form is straightforward and can be coded using basic HTML. The key is to set up a Java servlet to receive a submitted request and process the records using the servlet. This provides an easy mechanism for separating web content from the application logic.

In the example, a JSP document named `recipe01_19.jspx` contains a standard HTML form with a method of `POST` and an action of `/JakartaEERecipes/RecipeServlet`. The input form contains four fields, which map to database columns into which the data will eventually be inserted. The input tags contain the name of four corresponding fields (`recipeNumber`, `name`, `description`, and `text`), which will be passed to the form action when submitted. As you can see, the only reference to the Java code is the name of the servlet that is contained within the form `action` attribute.

The Java servlet named `RecipeServlet` is responsible for obtaining the request parameters that were submitted via the JSP document, validating them accordingly (not shown in the example), and inserting them into the database. When the page is submitted, `RecipeServlet` is invoked, and the request is sent to the `doPost()` method since the HTML action method is `POST`. Both the `doGet` and `doPost()` methods are really just wrapper methods for a processing method named `processRequest()`, which is responsible for most of the work.

The `processRequest()` method is responsible for obtaining the request parameters, inserting them into the database, and sending a response to the client. A `PrintWriter` object is declared and created by making a call to `response.getWriter()` first because this object will be used later to help form the response that is sent to the client. Next, an `int` value named result is set up and initialized to `-1`. This variable will be used for determining whether the SQL insert worked or failed. After those declarations, a `try-catch` block is opened, and the first line of the `try` block is a call to the `insertRow()` method, passing the request parameters as values. The `result` variable is going to accept the `int` value that is returned from the execution of the `insertRows()` method, indicating whether the insert was successful:

```
result = insertRow (request.getParameter("recipeNumber"),
                    request.getParameter("name"),
                    request.getParameter("description"),
                    request.getParameter("text"));
```

As such, a SQL insert statement is assigned to a String named `sql`, and it is set up using the `PreparedStatement` format. Each question mark in the SQL string corresponds to a parameter that will be substituted in the string when the SQL is executed:

```
String sql = "INSERT INTO RECIPES VALUES(" +
                    "RECIPES_SEQ.NEXTVAL,?,?,?,?)";
```

Next, `PreparedStatement` and int values are initialized, and then a `try-catch-finally` block is opened, which will contain the SQL insert code. Within the block, a `Connection` object is created by calling a helper class named `CreateConnection`. If you want to read more about this helper class, then you can read Chapter 5 on JDBC. For now, all you need to know is that `CreateConnection` will return a database connection that can then be used to work with the database. If for some reason the connection fails, the `catch` block will be executed, followed by the `finally` block. A `PreparedStatement` object is created from the successful connection, and the SQL string that contains the database insert is assigned to it. Each of the request parameter values, in turn, is then set as a parameter to the `PreparedStatement`. Lastly, the `PreparedStatement`'s `executeUpdate()` method is called, which performs an insert to the database. The return value of `executeUpdate()` is assigned to the result variable and then returned to the `processRequest()` method. Once the control is returned to `processRequest()`, the servlet response is created using a series of `PrintWriter` statements. If the insert was successful, then a message indicating success is displayed. Likewise, if unsuccessful, then a message indicating failure is displayed.

Developing database input forms with JSP is fairly easy to do. To preserve the MVC structure, using a Java servlet for handing the request and database logic is the best choice.

1-20. Looping Through Database Records Within a Page

Problem

You want to display the records from a database table on your JSP page.

Solution

Encapsulate the database logic in a Java class and access it from the JSP page. Use the JSTL `c:forEach` element to iterate through the database rows and display them on the page. Two Java classes would be used for working with the data in this situation. One of the classes would represent the table, which you are querying from the database, and it would contain fields for each column in that table. Another JavaBean class would be used to contain the database business logic for querying the database.

The example for this recipe will display the first and last names of each author contained within the AUTHORS database table. The following code is used to create the JSP document that will display the data from the table using a standard HTML-based table along with the JSTL <c:forEach> tag to loop through the rows:

```
<html xmlns:jsp="http://xmlns.jcp.org/JSP/Page"
    xmlns:c="http://xmlns.jcp.org/jsp/jstl/core"
    version="2.0">

    <jsp:directive.page contentType="text/html" pageEncoding="UTF-8"/>
    <jsp:useBean id="authorBean" scope="session" class="org.
    jakartaeerecipes.chapter01.recipe01_20.AuthorBean"/>
    <head>
        <title>Recipe 1-20: Looping Through Database Records within a Page
        </title>
    </head>
    <body>
        <h1>Authors</h1>
        <p>
            The authors from the books which Josh Juneau has worked on are
            printed below.
        </p>
        <table border="1">

        <c:forEach items="${authorBean.authorList}" var="author">
            <tr>
                <td> ${ author.first } ${ author.last }</td>
            </tr>
        </c:forEach>
        </table>
    </body>
</html>
```

As you can see, <c:forEach> is used to loop through the items contained within ${authorBean.authorList}. Each item within the list is an object of type Author. The following Java code is that of the Author class, which is used for holding the data contained within each table row:

```java
package org.jakartaeerecipes.chapter01.recipe01_20;

public class Author implements java.io.Serializable {
    private int id;
    private String first;
    private String last;

    public Author(){
        id = -1;
        first = null;
        last = null;
    }
...
    // Getters And Setters
...
}
```

Lastly, the JSP document makes reference to a JavaBean named AuthorBean, which contains the business logic to query the data and return it as a list to the JSP page. The following code is what is contained within the AuthorBean class:

```java
package org.jakartaeerecipes.chapter01.recipe01_20;

import java.sql.Connection;
import java.sql.PreparedStatement;
import java.sql.ResultSet;
import java.sql.SQLException;
import java.util.ArrayList;
import java.util.List;
import org.jakartaeerecipes.common.CreateConnection;
import org.jakartaeerecipes.entity.BookAuthor;

public class AuthorBean implements java.io.Serializable {

    public static Connection conn = null;
    private List<Author> authorList = null;

    public AuthorBean(){

    }
```

```java
public List queryAuthors(){
    String sql = "SELECT ID, FIRSTNAME, LASTNAME FROM BOOK_AUTHOR";
    List <Author> authorList = new ArrayList<Author>();
    PreparedStatement stmt = null;
    ResultSet rs = null;
    int result = -1;
    try {
        CreateConnection createConn = new CreateConnection();
        conn = createConn.getConnection();
        stmt = (PreparedStatement) conn.prepareStatement(sql);

        // Returns row-count or 0 if not successful
        rs = stmt.executeQuery();
        System.out.println("executing statement");
        while (rs.next()){
            Author author = new Author();
            author.setId(rs.getInt("ID"));
            author.setFirst((rs.getString("FIRSTNAME")));
            author.setLast(rs.getString("LASTNAME"));
            authorList.add(author);
            System.out.println("got author: " + author);
        }

    } catch (SQLException e) {
        e.printStackTrace();
    } finally {
        if (stmt != null) {
            try {
                stmt.close();
            } catch (SQLException ex) {
                ex.printStackTrace();
            }
        }

    }
    return authorList;
}
```

```
public List getAuthorList(){
    authorList = queryAuthors();
    System.out.println("authorlist: " + authorList);
    return authorList;
}
}
```

The names of the authors contained within the records in the table will be displayed on the page.

How It Works

Almost any enterprise application performs some sort of database querying. Oftentimes results from a database query are displayed in a table format. The example in this recipe demonstrates how to query a database and return the results to a JSP page for display in a standard HTML table. The JSP page in this example makes use of the JSTL c:forEach element to iterate through the results of the database query. Note that there is more than one way to develop this type of database query using JSP; however, the format demonstrated in this recipe is most recommended for use in a production enterprise environment.

As mentioned previously, the JSP page in this recipe uses a combination of the jsp:useBean element and the c:forEach element to iterate over the results of a database query. The logic for querying the database resides within a server-side JavaBean class that is referenced within the jsp:useBean element on the page. In the example, the JavaBean is named AuthorBean, and it is responsible for querying a database table named AUTHORS and populating a list of Author objects with the results of the query. When the c:forEach element is evaluated with the items attribute set to ${authorBean. authorList }, it calls upon the JavaBean method named getAuthorList() because JSP expressions always append get() to a method call behind the scenes and also capitalize the first letter of the method name within the call. When the getAuthorList() method is called, the authorList field is populated via a call to queryAuthors(). The queryAuthors() method utilizes a Java Database Connectivity (JDBC) database call to obtain the authors from the AUTHORS table. A new Author object is created for each row returned by the database query, and each new Author object is, in turn, added to the authorList. In the end, the populated authorList contains a number of Author objects, and it is returned to the JSP page and iterated over utilizing the c:forEach element.

The `c:forEach` element contains an attribute named `var`, and this should be set equal to a string that will represent each element in the list that is being iterated over. The `var` is then used between the opening and closing `c:forEach` element tags to reference each element in the list, printing out each author's first and last names.

This recipe provides some insight on how to combine the power of JSTL tags with other technologies such as JDBC to produce very useful results. To learn more about the different JSTL tags that are part of JSP, please visit the online documentation at `www.oracle.com/technetwork/java/jstl-137486.html`. To learn more about JDBC, please read Chapter 5 of this book.

1-21. Handling JSP Errors

Problem

You want to display a nicely formatted error page if a JSP page encounters an error.

Solution

Create a standard error page, and forward control to the error page if an exception occurs within the JSP page. The following JSP document, in JSP format (not JSPX), demonstrates a standard error page to display if an error occurs within a JSP application. If an exception occurs within any JSP page in the application, the following error page will be displayed.

Note   The example in the solution for this recipe uses the JSTL `fmt` library, which provides convenient access to formatting capabilities that allow for localization of text as well as date and number formatting. Text localization capabilities allow locales to be set so that text can be formatted into different languages, depending upon the user locale. Tags used for date manipulation make it easy for developers to format dates and times easily within a JSP page and also provide a way to parse dates and times for data input. Lastly, number-formatting tags provide a way to format and parse numeric data within pages. To learn more about the JSTL `fmt` tag library, please refer to the online documentation at `https://jakarta.ee/specifications/platform/8/apidocs/javax/servlet/jsp/jstl/fmt/package-summary.html`.

```
<%@page contentType="text/html" pageEncoding="UTF-8"%>
<%@ page isErrorPage="true" %>
<%@ taglib uri="http://xmlns.jcp.org/jsp/jstl/core"
    prefix="c" %>
<%@ taglib uri="http:/xmlns.jcp.org/jsp/jstl/fmt"
    prefix="fmt" %>
<!DOCTYPE html>
<html>
    <head>
        <meta http-equiv="Content-Type" content="text/html; charset=UTF-8">
        <title>JSP Error Page</title>
    </head>
    <body>
        <h1>Error Encountered</h1>
        <br/>
        <br/>
        <p>
            The application has encountered the following error:
            <br/>
            <fmt:message key="ServerError"/>: ${pageContext.errorData.
             statusCode}

        </p>
    </body>
</html>
```

For example, the following JSP would create an error (NullPointerException) if the parameter designated as param is null. If this occurs, the indicated error page would be displayed:

```
<html xmlns:jsp="http://xmlns.jcp.org/JSP/Page"
    xmlns:c="http://xmlns.jcp.org/jsp/jstl/core"
    version="2.0">

    <jsp:directive.page contentType="text/html" pageEncoding="UTF-8"/>
    <jsp:directive.page errorPage="recipe01_21_errorPage.jsp"/>
```

```
<head>
    <title>Recipe 1-21: Handling JSP Errors</title>
</head>
<body>
    <h1>There is an error on this page</h1>
    <p>
        This will produce an error:
        <jsp:scriptlet>
         if (request.getParameter("param").equals("value")) {
            System.out.println("test");
         }
        </jsp:scriptlet>
    </p>
</body>

</html>
```

How It Works

One of the most annoying issues for users while working with applications is when an error is thrown. A nasty, long stack trace is often produced, and the user is left with no idea how to resolve the error. It is better to display a nice and user-friendly error page when such an error occurs. The JSP technology allows an error page to be designated by adding a page directive to each JSP page that may produce an error. The directive should designate an error page that will be displayed if the page containing the directive produces an error.

The second JSP document in the solution to this recipe demonstrates a JSP page that will throw an error if the parameter being requested within the page is null. If this were to occur and there was no error page specified, then a `NullPointerException` error message would be displayed. However, this JSP indicates an error page by designating it within a page directive using the following syntax:

```
<jsp:directive.page errorPage="recipe01_21_errorPage.jsp"/>
```

When an error occurs on the example page, `recipe01_21.errorPage.jsp` is displayed. The first JSP document listed in the solution to this recipe contains the sources for the `recipe01_21.errorPage.jsp` page. It is flagged as an error page because it includes a page directive indicating as such:

```
<%@ page isErrorPage="true" %>
```

An error page is able to determine the error code, status, exception, and an array of other information by using the pageContext implicit object. In the example, the `${pageContext.errorData.statusCode}` expression is used to display the status code of the exception. Table 1-7 displays the other possible pieces of information that can be gleaned from the pageContext object.

Table 1-7. *pageContext Implicit Object Exception Information*

Expression	Value
pageContext.errorData	Provides access to the error information
pageContext.exception	Returns the current value of the exception object
pageContext.errorData.requestURI	Returns the request URI
pageContext.errorData.servletName	Returns the name of the servlet invoked
pageContext.errorData.statusCode	Returns the error status code
pageContext.errorData.throwable	Returns the throwable that caused the error

Providing user-friendly error pages in any application can help create a more usable and overall more functional experience for the end user. JSP and Java technology provide robust exception handling and mechanisms that can be used to help users and administrators alike when exceptions occur.

1-22. Disabling Scriptlets in Pages

Problem

You want to ensure that Java code cannot be embedded into JSP pages within your web application.

Solution

Set the scripting-invalid element within the web deployment descriptor to true. The following excerpt from a web.xml deployment descriptor demonstrates how to do so:

```
<jsp-config>
    <jsp-property-group>
        <scripting-invalid>true</scripting-invalid>
    </jsp-property-group>
</jsp-config>
```

How It Works

When working in an environment that encourages the use of the Model-View-Controller architecture, it can be useful to prohibit the use of scriptlets within JSP pages and documents. When JSP 2.1 was released, it provided solutions to help developers move Java code out of JSP pages and into server-side Java classes where it belonged. In the early years of JSP, pages were cluttered with scriptlets and markup. This made it difficult for developers to separate business logic from content, and it was hard to find good tools to help develop such pages effectively. JSP 2.1 introduced tags, which make it possible to eliminate the use of scriptlets within JSP pages, and this helps maintain the use of the MVC architecture.

To prohibit the use of scriptlets within JSP pages in an application, add the jsp-config element within the web.xml file of the application of which you want to enforce the rule. Add a subelement of jsp-property-group along with the scripting-invalid element. The value of the scripting-invalid element should be set to true.

1-23. Ignoring EL in Pages

Problem

You want to turn off EL expression translation within your JSP page so that older applications will be able to pass through expressions verbatim.

Solution #1

Escape the EL expressions within the page by using the \ character before any expressions. For instance, the following expressions will be ignored because the \ character appears before them:

```
\${elBean.myProperty}
\${2 + 4}
```

Solution #2

Configure a JSP property group within the web.xml file for the application. Within the web.xml file, a <jsp-property-group> element can contain child elements that characterize how the JSP page evaluates specified items. By including an <el-ignored>true</el-ignored> element, all EL within the application's JSP documents will be ignored and treated as literals. The following excerpt from web.xml demonstrates this feature:

```
<jsp-property-group>
     <el-ignored>true</el-ignored>
 </jsp-property-group>
```

Solution #3

Include a page directive including the isELIgnored attribute, and set it to true. The following page directive can be placed at the top of a given JSP document to allow each EL expression to be treated as a literal:

```
<jsp:directive.page isELIgnored="true"/>
```

or in a standard JSP:

```
<%@ page isELIgnored="true" %>
```

How It Works

There may be a situation in which the evaluation of JSP EL expressions should be turned off. This occurs most often in cases of legacy applications using older versions of JSP technology; EL expressions were not yet available. There are a few different ways to turn off the evaluation of EL expressions, and this recipe demonstrates each of them.

In the first solution to this recipe, the escape technique is demonstrated. An EL expression can be escaped by placing the \ character directly before the expression, as shown in the example. Doing so will cause the JSP interpreter to treat the expression as a string literal, and the output on the page will be the expression itself, rather than its evaluation. The second solution to this recipe demonstrates adding a jsp-property-group to the web.xml deployment descriptor in order to ignore EL. All EL within an application will be ignored by including the isELIgnored element and providing a true value for it. Lastly, the final solution demonstrates how to ignore EL on a page-by-page basis by including a page directive with the isELIgnored attribute set to true.

Each of the different solutions for ignoring EL allows coverage to different parts of the application. The solution you choose should depend upon how broadly you want to ignore EL throughout an application.

CHAPTER 2

JavaServer Faces Fundamentals

In 2004 Sun Microsystems introduced a Java web framework called JavaServer Faces (JSF) in an effort to help simplify web application development. It is an evolution of the JavaServer Pages (JSP) framework, adding a more organized development life cycle and the ability to more easily utilize modern web technologies.

JSF uses XML files for view construction and uses Java classes for application logic, making it adhere to the Model-View-Controller (MVC) architecture. JSF is request-driven, and each request is processed by a special servlet named the `FacesServlet`. The `FacesServlet` is responsible for building the component trees, processing events, determining which view to process next, and rendering the response. JSF 1.x used a special resource file named the `faces-config.xml` file for specifying application details such as navigation rules, registering listeners, and so on. While the `faces-config.xml` file can still be used in JSF 2.x, the more modern releases of JSF have focused on being easy to use, minimizing the amount of XML configuration, and utilizing annotations in place of XML where possible.

The framework is very powerful, including easy integration with technologies such as Ajax and making it effortless to develop dynamic, and even stateless, content. JSF works well with databases, using JDBC, EJB, or REST technology to work with the backend. Java classes known as JSF *controllers* are used for application logic and support the dynamic content within each view. They can adhere to different life spans depending upon the scope that is used. Views can invoke methods within the controllers to perform actions such as data manipulation and form processing. Utilizing Contexts and Dependency Injection (CDI), properties can also be declared within the controllers and

95

exposed within the views, providing a convenient way to pass request values. JSF allows developers to customize their applications with preexisting validation and conversion tags that can be used on components with the view. It is also easy to build custom validators, as well as custom components.

This chapter includes recipes that will be useful for those who are getting started with JSF and also those who are looking to beef up their basic knowledge using the latest features of the framework. You will learn how to create controllers, work with standard components, and handle page navigation. There are also recipes that cover useful techniques such as building custom validators and creating bookmarkable URLs. The recipes are refined to include the most current techniques and provide the most useful methodologies for using them. After studying the recipes in this chapter, you will be ready to build standard JSF applications, sprinkling in some custom features as well.

Note   Many people prefer to work within an integrated development environment (IDE) for increased productivity. To get started with learning how to create a new JSF project and manage it with the Apache NetBeans IDE, please see the appendix of this book.

2-1. Writing a Simple JSF Application
Problem

You want to get up and running quickly by creating a simple JSF application.

Solution #1

Create a simple JSF web application that is comprised of a single XHTML page and a single JSF controller. The application in this recipe simply displays a message that is initialized within a JSF controller.

Note   It is recommended that you utilize a Java IDE to make life easier. If you have not yet created a JSF application and are interested in learning how to create one from scratch with an IDE, then please see Solution #2 to this recipe. This book features the Apache NetBeans IDE, a cutting-edge Java development environment that is usually the first to support new Java features. However, there are many excellent IDE choices. You can choose the IDE you want and follow along with its instructions for working with JSF.

Displaying a JSF Controller Field Value

The following code makes up the XHTML view that will be used to display the JSF managed bean field value:

```
<html xmlns="http://www.w3.org/1999/xhtml"
    xmlns:f="http://xmlns.jcp.org/jsf/core"
    xmlns:h="http://xmlns.jcp.org/jsf/html">
  <h:head>
      <meta http-equiv="Content-Type" content="text/html;
      charset=UTF-8"/>
      <title>Recipe 2-1:  A Simple JSF Application</title>
  </h:head>
  <h:body>
      <p>
          This simple application utilizes a request-scoped JSF managed bean
          to display the message below. If you change the message within the
          managed bean's constructor and then recompile the application, the
          new message appears.
          <br/>
          <br/>
          #{helloWorldController.hello}
          <br/>
          or
          <br/>
```

```
            <h:outputText id="helloMessage" value="#{helloWorldController.
            hello}"/>
        </p>
    </h:body>
</html>
```

As you can see, the JSF page utilizes a JSF expression, #{helloWorldController.hello}. Much like JSP technology, a backing JavaBean, originally referred to as a *JSF managed bean,* but since JSF 2.0+ as the *controller class,* is referenced in the expression along with the field to expose.

Examining the JSF Controller

The following code is that of HelloWorldController, the JSF controller for this recipe example:

```
package org.jakartaeerecipes.chapter02.recipe02_01;

import java.io.Serializable;
import javax.annotation.PostConstruct;
import javax.inject.Named;
import javax.enterprise.context.RequestScoped;

@Named(value = "helloWorldController")
@RequestScoped
public class HelloWorldController implements Serializable {

    private String hello;

    /**
     * Creates a new instance of HelloWorldController
     */
    public HelloWorldController() {

    }

    @PostConstruct
    public void init(){
        System.out.println ("Instantiated helloWorldController");
```

```
        hello = "Hello World";
    }

    /**
     * @return the hello
     */
    public String getHello() {
        return hello;
    }

    /**
     * @param hello the hello to set
     */
    public void setHello(String hello) {
        this.hello = hello;
    }
}
```

Note   Prior to JSF 2.0, in order to enable the JSF servlet to translate the XHTML page, you needed to ensure that the web.xml file contained a servlet element indicating the javax.faces.webapp.FacesServlet class and its associated servlet-mapping URL. Since the release of JSF 2.0, if using a Servlet 3.x container, the FacesServlet is automatically mapped for you, so there is no requirement to adjust the web.xml configuration.

The listing that follows is an excerpt taken from the web.xml file for the sources to this book, and it demonstrates the features that must be added to the web.xml file in order to make the JSF application function properly in a pre–JSF 2.0 environment:

```
...
<servlet>
    <servlet-name>Faces Servlet</servlet-name>
    <servlet-class>javax.faces.webapp.FacesServlet</servlet-class>
    <load-on-startup>1</load-on-startup>
  </servlet>
    ...
```

```
<servlet-mapping>
  <servlet-name>Faces Servlet</servlet-name>
  <url-pattern>/faces/*</url-pattern>
</servlet-mapping>
...
<welcome-file-list>
  <welcome-file>faces/index.xhtml</welcome-file>
</welcome-file-list>
```

Let's take a deeper look at the web.xml configuration for a JSF application. It is not very complex, but a few elements could use some explanation. The javax.faces.webapp.FacesServlet servlet can optionally be declared within the web.xml file. If declared, the declaration must contain a servlet-name; the servlet-class element, which lists the fully qualified class name; and a load-on-startup value of *1* to ensure that the servlet is loaded when the application is started up by the container. The web.xml file must then map that servlet to a given URL within a servlet-mapping element. The servlet-mapping element must include the servlet-name, which is the same value as the servlet-name element that is contained in the servlet declaration, and a url-pattern element, which specifies the URL that will be used to map JSF pages with the servlet. When a URL is specified that contains the /faces/ mapping, the FacesServlet will be used to translate the view.

To load the application in your browser, visit http://localhost:8080/JakartaEERecipes/faces/chapter02/recipe02_01.xhtml, and you will see the following text:

This simple application utilizes a request-scoped JSF controller class to display the message below. If you change the "hello" variable within the controller class's constructor and then recompile and run the application, the new message appears.

```
Hello World
or
Hello World
```

Solution #2

Use an IDE, such as Apache NetBeans, to create a JSF application. To get started with Apache NetBeans, first download the most recent release from the https://netbeans.apache.org web site. The examples in this solution make use of Apache NetBeans 11.x. For more information about downloading and installing Apache NetBeans, please see the appendix of this book. Once installed, create a new project by clicking the "File" ➤ "New Project" menu.

Follow the directions in the book's appendix (in the "Creating an Apache NetBeans Java Web Project" section). Once completed, the index.xhtml file will open in the editor, which will be the default landing page for your application. Modify the index.xhtml file by making the page the same as the JSF view that is listed in Solution #1's "Displaying a JSF Controller Field Value" section. Once done, add the controller class to your application that will be used to supply the business logic for the index.xhtml page. To create the controller class, right-click the Source Packages navigation menu for your project, and choose "New" ➤ "JSF Controller Class" from the context menu. This will open the "New JSF Controller Class" dialog (Figure 2-1), which will allow you to specify several options for your controller, including the name, location, and scope.

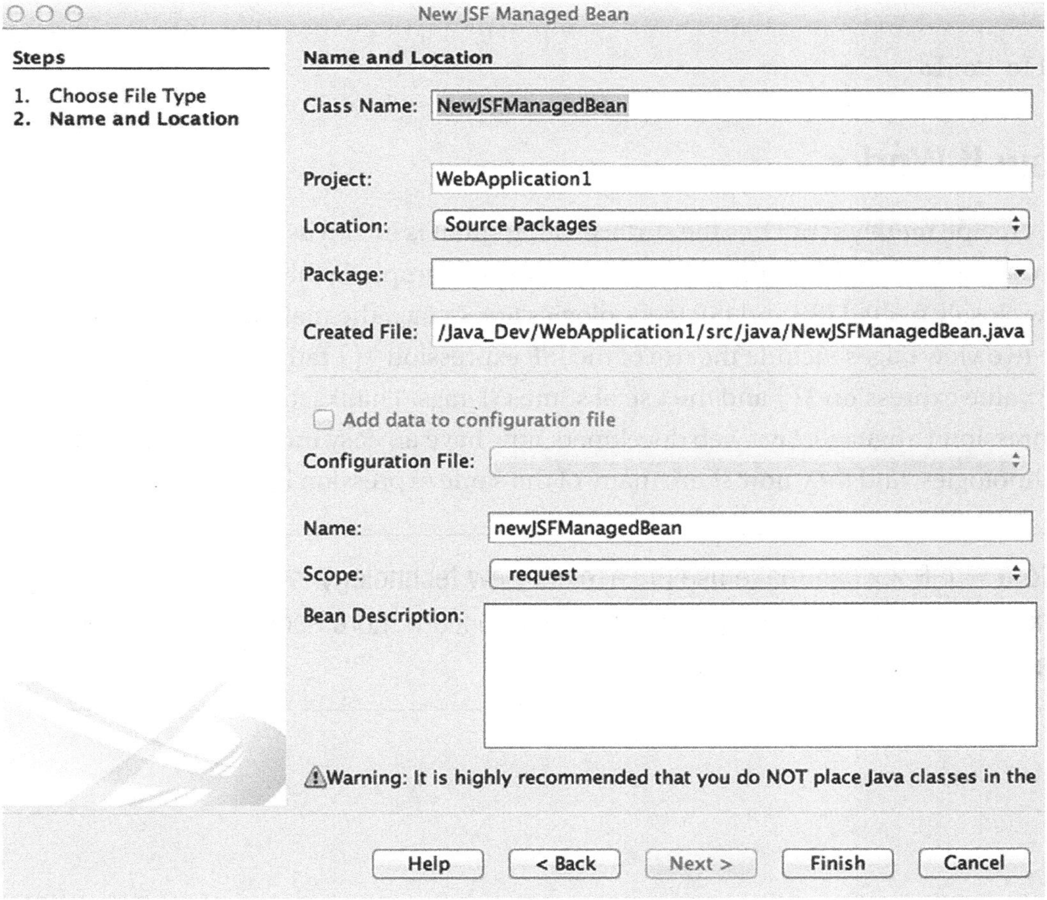

Figure 2-1. *New JSF controller class via the "New JSF Controller Class" dialog*

For the purposes of this recipe, change the name of the class to `HelloWorldController`, and leave the rest of the options at their defaults; then click Finish. Copy and paste the code from Solution #1's "Examining the JSF Controller" section into the newly created controller class. Once finished, right-click the application project from the Project navigation menu and choose Deploy to deploy your application.

To load the application in your browser, visit `http://localhost:8080/WebApplication1/faces/index.xhtml`, and you will see the following text:

```
This simple application utilizes a request-scoped JSF controller to
display the message below. If you change the "hello" variable within the
controller's constructor and then recompile and run the application, the
new message appears.
```

```
Hello World
or
Hello World
```

How It Works

This recipe merely scratches the surface of JSF, but it is meant as a starting point to guide you along the path of becoming a JSF expert. The example in this recipe demonstrates how closely related JSF and JSP technologies are. In fact, the main differences between the two view pages include the use of the JSF expression #{} rather than the standard JSP value expression ${} and the use of some JSF tags. Thanks to the JSP 2.0 Unified Expression Language, Java web developers now have an easy transition between the two technologies, and they now share many of the same expression language features.

Note   JSF 2.x can make use of Facelets view technology to produce even more sophisticated and organized designs. To learn more about Facelets view technology, please refer to Chapter 3.

Breaking Down a JSF Application

Now for the real reason you are reading this recipe...the explanation for building a JSF application! A JSF application is comprised of the following parts:

- If using or maintaining JSF applications written using JSF 1.x, the `web.xml` deployment descriptor that is responsible for mapping the `FacesServlet` instance to a URL path.

- One or more web pages on which JSF components are used to provide the page layout (may or may not utilize Facelets view technology). Typically these web pages are referred to as "views."

- JSF component tags within the views.

- One or more controller classes, which are simple, lightweight container-managed objects that are responsible for supporting page constructs and basic services.

- Optionally, one or more configuration files such as `faces-config.xml` that can be used to define navigation rules and configure beans and other custom objects.

- Optionally, supporting objects such as listeners, converters, or custom components.

- Optionally, custom tags for use on a JSF view.

LIFE CYCLE OF A JSF APPLICATION

The JSF view processing life cycle contains six stages. These stages are as follows:

1. Restore View

2. Apply Request Values

3. Process Validations

4. Update Model Values

5. Invoke Application

6. Render Response

Restore View is the first phase in the JSF life cycle, and it is responsible for constructing the view. The component tree then applies the request parameters to each of the corresponding component values using the component tree's decode method. This occurs during the Apply Request Values phase. During this phase, any value conversion errors will be added to FacesContext for display as error messages during the Render Response phase. Next, all of the validations are processed. During the Process Validations phase, each component that has a registered validator is examined, and local values are compared to the validation rules. If any validation errors arise, the Render Response phase is entered, rendering the page with the corresponding validation errors.

If the Process Validations phase exits without errors, the Update Model Values phase begins. During this phase, controller class properties are set for each of the corresponding input components within the tree that contains local values. Once again, if any errors occur, then the Render Response phase is entered, rendering the page with the corresponding errors displayed. After the successful completion of the Update Model Values phase, the application-level events are handled during the Invoke Application phase. Such events include page submits or redirects to other pages. Finally, the Render Response phase occurs, and the page is rendered to the user. If the application is using JSP pages, then the JSF implementation allows the JSP container to render the page.

The example in this recipe uses the minimum number of these parts. To run the example, you will need to ensure that the web.xml file contains the proper JSF configuration if running in a pre–JSF 2.*x* environment. You will need to have a controller declaring the field that is exposed on the JSF view along with the necessary accessor methods to make it work properly. And lastly, you will need to have the XHTML JSF view page containing the JSF expression that exposes the field that is declared within the controller class.

A JSF controller class is a lightweight, container-managed object that is associated with a JSF view. The controller class is much like a JSP JavaBean in that it provides the application logic for a particular page so that Java code does not need to be embedded into the view code. Components (aka JSF tags) that are used within a JSF view are mapped to server-side fields and methods contained within the JSF controller. Controller classes are indeed the controllers for the view logic. In the example, the JSF controller class is named HelloWorldController, and a field named hello is declared, exposing itself to the public via the getHello() and setHello() methods. The JSF controller class is instantiated and initialized when a view that contains a reference to the bean is requested, and the controller class scope determines the life span of the bean. In the case of this example, the controller class contains a request scope, via the `javax.enterprise.context.RequestScoped` annotation. Therefore, its life span is that of a single request, and it is re-instantiated each time a request is made. In this case, when the page in the example is reloaded. To learn more about the scope and annotations that are available for a controller class, please see Recipe 2-2.

JSF technology utilizes a web view declaration framework known as Facelets. Facelets uses a special set of XML tags, similar in style to the standard JSF tags, to help build componentized web views. While this example does not use Facelets, it is a vital part of JSF view technology. Facelets pages typically use XHTML, which is an HTML page that is comprised of well-formed XML components. The example JSF view in this recipe is well structured, and it contains two JSF EL expressions that are responsible for instantiating the controller class and displaying the content for the `hello` field. When the EL expression `#{helloWorldController.hello}` is translated by the `FacesServlet`, it makes the call to the `HelloWorldController`'s `getHello()` method.

Lots of information was thrown at you within this introductory recipe. The simple example in this recipe provides a good starting point for working with JSF technology. Continue with the recipes in this chapter to gain a broader knowledge of each component that is used for developing JavaServer Faces web applications.

2-2. Writing a Controller Class
Problem

You want to reference field values contained within a server-side Java class from your JSF application web views.

Solution

Develop a JSF controller class, a lightweight container-managed component, which will provide the application logic for use within your JSF application web pages. The example in this recipe is comprised of a JSF view and a JSF controller class. The application calculates two numbers that are entered by the user and then adds, subtracts, multiplies, or divides them depending upon the user's selection. The following code is the controller class that is responsible for declaring fields for each of the numbers that will be entered by the user, as well as a field for the result of the calculation. The controller class is also responsible for creating a list of Strings that will be displayed within an h:selectOneMenu element within the JSF view and retaining the value that is chosen by the user.

Although it may seem as though this controller class is doing a lot of work, it actually is very simple to make it happen! The controller class is really a beefed-up Plain Old Java Object (POJO) that includes some methods that can be called from JSF view components.

Controller Class

The following code is for the controller class that is used for the calculation example. The class is named CalculationController, and it is referenced as calculationController from within the JSF view.

Note   JSF uses convention over configuration for its naming conventions. By default, JSF views can contain EL that references a controller class by specifying the class name with the first character in lowercase.

```
package org.jakartaeerecipes.chapter02.recipe02_02;

import java.io.Serializable;
import java.util.ArrayList;
import java.util.List;
import javax.enterprise.context.SessionScoped;
import javax.faces.application.FacesMessage;
import javax.faces.context.FacesContext;
import javax.faces.model.SelectItem;
import javax.inject.Named;

@Named
@SessionScoped
public class CalculationController implements Serializable {

    private int num1;
    private int num2;
    private int result;
    private String calculationType;
```

```java
private static final String ADDITION = "Addition";
private static final String SUBTRACTION = "Subtraction";
private static final String MULTIPLICATION = "Multiplication";
private static final String DIVISION = "Division";
List<SelectItem> calculationList;

/**
 * Creates a new instance of CalculationController
 */
public CalculationController() {
    // Initialize variables
    num1 = 0;
    num2 = 0;
    result = 0;
    calculationType = null;
    // Initialize the list of values for the SelectOneMenu
    populateCalculationList();
    System.out.println("initialized the bean!");
}

. . .
/**
 * Getters and Setters
 */
. . .

public List<SelectItem> getCalculationList(){
    return calculationList;
}

private void populateCalculationList(){
    calculationList = new ArrayList<>();
    calculationList.add(new SelectItem(ADDITION));
    calculationList.add(new SelectItem(SUBTRACTION));
    calculationList.add(new SelectItem(MULTIPLICATION));
    calculationList.add(new SelectItem(DIVISION));
}
```

```java
    public void performCalculation() {
        switch (getCalculationType()) {
            case ADDITION:
                setResult(num1 + num2);
                break;
            case SUBTRACTION:
                setResult(num1 - num2);
                break;
            case MULTIPLICATION:
                setResult(num1 * num2);
                break;
            case DIVISION:
                try{
                    setResult(num1 / num2);
                } catch (Exception ex){
                    FacesMessage facesMsg = new FacesMessage(FacesMessage.
                    SEVERITY_ERROR, "Invalid Calculation", "Invalid
                    Calculation");
                    FacesContext.getCurrentInstance().addMessage(null,
                    facesMsg);
                }   break;
            default:
                break;
        }
    }
}
```

Next is the view, which is composed within an XHTML document and is well-formed XML.

JSF View

The view contains JSF components that are displayed as text boxes into which the user can enter information, a pick-list of different calculation types for the user to choose from, a component responsible for displaying the result of the calculation, and an h:commandButton component for submitting the form values:

```xml
<?xml version="1.0" encoding="UTF-8"?>
<!DOCTYPE html PUBLIC "-//W3C//DTD XHTML 1.0 Strict//EN"
"http://www.w3.org/TR/xhtml1/DTD/xhtml1-strict.dtd">
<html xmlns="http://www.w3.org/1999/xhtml"
    xmlns:f="http://xmlns.jcp.org/jsf/core"
    xmlns:h="http://xmlns.jcp.org/jsf/html">
  <h:head>
      <meta http-equiv="Content-Type" content="text/html;
      charset=UTF-8"/>
      <title>Recipe 2-2:  Writing a JSF Managed Bean</title>
  </h:head>
  <h:body>
      <f:view>

          <h2>Perform a Calculation</h2>
          <p>
              Use the following form to perform a calculation on two
              numbers.
              <br/>
              Enter
              the numbers in the two text fields below, and select a
              calculation to
              <br/>
              perform, then hit the "Calculate" button.
              <br/>
              <br/>
              <h:messages errorStyle="color: red" infoStyle="color:
              green" globalOnly="true"/>
              <br/>
              <h:form id="calculationForm">
                  Number1:
                  <h:inputText id="num1" value="#{calculationController.
                  num1}"/>
                  <br/>
```

```
Number2:
<h:inputText id="num2" value="#{calculationController.
num2}"/>
<br/>
<br/>
Calculation Type:
<h:selectOneMenu id="calculationType"
value="#{calculationController.calculationType}">
    <f:selectItems value="#{calculationController.
    calculationList}"/>
</h:selectOneMenu>
<br/>
<br/>
Result:
<h:outputText id="result"
value="#{calculationController.result}"/>
<br/>
<br/>
<h:commandButton action="#{calculationController.
performCalculation()}" value="Calculate"/>
        </h:form>
    </p>
  </f:view>
 </h:body>
</html>
```

The resulting JSF view looks like Figure 2-2 when displayed to the user.

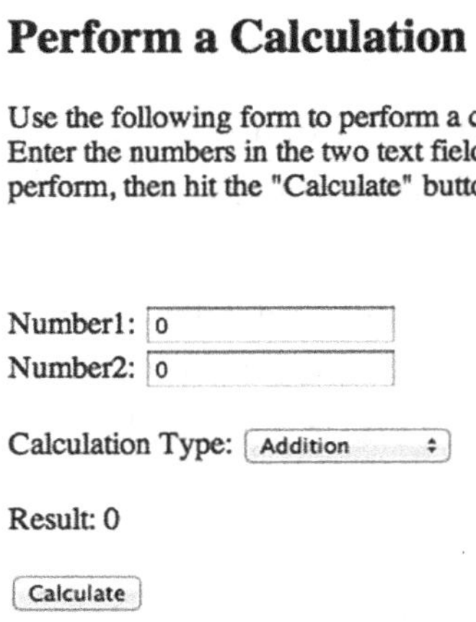

Perform a Calculation

Use the following form to perform a calculation on two numbers.
Enter the numbers in the two text fields below, and select a calculation to
perform, then hit the "Calculate" button.

Number1: `0`
Number2: `0`

Calculation Type: [Addition ⁢]

Result: 0

[Calculate]

Figure 2-2. *Resulting JSF view page*

How It Works

The JSF CDI controller class is responsible for providing the application logic for a
JSF-based web application. Much like the JavaBean is to a JSP, the controller class is
the backbone for a JSF view. They may also be referred to as *backing beans* or *managed
beans*, because there is typically one JSF controller class per JSF view. Controller
classes have changed a bit since the JSF technology was first introduced. There used
to be configuration required for each controller class within a `faces-config.xml`
configuration file and also within the `web.xml` file for use with some application servers.
Starting with the release of JSF 2.0, the controller class became easier to use, and coding
powerful JSF applications is easier than ever. This book, and Jakarta EE, focuses on
newer controller class technology.

The example for this recipe demonstrates many of the most important features
of a JSF controller class. The view components refer to the controller class as
`calculationController`. By default, a JSF controller class can be referred to within a
JSF view using the name of the bean class with a lowercase first letter. A controller class
must be annotated with `@Named` in order to mark it as an injectable CDI bean. Using the
`@Named` annotation, the string that is used to reference the bean from within a view can
be changed. In the example, `calculationController` is also used as the name passed
to the `@Named` annotation, but it could have easily been some other string. The `@Named`
annotation should be placed before the class declaration:

```
@Named(value="calculationController")
```

Scopes

The bean in the example will be initialized when it is first accessed by a session and destroyed when the session is terminated. It is a controller class that "lives" with the session. The scope of the bean is configured by an annotation on the class, just before the class declaration. There are different annotations that can be used for each available scope. In this case, the annotation is @SessionScoped, denoting that the controller class is session scoped. All of the possible controller class scopes are listed within Table 2-1.

Table 2-1. *Controller Class Scopes*

Scope Annotation	Description
@ApplicationScoped	Specifies that a bean is application scoped. Initialized when the application is started up. Destroyed when the application is shut down. Controller classes with this scope are available to all application constructs within the same application.
@RequestScoped	Specifies that a bean is request scoped in a web application context. Initialized when an HTTP request to the bean is made and destroyed when the request is complete.
@SessionScoped	Specifies that a bean is session scoped in a web application context. Initialized when first accessed within a session. Destroyed when the session ends. Available to all servlet requests that are made within the same session.
@ConversationScoped	Specifies that a bean is conversation scoped. A conversation is a series of HTTP requests and responses that occur in a step-by-step manner, in order to complete a process. This application scope is specific to web application contexts. Initialized when a conversation is started and destroyed when the conversation ends. Controllers with this scope are available throughout the life cycle of a conversation and belong to a single HTTP session. If the HTTP session ends, all conversation contexts that were created during the session are destroyed.

(continued)

Table 2-1. (*continued*)

Scope Annotation	Description
@Singleton	This is a pseudo-scope, meaning that it is not proxied as with other CDI scopes. This scope specifies that only one instance of the bean will exist for the entire application.
@Dependent	This is a pseudo-scope, meaning that it is not proxied as with other CDI scopes. Beans that use this scope behave differently than a controller class containing any of the other scopes.
@TransactionScoped	Life of a bean annotated with this scope indicates that the life span will exist for the duration of an active transaction. The first time a CDI bean uses a controller with this annotation in a session, the same instance will be used throughout the transaction.
@FlowScoped	Beans of this scope are used within the context of a JSF flow. The bean will be instantiated the first time it is accessed within the scope of a flow, and it will be destroyed once the flow is complete.
@ViewScoped	This scope indicates that the bean will remain available throughout the life of the JSF view.

The @Named annotation specifies to the application server container that the class is a CDI bean. Prior to JSF 2.0, a controller class had to be declared within the faces-config.xml file, and they were annotated with @ManagedBean until JSF 2.2+. The addition of annotations has made JSF controller class XML configuration-free. It is important to note that the controller class implements java.io.Serializable; all controller classes should be specified as serializable so that they can be persisted to disk by the container if necessary.

Fields declared within a controller should be specified as private in order to adhere to object-oriented methodology. To make a field accessible to the public and usable from JSF views, accessor methods should be declared for it. Any field that has a corresponding "getter" and "setter" is known as a JSF controller class *property*. Properties are available for use within JSF views by utilizing lvalue JSF EL expressions, meaning that the expression is contained within the #{ and } character sequences and that it is readable and writable. lvalue expressions can specify targets, whereas rvalue expressions cannot. For instance, to access the field num1 that is declared within the controller class, the JSF view can use the #{calculationController.num1} expression, as you can see in the JSF view code for the example.

Any public method contained within a JSF controller class is accessible from within a JSF view using the same EL expression syntax, that is, by specifying #{beanName.methodName} as the expression. In the example for this recipe, the performCalculation method of the controller class is invoked from within the JSF view using a h:commandButton JSF component. The component action is equal to the EL expression that will invoke the JSF controller class method. To learn more about JSF components and how to use them in view, please see Recipe 2-3 and Chapter 3:

```
<h:commandButton action="#{calculationController.performCalculation}"
value="Calculate"/>
```

Note   The input form tag for this example contains no action attribute. JSF forms do not contain action attributes since JSF components within the view are responsible for specifying the action method, rather than the form itself.

JSF controller classes are a fundamental part of the JSF web framework. They provide the means for developing dynamic, robust, and sophisticated web applications with the Java platform.

2-3. Building Sophisticated JSF Views with Components

Problem

You want to create a sophisticated user interface comprised of pre-bundled components.

Solution

Make use of bundled JSF components within your JSF views. JSF components contain bundled application logic and view constructs, including styles and JavaScript actions, that can be used within applications by merely adding tags to a view. In the following example, several JSF components are used to create a view that displays the authors for an Apress book and allows for a new author to be added to the list. The following code is the XHTML for the JSF view:

```
<!DOCTYPE html PUBLIC "-//W3C//DTD XHTML 1.0 Strict//EN"
"http://www.w3.org/TR/xhtml1/DTD/xhtml1-strict.dtd">
<html xmlns="http://www.w3.org/1999/xhtml"
      xmlns:f="http://xmlns.jcp.org/jsf/core"
      xmlns:h="http://xmlns.jcp.org/jsf/html">
    <h:head>
        <meta http-equiv="Content-Type" content="text/html;
        charset=UTF-8"/>
        <title>Recipe 2-3: Building Sophisticated JSF Views with
        Components</title>
    </h:head>
    <h:body>
        <h:form id="componentForm">
            <h1>JSF Components, Creating a Sophisticated Page</h1>
            <p>
                The view for this page is made up entirely of JSF standard
                components.
                <br/>As you can see, there are many useful components
                bundled with JSF out of the box.
                <br/>
            </p>
            <p>Book Recommendation:  Java 9 Recipes
                <br/>
                <h:graphicImage id="java9recipes" library="image"
                name="java9recipes.png"/>
                <br/>

                <h:dataTable id="authorTable" value="#{authorController.
                authorList}"
                              var="author">
                    <f:facet name="header">
                        Java 9 Recipes Authors
                    </f:facet>
                    <h:column>
                    <h:outputText id="authorName" value="#{author.first}
                    #{author.last}"/>
```

```
                    </h:column>
                </h:dataTable>
                <br/>
                <br/>
                <p>
                    Use the following form to add an author to the list.
                </p>
                <h:outputLabel for="newAuthorFirst" value="New Author
                First Name: "/>
                <h:inputText id="newAuthorFirst" value="#{authorController.
                newAuthorLast}"/>
                <br/>
                <h:outputLabel for="newAuthorLast" value="New Author Last
                Name: "/>
                <h:inputText id="newAuthorLast" value="#{authorController.
                newAuthorLast}"/>
                <br/>
                <h:inputTextarea id="bio" cols="20" rows="5"
                                 value="#{authorController.bio}"/>
                <br/>
                <br/>
                <h:commandButton id="addAuthor" action="#{authorController.
                addAuthor}"
                                 value="Add Author"/>
                <br/>
                <br/>
            </p>
        </h:form>
    </h:body>
</html>
```

This example utilizes a JSF controller class named AuthorController. The controller class declares a handful of properties that are exposed in the view, and it also declares and populates a list of authors that is displayed on the page within a JSF h:dataTable component:

```java
package org.jakartaeerecipes.chapter02.recipe02_03;

import java.io.Serializable;
import java.util.ArrayList;
import java.util.List;
import javax.enterprise.context.SessionScoped;
import javax.inject.Named;

@Named(value = "authorController")
@SessionScoped
public class AuthorController implements Serializable {

    private String newAuthorFirst;
    private String newAuthorLast;
    private String bio;
    private List <Author> authorList;

    /**
     * Creates a new instance of RecipeController
     */
    public AuthorController() {
        populateAuthorList();
    }

    private void populateAuthorList(){
        System.out.println("initializing authors");
        authorList = new ArrayList<>();
        authorList.add(new Author("Josh", "Juneau", null));
        authorList.add(new Author("Carl", "Dea", null));
        authorList.add(new Author("Mark", "Beaty", null));
        authorList.add(new Author("John", "O'Conner", null));
        authorList.add(new Author("Freddy", "Guime", null));
        System.out.println("AuthorList size:" + authorList.size());

    }

    public void addAuthor() {
        getAuthorList().add(
                new Author(this.getNewAuthorFirst(),
```

```java
                            this.getNewAuthorLast(),
                            this.getBio()));
    }

    /**
     * @return the authorList
     */
    public List<Author> getAuthorList() {
        return authorList;
    }

    /**
     * @param authorList the authorList to set
     */
    public void setAuthorList(List<Author> authorList) {
        this.authorList = authorList;
    }

    /**
     * @return the newAuthorFirst
     */
    public String getNewAuthorFirst() {
        return newAuthorFirst;
    }

    /**
     * @param newAuthorFirst the newAuthorFirst to set
     */
    public void setNewAuthorFirst(String newAuthorFirst) {
        this.newAuthorFirst = newAuthorFirst;
    }

    /**
     * @return the newAuthorLast
     */
```

```java
    public String getNewAuthorLast() {
        return newAuthorLast;
    }

    /**
     * @param newAuthorLast the newAuthorLast to set
     */
    public void setNewAuthorLast(String newAuthorLast) {
        this.newAuthorLast = newAuthorLast;
    }

    /**
     * @return the bio
     */
    public String getBio() {
        return bio;
    }

    /**
     * @param bio the bio to set
     */
    public void setBio(String bio) {
        this.bio = bio;
    }
}
```

Finally, the Author class is used to hold instances of Author objects that are loaded into the authorList. The following code is for the Author class:

```java
package org.jakartaeerecipes.chapter02.recipe02_03;

public class Author implements java.io.Serializable {
    private String first;
    private String last;
    private String bio;
```

```java
    public Author(){
        this.first = null;
        this.last = null;
        this.bio = null;
    }

    public Author(String first, String last, String bio){
        this.first = first;
        this.last = last;
        this.bio = bio;
    }

    /**
     * Getters and Setters
     */

}
```

The resulting web page would resemble the page shown in Figure 2-3.

JSF Components, Creating a Sophisticated Page

The view for this page is made up entirely of JSF standard components.
As you can see, there are many useful components bundled with JSF out of the box.

Book Recommendation: Java 9 Recipes

Java 9 Recipes Authors
Josh Juneau
Carl Dea
Mark Beaty
John O'Conner
Freddy Guime

Use the following form to add an author to the list.

New Author First Name:
New Author Last Name:

Add Author

Figure 2-3. *Sophisticated JSF view example*

How It Works

JSF views are comprised of well-formed XML, being a mixture of HTML and JSF component tags. Any well-formed HTML can be used within a JSF view, but the components are the means by which JSF communicates with controller class instances. There are components shipped with JSF that can be used for adding images to views, text areas, buttons, checkboxes, and much more. Moreover, there are several very good component libraries that include additional JSF components, which can be used within your applications. This recipe is meant to give you an overall understanding of JSF components and how they work. You can learn more details regarding JSF components and the use of external component libraries by reading the recipes in Chapter 3.

The first step toward using a component within a JSF view is to declare the tag library on the page. This is done within the HTML element at the top of the page. The example in this recipe declares both the JSF core component library and the JSF HTML component library within the HTML element near the top of the page. These two libraries are standard JSF component libraries that should be declared in every JSF view:

```
...
<html xmlns="http://www.w3.org/1999/xhtml"
      xmlns:f="http://xmlns.jcp.org/jsf/core"
      xmlns:h="http://xmlns.jcp.org/jsf/html">
...
```

Once a library is declared, a component from within that library can be used in the view by specifying the library namespace, along with the component you want to use. For instance, to specify an HTML element for displaying text, use the JSF `h:outputText` component tag, along with the various component attributes.

Prior to JSF 2.0, it was important to enclose a JSF view along with all of the components within the `f:view` tag. As of JSF 2.0, the tag is no longer required because the underlying Facelets view technology is part of every JSF view by default, so it takes care of specifying the view automatically. However, the `f:view` element can still be useful for specifying locale, content type, or encoding. Please see the online documentation for more information regarding the use of those features: `https://javaserverfaces. github.io/docs/2.3/vdldoc/index.html`.

The `<h:head>` and `<h:body>` tags can be used to specify the header and body for a JSF web view. However, using the standard HTML `<head>` and `<body>` tags is fine also. Some Java IDEs will automatically use `<h:head>` and `<h:body>` in place of the standard HTML tags when writing JSF views. An important note is that you must enclose any content that will be treated as an HTML input form with the `<h:form>` JSF tag. This tag encloses a JSF form and renders an HTML form using a `POST` method if none is specified. No `action` attribute is required for a JSF form tag because typically the JSF controller class action method is invoked using one of the JSF action components such as `h:commandButton` or `h:commandLink`.

Tip   Always specify an `id` for the `h:form` tag because the form `id` is added as a prefix to all JSF component tag `id`s when the page is rendered. For instance, if a form with an `id` of `myform` contained a component tag with an `id` of `mytag`, the component `id` will be rendered as `myform:mytag`. If you do not specify an `id`, then one will be generated for you automatically. If you want to use JavaScript to work with any of the page components, you will need to have an `id` specified for `h:form`, or you will never be able to access them programmatically.

The standard JSF component library contains a variety of components, and a few of them are utilized in the example. The `h:graphicImage` tag can be used to place an image on the page and utilize a JSF controller class if needed. The `h:graphicImage` tag is rendered into an HTML component, and as with all of the other JSF components, it accepts JSF EL expressions within its attributes, which allows for the rendering of dynamic images. In this recipe, a static image is specified with the `name`attribute, but an expression could also be used, making use of a JSF controller class field. The library attribute is used to specify the directory in which the resource, in this case an image, resides:

```
<h:graphicImage id="java9recipes" library="image" name="java9recipes.png"/>
```

The `h:outputLabel` tag is useful for reading controller class properties and displaying their values when the view is rendered. They are rendered as a label for a corresponding field within the view. The example utilizes static values for the `h:outputLabel` component, but they could include JSF expressions if needed. The `h:outputText` component is also useful for reading controller class properties and displaying their values. This component renders basic text on the page. The difference between `h:outputLabel` and `h:outputText` is that they are rendered into different HTML tags. Both components can accept JSF controller class expressions for their `value` attributes.

In the example, a couple of text fields are displayed on the page using the
h:inputText component, which renders an input field. The value attribute for
h:inputText can be set to a JSF controller class field, which binds the text field to
the corresponding controller class property. For instance, the example includes an
h:inputText component with a value of #{authorController.newAuthorFirst}, which
binds the component to the newAuthorFirst property within the AuthorController
class. If the field contains a value, then a value will be present within a text field when
the page is rendered. If a value is entered into the corresponding text field and the form
is submitted, the value will be set into the newAuthorFirst field using its setter method.
The h:inputText tag allows for both reading and writing of controller class properties
because it uses lvalue JSF EL expressions. The h:inputTextarea tag is very similar to
h:inputText in that it works the same way, but it renders a text area instead of a text
field.

The h:commandButton component is used to render a submit button on a page.
Its action attribute can be set to a JSF controller class method. When the button is
pressed, the corresponding controller class method will be executed, and the form
will be submitted. The request will be sent to the FacesServlet controller, and any
properties on the page will be set. Please see Recipe 2-1 for more details regarding the
JSF life cycle. The h:commandButton used in the example has an action attribute of
#{authorController.addAuthor}, which will invoke the addAuthor method within the
AuthorController class. As you can see from the method, when invoked it will add a
new Author object to the authorList, utilizing the values that were populated within the
corresponding h:inputText components for the newAuthorFirst, newAuthorLast, and
bio fields. The following excerpt from the example's JSF view lists the h:commandButton
component:

```
<h:commandButton id="addAuthor" action="#{authorController.addAuthor}"
                               value="Add Author"/>
```

The last component in the example that bears some explanation is the
h:dataTable. This JSF component is rendered into an HTML table, and it enables
developers to dynamically populate tables with collections of data from a controller
class. In the example, the value attribute is set to the controller class property of
#{authorController.authorList}, which maps to a List instance that is populated
with Author objects. The var attribute contains a String that will be used to reference
the different objects contained within each row of the table. In the example, the var
attribute is set to author, so referencing #{author.first} within the dataTable will

return the value for the current `Author` object's `first` property. The `dataTable` in the example effectively prints out the first and last names of each `Author` object within the `authorList`. This is just a quick overview of how the JSF `dataTable` component works. For more details, please refer to Recipe 2-12.

As you work more with constructing JSF views, you will become very familiar with the component library. The tags will become second nature, and you will be able to construct highly sophisticated views for your application. Adding external JSF component libraries into the mix along with using Ajax for updating components is the real icing on the cake!

2-4. Displaying Messages in JSF Pages
Problem

You have the requirement to display an information message on the screen for your application users.

Solution

Add the `h:messages` component to your JSF view and create messages as needed within the view's controller class using `FacesMessage` objects. The following JSF view contains an `h:messages` component tag that will render any messages that were registered with `FacesContext` within the corresponding page's controller class. It also includes an `h:message` component that is bound to an `h:inputText` field. The `h:message` component can display messages that are specific to the corresponding text field:

```
<!DOCTYPE html PUBLIC "-//W3C//DTD XHTML 1.0 Strict//EN" "http://www.
w3.org/TR/xhtml1/DTD/xhtml1-strict.dtd">
<html xmlns="http://www.w3.org/1999/xhtml"
      xmlns:f="http://xmlns.jcp.org/jsf/core"
      xmlns:h="http://xmlns.jcp.org/jsf/html">
    <h:head>
        <meta http-equiv="Content-Type" content="text/html;
        charset=UTF-8"/>
        <title>Recipe 2-4: Displaying Messages in JSF Pages</title>
    </h:head>
```

```
<h:body>
    <h:form id="componentForm">
        <h1>JSF Messages</h1>
        <p>
            This page contains a JSF message component below.  It will
            display messages from a JSF managed bean once the bean has
            been initialized.
        </p>
        <h:messages errorStyle="color: red" infoStyle="color: green"
        globalOnly="true"/>
        <br/>
        <br/>
        Enter the word Java here:
        <h:inputText id="javaText" value="#{messageController.
        javaText}"/>
        <h:message for="javaText"  errorStyle="color: red"
        infoStyle="color: green"/>
        <br/><br/>
        <h:commandButton id="addMessage" action="#{messageController.
        newMessage}"
                        value="New Message"/>

    </h:form>
</h:body>
</html>
```

The controller class in this example is named MessageController. It will create a
JSF message upon initialization, and then each time the newMessage method is invoked,
another message will be displayed. Also, if the text *java* is entered into the text field
that corresponds to the h:inputText tag, then a success message will be displayed for
that component. Otherwise, if a different value is entered into that field or if the field
is left blank, then an error message will be displayed. The following listing is that of
MessageController:

```java
package org.jakartaeerecipes.chapter02.recipe02_04;

import java.util.Date;
import javax.enterprise.context.SessionScoped;
import javax.faces.application.FacesMessage;
import javax.faces.context.FacesContext;
import javax.inject.Named;

@Named
@SessionScoped
public class MessageController implements java.io.Serializable {
    int hitCounter = 0;
    private String javaText;

    /**
     * Creates a new instance of MessageController
     */
    public MessageController() {
        javaText = null;
        FacesMessage facesMsg = new FacesMessage(FacesMessage.SEVERITY_INFO,
        "Managed Bean Initialized", null);

        FacesContext.getCurrentInstance().addMessage(null, facesMsg);
    }

    public void newMessage(){
        String hitMessage = null;
        hitCounter++;
        if(hitCounter > 1){
            hitMessage = hitCounter + " times";
        } else {
            hitMessage = hitCounter + " time";
        }
```

```
        Date currDate = new Date();
        FacesMessage facesMsg = new FacesMessage(FacesMessage.SEVERITY_
        ERROR,
                "You've pressed that button " + hitMessage + "!
                The current date and time: "
                + currDate, null);
        FacesContext.getCurrentInstance().addMessage(null, facesMsg);

        if (getJavaText().equalsIgnoreCase("java")){
            FacesMessage javaTextMsg = new FacesMessage(FacesMessage.
            SEVERITY_INFO, "Good Job, that is the correct text!", null);
            FacesContext.getCurrentInstance().addMessage("componentForm:
            javaText", javaTextMsg);
        } else {
            FacesMessage javaTextMsg = new FacesMessage(FacesMessage.
            SEVERITY_ERROR, "Sorry, that is NOT the correct text!", null);
            FacesContext.getCurrentInstance().addMessage("componentForm:
            javaText", javaTextMsg);
        }
    }

    /**
     * Getters and Setters
     */

}
```

The message will be displayed on the page in red text if it is an error message and in green text if it is an informational message. In this example, the initialization message is printed green, and the update message is printed in red.

How It Works

It is always a good idea to relay messages to application users, especially in the event that some action needs to be taken by the user. The JSF framework provides an easy API that allows messages to be added to a view from the JSF controller class. To use the API, add the h:message component to a view for displaying messages that are bound to specific components, and add the h:messages component to a view for displaying messages that are not bound to specific components. The h:message component contains a number of attributes that can be used to customize message output and other things. It can be bound to a component within the same view by specifying that component's id in the for attribute of h:message. The most important attributes for the h:message component are as follows:

- id: Specifies a unique identifier for the component

- rendered: Specifies whether the message is rendered

- errorStyle: Specifies the CSS styles to be applied to error messages

- errorClass: Indicates the CSS class to apply to error messages

- infoStyle: Specifies the CSS styles to be applied to informational messages

- infoClass: Indicates the CSS class to apply to informational messages

- for: Specifies the component for which the message belongs

For a list of all attributes available for the h:message component, please refer to the online documentation. In the example for this recipe, the h:message component is bound to the h:inputText component with an id of javaText. When the page is submitted, the newMessage method within the MessageController class is invoked. That method is used in this example for generating messages to display on the page. If the text entered within the javaText property matches Java, then a successful message will be printed on the page. To create a message, an instance of the javax.faces.application. FacesMessage class is generated, passing three parameters that correspond to message severity, message summary, and message detail. A FacesMessage object can be created without passing any parameters, but usually it is more productive to pass the message into the constructor at the time of instantiation. The general format for creating a FacesMessage object is as follows:

```
new FacesMessage(FacesMessage.severity severity, String summary, String
detail)
```

Passing a static field from the FacesMessage class specifies the message severity. Table 2-2 shows the possible message severity values along with their descriptions.

Table 2-2. *FacesMessage Severity Values*

Severity	Description
SEVERITY_ERROR	Indicates that an error has occurred
SEVERITY_FATAL	Indicates that a serious error has occurred
SEVERITY_INFO	Indicates an informational message rather than an error
SEVERITY_WARN	Indicates that an error may have occurred

In the example, if the value entered for the javaText property equals Java, then an informational message is created. Otherwise, an error message is created. In either case, once the message is created, then it needs to be passed into the current context using FacesContext.getCurrentInstance().addMessage(String componentId, FacesMessage message). In the example, the method is called, passing a component ID of componentForm:javaText. This refers to the component within the JSF view that has an ID of javaText (h:inputText component). The componentForm identifier belongs to the form (h:form component) that contains the h:inputText component, so in reality the h:inputText component is nested within the h:form component. To reference a nested component, combine component IDs using a colon as a delimiter. The following is an excerpt from the example, demonstrating how to create a message and send it to the h:message component:

```
FacesMessage javaTextMsg = new FacesMessage(FacesMessage.SEVERITY_ERROR,
                "Sorry, that is NOT the correct text!", null);
FacesContext.getCurrentInstance().addMessage("componentForm:javaText",
javaTextMsg);
```

The h:messages component can be used for displaying all messages that pertain to a view, or it can be used for displaying only non–component-related messages by using the globalOnly attribute. All other attributes for h:messages are very similar to the h:message component. By indicating a true value for the globalOnly attribute, you are telling the component to ignore any component-specific messages. Therefore, any FacesMessage that is sent to a specific component will not be displayed by h:messages.

In the example, the message that is displayed by h:messages is generated in the same manner as the component-specific message, with the exception of specifying a specific component to which the message belongs. The following excerpt demonstrates sending an error message to the h:messages component. Note that the last argument that is sent to the FacesMessage call is a null value. This argument should be the clientId specification, and by setting it to null, you are indicating that there is no specified client identifier. Therefore, the message should be a global message rather than tied to a specific component:

```
FacesMessage facesMsg = new FacesMessage(FacesMessage.SEVERITY_ERROR,
                "You've pressed that button " + hitMessage + "!  The
                current date and time: " + currDate, null);
FacesContext.getCurrentInstance().addMessage(null, facesMsg);
```

Displaying the appropriate message at the right time within an application is very important. By utilizing FacesMessages objects and displaying them using either the h:message or h:messages component, you can ensure that your application users will be well informed of the application state.

2-5. Updating Messages Without Recompiling

Problem

Rather than hard-coding messages into your controller classes, you want to specify the messages within a properties file so that they can be edited on the fly.

Solution

Create a resource bundle or properties file, and specify your messages within it. Then retrieve the messages from the bundle and add them to the FacesMessages objects rather than hard-coding a String value. In the example that follows, a resource bundle is used to specify a message that is to be displayed on a page. If you need to change the message at any time, simply modify the resource bundle and reload the page in the browser without the need to redeploy the entire application or change any code.

The following code is for a JSF view that contains the h:messages component for displaying the message from a corresponding controller class:

```
<!DOCTYPE html PUBLIC "-//W3C//DTD XHTML 1.0 Strict//EN"
"http://www.w3.org/TR/xhtml1/DTD/xhtml1-strict.dtd">
<html xmlns="http://www.w3.org/1999/xhtml"
    xmlns:f="http://xmlns.jcp.org/jsf/core"
    xmlns:h="http://xmlns.jcp.org/jsf/html">
  <h:head>
      <meta http-equiv="Content-Type" content="text/html; charset=UTF-8"/>
      <title>Recipe 2-5: Specifying Updatable Messages</title>
  </h:head>
  <h:body>
      <h:form id="componentForm">
          <h1>Utilizing a resource bundle</h1>
          <p>
              The message below is displayed from a resource bundle.
              The h:outputText component has been added to the page only
              to instantiate the bean for this example. To change the
              message, simply modify the corresponding message within the
              bundle and then refresh the page.
          </p>
          <h:outputText id="exampleProperty" value="#{exampleController.
          exampleProperty}"/>
          <br/>
          <h:messages errorStyle="color: red" infoStyle="color: green"
          globalOnly="true"/>
      </h:form>
  </h:body>
</html>
```

Next, the controller class is responsible for creating the message and sending it to the h:messages component via the FacesContext. The following source is for ExampleController, which is the controller class for the JSF view in this example:

```
package org.jakartaeerecipes.chapter02.recipe02_05;

import java.util.ResourceBundle;
import javax.enterprise.context.RequestScoped;

import javax.faces.application.FacesMessage;
import javax.faces.context.FacesContext;
import javax.inject.Named;

@Named(value="exampleController")
@RequestScoped
public class ExampleController {
    private String exampleProperty;

    /**
     * Creates a new instance of ExampleController
     */
    public ExampleController() {
        exampleProperty = "Used to instantiate the bean.";
        FacesMessage facesMsg = new FacesMessage(FacesMessage.SEVERITY_INFO,
                ResourceBundle.getBundle("/org/jakartaeerecipes/chapter02/
                Bundle").getString("ExampleMessage"), null);
        FacesContext.getCurrentInstance().addMessage(null, facesMsg);
    }

    . . .

}
```

The resource bundle, which contains the message, is read by the controller class to obtain the message. If you want to update the message, you can do so without recompiling any code.

```
# This file is an example resource bundle
ExampleMessage=This message can be changed by updating the message bundle!
```

When the page is loaded, the h:outputText component instantiates ExampleController, which in turn creates the FacesMessage object that is used to display the message on the screen.

How It Works

Oftentimes it is useful to have the ability to update custom system or user messages rather than hard-coding them. This could be useful in the case that some custom information that is contained within a particular message may have the possibility of changing in the future. It'd be nice to simply update the message in text format rather than editing the code, recompiling, and redeploying your application. It is possible to create undateable messages using a resource bundle. A resource bundle is simply a properties file, which contains name-value pairs. When adding custom messages to a bundle, name the message appropriately and then add the custom message as the value portion of the property. An application can then look up the property by name and utilize its value. In this case, the value is a `String` that will be used to create a `FacesMessage` instance.

In the example, the bundle contains a property named `ExampleMessage`, along with a corresponding value. When the JSF view is loaded into the browser, the `ExampleController` class is instantiated, causing its constructor to be executed. A `FacesMessage` instance is created, generating a message of type `FacesMessage.SEVERITY_INFO`, and it reads the resource bundle and obtains the value for the `ExampleMessage` property. The following excerpt demonstrates how to obtain a specified message value from the resource bundle:

```
ResourceBundle.getBundle("/org/jakartaeerecipes/chapter02/Bundle").
getString("ExampleMessage"), null);
```

After the message is created, it is added to the current instance of `FacesContext` and, subsequently, displayed on the page when it is rendered. Using a resource bundle to specify your messages can make life much easier because you'll no longer be required to recompile code in order to update such messages.

2-6. Navigation Based upon Conditions

Problem

Your JSF application contains multiple pages, and you want to set up navigation between them.

Solution

Utilize one of the following techniques for performing navigation within JSF applications:

- Utilize explicit navigation through the use of a JSF controller class method along with a corresponding `faces-config.xml` configuration file to control the navigation for your application.

- Use implicit navigation for specifying the next view to render from within the controller class, returning the name of the view in String format from an action method.

- Use implicit navigation by specifying the name of the view to render as the `action` attribute of a component tag, bypassing the controller class altogether.

The example in this recipe consists of four JSF views, and each one contains `h:commandButton` components that invoke navigation to another view. The `h:commandButton` components are linked to controller class methods that are present within the view's corresponding controller class named `NavigationController`. The first view listed here contains two `h:commandButton` components, each of which invokes a method within the controller class named `NavigationController`. The first button utilizes explicit JSF navigation, and the second uses implicit navigation:

```
<?xml version="1.0" encoding="UTF-8"?>
<!DOCTYPE html PUBLIC "-//W3C//DTD XHTML 1.0 Strict//EN" "http://www.
w3.org/TR/xhtml1/DTD/xhtml1-strict.dtd">
<html xmlns="http://www.w3.org/1999/xhtml"
    xmlns:f="http://xmlns.jcp.org/jsf/core"
    xmlns:h="http://xmlns.jcp.org/jsf/html">
  <h:head>
    <meta http-equiv="Content-Type" content="text/html; charset=UTF-8"/>
    <title>Recipe 2-6</title>
  </h:head>
  <h:body>
    <h:form id="componentForm">
      <h1>JSF Navigation - Page 1</h1>
```

```
        <p>
            Clicking the submit button below will take you to Page #2.
        </p>

        <br/>
        <h:commandButton id="navButton" action="#{navigationController.
        pageTwo}"
                            value="Go To Page 2"/>
        <br/>
        <br/>
        <h:commandButton id="navButton2" action="#{navigationController.
        nextPage}"
                            value="Implicitly Navigate to Page 3"/>

    </h:form>
  </h:body>
</html>
```

The source for the second JSF view is very similar, except that a different controller class method is specified within the action attribute of the view's h:commandButton component:

```
<?xml version="1.0" encoding="UTF-8"?>
<!DOCTYPE html PUBLIC "-//W3C//DTD XHTML 1.0 Strict//EN"
"http://www.w3.org/TR/xhtml1/DTD/xhtml1-strict.dtd">
<html xmlns="http://www.w3.org/1999/xhtml"
     xmlns:f="http://xmlns.jcp.org/jsf/core"
     xmlns:h="http://xmlns.jcp.org/jsf/html">
  <h:head>
      <meta http-equiv="Content-Type" content="text/html; charset=UTF-8"/>
      <title>Recipe 2-6 JSF Navigation</title>
  </h:head>
  <h:body>
      <h:form id="componentForm">
          <h1>JSF Navigation - Page 2</h1>
```

```
<p>
    Clicking the submit button below will take you to Page #1.
</p>

<br/>
<h:commandButton id="navButton" action="#{navigationController.
pageOne}"
                    value="Go To Page 1"/>
    </h:form>
    </h:body>
</html>
```

The third JSF view contains a h:commandButton component that invokes a controller class action and utilizes conditional navigation, rendering pages depending upon a conditional outcome within the faces-config.xml:

```
<?xml version="1.0" encoding="UTF-8"?>
<!DOCTYPE html PUBLIC "-//W3C//DTD XHTML 1.0 Strict//EN" "http://www.
w3.org/TR/xhtml1/DTD/xhtml1-strict.dtd">
<html xmlns="http://www.w3.org/1999/xhtml"
    xmlns:f="http://xmlns.jcp.org/jsf/core"
    xmlns:h="http://xmlns.jcp.org/jsf/html">
    <h:head>
        <meta http-equiv="Content-Type" content="text/html; charset=UTF-8"/>
        <title>Recipe 2-6 JSF Navigation</title>
    </h:head>
    <h:body>
        <h:form id="componentForm">
            <h1>JSF Navigation - Page 3</h1>
            <p>
                The button below will utilize conditional navigation to
                take a user to the next page. The application will use
                authentication to test conditional navigation.
            </p>
```

```
            <br/>
            <h:commandButton id="loginButton"
            action="#{navigationController.login}"
                            value="Login Action"/>
        </h:form>
    </h:body>
</html>
```

Lastly, the fourth JSF view in the navigational example application contains an h:commandButton that invokes a method and uses implicit navigation to return to the third JSF view, specifying the view name within the action attribute directly and bypassing the controller class altogether:

```
<?xml version="1.0" encoding="UTF-8"?>

<!DOCTYPE html PUBLIC "-//W3C//DTD XHTML 1.0 Strict//EN"
"http://www.w3.org/TR/xhtml1/DTD/xhtml1-strict.dtd">
<html xmlns="http://www.w3.org/1999/xhtml"
    xmlns:f="http://xmlns.jcp.org/jsf/core"
    xmlns:h="http://xmlns.jcp.org/jsf/html">
    <h:head>
        <meta http-equiv="Content-Type" content="text/html;
        charset=UTF-8"/>
        <title>Recipe 2-6 JSF Navigation</title>
    </h:head>
    <h:body>
        <h:form id="componentForm">
            <h1>JSF Navigation - Page 4</h1>
            <p>
                Clicking the submit button below will take you to Page #1
                using conditional navigation rules.
            </p>

            <br/>
            <h:commandButton id="navButton2" action="recipe02_06c"
                            value="Implicitly Navigate to Page 3"/>
```

```
        </h:form>
    </h:body>
</html>
```

Now let's take a look at the source listing for `NavigationController`. It contains the methods that are specified within each page's `h:commandButton` action attribute. Some of the methods return a `String` value, and others do not. However, after the methods are invoked, then the `FacesServlet` processes the request, and the `faces-config.xml` configuration file is traversed, if needed, to determine the next view to render:

```
package org.jakartaeerecipes.chapter02.recipe02_06;

import javax.inject.Named;
import javax.enterprise.context.RequestScoped;

@Named(value = "navigationController")
@RequestScoped
public class NavigationController implements java.io.Serializable{

    private boolean authenticated = false;

    /**
     * Creates a new instance of NavigationController
     */
    public NavigationController() {
    }

    public String pageOne(){
        return "PAGE_1";
    }

    public String pageTwo(){
        return "PAGE_2";
    }

    /**
     * Utilizing implicit navigation, a page name can be returned from an
     * action method rather than listing a navigation-rule within faces-
       config.xml
     * @return
```

```java
     */
    public String nextPage(){
        // Perform some task, then implicitly list a page to render

        return "recipe02_06c";
    }

    /**
     * Demonstrates the use of conditional navigation
     */
    public void login(){
        // Perform some tasks, if needed, and then
        // set the Authenticated boolean
        setAuthenticated(true);
        System.out.println("Here");
    }

    /**
     * @return the authenticated
     */
    public boolean isAuthenticated() {
        return authenticated;
    }

    /**
     * @param authenticated the authenticated to set
     */
    public void setAuthenticated(boolean authenticated) {
        this.authenticated = authenticated;
    }
}
```

At the heart of navigation is the faces-config.xml file. It specifies which view should be displayed after a corresponding outcome. Two of the navigation-rules use standard JSF navigation, and the last navigation-rule makes use of conditional navigation:

```xml
<?xml version='1.0' encoding='UTF-8'?>

<!-- =========== FULL CONFIGURATION FILE =============================== -->

<faces-config version="2.3"
              xmlns="http://xmlns.jcp.org/xml/ns/javaee"
              xmlns:xsi="http://www.w3.org/2001/XMLSchema-instance"
              xsi:schemaLocation="http://xmlns.jcp.org/xml/ns/javaee
              http://xmlns.jcp.org/xml/ns/javaee/web-facesconfig_2_3.xsd">
    <navigation-rule>
        <from-view-id>/chapter02/recipe02_06a.xhtml</from-view-id>
        <navigation-case>
            <from-outcome>PAGE_2/from-outcome>
            <to-view-id>/chapter02/recipe02_06b.xhtml</to-view-id>
        </navigation-case>
    </navigation-rule>

    <navigation-rule>
        <from-view-id>/chapter02/recipe02_06b.xhtml</from-view-id>
        <navigation-case>
            <from-outcome>PAGE_1</from-outcome>
            <to-view-id>/chapter02/recipe02_06a.xhtml</to-view-id>
        </navigation-case>
    </navigation-rule>

    <navigation-rule>
        <navigation-case>
            <from-action>#{navigationController.login}</from-action>
            <if>#{navigationController.authenticated}</if>
            <to-view-id>/chapter02/recipe02_06d.xhtml</to-view-id>
            <redirect/>
        </navigation-case>
    </navigation-rule>
</faces-config>
```

How It Works

One of the most daunting tasks when building a web application is to determine the overall page navigation. Many web frameworks have instituted XML configuration files for organizing page navigation. This is one technique used by the JavaServer Faces web framework, and the navigational XML is placed within a JSF application's `faces-config.xml` configuration file. When using standard navigation, JSF utilizes navigation rules to determine which view to render based upon the outcome of page actions. If using standard JSF navigation, when a page action occurs, the controller class method that is associated with the action can return a `String` value. That value is then evaluated using the navigational rules that are defined within the `faces-config.xml` file and used to determine which page to render next.

The standard navigation infrastructure works well in most cases, but in some instances it makes more sense to directly list the next page to be rendered within the controller class, rather than making a navigation rule in the configuration file. When a controller class action is invoked, it can return the name of a view, without the `.xhtml` suffix. Such navigation was introduced with the release of JSF 2.0, and it is known as *implicit navigation*. As shown in the fourth example for the solution, you can also perform implicit navigation by specifying the name of a view without the suffix for an `action` attribute of the component tag.

Yet another type of navigation was introduced with JSF 2.0, taking navigation to the next level by allowing the use of JSF EL expressions within the `faces-config.xml` navigation rules. Conditional navigation allows for an `<if>` element to be specified within the navigational rule, which corresponds to a JSF EL condition. If the condition evaluates to `true`, then the specified view is rendered.

Navigation rules are constructed in XML residing within the `faces-config.xml` descriptor, and each rule has a root element of `navigation-rule`. Within each rule construct, the `from-view-id` element should contain the name of the view from which the action method was invoked. A series of `navigation-cases` should follow the `from-view-id` element. Each `navigation-case` contains a `from-outcome` element, which should be set to a `String` value corresponding to the `String` value that is returned from a subsequent action method. For instance, when the `pageOne` method is invoked in the example, the `String` `"PAGE_1"` is returned, and it should be specified within the `from-outcome` element within a `navigation-case` in the `faces-config.xml` file. Lastly, the `to-view-id` element should follow the `from-outcome` element within the `navigation-case`, and it should specify which view to render if the `String` in `from-outcome` is returned from the action method. The following excerpt shows the standard navigation rule that allows for navigation from page 1 to page 2 of the application:

```
<navigation-rule>
        <from-view-id>/chapter02/recipe02_06a.xhtml</from-view-id>
        <navigation-case>
            <from-outcome>PAGE_1</from-outcome>
            <to-view-id>/chapter02/recipe02_06b.xhtml</to-view-id>
        </navigation-case>
</navigation-rule>
```

Implicit navigation does not require any XML navigation rules to be declared. The action method that is invoked via an `h:commandButton` returns a `String` that is equal to the name of the view that should be rendered next. In the example, the second `h:commandButton` on view 1 invokes the `nextPage` controller class method, which returns the name of the next view that should be rendered:

```
public String nextPage(){
        // Perform some task, then implicitly list a page to render

        return "recipe02_06c";
}
```

If you want to use implicit navigation, you can bypass the controller class altogether and specify the name of the view that you want to render directly within the `action` attribute of `h:commandButton` or `h:commandLink`. The fourth JSF view in the example demonstrates this technique.

The third view in the example, named `recipe02_06c.xhtml`, demonstrates conditional navigation. Its `h:commandButton` action invokes the login method within the `NavigationController` class. That method does not contain much business logic in this example, but it does set the bean's `authenticated` field equal to `true`. Imagine that someone entered an incorrect password and failed to authenticate; in such a case, the `authenticated` field would be set to `false`. After the `login` method is executed, the `faces-config.xml` file is parsed to determine the next view to render, and the conditional navigation rule utilizes JSF EL to specify the navigation condition. The `from-action` element is set equal to the JSF EL that is used to invoke the login method, and an `<if>`

element is specified, referencing the `navigationController.authenticated` field via JSF
EL. If that field is equal to `true`, then the view specified within the `to-view-id` element
will be rendered. Note that the `<redirect/>` is required to tell JSF to redirect to the view
listed in the `<to-view-id>` element since JSF uses a redirect rather than a forward:

```
<navigation-rule>
       <navigation-case>
            <from-action>#{navigationController.login}</from-action>
            <if>#{navigationController.authenticated}</if>
            <to-view-id>/chapter02/recipe02_06d.xhtml</to-view-id>
            <redirect/>
       </navigation-case>
    </navigation-rule>
</faces-config>
```

Standard JSF navigation allows enough flexibility for most cases, and its architecture
is much more sophisticated than other web frameworks. However, in JSF 2.0, two new
navigational techniques known as *implicit* and *conditional navigation* were introduced. With
the addition of the new techniques, JSF navigation is more robust and easier to manage.

2-7. Validating User Input

Problem

You want to add the ability for your application to validate any data that is entered into a
JSF form.

Solution

Register a JSF validator on any text field components or other input components that
need to be validated. Use predefined JSF validators where applicable, and create
custom validator classes when needed. The example for this recipe utilizes predefined
validators for two `h:inputText` components in order to ensure that the values entered
into them are of proper length. A custom validator is added to a third text field, and
it is responsible for ensuring that the text contains a specified `String`. The three
fields make up an employee input form, and when an employee is entered and the
data validates successfully, a new `Employee` object is created and added to a list of

employees. An h:dataTable element in the view is used to display the list of employees if there are any. This is perhaps not the most true-to-life example, but you can apply the basic philosophy to validate real-world needs within your own applications.

The following listing is for the JSF view that constructs the employee input form, including the validation tags for each input text field:

```
<html xmlns="http://www.w3.org/1999/xhtml"
    xmlns:f="http://xmlns.jcp.org/jsf/core"
    xmlns:h="http://xmlns.jcp.org/jsf/html">
  <h:head>
      <meta http-equiv="Content-Type" content="text/html; charset=UTF-8"/>
      <title>Recipe 2-7: Validating Data</title>
  </h:head>
  <h:body>
      <h:form id="employeeForm">
          <h1>Java Developer Employee Information</h1>
          <br/>
          <h:messages globalOnly="true" errorStyle="color: red"
          infoStyle="color: green"/>
          <br/>
          <h:dataTable id="empTable" var="emp"
                      border="1" value="#{employeeController.employeeList}"
                      rendered="#{employeeController.employeeList.
                      size() > 0}">
              <f:facet name="header">
                  Current Employees
              </f:facet>
              <h:column id="empNameCol">
                  <f:facet name="header">Employee</f:facet>
                  <h:outputText id="empName" value="#{emp.employeeFirst}
                  #{emp.employeeLast}"/>
              </h:column>
              <h:column id="titleCol">
                  <f:facet name="header">Title</f:facet>
                  <h:outputText id="title" value="#{emp.employeeTitle}"/>
              </h:column>
```

```
            </h:dataTable>
            <p>
                Please use the form below to insert employee information.
            </p>
            <h:panelGrid columns="3">
                <h:outputLabel for="employeeFirst" value="First: " />
                <h:inputText id="employeeFirst"
                value="#{employeeController.employeeFirst}">
                    <f:validateLength minimum="3" maximum="30"/>
                </h:inputText>
                <h:message for="employeeFirst" errorStyle="color:red"/>

                <h:outputLabel for="employeeLast" value="Last: "  />
                <h:inputText id="employeeLast" value="#{employeeController.
                employeeLast}">
                    <f:validateLength minimum="3" maximum="30"/>
                </h:inputText>
                <h:message for="employeeLast" errorStyle="color:red"/>

                <h:outputLabel for="employeeTitle" value="Title (Must be a
                Java Position): "/>
                <h:inputText id="employeeTitle"
                value="#{employeeController.employeeTitle}">
                    <f:validator validatorId="employeeTitleValidate" />
                </h:inputText>
                <h:message for="employeeTitle" errorStyle="color:red"/>

            </h:panelGrid>
            <h:commandButton id="employeeInsert"
            action="#{employeeController.insertEmployee}"
                        value="Insert Employee"/>
        </h:form>
    </h:body>
</html>
```

The third h:inputText component in the view utilizes a custom validator. The f:validator tag is used to specify a custom validator, and its validatorId attribute is used to specify a corresponding validator class. The following listing is the Java code for a class named EmployeeTitleValidate, the custom validation class for the text field:

```
package org.jakartaeerecipes.chapter02.recipe02_07;

import java.util.Date;
import java.util.Locale;
import java.util.ResourceBundle;
import javax.faces.application.FacesMessage;
import javax.faces.component.UIComponent;
import javax.faces.context.FacesContext;
import javax.faces.validator.FacesValidator;
import javax.faces.validator.Validator;
import javax.faces.validator.ValidatorException;

@FacesValidator("employeeTitleValidate")
public class EmployeeTitleValidate implements Validator {

    @Override
    public void validate(FacesContext facesContext, UIComponent
    uiComponent, Object value)
            throws ValidatorException {

        checkTitle(value);

    }

    private void checkTitle(Object value) {
        String title = value.toString();
        if (!title.contains("Java")) {
            String messageText = "Title does not include the word Java";
            throw new ValidatorException(new FacesMessage(FacesMessage.
            SEVERITY_ERROR, messageText, messageText));
        }
    }
}
```

Note   As of JSF 2.3, it has been possible to inject resources such as FacesContext into validator classes. User-generated validator classes are also injectable into other resources.

Now let's take a look at the JSF controller class for the JSF view that contains the validation tags. The controller class is named EmployeeController, and the action method, insertEmployee, is used to add new Employee objects containing valid data to an ArrayList:

```
package org.jakartaeerecipes.chapter02.recipe02_07;

import java.io.Serializable;
import java.util.ArrayList;
import java.util.List;
import javax.enterprise.context.SessionScoped;

import javax.faces.application.FacesMessage;
import javax.faces.context.FacesContext;
import javax.inject.Named;

@Named(value="employeeController")
@SessionScoped
public class EmployeeController implements Serializable {

    private String employeeFirst;
    private String employeeLast;
    private String employeeTitle;

    private List <Employee> employeeList;

    public EmployeeController(){
        employeeFirst = null;
        employeeLast = null;
        employeeTitle = null;
        employeeList = new ArrayList();
    }
```

```java
public void insertEmployee(){
    Employee emp = new Employee(employeeFirst,
                                employeeLast,
                                employeeTitle);
    employeeList.add(emp);
    FacesMessage facesMsg = new FacesMessage(FacesMessage.SEVERITY_INFO,
    "Employee Successfully Added", null);
    FacesContext.getCurrentInstance().addMessage(null, facesMsg);
}
. . .
    /**
     * Getters and Setters
     */
. . .
}
```

In the end, the validators will raise exceptions if a user attempts to enter an employee first or last name using an invalid length or a title that does not contain the word *Java*. When user input validation fails, error messages are displayed next to the components containing the invalid entries.

How It Works

The JSF framework contains many features that make it more convenient for developers to customize their applications. Validators are one of those features, because they can be used to solidify application data and ensure data is correct before storing in a database or other data stores. The JSF framework ships with a good deal of validators that are already implemented. To use these predefined validators, simply embed the appropriate validator tag within a component tag in a view to validate that component's data values. Sometimes there are cases where the standard validators will not do the trick. In such cases, JSF provides a means for developing custom validator classes that can be used from within a view in the same manner as the predefined validators.

In the example for this recipe, two of the h:inputText components contain standard JSF validators used to validate the length of the values entered. The f:validateLength tag can be embedded into a component for String length validation, and the tag's minimum and maximum attributes can be populated with the minimum and maximum

String length, respectively. As mentioned previously, JSF ships with a good number of these predefined validators. All that the developer is required to do is embed the validator tags within the components that they want to validate. Table 2-3 lists all standard validator tags and what they do. For a detailed look at each of the validator attributes, please see the online documentation.

Table 2-3. *Standard Validators*

Validator Tag	Description
validateLength	Checks the length of a String
validateLongRange	Checks the range of a numeric value
validateDoubleRange	Checks the range of a floating-point value
validateRequired	Ensures the input field is not empty (also an alternative to using the required attribute on an input field component tag)
validateRegex	Validates the component against a given regular expression pattern

Oftentimes, there is a need for some other type of validation to take place for a specified component. In such cases, developing a custom validator class may be the best choice. Many developers shy away from writing their own validators because it seems to be a daunting task at first glance. However, JSF 2.0 took great strides toward making custom validator classes easier to write and understand.

To create a custom validator class, implement the `javax.faces.validator. Validator` interface. Annotate the validator class with the `@FacesValidator` annotation, specifying the string you want to use for registering your validator within the `f:validator` tag. In the example, the name used to reference the validator class is `employeeTitleValidate`. The only requirement is that the validator class overrides the `validate` method, which is where the custom validation takes place. The validate method contains the following signature:

```
public void validate(FacesContext facesContext, UIComponent uiComponent,
Object value)
          throws ValidatorException
```

Utilizing the parameters that are passed into the method, you can obtain the current `FacesContext`, a handle on the component being validated, as well as the component's value. In the example, a helper method is called from within the `validate` method, and

150

it is used to check the component's value and ensure that the word *Java* is contained somewhere within it. If it does not validate successfully, a `ValidatorException` is created and thrown. The message that is placed within the `ValidatorException` is what will appear next to the component being validated if the validation fails. The following excerpt from the validation class demonstrates creating and throwing a `ValidatorException`:

```
throw new ValidatorException(new FacesMessage(FacesMessage.SEVERITY_ERROR,
                 messageText, messageText));
```

So when does the validation occur? That is the key to the validator, isn't it? The answer is immediately, before the request is sent to the controller class action method. Any validation occurs during the *Process Validations* phase, and if one or more components being validated within a view throw a `ValidatorException`, then the processing stops, and the request is not sent to the action method. When the user clicks the submit button, the validation takes place first, and if everything is OK, then the request is passed to the action method.

Note   A means of validating that an input component simply contains a value is to use the `required` attribute. The `required` attribute of input component tags can be set to `true` in order to force a value to be entered for that component.

The validation of components within a JSF view using standard validators can really save a developer some time and increase the usability and precision of an application's data. The ability to create custom validators allows validation to be performed for any scenario. Be constructive, use validation on all of your application's input forms, and create custom validators to perform validation using unique techniques. Your application users will appreciate it!

2-8. Evaluation of Page Expressions Immediately

Problem

You want to have some of your JSF component values evaluated immediately, rather than waiting until the form is submitted.

Solution

Specify true for the component tag's immediate attribute, and also specify the component's onchange attribute and set it equal to submit(). This will cause the input form to be submitted immediately when the value for the component is changed, and JSF will skip the Render Response phase when doing so and execute all components that specify an immediate attribute set to true during the Apply Request Values JSF life-cycle phase. The example for this recipe uses an employee form. Instead of waiting until the form is submitted, the first and last h:inputText components will be evaluated and validated during the Apply Request Values phase immediately when their values change. The following source is for the JSF view named recipe02_08.xhtml:

```
<html xmlns="http://www.w3.org/1999/xhtml"
    xmlns:f="http://xmlns.jcp.org/jsf/core"
    xmlns:h="http://xmlns.jcp.org/jsf/html">
    <h:head>
        <meta http-equiv="Content-Type" content="text/html; charset=UTF-8"/>
        <title>Recipe 2-8 Immediate View Evaluation</title>
    </h:head>
    <h:body>
        <h:form id="employeeForm">
            <h1>Java Developer Employee Information</h1>
            <br/>
            <h:messages globalOnly="true" errorStyle="color: red"
            infoStyle="color: green"/>
            <br/>
            <h:dataTable id="empTable" var="emp"
                        border="1" value="#{employeeController.employeeList}"
                        rendered="#{employeeController.employeeList.
                        size() > 0}">
                <f:facet name="header">
                    Current Employees
                </f:facet>
                <h:column id="empNameCol">
                    <f:facet name="header">Employee</f:facet>
```

```
            <h:outputText id="empName" value="#{emp.employeeFirst}
            #{emp.employeeLast}"/>
        </h:column>
        <h:column id="titleCol">
            <f:facet name="header">Title</f:facet>
            <h:outputText id="title" value="#{emp.employeeTitle}"/>
        </h:column>

</h:dataTable>
<p style="width: 40%;">
    Please use the form below to insert employee information.
    The first and last text fields will result in immediate
    evaluation during the apply request values phase, whereas
    the text field in the middle will result in standard
    evaluation and be validated during the invoke application
    phase.
    <br/><br/>
    To test, try inserting just one character in the first text
    field and then tab to the next field.  You should see an
    immediate result.
</p>
<h:panelGrid columns="3">
    <h:outputLabel for="employeeFirst" value="First: " />
    <h:inputText id="employeeFirst" immediate="true"
    onchange="submit()" value="#{employeeController.
    employeeFirst}">
        <f:validateLength minimum="3" maximum="30"/>
    </h:inputText>
    <h:message for="employeeFirst" errorStyle="color:red"/>

    <h:outputLabel for="employeeLast" value="Last: "   />
    <h:inputText id="employeeLast" value="#{employeeController.
    employeeLast}">
```

```
                <f:validateLength minimum="3" maximum="30"/>
            </h:inputText>
            <h:message for="employeeLast" errorStyle="color:red"/>

            <h:outputLabel for="employeeTitle" value="Title (Must be a
            Java Position): "/>
            <h:inputText id="employeeTitle" immediate="true"
            value="#{employeeController.employeeTitle}">
                <f:validator validatorId="employeeTitleValidate" />
            </h:inputText>
            <h:message for="employeeTitle" errorStyle="color:red"/>

        </h:panelGrid>
        <h:commandButton id="employeeInsert"
        action="#{employeeController.insertEmployee}"
                        value="Insert Employee"/>
    </h:form>
  </h:body>
</html>
```

As you can see, the h:inputText components with ids of employeeFirst and employeeTitle specify both the immediate="true" and the onchange="submit()" attributes. These two attributes cause the components to be validated and evaluated immediately rather than when the h:commandButton action is invoked.

How It Works

Event handling that occurs immediately can be useful in cases where you do not want to validate the entire form in order to process input but, rather, when you want chosen components to be validated immediately. As mentioned in Recipe 2-1, when a JSF view is processed, a number of phases are executed. As such, when a form is submitted, the Invoke Application phase initiates the event handlers for view components, and validation occurs. When the immediate attribute for a component is set to true, the event handlers for that component execute during the Apply Request Values phase, which occurs before the Process Validations phase, where component validation normally occurs. This allows for an immediate validation response for the specified components, resulting in immediate error messages if needed.

As mentioned previously, specify the `immediate` attribute for a component and set it to `true` if you want to have that component evaluated immediately. This will cause the component to be evaluated and validated during the Apply Request Values phase. The real fun comes into play when you also specify the `onclick` attribute and set it equal to `submit()`, causing the form to be submitted when the value for the component changes. Specifying attributes as such will cause any component within the view that has an `immediate` attribute set to `true` to be validated when the component value changes.

Note   The immediate attribute can also be useful when used on a `commandButton` component in such instances where you do not want any form processing to take place, such as if you want to set up a cancel button or another button to bypass form processing.

2-9. Passing Page Parameters to Methods

Problem

You want to pass parameters to controller class methods from within a JSF view via Expression Language (EL).

Solution

Use a standard JSF EL expression to invoke a controller class method, and enclose the parameters that you want to pass to the method within parentheses. In the example for this recipe, an `h:dataTable` component is used to display a list of `Author` objects in a view. Each row within the `h:dataTable` contains an `h:commandLink` component, which invokes a JSF controller class method when selected. The `h:commandLink` displays the current row's author name and invokes the `AuthorController` class `displayAuthor` method when clicked, passing the last name for the author being displayed in the current row. In the `displayAuthor` method, the list of authors is traversed, finding the element that contains the same last name as the parameter, which is passed into the method. The current author is then displayed in a subsequent page, which is rendered using implicit navigation.

The following source is for the JSF view entitled recipe02_09a.xhtml, which displays the list of authors using an h:dataTable component:

```
<html xmlns="http://www.w3.org/1999/xhtml"
    xmlns:f="http://xmlns.jcp.org/jsf/core"
    xmlns:h="http://xmlns.jcp.org/jsf/html">
    <h:head>
        <meta http-equiv="Content-Type" content="text/html; charset=UTF-8"/>
        <title>Recipe 2-9: Passing Page Parameters to Methods</title>
    </h:head>
    <h:body>
        <h:form id="componentForm">
            <h1>Author List</h1>
            <p>
                Below is the list of authors.  Click on the author's last
                name for more information regarding the author.
            </p>

            <h:graphicImage id="java9recipes" style="width: 10%; height:
            20%" library="image" name="java9recipes.png"/>
            <br/>
            <h:dataTable id="authorTable" border="1"
            value="#{authorTableController.authorList}"
                        var="author">
                <f:facet name="header">
                    Java 9 Recipes Authors
                </f:facet>
                <h:column>
                <h:commandLink id="authorName" action=
                "#{authorTableController.displayAuthor(author.last)}"
                            value="#{author.first} #{author.last}"/>
                </h:column>
            </h:dataTable>
            <br/>
            <br/>
```

```
          </h:form>
     </h:body>
</html>
```

The next listing is that of the controller class for the preceding JSF view. The controller class populates an `ArrayList` with `Author` objects upon instantiation:

```
package org.jakartaeerecipes.chapter02.recipe02_09;

import java.io.Serializable;
import java.util.ArrayList;
import java.util.List;
import javax.enterprise.context.SessionScoped;
import javax.inject.Named;

@Named(value = "authorTableController")
@SessionScoped
public class AuthorController implements Serializable {

    private List<Author> authorList = null;
    private final String juneauBio = "This is Josh Juneau's Bio";
    private final String deaBio = "This is Carl Dea's Bio";
    private final String beatyBio = "This is Mark Beaty's Bio";
    private final String oConnerBio = "This is John O'Connor's Bio";
    private final String guimeBio = "This is Freddy Guime's Bio";
    private Author current;
    private String authorLast;
    /**
     * Creates a new instance of AuthorController
     */
    public AuthorController() {
        super();
        authorLast = null;
        populateAuthorList();
    }
```

```
    private void populateAuthorList() {

        if(authorList == null){
            System.out.println("initializing authors list");
            authorList = new ArrayList<>();
            authorList.add(new Author("Josh", "Juneau", juneauBio));
            authorList.add(new Author("Carl", "Dea", deaBio));
            authorList.add(new Author("Mark", "Beaty", beatyBio));
            authorList.add(new Author("John", "O'Conner", oConnerBio));
            authorList.add(new Author("Freddy", "Guime", guimeBio));
        }
    }

    public String displayAuthor(String last){
        for(Author author:authorList){
            if(author.getLast().equals(last)){
                current = author;
                break;
            }
        }
        return "recipe02_09b";
    }
. . .
    /**
     * Getters and Setters
     */
. . .
}
```

The Author class is the same Author Plain Old Java Object (POJO) that was utilized in Recipe 2-3. For the source of the Author class, please refer to that recipe. Lastly, the following code is for a JSF view entitled recipe02_09b.xhtml, the detail view for each author. When an author name is clicked from the h:dataTable component in the first view, the component's corresponding controller class method is invoked, and then this view is rendered to display the selected author's information:

```
<html xmlns="http://www.w3.org/1999/xhtml"
      xmlns:f="http://xmlns.jcp.org/jsf/core"
      xmlns:h="http://xmlns.jcp.org/jsf/html">
    <h:head>
        <meta http-equiv="Content-Type" content="text/html;
        charset=UTF-8"/>
        <title>Recipe 2-9: Passing Page Parameters to Methods</title>
    </h:head>
    <h:body>
        <h:form id="componentForm">
            <h1>#{authorTableController.current.first}
            #{authorTableController.current.last}</h1>
            <p>
                <h:graphicImage id="java9recipes" library="image"
                style="width: 10%; height: 20%" name="java9recipes.png"/>
                <br/>
                #{authorTableController.current.bio}
            </p>

            <h:link value="Go Back to List" outcome="recipe02_09a"/>

        </h:form>
    </h:body>
</html>
```

How It Works

The release of JSF 2.0 contained many enhancements that made the life of JSF developers much easier than before. The ability to pass parameters to controller class methods from within JSF views is one such enhancement. As you can see from the example for this recipe, it is possible to pass parameters to a method within a JSF EL construct in the same manner that you would call any method with parameters in Java: by enclosing the argument(s) within parentheses after the method name. It cannot get much simpler than that!

Let's take a look at the lines of code that make this example work. The first JSF view displays a table of author names, and each name is displayed using an h:commandLink component. The value attribute for the h:commandLink component is set to the author name, and the action attribute is set to the JSF EL, which invokes a controller class action method named displayAuthor. Notice that within the call to the controller class method, the EL for the author's last name is passed as a String parameter:

```
<h:dataTable id="authorTable" border="1" value="#{authorTableController.
authorList}"
                        var="author">
    <f:facet name="header">
            Java 9Recipes Authors
    </f:facet>
    <h:column>
            <h:commandLink id="authorName" action="#{authorTable
            Controller.displayAuthor(author.last)}"
                        value="#{author.first} #{author.last}"/>
    </h:column>
</h:dataTable>
```

The displayAuthor method within the controller class accepts a String parameter value, which is the author's last name, and then finds an Author object within the list of authors that contains the same last name. When found, a class field named current is set equal to the Author object for the matching List element. The subsequent JSF view then displays content utilizing the current Author information.

Note   The h:link component can be used to add an HTML anchor element to the view. The outcome attribute should list the name of the view to which the anchor element should point.

Prior to JSF 2.0, developers were unable to pass parameters to controller class methods from within a view. This made it a bit more difficult to perform such techniques and usually involved a bit more code.

2-10. Operators and Reserved Words in Expressions

Problem

You want to perform some arithmetic and combine expressions within your JSF views.

Solution

JSF EL expressions can contain arithmetic using standard arithmetic operators. It is also possible to combine two or more expressions utilizing some of the JSF EL reserved words. In the following example, some JSF EL expressions are used to display mathematical results on a page. The usage of both arithmetic and reserved words is within the expressions:

```
<html xmlns="http://www.w3.org/1999/xhtml"
    xmlns:f="http://xmlns.jcp.org/jsf/core"
    xmlns:h="http://xmlns.jcp.org/jsf/html"
    xmlns:c="http://xmlns.jcp.org/jsp/jstl/core">
<h:head>
    <meta http-equiv="Content-Type" content="text/html; charset=UTF-8"/>
    <title>Recipe 2-10:  Arithmetic and Reserved Words</title>
</h:head>
<h:body>
    <h:form id="componentForm">
        <h1>JSF Arithmetic and Reserved Words in EL</h1>
        <p>
            The following examples use JSF EL to perform some arithmetic.
        </p>
        1 + 1 = #{1 + 1}
        <br/>
        <h:outputText value="20 / 5 = #{20 / 5}"/>
        <br/>

        <h:outputText rendered="#{1 + 1 eq 2}" value="1 + 1 DOES equal 2"/>
        <br/>
        <h:outputText rendered="#{5 * 4 != 20}" value="Is 5 * 4 equal
        to 20?"/>
```

```
            <br/>
            <h:outputText rendered="#{5 * 5 eq 25 and 1 + 1 eq 2}"
            value="Combining some expressions"/>
            <br/>
            <c:if test="#{evaluationController.expr1()}">
                This will be displayed if expr1() evaluates to true.
            </c:if>
            <br/>
            <c:if test="#{evaluationController.expr2() or
            evaluationController.field1}">
                This will be displayed if expr2() or field1 evaluates to true.
            </c:if>
        </h:form>
    </h:body>
</html>
```

Some of the expressions contain controller class references for a bean named EvaluationController. The listing for this controller class is as follows:

```
package org.jakartaeerecipes.chapter02.recipe02_10;

import javax.enterprise.context.RequestScoped;
import javax.inject.Named;

@Named(value = "evaluationController")
@RequestScoped
public class EvaluationController {

    private boolean field1 = true;

    /**
     * Creates a new instance of EvaluationController
     */
    public EvaluationController() {
    }

    public boolean expr1(){
        return true;
    }
```

```
    public boolean expr2(){
        return false;
    }

    /**
     * @return the field1
     */
    public boolean isField1() {
        return field1;
    }

    /**
     * @param field1 the field1 to set
     */
    public void setField1(boolean field1) {
        this.field1 = field1;
    }
}
```

The resulting page will look as follows:

```
The following examples use JSF EL to perform some arithmetic.
1 + 1 = 2
20 / 5 = 4.0
1 + 1 DOES equal 2

Combining some expressions
This will be displayed if expr1() evaluates to true.
This will be displayed if expr1() or field1 evaluates to true.
```

How It Works

It is possible to use standard arithmetic and combine expressions using reserved words within JSF EL expressions. All standard arithmetic operators are valid within EL, but a couple of things are different. For instance, instead of writing an expression such as #{1 + 1 = 2}, you could use the eq reserved characters so that the expression reads #{1 + 1 eq 2}. Similarly, the != symbol could be used to specify that some value is not equal to another value, but rather, in this example, the ne reserved word is used. Table 2-4 describes all such reserved words.

Table 2-4. *JSF EL Reserved Words*

Reserved Word	Description
and	Combines two or more expressions
div	Used to divide
empty	Used to refer to an empty list
eq	Equal to
false	Boolean false
ge	Greater than or equal to
gt	Greater than
instanceof	Used to evaluate whether an object is an instance of another
le	Less than or equal to
lt	Less than
mod	Modulus
ne	Not equal
not	Used for negation
null	Evaluates a null value
or	Combines two or more expressions
true	Boolean true

Table 2-5 lists the available operators that can be used within JSF EL expressions, in order of precedence.

Table 2-5. *Operators for Use in Expressions*

Operator
[]
()
- (unary), not, !, empty
*, /, div, %, mod
+, - (binary)
<, >, <=, >=, lt, gt, le, ge
==, !, eq, ne
&&, and
||, or
?, :

2-11. Creating Bookmarkable URLs
Problem

You want to enable your application to allow URLs that will be linked to display specific objects. For instance, you want to use a GET URL such as `http://myserver.com/JakartaEERecipes/chapter02/chapter02_11.xhtml?last=juneau` in order to display a page containing information on the author with the specified last name.

Solution

Add view parameters to a JSF view for which you want to create a bookmarkable URL by defining the parameter in an `f:viewParam` tag, which is a sub-tag of the `f:metadata` tag. Doing so will allow a page to become accessible via a URL that contains request parameters which can be used for record identification. In this example, the view contains a view parameter, via the `f:viewParam` tag, that allows for the specification of an author's last name when the view is requested. In the following example, the controller class that was created in Recipe 2-9 has been modified to include a new property named `authorLast` in order to accommodate the new view parameter.

The sources for the view named recipe02_11.xhtml are listed next. They are very similar to the view named recipe02_09b.xhtml, except that they include an f:viewParam element, which is enclosed between opening and closing f:metadata elements:

```
<html xmlns="http://www.w3.org/1999/xhtml"
    xmlns:f="http://xmlns.jcp.org/jsf/core"
    xmlns:h="http://xmlns.jcp.org/jsf/html">
    <h:head>
        <meta http-equiv="Content-Type" content="text/html; charset=UTF-8"/>
        <title>Recipe 2-11: Creating Bookmarkable URLs</title>

    </h:head>
    <h:body>

        <f:metadata>
            <f:viewParam name="authorLast" value="#{authorTableController.
            authorLast}"/>
        </f:metadata>
        <h:form id="componentForm">
            <h1>#{authorTableController.current.first}
            #{authorTableController.current.last}</h1>
            <p>
                <h:graphicImage id="java9recipes" library="image"
                style="width: 10%; height: 20%" name="java9recipes.png"/>
                <br/>
                #{authorTableController.current.bio}
            </p>

            <h:link value="Go Back to List" outcome="recipe02_09a"/>

        </h:form>

    </h:body>
</html>
```

The code for the `AuthorController` class which is pertinent to this example is listed next:

```
...
public class AuthorController implements Serializable {

    ...
    private String authorLast;
    ...

    /**
     * Getters and Setters
     */

}
```

As mentioned previously, a property named `authorLast` has been included in this controller. This property makes it possible for the JSF view listed in the example to accept a request parameter named `authorLast` via a GET URL and pass it to the bean when the page is requested. In the end, the URL for accessing the view and requesting the details for the author Josh Juneau would be as follows:

```
http://my-server.com/JakartaEERecipes/chapter02/chapter02_11.
xhtml?authorLast=Juneau
```

How It Works

JSF 2.0 introduced the ability to include view parameters, adding the ability for views to accept request parameters. Utilizing a GET-based URL, a request parameter can be appended to the end along with its value, and a view containing the new view parameter can then pass the parameter to a controller class before the response is rendered. The bean can then accept the parameter value and query a database or search through some other collection of data to find a record that matches the given value before rendering the response.

To include one or more view parameters within a view, you must add opening and closing `f:metadata` elements to the view and embed the number of `f:viewParam` elements between them. The `f:viewParam` element includes two attributes that must have values, those being the `name` and `value` attributes. The `name` attribute specifies the name of the request parameter as you would like it to appear within the bookmarkable URL, and the `value` attribute specifies the controller class field that should be mapped to that request parameter. In the example for this recipe, the JSF view contains a view parameter named `authorLast`, and the associated `authorLast` field within the controller class contains a setter method, which is invoked when the page is requested. The following excerpt from the view demonstrates the lines for adding the metadata and view parameter:

```
<f:metadata>
    <f:viewParam name="authorLast" value="#{authorTableController.
    authorLast}"/>
</f:metadata>
```

With the addition of the view parameter, the page can be requested with a URL containing the `authorLast` request parameter as follows:

```
http://my-server.com/JakartaEERecipes/chapter02/chapter02_11.
xhtml?authorLast=Juneau
```

When the page is requested, the view parameter's value invokes the `setAuthorLast` method within the controller class, which then searches for an author record that contains a last name equal to the given request parameter value:

```
...
public void setAuthorLast(String authorLast) {
        displayAuthor(authorLast);
    }
...
```

The addition of view parameters to JSF 2.0 made it easy to create bookmarkable URLs. This allows applications to be more flexible and produce results immediately without requiring a user to navigate through several pages before producing a result.

2-12. Displaying Lists of Objects

Problem

You want to display a list of objects within your rendered JSF page.

Solution

Use a JSF h:dataTable component to display the list of objects, iterating over each object in the list and displaying the specified values. The h:dataTable component is very customizable and can be configured to display content in a variety of layouts. The following JSF view contains two h:dataTable components that are used to display the authors for the *Java 9 Recipes* book using controller classes developed in previous recipes. The first table in the view is straightforward and displays the names of each author. It has been formatted to display alternating row colors. The second table contains two rows for each corresponding list element, displaying the author names on the first row and their bios on the second:

```
<html xmlns="http://www.w3.org/1999/xhtml"
    xmlns:f="http://xmlns.jcp.org/jsf/core"
    xmlns:h="http://xmlns.jcp.org/jsf/html">
  <h:head>
      <meta http-equiv="Content-Type" content="text/html; charset=UTF-8"/>
      <title>Recipe 2-12: Displaying Lists of Objects</title>

      <link href="#{facesContext.externalContext.requestContextPath}/css/
      styles.css"
          rel="stylesheet" type="text/css" />

  </h:head>
  <h:body>

      <h:form id="componentForm">
          <p>

              <h:graphicImage id="java9recipes" style="width: 10%;
              height: 20%" library="images" name="java9recipes.png"/>
              <br/>
```

```
            #{authorTableController.current.bio}
    </p>

    <h:dataTable id="authorTable" border="1"
                 value="#{authorTableController.authorList}"
                 styleClass="authorTable"
                 rowClasses="authorTableOdd, authorTableEven"
                 var="author">
        <f:facet name="header">
            Java 9 Recipes Authors
        </f:facet>
        <h:column>
        <h:outputText id="authorName" value="#{author.first}
        #{author.last}"/>
        </h:column>
    </h:dataTable>
    <br/><br/>
    <h:dataTable id="authorTable2" border="1"
    value="#{authorTableController.authorList}"
                 var="author" width="500px;">
        <f:facet name="header">
            Java 9 Recipes Authors
        </f:facet>
        <h:column>
            <h:panelGrid columns="2" border="1" width="100%">
                <h:outputText id="authorFirst" value="#{author.
                first}" style="width: 50%"/>
                <h:outputText id="authorLast" value="#{author.
                last}" style="width:50%"/>

            </h:panelGrid>
            <h:outputText id="authorBio" value="#{author.bio}"/>
        </h:column>
    </h:dataTable>
```

```
      </h:form>

    </h:body>
</html>
```

The example utilizes a cascading style sheet (CSS) to help format the colors on the table. The source for the style sheet is as follows:

```
.authorTable{
        border-collapse:collapse;
}
.authorTableOdd{
        text-align:center;
        background:none repeat scroll 0 0 #CCFFFF;
        border-top:1px solid #BBBBBB;
}

.authorTableEven{
        text-align:center;
        background:none repeat scroll 0 0 #99CCFF;
        border-top:1px solid #BBBBBB;
}
```

The resulting page should look similar to Figure 2-4.

Java 9 Recipes Authors
Josh Juneau
Carl Dea
Mark Beaty
John O'Conner
Freddy Guime

Java 9 Recipes Authors		
Josh	Juneau	
This is Josh Juneau's Bio		
Carl		Dea
This is Carl Dea's Bio		
Mark		Beaty
This is Mark Beaty's Bio		
John	O'Conner	
This is John O'Connor's Bio		
Freddy		Guime
This is Freddy Guime's Bio		

Figure 2-4. *JSF DataTable component examples*

How It Works

A JSF h:dataTable component can be used to display lists of objects within a page. When rendered, an HTML table is constructed, populating the cells of the table with the data for each list element or record of data. The h:dataTable can iterate over a collection of data, laying it out in a columnar format including column headers and the ability to customize the look using cascading style sheets (CSSs). The component contains a number of important attributes, as listed in Table 2-6. Perhaps the most important of them are the value and var attributes. The value attribute specifies the collection of data to iterate, and the var attribute lists a String that will be used to reference each individual row of the table. The collection usually comes from the controller class, such as in the example for this recipe. The legal data types for the value attribute are Array, DataModel, List, and Result. The var attribute is used within each column to reference a specific field within an object for the corresponding row.

Table 2-6. *DataTable Attributes*

Attribute	Description
id	ID for the component.
border	An integer indicating border thickness; 0 is default.
bgcolor	Background color of the table.
cellpadding	Padding between the cell wall and its contents.
cellspacing	Spacing within the cells.
width	Overall width of the table, specified in pixels or percentages.
first	The first entry in the collection to display.
rows	Total number of rows to display.
styleClass, captionClass, headerClass, footerClass, rowClasses, columnClasses	CSS attributes.
rendered	Boolean value indicating whether the component will be rendered.

The h:dataTable can contain any number of columns, and each is specified within the h:dataTable component in the JSF view. The h:column nested element encloses the output for each column. A column can contain just about any valid component or HTML, even embedded dataTables. An h:column normally does not have any attributes specified, but it always contains an expression or hard-coded value for display.

Normally, columns within an HTML table contain headers. You can add headers to the h:dataTable or individual columns by embedding an f:facet element within the h:dataTable and outside of the column specifications or within each h:column by specifying the name attribute as header. The f:facet element can also specify caption for the name attribute in order to add a caption to the table. The following excerpt from the example demonstrates an h:dataTable that includes each of these features:

```
<h:dataTable id="authorTable" border="1"
                         value="#{authorTableController.authorList}"
                         styleClass="authorTable"
                         rowClasses="authorTableOdd, authorTableEven"
                         var="author">
    <f:facet name="header">
        Java 9 Recipes Authors
    </f:facet>
    <h:column>
        <h:outputText id="authorName" value="#{author.first} #{author.last}"/>
    </h:column>
</h:dataTable>
```

In the example, you can see that the h:dataTable value attribute is listed as #{authorTableController.authorList}, a List of Author objects declared within the controller class. The var attribute establishes a variable named author that refers to the current author who is being processed from the author list. The author variable can then be accessed from within each h:column, displaying the data associated with the current list element.

An important piece of the puzzle to help make tables easier to read and follow is the CSS that can be used to style the table. The h:dataTable supports various attributes that allow you to apply externally defined CSS classes to your table, specifically, the styleClass, captionClass, headerClass, footerClass, rowClasses, and columnClasses attributes. Each of them can contain a CSS class specification for formatting. The example demonstrates this feature.

2-13. Developing with HTML5

Problem

You would like to develop your view composed using standard HTML5 markup, rather than JSF tags. Furthermore, you would like to take advantage of the JSF life cycle and managed bean/controller class architecture.

Solution

Utilize the HTML-friendly markup for use within JSF views. By using HTML5 within JSF views directly, you can take advantage of the entire JSF stack while coding views in pure HTML5. To use this solution, HTML5 tags have the ability to access the JSF infrastructure via the use of a new `taglib` URI specification `jsf="http://xmlns.jcp.org/jsf"`, which can be utilized within JSF views beginning with JSF 2.2 and beyond. In views that specify the new `taglib` URI, HTML tags can utilize attributes that expose the underlying JSF architecture.

In the following example view, HTML5 tags are used to compose an input form that is backed by a JSF managed bean. To visit the sources for this example, please visit the view `recipe02_13.xhtml` within the sources for the book:

```
<?xml version="1.0" encoding="UTF-8"?>
<!DOCTYPE html PUBLIC "-//W3C//DTD XHTML 1.0 Strict//EN"
"http://www.w3.org/TR/xhtml1/DTD/xhtml1-strict.dtd">
<html xmlns="http://www.w3.org/1999/xhtml"
    xmlns:jsf="http://xmlns.jcp.org/jsf">
  <head jsf:id="head">
    <meta http-equiv="Content-Type" content="text/html;
    charset=UTF-8"/>

  </head>
  <body jsf:id="body">
    <form jsf:id="form" jsf:prependId="false">
      <input type="email" jsf:id="value1" value="#{ajaxBean.value1}">
      </input>
      <br/><br/>
      <input type="text" jsf:id="value2" value="#{ajaxBean.value2}">
```

```
        </input>
        <br/>
        <br/>
        <input type="submit" jsf:id="status" jsf:value="#{ajaxBean.status}"
               jsf:action="#{ajaxBean.process()}" value="Process"/>
        <label for="status">Message: </label>
        <output jsf:id="status">#{ajaxBean.status}</output>
    </form>
  </body>
</html>
```

Note   This feature is only available to views written in Facelets. It is not available to views written in JSP.

How It Works

The JSF 2.2 release added the ability to utilize HTML5 markup within JSF views. As a matter of fact, the markup is not limited to HTML5; it can also include HTML4 and so on. The addition of a `taglib` URI makes this possible, because it allows existing HTML tags to be bound to the JSF life cycle via the use of new namespace attributes. It is now possible to develop entire JSF views without using any JSF tags at all.

To utilize the new namespace attributes, your JSF view must import the `taglib` URI `jsf="http://xmlns.jcp.org/jsf"`. The new `taglib` can then be referenced as attributes within existing HTML tags, setting the underlying JSF attributes that are referenced. For instance, to utilize an HTML input tag with JSF, you would add the `jsf:id` attribute and set it equal to the JSF ID that you want to assign to that component. You would then set an attribute of `jsf:value` equal to the managed bean value.

Note   There is no need to import the `http://xmlns.jcp.org/jsf/html` `taglib` because you are no longer utilizing JSF component tags in the view.

2-14. Creating Page Templates

Problem

You want to make each of the JSF views within your application follow the same structure. Moreover, you want to have the ability to reuse the same layout for each view.

Solution

Create a page template using the Facelets view definition language. Facelets ships as part of JavaServer Faces, and you can use it to create highly sophisticated layouts for your views in a proficient manner. The template demonstrated in this recipe will be used to define the standard layout for all pages within an application. The demo application for this chapter is for a bookstore web site. The site will display a number of book titles on the left side of the screen, a header at the top, a footer at the bottom, and a main view in the middle. When a book title is clicked in the left menu, the middle view changes, displaying the list of authors for the selected book.

To create a template, you must develop an XHTML view file and then add the appropriate HTML/JSF/XML markup to it. Content from other views will displace the `ui:insert` elements in the template once the template has been applied to one or more JSF views. The following source is that of a template named `custom_template.xhtml`; this is the template that will be used for all views within the application:

```
<html xmlns="http://www.w3.org/1999/xhtml"
    xmlns:ui="http://xmlns.jcp.org/jsf/facelets"
    xmlns:h="http://xmlns.jcp.org/jsf/html">

<h:head>
    <meta http-equiv="Content-Type" content="text/html; charset=UTF-8" />
    <h:outputStylesheet library="css" name="default.css"/>
    <h:outputStylesheet library="css" name="cssLayout.css"/>
    <h:outputStylesheet library="css" name="styles.css"/>
    <title>#{faceletsAuthorController.storeName}</title>
</h:head>

<h:body>
```

```
    <div id="top">
        <h2>#{faceletsAuthorController.storeName}</h2>
    </div>
    <div>
        <div id="left">
            <h:form id="navForm">
                <h:commandLink action="#{faceletsAuthorController.
                populateJavaRecipesAuthorList}" >Java 9 Recipes
                </h:commandLink>
                <br/>
                <br/>
                <h:commandLink action="#{faceletsAuthorController.
                populateJakartaEERecipesAuthorList}">Java EE 8 Recipes
                </h:commandLink>
            </h:form>
        </div>
        <div id="content" class="left_content">
            <ui:insert name="content">Content</ui:insert>
        </div>
    </div>
    <div id="bottom" style="position: absolute;width: 100%;bottom: 20px;">
        Written by Josh Juneau, Apress Author
    </div>

    </h:body>

</html>
```

The template defines the overall structure for the application views. However, it uses a CSS to declare the formatting for each of the <div> elements within the template. The style sheet, entitled default.css, should be contained within a resources directory in the application so that it will be accessible to the views. Please refer to Recipe 2-16 for more details on the resources directory.

Note   The CSSs can be automatically generated for you if using the NetBeans IDE.

There are also a couple of JSF EL expressions utilized within the template. The EL references a JSF controller by the name of `AuthorController`, which is referenced by `faceletsAuthorController`. While the source for this class is very important for the overall application, you'll wait to look at that code until Recipe 2-15 since it does not play a role in the application template layout.

How It Works

To create a unified application experience, all of the views should be coherent in that they look similar and function in a uniform fashion. The idea of developing web page templates has been around for a number of years, but unfortunately many template implementations contain duplicate markup on every application page. While duplicating the same layout for every separate web page works, it creates a maintenance nightmare. What happens when there is a need to update a single link within the page header? Such a conundrum would cause a developer to visit and manually update every web page for an application if the template was duplicated on every page. The Facelets view definition language provides a robust solution for the development of view templates, and it is one of the major bonuses of working with the JSF technology.

Facelets provides the ability for a single template to be applied to one or more views within an application. This means a developer can create one view that constructs the header, footer, and other portions of the template, and then this view can be applied to any number of other views that are responsible for containing the main view content. This technique mitigates issues such as changing a single link within the page header, because now the template can be updated with the new link, and every other view within the application will automatically reflect the change.

To create a template using Facelets, create an XHTML view, declare the required namespaces, and then add HTML, JSF, and Facelets tags accordingly to design the layout you desire. The template can be thought of as an "outer shell" for a web view in that it can contain any number of other views within it. Likewise, any number of JSF views can have the same template applied, so the overall look and feel of the application will remain constant. Figure 2-5 provides a visual representation, demonstrating the concept of an application template.

Figure 2-5. *Visual representation of a Facelets template and client*

You may have noticed from the view listing in the solution to this recipe that there are some tags toting the ui: prefix. Those are the Facelets tags that are responsible for controlling the view layout. To utilize these Facelets tags, you'll need to declare the XML namespace for the Facelets tag library in the <html> element within the template. Note that the XML namespace for the standard JSF tag libraries is also specified here:

```
<html xmlns="http://www.w3.org/1999/xhtml"
      xmlns:ui="http://xmlns.jcp.org/jsf/facelets"
      xmlns:h="http://xmlns.jcp.org/jsf/html">
...
```

Note   The Facelets template must include the <html>, <head> or <h:head>, and <body> or <h:body>, elements because they are what define the overall layout for each view that uses it. Each view that makes use of a Facelets template is known as a *composition*. One template can be used by multiple compositions or views. In actuality, everything outside of the <ui:composition> opening and closing tags within a composition is ignored. You'll learn more about that in the next recipe!

Facelets contains a number of special tags that can be used to help control page flow and layout. Table 2-7 in Recipe 2-15 lists the Facelets tags that are useful for controlling page flow and layout. The only Facelets tag that is used within the template for this recipe example is ui:insert. The ui:insert tag contains a name attribute, which is set to the name of the corresponding ui:define element that will be included in the view. Taking a look at the source for this recipe, you can see the following ui:insert tag:

```
<ui:insert name="content">Content</ui:insert>
```

If a view that uses the template, aka template client, specifies a ui:define tag with the same name as the ui:insert name, then any content that is placed between the opening and closing ui:define tags will be inserted into the view in that location. However, if the template client does not contain a ui:define tag with the same name as the ui:insert tag, then the content between the opening and closing ui:insert tags within the template will be displayed.

In summary, a Facelets template consists of HTML and JSF markup, and it is used to define a page layout. Sections of the template can specify where page content will be displayed through the usage of the ui:insert tag. Any areas within the template that contain a ui:insert tag can have content inserted into them from a template client.

2-15. Applying Templates
Problem

You have created a template for use within your JSF web views, and you want to apply it to the views of your application.

Solution

Use the ui:composition tag within each view that will utilize the template. The ui:composition tag should be used to invoke the template, and ui:define tags should be placed where content should be inserted. The following listings demonstrate how Facelets templates are applied to various views.

View #1: recipe02_15a.xhtml

recipe02_15a.xhtml is the markup for a view within the bookstore application that is
used to display the authors for the *Java 9 Recipes* book. The template that was created
in Recipe 2-14 is applied to the view, and individual ui:define tags are used within the
view to specify the content that should be inserted into the page/view:

```
<html xmlns="http://www.w3.org/1999/xhtml"
      xmlns:ui="http://xmlns.jcp.org/jsf/facelets"
      xmlns:f="http://xmlns.jcp.org/jsf/core"
      xmlns:h="http://xmlns.jcp.org/jsf/html">

    <body>

        <ui:composition template="./layout/custom_template.xhtml">

            <ui:define name="top">

            </ui:define>

            <ui:define name="left">

            </ui:define>

            <ui:define name="content">
                <h:form id="componentForm">
                    <h1>Author List for Java 9 Recipes</h1>
                    <p>
                        Below is the list of authors.  Click on the
                        author's last name for more information regarding
                        the author.
                    </p>

                    <h:graphicImage id="javarecipes" style="width: 100px;
                    height: 120px" library="image" name="java9recipes.png"/>
                    <br/>
                    <h:dataTable id="authorTable" border="1" value=
                    "#{faceletsAuthorController.authorList}"
                                var="author">
```

```
                    <f:facet name="header">
                        Java 9 Recipes Authors
                    </f:facet>
                    <h:column>
                        <h:commandLink id="authorName" action="#{facele
                        tsAuthorController.displayAuthor(author.last)}"
                                       value="#{author.first} #{author.
                                       last}"/>
                    </h:column>
                </h:dataTable>
                <br/>
                <br/>

            </h:form>
        </ui:define>

        <ui:define name="bottom">
            bottom
        </ui:define>

    </ui:composition>


    </body>
</html>
```

View #2: recipe02_15b.xhtml

recipe02_15b.xhtml contains the sources for the second view within the bookstore application. It is used to list the authors for the *Java EE 8 Recipes* book. Again, note that the template has been applied to the view by specifying the template attribute within the ui:composition tag:

```
<html xmlns="http://www.w3.org/1999/xhtml"
      xmlns:ui="http://xmlns.jcp.org/jsf/facelets"
      xmlns:f="http://xmlns.jcp.org/jsf/core"
      xmlns:h="http://xmlns.jcp.org/jsf/html">
```

```
<body>

    <ui:composition template="./layout/custom_template.xhtml">

        <ui:define name="top">

        </ui:define>

        <ui:define name="left">

        </ui:define>

        <ui:define name="content">
            <h:form id="componentForm">
                <h1>Author List for Java EE 8 Recipes</h1>
                <p>
                    Below is the list of authors.  Click on the
                    author's last name for more information regarding
                    the author.
                </p>

                <h:graphicImage id="javarecipes" library="image" style=
                "width: 100px; height: 120px" name="java9recipes.png"/>
                <br/>
                <h:dataTable id="authorTable" border="1" value=
                "#{faceletsAuthorController.authorList}"
                            var="author">
                    <f:facet name="header">
                        Java 9 Recipes Authors
                    </f:facet>
                    <h:column>
                        <h:commandLink id="authorName" action="#{facele
                        tsAuthorController.displayAuthor(author.last)}"
                                    value="#{author.first}
                                    #{author.last}"/>
                    </h:column>
                </h:dataTable>
                <br/>
                <br/>
```

```
            </h:form>
        </ui:define>

        <ui:define name="bottom">
            bottom
        </ui:define>

    </ui:composition>

  </body>
</html>
```

View #3: recipe02_15c.xhtml

Recipe02_15c.xhtml contains the sources for another view listing that is part of the bookstore application. This view is responsible for displaying the individual author detail. Again, the template is applied to this page:

```
<html xmlns="http://www.w3.org/1999/xhtml"
    xmlns:f="http://xmlns.jcp.org/jsf/core"
    xmlns:ui="http://xmlns.jcp.org/jsf/facelets"
    xmlns:h="http://xmlns.jcp.org/jsf/html">
  <h:head>
      <meta http-equiv="Content-Type" content="text/html; charset=UTF-8"/>
      <title>Recipe 2-15: Facelets Page Template</title>
  </h:head>
  <h:body>
      <ui:composition template="./layout/custom_template.xhtml">
          <ui:define name="top">
          </ui:define>
          <ui:define name="left">
          </ui:define>
          <ui:define name="content">
              <h:form id="componentForm">
                  <h1>#{faceletsAuthorController.current.first}
                  #{faceletsAuthorController.current.last}</h1>
```

```
            <p>
                <h:graphicImage id="java9recipes" library="image"
                style="width: 100px; height: 120px"
                name="java9recipes.png"/>
                <br/>
                #{faceletsAuthorController.current.bio}
            </p>
        </h:form>
    </ui:define>

    <ui:define name="bottom">
        bottom
    </ui:define>

    </ui:composition>
    </h:body>
</html>
```

Managed Bean Controller: AuthorController

Of course, all the business logic and navigation is occurring from within a JSF controller class. AuthorController is the bean that handles all the logic for the bookstore application. Note that the @Named annotation specifies a String value of faceletsAuthorController, which is used to reference the bean from within the views:

```
package org.jakartaeerecipes.chapter02.recipe02_15;

import java.io.Serializable;
import java.util.ArrayList;
import java.util.List;
import javax.annotation.PostConstruct;
import javax.enterprise.context.SessionScoped;
import javax.inject.Named;

@Named(value = "faceletsAuthorController")
@SessionScoped
```

```java
public class AuthorController implements Serializable {

    private List<Author> authorList;
    private String storeName = "Acme Bookstore";

    private final String juneauBio =
            "Josh Juneau has been developing software"
            + . . .";
    private final String deaBio = "This is Carl Dea's Bio";
    private final String beatyBio = "This is Mark Beaty's Bio";
    private final String oConnerBio = "This is John O'Connor's Bio";
    private final String guimeBio = "This is Freddy Guime's Bio";
    private Author current;
    private String authorLast;

    /**
     * Creates a new instance of RecipeController
     */
    public AuthorController() {

    }

    /**
     * Methods that are annotated with @PostConstruct are invoked when the
     * controller class is created.
     */
    @PostConstruct
    public void init(){
        populateJavaRecipesAuthorList();
    }

    public String populateJavaRecipesAuthorList() {

        authorList = null;

        authorList = new ArrayList<>();
        authorList.add(new Author("Josh", "Juneau", juneauBio));
        authorList.add(new Author("Carl", "Dea", deaBio));
        authorList.add(new Author("Mark", "Beaty", beatyBio));
```

```java
        authorList.add(new Author("John", "O'Conner", oConnerBio));
        authorList.add(new Author("Freddy", "Guime", guimeBio));
        return "recipe02_15a;
    }

    public String populateJakartaEERecipesAuthorList() {
        System.out.println("initializing authors list");
        authorList = new ArrayList<>();
        authorList.add(new Author("Josh", "Juneau", juneauBio));
        return "recipe02_15b";

    }

    public String displayAuthor(String last) {
        for (Author author : authorList) {
            if (author.getLast().equals(last)) {
                current = author;
            }
        }
        return "recipe02_15c";
    }

    /**
     * Getters and Setters
     */

}
```

In the end, the overall application will look like Figure 2-6. To run the application from the sources, deploy the web archive (WAR) file distribution to your application server, and then load the following URL into your browser: http://your-server:port_number/JakartaEERecipes/faces/chapter02/chapter02_15a.xhtml.

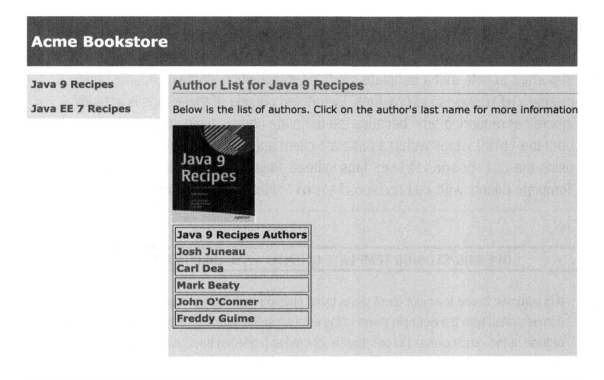

Figure 2-6. *Application using a Facelets template*

How It Works

Applying a Facelets template to individual views within a JSF application is quite easy. Views that make use of a template are known as *template clients*. As mentioned in Recipe 2-14, a view template can specify individual ui:insert tags, along with the name attribute, in any location on the template where view content could be inserted. The name attribute within the ui:insert tag will pair up with the name attribute within the ui:define tag in the template client in order to determine what content is inserted.

Note As noted in Recipe 2-14, each view that uses a Facelets template can be referred to as a *composition*. It can also be referred to as a *template client*. It is important to note that a template client, or composition, contains opening and closing `<ui:composition>` tags. Everything outside of those tags is actually ignored at rendering time because the template body is used instead. You can also omit the `<html>` tags within a template client and just open and close the view using the `<ui:composition>` tags instead. Please see the "Opening/Closing Template Clients with `<ui:composition>`" sidebar for an example.

OPENING/CLOSING TEMPLATE CLIENTS WITH <UI:COMPOSITION>

It is common to see template client views using opening and closing `<html>` tags, as demonstrated with the example views in the solution to this recipe. However, since everything outside of the `<ui:composition>` tags is ignored at rendering time, you can omit those tags completely. It is sometimes useful to open and close a template client with the `<ui:composition>` tag. However, some page editors will be unable to work with the code or errors will be displayed because the view does not include the `<html>` element at its root. Here's an example of using `<ui:composition>` as the opening and closing elements of a template client:

```
<ui:composition xmlns="http://www.w3.org/1999/xhtml"
      xmlns:ui="http://xmlns.jcp.org/jsf/facelets"
      xmlns:f="http://xmlns.jcp.org/jsf/core"
      xmlns:h=http://xmlns.jcp.org/jsf/html
      template="./layout/custom_template.xhtml">

<<same as code per the view samples in the solution to this recipe>>

  </ui:composition>
```

Use the technique that suits your application the best! Remember, JSF and Facelets will treat each view the same, and you can save a few lines of code specifying `<ui:composition>` as the root.

Applying Templates

A template can be applied to a view by specifying it within the template attribute within the view's `ui:composition` tag. For instance, all the views within this example specify the same template, as you can see in the following excerpt:

```
<ui:composition template="./layout/custom_template.xhtml">
```

The name of the template in the example is `custom_template.xhtml`, and the path to the template is `./layout/`. The `ui:composition` tag should encapsulate all other markup within a Facelets view. All views that are to use the template must specify the `ui:composition` tag. A number of other useful Facelets template tags come along with Facelets, as described in Table 2-7.

Table 2-7. *Facelets Page Control and Template Tags*

Tag	Description
ui:component	Defines a template component and specifies a file name for the component
ui:composition	Defines a page composition and encapsulates all other JSF markup
ui:debug	Creates a debug component, which captures debugging information, namely, the state of the component tree and the scoped variables in the application, when the component is rendered
ui:define	Defines content that is inserted into a page by a template
ui:decorate	Decorates pieces of a page
ui:fragment	Defines a template fragment, much like ui:component, except that all content outside of tag is not disregarded
ui:include	Allows another XHTML page to be encapsulated and reused within a view
ui:insert	Inserts content into a template
ui:param	Passes parameters to an included file or template
ui:repeat	Iterates over a collection of data
ui:remove	Removes content from a page

The ui:define tag encloses content that will be inserted into the template at the location of the template's ui:insert tags. The ui:define tag is matched to a template's ui:insert tag based on the value of the name attribute that is common to each tag. As you can see from the first view listing in this example, the first ui:define tag specifies top for the name attribute, and this will correspond to the template ui:insert tag with a name attribute equal to top. But the template does not specify such a tag! That is OK; there does not have to be a one-to-one match between the ui:define and ui:insert tags. A view can specify any number of ui:define tags, and if they do not correspond to any of the ui:insert tags within the template, then they are ignored. Likewise, a template can specify any number of ui:insert tags, and if they do not correspond to a ui:define tag within the template client view, then the content that is defined within the template in that location will be displayed.

Looking at the same view, another ui:define tag contains a name attribute value equal to content, and this tag does correspond with a ui:insert tag within the template that also has a name attribute value of content. The following excerpt is taken from the template, and it shows the ui:insert tag that corresponds to the view's ui:define tag with the same name attribute. You can see the full listing for the template in Recipe 2-14.

```
<div id="content" class="left_content">
        <ui:insert name="content">Content</ui:insert>
</div>
```

The following excerpt, taken from recipe02_01a.xhtml, is the corresponding ui:define tag that will be inserted into the template at this location:

```
<ui:define name="content">
                <h:form id="componentForm">
                    <h1>Author List for Java 9 Recipes</h1>
                    <p>
                        Below is the list of authors.  Click on the
                        author's last name for more information regarding
                        the author.
                    </p>

                    <h:graphicImage id="javarecipes" style="width: 10%;
                    height: 20%" library="image" name="java9recipes.png"/>
                    <br/>
```

```
<h:dataTable id="authorTable" border="1" value=
"#{faceletsAuthorController.authorList}"
            var="author">
    <f:facet name="header">
        Java 9 Recipes Authors
    </f:facet>
    <h:column>
        <h:commandLink id="authorName" action="#{facele
        tsAuthorController.displayAuthor(author.last)}"
                    value="#{author.first}
                    #{author.last}"/>
    </h:column>
</h:dataTable>
<br/>
<br/>

    </h:form>
</ui:define>
```

As you can see, it can be very powerful to define a view template that can be applied to several views within an application. Facelets templating provides a very powerful solution for defining such a template, allowing for consistent page layout and reusable page code.

2-16. Adding Resources into the Mix
Problem

You want to include resources, such as CSS, images, and JavaScript code, within your views that are accessible for use from every view within your application. For instance, rather than hard-coding a URL to an image, you want to reference the image location and have the application dynamically create the URL to the image location at runtime.

Solution

Create a resources directory and, optionally, subfolders within the resources directory to contain the resources that your application will utilize. Any CSS files, images, and so on that are placed within subdirectories in the resources folder can be referenced within a JSF view via a JSF component's library attribute, rather than specifying the full path to the resource. In the following example, a cascading style sheet is used to style the table of authors within the application. For this recipe, you will use the styles.css sheet that was applied to the h:dataTable in an earlier recipe. The style sheet declaration will reside within the custom_template.xhtml template, and you will use an h:outputStylesheet component rather than a <link> tag. As a matter of fact, all of the <link> tags will be removed and replaced with h:outputStylesheet components to take advantage of the resources folder. The directory structure should look like Figure 2-7 when set up correctly.

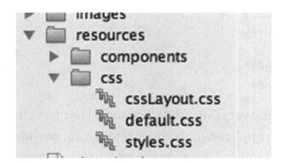

Figure 2-7. *Utilizing the resources directory*

The following listing is the updated custom_template.xhtml, because it now utilizes the h:outputStylesheet component rather than the <link> tag. Note that the library attribute is specified as css:

```
<html xmlns="http://www.w3.org/1999/xhtml"
    xmlns:ui="http://xmlns.jcp.org/jsf/facelets"
    xmlns:f="http://xmlns.jcp.org/jsf/core"
    xmlns:h="http://xmlns.jcp.org/jsf/html">

    <body>

        <ui:composition template="./layout/custom_template.xhtml">
            <ui:define name="content">
                <h:form id="componentForm">
```

```
<h1>Author List for Java 9 Recipes</h1>
<p>
    Below is the list of authors. Click on the author's
    last name for more information regarding the
    author.
</p>

<h:graphicImage id="javarecipes"
                library="image" style="width: 100px;
                height: 120px"
                name="java9recipes.png"/>
<br/>
<h:dataTable id="authorTable" border="1"
value="#{faceletsAuthorController.authorList}"
            styleClass="authorTable"
            rowClasses="authorTableOdd, authorTableEven"
            var="author">
    <f:facet name="header">
        Java 9 Recipes Authors
    </f:facet>
    <h:column>
        <h:commandLink id="authorName" action="#{facele
        tsAuthorController.displayAuthor(author.last)}"
                    value="#{author.first}
                    #{author.last}"/>
    </h:column>
</h:dataTable>
<br/>
<br/>

        </h:form>
    </ui:define>

</ui:composition>

</body>
</html>
```

The h:dataTable component that is used to list the authors within the views of the Acme Bookstore application can now make use of the styles that are listed within styles.css. The following excerpt from the XHTML document named recipe02_16. xhtml demonstrates the h:dataTable component with the styles applied:

```
<h:dataTable id="authorTable" border="1" value="#{faceletsAuthorController.
authorList}"
                                styleClass="authorTable"
                                rowClasses="authorTableOdd,
                                authorTableEven"
                                var="author">
        <f:facet name="header">
            Java 9 Recipes Authors
        </f:facet>
        <h:column>
                <h:commandLink id="authorName"
                    action="#{faceletsAuthorController.
                    displayAuthor(author.last)}"
                     value="#{author.first} #{author.last}"/>
        </h:column>
    </h:dataTable>
```

The table should now look like Figure 2-8 when rendered on a page.

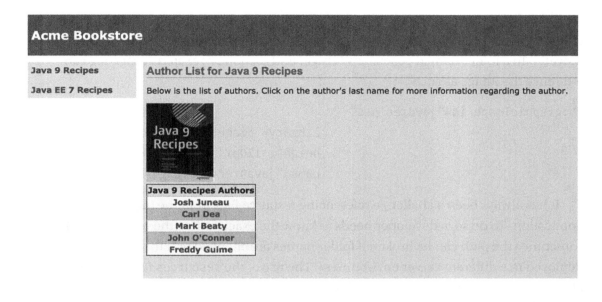

Figure 2-8. *Author table with styles applied*

How It Works

It is easy to add a resource to a JSF application because there is no need to worry about referring to a static path when declaring the resource. Since the release of JSF 2.0, the resources folder can be used to list subfolders, also known as *libraries*, into which the resources can be placed. The JSF components that can use resources now have the library attribute baked into them. This allows a specific library to be specified for such components so that the component will know where to find the resources that it requires.

To use the new resources folder, create a folder at the root of an application's web directory and name it resources. That resources folder can then contain subfolders, which will become the libraries that can be utilized within the JSF components. For instance, subfolders can be named css and images, and then those names can be specified for the library attribute of JSF components that utilize such resources. In the example, cascading style sheets are placed into the resources/css folder, and then they are referenced utilizing the h:outputStylesheet component and specifying the css library as follows:

```
<h:outputStylesheet library="css" name="default.css"/>
```

Other resources can be placed within such libraries. The h:graphicImage component also contains the library attribute, so the images for the books can be moved into a folder named resources/image, and then the h:graphicImage tag can reference the image as such:

```
<h:graphicImage id="javarecipes"
                          library="image" style="width: 100px;
                          height: 120px"
                          name="java9recipes.png"/>
```

It has always been a challenge referencing resource files from the pages of a web application. To do so, a developer needs to know the exact path to the resource, and sometimes the path can be broken if folder names are changed or if the application is deployed in a different server environment. The use of the resources folder in JSF 2.0 along with the new library attribute has greatly reduced the complexity of managing such resources.

2-17. Handling Variable-Length Data

Problem

You are interested in iterating over a collection of data using a technique other than an h:dataTable component because you want to use standard HTML table markup for each row and column of the table.

Solution

Use the Facelets ui:repeat tag for iterating over a collection of data rather than the h:dataTable component. Doing so allows for the same style of collection iteration, but it does not force the use of the h:dataTable component elements. For this recipe, the Acme Bookstore application has been rewritten so that it now contains the ability to list each author's books separately on their bio page. When an author name is chosen from the book listing or when an author is searched, then the bio page will appear, and the author's bio is displayed along with each of the books that the author has written.

Note   The example for this recipe has been rewritten to make the application more robust. A new Book class has been created so that each book is now its own object. The Author class has been rewritten so that one or more Book objects can now be added to each Author object. The AuthorController has been rewritten so that the new Book and Author objects can be used to populate the author listing tables, and a new method has been added that allows for the initialization of each Book and Author object. To use the new classes, the application template (custom_template_neworg.xhtml), search component (search_neworg.xhtml), and each of the application views have been rewritten. Please refer to the sources in the org.jakartaeerecipes.chapter02. recipe02_17 package and the recipe's corresponding XHTML documents for complete listings.

The ui:repeat tag is used to iterate over a collection of the selected author's books within the author bio view, named recipe02_05c.xhtml. The author bio page can be reached by selecting an author from a listing of authors or searching for an author using the search component. The following code shows the view, recipe02_17c.xhtml, which is the bio view:

```
<html xmlns="http://www.w3.org/1999/xhtml"
    xmlns:f="http://xmlns.jcp.org/jsf/core"
    xmlns:ui="http://xmlns.jcp.org/jsf/facelets"
    xmlns:h="http://xmlns.jcp.org/jsf/html">
  <h:head>
    <meta http-equiv="Content-Type" content="text/html; charset=UTF-8"/>
    <title>Recipe 2-17: Facelets Page Template</title>
  </h:head>
  <h:body>
    <ui:composition template="./layout_enhanced/custom_template_search_
    neworg.xhtml">
      <ui:define name="content">
        <h:form id="componentForm">
          <h1>#{uiRepeatAuthorController.current.first}
          #{uiRepeatAuthorController.current.last}</h1>
```

```
            <p>
                #{uiRepeatAuthorController.current.bio}
            </p>

            <br/>
            <h1>Author's Books</h1>

            <table>
            <ui:repeat id="bookList" var="book" value="#{uiRepeat
            AuthorController.current.books}">
                <tr>
                    <td>
                        <h:graphicImage id="bookImage"
                                        library="image"
                                        style="width: 100px;
                                        height: 120px"
                                        name="#{book.image}"/>
                    </td>
                </tr>
                <tr>
                    <td>
                        <strong>#{book.title}</strong>
                    </td>
                </tr>
            </ui:repeat>
            </table>
        </h:form>
      </ui:define>

    </ui:composition>
  </h:body>
</html>
```

Each Author object contains a list of books that an author has written, and when the bio page is rendered, it looks like Figure 2-9, displaying the list of books that the author has written using the ui:repeat tag.

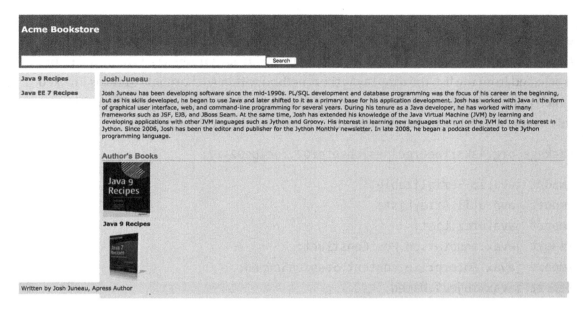

Figure 2-9. *Displaying a collection of objects with ui:repeat*

How It Works

The Facelets `ui:repeat` tag is a nice alternative to the `h:dataTable` component if you need to have more control over the HTML table that is rendered. The `h:dataTable` component is powerful in that it makes it easy to iterate over a collection of objects and display them within a page. However, sometimes it is useful to control the layout a bit more, and `ui:repeat` provides that level of control.

The `ui:repeat` tag has a handful of attributes that need to be specified in order to bind the tag to a collection of data within a managed bean. Specifically, the `value` and `var` attributes, much like those of the `h:dataTable` component, are used to specify the collection to iterate over and the variable that will be used to refer to a single object within the collection, respectively. In the example, the `value` attribute is set to `#{uiRepeatAuthorController.current.books}`, which is a collection of `Book` objects that is attached to the currently selected `Author`, and the `var` attribute is set to the value `book`.

The markup and JSF tags placed between the opening and closing `ui:repeat` tags will be processed for each iteration over the collection of objects. In the example, two table rows are placed inside `ui:repeat`; one row contains the book cover image, and the other contains the name of the book. The `Book` object fields are referenced within `ui:repeat` using the value of the `var` attribute, `book`.

201

In the example for this recipe, the views that display the complete author list for each of the books use a List named authorList. The authorList is declared within the AuthorController managed bean and populated with Author objects. When an author is selected from the list, the displayAuthor method within AuthorController is invoked, which populates the current Author object. Let's take a look at the AuthorController for this recipe, which has been rewritten since its use within previous recipes:

```
package org.jakartaeerecipes.chapter02.recipe02_17;

import java.io.Serializable;
import java.util.ArrayList;
import java.util.List;
import javax.annotation.PostConstruct;
import javax.enterprise.context.SessionScoped;
import javax.inject.Named;

@Named(value = "uiRepeatAuthorController")
@SessionScoped
public class AuthorController implements Serializable {

    private List<Author> authorBookList;
    private List<Author> authorList;
    private List<Author> completeAuthorList;
    private String storeName = "Acme Bookstore";

    private String juneauBio =
            "Josh Juneau has been developing software"
            . . .;
    private String deaBio = "This is Carl Dea's Bio";
    private String beatyBio = "This is Mark Beaty's Bio";
    private String oConnerBio = "This is John O'Connor's Bio";
    private String guimeBio = "This is Freddy Guime's Bio";
    private Author current;
    private String authorLast;

    /**
     * Creates a new instance of RecipeController
     */
    public AuthorController() {
```

```java
}

@PostConstruct
public void init(){
    populateAuthors();
    populateJavaRecipesAuthorList();
    populateCompleteAuthorList();
}
private void populateAuthors(){
    Book book1 = new Book("Java 9 Recipes", "java9recipes.png");
    Book book2 = new Book("Java EE 8 Recipes", "jakartaeerecipes.png");
    Book book3 = new Book("Java FX 2.0: Introduction By Example",
    "javafx.png");
    authorBookList = new ArrayList<Author>();

    Author author1 = new Author("Josh", "Juneau", juneauBio);
    author1.addBook(book1);
    author1.addBook(book2);
    authorBookList.add(author1);

    Author author2 = new Author("Carl", "Dea", deaBio);
    author2.addBook(book1);
    author2.addBook(book3);
    authorBookList.add(author2);

    Author author3 = new Author("Mark", "Beaty", beatyBio);
    author3.addBook(book1);
    authorBookList.add(author3);

    Author author4 = new Author("John", "O'Conner", oConnerBio);
    author4.addBook(book1);
    authorBookList.add(author4);

    Author author5 = new Author("Freddy", "Guime", guimeBio);
    author5.addBook(book1);
    authorBookList.add(author5);
}
```

```java
/**
 * Searches through all Author objects and populates the authorList
 * with only those authors who were involved with the Java 9 Recipes book
 * @return
 */
public String populateJavaRecipesAuthorList() {
    authorList = new ArrayList<>();
    authorBookList.forEach((author) -> {
        List<Book>books = author.getBooks();
        books.stream().filter((book) -> (book.getTitle()
                .equals("Java 7 Recipes"))).forEachOrdered((_item) -> {
            authorList.add(author);
        });
    });
    return "recipe02_05a";
}

/**
 * Searches through all Author objects and populates the authorList
 * with only those authors who were involved with the Java EE 8 Recipes
   book
 * @return
 */
public String populateJakartaEERecipesAuthorList() {
    authorList = new ArrayList<>();
    for(Author author:authorBookList){
        List<Book>books = author.getBooks();
        for(Book book:books){
            if(book.getTitle().equals("Java EE 8 Recipes")){
                authorList.add(author);
            }
        }
    }
    return "recipe02_05b";
}
```

```java
/**
 * Populates completeAuthorList with each existing Author object
 * @return
 */
private void populateCompleteAuthorList() {
    completeAuthorList = new ArrayList();
    for(Author author:authorBookList){
        completeAuthorList.add(author);
    }

}

public String displayAuthor(String last) {
    for (Author author : authorList) {
        if (author.getLast().equals(last)) {
            current = author;
        }
    }
    return "recipe02_05c";
}

/**
 * @return the authorList
 */
public List getauthorList() {
    return authorList;
}

/**
 * Getters and Setters
 */

}
```

When displayAuthor is invoked, the current Author object is populated with the currently selected author, and the bio page is rendered. The bio page source is listed in the solution to this recipe. Each Author object contains a List of Book objects that correspond to the books that particular author has written. The ui:repeat tag is used to iterate over this list of books.

The ui:repeat tag can be effective in various use cases. When deciding to use h:dataTable or ui:repeat, it is best to determine whether customization is going to be imperative. For those situations where more control is desired, ui:repeat is certainly the best choice.

2-18. Invoking Controller Class Actions on Life-Cycle Phase Events

Problem

You want to automatically invoke a controller class action when a specific JSF life-cycle phase event occurs. For instance, when a view is loading, you want to invoke a controller class action that performs a conditional verification based upon the user who is visiting the page.

Solution

Utilize a JSF view action by adding the f:viewAction facet to the JSF view. Use the facet to specify the controller class action to invoke, as well as when to invoke the action. In the following excerpt from the view chapter02/recipe02_18.xhtml, a controller class method action named validateUser is invoked:

```
<f:metadata>
        <f:viewAction action="#{viewActionManagedBean.validateUser()}"/>
</f:metadata>
```

How It Works

In JSF 2.1 and prior, it was difficult to invoke action methods within a controller class unless they were bound to a command component. Sometimes it makes sense to invoke a method when the page is loading, after the page has been fully loaded, and so on. In the past, this was done by using a preRenderView event listener, which invokes a method contained within a managed bean before the view is rendered. Utilization of the preRenderView event listener works, but it does not provide the level of control that is required to invoke a method during different phases of the view life cycle. The preRenderView also requires developers to programmatically check the request type and work with the navigation handler.

In the JSF 2.2 release, a new technique can be used to invoke action methods within a controller class during specified life-cycle events that occur within the view. A new tag, f:viewAction, can be bound to a view, and it can be incorporated into the JSF life cycle in both non-JSF (initial) and JSF (postback) requests. To use the tag, it must be a child of the metadata facet. View parameters can be specified within the metadata facet as well, and they will become available from within the controller class when the action method is invoked.

In the example, the action method named validateUser is invoked using the viewAction. In the example method, a String is returned, which enables implicit navigation based upon the action method results. If null is returned, the navigation handler is invoked, but the same view will be rendered again so long as there are no navigation condition expressions that change the navigation. If a String-based view name is returned, then the navigation handler will render that view once the method has completed. This can come in handy for situations such as authentication handling, where an action method is used to check the user's role and then the appropriate view is rendered based upon the authenticated user role:

```
public String validateUser() {
        String viewName;
        System.out.println("Look in the server log to see this message");
        // Here we would perform validation based upon the user visiting the
        // site to ensure that they had the appropriate permissions to view
        // the selected view.  For the purposes of this example, this
        // conditional logic is just a prototype.
        if (visitor.isAdmin()){
            // visit the current page
            viewName = null;
            System.out.println("Current User is an Admin");
        } else {
            viewName = "notAdmin";
            System.out.println("Current User is NOT an Admin");
        }
        return viewName;
    }
```

As mentioned previously, f:viewAction facet can be customized to allow the action method to be invoked at different stages within the view life cycle. By default, the viewAction will be initiated before postback because the specified action method is expected to execute whether the request was Faces or non-Faces. However, this can be changed by setting the onPostback attribute of the f:viewAction tag to true:

```
<f:viewAction action="#{viewActionManagedBean.validateUser()}"
onPostback="true"/>
```

If you need to get even more granular and invoke a view action during a specified life-cycle phase, it is possible by setting the phase attribute to the phase required. Table 2-8 specifies the different phases along with their phase value.

Table 2-8. *JSF Life-Cycle Phases*

Phase	Tag Value
Restore View	RESTORE_VIEW
Apply Request Values	APPLY_REQUEST_VALUES
Process Validations	PROCESS_VALIDATIONS
Update Model Values	UPDATE_MODEL_VALUES
Invoke Application	INVOKE_APPLICATION
Render Response	RENDER_RESPONSE

The following example demonstrates the f:viewAction facet that will cause the action to be invoked during the Process Validations phase:

```
<f:viewAction action="#{viewActionManagedBean.validateUser()}"
                phase="PROCESS_VALIDATIONS"/>
```

CHAPTER 3

Advanced JavaServer Faces

The JSF framework allows developers to build applications utilizing a series of views, and each view consists of a series of components. The framework is kind of like a puzzle in that each piece must fit into its particular place in order to make things work smoothly. Sprinkled into those pieces of the puzzle are advanced capabilities that are used for helping to create a seamless user interface experience.

Components are just one piece of the puzzle. Components are the building blocks that make up JSF views. One of the strengths of using the JSF framework is the abundance of components that are available for use within views. To developers, components can be tags that are placed within the XHTML views. Components resemble standard HTML tags; they contain a number of attributes, an opening tag and a closing tag, and sometimes components that are to be embedded inside of others. Components can also be written in Java code, and their tags can be bound to Java code that resides within a JSF CDI controller.

A number of components come standard with the JSF framework. Some of the recipes in this chapter will cover some widely used standard components in detail, and the chapter will provide examples that will allow you to begin using components in your applications right away.

Another important piece of the JSF user interface puzzle is seamless integration with the backend business logic. A task that can be run in the background, independent of other running tasks, is known as an *asynchronous* task. JavaScript is the most popular modern browser language that is used to implement asynchronous tasking in web applications. Ajax is a set of technologies that allows you to perform asynchronous tasks using JavaScript in the background, sending responses from the client browser to the server and then sending a response back to the client. That response is used to

209

update the page's Document Object Model (DOM). Enhancing an application to make use of such asynchronous requests and responses can greatly improve the overall user experience. The JSF framework allows developers to create rich user experiences via the use of technologies such as Ajax and HTML5. Much of the implementation detail behind these technologies can be abstracted away from the JSF developer using JSF components. As such, the developer needs to worry only about how to use a JSF component tag and relate it to a server-side property.

This chapter delves into using Ajax with the JSF web framework. Along the way, you will learn how to spruce up applications and make the user interface richer and more user-friendly so that it behaves more like that of a desktop application. You'll also learn how to listen to different component phases and system events, allowing further customization of application functionality.

Note   This chapter contains examples using the third-party component library PrimeFaces. It is recommended to use the most recent releases of third-party libraries in order to ensure that your application contains stable and secure sources.

Before tackling the recipes, though, the following section provides a brief overview of the standard JSF components and associated common component tags. This will help you get the most out of the recipes.

Component and Tag Primer

Table 3-1 lists the components that are available with a clean install of the JSF framework.

Table 3-1. *JSF HTML Components*

Component	Tag	Description
UIColumn	h:column	Represents a column of data in the dataTable component
UICommand	h:commandButton	Submits a form
	h:commandLink	Links pages or actions
	h:commandScript	Provides ability to call an arbitrary server-side method via Ajax from a JSF view
UIData	h:dataTable	Represents a table used for iterating over collections of data
UIForm	h:form	Represents an input form
UIGraphic	h:graphicImage	Displays an image
UIInput	h:inputHidden	Includes a hidden variable in a form
	h:inputSecret	Allows text entry without displaying the actual text
	h:inputText	Allows text entry
	h:inputTextarea	Allows multiline text entry
UIOutcomeTarget	h:link	Links to another page or location
UIMessage	h:message	Displays a localized message
UIMessages	h:messages	Displays localized messages
UIOutput	h:outputFormat	Displays a formatted localized message
	h:outputLabel	Displays a label for a specified field
	h:outputLink	Displays text and links to another page or location
UIPanel	h:panelGrid	Displays a table
	h:panelGroup	Groups components

(*continued*)

Table 3-1. (*continued*)

Component	Tag	Description
UISelectBoolean	h:selectBooleanCheckbox	Displays a (Boolean) checkbox choice
UISelectItem	h:selectItem	Represents one item in a list of items for selection
UISelectItems	h:selectItems	Represents a list of items for selection
UISelectMany	h:selectManyCheckbox	Displays a group of checkboxes that allow multiple user choices
	h:selectManyListbox	Allows a user to select multiple items from a list
	h:selectManyMenu	Allows a user to select multiple items from a drop-down menu
UISelectOne	h:selectOneListbox	Allows a user to select a single item from a list
	h:selectOneMenu	Allows a user to select a single item from a drop-down menu
	h:selectOneRadio	Allows a user to select one item from a set

JSF provides a number of core tags that can be used to provide more functionality for the components. For example, these tags can be embedded inside JSF component tags and specify rules that can be used to convert the values that are displayed or used as input for the component. Other uses of the core tags are to provide a list of options for a select component, validate input, and provide action and event listeners. Table 3-2 describes the JSF core tags.

Table 3-2. *JSF Core Tags*

Tag	Function
f:actionListener	Registers an action listener method with a component
f:phaseListener	Registers a PhaseListener to a page
f:setPropertyAction Listener	Registers a special form submittal action listener
f:valueChangeListener	Registers a value change listener with a component
f:converter	Registers an arbitrary converter with a component
f:convertDateTime	Registers a DateTimeConverter instance with a component
f:convertNumber	Registers a NumberConverter with a component
f:facet	Adds a nested component to particular enclosing parents
f:metadata	Registers a particular facet with a parent component
f:selectItem	Encapsulates one item in a list
f:selectItems	Encapsulates all items of a list
f:websocket	Provides ability to receive messages into a view via WebSockets
f:validateDoubleRange	Registers a DoubleRangeValidator with a component
f:validateLength	Registers a LengthValidator with a component
f:validateLongRange	Registers a LongRangeValidator with a component
f:validator	Registers a custom validator with a component
f:validateRegex	Registers a RegExValidator with a component (JSF 2.0)
f:validateBean	Delegates validation of a local value to a BeanValidator (JSF 2.0)
f:validateWholeBean	Delegates validation of an entire bean or class
f:validateRequired	Ensures that a value is present in a parent component

Note   The common sources and the completed classes to run the application for this chapter are contained within the org.jakartaeerecipes.chapter03 package, and one or more recipes throughout this chapter will utilize classes contained within that package.

Common Component Tag Attributes

Each standard JSF component tag contains a set of attributes that must be specified in order to uniquely identify it from the others, register the component to a controller class, and so on. There is a set of attributes that are common across each component tag, and this section lists those attributes, along with a description of each. *All attributes besides id can be specified using JSF EL:*

- binding: A controller class property can be specified for this attribute, and it can be used to bind the tag to a component instance within a controller class. Doing so allows you to programmatically control the component from within the controller class.

- id: This attribute can be set to uniquely identify the component. If you do not specify a value for the id attribute, then JSF will automatically generate one. Each component within a view must have a unique id attribute, or an error will be generated when the page is rendered. *I recommend you manually specify a value for the id attribute on each component tag, because then it will be easy to statically reference the tag from a scripting language or a controller class if needed. If you let JSF automatically populate this attribute, it may be different each time, and you will never be able to statically reference the tag from a scripting language.*

- immediate: This attribute can be set to true for input and command components in order to force the processing of validations, conversions, and events when the request parameter values are applied.

- rendered: The rendered attribute can be used to specify whether the component should be rendered onscreen. This attribute is typically specified as a JSF EL expression that is bound to a controller class property yielding a Boolean result. The EL expression must be an rvalue expression, meaning that it is read-only and cannot set a value.

- style: This attribute allows a CSS style to be applied to the component. The specified style will be applied when the component is rendered as output.

- `styleClass`: This attribute allows a CSS style class to be applied to the component. The specified style will be applied when the component is rendered as output.

- `value`: This attribute identifies the value of a given component. For some components, the `value` attribute is used to bind the tag to a CDI property. In this case, the value specified for the component will be read from, or set within, the CDI property. Other components, such as the `commandButton` component, use the `value` attribute to specify a label for the given component.

Common JavaScript Component Tags

Table 3-3 lists a number of attributes that are shared by many of the components, which enable JavaScript functionality to interact with the component.

Table 3-3. *Common Component Attributes*

Attribute	Description
onblur	JavaScript code that should be executed when the component loses focus
onchange	JavaScript code that should be executed when the component loses focus and the value changes
ondblclick	JavaScript code that should be executed when the component has been clicked twice
onfocus	JavaScript code that should be executed when the component gains focus
onkeydown	JavaScript code that should be executed when the user presses a key down and the component is in focus
onkeypress	JavaScript code that should be executed when the user presses a key and the component is in focus
onkeyup	JavaScript code that should be executed when key press is completed and the component is in focus
onmousedown	JavaScript code that should be executed when the user clicks the mouse button and the component is in focus

(*continued*)

Table 3-3. (*continued*)

Attribute	Description
onmouseout	JavaScript code that should be executed when the user moves mouse away from the component
onmouseover	JavaScript code that should be executed when the user moves mouse onto the component
onmousemove	JavaScript code that should be executed when the user moves mouse within the component
onmouseup	JavaScript code that should be executed when the mouse button click is completed and the component is in focus
onselect	JavaScript code that should be executed when the component is selected by the user

Binding Components to Properties

All JSF components can be bound to controller class properties. Do so by declaring a property for the type of component you want to bind within the CDI controller class and then by referencing that property using the component's binding attribute. For instance, the following dataTable component is bound to a CDI property and then manipulated from within the bean:

In the view:

```
<h:dataTable id="myTable" binding="#{myBean.myTable}" value="#{myBean.myTableCollection}"/>
```

In the controller:

```
// Provide getter and setter methods for this property
private javax.faces.component.UIData myTable;
...
myTable.setRendered(true);
...
```

Binding can prove to be very useful in some cases, especially when you need to manipulate the state of a component programmatically before re-rendering the view.

3-1. Creating an Input Form

Problem

You want to add input fields to a form within your application.

Solution

Create an input form by enclosing child input components within a parent form component. There are four JSF components that will allow for text entry as input. Those components are inputText, inputSecret, inputHidden, and inputTextarea. Any or all of these components can be placed within a form component in order to create an input form that accepts text entry.

In the example for this recipe, you will create an input form that will be used to sign up for the Acme Bookstore newsletter. The user will be able to enter their first and last names, an email address, a password, and a short description of their interests.

The View: recipe03_01.xhtml

The following code is for the view recipe03_01.xhtml, which constructs the layout for the input form:

```
<html xmlns="http://www.w3.org/1999/xhtml"
    xmlns:ui="http://xmlns.jcp.org/jsf/facelets"
    xmlns:f="http://xmlns.jcp.org/jsf/core"
    xmlns:h="http://xmlns.jcp.org/jsf/html">

  <body>

      <ui:composition template="layout/custom_template_search.xhtml">
          <ui:define name="content">
              <h:messages globalOnly="true"  errorStyle="color: red"
              infoStyle="color: green"/>
              <h:form id="contactForm">
                  <h1>Subscribe to Newsletter</h1>
```

```
            <p>
                Enter your information below in order to be added
                to the Acme Bookstore newsletter.
            </p>

            <br/>
            <label for="first">First: </label>
            <h:inputText id="first" size="40"
            value="#{contactController1.current.first}"/>
            <br/>
            <label for="last">Last: </label>
            <h:inputText id="last" size="40"
            value="#{contactController1.current.last}"/>
            <br/>
            <label for="email">Email: </label>
            <h:inputText id="email" size="40"
            value="#{contactController1.current.email}"/>
            <br/>
            <label for="password">Enter a password for site
            access:</label>
            <h:inputSecret id="password" size="40"
            value="#{contactController1.current.password}"/>
            <br/><br/>
            <label for="description">Enter your book interests
            </label>
            <br/>
            <h:inputTextarea id="description" rows="5" cols="100"
            value="#{contactController1.current.description}"/>
            <br/>
            <h:commandButton id="contactSubmit"
            action="#{contactController1.subscribe}" value="Save"/>
        </h:form>
    </ui:define>
  </ui:composition>

  </body>
</html>
```

Note   As you can see from the example, HTML can be mixed together with
JSF component tags. An HTML label tag is used to specify a label for each input
component in this recipe. In Recipe 3-3, you will learn about the JSF component
that is used to render a label.

To learn more about how the `commandButton` component works, please see
Recipe 3-2.

Controller Class: ContactController.java

Each view that contains an input form needs to have an associated controller class,
right? The controller class in this case is `RequestScoped`, and the name of the class is
`ContactController`. An excerpt from the listing for the `ContactController` class is as
follows:

```
import java.util.*;
import javax.enterprise.context.RequestScoped;
import javax.faces.application.FacesMessage;
import javax.faces.component.UIComponent;
import javax.faces.context.FacesContext;
import javax.faces.event.ValueChangeEvent;
import javax.faces.model.SelectItem;
import javax.faces.validator.ValidatorException;
import javax.inject.Inject;
import javax.inject.Named;

@RequestScoped
@Named(value = "contactController")
public class ContactController implements java.io.Serializable {
    private Contact current;

    /**
     * Creates a new instance of ContactController
     */
    public ContactController() {

    }
```

```
/**
 * Obtains the current instance of the Contact object
 * @return Contact
 */
public Contact getCurrent(){
    if (current == null){
        current = new Contact();
    }
    return current;
}

/**
 * Adds a subscriber to the newsletter
 * @return String
 */
public String subscribe(){
    // No implementation yet, will add to a database table in Chapter 7
    FacesMessage facesMsg = new FacesMessage(FacesMessage.SEVERITY_
    INFO,
            "Successfully Subscribed to Newsletter for " +
            getCurrent().getEmail(), null);
    FacesContext.getCurrentInstance().addMessage(null, facesMsg);
    return "SUBSCRIBE";
}

/**
 * Navigational method
 * @return String
 */
public String add(){
    return "ADD_SUBSCRIBER";
}
}
```

Note At this time, nothing happens when the submit button is clicked other than a nice "Success" message being displayed on the screen. Later in the book, you will revisit the subscribe method and add the code for creating a record within an underlying database. The input screen should look like Figure 3-1 when rendered.

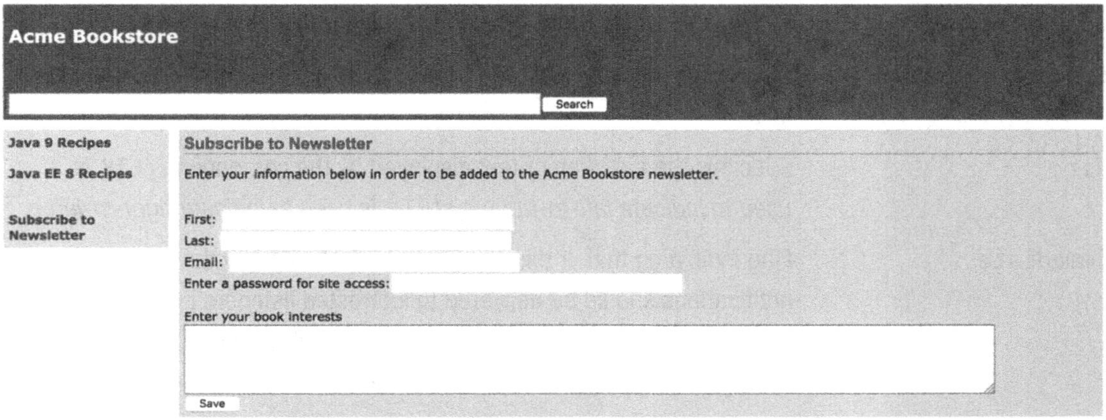

Figure 3-1. *JSF input form for subscribing to the Acme Bookstore newsletter*

How It Works

The JavaServer Faces framework ships with a slew of standard components that can be utilized within JSF views. There are four standard components that can be used for capturing text input: inputText, inputSecret, inputHidden, and inputTextarea. These component tags, as well as all of the other standard JSF component tags, share a common set of attributes and some attributes that are unique to each specific tag. To learn more about the common attributes, please see the related section in the introduction to this chapter. In this recipe, I will go over the specifics for each of these input components. The form component, specified via the h:form tag, is used to create an input form within a JSF view. Each component that is to be processed within the form should be enclosed between the opening and closing h:form tags. Each form typically contains at least one command component, such as a commandButton. A view can contain more than one form component, and only those components that are contained within the form will be processed when the form is submitted.

Each of the input tags supports the list of attributes that is shown in Table 3-4, in addition to those already listed as common component attributes in the introduction to this chapter.

Table 3-4. *Input Component Tag Attributes*

Attribute	Description
converter	Allows a converter to be applied to the component's data.
converterMessage	Specifies a message that will be displayed when a registered converter fails.
dir	Specifies the direction of text displayed by the component. *(*LTR *is used to indicate left-to-right, and* RTL *is used to indicate right-to-left.)*
immediate	Flag indicating that, if this component is activated by the user, notifications should be delivered to interested listeners and actions immediately (i.e., during the Apply Request Values phase) rather than waiting until the Invoke Application phase.
label	Specifies a name that can be used for component identification.
lang	Allows a language code to be specified for the rendered markup.
required	Accepts a Boolean to indicate whether the user must enter a value for the given component.
requiredMessage	Specifies an error message to be displayed if the user does not enter a value for a *required* component.
validator	Allows a validator to be applied to the component.
valueChangeListener	Allows a controller class method to be bound for event-handling purposes. The method will be called when there is a change made to the component.

The inputText component is used to generate a single-line text box within a rendered page. The inputText component value attribute is most commonly bound to a controller class property so that the values of the property can be retrieved or set when a form is processed. In the recipe example, the first inputText component is bound to the controller class property named first. The EL expression #{contactController.current.first} is specified for the component `value`, so if the controller class's `first` property contains a value, then it will be displayed within the `inputText` component. Likewise, when the form is submitted, then any value that has been entered within the component will be saved within the `first` property in the controller class.

The `inputSecret` component is used to generate a single-line text box within a rendered page, and when text is entered into the component, then it is not displayed; rather, asterisks are displayed in place of each character typed. This component makes it possible for a user to enter private text, such as a password, without it being displayed on the screen for others to read. The `inputSecret` component works identically to the `inputText` component, other than hiding the text with asterisks. In the example, the value of the `inputSecret` component is bound to a controller class property named `password` via the `#{contactController.current.password}` EL expression.

The `inputTextarea` component is used to generate a multiline text box within a rendered page. As such, this component has a couple of additional attributes that can be used to indicate how large the text area should be. The `inputTextarea` has the `rows` and `cols` attributes, which allow a developer to specify how many rows (height) and how many columns (wide) of space the component should take up on the page, respectively. Other than those two attributes, the `inputTextarea` component works in much the same manner as the `inputText` component. In the example, the `value` attribute of the `inputTextarea` component is specified as `#{contactController.current.description}`, so the `description` property will be populated with the contents of the component when the form is submitted.

The input component I have not yet discussed is the `inputHidden` component. This component is used to place a hidden input field into the form. It works in the same manner as the `inputText` component, except that it is not rendered on the page for the user to see. The value for an `inputHidden` component can be bound to a controller class property in the same way as the other components. You can use such a component for passing a hidden token to and from a `form`.

As you can see, the days of passing and receiving request parameters within JSP pages are over. Utilizing the JSF standard input components, it is possible to bind values to controller class properties using JSF EL expressions. This makes it much easier for developers to submit values from an input form for processing. Rather than retrieving parameters from a page, assigning them to variables, and then processing, the JSF framework takes care of that overhead for you.

3-2. Invoking Actions from Within a Page

Problem

You want to trigger a server-side method to be invoked from a button or link on one of your application pages.

Solution

Utilize the `commandButton` or `commandLink` component within your view to invoke action methods within a controller class. The command components allow for the user invocation of actions within controller classes. Command components bind buttons and links on a page directly to action methods, allowing developers to spend more time thinking about the development of the application and less time thinking about the Java servlet-processing life cycle.

In the example for this recipe, a button and a link are added to the newsletter page for the Acme Bookstore. The button that will be added to the page will be used to submit the input form for processing, and the link will allow a user to log into the application and manage their subscription and bookstore account.

Note   This recipe will not cover any authentication or security features; it focuses only on invoking actions within controller classes. For more information regarding authentication, please see Chapter 16.

The View: recipe03_02.xhtml

The following code is for the newsletter subscription view including the command components. The sources are for the file named `recipe03_02.xhtml`:

```
<html xmlns="http://www.w3.org/1999/xhtml"
      xmlns:ui="http://xmlns.jcp.org/jsf/facelets"
      xmlns:f="http://xmlns.jcp.org/jsf/core"
      xmlns:h="http://xmlns.jcp.org/jsf/html">
```

```
<body>

    <ui:composition template="layout/custom_template_search.xhtml">
        <ui:define name="content">
            <h:messages globalOnly="true"  errorStyle="color: red"
            infoStyle="color: green"/>
            <h:form id="contactForm">
                <h1>Subscribe to Newsletter</h1>
                <p>
                    Enter your information below in order to be added
                    to the Acme Bookstore newsletter.
                </p>

                <br/>
                <label for="first">First: </label>
                <h:inputText id="first" size="40"
                value="#{contactController.current.first}"/>
                <br/>
                <label for="last">Last: </label>
                <h:inputText id="last" size="40"
                value="#{contactController.current.last}"/>
                <br/>
                <label for="email">Email: </label>
                <h:inputText id="email" size="40"
                value="#{contactController.current.email}"/>
                <br/>
                <label for="password">Enter a password for site
                access:</label>
                <h:inputSecret id="password" size="40"
                value="#{contactController.current.password}"/>
                <br/><br/>
                <label for="description">Enter your book interests
                </label>
                <br/>
                <h:inputTextarea id="description" rows="5" cols="100"
                value="#{contactController.current.description}"/>
```

```
            <br/>
            <h:commandButton id="contactSubmit"
            action="#{contactController.subscribe}" value="Save"/>
            <br/><br/>
            <h:commandLink  id="manageAccount"
            action="#{contactController.manage}" value="Manage
            Subscription"/>
        </h:form>
      </ui:define>
    </ui:composition>

  </body>
</html>
```

Controller Class: ContactController.java

The controller class that contains the action methods is named `ContactController`, which was created in Recipe 3-1. The following code excerpt is taken from the `ContactController` class, and it shows the updates that have been made to the methods for this recipe:

Note   The complete implementation of `ContactController` resides within the package `org.jakartaeerecipes.chapter03`.

```
...
  /**
   * Adds a subscriber to the newsletter
   * @return String
   */
  public String subscribe(){
      // Using a list implementation for now,
      // but will add to a database table in Chapter 7
```

```java
        // Add the current contact to the subscription list
        subscriptionController.getSubscriptionList().add(current);
        FacesMessage facesMsg = new FacesMessage(FacesMessage.SEVERITY_
        INFO,
                "Successfully Subscribed to Newsletter for " +
                getCurrent().getEmail(), null);
        FacesContext.getCurrentInstance().addMessage(null, facesMsg);
        return "SUBSCRIBE";
    }

    /**
     * Navigational method
     * @return String
     */
    public String add(){
        return "ADD_SUBSCRIBER";
    }

    /**
     * This method will allow a user to navigate to the manageAccount view.
     * This method will be moved into another controller class that focuses
       on
     * authentication later on.
     * @return
     */
    public String manage(){
        return "/chapter03/manageAccount";
    }
```
...

When the view is rendered, the resulting page looks like Figure 3-2.

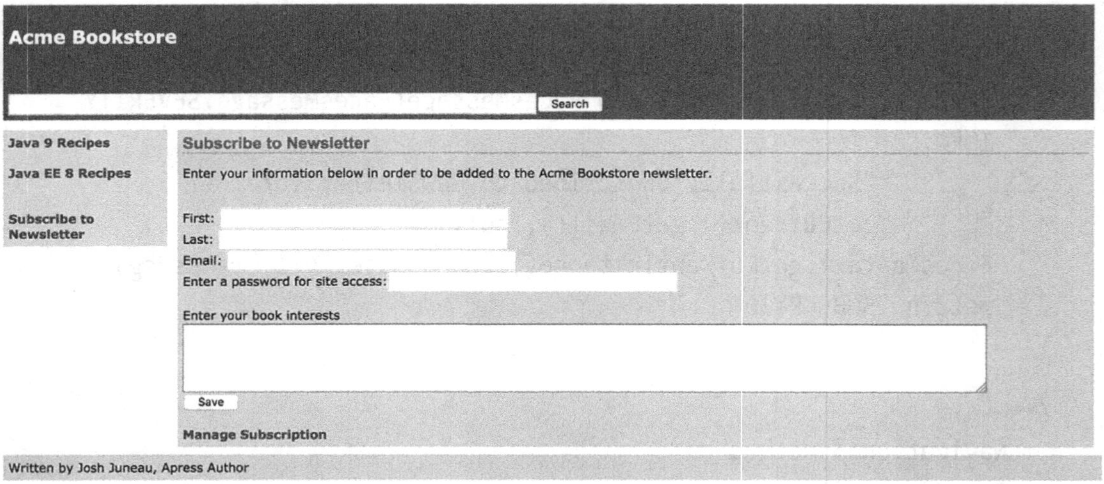

Figure 3-2. *Utilizing command components within a view*

How It Works

The command components make working with JSF vastly different from using JSP technology. In many of the other technologies, form actions are used to handle request parameters and perform any required business logic with them. With the JSF command components, Java methods can be bound directly to a button or a link and invoked when the components are activated (button or link clicked). In the example for this recipe, both the `commandButton` and `commandLink` components are utilized. The `commandButton` component is used to submit the form request parameters for processing, and the `commandLink` component is bound to an action method that performs a redirect to another application page.

The command components have a handful of attributes that are of note. Those attributes, along with a description of each, are listed in Table 3-5 and Table 3-6.

Table 3-5. *commandButton Component Additional Attributes*

Attribute	Description
`action`	EL that specifies a controller class action method that will be invoked when the user activates the component.
`actionListener`	EL that specifies a controller class action method that will be notified when this component is activated. The action method should be public and accept an `ActionEvent` parameter, with a return type of `void`.
`class`	CSS style class that can be applied to the component.
`dir`	Direction indication for text (LTR, left-to-right; RTL, right-to-left).
`disabled`	A Boolean to indicate whether the component is disabled.
`image`	Absolute or relative URL to an image that will be displayed on the button.
`immediate`	Flag indicating that, if this component is activated by the user, notifications should be delivered to interested listeners and actions immediately (i.e., during the Apply Request Values phase) rather than waiting until the Invoke Application phase.
`label`	Name for the component.
`lang`	Code for the language used for generating the component markup.
`readonly`	Boolean indicating whether the component is read-only.
`rendererType`	Identifier of renderer instance.
`tabindex`	Index value indicating the number of tab button presses it takes to bring the component into focus.
`title`	Tooltip that will be displayed when the mouse hovers over the component.
`transient`	Boolean indicating whether the component should be included in the state of the component tree.
`type`	Indicates type of button to create. Values are `submit` (default), `reset`, and `button`.

Table 3-6. *commandLink Component Additional Attributes*

Attribute	Description
action	EL that specifies a controller class action method that will be invoked when the user activates the component.
accessKey	Access key value that will transfer the focus to the component.
cords	Position and shape of the hotspot on the screen.
dir	Direction indication for text (LTR, left-to-right; RTL, right-to-left).
disabled	Specifies a Boolean to indicate whether the component is disabled.
hreflang	Language code of the resource designated by the hyperlink.
immediate	Flag indicating that, if this component is activated by the user, notifications should be delivered to interested listeners and actions immediately (i.e., during the Apply Request Values phase) rather than waiting until the Invoke Application phase.
lang	Code for the language used for generating the component markup.
rel	Relationship from the current document to the anchor specified by the hyperlink.
rev	Reverse anchor specified by this hyperlink to the current document.
shape	Shape of the hotspot on the screen.
tabindex	Index value indicating the number of tab button presses it takes to bring the component into focus.
target	Name of a frame where the resource retrieved via the hyperlink will be displayed.
title	Tooltip that will be displayed when the mouse hovers over the component.
type	Indicates type of button to create. Values are submit (default), reset, and button.
charset	Character encoding of the resource designated by the hyperlink.

The `commandButton` and `commandLink` components in the example for this recipe specify only a minimum number of attributes. That is, they both specify `id`, `action`, and `value` attributes. The `id` attribute is used to uniquely identify each of the components. The `action` attribute is set to the JSF EL, which binds the components to their controller class action methods. The `commandButton` component has an `action` attribute of `#{contactController.subscribe}`, which means that the `ContactController` class's `subscribe` method will be invoked when the button on the page is clicked. The `commandLink` has an `action` attribute of `#{contactController.manage}`, which means that the `ContactController` class's `manage` method will be invoked when the link is clicked. Each of the components also specifies a `value` attribute, which is set to the text that is displayed on the button or link when rendered.

As you can see, only a handful of the available attributes are used within the example. However, the components can be customized using the additional attributes that are available. For instance, an `actionListener` method can be specified, which will bind a controller class method to the component, and that method will be invoked when the component is activated. JavaScript functions can be specified for each of the attributes beginning with the word `on`, providing the ability to produce client-side functionality.

Command components vastly changed the landscape of Java web application development. They allow the incorporation of direct Java method access from within user pages and provide an easy means for processing request parameters.

3-3. Displaying Output
Problem

You want to display text from a controller class property within your application pages.

Solution

Incorporate JSF output components into your views. Output components are used to display static or dynamic text on a page, as well as the results of expression language arithmetic. The standard JSF component library contains five components that render output: `outputLabel`, `outputText`, `outputFormat`, `outputLink`, and `link`. The Acme Bookstore utilizes each of these components within the bookstore newsletter application façade.

The View: recipe03_03.xhtml

In the following example, the newsletter subscription view has been rewritten to utilize some of the output components:

```
<html xmlns="http://www.w3.org/1999/xhtml"
    xmlns:ui="http://xmlns.jcp.org/jsf/facelets"
    xmlns:f="http://xmlns.jcp.org/jsf/core"
    xmlns:h="http://xmlns.jcp.org/jsf/html">

    <body>

        <ui:composition template="layout/custom_template_search.xhtml">
            <ui:define name="content">
                <h:messages globalOnly="true"  errorStyle="color: red"
                infoStyle="color: green"/>
                <h:form id="contactForm">
                    <h1>Subscribe to Newsletter</h1>
                    <p>
                        <h:outputText  id="newsletterSubscriptionDesc"
                                    value="#{contactController.
                                    newsletterDescription}"/>
                    </p>

                    <br/>
                    <h:outputLabel for="first" value="First: "/>
                    <h:inputText id="first" size="40"
                    value="#{contactController.current.first}">
                        <f:validateRequired/>
                        <f:validateLength minimum="2" maximum="40"/>
                    </h:inputText>
                    <br/>
                    <h:outputLabel for="last" value="Last: "/>
                    <h:inputText id="last" size="40"
                    value="#{contactController.current.last}">
                        <f:validateRequired/>
                        <f:validateLength minimum="2" maximum="40"/>
                    </h:inputText>
```

```
<br/>
<h:outputLabel for="email" value="Email: "/>
<h:inputText id="email" size="40"
value="#{contactController.current.email}">
    <f:validateRequired/>
    <f:validateRegex pattern=""/>
</h:inputText>

<br/>
<h:outputLabel for="password" value="Enter a password
for site access: "/>
<h:inputSecret id="password" size="40"
value="#{contactController.current.password}">
    <f:validateRegex pattern=""/>
</h:inputSecret>
<br/><br/>
<h:outputLabel  for="description" value="Enter your
book interests"/>
<br/>
<h:inputTextarea id="description" rows="5" cols="100"
value="#{contactController.current.description}"/>
<br/>
<h:commandButton id="contactSubmit"
action="#{contactController.subscribe}" value="Save"/>
<br/><br/>
<h:commandLink id="manageAccount"
action="#{contactController.manage}" value="Manage
Subscription"/>
<br/><br/>
        </h:form>
    </ui:define>
</ui:composition>

</body>
</html>
```

Controller Class: ContactController.java

The ContactController controller class has been modified throughout the recipes within this chapter to incorporate new functionality as the recipes move forward. In this recipe, a new property has been added to the ContactController that contains the description of the newsletter.

Note   The hard-coded newsletter description is not a good idea for use in a production application. It is used in this example for demonstration purposes only. For a production application, utilization of resource bundles or database storage would be a more viable approach for storing Strings of text.

The following source excerpt from the ContactController class shows the code that is of interest in this example:

```
...
    private String newsletterDescription;

    public ContactController() {
        current = null;
        newsletterDescription = "Enter your information below in order to
        be " + "added to the Acme Bookstore newsletter.";
    }
...
    public String getNewsletterDescription() {
        return newsletterDescription;
    }

    public void setNewsletterDescription(String newsletterDescription) {
        this.newsletterDescription = newsletterDescription;
    }
...
```

The resulting page looks like Figure 3-3. Note that the text is the same, because it is merely reading the same text from a controller class property. Also note that there is now an additional link added to the bottom of the page, which reads Home.

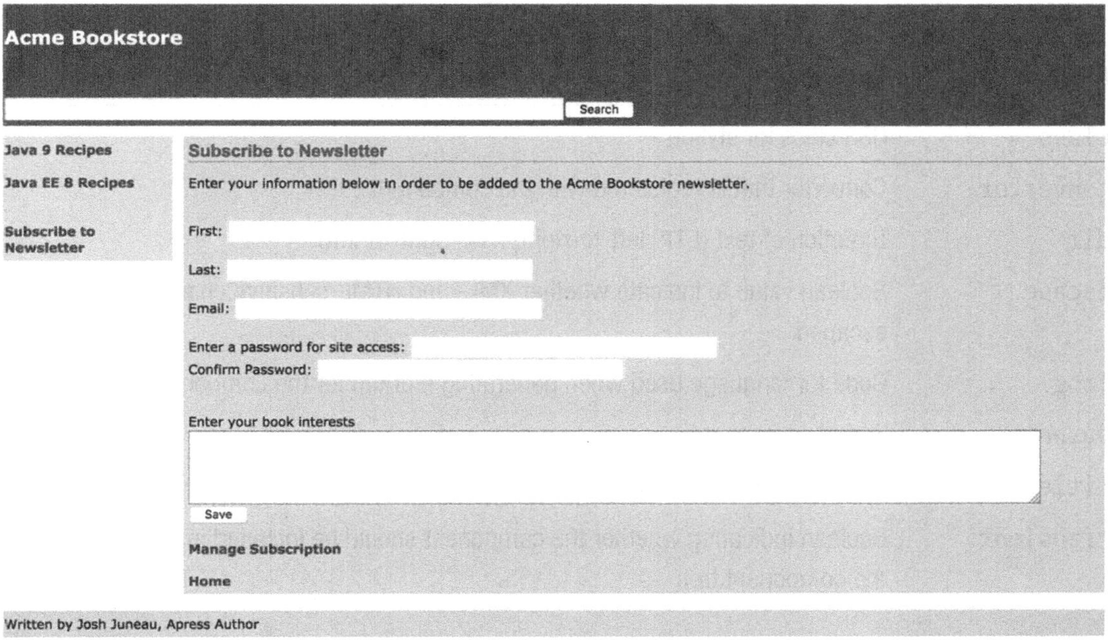

Figure 3-3. *Utilizing output components within a view*

How It Works

Output components can be used to display output that is generated within a controller class or to render a link to another resource. They can be useful in many cases for displaying dynamic output to a web view. The example for this recipe demonstrates three out of the five different output component types: outputText, outputLink, and outputLabel. Each of the components shares a common set of attributes, which are listed in Table 3-7.

Note The outputText component has become a bit less important since the release of JSF 2.0 because the Facelets view definition language implicitly wraps inline content with a similar output component. Therefore, the use of the outputText tag within JSF 2.0 is necessary only if you want to utilize some of the tag attributes for rendering, JavaScript invocation, or the like.

Table 3-7. *Common Output Component Attributes (Not Listed in Introduction)*

Attribute	Description
class	CSS class for styling
converter	Converter that is registered with the component
dir	Direction of text (LTR, left-to-right; RTL, right-to-left)
escape	Boolean value to indicate whether XML- and HTML-sensitive characters are escaped
lang	Code for language used when generating markup for the component
parent	Parent component
title	Tooltip text for the component
transient	Boolean indicating whether the component should be included in the state of the component tree

The outputText component in the example contains a value of #{contactController.newsletterDescription}, which displays the contents of the newsletterDescription property within ContactController. Only the common output component attributes can be specified within the h:outputText tag. Therefore, an attribute such as class or style can be used to apply styles to the text displayed by the component. If the component contains HTML or XML, the escape attribute can be set to true to indicate that the characters should be escaped.

The outputFormat component shares the same set of attributes as the outputText component. The outputFormat component can be used to render parameterized text. Therefore, if you require the ability to alter different portions of a String of text, you can do so via the use of JSF parameters (via the f:param tag). For example, suppose you wanted to list the name of books that someone has purchased from the Acme Bookstore; you could use the outputFormat component like in the following example:

```
<h:outputFormat value="Cart contains the books {0}, {1}, {2}"/>
    <f:param value="Java 9 Recipes"/>
    <f:param value="JavaFX 2.0: Introduction by Example"/>
    <f:param value="Java EE 8 Recipes"/>
</h:outputFormat>
```

The outputLink and outputLabel components can each specify a number of other attributes that are not available to the previously discussed output components. The additional attributes are listed in Table 3-8 (outputLink) and Table 3-9 (outputLabel). The outputLink component can be used to create an anchor or link that will redirect an application user to another page when the link is clicked. In the following example, the outputLink component is used to redirect a user to a view named home.xhtml. The value for the outputLink component can be set to a static page name, as per the example, or it can contain a JSF EL expression corresponding to a controller class property. It is also possible to pass parameters to another page using the outputLink component by nesting f:param tags between opening and closing h:outputLink tags as follows:

```
<h:outputLink id="homeLink" value="home.xhtml">
    <h:outputText value="User Home Page"/>
    <f:param name="username" value="#{contactController.current.email}"/>
 </h:outputLink>
```

The previous example would produce a link with the text *User Home Page* when rendered on the page. It would produce the following HTML link, where emailAddress corresponds to the EL expression of #{contactController.current.email}:

```
<a href="home.xhtml?username=emailAddress">Home Page</a>
```

Similarly, rather than displaying a link as text on the page, an image can be used by embedding a graphicImage component.

The outputLabel component renders an HTML <label> tag, and it can be used in much the same way as the outputText component. In the example, the outputLabel component values are all using static text, but they could also utilize JSF EL expressions to make use of controller class property values if that is more suitable for the application.

Table 3-8. *outputLink Additional Attributes*

Attribute	Description
accessKey	Access key value that will transfer the focus to the component.
binding	ValueExpresssion linking this component to a property in a backing bean.
charset	The character encoding of the resource designated by this hyperlink.
cords	Position and shape of the hotspot on the screen.
dir	Direction indication for text (LTR, left-to-right; RTL, right-to-left).
disabled	Specifies a Boolean to indicate whether the component is disabled.
fragment	Identifier for the page fragment that should be brought into focus when the target page is rendered.
hreflang	Language code of the resource designated by the hyperlink.
lang	Code for the language used for generating the component markup.
rel	Relationship from the current document to the anchor specified by the hyperlink.
rev	Reverse anchor specified by this hyperlink to the current document.
shape	Shape of the hotspot on the screen.
tabindex	Index value indicating the number of tab button presses it takes to bring the component into focus.
target	Name of a frame where the resource retrieved via the hyperlink will be displayed.
title	Tooltip that will be displayed when the mouse hovers over the component.
type	Type of button to create. Values are submit (default), reset, and button.

Table 3-9. *outputLabel Additional Attributes*

Attribute	Description
accessKey	Access key value that will transfer the focus to the component.
binding	ValueExpresssion linking this component to a property in a backing bean.
dir	Direction indication for text (LTR, left-to-right; RTL, right-to-left).
escape	Flag indicating that characters that are sensitive in HTML and XML markup must be escaped.
for	Client identifier of the component for which this element is a label.
lang	Code for the language used for generating the component markup.
tabindex	Index value indicating the number of tab button presses it takes to bring the component into focus.
title	Tooltip that will be displayed when the mouse hovers over the component.
type	Type of button to create. Values are submit (default), reset, and button.

The last output component that I'll cover in this recipe is the link component. It was introduced to JSF in release 2.0, and it makes the task of adding links to a page just a bit easier. Both the outputLink and link components produce similar results, but link has just a couple of different attributes that make it react a bit differently. The value attribute of the h:link tag specifies the label or text that should be used when the link is rendered on the page, and the outcome attribute specifies the page that should be linked to. The following example of the link component produces the same output as the outputLink component in the example for this recipe:

```
<h:link id=""homeLink"" value=""Home"" outcome=""home""/>
```

Parameters and images can also be embedded within the h:link tag, in the same manner as with outputLink. The link component also contains some custom attributes, as listed in Table 3-10.

Table 3-10. *link Component Additional Attributes*

Attribute	Description
charset	Character encoding of the resource that is designated by the hyperlink.
cords	Position and shape of the hotspot on the screen, usually used when generating maps or images containing multiple links.
disabled	Flag to indicate that the component should never receive focus.
fragment	Identifier for the page fragment that should be brought into focus when the link is clicked. The identifier is appended to the # character.
hreflang	Language of the resource designated by this link.
includeviewparams	Boolean indicating whether to include page parameters when redirecting.
outcome	Logical outcome used to resolve a navigational case.
rel	Relationship from the current document to the resource specified by link.
rev	Reverse link from the anchor specified from this link to the current document.
shape	Shape of the hotspot on the screen.
target	Name of the frame in which the resource linked to is to be displayed.
type	Content type of resource that is linked to.

This recipe provided a high-level overview of the JSF standard output components. In JSF 2.0+, it is important to note that you can simply include a JSF EL expression without using an output component to display text within a page. However, these components can still be quite useful under certain circumstances, making them an important set of components to have within your arsenal.

3-4. Adding Form Validation

Problem

To ensure that valid data is being submitted via your form, you need to incorporate some validation on your input fields.

Solution #1

Utilize prebuilt JSF validator tags on the view's input components where possible. JSF ships with a handful of prebuilt validators that can be applied to components within a view by embedding the validator tag within the component you want to validate. The following code excerpt is taken from a JSF view that defines the layout for the newsletter subscription page of the Acme Bookstore application. The sources can be found in the view named recipe03_04.xhtml, and the excerpt demonstrates applying prebuilt validators to some inputText components:

```
...
<h:outputLabel for="first" value="First: "/>
<h:inputText id="first" size="40" value="#{contactController.current.first}">
    <f:validateLength minimum="1" maximum="40"/>
 </h:inputText>
<br/>
<h:message id="firstError"
                   for="first"
                   errorStyle="color:red"/>
<br/>
<h:outputLabel for="last" value="Last: "/>
<h:inputText id="last" size="40" value="#{contactController.current.last}">
    <f:validateLength minimum="1" maximum="40"/>
</h:inputText>
<br/>
<h:message id="lastError"
                   for="last"
                   errorStyle="color:red"/>
<br/>
...
```

In the preceding code excerpt, you can see that the f:validateLength validator tags have been embedded in different inputText components. When the form is submitted, these validators will be applied to the values within the inputText component fields and will return an error message if the constraints have not been met.

Solution #2

Utilize JSF bean validation by annotating controller class fields with validation annotations. It is possible to perform validation from within the controller class by annotating the property field declaration with the validation annotations that are needed. When the form is submitted, then the bean validation will be performed.

Note   An f:validateBean tag can be embedded within the component in the view if making use of validationGroups in order to delegate the validation of the local value to the Bean Validation API. If using f:validateBean, the validationGroups attribute will serve as a filter that instructs which constraints should be enforced.

The following code excerpt is taken from the JSF view that defines the layout for the newsletter subscription page of the Acme Bookstore application. The sources can be found in the view named recipe03_04.xhtml:

```
...
<h:outputLabel for="email" value="Email: "/>
<h:inputText id="email" size="40" value="#{contactController.current.
email}"/>
<br/>
<h:message id="emailError"
                    for="email"
                    errorStyle="color:red"/>
...
```

Next is an excerpt from the ContactController controller class that demonstrates applying a validator annotation to the email property field declaration:

```
...
@Pattern(regexp = "[a-zA-Z0-9]+@[a-zA-Z0-9]+\\.[a-zA-Z0-9]+", message =
"Email format is invalid.")
    private String email;
...
```

When the form is submitted, the validation on the `email` field will occur. If the value entered into the `inputText` component does not validate against the regular expression noted in the annotation, then the error message will be displayed within the corresponding `messages` component.

Solution #3

Create a custom validator method within a controller class, and register that method with an input component by specifying the appropriate EL for the component's `validator` attribute. In this scenario, the controller class does not need to implement the `Validator` interface. The following code excerpt is taken from the JSF view that defines the layout for the newsletter subscription page of the Acme Bookstore application. The sources can be found in the view named `recipe03_04.xhtml`, and the excerpt demonstrates a custom validator method to a component by specifying it for the `validator` attribute:

```
...
<h:outputLabel for="password" value="Enter a password for site access: "/>
<h:inputSecret id="password" size="40" redisplay="true"
value="#{contactController.current.password}"/>
<br/>
<h:outputLabel for="passwordConfirm" value="Confirm Password: "/>
<h:inputSecret id="passwordConfirm" size="40" redisplay="true"
                       validator="#{contactController.
                       validatePassword}"/>
<br/>
<h:message id="passwordConfirmError"
                   for="passwordConfirm"
                   style="color:red"/>
...
```

> **Note**   If you are thinking outside of the box, you'll see that the previous code fragment would be an excellent choice for creating into a composite component! If a composite component is created, then it would be as simple as adding a tag such as `<custom:passwordValidate>` to your form.

The `validator` attribute specifies the `validatePassword` method within the `ContactController` controller class. The following excerpt is taken from `ContactController`, and it shows the validator method's implementation:

```
...
/**
    * Custom validator to ensure that password field contents match
    * @param context
    * @param component
    * @param value
    */
    public void validatePassword(FacesContext context,
                                 UIComponent component,
                                 Object value){
        Map map = context.getExternalContext().getRequestParameterMap();
        String passwordText = (String) map.get(("contactForm:password"));
        String confirmPassword = value.toString();

        if (!passwordText.equals(confirmPassword)) {
            throw new ValidatorException(new FacesMessage("Passwords do not
            match"));
        }
    }
...
```

When the form is submitted, the `validatePassword` method will be invoked during the Process Validations phase. The method will read the values of both the `password` and `passwordConfirm` fields, and an exception will be thrown if they do not match. For example, if the input form for the newsletter subscription page is submitted without any values, then the page should be re-rendered and look like Figure 3-4.

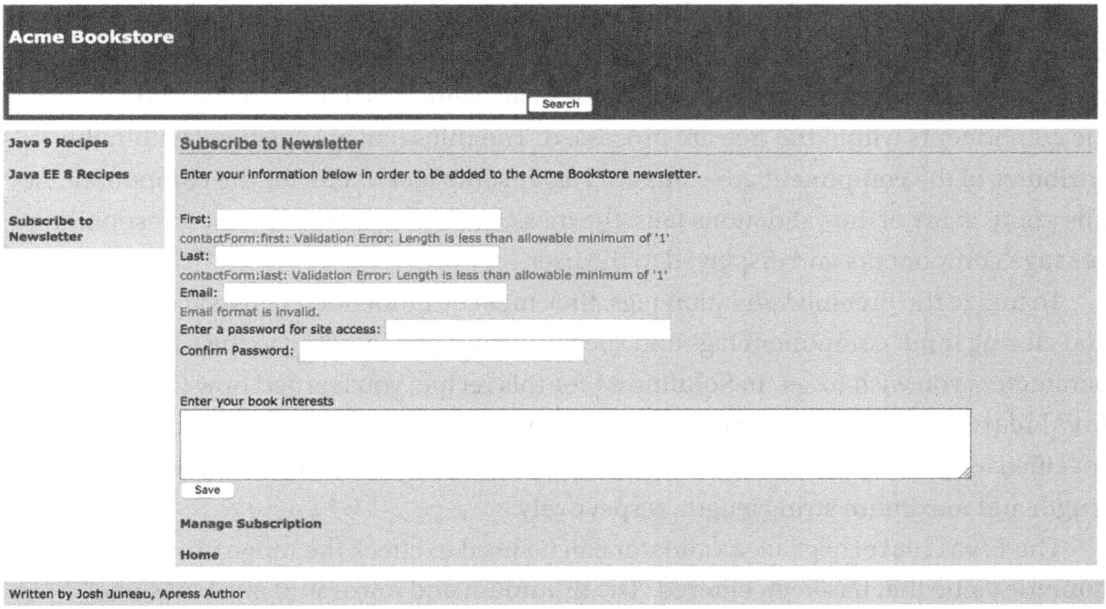

Figure 3-4. *Validation errors on input fields*

How It Works

There are a few different ways in which to apply validation to form input fields. The easiest way to apply validation to an input component is to utilize the prebuilt validator tags that ship with JSF. There are prebuilt tags for validating data for a specified length, range, and so on. Please see Table 3-2 in the introduction to this chapter for the complete list of validator tags. You can also choose to apply validation to input components using bean validation. Bean validation requires validation annotations to be placed on the property declaration within the controller class. Yet another possible way to perform validation is to create a custom validation method and specify the method within the input component's `validator` attribute. This section will provide a brief overview of each prebuilt validation tag, cover the basics of bean validation, and demonstrate how to build a custom validation method.

Note   It is possible to create a class that implements the `Validator` interface to perform validation.

No matter which validation solution you choose to implement, the validation occurs during the Process Validations phase of the JSF life cycle. When a form is submitted, via a command component or an Ajax request, all validators that are registered on the components within the tree are processed. The rules that are specified within the attributes of the component are compared against the local value for the component. At this point, if any of the validations fails, the messages are returned to the corresponding `message` components and displayed to the user.

To utilize the prebuilt validation tags, they must be embedded between opening and closing input component tags and specify attributes according to the validation parameters you wish to set. In Solution #1 for this recipe, you learned how to use the `f:validateLength` validator tag, which allows validation of component data for a specified length. The `minimum` and `maximum` attributes are set to the minimum string length and maximum string length, respectively.

The `f:validateLongRange` validator can be used to check the range of a numeric value that has been entered. The minimum and maximum attributes of `f:validateLongRange` are used to determine whether the value entered falls within the lower and upper bounds, respectively.

Similar to `f:validateLongRange` is the `f:validateDoubleRange` validator, which is used to validate the range of a floating-point value. Again, the minimum and maximum attributes of `f:validateDoubleRange` are used to determine whether the value entered falls within the lower and upper bounds, respectively.

The `f:validateRequired` validator is used to ensure that an input field is not empty. No attributes are needed with this validator; simply embed it within a component tag to ensure that the component will not contain an empty value.

Another validator that ships with JSF is the `f:validateRegex` validator. This validator uses a regular expression pattern to determine whether the value entered matches the specified pattern. The validator's pattern attribute is used to specify the regular expression pattern, as shown in the example for Solution #1 to this recipe.

In Solution #2, JSF bean validation is demonstrated. Bean validation allows you to annotate a controller class field with constraint annotations that indicate the type of validation that should be performed. The validation automatically occurs on the annotated fields when a form that contains input components referencing them is submitted. A handful of standard constraint annotations can be applied to bean fields, as listed in Table 3-11. Each annotation accepts different attributes; please see the online documentation at `https://docs.jboss.org/hibernate/beanvalidation/spec/2.0/api/` for more details.

Table 3-11. *Constraint Annotations Used for Bean Validation*

Annotation	Description
@AssertFalse	The annotated element must be false.
@AssertTrue	The annotated element must be true.
@DecimalMax	The annotated element must be a decimal that has a value less than or equal to the specified maximum.
@DecimalMin	The annotated element must be a decimal that has a value greater than or equal to the specified minimum.
@Digits	The annotated element must be a number within the accepted range.
@Email	The annotated element must adhere to the format of an email address.
@Future	The annotated element must be a date in the future.
@Max	The annotated element must be a number that has a value less than or equal to the specified maximum.
@Min	The annotated element must be a number that has a value greater than or equal to the specified minimum.
@Negative	The annotated element must be a negative number.
@NotBlank	The annotated element must not be null or blank after removing any trailing or leading whitespace.
@NotEmpty	The annotated element must not be null or empty.
@NotNull	The annotated element must not be null.
@Null	The annotated element must be null.
@Past	The annotated element must be a date in the past.
@Pattern	The annotated element must match the pattern specified in the annotation's regular expression.
@Positive	The annotated element must be a positive number.
@Size	The annotated element must be between the specified boundaries.

When using bean validation, the input component that references an annotated bean field can contain an `f:validateBean` tag to customize behavior. The `f:validateBean` tag's `validationGroups` annotation can be used to specify validation groups that can be used for validating the component. For instance, such a solution may resemble something like the following:

```
<h:inputText id="email" value="#{contactController.email}">
    <f:validateBean validationGroups="org.jakartaeerecipes.validation.
    groups.EmailGroup"/>
</h:inputText>
```

Note   Validation groups define a subset of constraints that can be applied for validation. A validation group is represented by an empty Java interface. The interface name can then be applied to annotation constraints within a bean class in order to assign such constraints to a particular group. For instance, the following field that is annotated with @Size specifies a group of `EmailGroup.class`:

```
@Size(min=2, max=30, groups=EmailGroup.class)
private String email;
```

When utilizing the `f:validateBean` tag, any constraint annotations that are contained within the specified group will be applied to the field for validation.

When using bean validation, a custom error message can be displayed if the validation for a field fails. To add a custom message, include the `message` attribute within the annotation, along with the error message that you want to have displayed. As a best practice, error messages should be pulled from a message bundle (`https://docs.oracle.com/javase/tutorial/i18n/resbundle/concept.html`) so that they can be updated without the need to change code.

The example for Solution #3 demonstrates the use of a custom validator method in order to perform validation on an input component. The input component's `validator` attribute can reference a controller class method that has no return type and accepts a `FacesContext`, a `UIComponent`, and an `Object`. The method can utilize the parameters to gain access to the current `FacesContext`, the `UIComponent` that is being validated, and the current value that is contained in the object, respectively. The validation logic can throw a `javax.faces.validator.ValidatorException` if the value does not pass validation and then return a message to the user via the exception. In the example, the method named `validatePassword` is used to compare the two password field contents to ensure that they match. The first two lines of code within the method are used to obtain the value of the component with the `id` of `password` and save it into a local variable. The actual validation logic compares that value against the incoming parameter's `Object` value, which is the current value of the component being validated, to determine whether there is a match. If not, then a `ValidationException` is thrown with a corresponding message. That message will then be displayed within the `messages` component that corresponds to the component being validated.

As mentioned at the beginning of this recipe, there are a few ways to validate input. None of them is any better than the other; their usage depends upon the needs of your application. If you are going to be changing validation patterns often, then you may want to stick with the prebuilt validator tags so that you do not need to recompile code in order to change the validation. On the other hand, if you know that your validation will not change, then it may be easier for you to work with the bean validation technique.

3-5. Validating Input with Ajax
Problem

You want to validate the values that are entered into text fields of a form, but you want them to be evaluated immediately, rather than after the form is submitted.

Solution

Perform validation on the field(s) by embedding the `f:ajax` tag within each component whose values you want to validate. Specify appropriate values for the `event` and `render` attributes so that the Ajax validation will occur when the field(s) loses focus, and any validation errors will be identified immediately. The following listing is the JSF view for the newsletter subscription page of the Acme Bookstore application. It has been updated to utilize Ajax validation so that the validation occurs immediately, without the need to submit the form before corresponding errors are displayed:

```
<ui:composition xmlns="http://www.w3.org/1999/xhtml"
                xmlns:ui="http://xmlns.jcp.org/jsf/facelets"
                xmlns:f="http://xmlns.jcp.org/jsf/core"
                xmlns:h="http://xmlns.jcp.org/jsf/html"
```

```
                template="layout/custom_template_search.xhtml">
    <ui:define name="content">
        <h:messages globalOnly="true"  errorStyle="color: red"
        infoStyle="color: green"/>
        <h:form id="contactForm">
            <h1>Subscribe to Newsletter</h1>
            <p>
                <h:outputText id="newsletterSubscriptionDesc"
                            value="#{ch3ContactController.
                            newsletterDescription}"/>
            </p>

            <br />
            <h:panelGrid columns="2" bgcolor="" border="0">
                <h:panelGroup>
                    <h:outputLabel for="first" value="First: "/>
                    <h:inputText id="first" size="40"
                    value="#{ch3ContactController.current.first}">
                        <f:validateLength minimum="1" maximum="40"/>
                        <f:ajax event="blur" render="firstError"/>
                    </h:inputText>
                </h:panelGroup>
                <h:panelGroup>

                    <h:outputLabel for="last" value="Last: "/>
                    <h:inputText id="last" size="40"
                    value="#{ch3ContactController.current.last}">
                        <f:validateLength minimum="1" maximum="40"/>
                        <f:ajax event="blur" render="lastError"/>
                    </h:inputText>
                </h:panelGroup>

                <h:message id="firstError"
                        for="first"
                        errorStyle="color:red"/>
```

```
<h:message id="lastError"
         for="last"
         errorStyle="color:red"/>
<h:panelGroup>
    <h:outputLabel for="email" value="Email: "/>
    <h:inputText id="email" size="40"
    value="#{ch3ContactController.current.email}">
        <f:ajax event="blur" render="emailError"/>
    </h:inputText>
</h:panelGroup>
<h:panelGroup/>
<h:message id="emailError"
         for="email"
         errorStyle="color:red"/>
<h:panelGroup/>

<h:selectOneRadio title="Gender" id="gender"
value="#{ch3ContactController.current.gender}">
    <f:selectItem  itemValue="M" itemLabel="Male"/>
    <f:selectItem itemValue="F" itemLabel="Female"/>
</h:selectOneRadio>
<h:panelGroup>
    <h:outputLabel for="occupation" value="Occupation: "/>
    <h:selectOneMenu id="occupation"
    value="#{ch3ContactController.current.occupation}">
        <f:selectItems value="#{ch3ContactController.
        occupationList}"/>
    </h:selectOneMenu>
</h:panelGroup>
<h:message id="genderError"
         for="gender"
         errorStyle="color:red"/>
```

```
        </h:panelGrid>
        <br />
        <h:outputLabel for="description" value="Enter your book
        interests"/>
        <br />
        <h:inputTextarea id="description" rows="5" cols="75"
        value="#{ch3ContactController.current.description}"/>

        <br />
        <h:panelGrid columns="2">
            <h:outputLabel for="password" value="Enter a password for
            site access: "/>
            <h:inputSecret id="password" size="40"
            value="#{ch3ContactController.current.password}">
                <f:validateRequired/>
                <f:ajax event="blur" render="passwordError"/>
            </h:inputSecret>

            <h:outputLabel for="passwordConfirm" value="Confirm
            Password: "/>
            <h:inputSecret id="passwordConfirm" size="40"
            value="#{ch3ContactController.passwordConfirm}"
                        validator="#{ch3ContactController.
                        validatePassword}">
                <f:ajax event="blur" render="passwordConfirmError"/>
            </h:inputSecret>
        </h:panelGrid>
        <h:message id="passwordError"
                for="password"
                style="color:red"/>
        <br />
        <h:message id="passwordConfirmError"
                for="passwordConfirm"
                style="color:red"/>
        <br />
        <hr/>
        <br />
```

```
<h:panelGrid columns="3">
    <h:panelGroup>
        <h:outputLabel for="newsletterList"
        value="Newsletters:" style=" "/>
        <h:selectManyListbox id="newsletterList"
        value="#{ch3ContactController.current.newsletterList}">
            <f:selectItems value="#{ch3ContactController.
            newsletterList}"/>
        </h:selectManyListbox>
    </h:panelGroup>
    <h:panelGroup/>
    <h:panelGroup>
        <h:panelGrid columns="1">
            <h:panelGroup>
                <h:outputLabel for="notifyme" value="Would you
                like to receive other promotional email?"/>
                <h:selectBooleanCheckbox id="notifyme"
                value="#{ch3ContactController.current.
                receiveNotifications}"/>
            </h:panelGroup>
            <h:panelGroup/>
            <hr/>
            <h:panelGroup/>
            <h:panelGroup>
                <h:outputLabel for="notificationTypes"
                value="What type of notifications are you
                interested in receiving?"/>
                <br />
                <h:selectManyCheckbox id="notifyTypes"
                value="#{ch3ContactController.current.
                notificationType}">
                    <f:selectItems value="#
                    {ch3ContactController.notificationTypes}"/>
```

```
                    </h:selectManyCheckbox>
                </h:panelGroup>
            </h:panelGrid>
        </h:panelGroup>
    </h:panelGrid>
    <hr/>
    <br />

    <h:commandButton id="contactSubmit" action="#{ch3Contact
    Controller.subscribe}" value="Save"/>
    <h:panelGrid  columns="2" width="400px;">
        <h:commandLink id="manageAccount" action="#{ch3Contact
        Controller.manage}" value="Manage Subscription"/>

        <h:outputLink id="homeLink" value="home.xhtml">Home</
        h:outputLink>
    </h:panelGrid>
</h:form>
</ui:define>
</ui:composition>
```

Once the input components have been "Ajaxified" by embedding the f:ajax tag within them, then tabbing through the fields (causing the onBlur event to occur for each field) will result in a form that resembles Figure 3-5.

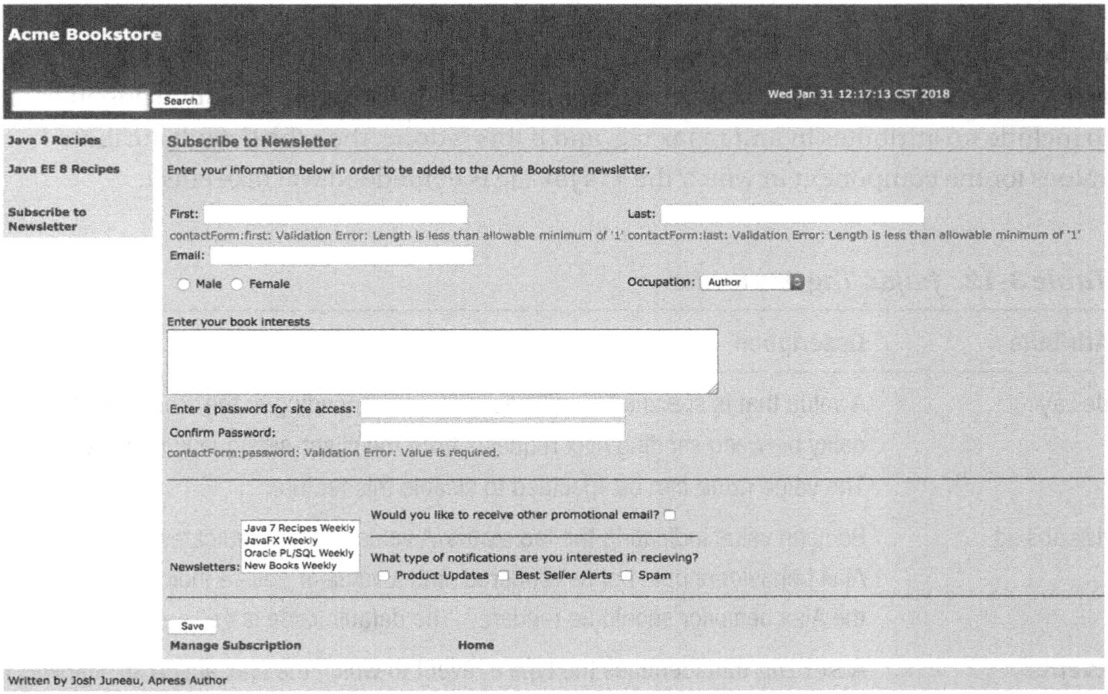

Figure 3-5. *Ajax validation using the f:ajax tag*

How It Works

In releases of JSF prior to 2.0, performing immediate validation required the manual coding of JavaScript or a third-party component library. The `f:ajax` tag was added to the JSF arsenal with the release of 2.0, bringing with it the power to easily add immediate validation (and other asynchronous processes) to JSF views using standard or third-party components. The `f:ajax` tag can be embedded within any JSF input component in order to immediately enhance the component, adding Ajax capabilities to it. This provides many benefits to the developer in that there is no longer a need to manually code JavaScript to perform client-side validation. It also allows validation to occur on the server (in Java code within a JSF controller class) asynchronously, providing seamless interaction between the client and server and generating an immediate response to the client. The result is a rich modern web application that behaves in much the same manner as a native desktop application. Validation can now occur instantaneously in front of an end user's eyes without the need to perform several page submits in order to repair all of the possible issues.

To use the `f:ajax` tag, simply embed it within any JSF component. There are a number of attributes that can be specified with `f:ajax`, as described in Table 3-12. If an attribute is not specified, then the default values are substituted. It is quite possible to include no attributes in an `f:ajax` tag, and if this is done, then the default attribute values for the component in which the `f:ajax` tag is embedded will take effect.

Table 3-12. *f:ajax Tag Attributes*

Attribute	Description
delay	A value that is specified in milliseconds, corresponding to the amount of delay between sending Ajax requests from the client-side queue to the server. The value none can be specified to disable this feature.
disabled	Boolean value indicating the tag status. A value of `true` indicates that the Ajax behavior should not be rendered, and a value of `false` indicates that the Ajax behavior should be rendered. The default value is `false`.
event	A `String` that identifies the type of event to which the Ajax action shall apply. If specified, it must be one of the supported component events. The default value is the event that triggers the Ajax request for the parent component of the Ajax behavior. The default event is `action` for `ActionSource` components and is `valueChange` for `EditableValueHolder` components.
execute	A collection that identifies a list of components to be executed on the server. A space-delimited `String` of component identifiers can be specified as the value for this attribute, or a `ValueExpression` (JSF EL) can be specified. The default value is `@this`, meaning the parent component of the Ajax behavior.
immediate	Boolean value indicating whether the input values are processed early in the life cycle. If `true`, then the values are processed, and their corresponding events will be broadcast during the Apply Request Values phase; otherwise, the events will be broadcast during the Invoke Application phase.
listener	Name of the listener method that is called when an `AjaxBehaviorEvent` has been broadcast for the listener.
onevent	Name of the JavaScript function used to handle UI events.

(continued)

Table 3-12. (*continued*)

Attribute	Description
onerror	Name of the JavaScript function used to handle errors.
resetValues	If true, then this particular Ajax transaction will reset the values.
render	Collection that identifies the components to be rendered on the client when the Ajax behavior is complete. A space-delimited String of component identifiers can be specified as the value for this attribute, or a ValueExpression (JSF EL) can be specified. The default value is @none, meaning that no components will be rendered when the Ajax behavior is complete.

The execute and render attributes of the f:ajax tag can specify a number of keywords to indicate which components are executed on the server for the Ajax behavior or which are rendered again after the Ajax behavior is complete, respectively. Table 3-13 lists the values that can be specified for both of these two attributes.

Table 3-13. *f:ajax Tag execute and render Attribute Values*

Attribute Value	Description
@all	All component identifiers are executed on the server, and all component identifiers are re-rendered once Ajax behavior is complete.
@form	The form that encloses the component.
@none	No component identifiers (default for the render attribute).
@this	The Ajax behavior parent component.
@child(n)	The nth child of the base component.
@composite	Closest composite component ancestor of the base component.
@id(id)	All component descendants of the base component with the specified id.
@namingcontainer	Closest NamingContainer ancestor of the base component.
@next	Next component in view after the base component.

(*continued*)

Table 3-13. (*continued*)

Attribute Value	Description
@parent	Parent of the base component.
@previous	Previous component to the base component.
@root	UIViewRoot.
Component IDs	Space-separated list of individual component identifiers.
JSF EL	Expression that resolves to a collection of string identifiers.

In the example for this recipe, an `f:ajax` tag has been embedded inside many of the input components within the form. Each of those components has been Ajaxified, in that the data entered as the values for the components will now have the ability to be processed using the JavaScript resource library associated with JSF. Behind the scenes, the `jsf.ajax.request()` method of the JavaScript resource library will collect the data for each component that has been Ajaxified and post the request to the JavaServer Faces life cycle. *In effect, the data is sent to the controller class property without submitting the page in a traditional fashion.* Notice that the event attribute specifies a JavaScript event that will be used to trigger the Ajax behavior. The JavaScript events that can be specified for the event attribute are those same JavaScript event attributes that are available on the parent component's tag, but the on prefix has been removed. For instance, if you want to perform an Ajax behavior on an `inputText` component when it loses focus, you would specify `blur` for the `f:ajax` event attribute rather than `onBlur`. Applying this concept to the example, when a user leaves the first or last name field, they will be validated using their associated `f:validate` tags immediately because the `f:ajax` tag has been embedded in them and the event on the `f:ajax` tag is specified as `blur`. When the Ajax behavior (the validation in this case) is complete, then the components whose identifiers are specified in the `f:ajax` render attribute will be re-rendered. In the case of the first and last `inputText` fields, their associated message components will be re-rendered, displaying any errors that may have occurred during validation.

UTILIZING AN ACTION LISTENER

It is possible to bind an action listener to an f:ajax tag so that when the invoking action occurs, the listener method is invoked. Why would you want to bind an action listener? There are any reasons to do so. For instance, suppose you wanted to capture the text that a user is typing into a text field. You could do so by binding an action method within a controller class to the listener attribute of an inputText field's corresponding f:ajax tag and then obtaining the current component's value from the AjaxBehaviorEvent object within the action method. For instance, suppose that you wanted to test a password for complexity and display a corresponding message indicating whether a password was strong enough. The inputSecret component for the password could be modified to include an f:ajax tag with an event specification of keyup and a listener specified as #{ch3ContactController.passwordStrength}, as the following listing demonstrates:

Within the view:

```
<h:outputLabel for="password" value="Enter a password for site access: "/>
<h:inputSecret id="password" size="40"
        value="#{ch3ContactController.current.password}">
    <f:validateRequired/>
    <f:ajax event="keyup" listener="#{ch3ContactController.passwordStrength}"
                                        render="passwordStrengthMessage"/>
</h:inputSecret>
...
```

Within the controller:

```
. . .
private String passwordStrengthMessage;
. . .
public void passwordStrength(AjaxBehaviorEvent event){
        UIInput password = (UIInput) event.getComponent();
        boolean isStrong = false;
        String input = password.getValue().toString();

        if(input.matches("((?=.*\\d)(?=.*[a-z])(?=.*[A-Z]).{6,})")) {
            isStrong = true;
        }
```

```
        if(isStrong == true){
            setPasswordStrengthMessage("Password is strong");
        } else {
            setPasswordStrengthMessage("Password is weak");
        }
    }
```

The code in this example would create a listener event that, when a user types a value, would check the present entry to determine whether it met the given criteria for a secure password. A message would then be displayed to the user to let them know whether the password was secure.

Using the `f:ajax` tag makes it easy to add Ajax behavior to a JSF component. Before the `f:ajax` tag, special third-party JavaScript libraries were often used to incorporate similar behaviors within JSF views. `f:ajax` adds the benefit of allowing the developer to choose between using Ajax behaviors, without the need for coding a single line of JavaScript.

3-6. Submitting Pages Without Page Reloads

Problem

You want to enable your input form to have the ability to submit input fields for processing without reloading the page. In essence, you want your web application input form to react more like that of a desktop application rather than navigating from page to page in order to process data.

Solution

Embed an `<f:ajax/>` tag within the command component in the view so that the CDI controller class action is invoked without the page being submitted. Enable `f:ajax` to update the `messages` component in the view so that any errors or success messages that result from the processing can be displayed. In this example, the newsletter subscription page for the Acme Bookstore will be changed so that the form is submitted using Ajax, and the `commandButton` component is processed without submitting the form in a traditional manner. The following excerpt from the newsletter subscription form sources from `recipe03_06.xhtml`, which demonstrates how to add Ajax functionality to the `action` components within the form:

```
<h:commandButton id="contactSubmit" action="#{ch3ContactController.
subscribe}"
                value="Save">
   <f:ajax event="action" execute="@form" render="@all"/>
</h:commandButton>
<h:panelGrid  columns="2" width="400px;">
```

When the button or link is clicked, JavaScript will be used in the background to process the request so that the results will be displayed immediately without needing to refresh the page.

How It Works

The user experience for web applications has traditionally involved a point, click, and page refresh mantra. While this type of experience is not particularly a bad one, it is not as nice as the immediate response that is oftentimes presented within a native desktop application. The use of Ajax within web applications has helped create a more unified user experience, allowing a web application the ability to produce an "immediate" response much like that of a native desktop application. Field validation (covered in Recipe 3-5) is a great candidate for immediate feedback, but another area where immediate responses work well is when forms are being submitted.

The `f:ajax` tag can be embedded in an `action` component in order to invoke the corresponding action method using JavaScript behind the scenes. The `f:ajax` tag contains a number of attributes, covered in Table 3-12 (see Recipe 3-5), that can be used to invoke Ajax behavior given a specified event and re-render view components when that Ajax behavior is complete. Please refer to Table 3-13 to see the values that can be specified for the `execute` and `render` attributes of the `f:ajax` tag.

In the example for this recipe, the `commandButton` component with an identifier of `contactSubmit` contains an `f:ajax` tag that specifies the `event` attribute as `action`, the `execute` attribute as `@form`, and the `render` attribute as `@all`. This means that when the button is invoked, the `ch3ContactController.subscribe` method will be called asynchronously using JavaScript, and it will send all the input component values from the form to the server (controller class) for processing. When the Ajax behavior (`subscribe` method) is complete, all of the components within the view will be re-rendered. By re-rendering all the components in the view, this allows those message components to display any messages that have been queued up as a result of failed validation or a successful form submission. It is possible to process or render only specified components during an Ajax behavior; to learn more about doing so, please see Recipe 3-7.

Note   The event attribute has a default value of `action` when the `f:ajax` tag is embedded within a `UICommand` component. However, it is specified in the code for this example for consistency.

3-7. Making Partial-Page Updates

Problem

You want to execute only a section of a page using an Ajax event and then render the corresponding section's components when the Ajax behavior is complete.

Solution

Use the `f:ajax` tag to add Ajax functionality to the components that you want to execute and render when the Ajax behavior is completed. Specify only the component identifiers corresponding to those components, or `@form`, `@this`, or one of the other execute keywords, for the `f:ajax` tag `execute` attribute. Likewise, specify only the component identifiers for the corresponding `message` components within the `render` attribute.

Suppose that the Acme Bookstore wants to execute the submission of the newsletter subscription form values and update the form's global message only when the submission is complete. The following `commandButton` component would execute only the form in which it is placed and the component corresponding to the identifier `newsletterSubscriptionMsgs`:

```
<h:commandButton id="contactSubmit" action="#{ch3ContactController.
subscribe}" value="Save">
    <f:ajax event="action" execute="@form" render="newsletterSubscription
    Msgs"/>
</h:commandButton>
```

When the button is clicked, the current form component values will be processed with the request, and the `ContactController` controller class `subscribe()` method will be invoked. Once the `subscribe()` method is complete, the component within the form that contains an identifier of `newsletterSubscriptionMsgs` (in this case a messages component) will be re-rendered.

Note   In the case of the newsletter subscription form for the Acme Bookstore, a partial-page render upon completion is a bad idea. This is because the form will never be submitted if the values within the form do not validate correctly. In this case, if some of the form values do not validate correctly, then nothing will be displayed on the page when the save button is clicked because the `subscribe` method will never be invoked. If the `f:ajax` tag's `render` attribute is set to `@all`, then all of the components that failed validation will have a corresponding error message that is displayed. This example should demonstrate how important it is to process the appropriate portions of the page for the result you are trying to achieve.

How It Works

The `f:ajax` tag makes it simple to perform partial-page updates. To do so, specify the identifiers for those components that you want to execute for the `f:ajax execute` attribute. As mentioned in the example for this recipe, suppose you want to execute only a portion of a page, rather than all of the components on the given page. You could do so by identifying the components that you want to execute within the view, specifying them within the `f:ajax execute` attribute, and then rendering the corresponding message components when the Ajax behavior was completed. If nothing is specified for an `f:ajax` execute attribute, then the `f:ajax` tag must be embedded inside a component, in which case the parent component would be executed. Such is the default behavior for the `f:ajax` execute attribute. In the example, the execute attribute of the `f:ajax` tag specifies the `@form` keyword, rather than a specific component `id`. As mentioned previously, a number of keywords can be specified for both the execute and render attributes of the `f:ajax` tag. Those keywords are listed in Table 3-13, which describes that the `@form` keyword indicates that all components within the same form as the given `f:ajax` tag will be executed when the Ajax behavior occurs. Therefore, all fields within the newsletter subscription form in this example will be sent to the controller class for processing when the button is clicked.

The same holds true for the render attribute, and once the Ajax behavior has completed, any component specified for the render attribute of the `f:ajax` tag will be re-rendered. Thus, if a validation occurs when a component is being processed because of the result of an `f:ajax` method call, a corresponding validation failure message can be displayed on the page after the validation fails. Any component can be rendered again, and the same keywords that can be specified for the execute attribute can also be used for the render attribute. In the example, the `newsletterSubscriptonMsgs` component is rendered once the Ajax behavior is completed.

3-8. Applying Ajax Functionality to a Group of Components

Problem

You want to apply Ajax functionality to a group of input components, rather than to each component separately.

Solution

Enclose any components to which you want to apply Ajax functionality within an `f:ajax` tag. The `f:ajax` tag can be the parent to one or more JSF components, in which case each of the child components inherits the given Ajax behavior. Applying Ajax functionality to multiple components is demonstrated in the following code listing. In the following example excerpt, the newsletter subscription view of the Acme Bookstore application is adjusted so that each of the `inputText` components that contains a validator is enclosed by a single `f:ajax` tag. Given that each of the `inputText` components is embodied within the same f:ajax tag, the f:ajax render attribute has been set to specify the message component for each of the corresponding inputText fields in the group:

```
<ui:define name="content">
    <h:form id="contactForm">
        <h1>Subscribe to Newsletter</h1>
        <p>
            <h:outputText id="newsletterSubscriptionDesc"
                        value="#{ch3ContactController.
                        newsletterDescription}"/>
        </p>

        <br/>
        <h:messages id="newsletterSubscriptionMsgs" global Only="true"
        errorStyle="color: red" infoStyle="color: green"/>
        <br/>
        <f:ajax event="blur" render="firstError lastError emailError
        genderError passwordError passwordConfirmError">
            <h:panelGrid columns="2" bgcolor="" border="0">
                <h:panelGroup>
                    <h:outputLabel for="first" value="First: "/>
                    <h:inputText id="first" size="40"
                    value="#{ch3ContactController.current.first}">
                        <f:validateLength minimum="1" maximum="40"/>

                    </h:inputText>
                </h:panelGroup>
                <h:panelGroup>

                    <h:outputLabel for="last" value="Last: "/>
                    <h:inputText id="last" size="40"
                    value="#{ch3ContactController.current.last}">
                        <f:validateLength minimum="1" maximum="40"/>

                    </h:inputText>
                </h:panelGroup>
```

```
<h:message id="firstError"
          for="first"
          errorStyle="color:red"/>

<h:message id="lastError"
          for="last"
          errorStyle="color:red"/>
<h:panelGroup>
    <h:outputLabel for="email" value="Email: "/>
    <h:inputText id="email" size="40"
    value="#{ch3ContactController.current.email}">

    </h:inputText>
</h:panelGroup>
<h:panelGroup/>
<h:message id="emailError"
          for="email"
          errorStyle="color:red"/>
<h:panelGroup/>

<h:selectOneRadio title="Gender" id="gender"
value="#{ch3ContactController.current.gender}">
    <f:selectItem  itemValue="M" itemLabel="Male"/>
    <f:selectItem itemValue="F" itemLabel="Female"/>
</h:selectOneRadio>
<h:panelGroup>
    <h:outputLabel for="occupation" value="Occupation: "/>
    <h:selectOneMenu id="occupation"
    value="#{ch3ContactController.current.occupation}">
        <f:selectItems value="#{ch3ContactController.
        occupationList}"/>
    </h:selectOneMenu>
</h:panelGroup>
<h:message id="genderError"
          for="gender"
          errorStyle="color:red"/>

</h:panelGrid>
```

```
<br/>
<h:outputLabel for="description" value="Enter your book
interests"/>
<br/>
<h:inputTextarea id="description" rows="5" cols="75"
 value="#{ch3ContactController.current.description}"/>

<br/>
<h:panelGrid columns="2">
    <h:outputLabel for="password" value="Enter a password for
    site access: "/>
    <h:inputSecret id="password" size="40"
    value="#{ch3ContactController.current.password}">
        <f:validateRequired/>
        <f:ajax event="keyup" listener="#{ch3ContactController.
        passwordStrength}" render="passwordStrengthMessage"/>
    </h:inputSecret>

    <h:outputLabel for="passwordConfirm" value="Confirm
    Password: "/>
    <h:inputSecret id="passwordConfirm" size="40"
    value="#{ch3ContactController.passwordConfirm}"
                  validator="#{ch3ContactController.
                  validatePassword}">

    </h:inputSecret>
</h:panelGrid>
<h:panelGroup>
    <h:outputText id="passwordStrengthMessage"
    value="#{ch3ContactController.passwordStrengthMessage}"/>
    <h:message id="passwordError"
            for="password"
            style="color:red"/>
</h:panelGroup>
<br/>
```

```
<h:message id="passwordConfirmError"
          for="passwordConfirm"
          style="color:red"/>
<br/>
<hr/>
<br/>

<h:panelGrid columns="3">
    <h:panelGroup>
        <h:outputLabel for="newsletterList"
        value="Newsletters:" style=" "/>
        <h:selectManyListbox id="newsletterList"
        value="#{ch3ContactController.current.newsletterList}">
            <f:selectItems value="#{ch3ContactController.
            newsletterList}"/>
        </h:selectManyListbox>
    </h:panelGroup>
    <h:panelGroup/>
    <h:panelGroup>
        <h:panelGrid columns="1">
            <h:panelGroup>
                <h:outputLabel for="notifyme" value="Would you
                like to receive other promotional email?"/>
                <h:selectBooleanCheckbox id="notifyme"
                value="#{ch3ContactController.current.
                receiveNotifications}"/>
            </h:panelGroup>
            <h:panelGroup/>
            <hr/>
            <h:panelGroup/>
            <h:panelGroup>
                <h:outputLabel for="notificationTypes"
                value="What type of notifications are you
                interested in recieving?"/>
                <br/>
```

```
                        <h:selectManyCheckbox id="notifyTypes"
                        value="#{ch3ContactController.current.
                        notificationType}">
                                <f:selectItems value="#{ch3Contact
                                Controller.notificationTypes}"/>
                        </h:selectManyCheckbox>
                    </h:panelGroup>
                </h:panelGrid>
            </h:panelGroup>
        </h:panelGrid>
        <hr/>
        <br/>
    </f:ajax>
    <h:commandButton id="contactSubmit" action="#{ch3ContactController.
    subscribe}" value="Save">
        <f:ajax event="action" execute="@form" render="@all"/>
    </h:commandButton>
    <h:panelGrid  columns="2" width="400px;">
        <h:commandLink id="manageAccount" action="#{ch3Contact
        Controller.manage}" value="Manage Subscription">
            <f:ajax event="action" execute="@this" render="@all"/>
        </h:commandLink>
        <h:outputLink id="homeLink" value="home.xhtml">Home
        </h:outputLink>
    </h:panelGrid>
    </h:form>
</ui:define>
```

When the page is rendered, each component will react separately given their associated validations. That is, if validation fails for one component, only the message component that corresponds with the component failing validation will be displayed, although each component identified within the f:ajax render attribute will be re-rendered.

Note   As a result of specifying a global f:ajax tag, the password component can now execute two Ajax requests. One of the Ajax requests for the field is responsible for validating to ensure that the field is not blank, and the other is responsible for ensuring that the given password String is strong.

How It Works

Grouping multiple components with the same Ajax behavior has its benefits. For one, if the behavior needs to be adjusted for any reason, one change can now be made to the Ajax behavior, and each of the components in the group can benefit from the single adjustment. However, the f:ajax tag is smart enough to enable each component to still utilize separate functionality, such as validation or actions, so each can still have their own customized Ajax behavior. To group components under a single f:ajax tag, they must be added to the view as subelements of the f:ajax tag. That is, any child components must be enclosed between the opening and closing f:ajax tags. All of the enclosed components will then use Ajax to send requests to the server using JavaScript in an asynchronous fashion.

In the example for this recipe, a handful of the inputText components within the newsletter subscription view have been embodied inside an f:ajax tag so that their values will be validated using server-side bean validation when they lose focus. The f:ajax tag that is used to group the components has an event attribute set to blur, and its render attribute contains the String-based identifier for each of the message components corresponding to the components that are included in the group. The space-separated list of component ids is used to re-render each of the message components when the Ajax behavior is complete, displaying any errors that occur as a result of the validation.

3-9. Custom Processing of Ajax Functionality

Problem

You want to customize the Ajax processing for JSF components within a view in your application.

Solution

Write the JavaScript that will be used for processing your request, and utilize the
`jsf.ajax.request()` function along with one of the standard JavaScript event-handling
attributes for a JSF component. The following example is the JSF view for the newsletter
subscription page for the Acme Bookstore application. All of the `f:ajax` tags that were
previously used for validating `inputText` fields (Recipe 3-1) have been removed, and the
`onblur` attribute of each `inputText` component has been set to use the
`jsf.ajax.request()` method in order to Ajaxify the component. The following excerpt
is taken from the view named `recipe03_09.xhtml`, representing the updated newsletter
subscription JSF view:

...

```
<h:outputScript name="jsf.js" library="javax.faces"
target="head"/>
<h1>Subscribe to Newsletter</h1>
<p>
    <h:outputText id="newsletterSubscriptionDesc"
                  value="#{ch3ContactController.
                  newsletterDescription}"/>
</p>

<br/>
<h:messages id="newsletterSubscriptionMsgs"
globalOnly="true" errorStyle="color: red"
infoStyle="color: green"/>
<br/>

<h:panelGrid columns="2" bgcolor="" border="0">
    <h:panelGroup>
        <h:outputLabel for="first" value="First: "/>
        <h:inputText id="first" size="40"
        value="#{ch3ContactController.current.first}"
                  onblur="jsf.ajax.request(this,
                  event, {execute: 'first', render:
                  'firstError'});
```

```
                return false;">
                    <f:validateLength minimum="1"
                    maximum="40"/>
                </h:inputText>
            </h:panelGroup>
            <h:panelGroup>
                <h:outputLabel for="last" value="Last: "/>
                <h:inputText id="last" size="40"
                value="#{ch3ContactController.current.last}"
                            onblur="jsf.ajax.request(this,
                            event, {execute: 'last', render:
                            'lastError'});
             return false;">
                    <f:validateLength minimum="1"
                    maximum="40"/>
                </h:inputText>
            </h:panelGroup>

            <h:message id="firstError"
                    for="first"
                    errorStyle="color:red"/>

            <h:message id="lastError"
                    for="last"
                    errorStyle="color:red"/>
            <h:panelGroup>
                <h:outputLabel for="email" value="Email: "/>
                <h:inputText id="email" size="40"
                value="#{ch3ContactController.current.email}"
                            onblur="jsf.ajax.request(this,
                            event, {execute: 'email', render:
                            'emailError'});
             return false;"/>
            </h:panelGroup>
            <h:panelGroup/>
            <h:message id="emailError"
```

```
                        for="email"
                        errorStyle="color:red"/>
            <h:panelGroup/>
...
```

Note   The `<h:panelGroup/>` tag is used to add a placeholder panel group to the grid for spacing purposes.

Using this technique, the `inputText` components that specify Ajax behavior for the `onblur` event will asynchronously have their values validated when they lose focus. If any custom JavaScript code needs to be used, it can be added to the same inline JavaScript call to `jsf.ajax.request()`.

Note   Method calls to CDI controllers cannot be made using the `jsf.ajax.request()` technique, so it is not possible to invoke a listener explicitly with the Ajax request.

How It Works

The JavaScript API method `jsf.ajax.request()` can be accessed directly by a Facelets application, enabling a developer to have slightly more control than using the `f:ajax` tag. Behind the scenes, the `f:ajax` tag is converted into a call to `jsf.ajax.request()`, sending the parameters as specified via the tag's attributes. To use this technique, you must include the `jsf.js` library within the view. A JSF `outputScript` tag should be included in the view, specifying `jsf.js` as the script name and `javax.faces` as the `library`. The `jsf.js` script within this example will be placed in the head of the view, which is done by specifying `head` for the `target` attribute of the `outputScript` tag. The following excerpt from the example demonstrates what the tag should look like:

```
<h:outputScript name="jsf.js" library="javax.faces" target="head"/>
```

> **Note**   To avoid nested IDs, it is a good idea to specify the `h:form` attribute of `prependId="false"` when using `jsf.ajax.request()` manually. For instance, the form tag should look as follows:
>
> `<h:form prependId="false">`

The `jsf.ajax.request()` method can be called inline, as is the case with the example for this recipe, and it can be invoked from within any of the JavaScript event attributes of a given component. The format for calling the JavaScript method is as follows:

`jsf.ajax.request(component, event,{execute:'id or keyword', render:'id or keyword'});`

Usually when the request is made using an inline call, the `this` keyword is specified for the first parameter, signifying that the current component should be passed. The event keyword is passed as the second parameter, and it passes with it the current event that is occurring against the component. Lastly, a map of name-value pairs is passed, specifying the `execute` and `render` attributes along with the component identifiers or keywords that should be executed and rendered after the execution completes, respectively. For a list of the valid keywords that can be used, please refer to Table 3-2 within the introduction to this chapter.

> **Note**   You can also utilize the `jsf.ajax.request` method from within a controller class by specifying the `@ResourceDependency` annotation (`https://jakarta.ee/specifications/faces/2.3/apidocs/javax/faces/application/ResourceDependency.html`) as follows:
>
> `@ResourceDependency(name="jsf.js" library="javax.faces" target="head")`

3-10. Listening for System-Level Events

Problem

You want to invoke a method within your application whenever a system-level event occurs.

Solution

Create a system event listener class by implementing the SystemEventListener interface and overriding the processEvent(SystemEvent event) and isListenerForSource(Object source) methods. Implement these methods accordingly to perform the desired event processing. The following code listing is for a class named BookstoreAppListener, and it is invoked when the application is started up or when it is shutting down:

```
public class BookstoreAppListener implements SystemEventListener {

    @Override
    public void processEvent(SystemEvent event) throws
    AbortProcessingException {
        if(event instanceof PostConstructApplicationEvent){
            System.out.println("The application has been constructed...");
        }

        if(event instanceof PreDestroyApplicationEvent){
            System.out.println("The application is being destroyed...");
        }
    }

    @Override
    public boolean isListenerForSource(Object source) {
        return(source instanceof Application);
    }

}
```

Next, the system event listener must be registered in the `faces-config.xml` file. The following excerpt is taken from the `faces-config.xml` file for the Acme Bookstore application:

```
...
<application>

            <system-event-listener>
                    <system-event-listener-class>
                            org.jakartaeerecipes.
                            chapter03.recipe03_10.
                            BookstoreAppListener
                    </system-event-listener-class>
                    <system-event-class>
                            javax.faces.event.
                            PostConstructApplicationEvent
                    </system-event-class
            </system-event-listener>

            <system-event-listener>
                    <system-event-listener-class>
                            org.jakartaeerecipes.
                            chapter03.recipe03_10.
                            BookstoreAppListener
                    </system-event-listener-class>
                    <system-event-class>
                            javax.faces.event.
                            PreDestroyApplicationEvent
                    </system-event-class
        </system-event-listener>

    </application>
...
```

When the application is started, the message "The application has been constructed…" will be displayed in the server log. When the application is shutting down, the message "The application is being destroyed…" will be displayed in the server log.

How It Works

The ability to perform tasks when an application starts up can sometimes be useful. For instance, let's say you'd like to have an email sent to the application administrator each time the application starts. You can do this by performing the task of sending an email within a class that implements the `SystemEventListener` interface. A class that implements `SystemEventListener` must then override two methods, `processEvent(SystemEvent event)` and `isListenerForSource(Object source)`. The `processEvent()` method is where the real action occurs, because it is the method into which your custom code should be placed. Whenever a system event occurs, the `processEvent()` method is invoked. In this method, you will need to perform a check to determine what type of event has occurred so that you can process only those events that are pertinent. To determine the event that has occurred, perform an `instanceof()` check on the `SystemEvent` object. In the example, there are two `if` statements used to determine the type of event that is occurring and to print a different message for each. If the event type is of `PostConstructApplicationEvent`, then that means the application is being constructed. Otherwise, if the event type is of `PreDestroyApplicationEvent`, the application is about to be destroyed. The `PostConstructApplicationEvent` event is called just after the application has been constructed, and `PreDestroyApplicationEvent` is called just prior to the application destruction.

The other method that must be overridden within the `SystemEventListener` class is named `isListenerForSource()`. This method must return `true` if this listener instance is interested in receiving events from the instance referenced by the source parameter. Since the example class is built to listen for system events for the application, a `true` value is returned if the source parameter is an instance of `Application`.

After the system event listener class has been written, it needs to be registered with the application. In the example, you want to listen for both the `PostConstructApplicationEvent` and the `PreDestroyApplicationEvent`, so there needs to be a `system-event-listener` element added to the `faces-config.xml` file for each of these events. Within the `system-event-listener` element, specify the name of the event listener class within a `system-event-listener-class` element and the name of the event within a `system-event-class` element.

3-11. Listening for Component Events

Problem

You want to invoke a listener method when a specified component event is occurring. For instance, you want to listen for a component render event.

Solution

Embed an f:event tag within the component for which you want to listen for events. The f:event tag allows components to invoke controller class listener methods based upon the current component state. For instance, if a component is being rendered or validated, a specified listener method could be invoked. In the example for this recipe, an outputText component is added to the book view of the Acme Bookstore application to specify whether the current book is in the user's shopping cart. When the outputText component is being rendered, a component listener is invoked that checks the current state of the cart to see whether the book is contained within it. If it is in the cart, then the outputText component will render a message stating so; if not, then the outputText component will render a message stating that it is not in the cart.

The following excerpt is taken from a view named recipe03_10.xhtml, a derivative of the book view for the application. It demonstrates the use of the f:event tag within a component. Note that the outputText component contains no value attribute because the value will be set within the event listener:

```
...
<h:outputText id="isInCart" style="font-style: italic; color: ">
    <f:event type="preRenderComponent" listener="#{ch3CartController.
    isBookInCart}"/>
</h:outputText>
...
```

The CartController class contains a method named isBookInCart(ComponentSystemEvent). The f:event tag in the view references this listener method via the CartController controller name ch3CartController. The listener method is responsible for constructing the text that will be displayed in the outputText component:

```
public void isBookInCart(ComponentSystemEvent event) {
        UIOutput output = (UIOutput) event.getComponent();
        if (cart != null) {
            if (searchCart(authorController.getCurrentBook()
            .getTitle()) > 0) {
                output.setValue("This book is currently in your cart.");
            } else {
                output.setValue("This book is not in your cart.");
            }
        } else {
            output.setValue("This book is not in your cart.");
        }
    }
```

How It Works

Everything that occurs within JSF applications is governed by the JSF application life cycle. As part of the life cycle, JSF components go through different phases throughout their lifetimes. Listeners can be added to JSF components to perform different tasks when a given phase is beginning or ending. There are two pieces to the puzzle for creating a component listener: the tag that is embedded within the component for which your listener will perform tasks and the listener method itself. To add a listener to a component, the f:event tag should be embedded within the opening and closing tags of the component that will be interrogated. The f:event tag contains a handful of attributes, but only two of them are mandatory for use: type and listener. The type attribute specifies the type of event that will be listened for, and the listener attribute specifies the controller class listener method that will be invoked when that event occurs. The valid values that could be specified for the name attribute are preRenderComponent, postAddToView, preValidate, and postValidate. In addition to these event values, any Java class that extends javax.faces.event.ComponentSystemEvent can also be specified for the name attribute.

The listener method must accept a ComponentSystemEvent object. In the example, the listener checks to see whether the shopping cart is null, and if it is, then a message indicating an empty cart will be set for the outputText component's value. Otherwise, if the cart is not empty, then the method looks through the List of books in the cart to see whether the currently selected book is in the cart. A message indicating whether the book is in the cart is then added to the value of the outputText component. Via the listener, the actual value of the component was manipulated. Such a technique could be used in various ways to alter components to suit the needs of the situation.

3-12. Developing a Page Flow
Problem
You want to develop a flow of pages within your application that share information with one another.

Solution
Define a page flow using the faces flow technology, a solution that allows a defined set of views to be interrelated with one another to share a common set of data, and views outside of the flow do not have access to the flow's data. Flows also have their own set of navigational logic, so they are almost like a subprogram within an application. To enable an application to utilize faces flow, a <flow-definition> section should be added to the faces-config.xml file. The section can be empty, because the navigational logic can instead reside in a separate configuration file for the flow. The following faces-config. xml file demonstrates how to enable faces flow for an application:

```
<faces-config version="2.3"
        xmlns="http://xmlns.jcp.org/xml/ns/javaee"
        xmlns:xsi="http://www.w3.org/2001/XMLSchema-instance"
        xsi:schemaLocation="http://xmlns.jcp.org/xml/ns/javaee
        http://xmlns.jcp.org/xml/ns/javaee/web-facesconfig_2_3.xsd">
 ...
<flow-definition>
    </flow-definition>
    ...
</faces-config>
```

The views belonging to a flow should be separated from the rest of the application views and placed into a folder at the root of the application's web directory. The folder containing the flow views should be named the same as the flow identifier. Navigation and configuration code is contained within a separate XML configuration file that resides within the flow view directory, and the file is named `flowname-flow.xml`, where `flowname` is the flow identifier. The following configuration file demonstrates the configuration for a very basic flow identified by `exampleFlow`. You can find more information regarding the different elements that can be used within the flow configuration in the "How It Works" section:

```
<faces-config version="2.2" xmlns="http://xmlns.jcp.org/xml/ns/javaee"
          xmlns:xsi="http://www.w3.org/2001/XMLSchema-instance"
          xsi:schemaLocation="
      http://xmlns.jcp.org/xml/ns/javaee
      http://xmlns.jcp.org/xml/ns/javaee/web-facesconfig_2_2.xsd">

    <flow-definition id="exampleFlow">

    </flow-definition>

</faces-config>
```

The views belonging to the flow should reside within the flow folder alongside the flow configuration file. Each of the views can access a controller class that is dedicated to facilitating the flow. The flows share a context that begins when the flow is accessed and ends when the flow exits. The following view demonstrates the entry point to a flow named `exampleFlow`. This example view can be found in the book sources in the file `recipes03_12.xhtml`:

```
<ui:composition xmlns:ui="http://xmlns.jcp.org/jsf/facelets"
            xmlns:f="http://xmlns.jcp.org/jsf/core"
            xmlns:h="http://xmlns.jcp.org/jsf/html"
            template="layout/custom_template_search.xhtml">
    <ui:define name="content">
        <h:messages globalOnly="true"  errorStyle="color: red"
        infoStyle="color: green"/>
```

```
    <h:form id="flowForm">
        <p>
            Faces Flow Example
        </p>
        <h:commandButton value="Begin Flow" action="exampleFlow"/>
        <h:commandButton value="Stay Here" action="stay"/>

    </h:form>
  </ui:define>
</ui:composition>
```

Next, let's take a look at a view that is accessing the controller class that is dedicated to the flow. In the following view, the controller class named FlowBean is accessed to invoke a method, which will return an implicit navigational String directing the application to the next view in the flow. Notice that this view also accesses the facesContext.application.flowHandler, which I will discuss more in the "How It Works" section:

```
<h:body>
    <f:view>
        <h:form>
    <p>
        This is the first view of the flow.
        <br/><br/>
        Flow ID: #{facesContext.application.flowHandler.currentFlow.id}
        <br/>
        <h:commandLink value="Go to another view in the flow"
        action="#{flowBean.navMethod()}"/>
    </p>
        </h:form>
    </f:view>
</h:body>
```

Each subsequent view within the flow can also access the resources of the flow's controller class. Lastly, you'll look at the code that is contained within org. jakartaeerecipes.chapter03.FlowBean, which is the controller class that is dedicated to the flow:

```java
import javax.faces.flow.FlowScoped;
import javax.inject.Named;

@Named
@FlowScoped("exampleFlow")
public class FlowBean implements java.io.Serializable {

    private String flowValue;
    private String parameter1;
    /**
     * Creates a new instance of FlowBean
     */
    public FlowBean() {
    }

    /**
     * Initializes the flow
     */

    public void initializeIt(){
        System.out.println("Initialize the flow...");
    }
    /**
     * Finalizes the flow
     */

    public void finalizeIt(){
        System.out.println("Finalize the flow...");
    }

    public String navMethod(){
        return "intermediateFlow";
    }
```

```java
    public String testMethod(){
        return "intermediate";
    }

    public String endFlow(){
        return "endingFlow";
    }

    /**
     * @return the flowValue
     */
    public String getFlowValue() {
        return flowValue;
    }

    /**
     * @param flowValue the flowValue to set
     */
    public void setFlowValue(String flowValue) {
        this.flowValue = flowValue;
    }

    /**
     * @return the parameter1
     */
    public String getParameter1() {
        return parameter1;
    }

    /**
     * @param parameter1 the parameter1 to set
     */
    public void setParameter1(String parameter1) {
        this.parameter1 = parameter1;
    }
}
```

This solution provided a quick overview of the files that are required for creating a flow within a JSF application. In the next section, I'll cover the features in more detail.

How It Works

The concept of session management has been a difficult feat to tackle since the beginning of web applications. A *web flow* refers to a grouping of web views that are related and must have the ability to share information with each view within the flow. Many web frameworks have attempted to tackle this issue by creating different solutions that would facilitate the sharing of data across multiple views. Oftentimes, a mixture of session variables, request parameters, and cookies are used as a patchwork solution.

Since JSF 2.2, a solution has been adopted for binding multiple JSF views to each other, allowing them to share information among each other. This solution is referenced as *faces flow*; and it allows a group of interrelated views to belong to a *flow instance*, and information can be shared across all the views belonging to a flow instance. Flows contain separate navigation that pertains to the flow itself and not the entire application. As such, flow navigation can be defined in an XML format or via code. A flow contains a single point of entry, and it can be called from any point within an application.

Defining a Flow

As mentioned in the solution to this recipe, the `faces-config.xml` file for a JSF application that will utilize the flow feature must contain a `<flow-definition>` section. This section of the `faces-config.xml` file can contain information specific to one or more flows residing within an application. However, for the purposes of this recipe, the solution utilizes a separate XML configuration file for use with the flow. Either way will work; the syntax does vary just a bit because the XML configuration file that is flow-specific uses a new JSF `taglib` for accessing the flow-specific configuration tags.

Note   To learn more about using the `faces-config.xml` file for flow configuration, please refer to the online documentation (`https://docs.oracle.com/javaee/7/tutorial/jsf-configure003.htm`).

Even if a flow is not using the `faces-config.xml` file for defining the flow configuration, the `<flow-definition>` section must exist to tell the JSF runtime that flows are utilized within the application.

The flow-specific configuration file and all flow-related views should reside within the same folder, at the root of the application's web directory. The name of the folder should be the same as the flow identifier. As mentioned in the solution, the flow configuration file should be named `flowname-flow.xml`, where `flowname` is the same as the flow identifier.

The Flow Controller Class

A flow contains its own controller class annotated as `@FlowScoped`, which differs from `@SessionScoped` because the data can be accessed only by other views (`ViewNodes`) belonging to the flow. The `@FlowScoped` annotation relies upon Contexts and Dependency Injection (CDI), because `FlowScoped` is a CDI scope that causes the runtime to consider classes with the `@FlowScoped` annotation to be in the scope of the specified flow. A `@FlowScoped` bean maintains a life cycle that begins and ends with a flow instance. Multiple flow instances can exist for a single application, and if a user begins a flow within one browser tab and then opens another, a new flow instance will begin in the new tab. This solution resolves many lingering issues around sessions and standard browsers that allow users to open multiple tabs. To maintain separate flow instances, the `ClientId` is used by JSF to differentiate among multiple instances.

Each flow can contain an `initializer` and a `finalizer` (i.e., a method that will be invoked when a flow is entered and a method that will be invoked when a flow is exited, respectively). To declare an initializer, specify a child element named `<initializer>` within the flow configuration `<flow-definition>`. The initializer element can be an EL expression that declares the controller class initializer method, as such:

```
...
<initializer>#{flowBean.initializeIt}</initializer>
...
```

Similarly, a `<finalizer>` element can be specified within the flow configuration to define the method that will be called when the flow is exited. The following demonstrates how to set the finalizer to an EL expression declaring the controller class finalizer method:

```
...
<finalizer>#{flowBean.finalizeIt}></finalizer>
...
```

Flows can contain method calls and variable values that are accessible only via the flow nodes. These methods and variables should be placed within the `FlowScoped` bean and used the same as standard controller class methods and variables. The main difference is that any method or variable that is defined within a `FlowScoped` bean is available only for a single flow instance.

Navigating Flow View Nodes

Flows contain their own navigational rules, which can be defined within the `faces-config.xml` file or the individual flow configuration files. These rules can be straightforward and produce a page-by-page navigation, or they can include conditional logic. There are a series of elements that can be specified within the navigation rules, which will facilitate conditional navigation. Table 3-14 lists the different elements, along with an explanation of what they do.

Table 3-14. *Flow Navigational Elements*

Element	Description
view	Navigates to a standard JSF view.
switch	Represents one or more EL expressions that conditionally evaluate to `true` or `false`. If `true`, then navigation occurs to the specified view node.
flow-return	Outcome determined by the caller of the flow.
flow-call	Represents a call to another flow; creates a nested flow.
method-call	Arbitrary method call that can invoke a method that returns a navigational outcome.

The following navigational sequence is an example of a flow navigation that contains conditional logic using the elements listed in Table 3-14:

```
<flow-definition>

    <start-node>exampleFlow</j:start-node>

    <switch id="startNode">
        <navigation-case>
            <if>#{flowBean.someCondition}</if>
                <from-outcome>newView</from-outcome>
        </navigation-case>
    </switch>

    <view id="oneFlow">
        <vdl-document>oneFlow.xhtml</vdl-document>
    </view>

    <flow-return id="exit">
        <navigation-case>
            <from-outcome>exitFlow</from-outcome>
        </navigation-case>
    </flow-return>

    <finalizer>#{flowBean.finalizeIt}</finalizer>


</flow-definition>
```

Flow EL

Flows contain a new EL variable named facesFlowScope. This variable is associated with the current flow, and it is a map that can be used for storing arbitrary values for use within a flow. The key-value pairs can be stored and read via a JSF view or through Java code within a controller class. For example, to display the content for a particular map key, you could use the following:

```
The content for the key is:  #{facesFlowScope.myKey}
```

3-13. Broadcasting Messages from the Server to All Clients

Problem

Your organization has constructed a Jakarta EE application, and it is in use by a number of clients. You wish to have the ability to send a message from the server and have that message distributed to all of the clients at once.

Solution

Make use of the `f:websocket` tag, which was new with the release of JSF 2.3, to send a message to all listening clients. The following example includes a client view which contains a text box, a send button, and a `f:websocket` tag. The user can type a message into the text box and click the send button, and the typed message will be sent to all other clients that are currently listening on the same channel:

```
<html xmlns="http://www.w3.org/1999/xhtml"
    xmlns:ui="http://xmlns.jcp.org/jsf/facelets"
    xmlns:f="http://xmlns.jcp.org/jsf/core"
    xmlns:h="http://xmlns.jcp.org/jsf/html">
  <head>
  </head>

  <body>

      <ui:composition template="layout/custom_template_search.xhtml">
          <ui:define name="content">
              <h:messages globalOnly="true"  errorStyle="color: red"
              infoStyle="color: green"/>
              <h:form id="webSocketForm">
                  <script type="text/javascript">
                      function messageListener(message) {
                          document.getElementById("messageDiv").innerHTML
                          += message + "<br/>";
                      }
                  </script>
```

```
                        <p>
                            Websocket Integration Example
                        </p>
                        <p>
                            Enter text into the box below and press send
                            button.  This will send
                            a message to all connected clients.
                        </p>
                        <h:inputText id="websocketMessageText"
                        value="#{bookstoreController.messageText}"/>
                        <br/>
                        <h:commandButton id="sendMessage"
                        action="#{bookstoreController.sendMessage}"
                        value="Send">
                            <f:ajax/>
                        </h:commandButton>
                        <br/>
                        <f:websocket channel="messagePusher"
                        onmessage="messageListener" />

                        <div id="messageDiv"/>
                    </h:form>
                </ui:define>
            </ui:composition>
        </body>
    </html>
```

The following code shows the server-side code behind the messagePusher channel and the bookstoreController.sendMessage() method:

```
import java.util.Date;
import javax.enterprise.context.ApplicationScoped;
import javax.faces.push.Push;
import javax.faces.push.PushContext;
import javax.inject.Inject;
import javax.inject.Named;
```

```
@Named("bookstoreController")
@ApplicationScoped
public class BookstoreController {

    private Date dayAndTime = null;

    private int counter;

    @Inject
    @Push(channel="messagePusher")
    private PushContext push;

    private String messageText;
. . .
/**
    * Initiates a notification to all Websocket clients.  This method is
    used
    * for example 3-12.
    */
    public void sendMessage(){
        System.out.println("sending message");
        push.send(messageText);
        messageText = null;
    }
. . .
}
```

The resulting solution looks like the following. If one types and clicks send, all listening clients (on the same view) will receive the message.

How It Works

Websockets have become a standard protocol for client and server communication. There are a couple of different ways in which to implement Websocket solutions. One can utilize a framework such as Atmosphere to develop Websockets, or since the release of Java EE 7, the native Websocket support can be utilized. Both approaches are supported by the JSF Websocket. The support in JSF 2.3 includes both implementations, so it provides some flexibility. To enable this support, one must specify the `javax.faces.ENABLE_WEBSOCKET_ENDPOINT` context parameter in the `web.xml` deployment descriptor with a value of `true`, as follows:

```
<context-param>
    <param-name>javax.faces.ENABLE_WEBSOCKET_ENDPOINT</param-name>
    <param-value>true</param-value>
</context-param>
```

The `f:websocket` tag enables support for Websockets within JSF client views. The tag includes a required `channel` attribute, which is a `ValueExpression` used to list the channel on which the Websocket client will listen. The tag also includes a required `onmessage` attribute, which is also a `ValueExpression`, and it is used to list the name of a JavaScript function that is to be executed when the Websocket message is received. In the example, you can see that the channel is set to `messagePusher`, meaning that the server must send message(s) to the channel named `messagePusher` in order to successfully send to this client. The message attribute is set to `messageListener`, and if you look at the JavaScript source that has been added to the view, you can see that it contains a function named `messageListener`. This function is executed when the message is received. In this example, the function merely prints a message to the `div` with an ID of `messageDiv` in the view. The signature of the JavaScript function in this example accepts the message only. However, a JavaScript function could also accept a channel name and event argument, if needed.

The `f:websocket` tag contains a number of other useful attributes as well. While optional, the following parameters may be of use in certain circumstances:

- `onclose`: Specifies a JavaScript function to invoke when the message is closed.

- `scope`: Used to specify a limit as to where messages are propagated. If set to session, this attribute limits the messages to all client views with the same websocket channel in the current session only.

- `port`: Specifies the TCP port number other than the HTTP port, if needed.

Now let's take a look at the server-side implementation. The solution to this recipe uses a new PushContext, which is injected into an ApplicationScoped bean. This PushContext is used to send the message to all listening clients, and it can be injected into any CDI bean by including the @Push annotation, along with the context. The name of the channel can be specified via an optional channel attribute on the @Push annotation; otherwise, it will assume the same name as the PushContext identifier. In the example, the PushContext is simply named "push." This is the channel on which all clients must listen.

To send a message, call upon the send() method of the PushContext, passing the message to be broadcast. The message will be encoded as JSON and delivered to the message argument of the JavaScript function on the client which corresponds to the function named in the f:websocket onmessage attribute. The message can be composed of any number of containers, including a plain String, List, Map, Object, and so on.

3-14. Programmatically Searching for Components

Problem

You wish to use Expression Language or Java code to find a particular component or a set of components within a JSF view. There are a number of reasons why you may wish to obtain access to components, such as invoking the component programmatically or referencing them from another component within the view.

Solution #1

Make use of the JSF component search framework via the use of expression language or programmatically from Java code. In the following example, a JSF panelGrid component is updated via expression language using key JSF search terms. The f:ajax tag contains a render attribute that specifies @parent, indicating that the parent component should be re-rendered once the Ajax process is complete:

```
<h:panelGrid columns="2">
            <h:outputLabel for="password" value="Enter a password for
            site access: "/>
```

```
<h:inputSecret id="password" size="40"
value="#{ch3ContactController.current.password}">
    <f:validateRequired/>
    <f:ajax event="blur" render="@parent"/>
</h:inputSecret>
<h:panelGroup/>
<h:message id="passwordError"
        for="password"
        style="color:red"/>

<h:outputLabel for="passwordConfirm" value="Confirm
Password: "/>
<h:inputSecret id="passwordConfirm" size="40"
value="#{ch3ContactController.passwordConfirm}"
                validator="#{ch3ContactController.
                validatePassword}">
    <f:ajax    event="blur" render="@parent"/>
</h:inputSecret>
<h:panelGroup/>
<h:message id="passwordConfirmError"
        for="passwordConfirm"
        style="color:red"/>
</h:panelGrid>
```

Solution #2

Utilize the programmatic API to search for components from within a server-side CDI controller class. In the following solution, a button from a JSF view is used to invoke an action method in the CDI bean. The action method merely demonstrates the programmatic search expression API. In the action method, a component is looked up by explicit ID:

```
public void findById() {
    FacesContext context = FacesContext.getCurrentInstance();
    SearchExpressionContext searchContext = SearchExpressionContext.
                                    createSearchExpressionCo
                                    ntext(context, context.
                                    getViewRoot());
```

```
context.getApplication()
        .getSearchExpressionHandler()
        .resolveComponent(
            searchContext,
            "passwordConfirm",
            (ctx, target) -> out.print(target.getId())));
}
```

How It Works

For years, JSF developers had difficulty referencing JSF components within a view by ID. There are a couple of problems that can be encountered if attempting to simply look up a component by ID. First, if an ID is not explicitly assigned to a JSF component, then the FacesServlet assigns one automatically. In this situation, the ID is unknown until runtime, and therefore it is almost impossible to reference the component using EL or from within Java code. Second, even if a JSF component is assigned a static ID, then the nesting architecture of JSF views and the JSF component tree causes the IDs of each parent component to be prepended to the ID of the child component. This can cause for long and sometimes difficult to maintain component IDs. Moreover, even if a specified component is easy to identify by prepending parent IDs, some components, such as those nested in tables, will still have a dynamic ID assigned at runtime.

There have been a number of third-party libraries that have developed solutions to combat this problem. OmniFaces and PrimeFaces are some of the most widely used. The addition of the JSF search expression API to JSF proper significantly reduces the work that needs to be done in order to gain access to JSF components within a view. This is especially the case in the event that a component is nested deep within other components in a view or part of a dataTable as mentioned previously. The search expression API allows one to utilize keywords to help search the component tree in a dynamic manner, rather than hard-coding static IDs that may change down the road.

Prior to JSF 2.3, there were four abstract search keywords that could be used to obtain reference to components, those being "@all", "@this", "@form", and "@none". Moreover, one could only perform EL search expressions in the f:ajax tag. This was quite a limitation, and JSF 2.3 greatly expands this functionality. Please refer to Table 3-15 for the search keywords. The following features have been added to the search expression API:

- Keywords and search expressions can be used programmatically.

- Many more keywords have been added.

- Keywords accept arguments.

- Keywords are extendible and can be chained.

Table 3-15. *Search Keywords*

Keyword	Description
@child(n)	The nth child of the base component
@composite	Nearest composite component of the base
@id(id)	Nearest descendant of the base component with an id matching a specified value
@namingcontainer	Nearest naming container of the base component
@next	Next component in view following the base component
@parent	Parent of the base component
@previous	Previous component to the base
@root	The UIViewRoot

The solution demonstrates how to find components using the @parent keyword, but any of the others can be used and strung together in order to find desired components.

Another new feature with JSF 2.3 is the programmatic search expression API. This makes it possible to gain access to components from within the controller class. The second listing in the solution demonstrates how to use the programmatic API. To use the API, first create a SearchExpressionContext, which will later be passed as a parameter to help find the component. Second, call upon the `FacesContext` to gain reference to the application via getApplication(), and then invoke get`SearchExpressionHandler()`. `resolveComponent()`, passing the `SearchExpressionContext`, the search expression string, and the function to call when the component is found. This can be used to search for any component via a programmatic API.

CHAPTER 4

Eclipse Krazo

Java EE has progressed over the years from a servlet-centric platform to one that provides a number of different options for building web and enterprise applications. In the early days of Java EE, in those days referred to as J2EE, one would focus on developing servlets for building the frontend, as well as the integration and business layers. Things got a bit more dynamic when JavaServer Pages (JSP) came to fruition, as developers could begin to divide the workload between teams that would focus on the HTML markup and JSP tags to compose the frontend and those who would focus on the application logic. JavaServer Faces took it one step further by adhering to the Model-View-Controller pattern, whereby code logic was completely separated from page markup, creating three different tiers. This pattern makes development more logical and long-term maintenance much easier.

Although JSF provides a robust and mature environment for development of enterprise applications, the framework is somewhat rigid in that you must adhere to many of the JavaServer Faces philosophies. One example is that JSF contains a life cycle that must be followed. One can choose to bypass certain phases of that life cycle, but in the end there is still some level of control given to the Faces servlet. The Eclipse Krazo framework, formerly known as "MVC," was introduced during the same time frame as Java EE 8 was being developed. The framework takes the Model-View-Controller focus one step further. It allows developers to adhere to the three-tier architecture without forcing certain behavior.

The MVC framework was originally intended to be included with Java EE 8 under JSR 371, but later in an effort to minimize the number of new specifications for inclusion, it was removed from the platform. However, Oracle handed off the ownership of MVC 1.0 to the community, which later transferred the specification to the Eclipse Foundation. As mentioned previously, the project name was also changed to Eclipse Krazo.

© Josh Juneau 2020
J. Juneau, *Jakarta EE Recipes*, https://doi.org/10.1007/978-1-4842-5587-2_4

Throughout this chapter, I will discuss the configuration for an Eclipse Krazo application; how to develop controllers, models, and views; and how to tie it all together. The framework was built on top of JAX-RS, so many of the key components are the same. Therefore, you'll learn a bit about the fundamentals of the JAX-RS API in this chapter as well. As part of Eclipse EE4J, Krazo is a key framework for building applications on the Jakarta EE platform. As I always state, if you have more tools in the shed, you will be able to accomplish a larger variety of tasks. The same holds true about application development, and frameworks such as JSF are great for development of some applications, but Eclipse Krazo may be even better for developing others. After reading this chapter, you will have a better understanding of the differences that Eclipse Krazo has to offer. You should be able to dive in developing with the Eclipse Krazo framework as I will walk through the development of an Eclipse Krazo application from start to finish, using the Apache NetBeans IDE for development.

4-1. Configure an Application for the Eclipse Krazo Framework

Problem

You wish to create an Eclipse Krazo application project. Therefore, you need to configure the project to work with the Eclipse Krazo API.

Solution

Add the appropriate configuration files to the project and configure JAX-RS accordingly. In this chapter, I will cover the use of Maven as the project build system, but you could easily configure using another build system, such as Gradle. Configuration of an Eclipse Krazo application is very much similar to that of an application that uses the JAX-RS specification. To begin, let's create a new project in Apache NetBeans. Create a Maven web application project, and name it Bookstore, as shown in Figure 4-1.

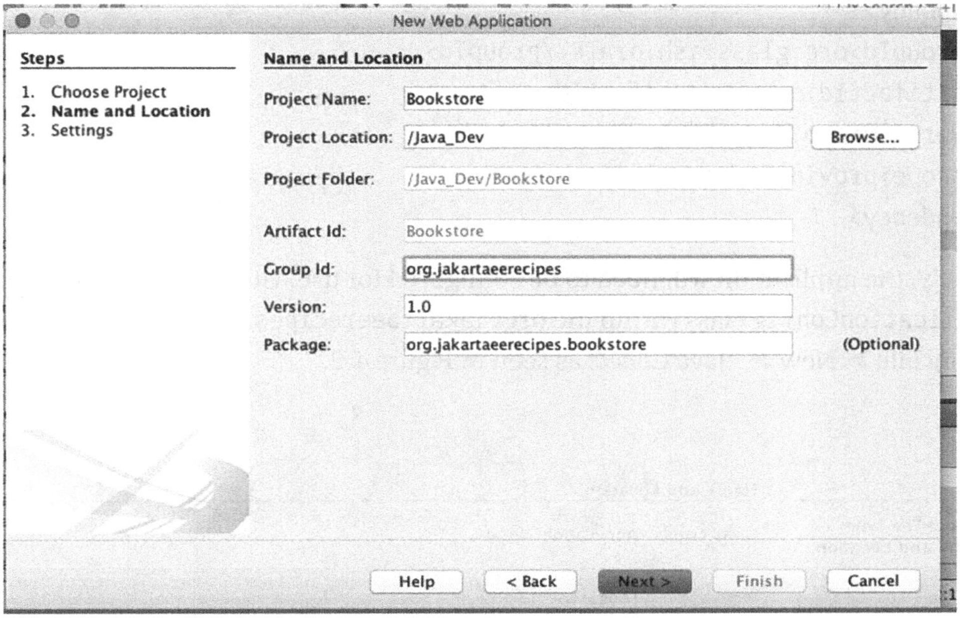

Figure 4-1. *New Maven web application*

Next, be sure to choose a Java EE 7–, Java EE 8–, or Jakarta EE–compliant application server for deployment, and then select Java EE 7 or Java EE 8 as the Java EE version. Click "Finish" to create the project. Once the project has been created, generate a beans.xml file. To do this, right-click the project, click "New" ➤ "beans.xml (CDI Configuration File)," accept the defaults to create it within WEB-INF and keep the name beans.xml, and finally click "Finish."

Next, add the required dependencies to the POM file. To do so, right-click the project and choose "Open POM" from the contextual menu. Once the POM file opens, add the dependencies for the Eclipse Krazo API:

```
<dependency>
    <groupId>javax.mvc</groupId>
    <artifactId>javax.mvc-api</artifactId>
    <version>1.0-pfd</version>
    <scope>provided</scope>
</dependency>
```

```
<dependency>
    <groupId>org.glassfish.ozark</groupId>
    <artifactId>ozark</artifactId>
    <version>1.0.0-m02</version>
    <scope>provided</scope>
</dependency>
```

Lastly, the application will need to be configured for use with JAX-RS. To do so, create an ApplicationConfig class within the org.jakartaeerecipes.bookstore package by selecting File ➤ New ➤ "Java Class", as seen in Figure 4-2.

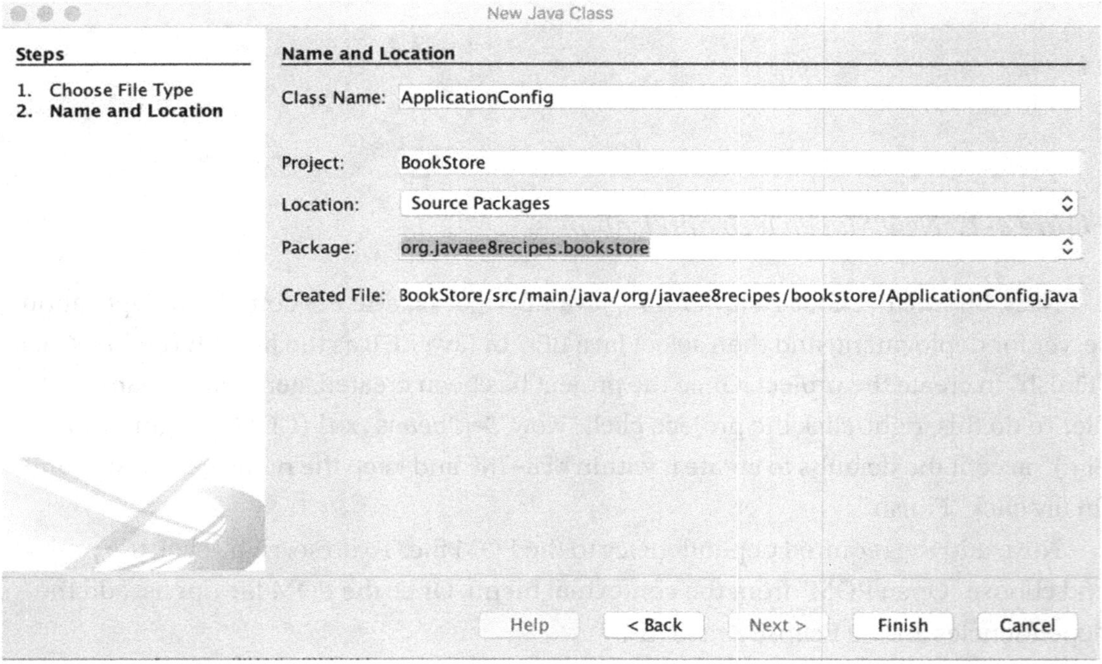

Figure 4-2. *Create ApplicationConfig class*

The ApplicationConfig class is used to map the RESTful web services to a URI. The @ApplicationPath annotation is used to configure the path for URI. The following code shows the sources for this class:

```
import java.util.HashMap;
import java.util.Map;
import javax.mvc.security.Csrf;
```

```
import javax.ws.rs.ApplicationPath;
import javax.ws.rs.core.Application;

@ApplicationPath("controller")
public class ApplicationConfig extends Application {

    @Override
    public Map<String, Object> getProperties() {
        final Map<String, Object> map = new HashMap<>();
        map.put(Csrf.CSRF_PROTECTION, Csrf.CsrfOptions.EXPLICIT);
        return map;
    }

}
```

Once these configurations are complete, you are ready to begin coding an Eclipse Krazo application.

How It Works

The Eclipse Krazo framework requires a number of easy configurations made to a project in order to pull in the required dependencies and to configure CDI and JAX-RS properly. In this recipe, I showed how to make these configurations, so now let's see why we need to make them. As mentioned previously, the JAX-RS configuration should reside within a class that extends `javax.ws.rs.core.Application`, which defines components and metadata for a JAX-RS application. The Eclipse Krazo framework builds upon the JAX-RS API, so this configuration is mandatory in order to provide the ability to generate controller classes (see Recipe 4-3 for more details).

In the solution, I named the class which extends the `javax.ws.rs.core.Application` class `ApplicationConfig`. As you see from the code, by extending the `Application` class, we can override the `getProperties()` method to provide application-specific configuration. In this case, I added CSRF (Cross-Site Request Forgery) Protection, which is a standard Eclipse Krazo security feature (see Recipe 4-8). The `getProperties()` method should return a `Map<String, Object>`. Lastly, the class should be annotated with `@ApplicationPath`, and the URI mapping for the controllers (or JAX-RS classes) should be passed as a String. In this case, the path is "controller," and the URL for accessing controller classes should translate to `http://localhost:8080/BookStore/controller/`.

The dependencies for Eclipse Krazo must be referenced within the Maven POM file. In this case, there are two dependencies, with the expectation that the Java EE 7 or Java EE 8 full or web profile is also a dependency.

Note   There are different profiles available for Java EE 7 and Java EE 8, and there will also be different profiles available for Jakarta EE. The web profile contains a smaller number of dependencies for developing web projects, whereas the full profile contains all Java EE or Jakarta EE dependencies.

The required dependencies for Eclipse Krazo are `javax.mvc-api` and `krazo`, which is the reference implementation. Lastly, ensure that you create a `beans.xml` configuration file for CDI. This configuration file allows one to specify how CDI beans are discovered. For the purposes of this example, accept the default discovery mode of annotated, as follows:

```
<?xml version="1.0" encoding="UTF-8"?>
<beans xmlns="http://xmlns.jcp.org/xml/ns/javaee"
       xmlns:xsi="http://www.w3.org/2001/XMLSchema-instance"
       xsi:schemaLocation="http://xmlns.jcp.org/xml/ns/javaee http://xmlns.
       jcp.org/xml/ns/javaee/beans_1_1.xsd"
       bean-discovery-mode="annotated">
</beans>
```

This recipe walked through the configurations required to create an Eclipse Krazo project. In the following recipes, I will cover how to build out the project into a fully functional web application.

4-2. Making Data Available for the Application Problem

You need to obtain existing data for your application, and you'd like to easily make the data available for your web views.

Solution #1

Utilize the Java Persistence API (JPA) along with Enterprise JavaBeans (EJBs) to provide data to your application. First, create entity classes which will map each of your database tables to a corresponding Java object. Please see Chapter 8 for more details on generating entity classes. For the purposes of the application that is being developed for this chapter, entity classes will be generated for a number of the tables being used throughout this book. In this solution, only a single entity class will be generated in order to demonstrate. However, if you look at the sources for the example application, then you will find an entity class for each of the tables that are used within the application.

Since the application will be used for the purposes of an online bookstore, the database tables that are used along with the application pertain to authors and books. In this solution, we will generate the entity class for the AUTHOR database table. As a brief primer, an entity class maps each column of a database table to a corresponding class member. The following code is for the BookAuthor entity class:

```
package org.jakartaeerecipes.bookstore.entity;

import java.io.Serializable;
import java.math.BigDecimal;
import java.util.List;
import java.util.Set;
import javax.persistence.*;
import javax.validation.constraints.NotNull;
import javax.validation.constraints.Size;

@Entity
@Table(name = "BOOK_AUTHOR")
public class BookAuthor implements Serializable {

    private static final long serialVersionUID = 1L;

    @Id
    @Basic(optional = false)
    @Column(name = "ID")
    private BigDecimal id;
```

```java
@Size(max = 30)
@Column(name = "LASTNAME")
private String last;

@Size(max = 30)
@Column(name = "FIRSTNAME")
private String first;

@Lob
@Column(name = "BIO")
private String bio;

@ManyToMany
@JoinTable(name="AUTHOR_WORK",
        joinColumns=
        @JoinColumn(name="AUTHOR_ID", referencedColumnName="ID"),
        inverseJoinColumns=
        @JoinColumn(name="BOOK_ID", referencedColumnName="ID"))
private Set<Book> books;

public BookAuthor() {
}

public BookAuthor(BigDecimal id) {
    this.id = id;
}
```
. . .
```java
// getters and setters
```
. . .
```java
@Override
public int hashCode() {
    int hash = 0;
    hash += (id != null ? id.hashCode() : 0);
    return hash;
}
```

```java
    @Override
    public boolean equals(Object object) {
        if (!(object instanceof BookAuthor)) {
            return false;
        }
        BookAuthor other = (BookAuthor) object;
        if ((this.id == null && other.id != null) || (this.id != null &&
        !this.id.equals(other.id))) {
            return false;
        }
        return true;
    }

    @Override
    public String toString() {
        return "org.jakartaeerecipes.bookstore.entity.BookAuthor[ id="
        + id + " ]";
    }
}
```

Once the entity classes for each database table have been created, develop EJB façade (session bean) classes for each of them. To do this, first generate a package to hold all of the EJB session bean classes. In this case, create a package named `org.jakartaeerecipes.bookstore.session`. Next, create a session bean class for each of the entity classes that have been created. To create the session bean for the `BookAuthor` class, create a class within the newly created package, or if using Apache NetBeans, right-click the new package and select "New" ➤ "Session Beans from Entity Classes." Name the bean `BookAuthorFacade`. If using Apache NetBeans, two classes will be generated, one of them is an abstract class named `AbstractFacade`. This abstract class will be extended by each of the session beans that are created for the application. It contains a set of common methods that can be used throughout all of the session beans. If creating a session bean from scratch, you'll need to create these methods for each bean or use a similar technique to provide a common implementation for beans to use, similar to the `AbstractFacade`.

No matter which technique you choose, you will need to generate a persistence unit for your application. This is an XML configuration file that is used to contain connection configuration for your database. Typically, the persistence unit contains Java Naming and Directory Interface (JNDI) information for connecting to a data source that has been defined within an application server container. In this case, create a persistence unit by right-clicking your project and choosing "Create Persistence Unit" if using Apache NetBeans. Choose an existing data source that has been configured for your database within Apache NetBeans.

The following code is that of the `AbstractFacade`, which is automatically generated by Apache NetBeans:

```
package org.jakartaeerecipes.bookstore.session;

import java.util.List;
import javax.persistence.EntityManager;

public abstract class AbstractFacade<T> {

    private Class<T> entityClass;

    public AbstractFacade(Class<T> entityClass) {
        this.entityClass = entityClass;
    }

    protected abstract EntityManager getEntityManager();

    public void create(T entity) {
        getEntityManager().persist(entity);
    }

    public void edit(T entity) {
        getEntityManager().merge(entity);
    }

    public void remove(T entity) {
        getEntityManager().remove(getEntityManager().merge(entity));
    }

    public T find(Object id) {
        return getEntityManager().find(entityClass, id);
    }
```

```
public List<T> findAll() {
    javax.persistence.criteria.CriteriaQuery cq = getEntityManager().
    getCriteriaBuilder().createQuery();
    cq.select(cq.from(entityClass));
    return getEntityManager().createQuery(cq).getResultList();
}

public List<T> findRange(int[] range) {
    javax.persistence.criteria.CriteriaQuery cq = getEntityManager().
    getCriteriaBuilder().createQuery();
    cq.select(cq.from(entityClass));
    javax.persistence.Query q = getEntityManager().createQuery(cq);
    q.setMaxResults(range[1] - range[0] + 1);
    q.setFirstResult(range[0]);
    return q.getResultList();
}

public int count() {
    javax.persistence.criteria.CriteriaQuery cq = getEntityManager().
    getCriteriaBuilder().createQuery();
    javax.persistence.criteria.Root<T> rt = cq.from(entityClass);
    cq.select(getEntityManager().getCriteriaBuilder().count(rt));
    javax.persistence.Query q = getEntityManager().createQuery(cq);
    return ((Long) q.getSingleResult()).intValue();
}
}
```

Next, let's take a look at the code that is generated for the BookAuthorFacade. This code is also automatically generated by Apache NetBeans, or it could be manually created if you wish:

```
@Stateless
public class BookAuthorFacade extends AbstractFacade<BookAuthor> {
    @PersistenceContext(unitName = "BookStore_1.0PU")
    private EntityManager em;
```

```
@Override
protected EntityManager getEntityManager() {
    return em;
}

public BookAuthorFacade() {
    super(BookAuthor.class);
}

}
```

Solution #2

Utilize RESTful web services to obtain data for your application. As mentioned in Solution #1, create entity classes which will map each of your database tables to a corresponding Java object. Once the entity classes have been created, develop REST service classes for each of them. If using an IDE such as Apache NetBeans, it will only take a few clicks to generate these RESTful web services, as most IDEs provide an auto-generation option. Otherwise, simply create a Plain Old Java Object (POJO) and annotate it accordingly to develop a RESTful service class.

To begin, create a new package and name it `org.jakartaeerecipes.bookstore.service`. Next, create the RESTful class inside the newly created package. In Apache NetBeans IDE, right-click the package and select "New..." ➤ "Web Services" ➤ "RESTful Web Services from Entity Classes" and then choose "Next." When the "New RESTful Web Services from Entity Classes" dialog is displayed, select the `org.jakartaeerecipes.entity.BookAuthor` class. On the next screen, change the Resource Package such that it is `org.jakartaeerecipes.bookstore.service`, as shown in Figure 4-3. Lastly, choose "Finish" to create the class.

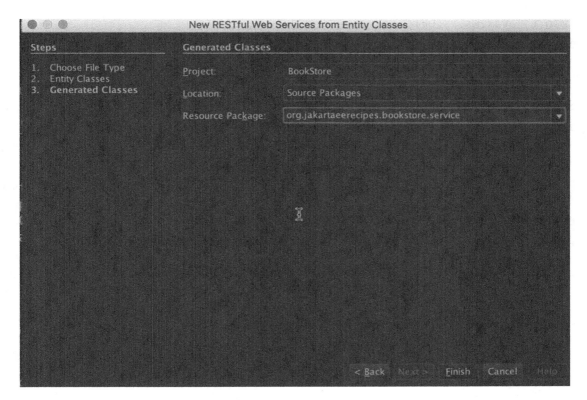

Figure 4-3. *Creating RESTful web service from entity class in Apache NetBeans IDE*

Similar to creation of an EJB, creation of a RESTful web service provides methods that can be used to perform create, read, update, and delete actions against a database. Furthermore, since these methods are annotated as REST services, they can be invoked via a REST client. The following code shows the RESTful web service class for the BookAuthor entity. This class is named BookAuthorFacadeREST by NetBeans IDE, or you can name it differently if generating from scratch:

```
package org.jakartaeerecipes.bookstore.service;

import java.math.BigDecimal;
import java.util.List;
import javax.ejb.Stateless;
import javax.persistence.EntityManager;
import javax.persistence.PersistenceContext;
import javax.ws.rs.Consumes;
import javax.ws.rs.DELETE;
```

```
import javax.ws.rs.GET;
import javax.ws.rs.POST;
import javax.ws.rs.PUT;
import javax.ws.rs.Path;
import javax.ws.rs.PathParam;
import javax.ws.rs.Produces;
import javax.ws.rs.core.MediaType;
import org.jakartaeerecipes.bookstore.entity.BookAuthor;

@Stateless
@Path("org.jakartaeerecipes.bookstore.entity.bookauthor")
public class BookAuthorFacadeREST extends AbstractFacade<BookAuthor> {

    @PersistenceContext(unitName = "BookStore_1.0PU")
    private EntityManager em;

    public BookAuthorFacadeREST() {
        super(BookAuthor.class);
    }

    @POST
    @Override
    @Consumes({MediaType.APPLICATION_XML, MediaType.APPLICATION_JSON})
    public void create(BookAuthor entity) {
        super.create(entity);
    }

    @PUT
    @Path("{id}")
    @Consumes({MediaType.APPLICATION_XML, MediaType.APPLICATION_JSON})
    public void edit(@PathParam("id") BigDecimal id, BookAuthor entity) {
        super.edit(entity);
    }

    @DELETE
    @Path("{id}")
    public void remove(@PathParam("id") BigDecimal id) {
        super.remove(super.find(id));
    }
}
```

```java
@GET
@Path("{id}")
@Produces({MediaType.APPLICATION_XML, MediaType.APPLICATION_JSON})
public BookAuthor find(@PathParam("id") BigDecimal id) {
    return super.find(id);
}

@GET
@Override
@Produces({MediaType.APPLICATION_XML, MediaType.APPLICATION_JSON})
public List<BookAuthor> findAll() {
    return super.findAll();
}

@GET
@Path("{from}/{to}")
@Produces({MediaType.APPLICATION_XML, MediaType.APPLICATION_JSON})
public List<BookAuthor> findRange(@PathParam("from") Integer from,
@PathParam("to") Integer to) {
    return super.findRange(new int[]{from, to});
}

@GET
@Path("count")
@Produces(MediaType.TEXT_PLAIN)
public String countREST() {
    return String.valueOf(super.count());
}

@Override
protected EntityManager getEntityManager() {
    return em;
}

}
```

To learn more about generating RESTful web services and the respective annotations, please see Chapter 13. Once a RESTful web service has been created, it can be called upon from other applications to obtain data in various formats, being XML, JSON, plain text, or some other medium. An Eclipse Krazo application can utilize a JAX-RS client to call upon RESTful web services to obtain data for the application. This can be achieved by generating a service class that contains the JAX-RS client and web service calls to obtain the data.

To begin, create a class within the org.jakartaeerecipes.bookstore.service package, and name it BookAuthorService. This will be a session-scoped CDI bean (see Chapter 11 for details on CDI), which will create a client upon bean construction, and then load data for use within the application, as needed. In the next recipe which covers Eclipse Krazo controllers, I'll demonstrate how to call upon this service class from within a controller class to obtain data. The following code shows the finished product for the BookAuthorService class:

```
package org.jakartaeerecipes.bookstore.service;

import java.util.List;
import javax.annotation.PostConstruct;
import javax.ejb.EJB;
import javax.enterprise.context.SessionScoped;
import javax.ws.rs.client.Client;
import javax.ws.rs.client.ClientBuilder;
import javax.ws.rs.core.GenericType;
import org.jakartaeerecipes.bookstore.entity.BookAuthor;

@SessionScoped
public class BookAuthorService implements java.io.Serializable {
    Client jaxRsClient;
    private List<BookAuthor> bookAuthorList;

    final String hostUri = "http://localhost:8080/BookStore/bookstore";

    public BookAuthorService(){

    }
```

```
@PostConstruct
public void init(){
    // Construct a JAX-RS Client
    jaxRsClient = ClientBuilder.newClient();
    loadData();
}

private void loadData(){

    bookAuthorList = jaxRsClient.target(hostUri + "/org.
    jakartaeerecipes.bookstore.entity.bookauthor/findAll")
            .request("application/xml")
            .get(new GenericType<List<BookAuthor>>() {
            }
            );
}

/**
 * @return the bookAuthorList
 */
public List<BookAuthor> getBookAuthorList() {
    if(bookAuthorList == null){
        loadData();
    }
    return bookAuthorList;
}

/**
 * @param bookAuthorList
 */
public void setBookAuthorList(List<BookAuthor> bookAuthorList) {
    this.bookAuthorList = bookAuthorList;
}
}
```

The service class can be used to load the data and obtain the set of data for our application. This class could be modified at a later time to provide RESTful web service methods for creating, updating, and removing data, as needed.

How It Works

Most enterprise applications do some work with data. Eclipse Krazo applications are no different, as data typically plays an important role. The way to obtain data for an Eclipse Krazo application is very much the same as it would be for many other Java web applications, and RESTful web services or EJBs are some great options. Keep in mind that these are not the only options for pulling data into an Eclipse Krazo application. Since the Eclipse Krazo framework provides a very fluid design pattern, it allows the developer to make many choices along the way. To that end, one could certainly use another methodology such as JDBC or a homegrown data access object (DAO) to orchestrate work with the database. This recipe shows two of the most standard approaches.

In Solution #1, I showed how one could create entity classes based upon existing (or new) database tables and then write an EJB façade used in tandem with the entity classes to work with the data. This is, by far, one of the most standard approaches for coercing data into Java objects, dating back to the J2EE days. Back in the days of J2EE, developers were required to write heavyweight EJB solutions and lots of XML in order to pull off the same feat that can be resolved nowadays using simple POJOs with annotations.

The use of EJBs goes hand in hand with the use of entity classes for mapping database tables to Java objects. To learn more about the use of entity classes, please refer to Chapter 6 where object-relational mapping is discussed. Once an entity class has been constructed, it is easy to create an EJB that can be used to work with the entity class to orchestrate the data. Since Chapter 8 is dedicated to the use of EJBs, you can look there for more information on creating and using them. The point of this particular recipe is to show how to use these options within an Eclipse Krazo application. One can bind the use of EJBs with the Eclipse Krazo controller classes to obtain data and manipulate it, as needed. In the next recipe, you will learn more about Eclipse Krazo controller classes.

Solution #2 shows how to also make use of entity classes for mapping Java objects to database tables, but instead uses RESTful service classes to obtain the data. The solution demonstrates how to create the RESTful web services that will provide the data, and it also shows how to create a JAX-RS client service class that can be used to call upon the RESTful web services to obtain data. Most likely with these two JAX-RS solutions, the JAX-RS web service and the JAX-RS client will not be part of the same application. Typically, one application or microservice will obtain the data from the database and provide it to other consumers via the JAX-RS web service, and other applications or microservices will act as consumers, using JAX-RS clients to obtain the data from the web service. I only demonstrated both the web service and the client in this application for the purposes of example.

Since Chapter 13 covers RESTful web services in entirety, I will point you to that chapter for more information. Let's focus on how we can glean the data from the web services using a JAX-RS client for our MVC application. Typically, an MVC controller (see the next recipe) will call upon the JAX-RS client to obtain the data for the application. In Solution #2, a simple client is created to obtain the list of `BookAuthor` entities from the web service and load them into a local list. The `BookAuthorService` class is a session-scoped CDI bean, so it is annotated with `@SessionScoped` (`javax.enterprise.context.SessionScoped`). Since this class may need to be saved to disk to store the session data, it must be made serializable. Next, declare a `javax.ws.rs.client.Client` and a `List<BookAuthor>` so that the client can be created and the list of `BookAuthor` objects can be stored in the session. The class should create the client and load the data when the bean is created, so one of the methods should be annotated with `@PostConstruct` so that it is automatically invoked upon bean construction. In this case, the `init()` method is invoked upon construction, allowing the client to make a RESTful service call to the `org.jakartaeerecipes.bookstore.entity.bookauthor` web service to obtain all of the records and store them into the `bookAuthorList`.

Although this recipe does not directly pertain to the Eclipse Krazo application methodology, it is an important piece of the puzzle for obtaining data for use with the application. In the next recipe, I will dive directly into the Eclipse Krazo controller class, which is the heart of the business logic for an Eclipse Krazo application.

4-3. Writing a Controller Class
Problem

You would like to orchestrate the navigation and business logic for an Eclipse Krazo application.

Solution

Develop Eclipse Krazo controller classes to provide the business logic and navigation logic behind the application. To get started, create a new package in which to store the controllers for the application. In this example, I've named the package `org.jakartaeerecipes.bookstore.controller`. Also create a package to hold classes that will be used as objects for transporting data within the application. Name this

package org.jakartaeerecipes.bookstore.container. Before the controller
class can be created, a container needs to be created within the newly created org.
jakartaeerecipes.bookstore.container package, and name it BookAuthorContainer.
This class is merely a SessionScoped CDI bean that will be used to hold instances of the
BookAuthor objects and expose them to the web views of the application. The sources for
BookAuthorContainer should look as follows:

```
package org.jakartaeerecipes.bookstore.container;

import java.util.List;
import javax.enterprise.context.SessionScoped;
import javax.inject.Inject;
import javax.inject.Named;
import org.jakartaeerecipes.bookstore.entity.BookAuthor;

@Named
@SessionScoped
public class BookAuthorContainer implements java.io.Serializable {

    private BookAuthor bookAuthor;

    private List<BookAuthor> bookAuthorList;

    public BookAuthorContainer(){

    }
    . . .
    // Getters and Setters
    . . .
}
```

Next, create a class named BookAuthorController inside of the
org.jakartaeerecipes.bookstore.controller package, and annotate the controller
class with the @Path("/bookAuthor") and @Controller annotations. Next, create a
public method with a return type of String and name it getBookAuthors, accepting
no arguments. Annotate the method with @GET and within this method query data for
loading the BookAuthor list, and return a String of "bookAuthor.jsp". The following
sources show the code for the BookAuthorController class:

```java
import java.util.List;
import javax.inject.Inject;
import javax.ws.rs.Path;
import javax.mvc.annotation.Controller;
import javax.ws.rs.GET;
import org.jakartaeerecipes.bookstore.entity.BookAuthor;
import org.jakartaeerecipes.bookstore.service.BookAuthorService;

@Path("/bookAuthor")
@Controller
public class BookAuthorController {

    @Inject
    private BookAuthorService bookAuthorService;

    public BookAuthorController(){
    }

    @GET
    public String getBookAuthors(){
        // obtain list of authors
        return "bookAuthor.jsp";
    }
}
```

If a URI containing the path indicated by the @Path annotation is loaded, the bookAuthor.jsp view will be loaded.

How It Works

An Eclipse Krazo controller class is used to bind business logic to the view, and process requests and responses. Controller classes are CDI controllers that contain a number of JAX-RS annotations, as the Eclipse Krazo controller façade is based upon the JAX-RS API. Every controller class is indicated as such via the javax.mvc.annotation. Controller annotation. The javax.ws.rs.Path annotation is applied at the controller class level to indicate which URI will be used to access controller class methods via the web application. For instance, this controller class can be accessible via a URI matching the following format since there is only one method:

`http://localhost:8080/BookStore/controller/bookAuthor`

It is important to note that the controller class is annotated like a JAX-RS class. Controllers in the Eclipse Krazo framework are implemented using the same annotations that are used to implement a JAX-RS RESTful web service class. That said, when the preceding URI is used to access the application, the `BookAuthor` CDI controller is invoked due to the application path being `/BookStore/` and the matching `@Path` annotation specifying `/bookAuthor` as the matching path. When invoked, the GET requests are handled by the `getBookAuthors()` method, as it is annotated with `@GET` without a specified path. The `@GET` annotation is used to indicate an HTTP GET method. Since this particular controller only has one controller method annotated with `@GET`, the default path is going to invoke the single method. If there were more than one method in the controller, each method would also need to be annotated with `@Path` to indicate the sub-path to invoke each method in turn. An Eclipse Krazo controller should utilize other HTTP methods such as `@PUT` and `@POST` for inserting or updating records in a database.

In the example, when the `getBookAuthors()` method is invoked, the `BookAuthorService` is called upon, invoking the `getBookAuthorList()` method and loading the local `bookAuthors` list. Next, data loaded into a list will be accessible via the view. The data loading processes are omitted from this recipe, but they are covered in greater detail in Recipe 4-4.

The last important detail to note is that the return value from the `getBookAuthorList()` method is the next view that will be rendered when the response is returned. The default return type for a controller method is text/html, but that can be changed via the `@Produces` annotation. A String returned from a controller method is the view path. In this case, the `bookAuthor.jsp` view is next to be loaded. It is possible to provide navigation to the next view in a number of different ways, and returning the name of the next view is the first technique.

A controller method can also have a return type of void, and in such cases the method must be annotated with `@View("returnViewName")`. As seen here, the String-based view name is passed as an attribute to the annotation. This technique makes it easy to separate navigational logic from business logic:

```
@GET
@View("bookAuthor.jsp")
public void getBookAuthors(){
    //obtain authors
}
```

The next technique involves returning a Viewable, which would look like the following lines of code. A Viewable provides flexibility, especially in cases where one wishes to implement a non-standard view engine:

```
@GET
public Viewable getBookAuthors(){
    //obtain authors
    return new Viewable("bookAuthor.jsp");
}
```

The final technique for controlling navigation is to return a JAX-RS response object, which provides a lot of information since it can include different response codes depending upon certain situations:

```
@GET
public Response getBookAuthors(){
    // obtain authors
    return Response.status(Response.Status.OK).entity("bookAuthor.jsp").
build();
}
```

As mentioned previously, Eclipse Krazo controller classes are very much the same as JAX-RS web service classes in that they use common annotations. In the example, the controller class is utilized as an Eclipse Krazo controller only, but it is possible for a controller class to become a hybrid class which also contains JAX-RS methods. To do this, move the @Controller annotation to each Eclipse Krazo method, rather than at the class level itself. The javax.mvc.annotation.View annotation can also be applied at either class or method level. As mentioned previously, it points to the view for the controller method.

The controller method defines the business logic for an Eclipse Krazo application. Controllers utilize JAX-RS annotations and provide plumbing for the request response life cycle. Lastly, controllers are responsible for returning responses including data to application views.

4-4. Using a Model to Expose Data to a View

Problem

You wish to obtain data from a data source and make it available for use within an application view.

Solution

Inject and make use of the Models API from within your controller class. In the following example, the method getBookAuthors(), which is invoked when the URI path to the controller is accessed, obtains data from a web service (see Recipe 4-2 for more information) and populates data for use in a view using a model:

```
import java.util.List;
import javax.inject.Inject;
import javax.mvc.Models;
import javax.ws.rs.Path;
import javax.mvc.annotation.Controller;
import javax.ws.rs.GET;
import org.jakartaeerecipes.bookstore.entity.BookAuthor;
import org.jakartaeerecipes.bookstore.service.BookAuthorService;

@Path("/bookAuthor")
@Controller
public class BookAuthorController {

    @Inject
    private Models models;

    @Inject
    private BookAuthorService bookAuthorService;

    public BookAuthorController(){
    }

    @GET
    public String getBookAuthors(){
        List<BookAuthor> bookAuthors = bookAuthorService.getBookAuthorList();
```

```
        models.put("bookauthors", bookAuthors);
        return "bookAuthor.jsp";
    }
}
```

The JSP view markup that is contained within the bookAuthor.jsp JSP view looks like the following:

```
<%@ page contentType="text/html;charset=UTF-8" language="java" %>
<%@ taglib prefix="c" uri="http://java.sun.com/jsp/jstl/core" %>
<!DOCTYPE html>
<html>
    <head>
        <meta http-equiv="Content-Type" content="text/html; charset=UTF-8">
        <title>Example of Eclipse Krazo Using JSP for View</title>
    </head>
    <body>
        <h1>Book Authors</h1>
        <table class="table table-striped">
                <colgroup>
                    <col style="width: 80%;" />
                </colgroup>
                <thead>
                    <tr>
                        <th class="text-left">Author</th>
                    </tr>
                </thead>
                <tbody>
                    <c:forEach var="bookAuthor" items="${bookauthors}">
                        <tr>

                            <td class="text-center">
                                ${bookAuthor.last}
                            </td>

                        </tr>
                    </c:forEach>
```

```
            </tbody>
        </table>
    </body>
</html>
```

Given the sample dataset, the results of the simple view will look like that in Figure 4-4.

Book Authors

Author

Juneau

Dea

Gennick

Figure 4-4. *Example of bookAuthor.jsp results*

How It Works

The Models API must be included in every implementation of the Eclipse Krazo framework. Essentially, the Models API provides a `javax.mvc.Models` map which is used to store a dataset with a key identifier as a key/value pair that is exposed to the next rendered view. The HashMap for the Models API adheres to the following format:

```
Map<String, Object> model = new HashMap<String, Object>();
```

In the example, the Models map is injected into the controller class using CDI `@Inject`. Once injected, the model can be used to store data for exposure. A `List<BookAuthor>` is placed into the Models map as follows:

```
models.put("bookauthors", bookAuthors);
```

The model is exposed to the view via the `bookauthors` key. In the example JSP view, the `${bookauthors}` expression is used within a JSTL `c:if` tag to display the records in a table:

```
<c:forEach var="bookAuthor" items="${bookauthors}">
    <tr>

        <td class="text-center">
            ${bookAuthor.last}
        </td>

    </tr>
</c:forEach>
```

As seen in the example, the Models API is very easy to utilize. However, it is not the preferred method for exposing data, as CDI is preferred. CDI is preferred in general because it allows for more flexibility than the Models API. Recipe 4-5 delves into utilizing CDI beans for exposing data.

4-5. Utilizing CDI for Exposing Data

Problem

You are interested in exposing data from a controller into a view, but you'd like to not make use of Eclipse Krazo Models to do so. Instead, you'd like to harness the power of CDI to expose data to views.

Solution

Utilize CDI models to return data to the view. The use of CDI is the preferred technique for exposing data to views. In this recipe, a CDI bean is injected into the controller, and then it is utilized to store data. This CDI bean is session scoped, so the data that is placed within the bean will last the entire web session. The following code is that of the CDI bean which is used to expose the data:

```
import java.util.List;
import javax.enterprise.context.SessionScoped;
import javax.inject.Named;
import org.jakartaeerecipes.bookstore.entity.Book;

@Named
@SessionScoped
public class BookContainer implements java.io.Serializable {
```

```
    private Book book;

    private List<Book> bookList;

    public BookContainer(){

    }
    . . .
    // Getters and setters

    . . .
}
```

Next, the controller class utilizes the CDI bean to store data and make it available to the view:

```
@Path("/book")
@Controller
public class BookController {
    @Inject
    private BookContainer bookContainer;

    public BookController() {
    }

    /**
     * Queries all books using the <code>BookService</code> and then
     * returns to the <code>book.jsp</code> JSP page.
     * @return
     */
    @GET
    public String getBooks(){
        Book book = new Book();
        book.setTitle("Jakarta EE Recipes");
        bookContainer.setBook(book);
        return "book.jsp";
}
```

The following markup is that of the book.jsp view. As you can see from the example, the view simply displays the name of the book that was loaded into the CDI bean:

```jsp
<%@page contentType="text/html" pageEncoding="UTF-8"%>
<!DOCTYPE html>
<html>
    <head>
        <meta http-equiv="Content-Type" content="text/html; charset=UTF-8">
        <title>Jakarta EE Recipes: Recipe 4-5</title>
    </head>
    <body>
        <h1>Book List</h1>
        The book that was loaded in BookController:  ${bookContainer.book.
        title}
    </body>
</html>
```

How It Works

The preferred technique for exposing data to the web views of an Eclipse Krazo application is to utilize Contexts and Dependency Injection (CDI) beans. CDI is a specification that binds many of the Java EE and Jakarta EE technologies together. CDI is a large specification that includes many details, but in-depth explanations of the specification are out of scope for this recipe. For more details on CDI, please refer to Chapter 11. One of the functions of CDI is to wire beans together, effectively making it possible for data and scope to be shared between classes and between the backend and front-facing views of an application.

For the purposes of the Eclipse Krazo framework, one of the core focuses is the ability to share contextual objects between the backend code and the frontend views. In this simple example, the CDI bean is merely a SessionScoped container named BookContainer. As seen in the code, the BookContainer class is annotated with @Named, which marks the class as a CDI bean and makes it available for injection into other classes using the class name with the first letter in lowercase. In this case, the bean will be injectable via the name bookContainer. The @Named annotation does accept a String-based alias, which can be used to call upon the class at injection time from a view. The BookContainer class is also annotated with @SessionScoped, which defines the scope of the bean. The other available scope possibilities are @RequestScoped, @ApplicationScoped, and @ConversationScoped.

The BookController utilizes a contextual proxy to the bean by injecting an instance of it using the @Inject annotation. The bean is used within the getBooks() method, as it accepts a Book instance for which the title and description have been populated. It is also possible to define different class fields within the CDI bean and populate them with data directly to expose it to a view or other classes. Once the data has been populated, the BookController bean can be accessed from a view using expression language, or the same instance of the bean can be injected into another class and made accessible. In this example, the controller method getBooks() simply returns the name of the next view to be loaded, books.jsp. The books.jsp JSP view accesses the title of the book by referring to the bean via the injection name ${bookController.book.title}.

CDI can be very powerful for managing contextual instances of classes within a Jakarta EE application. Using CDI to expose data to a view within an Eclipse Krazo application brings forth the same functionality as the use of the Models API, and it also allows data to be utilized in other classes, if needed.

4-6. Supplying Message Feedback to the User

Problem

You wish to display feedback to a user after a transaction occurs.

Solution

Utilize CDI beans to easily provide feedback to users in the form of messages displayed onscreen. In the following scenario, all books in a bookstore are loaded and displayed in the book.jsp view. A RequestScoped CDI bean entitled Messages is used to encapsulate the logic for storing informative or error messages. In the controller class, a message indicating the number of books that are loaded is set into the bean using the info field. This bean is then available for display within the view.

First, here is a look at the CDI bean named Messages:

```
import javax.enterprise.context.RequestScoped;
import javax.inject.Named;
import java.util.ArrayList;
```

```java
import java.util.Collections;
import java.util.List;

/**
 * This class encapsulates messages displayed to the users. There can be a
 * single info message and multiple error messages. Controllers can use this
 * class to queue messages for rendering. The class shows how named CDI beans
 * can be used as a model for the view. Whether to include some class like
 * this in the spec is not decided yet.
 */
@Named
@RequestScoped
public class Messages {

  private String info;

  private final List<String> errors = new ArrayList<>();

  public Messages addError(String error) {
    errors.add(error);
    return this;
  }

  public List<String> getErrors() {
    return Collections.unmodifiableList(errors);
  }

  public String getInfo() {
    return info;
  }

  public void setInfo(String info) {
    this.info = info;
  }

}
```

The code for the controller class used to load the book listing and provide the message is as follows:

```
@Inject
private Messages messages;
. . .
@GET
@Path("/books")
public String displayBookListing() {
    bookList = bookService.getBookList();
    bookContainer.setBookList(bookList);
    messages.setInfo("There are " + bookList.size() + " books in the
    library.");
    return "book.jsp";
}
```

The subsequent book.jsp view markup is as follows:

```
<%@page contentType="text/html" pageEncoding="UTF-8"%>
<!DOCTYPE html>
<html>
    <head>
        <meta http-equiv="Content-Type" content="text/html; charset=UTF-8">
        <link href="${pageContext.request.contextPath}/webjars/
        bootstrap/3.3.4/dist/css/bootstrap.css" rel="stylesheet">
        <script src="${pageContext.request.contextPath}/webjars/
        bootstrap/3.3.4/dist/js/bootstrap.js"></script>
        <title>Jakarta EE Recipes</title>
    </head>
    <body>
        <h1>Book List</h1>
        The book that was loaded in BookController:  ${bookContainer.book.
        title}
        <br/><br/>
        <c:if test="${messages.info != null}">
                <div class="alert alert-success" role="alert">
                    ${messages.info}
```

```
                </div>
            </c:if>
            <c:if test="${not empty messages.errors}">
                <div class="alert alert-danger" role="alert">
                    <ul class="list-unstyled">
                        <c:forEach var="error" items="${messages.errors}">
                            <li>${error}</li>
                        </c:forEach>
                    </ul>
                </div>
            </c:if>
        <br/>
        <table class="table table-striped">
            <colgroup>
                <col style="width: 80%;" />
            </colgroup>
            <thead>
                <tr>
                    <th class="text-left">Book</th>
                </tr>
            </thead>
            <tbody>
            <c:forEach var="book" items="${bookContainer.bookList}">
                <tr>

                    <td class="text-center">
                        ${book.title}
                    </td>

                </tr>
            </c:forEach>
            </tbody>
        </table>
    </body>
</html>
```

How It Works

CDI beans can be leveraged to easily display messages from a controller. As seen in Recipe 4-5, the CDI bean can be injected into a controller class, data can be set into the controller, and then it can be made available in subsequent views. In the example for this recipe, a message containing the number of books within the bookList is created as a String, and then it is assigned to the info field of the Messages bean:

```
messages.setInfo("There are " + bookList.size() + " books in the
library.");
```

When the book.jsp view is loaded, the message is displayed within the view using expression language in the ${messages.info} format. In the view, a <c:if> tag is used to conditionally display the informative message if it exists, or if the error message exists, then it will be displayed instead. If users are seeing an error message, it usually helps to have that message stand out in red text or bold text. If a user is seeing helpful information within a message, it may be helpful to see that message in green text or something of the like. In such cases, the Eclipse Krazo framework can leverage existing JavaScript APIs to provide nice message formatting. The example utilizes the Bootstrap JavaScript library to display messages nicely depending upon type.

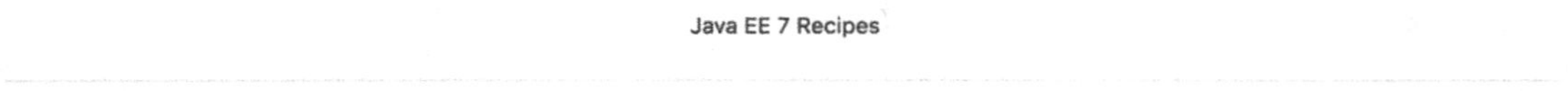

Book Listing

There are 2 books in the library.

Book

Java 9 Recipes

Java EE 7 Recipes

Figure 4-5. *Messages displayed nicely using Bootstrap*

4-7. Inserting and Updating Data
Problem

You wish to utilize a form to insert or update data.

Solution

Create controller methods that are annotated with @PUT or @POST, depending upon whether the methods will be utilized for inserting or updating, respectively. The following markup, excerpted from book.jsp, contains a form that is used to create a new book record. Make note that in the following example, the action invoked upon submit will initiate the RESTful web service that contains the "/create" path:

```
<form action="${pageContext.request.contextPath}/bookstore/book/create"
method="POST" class="form-inline">
            <div class="panel panel-default">
            <div class="panel-heading">
                <h3 class="panel-title">Book Information</h3>
            </div>
            <div class="panel-body">
                <div class="form-group">
                    <label for="subject">Title</label>
                    <input type="text" class="form-control"
                    id="title" name="title" placeholder="Title"
                            value="${book.title}" autofocus>
                </div>

            </div>
        </div>

        <br/><br/>
        <div class="form-group">
            <label for="description">Description:</label>
            <br/>
            <textarea cols="100" rows="4" class="form-control"
            id="description" name="description"
            placeholder="Description">
                ${book.description}
            </textarea>
        </div>
        <br/><br/>
        <button type="submit" class="btn btn-primary">Create</button>
    </form>
```

The submit action in the form invokes the controller method named `createItem()`, which obtains data that was submitted via a form and utilizes JAX-RS to insert into the database:

```
@POST
@Path("/create")
@Controller
public String createItem(@BeanParam @Valid Book form) {
    // Create new book

    // Obtain issue list to count records for ID population
    bookList = bookService.getBookList();
    form.setId(new BigDecimal(bookList.size() + 1));
    Book entity = new Book();
    entity.setId(form.getId());
    entity.setTitle(form.getTitle());
    entity.setDescription(form.getDescription());

    bookService.create(entity);

    return displayBookListing();
}
```

Once the method has been executed, the book listing is refreshed because the final line of `createItem()` invokes `displayBookListing()`, which executes the code as follows:

```
@GET
@Path("/books")
public String displayBookListing() {
    bookList = bookService.getBookList();
    bookContainer.setBookList(bookList);
    messages.setInfo("There are " + bookList.size() + " books in the
    library.");
    System.out.println("Issue count: " + bookList.size());
    return "book.jsp";
}
```

The resulting view, book.jsp, will display the newly created book within the listing of books, as seen in the previous recipe in Figure 4-5.

How It Works

The overall mantra of the Eclipse Krazo framework is complete control and ease of use. This example demonstrates exactly those ideals, as it demonstrates how the entire request-processing life cycle is handled by the developer, and the framework makes it easy to achieve. In order to create or update data, an HTML form is used to submit form data to a controller method. In this case, the form is written in JSP markup, and the submit action invokes a RESTful controller method entitled createItem(). The createItem() method contains a signature that returns a String for the next view to render after completion, and it accepts a parameter of type Book. Note that the parameter is annotated with @BeanParam and @Valid. The @BeanParam annotation indicates that the Book class contains some form parameter annotations to specify for fields. Specifically, in this case the Book entity class contains the following:

```
public class Book implements Serializable {
    private static final long serialVersionUID = 1L;
    // @Max(value=?)  @Min(value=?)//if you know range of your decimal
    fields consider using these annotations to enforce field validation
    @Id
    @GeneratedValue(strategy = GenerationType.SEQUENCE,
            generator = "book_s_generator")
    @SequenceGenerator(name = "book_s_generator", sequenceName = "book_s",
    allocationSize = 1)
    @Basic(optional = false)
// @NotNull
    @Column(name = "ID")
    private BigDecimal id;
    //@Size(max = 150)
    @FormParam(value="title")
    @Column(name = "TITLE")
    protected String title;
    //@Size(max = 500)
    @Column(name = "IMAGE")
```

335

```
private String image;
@FormParam(value="description")
@Lob
@Column(name = "DESCRIPTION")
private String description;
```

Therefore, the @BeanParam annotation will introspect the Book object for injection annotations and set them appropriately. The @Valid annotation indicates that Bean Validation processing should be invoked for this object. At method invocation time (form submit), the bean validation will take place and help to prevent erroneous data from being submitted.

Once initiated, the book listing is obtained from the BookService, which will be used to count the number of books. This number is used to increment a number to produce the primary key for the new record being created. The new Book entity is then created, values are set accordingly, and then the create() method is called to persist the data. Once persisted, the database is queried again via the call to displayBookListing(), and then the response is returned and the book.jsp view is displayed.

4-8. Applying a Different View Engine
Problem

Rather than utilizing a standard Eclipse Krazo view engine, you'd like to make use of another view type that is either already supported or not yet officially supported.

Solution #1

Make use of another view engine that has already been implemented for the MVC framework. There have been many different view engines already generated that are ready for use, and this example will demonstrate Facelets. Since Facelets ships with Eclipse Krazo, it is easy to add to a project. In order to do so, modify the web.xml to contain the Faces Servlet mapping by adding the following:

```
<servlet>
   <servlet-name>Faces Servlet</servlet-name>
   <servlet-class>javax.faces.webapp.FacesServlet</servlet-class>
```

```
    <load-on-startup>1</load-on-startup>
</servlet>
<servlet-mapping>
    <servlet-name>Faces Servlet</servlet-name>
    <url-pattern>*.xhtml</url-pattern>
</servlet-mapping>
```

Next, simply make use of .xhtml views within the application. The following method in BookController sends a response to hello.xhtml, which is written in Facelets:

```
<?xml version="1.0" encoding="UTF-8"?>
<!DOCTYPE html PUBLIC "-//W3C//DTD XHTML 1.0 Transitional//EN"
"http://www.w3.org/TR/xhtml1/DTD/xhtml1-transitional.dtd">
<html xmlns="http://www.w3.org/1999/xhtml"
    xmlns:h="http://xmlns.jcp.org/jsf/html"
    xmlns:c="http://java.sun.com/jsp/jstl/core">
    <h:head>
        <title>Facelets View</title>
        <meta name="viewport" content="width=device-width, initial-scale=1.0"/>
    </h:head>
    <h:body>
        <h:dataTable var="book" value="#{bookContainer.bookList}">
            <h:column>
                ${book.title}
            </h:column>
        </h:dataTable>
    </h:body>
</html>
```

Solution #2

Generate a new view engine by implementing the javax.mvc.engine.ViewEngine interface and incorporating logic to load and process the views of your choice. A ViewEngine is responsible for finding and loading views for an application, preparing

models, and rendering views to return control to the client. In the following code, a
ViewEngine has been implemented for the Pebble templating engine (https://github.
com/PebbleTemplates/pebble):

```
package org.jakartaeerecipes.bookstore.engine;

import com.mitchellbosecke.pebble.PebbleEngine;
import com.mitchellbosecke.pebble.error.PebbleException;
import com.mitchellbosecke.pebble.template.PebbleTemplate;
import java.io.IOException;
import java.io.StringWriter;
import java.io.Writer;
import java.net.URL;
import javax.enterprise.context.ApplicationScoped;
import javax.inject.Inject;
import javax.mvc.engine.ViewEngine;
import javax.mvc.engine.ViewEngineContext;
import javax.mvc.engine.ViewEngineException;
import javax.servlet.ServletContext;

@ApplicationScoped
public class PebbleViewEngine implements ViewEngine {

    @Inject
    private ServletContext servletContext;

    @Override
    public boolean supports(String view) {
        return view.endsWith(".html");
    }

    @Override
    public void processView(ViewEngineContext context) throws
    ViewEngineException {

        try {

            String viewName = "/WEB-INF/views/" + context.getView();
            URL template = servletContext.getResource(viewName);
```

```
        PebbleEngine engine = new PebbleEngine.Builder()
                .loader(new ServletLoader(servletContext)).build();

        PebbleTemplate compiledTemplate = engine.getTemplate(viewName);

        Writer writer = new StringWriter();

        compiledTemplate.evaluate(writer, context.getModels());

        context.getResponse().getWriter().write(writer.toString());

    } catch (IOException|PebbleException e) {
        throw new IllegalStateException(e);
    }

  }
}
```

Once the ViewEngine is created, simply begin generating views (or templates) using the markup for your view engine. The following sources are taken from the simple view pebbleTest.html:

```
<!DOCTYPE html>
<html>
        <head>
                <title>{{ websiteTitle }}</title>
        </head>
        <body>
                {{ content }}
        </body>
</html>
```

How It Works

The Eclipse Krazo framework is very flexible, allowing the developer to customize just about any of the functionality. One area where this comes in very handy is the choice of view (template) engine. Utilizing the ViewEngine interface, a developer can easily create a new ViewEngine to support just about any templating engine available. There are also a number of template engines that have already been implemented, supporting many of the most well-known templating engines in use. For example, there are engines available for download from Maven Central (`http://search.maven.org/#search%7Cga%7C1%7Cg%3A%22com.oracle.ozark.ext%22`), including the following:

- Thymeleaf

- Apache Velocity

- Mustache

- Handlebars

- FreeMarker

In order to utilize one or more of these engines (yes, you can use more than one in a single application), download the artifact from Maven Central and include it in your project. Then you can simply begin using the template engine of your choice, so long as the template pages adhere to the format that is specified within the `ViewEngine` implementation. In Solution #1, the Facelets view engine is used by simply modifying the web.xml to include a mapping to the Faces Servlet when a view file containing the suffix of `.xhtml` is loaded. The `ViewEngine` implementation for Facelets is automatically invoked when views containing that suffix are loaded, so no additional configuration is needed.

If interested in creating a new custom view engine, simply implement the `ViewEngine` interface. In Solution #2, a `ViewEngine` implementation for the Pebble templating engine is created. To implement this interface, one must override two methods, `supports()` and `processView()`. The `supports()` method is used to determine the path or file extension that must be supported by this engine. In this case, any file with the `.html` suffix will utilize the `PebbleViewEngine`. The `processView()` method is where much of the customization will occur, as this is where each view engine will perform customized processing in order to render the view. In the case of this example, the view name is first determined by calling upon the `context.getView()` method and appending the returned name to the String-based view path. Next, the `PebbleEngine` is created by utilizing the `PebbleEngine` builder API to load the injected `ServletContext`. This essentially allows the `PebbleEngine` to gain access to the views within the application. Once created, the engine is used to compile the currently visited view, returning a `PebbleTemplate`. Finally, the compiled template is evaluated using a `StringWriter` and passing in any Model values from the `ViewEngineContext`. Therefore, if anything has been loaded via the Models API in the controller, it is evaluated at this time and merged with the view. Lastly, the response writer is used to render the view.

CHAPTER 5

JDBC with Jakarta EE

The Java Database Connectivity (JDBC) API is a standard for accessing Relational Database Management Systems (RDBMSs) via Java. It has been in use for years and can be used when developing all types of Java applications, including desktop, stand-alone, and web. Almost every nontrivial application utilizes an RDBMS for storing and retrieving data. Therefore, it is important for application developers of all types to learn how to work with JDBC.

Enterprise application development has proven to be more productive for developers when working directly with Java objects as opposed to database access. While the JDBC API is still very mainstream for the development of enterprise applications and microservices, many developers have begun to adopt object-relational mapping programming interfaces as a standard. One of the easiest ways to map Java objects to database tables is to encapsulate JDBC logic into classes containing private methods for performing database access and exposing those methods using public methods that work with objects instead of SQL. This chapter contains recipes to demonstrate the technique of abstracting JDBC logic from ordinary business logic, sometimes referred to as creating data access objects.

The JDBC 4.2 release, included with Java SE 8, introduced some new features into the JDBC API to make working with databases a bit easier, and this chapter includes a recipe that covers one of those new features as well, the use of the REF_CURSOR. For a full list of the new features and enhancements with the JDBC 4.2 release, please visit the online documentation: `http://docs.oracle.com/javase/8/docs/technotes/guides/jdbc/jdbc_42.html`. After reviewing the recipes included in this chapter, you should be comfortable using JDBC within your Java web applications.

© Josh Juneau 2020
J. Juneau, *Jakarta EE Recipes*, https://doi.org/10.1007/978-1-4842-5587-2_5

Note   The Acme Bookstore application has been completely rewritten for this chapter in order to utilize an Oracle database rather than simple Java lists of data. Please run the `create_database.sql` script within your database prior to working with the examples from this chapter. Also, you will need to provide the necessary database connection properties for your database within the `db_props.properties` file and/or within the code examples for this chapter. If you are utilizing another database vendor, you should be able to adjust the SQL accordingly to work with that database. To access the Acme Bookstore application utilizing the database, be sure to deploy the `JakartaEERecipes` web application to your Eclipse GlassFish or Payara application server, and visit the URL `http://localhost:8080/JakartaEERecipes/faces/chapter05/home.xhtml`. This chapter will typically reference the Eclipse GlassFish server (aka GlassFish), although most of the references will be the same for the Payara server.

5-1. Obtaining Database Drivers and Adding Them to the CLASSPATH

Problem

You need to have the ability to utilize a database from your application, so you need to obtain drivers and configure the databases for your application.

Solution

Download the appropriate drivers for the database that you will be working with, and add them to the CLASSPATH for your application. In this solution, I will assume you are going to develop an enterprise-level web application and deploy it to the GlassFish application server. The application will utilize the Oracle database for persistence. In this case, it is recommended to download the most current Oracle database driver for Java Database Connectivity (JDBC). At the time of this writing, the driver is `ojdbc8.jar`, but you can find the latest online at `www.oracle.com/database/technologies/jdbc-ucp-122-downloads.html`. Optionally, it can be used as a Maven dependency via the following coordinates:

```
<!-- https://mvnrepository.com/artifact/com.oracle.jdbc/ojdbc8 -->
<dependency>
    <groupId>com.oracle.jdbc</groupId>
    <artifactId>ojdbc8</artifactId>
    <version>12.2.0.1</version>
</dependency>
```

The driver for your application may be different, depending upon which database you plan to use. For instance, to work with a PostgreSQL database, you would need to download the driver from the location `https://jdbc.postgresql.org/`.

Once you have downloaded the required drivers for your database, add them to the application CLASSPATH. If using an IDE, you can adjust the project properties for your application project accordingly to include the JAR that contains your database driver. If you are working from the command line or terminal, you can add the driver to your CLASSPATH by issuing one of the following commands, depending upon the OS platform you are using:

Use the following on Unix-based systems or OS X:

```
export CLASSPATH=/path-to-jar/ojdbc8.jar
```

Use the following on Windows:

```
set CLASSPATH=C:\path-to-jar\ojdbc8.jar
```

You should now be able to work with the database from your application, but in order to deploy to the GlassFish application server, you will need to make the database driver available for GlassFish. You can do this by copying the JAR containing the database driver into the GlassFish `lib` directory. The database driver JAR should be placed within a domain rather than at the application server level. Therefore, if your domain is named `domain1` (the default), then the path to where the JAR should be placed would be as follows:

```
GlassFish_Home/glassfish5/glassfish/domains/domain1/lib/databases
```

Restart the application server instance, and you are ready to deploy your database application.

How It Works

The first step to working with any database from an application is to configure the database driver for the specific vendor of your choice. Whether you decide to use MySQL, PostgreSQL, Oracle, Microsoft SQL, or another database, most enterprise-level databases have a JDBC driver available. This driver must be added to the application CLASSPATH and integrated development environment (IDE) project CLASSPATH if using one. If working from the command line or terminal, you will need to set the CLASSPATH each time you open a new session. If using an IDE, your settings can usually be saved so that you need to configure them only one time. After the driver for your database has been added to the application or project CLASSPATH, you are ready to begin working with the database.

When it comes time to deploy the application to a server, you will need to ensure that the server has access to the database driver. You can simply add the driver JAR for your database to the domain's lib directory and restart the server. Once you've done this, then you can either deploy your JDBC-based application or set up a database connection pool for your database. Please see Recipe 5-2 for more information on how to connect to your database from within an application using standard JDBC connectivity or how to set up a JDBC connection pool via the GlassFish or Payara application server.

5-2. Connecting to a Database

Problem

You need to connect to a database so that your application can perform database transactions.

Solution #1

Perform a JDBC connection to the database from within your application. Do this by creating a new Connection object, and then load the driver that you need to use for your particular database. Once the Connection object is ready, call its getConnection() method. The following code demonstrates how to obtain a connection to an Oracle database:

```
public final static class OracleConnection {

    private final String hostname = "myHost";
    private final String port = "1521";
    private final String database = "myDatabase";
    private final String username = "user";
    private final String password = "password";

    public static Connection getConnection() throws SQLException {
        Connection conn = null;
        String jdbcUrl = "jdbc:oracle:thin:@" + this.hostname + ":"
                + this.port + ":" + this.database;
        conn = DriverManager.getConnection(jdbcUrl, username, password);
        System.out.println("Successfully connected");
        return conn;
    }
}
```

The method portrayed in this example returns a `Connection` object that is ready to be used for database access.

Solution #2

Configure a database connection pool within an application server, and connect to it from your application. Use a `DataSource` object to create a connection pool. The `DataSource` object must have been properly implemented and deployed to an application server environment. After a `DataSource` object has been implemented and deployed, it can be used by an application to obtain a connection to a database.

Note   A connection pool is a cluster of identical database connections that are allocated by the application server (container-managed connection pool) to be utilized by applications for individual client sessions.

To create a connection pool using the GlassFish administrative console, first log into the console using the credentials that were specified upon installation, by visiting `http://localhost:4848` (assuming you are on the same machine as the server and that your GlassFish installation is using the default port numbers). Once successfully logged into the console, click the JDBC menu under Resources, and then expand the JDBC Connection Pools menu, as shown in Figure 5-1.

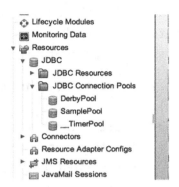

Figure 5-1. *Displaying the JDBC connection pools within GlassFish administrative console*

Click the New button on the JDBC Connection Pools screen, and it will then navigate you to the New JDBC Connection Pool (Step 1 of 2) screen. There, you can name the pool, select a resource type, and select a database driver vendor. For this example, I am using Oracle Database 12c. Therefore, the entries should be specified like those shown in Figure 5-2, although you could change the pool name to something you like better.

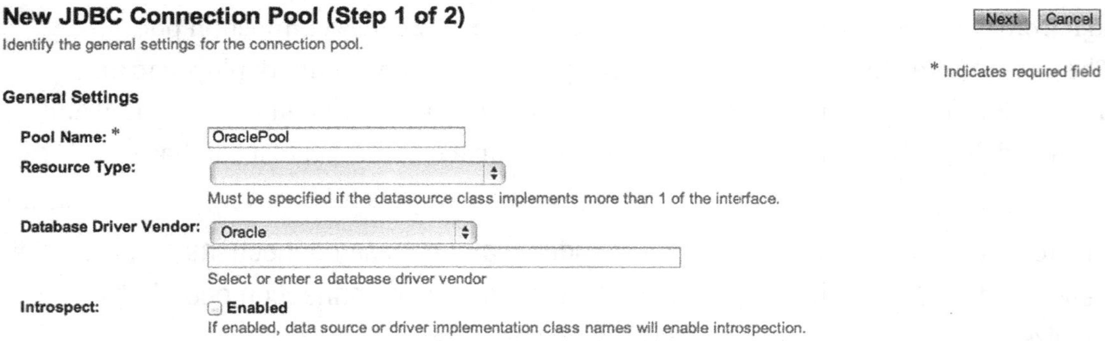

New JDBC Connection Pool (Step 1 of 2)   Next   Cancel
Identify the general settings for the connection pool.

                                                                      * Indicates required field

General Settings

Pool Name: *   OraclePool

Resource Type: [▲▼]
                           Must be specified if the datasource class implements more than 1 of the interface.

Database Driver Vendor: [Oracle   ▲▼]
                           [   ]
                           Select or enter a database driver vendor

Introspect: ☐ **Enabled**
                           If enabled, data source or driver implementation class names will enable introspection.

Figure 5-2. *Creating a GlassFish JDBC connection pool*

When the next screen opens, it should automatically contain the mappings for your Oracle database DataSource Classname as oracle.jdbc.pool.OracleDataSource. If it does not look like Figure 5-3, then you may not yet have the ojdbc8.jar database driver in the application server **lib** directory. Be sure to check the Enabled checkbox next to the Ping option.

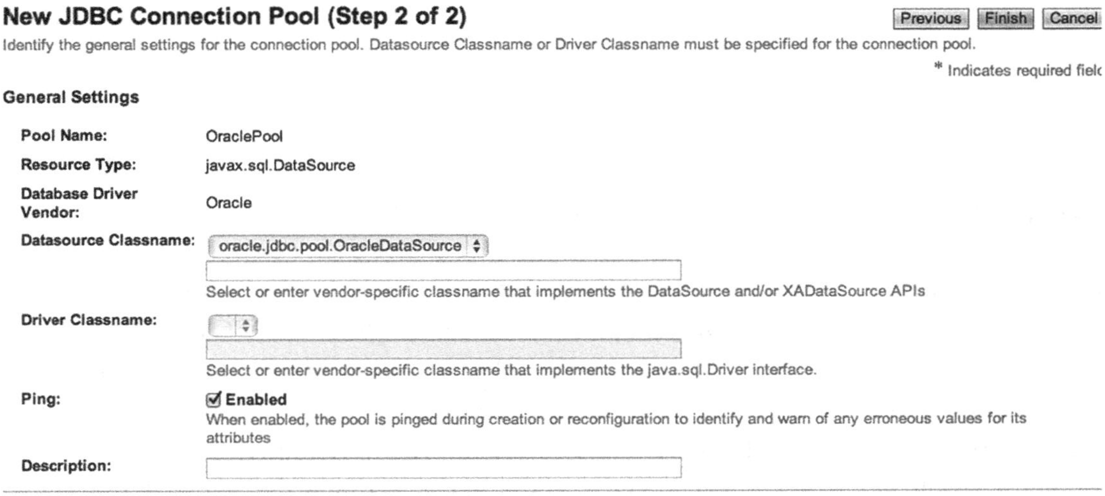

Figure 5-3. *Data source class name automatically populates*

Lastly, go down to the bottom of the second screen, and check all the properties within the Additional Properties table with the exception of User, Password, and URL. Please specify the information for these properties according to the database you will be connecting against, as shown in Figure 5-4. Once you populated them accordingly, click the Finish button.

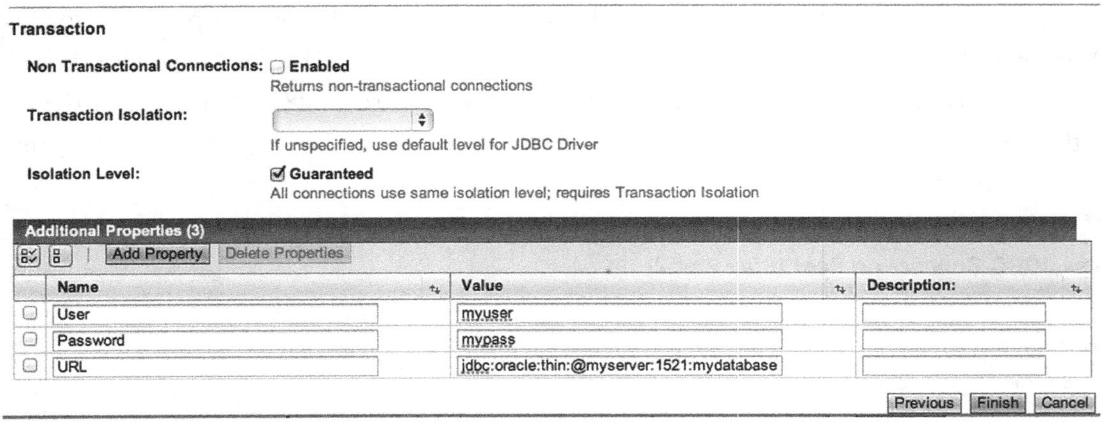

Transaction

Non Transactional Connections: ☐ Enabled
Returns non-transactional connections

Transaction Isolation: [⬍]
If unspecified, use default level for JDBC Driver

Isolation Level: ☑ Guaranteed
All connections use same isolation level; requires Transaction Isolation

Additional Properties (3)

[☰✓] [☰] | Add Property   Delete Properties

	Name	Value	Description:
☐	User	myuser	
☐	Password	mypass	
☐	URL	jdbc:oracle:thin:@myserver:1521:mydatabase	

Previous   Finish   Cancel

Figure 5-4. *Populating the additional properties for your database*

After clicking Finish, you should see a message indicating that the "ping" has succeeded. Now you can set up your JDBC resource by clicking the JDBC Resources menu within the left tree menu. When the JDBC Resources screen appears, click the New... button. Enter a JNDI name for your resource, beginning with `jdbc/`, and then select the pool name for the database connection pool you just created. The screen should resemble Figure 5-5. Once you've populated it accordingly, click the OK button to complete the creation of the resource.

Note   JNDI is the communication technology that allows applications to communicate with services by name within an application server container (`https://jakarta.ee/specifications/platform/8/platform-spec-8.html#java-naming-and-directory-interface-jndi`).

New JDBC Resource   OK   Cancel

Specify a unique JNDI name that identifies the JDBC resource you want to create. The name must contain only alphanumeric, underscore, dash, or dot characters.

JNDI Name: * jdbc/OracleConnection

Pool Name: OraclePool ◆
Use the JDBC Connection Pools page to create new pools

Description:

Status: ☑ Enabled

Additional Properties (0)

Add Property   Delete Properties

Name	Value	Description:
No items found.		

Figure 5-5. *Creating a JDBC resource*

You can use the following code to obtain a database connection via a `DataSource` object:

```
public static Connection getDSConnection() {
    Connection conn = null;
    try {
        Context ctx = new InitialContext();
        DataSource ds = (DataSource)ctx.lookup("jdbc/OracleConnection");
        conn = ds.getConnection();
    } catch (NamingException | SQLException ex) {
        ex.printStackTrace();
    }
        return conn;
}
```

Notice that the only information required in the `DataSource` implementation is the name of a valid `DataSource` object. All the information that is required to obtain a connection with the database is managed within the application server.

How It Works

You have a couple of options for creating database connections for use within Java applications. If you are writing a stand-alone or desktop application, usually a standard JDBC connection is the best choice. However, if working with an enterprise-level or web-based application, DataSource objects may be the right choice. Solution #1 for this recipe covers the former option, and it is the easiest way to create a database connection in a stand-alone environment. I will cover the creation of a JDBC Connection via Solution #1 first.

Once you've determined which database you are going to use, you will need to obtain the correct driver for the database vendor and release of your choice. Please see Recipe 5-1 for more information on obtaining a driver and placing it into your CLASSPATH for use. Once you have the JAR file in your application CLASSPATH, you can use a JDBC DriverManager to obtain a connection to the database.

Note As of JDBC version 4.0, drivers that are contained within the CLASSPATH are automatically loaded into the DriverManager object. If you are using a JDBC version prior to 4.0, the driver will have to be manually loaded.

To obtain a connection to your database using the DriverManager, you need to pass a String containing the JDBC URL to it. The JDBC URL consists of the database vendor name, along with the name of the server that hosts the database, the name of the database, the database port number, and a valid database username and password that has access to the schema you want to work with. Many times, the values used to create the JDBC URL can be obtained from a properties file so that the values can be easily changed if needed. To learn more about using a properties file to store connection values, please see Recipe 5-4. The code that is used to create the JDBC URL for Solution #1 looks like the following:

```
String jdbcUrl = "jdbc:oracle:thin:@" + this.hostname + ":" +
this.port + ":" + this.database;
```

Once all the variables have been substituted into the String, it will look something like the following:

```
jdbc:oracle:thin:@hostname:1521:database
```

Once the JDBC URL has been created, it can be passed to the DriverManager. getConnection() method to obtain a java.sql.Connection object. If incorrect information has been passed to the getConnection() method, a java.sql. SQLException will be thrown; otherwise, a valid Connection object will be returned.

Note   The prefix of the `jdbcurl` connection string in the example, `jdbc:oracle:thin`, indicates that you will be using the Oracle drivers, which are located within the `ojdbc8.jar`. `DriverManager` makes the association.

If running on an application server, such as GlassFish, the preferred way to obtain a connection is to use a `DataSource`. To work with a `DataSource` object, you need to have an application server to deploy it to. Any compliant Java application server such as Apache TomEE, GlassFish, Oracle WebLogic, or Open Liberty will work. Microservices containers such as Payara Micro will also work with the `DataSource`. Most of the application servers contain an administrative web interface that can be used to easily deploy a `DataSource` object, such as demonstrated via GlassFish in Solution #2 to this recipe. However, you can manually deploy a `DataSource` object by using code that will look like the following:

```
org.jakartaeerecipes.chapter5.recipe05_02.FakeDataSourceDriver ds =
new org.jakartaeerecipes.chapter5.recipe05_02.FakeDataSourceDriver();
ds.setServerName("my-server");
ds.setDatabaseName("JakartaEERecipes");
ds.setDescription("Database connection for Jakarta EE 8 Recipes");
```

This code instantiates a class that represents a new `DataSource` driver class, and then it sets properties based upon the database you want to register. `DataSource` code such as that demonstrated here is typically used when registering a `DataSource` in an application server or with access to a JNDI server. Application servers usually do this work behind the scenes if you are using a web-based administration tool to deploy a `DataSource`. Most database vendors will supply a `DataSource` driver along with their JDBC drivers, so if the correct JAR resides within the application or server `CLASSPATH`, it should be recognized and available for use. Once a `DataSource` has been instantiated and configured, the next step is to register the `DataSource` with a JNDI naming service.

The following code demonstrates the registration of a `DataSource` with JNDI:

```
try {
    Context ctx = new InitialContext();
    DataSource ds =
    (DataSource) ctx.bind("jdbc/OracleConnection");
```

```
} catch (NamingException ex) {
    ex.printStackTrace();
}
```

Once the DataSource has been deployed, any application that has been deployed to the same application server will have access to it. The beauty of working with a DataSource object is that your application code doesn't need to know any connection information, such as user credentials, for the database; it needs to know only the name of the DataSource. By convention, the name of the DataSource begins with a jdbc/ prefix, followed by an identifier. To look up the DataSource object, an InitialContext object is used. The InitialContext looks at all the DataSources available within the application server, and it returns a valid DataSource if it is found; otherwise, it will throw a java.naming.NamingException exception. In Solution #2, you can see that the InitialContext returns an object that must be cast as a DataSource:

```
Context ctx = new InitialContext();
DataSource ds = (DataSource)ctx.lookup("jdbc/OracleConnection");
```

If the DataSource is a connection pool cache, the application server will send one of the available connections within the pool when an application requests it. The following line of code returns a Connection object from the DataSource:

```
Connection conn = ds.getConnection();
```

Of course, if no valid connection can be obtained, a java.sql.SQLException is thrown. The DataSource technique is preferred over manually specifying all details and passing to the DriverManager because database connection information is stored in only one place: the application server or microservices container, not within each application. Once a valid DataSource is deployed, it can be used by many applications.

After a valid connection has been obtained by your application, it can be used to work with the database. To learn more about working with the database using a Connection object, please see the recipes within this chapter regarding working with the database.

5-3. Handling Database Connection Exceptions

Problem

A database activity in your application has thrown an exception. You need to handle that SQL exception so your application does not crash.

Solution

Use a try-catch block to capture and handle any SQL exceptions that are thrown by your JDBC connection or SQL queries. The following code demonstrates how to implement a try-catch block in order to capture SQL exceptions:

```
try {
// perform database tasks
} catch (java.sql.SQLException){
// perform exception handling
}
```

How It Works

A standard try-catch block can be used to catch java.sql.SQLException exceptions. Your code will not compile if these exceptions are not handled, and it is a good idea to handle them in order to prevent your application from crashing if one of these exceptions is thrown. Almost any work that is performed against a java.sql.Connection object will need to perform error handling to ensure that database exceptions are handled correctly. In fact, nested try-catch blocks are often required to handle all the possible exceptions. You need to ensure that connections are closed once work has been performed and the Connection object is no longer used. Similarly, it is a good idea to close java.sql.Statement objects for memory allocation cleanup.

Because Statement and Connection objects need to be closed, it is common to see try-catch-finally blocks used to ensure that all resources have been tended to as needed. It is not unlikely that you will see JDBC code that resembles the following style:

```
try {
    // perform database tasks
} catch (java.sql.SQLException ex) {
    // perform exception handling
```

```
} finally {
    try {
    // close Connection and Statement objects
    } catch (java.sql.SQLException ex){
    // perform exception handling
    }
}
```

As shown in the previous pseudo-code, nested try-catch blocks are often required in order to clean up unused resources. Proper exception handling sometimes makes JDBC code rather laborious to write, but it will also ensure that an application requiring database access will not fail, causing data to be lost.

5-4. Simplifying Connection Management
Problem

Your application requires the use of a database. To work with the database, you need to open a connection. Rather than code the logic to open a database connection every time you need to access the database, you want to simplify the connection process.

Solution

Write a class to handle all the connection management within your application. Doing so will allow you to call that class in order to obtain a connection, rather than setting up a new Connection object each time you need access to the database. Perform the following steps to set up a connection management environment for your JDBC application:

1. Create a class named CreateConnection.java that will encapsulate all the connection logic for your application.

2. Create a properties file to store your connection information. Place the file in a designated location so that the CreateConnection class can load it.

3. Use the CreateConnection class to obtain your database connections.

Note   If utilizing an application server, you can handle a similar solution via a container-managed connection pool. However, if the application is not deployed to an application server container, then building a connection management utility such as the one in this solution is a good alternative.

The following code is the org.jakartaeerecipes.chapter05.CreateConnection class that can be used for centralized connection management:

```
package org.jakartaeerecipes.chapter05;

import java.io.File;
import java.io.FileInputStream;
import java.io.FileNotFoundException;
import java.io.IOException;
import java.io.InputStream;
import java.nio.file.FileSystems;
import java.nio.file.Files;
import java.sql.Connection;
import javax.sql.DataSource;import java.sql.DriverManager;
import java.sql.SQLException;
import java.util.Properties;
import javax.naming.Context;
import javax.naming.InitialContext;
import javax.naming.NamingException;

public final class CreateConnection {

    static Properties props = new Properties();
    static String hostname = null;
    static String port = null;
    static String database = null;
    static String username = null;
    static String password = null;
    static String jndi = null;

    public CreateConnection() {

    }
```

```
public static void loadProperties() {
    // Return if the host has already been loaded
    if(hostname != null){
        return;
    }

    try(InputStream in = Files.newInputStream(FileSystems.getDefault().
    getPath(System.getProperty("user.dir")
            + File.separator + "db_props.properties"));) {
        // Looks for properties file in the root of the src directory
           in project

        System.out.println(FileSystems.getDefault().getPath(System.
        getProperty("user.dir")
                + File.separator + "db_props.properties"));
        props.load(in);

    } catch (IOException ex) {
        ex.printStackTrace();
    }

    hostname = props.getProperty("host_name");
    port = props.getProperty("port_number");
    database = props.getProperty("db_name");
    username = props.getProperty("username");
    password = props.getProperty("password");
    jndi = props.getProperty("jndi");
    System.out.println(hostname);
}

public static Connection getConnection() throws SQLException {
    Connection conn = null;
    String jdbcUrl = "jdbc:oracle:thin:@" + hostname + ":"
            + port + ":" + database;
    conn = DriverManager.getConnection(jdbcUrl, username, password);
    System.out.println("Successfully connected");
    return conn;
}
```

```java
public static Connection getDSConnection() {
    Connection conn = null;
    try {
        Context ctx = new InitialContext();
        DataSource ds = (DataSource) ctx.lookup(jndi);
        conn = ds.getConnection();
    } catch (NamingException | SQLException ex) {
        ex.printStackTrace();
    }
    return conn;
}

public static void main(String[] args) {
    Connection conn = null;
    try {
        CreateConnection.loadProperties();
        System.out.println("Beginning connection..");
        conn = CreateConnection.getConnection();
        //performDbTask();
    } catch (java.sql.SQLException ex) {
        ex.printStackTrace();
    } finally {
        if (conn != null) {
            try {
                conn.close();
            } catch (SQLException ex) {
                ex.printStackTrace();
            }
        }
    }

}
}
```

Next, the following lines of code are an example of what should be contained in the properties file that is used for obtaining a connection to the database. For this example, the properties file is named db_props.properties:

```
host_name=your_db_server_name
db_name=your_db_name
username=db_username
password=db_username_password
port_number=db_port_number
jndi=jndi_connection_string
```

Finally, use the CreateConnection class to obtain connections for your application. The following code demonstrates this concept:

```
Connection conn = null;
try {
    CreateConnection.loadProperties();
    System.out.println("Beginning connection..");
    conn = CreateConnection.getConnection();
    //performDbTask();
} catch (java.sql.SQLException ex) {
    System.out.println(ex);
} finally {
    if (conn != null) {
        try {
            conn.close();
        } catch (SQLException ex) {
            ex.printStackTrace();
        }
    }
}
```

Note   You could update this code to use the try-with-resources syntax in order to get rid of the finally block requirement. However, I'm showing this syntax to demonstrate how to ensure that a Connection object is closed, if you're not using try-with-resources.

To run the code for testing, execute the class `org.jakartaeerecipes.chapter05.CreateConnection.java` because it contains a main method for testing purposes.

How It Works

Obtaining a connection within a database application can be code intensive. Moreover, the process can be prone to error if you retype the code each time you need to obtain a connection. By encapsulating database connection logic within a single class, you can reuse the same connection code each time you require a connection to the database. This increases your productivity, reduces the chances of typing errors, and also enhances manageability because if you have to make a change, it can occur in one place rather than in several different locations.

Creating a strategic connection methodology is beneficial to you and others who might need to maintain your code in the future. Although data sources are the preferred technique for managing database connections when using an application server or JNDI, the solution to this recipe demonstrates how to use standard JDBC `DriverManager` connections. One of the security implications of using the `DriverManager` is that you will need to store the database credentials somewhere for use by the application. It is not safe to store those credentials in plain text anywhere, and it is also not safe to embed them in application code, which might be decompiled at some point in the future. As seen in the solution, a properties file that resides on disk is used to store the database credentials. Assume that this properties file will be encrypted at some point before deployment to a server.

As shown in the solution, the code reads the database credentials, host name, database name, and port number from the properties file. That information is then pieced together to form a JDBC URL that can be used by `DriverManager` to obtain a connection to the database. Once obtained, that connection can be used anywhere and then closed. Similarly, if using a `DataSource` that has been deployed to an application server, the properties file can be used to store the JNDI connection. That is the only piece of information that is needed to obtain a connection to the database using the `DataSource`. To the developer, the only difference between the two types of connections would be the method name that is called in order to obtain the `Connection` object, those being `getDSConnection()` or `getConnection()` in the example.

You could develop a JDBC application so that the code that is used to obtain a connection needs to be hard-coded throughout. Instead, this solution enables all the code for obtaining a connection to be encapsulated by a single class so that the developer does not need to worry about it. Such a technique also allows the code to be more maintainable. For instance, if the application was originally deployed using the DriverManager but then later had the ability to use a DataSource, very little code would need to be changed.

5-5. Querying a Database
Problem

You have a table that contains authors within the company database, and you want to query that table to retrieve the records.

Solution

Obtain a JDBC connection using one of the techniques covered in Recipe 5-2 or Recipe 5-4; then use the java.sql.Connection object to create a Statement object. A java.sql. Statement object contains the executeQuery method, which can be used to parse a String of text and use it to query a database. Once you've executed the query, you can retrieve the results of the query into a ResultSet object. The following example, excerpted from the org.jakartaeerecipes.chapter05.dao.AuthorDAO class, queries a database table named BOOK_AUTHOR and prints the results to the server log:

```
public void queryBookAuthor() {
        final String qry = "select id, first, last, bio from book_author";
        CreateConnection.loadProperties();
        try (Connection conn = CreateConnection.getConnection();
                Statement stmt = conn.createStatement();
                ResultSet rs = stmt.executeQuery(qry);) {

            while (rs.next()) {
                int author_id = rs.getInt("ID");
                String first_name = rs.getString("FIRST");
                String last_name = rs.getString("LAST");
```

```
            String bio = rs.getString("BIO");
            System.out.println(author_id + "\t" + first_name
                    + " " + last_name + "\t" + bio);
        }
    } catch (SQLException e) {
        e.printStackTrace();
    }

}
```

Executing this method against the database schema that ships with this book will produce the following results, considering that the BIO column is null for each author record:

```
Successfully connected
2    JOSH JUNEAU     null
3    CARL DEA     null
4    MARK BEATY     null
5    FREDDY GUIME     null
6    OCONNER JOHN     null
```

How It Works

One of the most commonly performed operations against a database is a query. Performing database queries using JDBC is quite easy, although there is a bit of boilerplate code that needs to be used each time a query is executed. First, you need to obtain a Connection object for the database and schema that you want to run the query against. You can do this by using one of the solutions in Recipe 5-2. Next, you need to form a query and store it in String format. The CreateConnection properties are then loaded via a call to the loadProperties() method, which ensures that the db_props. properties file is used to populate database connection information. Next, a try-with-resources clause is used to create the objects that are necessary for querying the database. Since the objects are instantiated within the try-with-resources, then they will be closed automatically once they are no longer being used. The Connection object is then used to create a Statement. Your query String will be passed to the Statement object's executeQuery method in order to actually query the database:

```
String qry = "select id, first, last, bio from book_author";
        CreateConnection.loadProperties();
        try (Connection conn = CreateConnection.getConnection();
                Statement stmt = conn.createStatement();
                ResultSet rs = stmt.executeQuery(qry);) {
. . .
```

As you can see, the Statement object's executeQuery method accepts a String and returns a ResultSet object. The ResultSet object makes it easy to work with the query results so that you can obtain the information you need in any order. If you take a look at the next line of code, a while loop is created on the ResultSet object. This loop will continue to call the ResultSet object's next method, obtaining the next row that is returned from the query with each iteration. In this case, the ResultSet object is named rs, so while rs.next() returns true, the loop will continue to be processed. Once all the returned rows have been processed, rs.next() will return a false to indicate that there are no more rows to be processed.

Within the while loop, each returned row is processed. The ResultSet object is parsed to obtain the values of the given column names with each pass. Notice that if the column is expected to return a String, you must call the ResultSet getString() method, passing the column name in String format. Similarly, if the column is expected to return an int, you'd call the ResultSet getInt() method, passing the column name in String format. The same holds true for the other data types. These methods will return the corresponding column values. In the example in the solution to this recipe, those values are stored into local variables:

```
int author_id = rs.getInt("ID");
String first_name = rs.getString("FIRST");
String last_name = rs.getString("LAST");
String bio = rs.getString("BIO");
```

Once the column value has been obtained, you can do what you want to do with the values you have stored within local variables. In this case, they are printed out using the System.out.println() method. Notice that there is a try-catch-finally block used in this example. A java.sql.SQLException could be thrown when attempting to query a database (for instance, if the Connection object has not been properly obtained or if the database tables that you are trying to query do not exist). You must provide exception handling to handle errors in these situations. Therefore, all database-processing code should be placed within a `try` block. The `catch` block then handles a `SQLException`, so if it is thrown, the exception will be handled using the code within the `catch` block. Sounds easy enough, right? It is, but you must do it each time you perform a database query. That means lots of boilerplate code. Inside the `finally` block, you will see that the `Statement` and `Connection` objects are closed if they are not equal to `null`.

Note   Performing these tasks also incurs the overhead of handling `java.sql.SQLException` when it is thrown. They might occur if an attempt is made to close a `null` object. It is always a good idea to close statements and connections if they are open. This will help ensure that the system can reallocate resources as needed and act respectfully on the database. It is important to close connections as soon as possible so that other processes can reuse them.

5-6. Performing CRUD Operations
Problem

You need to have the ability to perform standard database operations from within your enterprise application. That is, you need to have the ability to create, retrieve, update, and delete (CRUD) database records.

Solution

Create a `Connection` object and obtain a database connection using one of the solutions provided in Recipe 5-2; then perform the CRUD operation using a `java.sql.Statement` object that is obtained from the `java.sql.Connection` object. The following code, taken from `org.jakartaeerecipes.chapter05.recipe05_06.AuthorDAOStandard.java`, demonstrates how to perform each of the CRUD operations against the `BOOK_AUTHORS` table using JDBC, with the exception of the query (retrieve) since that is already covered in Recipe 5-5.

> **Note**   This recipe demonstrates the use of `String` concatenation for creating SQL statements rather than substitution variables with `PreparedStatements`. This is not a safe practice because the variables could potentially contain malicious values that may compromise your database. The solution to this recipe demonstrates the practice of creating SQL statements using `String` concatenation so that you can see the different options that are available. For information on using `PreparedStatement` objects and a safer alternative to `String` concatenation, please see Recipe 5-7.

```
private void performCreate(String first, String last, String bio) {
        String sql = "INSERT INTO BOOK_AUTHOR VALUES("
                + "BOOK_AUTHOR_S.NEXTVAL, "
                + "'" + last.toUpperCase() + "', "
                + "'" + first.toUpperCase() + "', "
                + "'" + bio.toUpperCase() + "')";
        try (Connection conn = CreateConnection.getConnection();
                PreparedStatement stmt = conn.prepareStatement(sql)) {
            // Returns row-count or 0 if not successful
            int result = stmt.executeUpdate();
            if (result > 0) {
                System.out.println("-- Record created --");
            } else {
                System.out.println("!! Record NOT Created !!");
            }
        } catch (SQLException e) {
            e.printStackTrace();
        }
    }

    private void performUpdate(String first, String last, String bio) {
        String sql = "UPDATE BOOK_AUTHOR "
                + "SET bio = '" + bio.toUpperCase() + "' "
                + "WHERE last = '" + last.toUpperCase() + "' "
                + "AND first = '" + first.toUpperCase() + "'";
```

```
    try (Connection conn = CreateConnection.getConnection();
            PreparedStatement stmt = conn.prepareStatement(sql)) {
        int result = stmt.executeUpdate();
        if (result > 0) {
            System.out.println("-- Record Updated --");

        } else {
            System.out.println("!! Record NOT Updated !!");
        }
    } catch (SQLException e) {
        e.printStackTrace();
    }
}

private void performDelete(String first, String last) {
    String sql = "DELETE FROM BOOK_AUTHOR WHERE LAST = '" + last.
toUpperCase() + "' "
            + "AND FIRST = '" + first.toUpperCase() + "'";
    try (Connection conn = CreateConnection.getConnection();
            PreparedStatement stmt = conn.prepareStatement(sql)) {
        int result = stmt.executeUpdate();
        if (result > 0) {
            System.out.println("-- Record Deleted --");
        } else {
            System.out.println("!! Record NOT Deleted!!");
        }
    } catch (SQLException e) {
        e.printStackTrace();
    }
}
```

Note   If you follow the code, you will notice that whenever a String of data is passed to the database, it is first changed to uppercase by calling the toUpperCase method on it. This is to help maintain a standard uppercase format for all data within the database.

Executing the following main method will produce the results that follow:

```
public static void main(String[] args) {
        AuthorDAO authorDao = new AuthorDAO();
        authorDao.queryBookAuthor();
        authorDao.performCreate("Joe", "Blow", "N/A");
        authorDao.performUpdate("Joe", "Blow", "Joes Bio");
        authorDao.queryBookAuthor();
        authorDao.performDelete("Joe", "Blow");
}
```

The results from running the main method should be similar to the following:

```
Successfully connected
2     JOSH JUNEAU     null
3     CARL DEA       null
4     MARK BEATY      null
5     FREDDY GUIME     null
6     OCONNER JOHN     null
Successfully connected
-- Record created --

Successfully connected
-- Record Updated --
Successfully connected
2     JOSH JUNEAU     null
3     CARL DEA       null
4     MARK BEATY      null
5     FREDDY GUIME     null
6     OCONNER JOHN     null
105    JOE BLOW     JOES BIO

Successfully connected
-- Record Deleted --
```

How It Works

The same basic code format is used for performing just about every database task. The format is as follows:

1. Obtain a connection to the database within the `try` clause.

2. Create a statement from the connection within the `try` clause.

3. Perform a database task with the statement.

4. Do something with the results of the database task.

5. Close the statement (and database connection if finished using it).

This step is done automatically for you if using the `try-with-resources` clause, as demonstrated in the solution to this recipe.

The main difference between performing a query using JDBC and using Data Manipulation Language (DML) is that you will call different methods on the `Statement` object, depending on which operation you want to perform. To perform a query, you need to call the `Statement executeQuery` method. To perform DML tasks, such as insert, update, and delete, call the `executeUpdate` method.

The `performCreate` method in the solution to this recipe demonstrates the operation of inserting a record into a database. To insert a record in the database, you will construct a SQL insert statement in `String` format. To perform the insert, pass the SQL string to the `Statement` object's `executeUpdate` method. If the insert is performed, an `int` value will be returned that specifies the number of rows that have been inserted. If the insert operation is not performed successfully, either a zero will be returned or a `SQLException` will be thrown, indicating a problem with the statement or database connection.

The `performUpdate` method in the solution to this recipe demonstrates the operation of updating record(s) within a database table. First, you will construct a SQL update statement in `String` format. Next, to perform the update operation, you will pass the SQL string to the `Statement` object's `executeUpdate` method. If the update is successfully performed, an `int` value will be returned, which specifies the number of records that were updated. If the update operation is not performed successfully, either a zero will be returned or a `SQLException` will be thrown, indicating a problem with the statement or database connection.

The last database operation that is covered in the solution is the delete operation. The `performDelete` method in the solution to this recipe demonstrates how to delete records from the database. First, you will construct a SQL delete statement in `String` format. Next, to execute the deletion, you will pass the SQL string to the `Statement` object's `executeUpdate` method. If the deletion is successful, an `int` value specifying the number of rows deleted will be returned. Otherwise, if the deletion fails, a zero will be returned, or a `SQLException` will be thrown, indicating a problem with the statement or database connection.

Almost every database application uses at least one of the CRUD operations at some point. This is foundational JDBC that you need to know if you are working with databases within Java applications. Even if you will not work directly with the JDBC API, it is good to know these basics.

5-7. Preventing SQL Injection
Problem

Your application performs database tasks. To reduce the chances of a SQL injection attack, you need to ensure that no unfiltered `Strings` of text are being appended to SQL statements and executed against the database.

Tip   Prepared statements provide more than just protection against SQL injection attacks. They also provide a way to centralize and better control the SQL used within an application, and performance benefits. Instead of creating multiple and possibly different versions of the same query, you can create the query once as a prepared statement and invoke it from many different places within your code. Any change to the query logic needs to happen only at the point that you prepare the statement.

Note   There have been data access objects (DAOs) created for each database table used by the Acme Bookstore application for this recipe. The DAO classes are used to perform CRUD operations against each of the tables for the Acme Bookstore application. The CRUD operations utilize `PreparedStatements` in order to add security and enhance the performance of the application.

Solution

Utilize PreparedStatements for performing the database tasks. PreparedStatements send a precompiled SQL statement to the DBMS rather than a clear-text String. The following code demonstrates how to perform a database query and a database update using a java.sql.PreparedStatement object. The following code excerpts are taken from a new data access object named org.jakartaeerecipes.chapter05.dao. AuthorDAO, which utilizes PreparedStatement objects rather than String concatenation for executing SQL statements:

. . .

```
    public Author performFind(int id) {
        String qry = "SELECT ID, LAST, FIRST, BIO "
                + "FROM BOOK_AUTHOR "
                + "WHERE ID = ?";

        Author author = null;
        CreateConnection.loadProperties();
        try (Connection conn = CreateConnection.getConnection();
                PreparedStatement stmt = conn.prepareStatement(qry)) {
            stmt.setInt(1, id);
            try (ResultSet rs = stmt.executeQuery();) {

                if (rs.next()) {
                    int author_id = rs.getInt("ID");
                    String first_name = rs.getString("FIRST");
                    String last_name = rs.getString("LAST");
                    String bio = rs.getString("BIO");
                    author = new Author(author_id,
                            first_name,
                            last_name,
                            bio);
                }
            }
```

```java
        } catch (SQLException e) {
            e.printStackTrace();
        }
        return author;

    }

    public List<Author> performFind(String first, String last) {
        String qry = "SELECT ID, LAST, FIRST, BIO "
                + "FROM BOOK_AUTHOR "
                + "WHERE LAST = ? "
                + "AND FIRST = ?";

        List authorList = new ArrayList();
        try (Connection conn = CreateConnection.getConnection();
                PreparedStatement stmt = conn.prepareStatement(qry)) {
            stmt.setString(1, last.toUpperCase());
            stmt.setString(2, first.toUpperCase());
            try (ResultSet rs = stmt.executeQuery();) {

                while (rs.next()) {
                    int author_id = rs.getInt("ID");
                    String first_name = rs.getString("FIRST");
                    String last_name = rs.getString("LAST");
                    String bio = rs.getString("BIO");
                    Author author = new Author(author_id,
                            first_name,
                            last_name,
                            bio);
                    authorList.add(author);
                }
            }
        } catch (SQLException e) {
            e.printStackTrace();
        }
        return authorList;

    }
```

```java
private void performCreate(String first, String last, String bio) {
    String sql = "INSERT INTO BOOK_AUTHOR VALUES("
            + "BOOK_AUTHOR_S.NEXTVAL, ?, ?, ?)";
    try (Connection conn = CreateConnection.getConnection();
            PreparedStatement stmt = conn.prepareStatement(sql)) {
        stmt.setString(1, last.toUpperCase());
        stmt.setString(2, first.toUpperCase());
        stmt.setString(3, bio.toUpperCase());

            // Returns row-count or 0 if not successful
            int result = stmt.executeUpdate();
            if (result > 0) {
                System.out.println("-- Record created --");
            } else {
                System.out.println("!! Record NOT Created !!");
            }

    } catch (SQLException e) {
        e.printStackTrace();
    }
}

private void performUpdate(int id, String first, String last, String
bio) {
    String sql = "UPDATE BOOK_AUTHOR "
            + "SET bio = ?,"
            + "   last = ?,"
            + "   first = ? "
            + "WHERE ID = ?";
    try (Connection conn = CreateConnection.getConnection();
            PreparedStatement stmt = conn.prepareStatement(sql)) {
        stmt.setString(1, bio.toUpperCase());
        stmt.setString(2, last.toUpperCase());
        stmt.setString(3, first.toUpperCase());
        stmt.setInt(4, id);
```

```
                int result = stmt.executeUpdate();
                if (result > 0) {
                    System.out.println("-- Record Updated --");

                } else {
                    System.out.println("!! Record NOT Updated !!");
                }

        } catch (SQLException e) {
            e.printStackTrace();
        }
    }

    private void performDelete(int id) {
        String sql = "DELETE FROM BOOK_AUTHOR WHERE ID = ?";
        try (Connection conn = CreateConnection.getConnection();
                PreparedStatement stmt = conn.prepareStatement(sql)) {
            stmt.setInt(1, id);

                int result = stmt.executeUpdate();
                if (result > 0) {
                    System.out.println("-- Record Deleted --");
                } else {
                    System.out.println("!! Record NOT Deleted!!");
                }

        } catch (SQLException e) {
            e.printStackTrace();
        }
    }
    ...
```

The methods displayed previously exhibit the use of PreparedStatement objects
rather than using standard JDBC Statement objects and String concatenation for
appending variables into SQL statements.

How It Works

While standard JDBC statements will get the job done, the harsh reality is that they can be insecure and difficult to work with. For instance, bad things can occur if a dynamic SQL statement is used to query a database and a user-accepted String is assigned to a variable and concatenated with the intended SQL String. In most ordinary cases, the user-accepted String would be concatenated, and the SQL String would be used to query the database as expected. However, an attacker could decide to place malicious code inside the String (aka *SQL injection*), which would then be inadvertently sent to the database using a standard Statement object. Using PreparedStatements prevents malicious Strings from being concatenated into a SQL string and passed to the DBMS. PreparedStatements use substitution variables rather than concatenation to make SQL strings dynamic. They are also precompiled, which means that a valid SQL string is formed prior to the SQL being sent to the DBMS. Moreover, PreparedStatements can help your application perform better because if the same SQL has to be run more than one time, it has to be compiled only once per session. After that, the substitution variables are interchangeable, but the PreparedStatement can execute the SQL very quickly.

Let's take a look at how a PreparedStatement works in practice. If you look at the example in the solution to this recipe, you can see that the database table BOOK_AUTHOR is being queried in the performFind() method, sending the author's ID as a substitution variable and retrieving the results for the matching record. The SQL string looks like the following:

```
String qry = "SELECT ID, LAST, FIRST, BIO "
                + "FROM BOOK_AUTHOR "
                + "WHERE ID = ?";
```

Everything looks standard with the SQL text except for the question mark (?) at the end of the string. Placing a question mark within a string of SQL signifies that a substitution variable will be used in place of that question mark when the SQL is executed.

The next step for using a PreparedStatement is to declare a variable of type PreparedStatement. You can see this with the following line of code:

```
PreparedStatement stmt = null;
```

Now that a `PreparedStatement` has been declared, it can be put to use. However, using a `PreparedStatement` may or may not cause an exception to be thrown. Therefore, any use of a `PreparedStatement` should occur within a `try-catch` block so that any exceptions can be handled gracefully. For instance, exceptions can occur if the database connection is unavailable for some reason or if the SQL string is invalid. Rather than crashing an application because of such issues, it is best to handle the exceptions wisely within a `catch` block. The following `try-catch` block includes the code that is necessary to send the SQL string to the database and retrieve results:

```
try (Connection conn = CreateConnection.getConnection();
        PreparedStatement stmt = conn.prepareStatement(qry)) {
    stmt.setInt(1, id);
    try (ResultSet rs = stmt.executeQuery();) {
    if (rs.next()) {
        int author_id = rs.getInt("ID");
        String first_name = rs.getString("FIRST");
        String last_name = rs.getString("LAST");
        String bio = rs.getString("BIO");
        author = new Author(author_id,
                                  first_name,
                                  last_name,
                                  bio);
    }
  }
} catch (SQLException e) {
    e.printStackTrace();
}
```

First, you can see that the `Connection` object is used to instantiate a `PreparedStatement` object. The SQL string is passed to the `PreparedStatement` object's constructor upon creation. Next, the `PreparedStatement` object is used to set values for any substitution variables that have been placed into the SQL string. As you can see, the `PreparedStatement setString()` method is used in the example to set the substitution variable at position 1 equal to the contents of the `id` variable. The positioning of the substitution variable is associated with the placement of the question mark (`?`) within the SQL string. The first question mark within the string is assigned to the first position, the second one is assigned to the second position, and so forth. The number of question marks must be equal to the number of substitution variables, or an error will be thrown. If there were more than one substitution variable to be assigned, there would be more than one call to the PreparedStatement setter methods, assigning each of the variables until each one has been accounted for. PreparedStatements can accept substitution variables of many different data types. For instance, if a Date value were being assigned to a substitution variable, a call to the setDate(position, variable) method would be in order. Please see the online documentation or your IDE's code completion for a complete set of methods that can be used for assigning substitution variables using PreparedStatement objects.

It is also possible to utilize named parameters, rather than indexes. To use this technique, provide a name prefixed with a colon for each substitution variable, rather than a question mark. The following lines of code demonstrate named parameters:

```
String qry = "SELECT ID, LAST, FIRST, BIO "
             + "FROM BOOK_AUTHOR "
             + "WHERE LAST = :last "
             + "AND FIRST = :first";

        List authorList = new ArrayList();
        try (Connection conn = CreateConnection.getConnection();
              PreparedStatement stmt = conn.prepareStatement(qry)) {
            stmt.setString("last", last.toUpperCase());
            stmt.setString("first", first.toUpperCase());
            try (ResultSet rs = stmt.executeQuery();) {
. . .
```

Once all the variables have been assigned, the SQL string can be executed. The PreparedStatement object contains an executeQuery() method that is used to execute a SQL string that represents a query.

The executeQuery() method returns a ResultSet object, which contains the results that have been fetched from the database for the particular SQL query. Next, the ResultSet can be traversed to obtain the values retrieved from the database. There are two different ways to retrieve the results from the ResultSet. Positional assignments can be used to retrieve the results by calling the ResultSet object's corresponding getter methods and passing the position of the column value, or the String identifier of the column value that you want to obtain can be passed to the getter methods. If passing the position, it is determined by the order in which the column names appear within the SQL string. In the example, String-based column identifiers are used to obtain the values. As you can see from the example, passing the column identifier to the appropriate getter method will retrieve the value. When the record values from the ResultSet are obtained, they are stored into local variables. Once all the variables have been collected for a particular author, they are stored into an Author object, which will eventually be returned from the method. Of course, if the substitution variable is not set correctly or if there is an issue with the SQL string, an exception will be thrown. This would cause the code that is contained within the catch block to be executed.

If you do not use the try-with-resources clause, as demonstrated in the solution, you should be sure to clean up after using PreparedStatements by closing the statement when you are finished using it. It is a good practice to put all the cleanup code within a finally block to be sure that it is executed even if an exception is thrown. For example, a finally block that is used to clean up unused Statement and Connection objects may look like the following:

```
finally {
    if (stmt != null) {
        try {
            stmt.close();
        } catch (SQLException ex) {
            ex.printStackTrace();
        }

    }
    if (conn != null) {
        try {
            conn.close();
            conn = null;
        } catch (SQLException ex) {
            ex.printStackTrace();
        }
    }
    return author;

}
```

You can see that the `PreparedStatement` object that was instantiated, `stmt`, is checked to see whether it is `NULL`. If not, it is closed by calling the `close()` method. Working through the code in the solution to this recipe, you can see that similar code is used to process database insert, update, and delete statements. The only difference in those cases is that the `PreparedStatement executeUpdate()` method is called rather than the `executeQuery()` method. The `executeUpdate()` method will return an `int` value representing the number of rows affected by the SQL statement.

The use of `PreparedStatement` objects is preferred over JDBC `Statement` objects. This is because they are more secure and perform better. They can also make your code easier to follow and easier to maintain.

5-8. Utilizing Java Objects for Database Access
Problem

Your application works with an underlying database for storing and retrieving data. You would prefer to code your business logic using Java objects, rather than working directly with JDBC and SQL for performing database activities.

Solution

Create a data access object (DAO) for each database table that will be used to perform the mundane JDBC and SQL work. Within the DAO, create façade methods that accept Java objects to represent a single record of data for the database table for which the DAO has been created. Use the Java objects to pass record data to and from the DAO, while the DAO breaks the objects apart and utilizes the data fields within standard SQL statements.

The following class excerpts demonstrate a data access object for the AUTHOR database table, which is used for storing book author data (a main method has been included merely for testing purposes within this DAO):

Note   For the full source listing, please refer to the `org.jakartaeerecipes.` `chapter05.dao.AuthorDAO` class, located in the JakartaEERecipes NetBeans project. Repetitive portions of the sources (`finally` blocks) have been removed from the following listing for brevity.

```
...
public class AuthorDAO implements java.io.Serializable {

    public AuthorDAO() {
    }

    public void queryBookAuthor() {
        String qry = "select id, first, last, bio from book_author";
        CreateConnection.loadProperties();
        try (Connection conn = CreateConnection.getConnection();
                Statement stmt = conn.createStatement();
                ResultSet rs = stmt.executeQuery(qry);) {

            while (rs.next()) {
                int author_id = rs.getInt("ID");
                String first_name = rs.getString("FIRST");
                String last_name = rs.getString("LAST");
                String bio = rs.getString("BIO");
                System.out.println(author_id + "\t" + first_name
                        + " " + last_name + "\t" + bio);
            }
        } catch (SQLException e) {
            e.printStackTrace();
        }

    }

    public List<Author> obtainCompleteAuthorList() {
        String qry = "select id, first, last, bio from book_author";
        List<Author> authors = new ArrayList();
        CreateConnection.loadProperties();
        try (Connection conn = CreateConnection.getConnection();
                Statement stmt = conn.createStatement();
                ResultSet rs = stmt.executeQuery(qry);) {
            while (rs.next()) {
                int author_id = rs.getInt("ID");
                String first_name = rs.getString("FIRST");
```

```java
                String last_name = rs.getString("LAST");
                String bio = rs.getString("BIO");
                Author author = new Author(author_id, first_name,
                        last_name, bio);
                authors.add(author);
            }
        } catch (SQLException e) {
            e.printStackTrace();
        }
        return authors;
    }

    public Author performFind(int id) {
        String qry = "SELECT ID, LAST, FIRST, BIO "
                + "FROM BOOK_AUTHOR "
                + "WHERE ID = ?";

        Author author = null;
        CreateConnection.loadProperties();
        try (Connection conn = CreateConnection.getConnection();
                PreparedStatement stmt = conn.prepareStatement(qry)) {
            stmt.setInt(1, id);
            try (ResultSet rs = stmt.executeQuery();) {

                if (rs.next()) {
                    int author_id = rs.getInt("ID");
                    String first_name = rs.getString("FIRST");
                    String last_name = rs.getString("LAST");
                    String bio = rs.getString("BIO");
                    author = new Author(author_id,
                            first_name,
                            last_name,
                            bio);
                }
            }
```

```java
        } catch (SQLException e) {
            e.printStackTrace();
        }
        return author;

    }

    public List<Author> performFind(String first, String last) {
        String qry = "SELECT ID, LAST, FIRST, BIO "
                + "FROM BOOK_AUTHOR "
                + "WHERE LAST = ? "
                + "AND FIRST = ?";

        List authorList = new ArrayList();
        try (Connection conn = CreateConnection.getConnection();
                PreparedStatement stmt = conn.prepareStatement(qry)) {
            stmt.setString(1, last.toUpperCase());
            stmt.setString(2, first.toUpperCase());
            try (ResultSet rs = stmt.executeQuery();) {

                while (rs.next()) {
                    int author_id = rs.getInt("ID");
                    String first_name = rs.getString("FIRST");
                    String last_name = rs.getString("LAST");
                    String bio = rs.getString("BIO");
                    Author author = new Author(author_id,
                            first_name,
                            last_name,
                            bio);
                    authorList.add(author);
                }
            }
        } catch (SQLException e) {
            e.printStackTrace();
        }
        return authorList;

    }
```

```
private void performCreate(String first, String last, String bio) {
    String sql = "INSERT INTO BOOK_AUTHOR VALUES("
            + "BOOK_AUTHOR_S.NEXTVAL, ?, ?, ?)";
    try (Connection conn = CreateConnection.getConnection();
            PreparedStatement stmt = conn.prepareStatement(sql)) {
        stmt.setString(1, last.toUpperCase());
        stmt.setString(2, first.toUpperCase());
        stmt.setString(3, bio.toUpperCase());

            // Returns row-count or 0 if not successful
            int result = stmt.executeUpdate();
            if (result > 0) {
                System.out.println("-- Record created --");
            } else {
                System.out.println("!! Record NOT Created !!");
            }

    } catch (SQLException e) {
        e.printStackTrace();
    }
}

private void performUpdate(int id, String first, String last,
String bio) {
    String sql = "UPDATE BOOK_AUTHOR "
            + "SET bio = ?,"
            + "    last = ?,"
            + "    first = ? "
            + "WHERE ID = ?";
    try (Connection conn = CreateConnection.getConnection();
            PreparedStatement stmt = conn.prepareStatement(sql)) {
        stmt.setString(1, bio.toUpperCase());
        stmt.setString(2, last.toUpperCase());
        stmt.setString(3, first.toUpperCase());
        stmt.setInt(4, id);

            int result = stmt.executeUpdate();
```

```java
            if (result > 0) {
                System.out.println("-- Record Updated --");

            } else {
                System.out.println("!! Record NOT Updated !!");
            }

        } catch (SQLException e) {
            e.printStackTrace();
        }
    }

    private void performDelete(int id) {
        String sql = "DELETE FROM BOOK_AUTHOR WHERE ID = ?";
        try (Connection conn = CreateConnection.getConnection();
                PreparedStatement stmt = conn.prepareStatement(sql)) {
            stmt.setInt(1, id);

                int result = stmt.executeUpdate();
                if (result > 0) {
                    System.out.println("-- Record Deleted --");
                } else {
                    System.out.println("!! Record NOT Deleted!!");
                }

        } catch (SQLException e) {
            e.printStackTrace();
        }
    }

    /**
     * Returns the next ID in the BOOK_AUTHOR_S sequence
     *
     * @return
     */
    public int getNextId() {
        String qry = "select book_author_s.currval as ID from dual";
```

```
    int returnId = -1;
    CreateConnection.loadProperties();
    try (Connection conn = CreateConnection.getConnection();
            Statement stmt = conn.createStatement();
            ResultSet rs = stmt.executeQuery(qry);) {

        while (rs.next()) {
            int author_id = rs.getInt("ID");
            returnId = author_id + 1;
        }
    } catch (SQLException e) {
        e.printStackTrace();
    }
    return returnId;

}

/**
 * Facade method for inserting Author objects into the BOOK_AUTHOR table
 *
 * @param author
 */
public void insert(Author author) {
    performCreate(author.getFirst(),
            author.getLast(),
            author.getBio());
}

/**
 * Facade method for updating Author objects in the BOOK_AUTHOR table
 *
 * @param author
 */
public void update(Author author) {
    this.performUpdate(author.getId(), author.getFirst(), author.
    getLast(), author.getBio());
}
```

```
/**
 * Facade method for deleting Author objects from the BOOK_AUTHOR table
 *
 * @param args
 */
public void delete(Author author) {
    performDelete(author.getId());
}

public static void main(String[] args) {
    AuthorDAO authorDao = new AuthorDAO();
    authorDao.queryBookAuthor();
    authorDao.performCreate("Joe", "Blow", "N/A");

    // Find any author named Joe Blow and store in authList
    List<Author> authList = authorDao.performFind("Joe", "Blow");
    // Update the BIO for any author named Joe Blow
    for (Author auth : authList) {
        auth.setBio("New Bio");
        authorDao.update(auth);
    }
    authorDao.queryBookAuthor();

    // Delete any author named Joe Blow
    for (Author auth : authList) {
        authorDao.delete(auth);
    }
}
}
```

How It Works

It can be advantageous for developers to separate different types of work into different classes within an application code base. In the same way that you separate web views from Java code within a Java web application, you should also separate JDBC from classes that are used to perform business logic. Have you ever had to maintain or debug a class that was riddled with business logic and SQL statements? It can be a nightmare! Simplifying code by breaking it down into smaller, more manageable pieces can oftentimes make maintenance and debugging much easier on a developer. The idea of separating JDBC and database-specific code from other business logic within an application falls within this same concept. Creating data access objects that are used solely for accessing the database can allow developers to code against Java objects rather than database tables.

A DAO is not a standard Java enterprise object. There is no framework that is used for creating DAOs. A DAO is simply a class that contains all of the JDBC code that is relevant for working with a single database table for your application. If there are twenty database tables that are required for use, then there should be that same number of DAOs. A DAO should contain minimally eight different methods. There should be at least one method for each of the four possible database transactions that could take place, those being CREATE, READ, UPDATE, and DELETE. These methods would contain specific JDBC code for connecting to the database, performing JDBC calls, and then closing the connection. The DAO should also contain four façade methods that will be used directly by classes containing the business logic. These methods should accept Java objects that correspond to the database table for which the DAO was written, and they should break down the object into separate fields and pass them to the JDBC methods to perform the actual database transaction.

In the solution to this recipe, the AuthorDAO class contains more than eight methods. This is because there is more than one way to search for author records within the database, and therefore, there is more than one find method within the class. A couple of different performFind() methods are available, each with a different method signature. These methods allow one to find an author based upon ID or by name. Once a matching author record is found in the database, the values for that record are retrieved using standard JDBC methods, and they are stored into the corresponding fields within a new Author object. In the end, either a list of Author objects or a single Author object is returned to the caller. These finder methods contain public modifiers, so a managed bean can call them directly to retrieve a list of Author objects or a single Author object.

The performCreate(), performUpdate(), and performDelete() methods are private, and therefore they can be accessed only by other methods within the same class. A CDI managed bean should not work directly with these private methods, nor will it be allowed to do so. Instead, there are public methods named insert, update, and delete, which are to be used by the CDI managed beans in order to access the private methods. The insert, update, and delete methods accept Author objects, and they perform the task of breaking down the `Author` object by field and passing the appropriate fields to their corresponding private methods in order to perform database activities. For instance, a bean can call the `AuthorDAO` insert method, passing an `Author` object. The insert method then calls the `performCreate` method, passing the fields of the `Author` object in their respective positions. Each of the CRUD operations can be performed in the same manner, allowing the business logic to interact directly with `Author` objects rather than deal with SQL.

5-9. Calling PL/SQL Stored Procedures

Problem

Some logic that is required for your application is written as a stored procedure residing in the database. You require the ability to invoke the stored procedure from within your application.

Solution

The following block of code shows the PL/SQL that is required to create the stored procedure that will be called by Java. The functionality of this stored procedure is very minor; it simply accepts a value and assigns that value to an `OUT` parameter so that the program can display it:

```
create or replace procedure dummy_proc (text IN VARCHAR2,
msg OUT VARCHAR2) as
begin
-- Do something, in this case the IN parameter value is assigned to the OUT
parameter
msg :=text;
end;
```

The `CallableStatement` in the following code executes this stored procedure that is contained within the database, passing the necessary parameters. The results of the `OUT` parameter are then displayed to the user:

```
CallableStatement cs = null;
try {
    cs = conn.prepareCall("{call DUMMY_PROC(?,?)}");
    cs.setString(1, "This is a test");
    cs.registerOutParameter(2, Types.VARCHAR);
    cs.executeQuery();
    System.out.println(cs.getString(2));
} catch (SQLException ex){
    ex.printStackTrace();
}
```

Running the example class for this recipe will display the following output, which is the same as the input. This is because the DUMMY_PROC procedure simply assigns the contents of the IN parameter to the OUT parameter:

```
This is a test
```

How It Works

It is not uncommon for an application to use database stored procedures for logic that can be executed directly within the database. To call a database stored procedure from Java, you must create a CallableStatement object, rather than using a PreparedStatement. In the solution to this recipe, a CallableStatement is used to invoke a stored procedure named DUMMY_PROC. The syntax for instantiating the CallableStatement is similar to that of using a PreparedStatement. Use the Connection object's prepareCall() method, passing the call to the stored procedure. The solution to this recipe demonstrates one technique for making a stored procedure call, that is, enclosing it in curly braces: {}.

```
cs = conn.prepareCall("{call DUMMY_PROC(?,?)}");
```

Once the CallableStatement has been instantiated, it can be used just like a PreparedStatement for setting the values of parameters. However, if a parameter is registered within the database stored procedure as an OUT parameter, you must call a special method, registerOutParameter, passing the parameter position and database type of the OUT parameter that you want to register. In the solution to this recipe, the OUT parameter is in the second position, and it has a VARCHAR type:

```
cs.registerOutParameter(2, Types.VARCHAR);
```

To execute the stored procedure, call the executeQuery() method on the CallableStatement. Once this has been done, you can see the value of the OUT parameter by making a call to the CallableStatement getXXX() method that corresponds to the data type:

```
System.out.println(cs.getString(2));
```

A NOTE REGARDING STORED FUNCTIONS

Calling a stored database function is essentially the same as calling a stored procedure. However, the syntax to prepareCall() is slightly modified. To call a stored function, change the call within the curly braces to entail a returned value using a ? character. For instance, suppose that a function named DUMMY_FUNC accepted one parameter and returned a value. The following code would be used to make the call and return the value:

```
cs = conn.prepareCall("{? = call DUMMY_FUNC(?)}");
cs.registerOutParameter(1, Types.VARCHAR);
cs.setString(2, "This is a test");
cs.execute();
```

A call to cs.getString(1) would then retrieve the returned value.

5-10. Querying and Storing Large Objects

Problem

The application you are developing requires the storage of Strings of text that can include an unlimited number of characters.

Solution

Because the size of the Strings that need to be stored is unlimited, it is best to use a character large object (CLOB) data type to store the data. The code in the following example demonstrates how to load a CLOB into the database and how to query it. The following excerpts are two methods from the org.jakartaeerecipes.chapter5.dao. ChapterDAO class.

Let's take a look at how to read a CLOB column value from the database. The readClob() method queries the database, reading the CHAPTER_NUMBER, TITLE, and DESCRIPTION columns from the CHAPTER database table. The length of the DESCRIPTION, which is the CLOB column, is printed to the command line along with the chapter number, title, and description:

```
public void readClob() {
        String qry = "select chapter_number, title, description from chapter";
        Clob theClob = null;
        CreateConnection.loadProperties();
        try (Connection conn = CreateConnection.getConnection();
                PreparedStatement stmt = conn.prepareStatement(qry)) {

            try (ResultSet rs = stmt.executeQuery();) {
                while (rs.next()) {
                    int chapterNumber = rs.getInt(1);
                    String title = rs.getString(2);
                    theClob = rs.getClob(3);
                    System.out.println("Clob length: " + theClob.length());
                    System.out.println(chapterNumber + " - " + title + ": ");
                    java.io.InputStream in =
                            theClob.getAsciiStream();
                    int i;
                    while ((i = in.read()) > -1) {
                        System.out.print((char) i);
                    }
                    System.out.println();
                }
            }
        } catch (IOException ex) {
            ex.printStackTrace();
        } catch (SQLException ex) {
            ex.printStackTrace();
        }
    }
```

The resulting output from running the method would look similar to the following, depending upon which records are stored in the database:

```
Clob length: 19
1 - Getting Started with Java 5:
chapter description
Clob length: 19
2 - Strings:
chapter description
Clob length: 19
3 - Numbers and Dates:
chapter description
Clob length: 19
4 - Data Structures, Conditionals, and Iteration:
chapter description
Clob length: 19
5 - Input and Output:
chapter description
Clob length: 19
6 - Exceptions, Logging, and Debugging:
chapter description
Clob length: 19
5 - Object-Oriented Java:
chapter description
Clob length: 19
8 - Concurrency:
chapter description
Clob length: 19
9 - Debugging and Unit Testing:
chapter description
Clob length: 19
10 - Unicode, Internationalization, and Currency Codes:
chapter description
```

What about inserting CLOB values into the database? The next method accepts values for each field within a record of the CHAPTER table, and it constructs the CLOB contents and lastly performs the insert:

```
private void performCreate(int chapterNumber, int bookId, String title,
String description) {
        String sql = "INSERT INTO CHAPTER VALUES("
                + "CHAPTER_S.NEXTVAL, ?, ?, ?, ?)";

        Clob textClob = null;
        CreateConnection.loadProperties();
        try (Connection conn = CreateConnection.getConnection();
                PreparedStatement stmt = conn.prepareStatement(sql)) {

            textClob = conn.createClob();
            textClob.setString(1, description);

            stmt.setInt(1, chapterNumber);
            stmt.setString(2, title.toUpperCase());
            stmt.setClob(3, textClob);
            stmt.setInt(4, bookId);
            // Returns row-count or 0 if not successful
            int result = stmt.executeUpdate();
            if (result > 0) {
                System.out.println("-- Record created --");
            } else {
                System.out.println("!! Record NOT Created !!");
            }
        } catch (SQLException e) {
            e.printStackTrace();
        }
    }
```

How It Works

If your application requires the storage of String values, you need to know how large those Strings might possibly become. Most databases have an upper boundary when it comes to the storage size of VARCHAR fields. For instance, Oracle database has an upper boundary of 4,000 bytes, and anything exceeding that length will be cut off. If you have large amounts of text that need to be stored, use a CLOB field in the database.

A CLOB is handled a bit differently from a String within Java code. In fact, it is actually a bit odd to work with the first couple of times you use it because you have to create a CLOB from a Connection.

Note   In reality, CLOBs and BLOBs (binary large objects) are not stored in the Oracle table where they are defined. Instead, a large object (LOB) locator is stored in the table column. Oracle might place the CLOB in a separate file on the database server. When Java creates the Clob object, it can be used to hold data for update to a specific LOB location in the database or to retrieve the data from a specific LOB location within the database.

Let's take a look at the performCreate() method that is contained in the solution to this recipe. As you can see, a Clob object is created using the Connection object's createClob() method. Once the Clob has been created, you set its contents using the setString() method by passing the position, which indicates where to place the String, and the String of text itself:

```
textClob = conn.createClob();
textClob.setString(1, "This will be the recipe text in clob format");
```

Once you have created and populated the Clob, you simply pass it to the database using the PreparedStatement setClob() method. In the case of this example, the PreparedStatement performs a database insert into the CHAPTER table by calling the executeUpdate() method as usual. Querying a Clob is fairly straightforward as well. As you can see in the readClob() method that is contained within the solution to this recipe, a PreparedStatement query is set up, and the results are retrieved into a ResultSet. The only difference between using a Clob and a String is that you must load the Clob into a Clob type. Calling the Clob object's getString() method will pass you a strange-looking String of text that denotes a Clob object. Therefore, calling the Clob object's getAsciiStream() method will return the actual data that is stored in the Clob. This technique is used in the solution to this recipe.

Although Clobs are fairly easy to use, they take a couple of extra steps to prepare. It is best to plan your applications accordingly and try to estimate whether the database fields you are using might need to be CLOBs because of size restrictions. Proper planning will prevent you from going back and changing standard String-based code to work with Clobs later.

5-11. Querying with a REF_CURSOR
Problem

Your database has implemented a REF_CURSOR datatype, which holds a query cursor value. You would like to have the ability to call upon a REF_CURSOR from your application and use the results just like a standard query.

Solution

Utilize a CallableStatement to call upon the database function or procedure that returns a REF_CURSOR, and register the returned value as Types.REF_CURSOR. The result will be returned as a ResultSet.class type, which can then be called upon like an ordinary query ResultSet to obtain the results. In the following example, a procedure named AUTHOR_PROC is called upon, which returns a REF_CURSOR. The results are then registered and parsed accordingly:

```
CallableStatement cstmt = conn.prepareCall("{AUTHOR_PROC(?)}");
cstmt.registerOutParameter(1, Types.REF_CURSOR);
cstmt.executeQuery();
ResultSet rs = cstmt.getObject(1, ResultSet.class);
while(rs.next()){
    System.out.println("Name="+ rs.getString(1));
}
```

How It Works

A REF_CURSOR is a database construct that allows one to generate a query string that can be passed by reference and called upon when needed. Oftentimes these constructs are returned from functions or procedures, and they allow for the ability to generate dynamic queries. As such, it can be quite useful to call upon a REF_CURSOR from within a Java application. The JDBC 4.2 release added the ability to call upon and work with REF_CURSORs.

The solution to this recipe demonstrates how to call upon a REF_CURSOR and obtain a ResultSet. The ResultSet can then be used to obtain access to the record data that is returned. Return a CallableStatement to call upon the REF_CURSOR by invoking the Connection prepareCall() method and passing a String containing the name of the database procedure or function that returns the REF_CURSOR using the following syntax:

```
CallableStatement cstmt = conn.prepareCall("{AUTHOR_PROC(?)}");
```

Once the CallableStatement has been generated, call upon the registerOutParameter(int) method and pass the REF_CUROR positional index, which in this case is 1, and the data type of the value being returned at that index. In this case, the data type is Types.REF_CURSOR:

```
cstmt.registerOutParameter(1, Types.REF_CURSOR);
```

Lastly, call upon the CallableStatment executeQuery() method, which will execute the query and return the result. The CallableStatement getObject(int) method can then be called upon, once again passing the position of the value being returned. In this case the position is 1 and the type is ResultSet.class, and this can be assigned to a ResultSet which can then be used to return the results of the REF_CURSOR query. As you can see from the example, a String value is expected:

```
ResultSet rs = cstmt.getObject(1, ResultSet.class);
while(rs.next()){
    System.out.println("Name="+ rs.getString(1));
}
```

The support for REF_CURSOR is a great addition for the JDBC API with release 4.2. REF_CURSORs provide the ability to create dynamic queries within SQL, and with the addition of the JDBC support, these dynamic SQL statements can now be utilized from Java applications.

CHAPTER 6

Object-Relational Mapping

For years, the Java Database Connectivity (JDBC) API was the standard for working with databases both web and desktop Java applications alike. Over the years, techniques for obtaining access to data stores and working with data within applications have evolved, and many organizations began to develop their own strategies for working with data in a more convenient way. Developers often find it easier to work with Java objects rather than Structured Query Language (SQL) for relational data. This chapter discusses some techniques that have been used in order to encapsulate SQL into separate utility classes and abstract it from developers so that they can work with Java objects rather than the SQL. Such strategies are known as *object-relational mapping* (ORM) strategies, and there are several well-known ORM strategies available from a multitude of organizations today.

Among the most well-known ORM strategies are Hibernate (`http://hibernate.org`), Oracle's TopLink (`www.oracle.com/technetwork/middleware/toplink/overview/index.html`), and EclipseLink (`http://wiki.eclipse.org/EclipseLink/UserGuide/JPA/Basic_JPA_Development`).

In an effort to standardize the industry, the Java Persistence API (JPA) has been deemed the strategy to use for moving forward with Java and Jakarta EE. JPA includes many features that were first introduced in ORM strategies such as Hibernate and TopLink. In fact, some of the top representatives from many of the different ORM projects formulated the Java Specification Requests (JSRs) for producing JPA, providing Java enterprise developers with a standard, efficient, and highly productive way to work with an underlying RDBMS from within Java applications. JPA allows developers to choose from a variety of Java persistence providers to utilize the configuration with which they are most comfortable, without the need to include multiple third-party libraries or customizations within the application. Some of the possible providers are as follows:

- EclipseLink (JPA default)

- Hibernate

- TopLink Essentials

J. Juneau, *Jakarta EE Recipes*, https://doi.org/10.1007/978-1-4842-5587-2_6

- KODO

- OpenJPA

Object-relational mapping is the process of mapping a Java object to a database table, such that each column of the database table maps to a single field or property within the Java object. Java objects that are used to map against database tables are referred to as *entity classes*, and this chapter will focus on the creation and use of entity classes. Recipes will cover areas such as creating classes and performing standard database transactions. You will learn how to configure a connection against a database, how to utilize JPA to persist and retrieve objects without using SQL, and how to relate objects to one another in a meaningful and productive manner.

Not only does ORM programming abstract the implementation details of working directly with a database from a developer, but it also provides a standard mechanism for deploying applications on databases from multiple vendors. JPA takes care of translating code into SQL statements, so once an application is written using JPA, it can be deployed using almost any underlying database.

Note   The recipes within this chapter may or may not be available for your use depending upon which JPA provider you choose. For instance, providers may include a different set of metadata annotations to use. Rather than list each annotation that is available for use in each recipe, I will direct you to very good resources for learning about all of the possible annotations that can be used along with each of the most widely used providers. While most of the annotations are common among all providers, there are a handful of custom annotations for each.

EclipseLink (use 2.7+ with Jakarta EE 8): `www.eclipse.org/eclipselink/api/2.7/org/eclipse/persistence/annotations/package-summary.html`

Hibernate (use 5.3+ with Jakarta EE 8): `https://docs.jboss.org/hibernate/orm/5.3/javadocs/`

TopLink JPA (Java Persistence API): `www.oracle.com/technetwork/middleware/ias/toplink-jpa-annotations-096251.html`

The sources for this chapter reside within the `org.jakartaeerecipes.chapter06` package. To run the examples from this chapter, deploy the application to the application server, and then visit the URL `http://localhost:8080/JakartaEERecipes/faces/chapter06/home.xhtml`. It should be noted that the examples for this chapter cannot be run within a web application without the use of other technologies such as Enterprise JavaBeans, which will be covered in Chapter 8. For that reason, many of the examples in this chapter utilize stand-alone Java classes for testing purposes.

6-1. Creating an Entity

Problem

You want to create a Java object that can be mapped to a database table such that the class can be used for persistence, rather than using JDBC.

Solution

Create an entity class against a particular database table. Declare persistent fields or properties for each of the columns in the underlying data table and use annotations to map the fields to a given column. Provide getters and setters for each of the persistent fields or properties that are declared within the entity so that other classes can access the contents.

The following code is an entity class named BookAuthor, which maps the BOOK_ AUTHOR database table to a standard Java object for use within the application:

```
package org.jakartaeerecipes.chapter06.entity;

import java.io.Serializable;
import java.math.BigDecimal;
import javax.persistence.*;
import javax.validation.constraints.NotNull;
import javax.validation.constraints.Size;
```

```java
/**
 * Chapter 6
 * Entity class for the BOOK_AUTHOR database table of the Acme Bookstore
   application
 * @author juneau
 */
@Entity
public class BookAuthor implements Serializable {
    private static final long serialVersionUID = 1L;
    @Id
    @Basic(optional = false)
    @NotNull
    @Column(name = "ID")
    private BigDecimal id;
    @Size(max = 30)
    @Column(name = "LAST")
    private String last;
    @Size(max = 30)
    @Column(name = "FIRST")
    private String first;
    @Lob
    @Column(name = "BIO")
    private String bio;

    public BookAuthor() {
    }

    public BookAuthor(BigDecimal id) {
        this.id = id;
    }

    public BigDecimal getId() {
        return id;
    }

    public void setId(BigDecimal id) {
        this.id = id;
    }
```

```
public String getLast() {
    return last;
}

public void setLast(String last) {
    this.last = last;
}

public String getFirst() {
    return first;
}

public void setFirst(String first) {
    this.first = first;
}

public String getBio() {
    return bio;
}

public void setBio(String bio) {
    this.bio = bio;
}

@Override

public int hashCode() {
    int hash = 0;
    hash += (id != null ? id.hashCode() : 0);          return hash;
}

@Override
public boolean equals(Object object) {
    // TODO: Warning - this method won't work in the case the id fields
        are not set
    if (!(object instanceof BookAuthor)) {
        return false;
    }
    BookAuthor other = (BookAuthor) object;
```

```
        if ((this.id == null && other.id != null) || (this.id != null &&
        !this.id.equals(other.id))) {
            return false;
        }
        return true;
    }

    @Override
    public String toString() {
        return "org.jakartaeerecipes.chapter06.entity.BookAuthor
        [ id=" + id + " ]";
    }

}
```

The entity itself cannot be used alone to access the database. Minimally, a persistence unit is required in order to connect with a database and perform transactions with the entity classes. To learn more about creating a persistence unit, please refer to Recipe 6-3.

How It Works

As an object-oriented developer, it sometimes makes more sense to work with objects that represent data, rather than working with variables of data and writing SQL to work directly with the underlying data store. The concept of mapping objects to database tables is better known as *object-relational mapping*. The Java Persistence API utilizes ORM for storing and retrieving data from a database via the usage of object classes known as *entity classes*. An entity class is a Java object that represents an underlying database table.

Note   Prior to EJB 3.0, XML files were used instead of annotations in order to manage metadata for entity classes. You can still use XML descriptors to manage metadata today, but I will not cover how to do so in this book. Most annotations can be used to selectively override default values within a class.

The entity class is usually named the same as the underlying database table, using camel-case lettering (capitalized first letters for all words) to separate different words within the table name. For instance, the BOOK_AUTHOR database table has a Java entity class named BookAuthor. The name of the entity can differ from the name of the underlying database table. However, it is a standard practice to name the entity class the same. In such cases where the name of the entity class has to differ from the database table, the @Table annotation can be used to annotate the entity class, providing the name of the underlying data table. Every entity class must be annotated as such by specifying the javax.persistence.Entity annotation. In the example, the BookAuthor entity class specifies only those annotations that are required. If the entity were to be named differently than the database table, the @Table annotation could be utilized as follows:

```
...
@Entity
@Table(name = "BOOK_AUTHOR")
...
```

An entity class must have a public or protected no-argument constructor. It is always a good idea to make an entity class Serializable by implementing the java.io.Serializable interface because doing so ensures that the entity class may be passed by value and persisted to disk, if needed. All entity classes must contain private or protected instance variables for each of the columns within the underlying database table, as well as variables for each relationship that the entity may have with other entities. (To read more about entity relationships, please take a look at Recipes 6-6, 6-7, and 6-8.) All database tables that will be mapped to Java entity classes must contain a primary key field, and the corresponding instance variable within the entity class that maps to the primary key column must be annotated with @Id. Each of the instance variables that maps to a database column can be annotated with @Column, specifying the name of the underlying database column. However, if no @Column annotation is specified, the name of the variable should match the database column name exactly, using camel-case lettering to separate words within the column name. To signify that a particular database column and its mapped instance variable cannot contain a NULL value, the variable can be annotated with @NotNull.

Another annotation worth mentioning that is used within the example for this recipe is @Size, which is used to specify the maximum size for a String variable. The size value should correspond to the database column size for the corresponding column. In addition, the @Lob annotation can be used to signify that the underlying database data type is a large object. There are other annotations that can be used to further customize an entity class; please see the link within the introduction to this chapter for the JPA provider that you are using in order to learn more about all of the annotations that can be used. Table 6-1 summarizes the most commonly used annotations when creating an entity class. Those annotations are covered within the solution to this recipe.

Table 6-1. *Commonly Used Annotations for Creating Entity Classes*

Annotation	Description
@Entity	Designates a Plain Old Java Object (POJO) class as an entity so that it can be used with JPA services
@Table	Specifies the name of the primary table associated with an entity (optional)
@Id	Designates one or more persistent fields or properties of the entity's primary key
@Basic	Configures the fetch type to LAZY
@Column	Associates a persistent attribute with a different name if the column name is awkward, incompatible with a preexisting data model, or invalid as a column name in your database

As mentioned in the solution for this recipe, an entity class cannot be used by itself. It is part of an overall solution for working with an underlying data source. Entity classes make it easy to map Java objects to database tables. They should be used in tandem with Enterprise JavaBean (EJB) classes (Chapter 7) and Contexts and Dependency Injection (CDI) or stand-alone with a persistence unit (Recipe 6-3) to perform database operations. A full Java EE solution utilizing the JSF framework can also use JSF managed beans to work directly with EJBs, or JAX-RS RESTful clients, which in turn conduct work via the entity classes.

Note   You may be wondering why the hashCode() and equals() methods are overridden in the example. The equals() method is present in every Java object, and it is used to determine object identity. Every entity class needs to contain an implementation of these methods in order to differentiate objects from one another. It is very possible for two entity objects to point to the same row in a database table. The equals() method can determine whether two entities both point to the same row. Moreover, all Java objects that are equal to one another should contain the same hashCode. In entity classes, it is important to override these methods to determine whether objects represent the same database table row.

6-2. Mapping Data Types

Problem

You are interested in mapping database table columns with entity class fields, but you are unsure which data types to declare for the fields within the class.

Note   Transient fields or properties cannot contain mapping annotations. A transient field or property is not persisted to the database.

Solution

Map database table column data types with their equivalent data types in the Java language specification when declaring instance variables for the columns within an entity class. The Jakarta EE container will convert the database value accordingly so long as the database column data type matches up to a Java data type that will contain the specified column's value. To demonstrate data type mapping, an entity class will be written for the Acme Bookstore's CONTACT database table. The CONTACT table has the following description:

```
SQL> desc contact
 Name                                      Type
 ----------------------------------------- ----------------------------
 ID                                        NOT NULL NUMBER
 FIRST                                     VARCHAR2(50)
 LAST                                      VARCHAR2(50)
 EMAIL                                     VARCHAR2(150)
 PASSWORD                                  VARCHAR2(30)
 DESCRIPTION                               CLOB
 OCCUPATION                                VARCHAR2(150)
 RECEIVENOTIFICATIONS                      VARCHAR2(1)
 GENDER                                    VARCHAR2(1)
```

The corresponding entity class is named Contact, and its class listing, shown next, demonstrates how to match each database column type to an appropriate Java data type:

```java
package org.jakartaeerecipes.chapter06.entity;
...

@Entity
@Table(name = "CONTACT")
public class Contact implements Serializable {
    private static final long serialVersionUID = 1L;

    @Id
    .@Basic(optional = false)
    @NotNull
    @Column(name = "ID")
    private BigDecimal id;
    @Size(max = 50)
    @Column(name = "FIRST")
    private String first;
    @Size(max = 50)
    @Column(name = "LAST")
    private String last;
    @Size(max = 150)
    @Column(name = "EMAIL")
    private String email;
    @Size(max = 30)
    @Column(name = "PASSWORD")
    private String password;
    @Lob
    @Column(name = "DESCRIPTION")
    private String description;
    @Size(max = 150)
    @Column(name = "OCCUPATION")
    private String occupation;
    @Size(max = 1)
    @Column(name = "RECEIVENOTIFICATIONS")
    private String receivenotifications;
```

```java
    @Size(max = 1)
    @Column(name = "GENDER")
    private String gender;

    public Contact() {
    }

    ...

// getters and setters

    ...

    @Override
    public int hashCode() {
        ...
    }

    @Override
    public boolean equals(Object object) {
        ...
    }

    @Override
    public String toString() {
        return "org.jakartaeerecipes.chapter06.entity.Contact[ id=" + id + " ]";
    }

}
```

It is important to specify the correct mapping data types because errors can occur down the line if not done correctly. Such is often the case with numerical data types.

How It Works

To create a Java class that will be used to represent a database table, you must map each of the table's columns to a class instance variable. In doing so, the variable must be assigned a data type that corresponds to that database column's data type. In some cases, more than one Java data type will map to a single database column's data type. In other cases, however, a database column's data type must match up to a specific Java data type. Table 6-2 lists the different Java data types and their associated database data types. If you are using another database for your work besides Oracle, please see the documentation for the database to rectify any discrepancies between the data types from those used by Oracle.

MySQL Data Mapping Documentation: `https://dev.mysql.com/doc/connector-j/5.1/en/connector-j-reference-type-conversions.html`

Table 6-2. *Oracle Database and Java Data Type Mapping*

Oracle Data Type	Java Data Type
BINARY_INTEGER, NATURAL, NATURALN, PLS_INTEGER, POSITIVE, POSITIVEN, SIGNTYPE, INT, INTEGER	int
CHAR, CHARACTER, VARCHAR2 LONG, STRING, VARCHAR	java.lang.String
RAW, LONG RAW	byte[]
DEC, DECIMAL, NUMBER	java.math.BigDecimal
DOUBLE PRECISION, FLOAT	double
SMALLINT	int
REAL	float
DATE	java.sql.Timestamp java.sql.Date
TIMESTAMP (or derivative)	java.sql.Timestamp
BOOLEAN	boolean
CLOB	java.sql.Clob
BLOB	java.sql.Blob
VARRAY	java.sql.Array
REF CURSOR	java.sql.ResultSet

Mapping data types correctly is a very important step in the creation of an entity class because an incorrect mapping can result in incorrect precision for numerical values and so forth. Utilizing the correct data types when mapping entity classes to the database table may vary depending upon database vendor, but Table 6-2 should be easily translated from Oracle data types to the data types for the RDBMS of your choice.

6-3. Creating a Persistence Unit

Problem

You want to use an entity class to perform database transactions. Therefore, you need to configure your application's database connectivity.

Solution

Create a persistence unit to configure a database connection, and then use the persistence unit to perform transactions with a given entity class. A persistence unit can use a database connection pool configured within an application server, or it can utilize a local JDBC configuration in order to obtain a database connection. In this example, I will demonstrate the use of the local JDBC configuration since the example will be run as a stand-alone application, rather than being deployed to an application server.

The following persistence unit is configured to create local JDBC connections, rather than using JPA for connections. However, you can learn more about configuring a persistence unit to work with database connection pools that are configured within an application server in the "How It Works" section of this recipe. The following code is from a file named `persistence.xml`, which is located in the `src\conf` directory for this chapter:

```xml
<?xml version="1.0" encoding="UTF-8"?>
<persistence version="2.0" xmlns="http://java.sun.com/xml/ns/
persistence" xmlns:xsi="http://www.w3.org/2001/XMLSchema-instance"
xsi:schemaLocation="http://java.sun.com/xml/ns/persistence http://java.sun.
com/xml/ns/persistence/persistence_2_0.xsd">
    <persistence-unit name="JakartaEERecipesLOCAL" transaction-
    type="RESOURCE_LOCAL">
        <class>org.jakartaeerecipes.chapter06.entity.BookAuthor</class>
        <properties>
            <property name="javax.persistence.jdbc.user" value="username"/>
            <property name="javax.persistence.jdbc.password"
            value="password"/>
```

```
        <property name="javax.persistence.jdbc.url"
        value="jdbc:oracle:thin:@hostname:port_number:dbname"/>
    </properties>
  </persistence-unit>
</persistence>
```

How It Works

To work with a database, an application needs to have the ability to connect to it. Usually a database connection pertains to a single username/password within a database. The persistence context XML file is where the connection information for the Java Persistence API resides, in our case a persistence.xml file. A persistence context can contain configuration for more than one connection to the database. Each connection configuration is referred to as a *persistence unit*, and each has a unique name that is used to identify the connection from within the application classes. The `persistence.xml` file can be packaged as part of a web archive (WAR) or enterprise archive (EAR) file, or it can be packed into a JAR file, which is, in turn, packaged with a WAR or EAR. If packaged with an EAR file, it should reside within the `META-INF` directory. If using a WAR file, the `persistence.xml` file should be packaged within the `resources/META-INF` directory. Lastly, if packaging into a JAR file, the JAR should reside within the `WEB-INF/lib` directory of a WAR or the library directory of an EAR.

As mentioned previously, each `persistence.xml` file can contain more than one database configuration, or persistence unit. Each persistence unit contains the type of JPA provider that will be used for the connection, the transaction type (`JTA` or `RESOURCE_LOCAL`), classes to be used for persistence (entity classes), and database connection specifics. In this section, I will break down the persistence unit that is configured for the recipe solution and describe each piece.

At the root of each persistence unit is the `persistence-unit` element, which contains the `name` and `transaction-type` attributes. Each persistence unit has a name; in the case of the example, it is `JakartaEERecipesLOCAL`, and this name is used to obtain a reference to the persistence unit from within application code. The `transaction-type` attribute of a persistence unit indicates whether Java Transaction API entity managers will be created (for use within an application server) or `Resource-Local` entity managers will be created (for use with stand-alone applications).

Next in the example you will see a series of classes listed within separate `class` elements. Within the `persistence-unit` element, zero or more classes can be identified for use with the persistence unit. These classes are the entity classes that will be mapped to the underlying database table. If using the `RESOURCE_LOCAL` transaction type, each entity class must be listed within the persistence unit. If using JTA (deployed to an application server within a WAR or EAR file), then the container takes care of identifying the entity classes, and they do not need to be listed in the persistence unit. If an entity class is not identified in the persistence unit and the transaction type is `RESOURCE_LOCAL`, then that entity class will not be available for use within the application.

Note   A persistence unit may also include an `<exclude-unlisted-classes>` element, which should be set to a Boolean value. This element is used to indicate whether classes must be listed using a `<class>` element within the persistence unit when using JTA, and it is `FALSE` by default. It may make sense to set this element to `TRUE` if two or more data sources are being used within an application and only specified entity classes should be used for each.

The `properties` element should contain subelements that define the connection to the database. Specifically, the user, password, and database URL are identified within sub-properties of the properties element. For `RESOURCE_LOCAL` persistence units, the following points are true:

- The property `javax.persistence.jdbc.username` should be used to identify the database username for the connection.

- The property `javax.persistence.jdbc.password` should identify the database user password for the connection.

- The property `javax.persistence.jdbc.url` should identify the database URL for the connection.

The properties for a Java Transaction API connection are different. In fact, for JTA, there can be no properties specified. Instead, an element named `jta-data-source` can be used to specify a JNDI name of a database connection that has been configured within the application server for use. For example, let's say the database connection is configured as `jdbc/OracleConnection` within the application server. Furthermore, let's assume you are deploying a WAR file to the GlassFish application server and you will use JTA instead of RESOURCE_LOCAL. If this is the case, the persistence unit may look like the following:

```
<persistence-unit name="JakartaEERecipesJTA" transaction-type="JTA">
    <jta-data-source>jdbc/OracleConnection</jta-data-source>
    <properties/>
</persistence-unit>
```

Note   There are no classes listed in the JTA example because the application server automatically identifies the entity classes for use with the persistence unit. However, there are circumstances for which it may be useful to list classes, as mentioned in the preceding note.

To use a persistence unit, an EntityManagerFactory object must first be obtained. An EntityManagerFactory object can be obtained by calling the Persistence.createEntityManagerFactory method and passing the string-based name of the persistence unit for which you want to obtain a connection. Once an EntityManagerFactory object has been obtained, an EntityManager object can be created and used to begin a database transaction. Obtaining a connection via a persistence unit would look similar to the following:

```
...
EntityManagerFactory emf = Persistence.createEntityManagerFactory("JakartaE
ERecipesLOCAL");
EntityManager em = emf.createEntityManager();
try {
    EntityTransaction entr = em.getTransaction();
    entr.begin();
    Query query = em.createNamedQuery("BookAuthor.findAll");
...
```

> **Note**   The preceding example uses the `createNamedQuery` method in order to substitute a named query rather than writing the Java Persistence Query Language (JPQL) inline. For more information, please see Recipe 6-9.

The `persistence.xml` configuration file contains the database connection information that will be utilized by an application to work with database(s). If you are working with JPA, you will become very familiar with creating a persistence unit, whether using local JDBC connections or an application server connection pool.

6-4. Using Database Sequences to Create Primary Key Values

Problem

Your database contains sequences that are used to generate primary key values for your database table records. Your application needs to use those database sequences in order to assign primary key values when creating and persisting objects.

Solution

Annotate an entity class's primary key field with a `SequenceGenerator` and then associate it with an entity generator in order to utilize a database sequence for populating a database table column value. In the following example, the `BookAuthor` entity has been updated to utilize the `BOOK_AUTHOR_S` database sequence for creating primary key values. As such, the `id` field has been annotated accordingly:

```
package org.jakartaeerecipes.chapter06.entity;

import java.io.Serializable;
import java.math.BigDecimal;
import javax.persistence.*;
import javax.validation.constraints.NotNull;
import javax.validation.constraints.Size;
```

```java
@Entity
@Table(name = "BOOK_AUTHOR")
public class BookAuthor implements Serializable {
    private static final long serialVersionUID = 1L;

    @Id
    @Basic(optional = false)@SequenceGenerator(name="book_author_s_
    generator",sequenceName="book_author_s",initialValue=1,
    allocationSize=1)
    @GeneratedValue(strategy=GenerationType.SEQUENCE,
    generator="book_author_s_generator")
    @NotNull
    @Column(name = "ID")
    private BigDecimal id;

    @Size(max = 30)
    @Column(name = "LAST")
    private String last;
    @Size(max = 30)
    @Column(name = "FIRST")
    private String first;
    @Lob
    @Column(name = "BIO")
    private String bio;

    public BookAuthor() {
    }

    ...
```

When a new BookAuthor object is persisted to the database, the next sequence value for BOOK_AUTHOR_S will be used as the primary key value for the new database record. The class org.jakartaeerecipes.chapter06.recipe06_04.SequenceTest.java can be run to test the sequence-generated primary key once the persistence context has been configured for the local JDBC database connection (see Recipe 6-3 for details). The following excerpt is taken from the SequenceTest class, and it demonstrates how to add a new BookAuthor object to the database:

```
...
EntityManagerFactory emf = Persistence.createEntityManagerFactory
("JakartaEERecipesLOCAL");
EntityManager em = emf.createEntityManager();
try {
    EntityTransaction entr = em.getTransaction();
    entr.begin();
    BookAuthor author = new BookAuthor();
    author.setFirst("JOE");
    author.setLast("TESTER");
    author.setBio("An author test account.");
    boolean successful = false;
    try {
        em.persist(author);
        successful = true;
    } finally {
        if (successful){
            entr.commit();
        } else {
            entr.rollback();
        }
    }
    Query query = em.createNamedQuery("BookAuthor.findAll");
    List authorList = query.getResultList();
    Iterator authorIterator = authorList.iterator();
    while (authorIterator.hasNext()) {
        author = (BookAuthor) authorIterator.next();
        System.out.print("Name:" + author.getFirst() + " " + author.getLast());
        System.out.println();
    }
} catch (Exception ex){
    ex.printStackTrace();;
} finally {
    em.close();
}
...
```

> **Note**   This example demonstrates the use of database transactions. Transactions allow for an entire sequence of processes to be performed at once. If a failure occurs in one of the processes, then all processes in the transaction fail, and changes to the database are rolled back. Otherwise, if all processes in the transaction complete successfully, then they are committed to the database. Transactions are very useful in situations where multiple database events depend upon one another.

How It Works

In many cases, it makes sense to generate primary key values for database table records via a database sequence. Utilizing JPA allows you to do so by incorporating the use of the `@SequenceGenerator` and `@GeneratedValue` annotations into an entity class. Every database table that is mapped to an entity class must have a primary key value, and using database sequences to obtain those values makes sense for many reasons. For instance, in some cases an application administrator will need to know what the next number, current number, or last number used for a primary key value might be. By using a database sequence, gathering information regarding the next, current, or last numbers is just a query away.

The `@SequenceGenerator` annotation should be placed directly before the declaration of the primary key field or property within the entity class, or it can be placed before the entity class declaration. Note that other annotations may be placed between the `@SequenceGenerator` annotation and the actual variable declaration. The `@SequenceGenerator` annotation accepts values regarding the database sequence that is to be used for primary key generation. More specifically, the annotation accepts the following attributes:

- `name` (required): The name of the generator (this name can be an arbitrary value)

- `sequenceName` (optional): The name of the database sequence from which to obtain the primary key value

- initialValue (optional): The initial value of the sequence object

- allocationSize (optional): The amount of increment when allocating numbers from the sequence

The @GeneratedValue annotation provides for the specification of the primary key generation strategy for the entity. Similar to the @SequenceGenerator attribute, it can be placed before the declaration of the primary key field or property within the entity class, or it can be placed before the entity class declaration. It is used to specify the means for which the entity class primary key will be generated. The three options are as follows:

- The entity class will generate its own primary key value before inserting a new record.

- The entity class will use a database sequence for the key generation.

- The entity class will generate keys via some other means.

The attributes that can be specified for the @GeneratedValue annotation are as follows:

- generator (optional): This is the name of the primary key generator to use as specified by the @SequenceGenerator annotation. This must match the name attribute that was supplied for the @SequenceGenerator annotation unless using a @TableGenerator. This defaults to the ID generator supplied by the persistence provider.

- strategy (optional): This is the primary key generation strategy that will be used by the persistence provider to generate the primary key for the annotated field or entity class. This defaults to AUTO if not supplied.

The strategy attribute of @GeneratedValue can accept four different javax. persistence.GenerationType Enum values:

- AUTO: Indicates that the persistence provider should choose an appropriate strategy for a particular database

- IDENTITY: Indicates that the persistence provider must assign primary keys for the entity using the database identity column

- SEQUENCE: Indicates that the persistence provider must assign primary keys for the entity using the database sequence column

- TABLE: Indicates that the persistence provider must assign primary keys for the entity using an underlying database table to ensure unique values are provided.

In the example for this recipe, the BOOK_AUTHOR_S database sequence is specified for the sequenceName attribute of the @SequenceGenerator annotation, and the name of the generator is book_author_s_generator. Note that the @GeneratedValue name attribute matches that of the @SequenceGenerator annotation; this is very important! Once specified, the entity class will automatically obtain the next value from the database sequence when a new object is persisted.

Note   There are other options for generating key values, such as AUTO, IDENTITY, and TABLE. These strategies can be valid in different situations. For more information on using other options, please refer to the online Jakarta EE documentation at `https://javaee.github.io/`.

6-5. Generating Primary Keys Using More Than One Attribute
Problem

A particular database table does not contain a primary key. Since use of the Java Persistence API (JPA) requires a primary key for mapping entity classes to database tables, you need to join the values of two or more of the table columns in order to create a primary key for each record.

Solution #1

Create a composite primary key by developing an embedded composite primary key class and denoting the composite key field within an entity using the javax. persistence.EmbeddedId and javax.persistence.IdClass annotations. Consider the AUTHOR_WORK database table that is used for the Acme Bookstore application. Suppose that the AUTHOR_WORK database table did not contain a primary key column. It would be possible to generate a primary key for each record based upon its BOOK_ID and AUTHOR_ ID columns. The following entity class is that for the AuthorWork entity. Instead of using the ID column as a primary key, it uses both the bookId and authorId columns together to formulate a composite primary key:

```
package org.jakartaeerecipes.chapter06.entity;

import java.io.Serializable;
import java.math.BigDecimal;
import java.math.BigInteger;
import javax.persistence.*;
import javax.validation.constraints.NotNull;
import org.jakartaeerecipes.chapter06.entity.key.AuthorWorkPKEmbedded;
import org.jakartaeerecipes.chapter06.entity.key.AuthorWorkPKNonEmbedded;

@Entity
@Table(name = "AUTHOR_WORK")
// (Named queries are covered in Recipe 6-9)
@NamedQueries({
    @NamedQuery(name = "AuthorWork.findAll", query = "SELECT a FROM
    AuthorWork a")})
public class AuthorWorkEmbedded implements Serializable {
    private static final long serialVersionUID = 1L;

    // You can use an embedded ID in-place of a standard Id if a table
    // contains more than one column to compose a primary key.  Comment
    // out along with the getters and setters to use a non-embeddable
       primary key.
    @EmbeddedId
    private AuthorWorkPKEmbedded embeddedId;

    public AuthorWorkEmbedded() {
    }

    public AuthorWorkEmbedded(BigInteger bookId, BigInteger authorId) {
        this.embeddedId = new AuthorWorkPKEmbedded(bookId, authorId);
    }
```

```
/**
 * @return the embeddedId
 */
public AuthorWorkPKEmbedded getEmbeddedId() {
    return embeddedId;
}

/**
 * @param embeddedId the embeddedId to set
 */
public void setEmbeddedId(AuthorWorkPKEmbedded embeddedId) {
    this.embeddedId = embeddedId;
}

}
```

To utilize an embedded primary key, you must create a class that contains the logic for mapping the primary key ID to the columns that are used to compose it. For this example, the AuthorWorkPKEmbedded class serves this purpose, which is shown here:

```
package org.jakartaeerecipes.chapter06.entity.key;

import java.io.Serializable;
import java.math.BigInteger;
import javax.persistence.Embeddable;

/**
 * Embeddable Primary Key class for AuthorWork
 *
 * @author juneau
 */
@Embeddable
public class AuthorWorkPKEmbedded implements Serializable {

    private BigInteger bookId;
    private BigInteger authorId;

    public AuthorWorkPKEmbedded() {
    }
```

```
    public AuthorWorkPKEmbedded(BigInteger bookId, BigInteger authorId){
        this.bookId = bookId;
        this.authorId = authorId;
    }
...
    // getters and setters
...
    public int hashCode() {
        return bookId.hashCode() + authorId.hashCode();
    }

    public boolean equals(Object obj) {
        if (obj == this) {
            return true;
        }
        if (!(obj instanceof AuthorWorkPKEmbedded)) {
            return false;
        }
        if (obj == null) {
            return false;
        }
        AuthorWorkPKEmbedded pk = (AuthorWorkPKEmbedded) obj;
        return (((bookId == ((AuthorWorkPKEmbedded) obj).getBookId()))
                && ((authorId == ((AuthorWorkPKEmbedded) obj).
                getAuthorId()))));
    }
}
```

Note   Although the preceding example is not an entity class, its member values are persisted. Even if the members are not designated as @Basic, they are still persisted.

Both the hashCode() and equals() methods must be present in composite key classes.

Solution #2

Create a composite primary key by developing a non-embedded composite primary key class, and denote two or more of the columns within the entity class with the `@Id` annotation. Also, if using a non-embedded primary key class, the entity class must be designated as such by utilizing the `@IdClass` annotation and specifying the non-embedded primary key class.

Consider the AUTHOR_WORK database table that is used for the Acme Bookstore application. Suppose that the AUTHOR_WORK database table did not contain a primary key column. It would be possible to generate a primary key for each record based upon its BOOK_ID and AUTHOR_ID columns since together they would formulate a unique value for each record. The following entity class is that for the AuthorWork entity. Instead of using the ID column as a primary key, it uses both the bookId and authorId columns together to formulate a composite primary key:

```
package org.jakartaeerecipes.chapter06.entity;

import java.io.Serializable;
import java.math.BigDecimal;
import java.math.BigInteger;
import javax.persistence.*;
import javax.validation.constraints.NotNull;
import org.jakartaeerecipes.chapter06.entity.key.AuthorWorkPKEmbedded;
import org.jakartaeerecipes.chapter06.entity.key.AuthorWorkPKNonEmbedded;

/**
 * Chapter 6 - Example of Non-Embedded Primary Key
 * @author juneau
 */

@IdClass(AuthorWorkPKNonEmbedded.class)
@Entity
@Table(name = "AUTHOR_WORK_LEGACY")
@NamedQueries({
    @NamedQuery(name = "AuthorWork.findAll", query = "SELECT a FROM
    AuthorWork a")})
public class AuthorWorkNonEmbedded implements Serializable {
    private static final long serialVersionUID = 1L;
```

```
    @Id
    @Column(name = "BOOK_ID")
    private BigInteger bookId;

    @Id
    @Column(name= "AUTHOR_ID")
    private BigInteger authorId;

    public AuthorWorkNonEmbedded() {
    }

    public AuthorWorkNonEmbedded(BigInteger bookId, BigInteger authorId) {
        this.bookId = bookId;
        this.authorId = authorId;
    }

. . .
// getters and setters
. . .

}
```

The associated non-embeddable primary key class is named AuthorWorkPKNonEmbedded. The code for this class is as follows:

```
package org.jakartaeerecipes.chapter06.entity.key;
import java.io.Serializable;
import java.math.BigInteger;

/**
 * Non-Embeddable Primary Key class for AuthorWork
 *
 * @author juneau
 */
public class AuthorWorkPKNonEmbedded implements Serializable {

    private BigInteger bookId;
    private BigInteger authorId;
```

```java
    public AuthorWorkPKNonEmbedded() {
    }
. . .
// getters and setters
. . .

    public int hashCode() {
        return bookId.hashCode() + authorId.hashCode();
    }

    public boolean equals(Object obj) {
        if (obj == this) {
            return true;
        }
        if (!(obj instanceof AuthorWorkPKEmbedded)) {
            return false;
        }
        if (obj == null) {
            return false;
        }
        AuthorWorkPKEmbedded pk = (AuthorWorkPKEmbedded) obj;
        return (((bookId == ((AuthorWorkPKEmbedded) obj).getBookId()))
                && ((authorId == ((AuthorWorkPKEmbedded) obj).getAuthorId()))));
    }
}
```

Note   Although the AuthorWorkPKNonEmbedded class is not an entity, its member values are persisted.

How It Works

There can be situations in which a database table may not contain a single primary key value to uniquely identify each row. Oftentimes this can be the case when working with legacy databases. In the Java Persistence API, all entity classes must contain a primary key that can be used to uniquely identify an object. To get around this obstacle when working with tables that do not contain a single primary key value, a composite primary key can be used to uniquely identify an object.

A composite primary key is composed of two or more fields or properties within an entity class that can be combined together to create a unique identifier. Think in terms of performing a database query and attempting to return a record that matches only certain criteria. In such a case, you often need to include multiple relationships within the SQL WHERE clause. Creating a composite primary key within an entity class is basically the same concept in that you are telling JPA to use all of the fields or properties designated within the composite key in order to uniquely identify an object.

There are a couple of different techniques, embeddable and non-embeddable, that can be used to develop a composite primary key. The two techniques are similar in that they each require the creation of a separate class to compose the primary key, but they differ by the way in which the primary key is denoted within the entity class. In fact, the separate primary key class in both techniques can be created almost identically, except that an embeddable primary key class must be annotated using @Embeddable, as demonstrated in Solution #1 to this recipe. An entity with an embeddable primary key class should contain only a single primary key, and the data type for the primary key should be the same as the embeddable primary key class. That is, the primary key class should be declared within the entity using a private modifier, along with all of the other persistent properties and fields, and it should be annotated with @Id to indicate that it is the primary key. The following excerpt from Solution #1 shows how this is done:

```
@EmbeddedId
private AuthorWorkPKEmbedded embeddedId;
```

The entity class containing an embedded primary key should contain a constructor that accepts one parameter for each of the persistent fields or properties used for the primary key. Within the constructor, a new instance of the embeddable primary key class should then be instantiated using the passed-in arguments. The entity class using an embeddable primary key should contain accessor methods for the primary key field or property. However, unlike most entity classes, the hashCode() and equals() methods are not present because they are within the primary key class instead. Now that I've gone over the logistics of an entity class that uses an embeddable primary key, let's take a look at the embeddable primary key class itself to see how it works.

423

A primary key class that is used for creating an embeddable primary key should contain declarations for each of the persistent fields or properties that will be used to compose the primary key for the associated entity class. Of course, these fields or properties should be made private, and there should be corresponding getters and setters for accessing the fields. The embeddable primary key class should be annotated with @Embeddable. It can contain two constructors: one that accepts no arguments and another optional constructor that accepts an argument for each of the persistent fields or properties that compose the primary key. Remember how the entity class that uses the embeddable primary key contains no hashCode() method? That is because it resides within the primary key class, and it simply adds together the hashCodes for each of the fields used to compose the primary key, and it returns the sum.

The most important piece of the primary key class is the equals() method since it is used to determine whether an object or database record uniquely matches the associated primary key. The equals() method should accept an argument of type Object, which will be the object that is being compared against the current primary key object. The object is then compared to determine whether it is equal to the current primary key object, and if so, a true is returned. If not equal, then the object is compared to determine whether it is the same type of class as the embeddable primary key class, and a false is returned if it is not the same type. A false is also returned if the object is NULL. Finally, if a Boolean has not yet been returned based upon the conditionals that have been tested, then the object is casted into the same type of object as the primary key class, and each of its fields or properties is compared against those in the current primary key class. If equal, then a true is returned; if not equal, then a false is returned. The following lines of code demonstrate the equals() method:

```
public boolean equals(Object obj) {
    if (obj == this) {
        return true;
    }
    if (!(obj instanceof AuthorWorkPKEmbedded)) {
        return false;
    }
    if (obj == null) {
        return false;
    }
```

```
AuthorWorkPKEmbedded pk = (AuthorWorkPKEmbedded) obj;
return (((bookId == ((AuthorWorkPKEmbedded) obj).getBookId()))
        && ((authorId == ((AuthorWorkPKEmbedded) obj).getAuthorId()))));
}
```

Solution #2 covers the use of a non-embedded primary key. The generation of a non-embeddable primary key is sometimes preferred over the use of an embedded primary key because some believe that the resulting entity class is easier to read. The overall construction of a non-embeddable primary key is basically the same, although there are a few subtle differences. For instance, when developing the primary key class for the non-embeddable primary key, there is no @Embeddable annotation on the class. Another difference that you may notice from the code in Solution #2 is that there is only one constructor used. Of course, an optional second constructor can still be created, accepting an argument for each of the persistent fields or properties that are used to compose the primary key.

Most differences take place within the entity class itself. To use a non-embedded composite primary key, the entity class must be annotated with @IdClass, naming the class that is used to construct the composite primary key. In the case of Solution #2, the @IdClass is as follows:

@IdClass(AuthorWorkPKNonEmbedded.class)

Another big difference in an entity class that uses a non-embeddable composite primary key is that instead of declaring one persistent field or property as an ID using the @Id annotation, the two or more fields or properties that are used to compose the primary key for the entity are declared directly within the entity, and each of them is annotated accordingly. The rest of the implementation is the same as an entity that uses an embedded composite primary key.

Which type of composite key you decide to use is completely a personal preference. Many people use a non-embeddable primary key to make the entity class easier to follow, in that it resembles a standard entity class more closely than an entity class using an embeddable composite primary key. In the end, both will produce the same result and allow entity classes to be created for those database tables that do not contain a single primary key field.

6-6. Defining a One-to-One Relationship

Problem

A database table that is used by your application contains data that has a one-to-one reference with data records from another table. As such, you want to create a one-to-one relationship between two entity objects within your application.

Solution

Create an association between the two tables that have a one-to-one relationship by declaring each of the entity classes themselves as persistent fields or properties within each other using an "owned" relationship, and annotate those fields with @OneToOne. For instance, let's say that each record within the AUTHOR database table can be associated to a record in another table named AUTHOR_DETAIL and vice versa. The AUTHOR_DETAIL table contains contact information for the author, so, in fact, these tables have a one-to-one relationship. To correlate them to each other from within the entity classes, specify the @OneToOne annotation on the field or property that is associated with the corresponding entity class. To have the ability to obtain the full author information from either table, a bidirectional one-to-one relationship needs to be created.

Note   A one-to-one mapping could be unidirectional or bidirectional.
A unidirectional mapping contains only an @OneToOne annotation on the owning entity for the corresponding entity class, whereas a bidirectional mapping contains a @ManyToOne, @OneToMany, or @ManyToMany annotation, depending upon the association.

A relationship is referred to as *owned* if one entity contains a reference to another entity object referring to the entity itself. On the other hand, a relationship where an entity refers to another entity by primary key value is known as an *unowned* relationship.

In this solution, the `Author` entity would contain a `@OneToOne` reference for the `AuthorDetail` entity to create a bidirectional one-to-one mapping. In this code excerpt from the `Author` entity, the `Author` entity is the owning entity:

```
...
@Entity
@Table(name = "AUTHOR")

public class Author implements Serializable {

    private static final long serialVersionUID = 1L;
    @Id
    @Basic(optional = false)
    @SequenceGenerator(name="author_s_generator",
sequenceName="author_s", initialValue=1, allocationSize=1)
    @GeneratedValue(strategy=GenerationType.SEQUENCE,
    generator="author_s_generator")
    @NotNull
    @Column(name = "ID")
    private BigDecimal id;

    @Size(max = 30)
    @Column(name = "LAST")
    private String last;

    @Size(max = 30)
    @Column(name = "FIRST")
    private String first;

    @Lob
    @Column(name = "BIO")
    private String bio;

    @OneToOne
    private AuthorDetail authorId;

    public Author() {
    }

    ...
```

An excerpt for the entity class for the AUTHOR_DETAIL table is shown next. Of course, it has the name of AuthorDetail, and it contains a reference to the Author entity class:

```
...
@Entity
@Table(name = "AUTHOR_DETAIL")

public class AuthorDetail implements Serializable {
    private static final long serialVersionUID = 1L;
    @Id
    @Basic(optional = false)
    @SequenceGenerator(name="author_detail_s_generator",sequenceName=
    "author_detail_s", initialValue=1, allocationSize=1)
    @GeneratedValue(strategy=GenerationType.SEQUENCE,
    generator="author_detail_s_generator")
    @NotNull
    @Column(name = "ID")
    private BigDecimal id;
    @Size(max = 200)
    @Column(name = "ADDRESS1")
    private String address1;
    @Size(max = 200)
    @Column(name = "ADDRESS2")
    private String address2;
    @Size(max = 250)
    @Column(name = "CITY")
    private String city;
    @Size(max = 2)
    @Column(name = "STATE")
    private String state;
    @Size(max = 10)
    @Column(name = "ZIP")
    private String zip;
    @Column(name = "START_DATE")
    @Temporal(TemporalType.DATE)
    private Date startDate;
```

```
@Lob
@Column(name = "NOTES")
private String notes;
@OneToOne(optional=false, mappedBy="authorDetail")
private Author authorId;

public AuthorDetail() {
}
...
```

How It Works

It is not uncommon in the world of relational databases to have one table that depends upon another table. In the case where a record from a table has a one-to-one correspondence to a record from another table, an entity class for one table should be configured to have a one-to-one correspondence with the entity class for the other table. Working with objects is a bit different from working with database records, but the concept is basically the same. Within the database, a unique identifier is used to correlate one table to another. For instance, in the case of this example, the AUTHOR_DETAIL table contains a field named AUTHOR_ID, and it must contain an ID from the AUTHOR database table in order to map the two records together. Owned entity relationships work a bit differently in that the entity object itself is used to map to another entity, rather than an ID number.

When creating a bidirectional one-to-one relationship between entity classes, each entity class must declare the other entity class as a persistent field or property and then designate the type of relationship using the @OneToOne annotation. The @OneToOne annotation is used to designate a one-to-one relationship between the entities. The @OneToOne annotation contains the following optional attributes:

- cascade: The operations (e.g., delete) that must be cascaded to the target of the association. Default: no operations.

- fetch: Whether the association should be lazily loaded or must be eagerly fetched. Default: EAGER.

- optional: Whether the association is optional. For instance, can the entity be persisted without the association? Default: true.

- mappedBy: The field that owns the relationship. Default: "".

In the solution to this recipe, the AuthorDetail entity specifies the @OneToOne annotation prior to the declaration of the Author field specifying the mappedBy and optional attributes. The mappedBy attribute is set to authorDetail, because this will be the mapping field, and the optional attribute is set to false. On the other hand, the Author entity specifies the @OneToOne annotation prior to the declaration of the AuthorDetail field, and there are no attributes specified. In practice, when these entities are used, a bidirectional mapping will be enforced. This means that an AuthorDetail object cannot exist without a corresponding Author object.

6-7. Defining One-to-Many and Many-to-One Relationships

Problem

You want to associate two entity classes to each other, such that one entity object can contain a reference to many of the other entity objects.

Solution

Define a relationship between the two entities by specifying the @OneToMany annotation on a field or property referencing the other entity class within the owning object and by specifying the @ManyToOne annotation on a field or property referencing the owning object within the non-owning entity. For instance, let's say you allow an Author object to contain many different addresses or AuthorDetail objects. In fact, an Author can contain as many addresses as needed. That being the case, there would be one Author object for every AuthorDetail object. Likewise, there could be many AuthorDetail objects for every Author object.

In the following code listings, I will demonstrate the one-to-many relationship between the Author and AuthorDetail objects. First, let's take a look at the Author object, which is otherwise referred to as the *owning* object. This entity class can contain a reference to many different AuthorDetail objects:

```
@Entity
@Table(name = "AUTHOR")

public class Author implements Serializable {

    private static final long serialVersionUID = 1L;
    @Id
    @Basic(optional = false)
    @SequenceGenerator(name="author_s_generator",sequenceName="author_s",
    initialValue=1, allocationSize=1)
    @GeneratedValue(strategy=GenerationType.SEQUENCE,
    generator="author_s_generator")
    @NotNull
    @Column(name = "ID")
    private BigDecimal id;
    @Size(max = 30)
    @Column(name = "LAST")
    private String last;
    @Size(max = 30)
    @Column(name = "FIRST")
    private String first;
    @Lob
    @Column(name = "BIO")
    private String bio;
    @OneToMany(mappedBy="author")
    private Set<AuthorDetail> authorDetail;

    public Author() {
    }
...
```

Next, I'll show the non-owning object, also known as the AuthorDetail class. There may be many AuthorDetail objects within a single Author object:

```
public class AuthorDetail implements Serializable {
    private static final long serialVersionUID = 1L;
    @Id
    @Basic(optional = false)
```

431

```java
@SequenceGenerator(name="author_detail_s_generator",sequenceName=
"author__detail_s", initialValue=1, allocationSize=1)
@GeneratedValue(strategy=GenerationType.SEQUENCE,
generator="author_detail_s_generator")
@NotNull
@Column(name = "ID")
private BigDecimal id;
@Size(max = 200)
@Column(name = "ADDRESS1")
private String address1;
@Size(max = 200)
@Column(name = "ADDRESS2")
private String address2;
@Size(max = 250)
@Column(name = "CITY")
private String city;
@Size(max = 2)
@Column(name = "STATE")
private String state;
@Size(max = 10)
@Column(name = "ZIP")
private String zip;
@Column(name = "START_DATE")
@Temporal(TemporalType.DATE)
private Date startDate;
@Lob
@Column(name = "NOTES")
private String notes;
@ManyToOne
private Author author;

public AuthorDetail() {
}
```

...

Note   To run the `org.jakartaeerecipes.chapter06.recipe06_07.`
`RecipeTest.java` example, please be sure to add both entity classes for this
example to the `persistence.xml` context file. Also, be sure to comment out any
other entities within the persistence context by the same name, because there
cannot be duplicate entities within a single persistence context.

How It Works

The most common database table relationship is the one-to-many or many-to-one
relationship, whereby a record in one table may relate to one or more records within
another table. Consider the scenario from the solution to this recipe, being that a single
AUTHOR table record may have one or more address records within the AUTHOR_DETAIL
table. Defining this relationship within the entity classes is easy, because annotations are
used to indicate the relationship.

When creating a one-to-many relationship within an entity, the entity that
corresponds to the table where one record can correlate to many in another table is
known as the *owning* entity. The entity that correlates to the database table that may
contain more than one record relating to the single record in the other table is known
as the *non-owning* entity. The owning entity class should declare a persistent field or
property for the entity to which it relates and may have more than one related object.
Since there may be more than one non-owning entity object, the owning entity must
declare a Set of the non-owning objects and indicate as such using the @OneToMany
annotation. The mappedBy attribute of the @OneToMany annotation should be set to the
name, which is used within the non-owning entity for declaration of the many-to-one
relationship. In the example, the Author entity contains a one-to-many relationship with
AuthorDetail. Therefore, the Author entity declares the relationship as follows:

```
@OneToMany(mappedBy="author")
private Set<AuthorDetail> authorDetail;
```

On the other end of the spectrum is the many-to-one relationship. In the example, more than one `AuthorDetail` object may relate to one `Author` object. Therefore, a many-to-one relationship should be defined within the `AuthorDetail` entity class for the `Author` entity. This is done by declaring a persistent field or property for the `Author` entity and signifying the relationship with the @ManyToOne annotation as follows:

```
@ManyToOne
private Author author;
```

When working with the entities, a `Set` containing one or more `AuthorDetail` objects should be persisted within a single `Author` object. The following code demonstrates how to use a one-to-many relationship within an application:

```
EntityManagerFactory emf = Persistence.createEntityManagerFactory("JakartaE
ERecipesLOCAL");
EntityManager em = emf.createEntityManager();
try {
    em.getTransaction().begin();
    Author author = new Author();
    author.setFirst("JOE");
    author.setLast("TESTER");
    author.setBio("An author test account.");
    Set detailSet = new HashSet<AuthorDetail>();
    AuthorDetail detail = new AuthorDetail();
    detail.setAddress1("Address 1");
    detail.setAddress2("Address 2");
    detail.setCity("NoMansLand");
    detail.setState("ZZ");
    detail.setZip("12345");
    detail.setNotes("This is a test detail");
    detailSet.add(detail);
    AuthorDetail detail2 = new AuthorDetail();
    detail.setAddress1("Address 1");
    detail.setAddress2("Address 2");
    detail.setCity("NoMansLand");
```

```
        detail.setState("ZZ");
        detail.setZip("12345");
        detail.setNotes("This is a test detail");
        detailSet.add(detail2);
        em.persist(author);
        em.getTransaction().commit();
} catch (Exception ex){
        ex.printStackTrace();
} finally{
                if (em != null){
                    em.close();
                }
}
```

The @OneToMany annotation contains the following optional attributes:

- cascade: The operations (e.g., delete) that must be cascaded to the target of the association. Default: no operations.

- fetch: Whether the association should be lazily loaded or must be eagerly fetched. Default: EAGER.

- orphanRemoval: Whether to apply the remove operation to entities that have been removed from the relationship and to cascade the remove operation to those entities. Default: false.

- targetedEntity: The entity class that is the target of the association. Default: "".

The @ManyToMany annotation contains the following optional attributes:

- cascade: The operations (e.g., delete) that must be cascaded to the target of the association. Default: no operations.

- fetch: Whether the association should be lazily loaded or must be eagerly fetched. Default: EAGER.

- targetedEntity: The entity class that is the target of the association. Default: "".

6-8. Defining a Many-to-Many Relationship

Problem

There are tables within your database that contain cases where multiple records from one table may correlate to multiple records from another. You want to define entity relationships for these tables.

Solution

Create a many-to-many association between the two tables by declaring a field or property within each entity class for a Set of objects corresponding to the entity class on the opposite end. Utilize the @ManyToMany annotation to specify the relationship, and mark the owning side of the relationship by specifying a mappedBy attribute on the non-owning entity's @ManyToMany annotation. Therefore, the class org.jakartaeerecipes. chapter06.recipe06_08.Book is the entity class corresponding to the BOOK database table, and it will contain the @ManyToMany annotation on a declaration for a Set of BookAuthor objects. A mapping table in the database will be "automagically" populated with the associated mappings from the entities. Shown next is the partial code for the Book class, the "owning" entity:

```
@Entity
@Table(name = "BOOK")
@NamedQueries({
    @NamedQuery(name = "Book.findAll", query = "SELECT b FROM Book b"),
})
public class Book implements Serializable {

    private static final long serialVersionUID = 1L;
    @Id
    @Basic(optional = false)
    @SequenceGenerator(name="book_s_generator",sequenceName="book_s",
    initialValue=1, allocationSize=1)
    @GeneratedValue(strategy=GenerationType.SEQUENCE,
    generator="book_s_generator")
    @NotNull
    @Column(name = "ID")
```

```
    private BigDecimal id;
    @Size(max = 150)
    @Column(name = "TITLE")
    private String title;
    @Size(max = 500)
    @Column(name = "IMAGE")
    private String image;
    @Lob
    @Column(name = "DESCRIPTION")
    private String description;
    @ManyToMany
    private Set<BookAuthorMany> bookAuthors;
```

The BookAuthor class is mapped to the Book class using the same concept. The only difference is that it contains a mappedBy attribute within the @ManyToOne annotation to signify the owning table relation:

```
@Entity
@Table(name = "BOOK_AUTHOR")
@NamedQueries({
    @NamedQuery(name = "BookAuthor.findAll", query = "SELECT b FROM
    BookAuthor b"),
    @NamedQuery(name = "BookAuthor.findById", query = "SELECT b FROM
    BookAuthor b WHERE b.id = :id"),
    @NamedQuery(name = "BookAuthor.findByLast", query = "SELECT b FROM
    BookAuthor b WHERE b.last = :last"),
    @NamedQuery(name = "BookAuthor.findByFirst", query = "SELECT b FROM
    BookAuthor b WHERE b.first = :first")})
public class BookAuthorMany implements Serializable {

    private static final long serialVersionUID = 1L;
    @Id
    @Basic(optional = false)
    @SequenceGenerator(name="book_author_s_generator",sequenceName=
    "book_author_s", initialValue=1, allocationSize=1)
    @GeneratedValue(strategy=GenerationType.SEQUENCE,
    generator="book_author_s_generator")
```

```
@NotNull
@Column(name = "ID")
private BigDecimal id;
@Size(max = 30)
@Column(name = "LAST")
private String last;
@Size(max = 30)
@Column(name = "FIRST")
private String first;
@Lob
@Column(name = "BIO")
private String bio;
@ManyToMany(mappedBy="bookAuthors")
private Set<Book> books;
```

Note   The BookAuthor entity has been named BookAuthorMany so that there are no conflicting entity classes within the JakartaEERecipes sources. No entities with duplicate names can exist within the same application.

How It Works

It is possible for databases to contain a many-to-many relationship between two or more different tables. In the case of the example in this recipe, a book may have many authors, and an author may have written many books. On that note, both the database table containing books and the database table containing authors are associated to each other via a many-to-many relationship. It is easy to associate entity classes to one another to form a many-to-many relationship via the use of the @ManyToMany annotation. The @ManyToMany annotation is used to signify that an entity contains a many-to-many association with the annotated persistent field or property.

To create the association, each entity within the many-to-many relationship should declare a field or property for a Set of the associated entity objects. In the case of the example, the Book entity should declare a Set of BookAuthor objects and vice versa. That declaration is then annotated with @ManyToMany, using any attributes that are deemed necessary to make the association. The @ManyToMany annotation contains the following optional attributes:

- targetEntity: The entity class that is the target of the association. This is necessary only if the collection-valued relationship property is not defined using Java generics.

- cascade: The operations that must be cascaded to the target of the association.

- fetch: Whether the association should be lazily loaded or eagerly fetched. The default is javax.persistence.FetchType.LAZY.

- mappedBy: The field that owns the relationship. This is not required if the relationship is unidirectional.

As such, when creating an object of either type, one may persist a Set of the associated entity objects using the persistent field or property that has been annotated with @ManyToMany. The following example demonstrates how to create an entity with a many-to-many relationship (excerpt from the org.jakartaeerecipes.chapter06. recipe06_08.RecipeTest class):

```
EntityManagerFactory emf = Persistence.createEntityManagerFactory("JakartaE
ERecipesLOCAL");
EntityManager em = emf.createEntityManager();
try {
    em.getTransaction().begin();
    Book book1 = new Book();
    book1.setTitle("New Book 1");
    Book book2 = new Book();
    book2.setTitle("New Book 2");

    BookAuthorMany author1 = new BookAuthorMany();
    author1.setFirst("JOE");
    author1.setLast("AUTHOR 1");
```

```
    BookAuthorMany author2 = new BookAuthorMany();
    author2.setFirst("MARYJJOE");
    author2.setLast("AUTHOR 2");

    Set authors = new HashSet();
    authors.add(author1);
    authors.add(author2);

    Set books = new HashSet();
    books.add(book1);
    books.add(book2);

    book1.setBookAuthor(authors);
    author1.setBooks(books);

    em.persist(author1);
    em.persist(book1);
    em.getTransaction().commit();
} catch (Exception ex){
    // Please use a logging framework, such as log4j in production
    System.err.println(ex);
} finally{
            if (em != null){
                em.close();
            }
}
```

When an entity object that contains a many-to-many association with another is created, a record is populated into a mapping table that contains the primary key from each associated table record. You can optionally specify the name of the mapping table by using the annotation @JoinTable and specifying the name of the table. If no @JoinTable annotation is used, then the mapping table name is derived from a concatenation of the two entity classes, beginning with the owning entity. Therefore, in the example, the mapping table name is BOOK_BOOK_AUTHOR, and it contains a field for storing the primary key from the associated records of each table.

6-9. Querying with Named Queries

Problem

Rather than issue SQL or Java Persistence Query Language (JPQL) queries to a persistence unit, you want to define one or more predefined queries for an entity class that can be called by name.

Solution

Specify a single named query or a group of named queries for an entity class. Provide a name for each of the named queries so that they can be called by that name. In this example, a group of named queries will be added to the BookAuthor entity class, and then a separate class may be used to query the entity class using the named queries. We will create an EntityManagerFactory and database connection based upon a persistence.xml file that obtains a local JDBC connection to the database. The following excerpt is taken from the BookAuthor entity, and it demonstrates how to associate named queries with an entity class:

```
@Entity
@Table(name = "BOOK_AUTHOR")
@NamedQueries({
    @NamedQuery(name = "BookAuthor.findAll", query = "SELECT b FROM
    BookAuthor b"),
    @NamedQuery(name = "BookAuthor.findById", query = "SELECT b FROM
    BookAuthor b WHERE b.id = :id"),
    @NamedQuery(name = "BookAuthor.findByLast", query = "SELECT b FROM
    BookAuthor b WHERE b.last = :last"),
    @NamedQuery(name = "BookAuthor.findByFirst", query = "SELECT b FROM
    BookAuthor b WHERE b.first = :first")})
public class BookAuthor implements Serializable {

    private static final long serialVersionUID = 1L;
    @Id
    @Basic(optional = false)
    @SequenceGenerator(name="book_author_s_generator",sequenceName="book_
    author_s", initialValue=1, allocationSize=1)
```

441

```
@GeneratedValue(strategy=GenerationType.SEQUENCE,
generator="book_author_s_generator")
@NotNull
@Column(name = "ID")
private BigDecimal id;
@Size(max = 30)
@Column(name = "LAST")
private String last;
@Size(max = 30)
@Column(name = "FIRST")
private String first;
@Lob
@Column(name = "BIO")
private String bio;

public BookAuthor() {
}
...
```

In another class, the named queries that have been registered with the BookAuthor entity can be called by name. The following excerpt from the org.jakartaeerecipes. chapter06.recipe06_09.RecipeTest class demonstrates how to invoke a named query:

```
EntityManagerFactory emf = Persistence.createEntityManagerFactory("JakartaE
ERecipesLOCAL");
EntityManager em = emf.createEntityManager();
try {
    EntityTransaction entr = em.getTransaction();
    entr.begin();
    Query query = em.createNamedQuery("BookAuthor.findAll");
    List authorList = query.getResultList();
    Iterator authorIterator = authorList.iterator();
    while (authorIterator.hasNext()) {
        BookAuthor author = (BookAuthor) authorIterator.next();
        System.out.print("Name:" + author.getFirst() + " " + author.getLast());
        System.out.println();
    }
```

```
} catch (Exception ex){
    System.err.println(ex);
}
```

How It Works

A named query is contained within an entity class, and it consists of a static JPQL query that is specified via metadata. A given entity class can include zero or more named queries or a group of named queries. A named query is expressed via the @NamedQuery annotation, which contains two attributes: name and query. The name attribute of the @NamedQuery annotation is used to specify a String-based name for the query, and the query attribute is used to specify the static JPQL query against the entity. If an entity contains a group of named query annotations, they can be grouped together using the @NamedQueries annotation. One or more @NamedQuery annotation specifications can exist within a single @NamedQueries annotation, separated by commas.

The JPQL within a named query can contain zero or more bind variables that can have values substituted when the named query is called. To utilize a named query, you must first obtain an active connection to the database. To learn more about obtaining an active connection to the database via an EntityManagerFactory, please refer to Recipe 6-3. Once an active database connection has been obtained, the EntityManager object's createNamedQuery method can be called, passing the string-based name of the named query that you would like to issue. A Query object is returned from the call, and it can be used to obtain the query results.

In the example for this recipe, you can see that the BookAuthor entity is queried, returning a List of BookAuthor objects. A simple while loop is used to iterate through the List of objects, printing the first and last names from each BookAuthor object to System.out (the server log), although use of a logging framework such as Log4j is encouraged.

6-10. Performing Validation on Entity Fields
Problem

You want to specify validation rules for specific fields within an entity class to prevent invalid data from being inserted into the database.

Solution

Include bean validation constraints within an entity class. Bean validation constraints are annotations that are applied to persistent fields or properties of an entity class. The bean validation mechanism provides a number of annotations that can be placed on fields or properties in order to validate data in different ways. In the following example, the AuthorWork entity has been enhanced to include bean validation for the id, address1, state, and zip fields:

```
...
@Entity
@Table(name = "AUTHOR_DETAIL")

public class AuthorDetailBeanValidation implements Serializable {
    private static final long serialVersionUID = 1L;
    @Id
    @Basic(optional = false)
    @SequenceGenerator(name="author_detail_s_generator",sequenceName=
    "author__detail_s", initialValue=1, allocationSize=1)
    @GeneratedValue(strategy=GenerationType.SEQUENCE,
    generator="author_detail_s_generator")
    @NotNull
    @Column(name = "ID")
    private BigDecimal id;
    @Size(max = 200)
    @Pattern(regexp="", message="Invalid Address")
    @Column(name = "ADDRESS1")
    private String address1;
    @Size(max = 200)
    @Column(name = "ADDRESS2")
    private String address2;
    @Size(max = 250)
    @Column(name = "CITY")
    private String city;
    @Size(max = 2)
    @Column(name = "STATE")
```

```
@Pattern(regexp="^(?-i:A[LKSZRAEP]|C[AOT]|D[EC]|F[LM]|G[AU]|HI|I[ADLN]|
K[SY]|LA|M[ADEHINOPST]|N[CDEHJMVY]|O[HKR]|P[ARW]|RI|S[CD]|T[NX]|UT|V[AI
T]|W[AIVY])$",
        message="Invalid State")
private String state;
@Size(max = 10)
@Column(name = "ZIP")
@Pattern(regexp="^\\d{5}\\p{Punct}?\\s?(?:\\d{4})?$",
        message="Invalid Zip Code")
private String zip;
@Column(name = "START_DATE")
@Temporal(TemporalType.DATE)
private Date startDate;
@Lob
@Column(name = "NOTES")
private String notes;
@ManyToOne
private AuthorBeanValidation author;
...
```

In an attempt to insert a value that does not conform to the validation rules, the object will not be persisted, and the message correlating to the bean validation annotation will be displayed.

How It Works

It is always a good idea to utilize a data validation strategy when working with user input, especially if the data will be persisted into a database or other data stores for later use. The Java Persistence API allows bean validation to occur within an entity class, whereby a developer can place validation rules directly on a persistent field or property. By default, the persistence provider automatically invokes validation processes on entities containing bean validation annotation constraints after the PrePersist, PreUpdate, and PreRemove life-cycle events occur. At that time, any value that does not adhere to the given validation constraint will cause the entity to stop persistence and display an associated message.

The details of bean validation are the same, whether it be on a Plain Old Java Object (POJO) or an entity class. In the case of an entity class, either the persistent field or property can be annotated with the desired bean validation constraint. To see a list of possible bean validation constraint annotations, please refer to Chapter 10.

In the example for this recipe, the @NotNull and @Pattern annotations are specified on persistent properties of the AuthorDetail entity. Specifically, the id field is annotated with @NotNull, and validation will fail in an attempt to enter a NULL value for that field. The state and zip fields contain a @Pattern annotation, along with a corresponding regular expression and failure message. If the values for those fields do not adhere to the regular expression that has been specified, then the message that is assigned to the message attribute of the @Pattern annotation will be displayed via a JSF view by the h:message component corresponding to the validated field. What if you want to apply a set of regular expression patterns to a given field or property? Such a feat can be done using the @Pattern.List syntax, whereby the list would contain a comma-separated list of @Pattern annotations. The following lines of code demonstrate this technique:

```
@Pattern.List({
    @Pattern(regexp="regex-pattern", message="Error Message"),
    @Pattern(regexp="another regex-pattern", message("Error Message 2")
})
```

Bean validation is a good way to ensure that invalid data is not submitted to a data store. However, most advanced desktop or web applications today use a couple tiers of validation to make the user experience more convenient. Many times, web applications use JavaScript field validation first so that users do not have to submit a page in order to see their validation errors displayed on the screen. If using JSF or other web frameworks, some components allow direct access to bean validation, in which cases an Ajax submission of a given field or property will occur behind the scenes, allowing the bean validation to take place without page submission. Whatever tact you take, bean validation within entity classes is important and should become a handy tool to add to your arsenal.

6-11. Generating Database Schema Objects Automatically

Problem

You are developing an application and want to automatically have your entity classes generated into tables within the underlying database.

Solution

Use the automatic schema generation that was introduced in EJB 3.2. Schema generation is determined by the object-relational metadata of the `persistence.xml` unit, unless custom scripts are provided for the generation. The application developer can package scripts as part of the persistence unit or can supply URLs to the location of the scripts for schema generation. The execution of such scripts can be carried out by the container itself, or the container may direct the persistence provider to take care of script execution. Table 6-3 in the "How It Works" section of this recipe lists the different `persistence.xml` or `EntityManagerFactory` properties that are used to configure schema generation. These properties are passed as a `Map` argument from the container to the `PersistenceProvider generateSchema` method or the `createContainerEntityManagerFactory` method.

To define the different objects that need to be generated, annotate entity classes accordingly. The standard entity class annotations (`@Table`, `@Id`, etc.) determine what objects are created and how they are structured. For more information regarding the specification of annotations within entity classes in order to generate schema objects, please refer to the annotations listed in Table 6-4 within the "How It Works" section of this recipe.

How It Works

Schema generation refers to the creation of underlying database tables, views, constraints, and other database artifacts. Prior to the Java EE 7 release, schema generation had been automated only via the use of an IDE such as NetBeans or Eclipse. However, the EE 7 release took a step toward breaking this dependency on an IDE by allowing schema generation to become automated by configuring an appropriate `persistence.xml` file for an application.

Schema generation can be applied directly to the database, or it can generate SQL scripts that can be manually applied to the database (or both), depending upon which options are configured for the application. Schema generation may occur prior to application deployment or when an `EntityManagerFactory` is created as part of the application deployment and initialization. To perform schema generation, the container may call the `PersistenceProvider generateSchema` method separately from and/or prior to the entity manager factory for the persistence unit. The `createContainerEntityManagerFactory` call can accept additional information to cause the generation of schema constructs to occur as part of the entity manager factory creation or initialization process. Furthermore, this information can determine whether the database is manipulated directly or whether SQL scripts are created, or both.

Note   Schema generation is also available outside of a managed container (e.g., web application server) in Java SE environments. To perform schema generation in a Java SE environment, the application may call the `Persistence generateSchema` method separately from and/or prior to the creation of the entity manager factory or may pass information to the `createEntityManagerFactory` method to cause schema generation to occur as part of the entity manager factory creation.

Table 6-3 lists the different schema generation properties that can be specified in the `persistence.xml` file in order to automate schema generation.

Table 6-3. *Schema Generation Properties*

Property	Purpose
`schema-generation-action`	Controls the action to be taken by the persistence provider with regard to object generation and destruction. **Values**: none, `create`, `drop-and-create`, and `drop`.
`schema-generation-target`	Controls whether schema is to be created within the database, whether Data Definition Language (DDL) scripts are to be created, or both. **Values**: `database`, `scripts`, and `database-and-scripts`.
`ddl-create-script-target`, `ddl-drop-script-target`	Controls target locations for writing scripts if the schema-generation-target specifies script generation. Writers are preconfigured for the persistence provider. **Values**: `java.io.Writer` (e.g., `MyWriter.class`) or URL strings.
`ddl-create-script-source`, `ddl-drop-script-source`	Specifies locations from which DDL scripts are to be read. Readers are preconfigured for the persistence provider. **Values**: `java.io.Reader` (e.g., `MyReader.class`) or URL strings.
`sql-load-script-source`	Specifies the file location of the SQL bulk load script. **Values**: `java.io.Reader` (e.g., `MyReader.class`) or URL string.
`schema-generation-connection`	JDBC connection to be used for performing schema generation.
`database-product-name`, `database-major-version`, `database-minor-version`	Needed if scripts are to be generated. Values are those obtained from JDBC `DatabaseMetaData`.
`create-database-schemas`	Whether the persistence provider needs to create schema in addition to creating database objects such as tables, sequences, constraints, and so on. **Values**: `true` and `false`.

Programmatically, schema generation is determined by a series of annotations that are placed in entity classes. The @Table annotation denotes an entity mapping to an underlying database table. By default, a table is generated for each top-level entity and includes columns based upon the specified attributes for that entity. Therefore, the @Column and @JoinColumn annotations are used for generating such columns for a table. Column ordering is not determined based upon the ordering of @Column or @JoinColumn annotations. If column ordering is important, then a Data Definition Language (DDL) script must be supplied for generating the table. Other annotations and annotation attributes, such as @Id, also play important roles in schema generation. Table 6-4 lists the different annotations that are involved in schema generation, along with a brief description and the elements that can be populated for further control over the generated schema.

Table 6-4. *Schema Generation Annotations*

Annotation	Description	Elements
@Table	Used for generating tables. By default, the table name is generated from the entity name, and the entity name is defaulted from the class name.	
@SecondaryTable	A secondary table is created to partition the mapping of entity state across multiple tables.	
@CollectionTable	A collection table is created for mapping of an element collection. The Column, AttributeOverride, and AssociationOverride annotations may be used to override CollectionTable mappings.	
@JoinTable	Used in mapping of associations. By default, join tables are created for the mapping of many-to-many relationships and unidirectional one-to-many relationships.	

(continued)

Table 6-4. (*continued*)

Annotation	Description	Elements
@TableGenerator	Used to store generated primary key values.	
@Column	Determines the name and configuration for a column within a table.	unique, nullable, columnDefinition, table, length, precision, scale, name
@MapKeyColumn	Specifies the mapping name of a key column of a map when the key is of basic type.	unique, nullable, columnDefinition, table, length, precision, scale
@Enumerated, @MapKeyEnumerated	Controls whether string- or integer-valued columns are generated for basic attributes of enumerated types and therefore impact the default column mapping of these types.	
@Temporal, @MapKeyTemporal	Controls whether date-, time-, or timestamp-valued columns are generated for basic attributes of temporal types and therefore impact the default column mappings for these types.	
@Lob	Specifies that a persistent attribute is to be mapped to a database large object type.	
@OrderColumn	Specifies the generation of a column that is used to maintain the persistent ordering of a list that is represented in an element collection, one-to-many, or many-to-many relationship.	name, nullable, columnDefinition

(*continued*)

Table 6-4. (*continued*)

Annotation	Description	Elements
@DiscriminatorColumn	Generated for the SINGLE_TABLE mapping strategy and may optionally be generated by the provider for use with the JOINED inheritance strategy.	
@Version	Specifies the generation of a column to serve as an entity's optimistic lock.	
@Id	Specifies a database primary key column. Use of the @Id annotation results in the creation of a primary key which consists of the corresponding column or columns.	
@EmbeddedId	Specifies an embedded attribute whose corresponding columns formulate a database primary key. Use of the @EmbeddedId annotation results in the creation of a primary key consisting of the corresponding columns.	
@GeneratedValue	Indicates a primary key that should have an automatically generated value. If a strategy is indicated, the provider must use it if it is supported by the target database.	
@JoinColumn	The @JoinColumn annotation is typically used for specifying a foreign key mapping.	name, referencedColumnName, unique, nullable, columnDefinition, table, foreignKey

(*continued*)

Table 6-4. (*continued*)

Annotation	Description	Elements
@MapKeyJoinColumn	Specifies foreign key mappings to entities that are map keys in element collections or relationships that consist of map values.	name, referencedColumnName, unique, nullable, columnDefinition, table, foreignKey
@PrimaryJoinKeyColumn	Specifies that a primary key column is to be used as a foreign key. This annotation is used in the specification of the JOINED mapping strategy and for joining a secondary table to a primary table in a one-to-one relationship mapping.	
@ForeignKey	Used within the JoinColumn, JoinColumns, MapKeyJoinColumn, MapKeyJoinColumns, PrimaryKeyJoinColumn, and PrimaryKeyJoinColumns annotations to specify or override a foreign key constraint.	
@SequenceGenerator	Creates a database sequence to be used for ID generation.	
@Index	Generates an index consisting of the specified columns.	
@UniqueConstraint	Generates a unique constraint for the given table.	

As per Table 6-4, there are a couple of annotations that have been created specifically to facilitate schema generation. The new annotations are @Index and @ForeignKey, where @Index is responsible for generating an index of the specified columns. @ForeignKey is used to define a foreign key on a table.

6-12. Mapping Date-Time Values

Problem

You wish to utilize the Date-Time API to persist Java LocalDate values to the database.

Solution

Use JPA 2.2 support for the Date-Time API to work with the LocalDate. Since the JPA 2.2 maintenance release supports the Java Date-Time API, it is possible to make use of the date and time objects that were introduced in Java 8 to persist without the need for the @Temporal annotation. The following entity class demonstrates how to achieve this feat:

```
public class Book implements Serializable {
    private static final long serialVersionUID = 1L;
    @Id
    @Basic(optional = false)
    @Column(name = "ID")
    private BigDecimal id;
    @Size(max = 150)
    @Column(name = "TITLE")
    protected String title;
    @Size(max = 500)
    @Column(name = "IMAGE")
    private String image;
    @Lob
    @Column(name = "DESCRIPTION")
    private String description;
    @Column(name = "PUBLISH_DATE")
    private LocalDate publishDate;
    @ManyToMany(mappedBy="books")
    private Set<BookAuthor> authors;
    @OneToMany(mappedBy="book", cascade=CascadeType.ALL)
    private List<Chapter> chapters = null;
```

```
    public Book() {
    }
. . .
}
```

As you can see, the entity class contains a `LocalDate` field that includes no special annotations.

How it Works

When Java 8 was initially released, Java EE and JPA did not have support for the updated Date-Time API. Therefore, in order to utilize the newer date and time objects, one had to develop a converter to perform automatic conversion between the new date and time objects and `java.util.Date`. Since JPA maintenance release 2.2, this issue has been mitigated, as the Java Date-Time API is officially supported, making it easier than ever before to persist fields that contain date and time values.

In order to map a database column that contains a date to a Java object, simply annotate the column with the `@Column` annotation, specifying the column name if you wish. The `@Temporal` annotation is no longer required. Apply one of the following data types to the class field:

- java.time.LocalDate

- java.time.LocalTime

- java.time.LocalDateTime

- java.time.OffsetTime

- java.time.OffsetDateTime

It is as simple as that! The JPA Date-Time support has provided the ability to utilize the API within Java EE applications without the requirement of a converter. It is also cut down on code because `@Temporal` is no longer required.

6-13. Using the Same Annotation Many Times

Problem

You wish to utilize the same annotation a number of different times within a given class. For instance, suppose that you would like to use more than one @PersistenceContext annotation within a single class.

Solution

Take advantage of the Java 8 repeatable annotation support that has been provided with JPA 2.2. This added support provides the ability to use repeatable annotations for a number of situations. In the following example, the @NamedQuery annotation is utilized more than one time in the same class. Prior to JPA 2.2, this would not work without first grouping the annotations together into a single container annotation:

```
@Entity
@Table(name = "EMPLOYEE")
@XmlRootElement

@NamedQuery(name = "Employee.findAll", query = "SELECT e FROM Employee e")
@NamedQuery(name = "Employee.findById", query = "SELECT e FROM Employee
e WHERE e.id = :id")
@NamedQuery(name = "Employee.findByFirst", query = "SELECT e FROM Employee
e WHERE e.first = :first")
@NamedQuery(name = "Employee.findByLast", query = "SELECT e FROM Employee
e WHERE e.last = :last")
@NamedQuery(name = "Employee.findByAge", query = "SELECT e FROM Employee
e WHERE e.age = :age")
@NamedStoredProcedureQuery(name = "createEmp", procedureName = "CREATE_EMP")
public class Employee implements Serializable {

    private static final long serialVersionUID = 1L;
    // @Max(value=?)  @Min(value=?)//if you know range of your decimal
fields consider using these annotations to enforce field validation
    @Id
```

```
@Basic(optional = false)
//@NotNull
@Column(name = "ID")
private BigDecimal id;
@Size(max = 30)
@Column(name = "FIRSTNAME")
private String first;
@Size(max = 30)
@Column(name = "LASTNAME")
private String last;
@Column(name = "AGE")
private BigInteger age;
@ManyToOne(optional = false)
@JoinColumn(name = "JOB_ID", nullable = false)
private Jobs job;
@Column(name = "STATUS")
private String status;

public Employee() {
}

. . .
}
```

How It Works

Repeatable annotation support came to the Java platform with the release of Java 8. This enables one to utilize the same annotation more than once within a portion of code. Annotations are not repeatable by default; the annotation class must be designated as such with the @Repeatable annotation. Therefore, not all annotations will be usable more than once within a class. The following annotations were made repeatable for the Java EE 8 release:

- AssociationOverride

- AttributeOverride

- Convert

- JoinColumn

- MapKeyJoinColumn

- NamedEntityGraph

- NamedNativeQuery

- NamedQuery

- NamedStoredProcedureQuery

- PersistenceContext

- PersistenceUnit

- PrimaryKeyJoinColumn

- SecondaryTable

- SqlResultSetMapping

As mentioned previously, annotations must be designated as repeatable by marking them with the @Repeatable annotation. Therefore, if you have created a custom annotation and you would like to make it repeatable, then you can do so.

CHAPTER 7

Jakarta NoSQL

Microservices and applications built for the cloud sometimes benefit from a non-centralized database, and many of the most commonly used are NoSQL databases. NoSQL means "Not Only SQL," and such databases do not follow the conventional Relational Database Management System (RDBMS) model. The first new specification that was created as part of the Eclipse Jakarta EE Specification Process is Jakarta NoSQL. Although Jakarta NoSQL was not released as part of Jakarta EE 8, it is quite stable and expected to be a part of the platform within the coming releases. Please keep track of the project on `https://projects.eclipse.org/proposals/jakarta-nosql`. This chapter provides a sneak preview of the Jakarta NoSQL specification, which includes two communication APIs: Diana and, a driver for most of the well-known NoSQL databases, the Jakarta NoSQL Database Driver.

There are a few different types of NoSQL databases that can be used. The API supports key-value, column, document, and graph database types. The Diana API consists of three different modules for working with these database types:

- diana-key-value

- diana-column

- diana-document

The diana-core module provides common functionality for each of these three APIs. This chapter will not dive deep into the functionality of these APIs, but rather, it will provide a brief overview for utilization of Jakarta NoSQL with one of the most widely used NoSQL databases, MongoDB. It will also briefly touch upon the use of key-value–oriented databases such as Hazelcast.

© Josh Juneau 2020
J. Juneau, *Jakarta EE Recipes*, https://doi.org/10.1007/978-1-4842-5587-2_7

> **Note** MongoDB is a document database, and it is helpful to know that while working with a document database, we refer to collections of data. A collection in a document database is analogous to a table in an RDBMS. To learn more about MongoDB, please refer to the online documentation: `https://docs.mongodb.com/manual/`.

This chapter will cover some high-level basics for using the Jakarta NoSQL specification. As the specification is not part of the Jakarta EE 8 release, portions of it are subject to change prior to its inclusion with the Jakarta EE platform.

7-1. Configuring for Jakarta NoSQL
Problem

You would like to configure your Jakarta EE application to work with a NoSQL database, rather than a traditional Relational Database Management System.

Solution

Add the appropriate dependencies to your project, depending upon the type of NoSQL database that you wish to utilize. Next, create a class to load the database and enable it for use within the application. In this example, a document database will be configured using MongoDB.

The first dependency that is required for working with Jakarta NoSQL is Artemis, which is the core API.

> **Note** Please refer to the Artemis documentation at `https://github.com/eclipse/jnosql-artemis`.

```
<dependency>
    <groupId>org.jnosql.artemis</groupId>
    <artifactId>artemis-core</artifactId>
    <version>version</version>
</dependency>
```

The Artemis dependency that pertains to the type of database in use is also required. There are four Artemis dependency types:

- artemis-document

- artemis-key-value

- artemis-column

- artemis-graphing

Next, the API for the database type will need to be added to the project. The following excerpts show the Maven dependencies for each of the Diana APIs. Only one of the following dependencies is required to work with the API in a project, depending upon which type of NoSQL database is being used:

```
<--diana-document -->
<dependency>
    <groupId>org.jnosql.diana</groupId>
    <artifactId>diana-document</artifactId>
    <version>0.0.5</version>
</dependency>

<!-- diana-key-value -->
<dependency>
    <groupId>org.jnosql.diana</groupId>
    <artifactId>diana-key-value</artifactId>
    <version>0.0.5</version>
</dependency>

<!-- diana-column -->
<dependency>
    <groupId>org.jnosql.diana</groupId>
    <artifactId>diana-column</artifactId>
    <version>0.0.5</version>
</dependency>
```

There is a required driver dependency for supporting most NoSQL databases, and it is provided by Eclipse Jakarta NoSQL. Depending upon which type of database is being used, the correct driver needs to be pulled into the project. A list of each driver is located on GitHub: https://github.com/eclipse/jnosql-diana-driver.

461

In the following POM excerpt, the mongodb driver is being utilized:

```
<dependency>
    <groupId>org.jnosql.diana</groupId>
    <artifactId>diana-document</artifactId>
    <version>0.0.5</version>
</dependency>
<dependency>
    <groupId>org.jnosql.diana</groupId>
    <artifactId>mongodb-driver</artifactId>
    <version>0.0.5</version>
</dependency>
```

Lastly, provide the appropriate configuration via a properties file on the CLASSPATH or as hard-coded values. The configuration should include the host name, port number, and possibly credentials. In this case, hard-coded values are added to configure the database within a class. In the following source code, a class named DocumentCollectionManagerProducer is used to get the database configured and generate a DocumentCollectionManager, which can be used to work with the data:

```
import java.util.Collections;
import java.util.Map;
import javax.annotation.PostConstruct;
import javax.enterprise.context.ApplicationScoped;
import javax.enterprise.inject.Produces;
import org.jnosql.diana.api.Settings;
import org.jnosql.diana.api.document.DocumentCollectionManager;
import org.jnosql.diana.api.document.DocumentCollectionManagerFactory;
import org.jnosql.diana.api.document.DocumentConfiguration;
import org.jnosql.diana.mongodb.document.MongoDBDocumentConfiguration;

@ApplicationScoped
public class DocumentCollectionManagerProducer {

    // Set the name of the database
  private static final String COLLECTION = "acmepools";

  private DocumentConfiguration configuration;
```

```
private DocumentCollectionManagerFactory managerFactory;

@PostConstruct
public void init() {
  configuration = new MongoDBDocumentConfiguration();
  Map<String, Object> settings = Collections.singletonMap("mongodb-
  server-host-1", "localhost:27017");
  managerFactory = configuration.get(Settings.of(settings));
}

@Produces
public DocumentCollectionManager getManager() {
  return managerFactory.get(COLLECTION);

}
}
```

The DocumentCollectionManagerProducer can be injected into a class, and the DocumentCollectionManager can then be called upon to work with the data.

How It Works

As with any database configuration for an application, a NoSQL database requires a bit of setup. The configuration that is necessary for a NoSQL application can be equated to the DriverManager or EntityManager configuration for JDBC or JPA.

To begin, there are a number of dependencies, but the nice thing is that the Jakarta NoSQL specification contains all of them, so there is no need to rummage around the Web or Maven Central to find them. In order to incorporate the appropriate dependencies for use with NoSQL, you must also know which type of database is being used. There are different dependencies for each of the NoSQL database types, as mentioned in the previous section.

The communication layer (aka the Diana API) defines three modules: diana-key-value, diana-column, and diana-document. Each of these modules corresponds to the respective NoSQL database type. The NoSQL mapping databases are not covered by the Diana module, as they are already handled by Apache TinkerPop (https://tinkerpop.apache.org/).

Note   Apache TinkerPop is a graph computing framework for both graph databases and graph analytic systems.

Each of the database types requires a necessary setting to be put into place, such as database host and port. In a document-, column-, or key-value–oriented database, these settings can be placed into a configuration file and then put onto the CLASSPATH. They can also be hard-coded within an application, as follows:

```
Map<String, Object> map = new HashMap<>();
map.put("mongodb-server-host-1", "localhost:27017");
```

The next API, also known as Artemis, is used for mapping NoSQL database data to Java classes, much like object-relational mapping with standard databases. The artemis-configuration dependency is required to use the mapping API, as well as the corresponding Artemis driver for the database type that is in use. In the case of using a document database, the artemis-document dependency is used. The important piece of the configuration is to initialize the database by providing the host, port, username, and password (if required). There are various methodologies which could be followed for initializing the database, from using a main method in a Java SE application to using an @ApplicationScoped CDI bean in an enterprise application.

In the example, an @ApplicationScoped bean contains the initialization of the database within a method annotated with @PostConstruct. Any methods designated as @PostConstruct are executed directly after the bean has been initialized. Since the bean in the example is application scoped, it is started up when the application starts. In this case, a DocumentConfiguration is instantiated from MongoDbDocumentConfiguration. A Map is then used to store some configuration settings, which could alternatively be placed into a properties file on the CLASSPATH. The Map of settings is then set into the DocumentConfiguration, and a DocumentCollectionManagerFactory is returned. This manager will be used by the application to perform database interactions.

7-2. Writing a Query for a Document Database Problem

You have configured an application to utilize a document-based NoSQL database, and now you wish to obtain data by creating a query.

Solution

Utilize the DocumentCollectionManager or a DocumentTemplate that was generated as part of the configuration (Recipe 7-1) to initiate a query against a collection. In this example, the DocumentTemplate is injected into a managed bean, and it is used to query the collection of Pool within the acmepools database. The following example shows an excerpt of the code for a query within the managed bean:

```
import org.jnosql.artemis.document.DocumentTemplate;
import org.jnosql.diana.api.document.Document;
import org.jnosql.diana.api.document.DocumentEntity;
import org.jnosql.diana.api.document.DocumentQuery;
import static org.jnosql.diana.api.document.query.DocumentQueryBuilder.
select;
. . .
@Inject
    DocumentTemplate documentTemplate;
. . .
DocumentQuery query = select().from("Pool")
                .where("_id").eq(id).build();
```

This particular query selects from the Pool collection where the _id is equal to the provided value. To obtain the value from the query, it can be passed to an injected DocumentTemplate instance, which will return an optional result:

```
. . .
Optional<Customer> customerOptional = documentTemplate.singleResult(query);
        System.out.println("Entity found: " + customerOptional.get());
```

How It Works

When querying with the Jakarta NoSQL API, it has a very similar feel to utilizing the CriteriaQuery API. To create a DocumentQuery, use the DocumentQueryBuilder by importing the static org.jnosql.diana.api.document.query.DocumentQueryBuilder. select and then "building" a query by calling upon the builder methods. In the example, the query simply selects from the Pool collection where the _id is equal to the id parameter. Tables 7-1 and 7-2 show the various builder methods that can be utilized to help generate queries for a document database.

Table 7-1. *DocumentQuery.DocumentFrom Methods*

Builder Method	Description
`limit`	Defines max number of results to retrieve
`orderBy(String name)`	Determines the order by which results will be displayed
`skip(long skip)`	Defines position of the first retrieved result
`where(String name)`	Starts new condition defining the column name

Table 7-2. *DocumentQuery.DocumentWhere Methods*

Builder Method	Description
`between`	Creates between condition
`eq`	Creates an equal condition
`gt`	Creates greater than condition
`gte`	Creates greater than or equal condition
`in`	Creates in condition
`like`	Creates like condition
`lt`	Creates less than condition
`lte`	Creates less than or equal condition
`not`	Creates the not equal condition

Given the number of different builders that can be used to obtain information, there are plenty of ways to retrieve the data that is required from your collection. If no builder methods are applied to a query at all, then all records of the collection will be retrieved. Such a case is presented with the following example:

```
DocumentQuery query = select().from("Pool").build();
List<DocumentEntity> entities = manager.getManager().select(query);
```

> **Note**   If using a different type of NoSQL database, there are similar builder techniques that can be used for retrieving the data. For more information on using Jakarta NoSQL to query each of the types of NoSQL databases, please refer to the documentation: `www.jnosql.org/getting_started.html`.

One can either inject a `DocumentTemplate` into a CDI bean as shown in the example or obtain it from an `SeContainer` if using in a Java SE environment. Taking a look at the latter, one can obtain an `SeContainer` by calling upon an `SeContainerInitializer` and then obtain a `DocumentTemplate` from that container by passing `DocumentTemplate.class` to the container `select()` method:

```
try (SeContainer se = SeContainerInitializer.newInstance().initialize()){
    DocumentTemplate documentTemplate = se.select(DocumentTemplate.class).
    get();
    DocumentQuery query = select().from("Pool").build();

    List<Pool> results = documentTemplate.select(query);

    . . .
}
```

The Jakarta NoSQL specification allows one to query document-oriented NoSQL databases, as well as other types of NoSQL databases, in a standardized manner.

7-3. Inserting, Updating, and Deleting from a Document-Oriented Database

Problem

You wish to utilize your application to perform standard CRUD operations against a document-oriented NoSQL database.

Solution

Utilize the `DocumentCollectionManagerFactory` that was generated as part of the configuration (Recipe 7-1) to obtain a manager which can be used for creating, reading, updating, or deleting data from the document-oriented database.

Inserting

There are a couple of different techniques that can be used for generating new entities within a document-oriented database: utilization of the DocumentTemplate or utilization of a DocumentEntity.

When using a DocumentTemplate to create an entity, the workflow is very similar to that of the Jakarta Persistence API along with the Criteria API. Taking a look at the following code, which was excerpted from the AcmePoolsService class within the AcmePoolsNoSql project, one can see that objects are created using plain Java, and then they are inserted into the database using the document template. In this case, the DocumentTemplate has been injected into the CDI bean:

```
Random random = new Random();
Long id = random.nextLong();

Customer customer = new Customer("Josh", "Juneau", "123 AcmeWay",
"JavaLand", "JJ", "12345");

Pool pool = new Pool(id, 32.0, 16.0, customer);

Pool savedPool = documentTemplate.insert(pool);
```

Use the DocumentEntity construct along with a DocumentCollectionManager Factory to generate a new entity for addition to an existing collection of data, and then use the manager to insert the entity. In the following example, a new entity is created and added to the existing pool collection of data:

```
DocumentEntity documentEntity = DocumentEntity.of("Pool");
documentEntity.add(Document.of("_id", id));
documentEntity.add(Document.of("length", 30.0));
documentEntity.add(Document.of("width", 15.0));
DocumentEntity saved = manager.getManager().insert(documentEntity);
```

Updating

To update an entity, modify the DocumentEntity instance and then pass it to the DocumentCollectionManagerProducer update() method:

```
DocumentEntity saved = manager.getManager().insert(documentEntity);
```

```
//Update Document
saved.add(Document.of("Customer", "Juneau"));
DocumentEntity updated = manager.getManager().update(saved);
```

Deleting

The DocumentDeleteQuery interface can be used to easily delete an entity from a collection of data:

```
DocumentDeleteQuery delete = delete().from("Pools").where("length").
gte(36.0).build();
        manager.getManager().delete(delete);
```

How It Works

Whether utilizing a DocumentTemplate or a DocumentCollectionManager, the Jakarta NoSQL API is a pleasure to use for performing CRUD operations against a NoSQL database. The DocumentTemplate can be used to perform transactions against org. jnosql.artemis.Entity classes, much like the Java Persistence API. When utilizing a DocumentCollectionManager, persistence methods can be called upon to invoke behavior, passing DocumentEntity objects or DocumentQuery objects.

A DocumentTemplate can either be injected via CDI or created from an SEContainer instance. Once created, it can be used to perform operations with entity classes. In the example for inserting, the Pool entity was created and then inserted using the DocumentTemplate.insert() method. Table 7-3 shows the different methods available via a DocumentTemplate.

Table 7-3. *Methods of the DocumentTemplate Interface*

Method	Description
insert(T entity)	Inserts an entity into a collection
insert(T entity, Duration)	Inserts an entity with time to live
insert(Iterable<T> entities)	Saves a collection of entities
insert(Iterable<T> entities, Duration)	Saves a collection of entities with time to live
update(T entity)	Updates an entity
update(Iterable<T> entities)	Updates a collection of entities
delete(DocumentDeleteQuery)	Deletes an entity obtained via query
select(DocumentQuery)	Selects entities from a query
query(String query)	Executes a query
singleResult(String query)	Executes a query and returns a single unique result
prepare(String query)	Creates a PreparedStatement from a query.
find(T entity, ID)	Find an entity class by ID
delete(T entity, ID)	Delete an entity class by ID
count(String documentCollection)	Returns the number of elements in a document collection
count(T entityType)	Returns the number of elements in a document collection
singleResult(DocumentQuery)	Executes a query and returns a single unique result

The remainder of the examples in this recipe demonstrated various persistence transactions utilizing a DocumentCollectionManager. This, too, can be injected via CDI or created from an SeContainer instance. In a Jakarta EE application, typically the configuration will take place within a single @ApplicationScoped bean, which @Produces a DocumentCollectionManager (see Recipe 7-1).

When using a DocumentCollectionManager, call upon the various persistence methods, passing either DocumentQuery or DocumentEntity objects.

In the examples, a DocumentEntity for a Pool is constructed, and inserted using the DocumentCollectionManager. Taking a different approach in the next example, a DocumentDeleteQuery is constructed to delete an entity from the Pool collection. The DocumentCollectionManager delete() method is then invoked, passing the DocumentDeleteQuery object. Table 7-4 shows the methods available on a DocumentCollectionManager.

Table 7-4. *Methods of the DocumentCollectionManager Interface*

Method	Description
close()	Closes a resource
delete(DocumentDeleteQuery)	Deletes an entity obtained via a query
insert(DocumentEntity)	Inserts an entity
insert(DocumentEntity, Duration)	Inserts an entity with time to live
insert(Iterable<DocumentEntity>)	Inserts a collection of DocumentEntity
insert(Iterable<DocumentEntity>, Duration)	Inserts a collection of DocumentEntity with time to live
select(DocumentQuery)	Selects one or more entities from a collection using a DocumentQuery
singleResult(DocumentQuery)	Selects a single unique result from a collection using a DocumentQuery
update(DocumentEntity)	Updates an entity
update(Iterable<DocumentEntity>)	Updates a collection of DocumentEntity

Either way you choose to perform CRUD operations, the API is straightforward. The choice of which option to use is in the hands of the developer. It is time to choose the best tool for the job.

7-4. Working with a Key-Value Database

Problem

You wish to place values into a key-value database and also retrieve them at a later point. For example, you wish to utilize Hazelcast with the Jakarta NoSQL API.

Solution

Configure your application to work with a key-value NoSQL database. Once configured, utilize a `KeyValueConfiguration` to generate a `BucketManagerFactory`. The `BucketManagerFactory` can then be used to work with key/value pairs.

The following dependency will need to be added to your project in order to support Hazelcast with Jakarta NoSQL, along with the standard artemis-core dependency:

```
<dependency>
    <groupId>org.jnosql.diana</groupId>
    <artifactId>hazelcast-driver</artifactId>
    <version>version</version>
</dependency>
```

Note   Hazelcast is an open source in-memory data grid based on Java.

Once the dependency has been added, configuration can take place. The following sample source code demonstrates key-value database configuration:

```
KeyValueConfiguration configuration = new HazelcastKeyValueConfiguration();
BucketManagerFactory managerFactory = configuration.get();
BucketManager bucketManager = managerFactory.getBucketManager("Pools");
```

A Plain Old Java Object (POJO) can be used to contain the data, and the `BucketManager` is used to perform the transactions. In the following case, a `Pool` object has been populated, and a `BucketManager` is being used to insert the object into the database:

```
KeyValueEntity entity = KeyValueEntity.of(pool.getLength(), pool.Id);
bucketManager.put(entity);
```

How It Works

To refer back to Recipe 7-2, the key-value–oriented database configuration is very similar to document oriented. Typically in a Jakarta EE application, one would create an @ApplicationScoped bean in which to place the configuration of type KeyValueConfiguration. The bean also contains a manager, just like the document-oriented database. However, this manager is a BucketManager, and it will be the basis for performing transactions against the database. In a Java SE environment, the BucketManager can be obtained from the SEContainer instance. In an enterprise environment, the BucketManager can be injected via CDI.

In order to perform transactions against a key-value NoSQL database, utilize the various methods that are available when calling upon the BucketManager. Table 7-5 lists some methods of the BucketManager interface.

Table 7-5. *BucketManager Methods*

Method	Description
close()	Close the resource
delete(Iterable keys)	Removes entities from keys
delete(K key)	Remofes entity from a key
get(Iterable keys)	Finds a list of values, given keys
get(K key)	Finds a value, given a key
prepare(String query)	Executes a query and returns the result
put(Iterable entities)	Saves the iterable of keys
put(KeyValueEntity entity)	Saves the KeyValueEntity
put(K key, V value)	Associates the specified value with a key

Utilization of a key-value NoSQL database can prove to make code easy to maintain and provides for a well-performing application. The Jakarta NoSQL API is a powerful means for working with key-value databases.

CHAPTER 8

Enterprise JavaBeans

Enterprise JavaBeans were created in order to separate the view layer from the database access and business layers. EJBs are where all of the database (`EntityManager`) access and business logic can take place within a Jakarta EE application, and they have become significantly easier to use over the past few releases. EJBs are used to coordinate database tasks with entities, and JSF CDI controllers (aka controller classes) are used to interact directly with the JSF views or web pages. CDI beans are used to provide a façade between the view layer and the business layer.

EJBs are deployed to an application server container, which manages the bean life cycle. The container also provides features such as transaction management and security for EJBs. EJBs are portable, meaning that they can be deployed to different application server containers. This adds benefit for EJB developers because a single EJB can be utilized across multiple applications. EJBs also alleviate the issue of modifying applications to work with multiple databases due to the use of Java Persistence Query Language (covered in Chapter 9) rather than routine SQL is used to perform database operations. Therefore, if an application is developed on one database, it can be ported to another without the need to rewrite any SQL.

There are three types of EJBs that can be used: stateless, stateful, and message-driven. This chapter will cover the first two, and message-driven beans (MDBs) will be covered in Chapter 12 where the Java Message Service (JMS) is covered. Stateless session beans are used most often, because they are used for quick transactions and do not maintain any conversational state. Stateful beans, on the other hand, are to be used in situations where a conversational state across multiple client requests is required.

This chapter includes recipes to familiarize you with stateful and stateless session beans. You will learn how to access EJBs from a JSF CDI controller client and display content within a JSF view or web page that the EJB has queried from the database. There are also recipes covering useful tactics such as using bean `Timers` and creating singleton session beans.

© Josh Juneau 2020

J. Juneau, *Jakarta EE Recipes*, https://doi.org/10.1007/978-1-4842-5587-2_8

> **Note**   In recent times, EJBs may be considered older technology because CDI
> beans can now be used in their place. However, EJBs are a widely adopted
> technology that remains a viable option. At the time of the Jakarta EE 8 release,
> EJB usage is still dominant as CDI is not yet a complete replacement.

8-1. Obtaining an Entity Manager

Problem

You have created a persistence unit for your database connection, and you want to use it
to obtain a connection for working with the database.

Solution #1

Create an EntityManagerFactory object utilizing a local JDBC connection by calling the
javax.persistence.Persistence createEntityManagerFactory method and passing
the name of the JakartaEERecipesLOCAL persistence unit. Obtain an EntityManager
object from the factory object that has been created, and then utilize the EntityManager
object as needed to work with the database entities. The following lines of code
demonstrate how to accomplish the creation of an EntityManager object using a local
JDBC connection:

```
EntityManagerFactory emf = Persistence.createEntityManagerFactory("JakartaE
ERecipesLOCAL");
 EntityManager em = emf.createEntityManager();
```

> **Note**   For further reference regarding the creation of a persistence unit, please
> see Recipe 8-3.

Solution #2

Inject `EntityManager` into EJB when using a database connection within an environment utilizing Java Naming and Directory Interface (JNDI), such as an application server. To do so, declare a private field of the `EntityManager` type, and annotate it using `@PersistenceContext`. Pass the name of the relevant persistence unit to the `@PersistenceContext` annotation. The following lines of code demonstrate how this technique is performed. In an application, these lines of code would reside within an EJB for an entity class:

```
@PersistenceContext(unitName = "JakartaEERecipes")
  private EntityManager em;
```

How It Works

Before an entity class can be used to persist an object or obtain query results, an entity manager must be created from the persistence unit database connection configuration. The way in which you achieve the creation of an entity manager will differ depending upon the type of database connection you are using. For instance, if you are creating an entity manager from a local JDBC connection, then there is a little more work to be done because an `EntityManagerFactory` must be used to obtain the `EntityManager` object. On the other hand, if you are creating a container-managed entity manager from a database connection that is registered with an application server via JNDI, then much of the work is done for you behind the scenes via metadata annotations.

In the first solution to this recipe, a persistence unit pertaining to a local JDBC connection is used to obtain an `EntityManager` object. As mentioned previously, within an EJB, an `EntityManagerFactory` object must first be obtained by calling the `javax.persistence.Persistence` class's `createEntityManagerFactory` method and passing the string-based persistence unit name to the method. From there, an `EntityManager` object can be instantiated by invoking the `EntityManagerFactory`'s `createEntityManager` method.

In the second solution to this recipe, a container-managed `EntityManager` object instance is obtained. If an application is deployed to an enterprise application server container such as Oracle's GlassFish or Payara, this is the preferred way to obtain an `EntityManager`. Utilizing container-managed entity managers makes JPA development easier because a Jakarta EE container manages the life cycle of container-managed entity managers. Moreover, container-managed entity managers are automatically propagated to all application components within a single Java Transaction API (JTA) transaction. To obtain a container-managed entity manager, declare an `EntityManager` field within an EJB and simply annotate it with `@PersistenceContext`, passing the string-based name of the persistence unit to the annotation. Doing so injects the entity manager into the application component.

After performing either of these solutions, the newly obtained `EntityManager` object is ready to be utilized. The most often used `EntityManager` methods are `createQuery`, `createNamedQuery`, `find`, and `persist`. You will learn more about utilizing the `EntityManager` in the following recipes.

8-2. Developing a Stateless Session Bean
Problem

You want to create a class that can be used to perform tasks for a client, but the application does not require the bean to retain any state between transactions. Additionally, you want to have the ability to interact with a database from within the class.

Solution #1

Create a stateless session bean for the entity class for which you'd like to perform tasks. Create an `EntityManager` object from a persistence unit, and initiate tasks against the database using the entity classes. In the following solution, a stateless session bean is created for working with the Book entity:

```
package org.jakartaeerecipes.chapter08.session;

import javax.ejb.Stateless;
import javax.persistence.EntityManager;
import javax.persistence.PersistenceContext;
import org.jakartaeerecipes.chapter08.entity.Book;

/**
 * Stateless Session Bean for the Book entity
 * @author juneau
 */
```

```java
@Stateless
public class BookFacade {
    @PersistenceContext(unitName = "JakartaEERecipes")
    private EntityManager em;

    protected EntityManager getEntityManager() {
        return em;
    }

    public BookFacade() {

    }

    /**
     * Create a book object
     * @param book
     */
    public void create(Book book){
        em.persist(book);
    }

    /**
     * Update a book object
     * @param book
     */
    public void edit(Book book){
        em.merge(book);
    }

    /**
     * Remove a book object
     * @param book
     */
    public void remove(Book book){
        em.remove(book);
    }
```

```
    /**
     * Return a Book object based upon a given title.  This assumes that
       there are no duplicate titles in the database.
     * @param title
     * @return
     */
    public Book findByTitle(String title){
        Book returnValue = null;
      try{
      returnValue = (Book) em.createQuery("select object(o) from Book o " +
                              "where o.title = :title")
                              .setParameter("title", title.toUpperCase())
                              .getSingleResult();
      } catch (NoResultException ex){
          ex.printStackTrace();
      }
      return returnValue;
    }

}
```

In the example session bean, the create, edit, and remove methods can be called via a client to perform CRUD operations with the database. The findByTitle() method can be called via a client to obtain a Book object from the database.

Solution #2

Create a stateless session bean for the entity class for which you'd like to perform tasks, and extend an abstract class that encapsulates standard operations from the session bean. Create an EntityManager object from a persistence unit, and initiate tasks against the database using the entity classes. In the following solution, a stateless session bean is created for working with the Book entity. It extends a class named AbstractFacade, which contains implementations for most of the commonly used tasks within EJBs.

First, let's take a look at the BookFacade class, the stateless session bean:

```java
package org.jakartaeerecipes.chapter08.session;

import javax.ejb.Stateless;
import javax.persistence.EntityManager;
import javax.persistence.PersistenceContext;
import org.jakartaeerecipes.chapter08.entity.Book;

/**
 * Stateless Session Bean for the Book entity
 * @author juneau
 */
@Stateless
public class BookFacade extends AbstractFacade<Book> {
    @PersistenceContext(unitName = "JakartaEERecipes")
    private EntityManager em;

    @Override
    protected EntityManager getEntityManager() {
        return em;
    }

    public BookFacade() {
        super(Book.class);
    }

    /**
     * Return a Book object based upon a given title.  This assumes that there
     * are no duplicate titles in the database.
     * @param title
     * @return
     */
    public Book findByTitle(String title){
        return (Book) em.createQuery("select object(o) from Book o " +
                            "where o.title = :title")
                            .setParameter("title", title.toUpperCase())
                            .getSingleResult();
    }

}
```

As you can see, there is only a single method implemented within the EJB, which is the findByTitle() method. However, other CRUD functionality such as create, update, and remove for the Book entity can also be performed via the BookFacade session bean because it extends AbstractFacade. The AbstractFacade class is an abstract class that implements the most commonly used EJB methods. It accepts an entity class type specified as a generic, and its implementation is as follows.

Note   The following code was automatically generated via the Apache NetBeans IDE along with the BookFacade session bean after creating a stateless session bean for the Book entity class.

```
package org.jakartaeerecipes.chapter08.session;

import java.util.List;
import javax.persistence.EntityManager;

/**
 * Abstract Facade for Session Beans
 */
public abstract class AbstractFacade<T> {
    private Class<T> entityClass;

    public AbstractFacade(Class<T> entityClass) {
        this.entityClass = entityClass;
    }

    protected abstract EntityManager getEntityManager();

    public void create(T entity) {
        getEntityManager().persist(entity);
    }

    public void edit(T entity) {
        getEntityManager().merge(entity);
    }
```

```java
public void remove(T entity) {
    getEntityManager().remove(getEntityManager().merge(entity));
}

public T find(Object id) {
    return getEntityManager().find(entityClass, id);
}

public List<T> findAll() {
    javax.persistence.criteria.CriteriaQuery cq = getEntityManager().
    getCriteriaBuilder().createQuery();
    cq.select(cq.from(entityClass));
    return getEntityManager().createQuery(cq).getResultList();
}

public List<T> findRange(int[] range) {
    javax.persistence.criteria.CriteriaQuery cq = getEntityManager().
    getCriteriaBuilder().createQuery();
    cq.select(cq.from(entityClass));
    javax.persistence.Query q = getEntityManager().createQuery(cq);
    q.setMaxResults(range[1] - range[0]);
    q.setFirstResult(range[0]);
    return q.getResultList();
}

public int count() {
    javax.persistence.criteria.CriteriaQuery cq = getEntityManager().
    getCriteriaBuilder().createQuery();
    javax.persistence.criteria.Root<T> rt = cq.from(entityClass);
    cq.select(getEntityManager().getCriteriaBuilder().count(rt));
    javax.persistence.Query q = getEntityManager().createQuery(cq);
    return ((Long) q.getSingleResult()).intValue();
}

}
```

All of the methods declared in the AbstractFacade are available to the BookFacade since it extends the class. One of the biggest benefits of using an abstract class to implement the standard CRUD functionality is that it can be applied across many different EJBs, rather than written from scratch each time.

How It Works

A Java class that is used to encapsulate the business logic and data access for an application is also known as a *session bean*. More specifically, session beans typically correspond to entity classes, whereas there is usually one bean per entity, although this is not a requirement and there are instances in which such an implementation does not work well. Any database transactions for an application should be encapsulated within a session bean class that is responsible for business process implementations, and clients should then make calls to the session beans in order to invoke those business processes. A stateless session bean does not retain any state, meaning that variables within the bean are not guaranteed to retain their values across invocations. An application server container maintains a pool of session beans for use by its clients, and when a client invokes a bean, then one is taken from the pool for use. Beans are returned to the pool immediately after the client is finished with the invoking task. Therefore, stateless session beans are thread-safe, and they work very well within a concurrent user environment.

Stateless session beans should contain a no-argument constructor, and they are instantiated by an application server container at application startup. To signify that a session bean is stateless, the class should be annotated with @Stateless, optionally passing a String-based name parameter for the bean. If no name parameter is specified within the @Stateless annotation, then the name of the bean is used. A stateless session bean should not be final or abstract; therefore, all methods within the bean should contain an implementation. They can extend other session beans or POJOs in order to extend functionality. In pre–EJB 3.1 environments, there was a requirement for session beans to implement business interfaces that contained method signatures for those methods that were to be made public for client use. However, it is no longer a requirement for a session bean to implement a business interface, and indeed the solutions to this recipe do not demonstrate the use of business interfaces (see Recipe 8-4 for a concrete example).

Zero or more variables can be declared within a stateless session bean, although the contents of those variables are not guaranteed for retention across client calls. It is typical for a stateless session bean to contain at least one `EntityManager` connection, although it is possible for a bean to contain zero or more connections. For instance, in some cases session beans do not have a need to persist data, and in such cases no database connection would be needed. In other instances, there may be a need for a session bean to have the ability to work with multiple databases, in which case multiple database connections would be necessary. In the example for this recipe, a single database connection is declared as an `EntityManager` object, corresponding to the `JakartaEERecipes` persistence unit. It is possible to make use of standard JDBC persistence units, as well as standard JDBC `DataSource` objects within a session bean. The use of a standard JDBC `DataSource` declaration may look like the following:

```
@Resource(name="jdbc/MyDataSource")
private DataSource dataSource;
```

As mentioned previously, stateless session beans can implement business interfaces, although it is not required. The business interfaces that can be implemented via a stateless session bean can be local, remote, or web service endpoints. A local business interface is designed for clients of stateless session beans that exist within the same container instance as the session bean itself. Designating a business interface with the `@Local` annotation specifies a local interface. Remote business interfaces are designed for use by clients that reside outside of the session bean's container instance. A remote business interface is denoted by the `@Remote` annotation.

Stateless session beans contain "callback methods" that will be invoked by the container automatically when certain life-cycle events occur. Specifically, stateless session beans can make use of two callbacks: `PostConstruct` and `PreDestroy`. After the container constructs a stateless session bean and resources have been injected, any method within the bean that is denoted with a `@PostConstruct` annotation will be invoked. Similarly, when the container decides that a bean should be removed from the pool or destroyed, then any method denoted with a `@PreDestroy` annotation will be invoked before the bean is destroyed. Callback methods can be very useful for instantiating database connections and so forth.

LIFE CYCLE OF A STATELESS SESSION BEAN

Stateless session beans have the following life cycle:

1. A container creates a stateless session bean using the default no-argument constructor.

2. Resources are injected as necessary (i.e., database connections).

3. A managed pool of beans is generated, and multiple instances of the session bean are placed into the pool.

4. An idle bean is taken from the pool when the invocation request is received from a client. If all beans in a pool are currently in use, more beans are instantiated until the maximum specified amount of beans has been reached.

5. The business method invoked by the client is executed.

6. The bean is returned to the pool after the business method process is complete.

7. The bean is destroyed from the pool on an as-needed basis.

In the first solution to this recipe, a stateless session bean is listed that does not implement any interfaces or extend any other classes. Such a stateless session bean is very typical, and it is not uncommon to see it in EJB 3.1+ applications. The bean in the solution declares an EntityManager object, and the application server container performs the creation of the EntityManager automatically and injects it into the bean since the @PersistenceContext annotation is specified. The annotation must designate a persistence unit name to tell the container the type of EntityManager to inject. In the case where a bean needs access to multiple database connections, then more than one EntityManager object may be declared, specifying different names for each persistence unit corresponding to the different connections that are required by the bean. A no-argument constructor is specified as per the guidelines for stateless session beans. The solution also contains one business method implementation, findByTitle(), which accepts a String argument and queries the Book entity for the specified book title. If found, the matching Book object is returned to the caller. The findByTitle() method demonstrates the typical usage of an EntityManager object for working with a database from within a session bean.

In the second solution to the recipe, the `BookFacade` stateless session bean extends a class named `AbstractFacade`. The `AbstractFacade` class contains a number of method implementations that are commonly used within session bean classes. For instance, the `create` method within `AbstractClass` can be used to persist an object (insert into the database), and the edit method can be used to update an object. Solution #2 demonstrates a good technique that can be used to encapsulate commonly used business logic into a separate class so that it can be extended to multiple different beans. Consider that the application may contain several different stateless session beans that corresponded to several different entity classes, and each of those beans would need to contain `create`, `edit`, and `remove` methods. It is much easier to simply extend a single class that contains this functionality, rather than rewriting in each separate session bean class.

Stateless session beans are highly performant objects that are used to encapsulate the business logic and data access corresponding to an application entity. While most times a single session bean is written for each entity class, this is not a mandatory rule. Stateless session beans should be considered first when deciding upon which type of bean to use for encapsulating the logic for a particular application process. If a conversational state between the client and the bean is not required (no state needs to be maintained), then stateless session beans are the best choice since they provide the most concurrency and best performance. If, however, state is required, then consider the use of stateful session beans.

8-3. Developing a Stateful Session Bean
Problem

You want to develop a session bean that has the capability of maintaining a conversational state with the client. For instance, you want the client to have the ability to perform a multistep process without the state of the session bean being lost between requests.

Solution

Create a stateful session bean and implement the business logic pertaining to the entity class of your choice. Consider that a customer is browsing the pages of the Acme Bookstore application and wants to add a book to a shopping cart. The cart would need to be maintained within a stateful session bean since it would be required to maintain state until the customer decides to make a purchase, cancel an order, or close the browser.

The following class is that of OrderFacade, the stateful session bean that maintains a visitor's shopping cart and purchases:

```
package org.jakartaeerecipes.chapter08.session;

import java.util.concurrent.TimeUnit;
import javax.ejb.PostActivate;
import javax.ejb.PrePassivate;
import javax.ejb.Remove;
import javax.ejb.Stateful;
import javax.ejb.StatefulTimeout;
import org.jakartaeerecipes.chapter08.object.Cart;

@Stateful
@StatefulTimeout(unit = TimeUnit.MINUTES, value = 30)
public class OrderFacade {

    private Cart cart;

    @SuppressWarnings("unused")
    @PrePassivate
    private void prePassivate() {
        System.out.println("In PrePassivate method");
    }

    @SuppressWarnings("unused")
    @PostActivate
    private void postActivate() {
        System.out.println("In PostActivate method");
    }

    public Cart getCart() {
        if(cart == null)
            cart = new Cart();
        return cart;
    }

    public void setCart(Cart cart) {
        this.cart = cart;
    }
```

```
    public void completePurchase() {
        System.out.println("Not yet implemented..");
    }

    @Remove
    public void destroy() {
        System.out.println("Destroying OrderFacade...");
    }
}
```

A client can make calls to a stateful session bean in the same manner as with a stateless session bean (see Recipe 8-2). That is, a client can access the methods of the stateful session bean via a business interface or controller class/CDI bean. In this example, the CartController JSF CDI bean will access the stateful session bean. The following code for CartController demonstrates how to access the OrderFacade. The main point of access to the EJB takes place within the getCart() method:

```
@Named(name = "cartController")    // Specifies a CDI bean
@SessionScoped                     // Specifies a session scoped bean
public class CartController implements Serializable {

    private Item currentBook = null;

    @EJB        // Injects EJB
    OrderFacade orderFacade;

    @Inject     // Injects specified CDI bean controller
    private AuthorController authorController;

    /**
     * Creates a new instance of CartController
     */
    public CartController() {
    }

    public String addToCart() {
        if (getCart().getBooks() == null) {
            getCart().addBook(getAuthorController().getCurrentBook(), 1);
        } else {
```

```
            getCart().addBook(getAuthorController().getCurrentBook(),
                    searchCart(getAuthorController().getCurrentBook().
                    getTitle()) + 1);
        }
        FacesMessage facesMsg = new FacesMessage(FacesMessage.SEVERITY_INFO,
                "Succesfully Updated Cart", null);
        FacesContext.getCurrentInstance().addMessage(null, facesMsg);
        return null;
    }

    /**
     * Determines if a book is already in the shopping cart
     * If no book with the specified title is present, then
     * 0 is returned.
     *
     * @param title
     * @return
     */
    public int searchCart(String title) {
        int count = 0;

        for (Item item : getCart().getBooks()) {
            if (item.getBook().getTitle().equals(title)) {
                count++;
            }
        }
        return count;
    }

    public String viewCart() {
        if (getCart() == null) {
            FacesMessage facesMsg = new FacesMessage(FacesMessage.SEVERITY_
            INFO,
                    "No books in cart...", null);
            FacesContext.getCurrentInstance().addMessage(null, facesMsg);
        }
```

```java
        return "/chapter08/cart";
    }

    public String continueShopping() {
        return "/chapter08/book";
    }

    public String editItem(String title) {
        for (Item item : getCart().getBooks()) {
            if (item.getBook().getTitle().equals(title)) {
                currentBook = item;
            }
        }
        return "/chapter08/reviewItem";

    }

    public String updateCart(String title) {
        Item foundItem = null;
        if (currentBook.getQuantity() == 0) {
            for (Item item : getCart().getBooks()) {
                if (item.getBook().getTitle().equals(title)) {
                    foundItem = item;
                }
            }
        }
        getCart().getBooks().remove(foundItem);
        FacesMessage facesMsg = new FacesMessage(FacesMessage.SEVERITY_INFO,
                "Succesfully Updated Cart", null);
        FacesContext.getCurrentInstance().addMessage(null, facesMsg);
        return "/chapter08/cart";
    }

    /**
     * @return the cart
     */
```

```java
public Cart getCart() {
    return orderFacade.getCart();
}

/**
 * @return the currentBook
 */
public Item getCurrentBook() {
    return currentBook;
}

/**
 * @param currentBook the currentBook to set
 */
public void setCurrentBook(Item currentBook) {
    this.currentBook = currentBook;
}

public void isBookInCart(ComponentSystemEvent event) {
    UIOutput output = (UIOutput) event.getComponent();
    if (getCart() != null) {
        if (searchCart(getAuthorController().getCurrentBook().
        getTitle()) > 0) {
            output.setValue("This book is currently in your cart.");
        } else {
            output.setValue("This book is not in your cart.");
        }
    } else {
        output.setValue("This book is not in your cart.");
    }
}

public void updateRowData(RowEditEvent e) {
    System.out.println("Perform editing logic here...");
    currentBook = (Item)e.getObject();
    // Call the updateCart method, passing the title of the current book.
    updateCart(((Item)e.getObject()).getBook().getTitle());
}
```

```
/**
 * @return the authorController
 */
public AuthorController getAuthorController() {
    return authorController;
}

/**
 * @param authorController the authorController to set
 */
public void setAuthorController(AuthorController authorController) {
    this.authorController = authorController;
}
}
```

How It Works

A stateful session bean is a Java class that is used to encapsulate business logic for an application. In most cases, a stateful bean has a one-to-one correspondence with an entity class, in that the bean handles all of the database calls regarding one particular entity. Programmatically, a stateful session bean is very similar to a stateless session bean in that regard. However, stateful session beans are guaranteed to maintain a conversational state with a client, whereas a stateless session bean is not. That said, the application server container handles stateful session beans differently, and they have a much different life cycle than stateless session beans. The application server container maintains a pool of the stateful session beans for client use, but there is a one-to-one mapping between a client and a bean in that when a client invokes a stateful bean, it will not release that bean back to the pool while it is still active. Therefore, stateful session beans can be less efficient than stateless, and they can take up a larger memory footprint than stateless session beans because if there are a large number of active sessions using a stateful bean, then there will be a large number of stateful beans retained in memory remaining active for those sessions.

To make a stateful session bean, the class must be designated as such by annotating it with @Stateful. The optional name parameter of the @Stateful annotation can be used to specify a string-based name for the bean. Similar to stateless session beans, a stateful session bean can implement a business interface, but as of EJB 3.1, it is not mandatory. In the example for this recipe, no business interface is used; therefore, any method within the bean that has a public modifier will be available for use by a client. Any variables that are used to store conversational state must be Java primitive types or `Serializable`. When an instance variable is used to store data, it will be maintained throughout the life cycle of the conversation.

Every stateful session bean must also contain a method that will be called when the bean client removes it. The state of the bean will be maintained until the @Remove method is called. The container will invoke the method annotated with @Remove when this occurs, and the bean will be removed after the @Remove method completes.

LIFE CYCLE OF STATEFUL SESSION BEANS

Stateful session beans have the following life cycle:

1. The container creates new bean instances utilizing the default constructor whenever a new client session is started.

2. Resources are injected into the bean.

3. The bean instance is stored in memory.

4. The method invoked by the client is executed.

5. The bean waits and executes any subsequent requests.

6. The bean is *passivated* or removed from active memory into temporary storage if the client remains idle for a period of time.

7. The client invocation of a passivated bean will bring it back into memory from temporary storage.

8. Failure of the client to invoke a passivated bean instance for a period of time will cause the bean to be destroyed.

9. If a client requests the removal of a bean instance, then it is activated if necessary and then destroyed.

Stateful session beans are stored in memory for a period of time. If the client does not request a stateful bean for use again after a period of time, then the container passivates it. Passivation is the process of taking a stateful session bean out of active memory and storing it into a temporary location on disk. The container does this by serializing the entire bean instance and moving it into permanent storage on disk. A bean is then activated later if a client invokes it, and activation is the opposite of passivation.

Another way to passivate a stateful session bean on a timed basis is by annotating the class using @StatefulTimeout. This annotation allows the developer to choose how long to maintain the state of the bean. In the case of the example for this recipe, the state is maintained for 30 minutes before the bean is passivated:

```
@StatefulTimeout(unit = TimeUnit.MINUTES, value = 30)
```

Stateful session beans have more callback methods than stateless session beans. Callback methods can be used to perform operations at a certain point in the bean's life cycle. Specifically, the following annotations can be placed before method signatures in order to mark them for execution when the given bean life-cycle event occurs: @PostConstruct, @PrePassivate, @PostActivate, and @PreDestroy. The @PostConstruct annotation denotes that the annotated method will be executed by the container as an instance is created. @PrePassivate denotes that the annotated method will be executed by the container before passivation occurs. @PostActivate denotes that the annotated method should be executed after activation or, in other words, once a bean becomes active again. Lastly, methods annotated with @PreDestroy will be executed by the container just before the bean is destroyed.

If your session bean needs the ability to retain state throughout a conversation, then you will need to make use of a stateful session bean. However, it is important to make use of stateful session beans sparingly since they are less efficient than stateless session beans and they require a larger memory footprint on the application server.

8-4. Utilizing Session Beans with JSF
Problem

You want to develop a web-based client for a session bean that resides within the same container as the session bean itself.

Solution

Write a Java client and work directly with the session bean of your choice. The following code demonstrates a JSF CDI controller that interacts directly with a stateless session bean. The JSF CDI bean, named BookController, is the client class for the BookFacade

EJB session bean. You will see from the code that the bean is able to interact directly with the EJB session bean public methods via the declaration of a property pertaining to the BookFacade class:

```
package org.jakartaeerecipes.chapter08.jsf;

import java.math.BigDecimal;
import java.util.List;
import java.util.Map;
import javax.ejb.EJB;
import javax.enterprise.context.SessionScoped;
import javax.inject.Inject;
import javax.inject.Named;
import org.jakartaeerecipes.chapter08.entity.Book;
import org.jakartaeerecipes.chapter08.entity.BookAuthor;
import org.jakartaeerecipes.chapter08.session.BookFacade;

@Named(value="bookController")
@SessionScoped
public class BookController implements java.io.Serializable {

    @EJB
    BookFacade ejbFacade;

    private List<Book> completeBookList = null;
    private List<Map> customBookList = null;
    private List<Book> booksByAuthor = null;
    private List<Book> nativeBookList = null;
    private List<Book> namedNativeBookList = null;

    @Inject
    private AuthorController authorController;

    public BookController(){

    }
```

```java
public List<Book> getCompleteBookList() {
    completeBookList = ejbFacade.findAll();
    return completeBookList;
}

public List<Map> getCustomBookList(){
    customBookList = ejbFacade.obtainCustomList();
    return customBookList;
}

public void setCompleteBookList(List<Book> completeBookList) {
    this.completeBookList = completeBookList;
}

public String populateBookList(BigDecimal bookId){
    String returnValue = authorController.populateAuthorList(bookId);
    return returnValue;
}

public String findBooksByAuthor(BookAuthor author){
    setBooksByAuthor(ejbFacade.findBooksByAuthor(author));
    return "/chapter08/recipe08_2b.xhtml";
}

/**
 * @return the booksByAuthor
 */
public List<Book> getBooksByAuthor() {
    return booksByAuthor;
}

/**
 * @param booksByAuthor the booksByAuthor to set
 */
public void setBooksByAuthor(List<Book> booksByAuthor) {
    this.booksByAuthor = booksByAuthor;
}
```

```java
    public List<Book> getNativeBookList() {
        nativeBookList = ejbFacade.obtainNativeList();
        return nativeBookList;
    }

    /**
     * @param nativeBookList the nativeBookList to set
     */
    public void setNativeBookList(List<Book> nativeBookList) {
        this.nativeBookList = nativeBookList;
    }

    /**
     * @return the namedNativeBookList
     */
    public List<Book> getNamedNativeBookList() {
        namedNativeBookList = ejbFacade.obtainNamedNativeList();
        return namedNativeBookList;
    }

    /**
     * @param namedNativeBookList the namedNativeBookList to set
     */
    public void setNamedNativeBookList(List<Book> namedNativeBookList) {
        this.namedNativeBookList = namedNativeBookList;
    }
}
```

As you can see from the example, it is also possible for one JSF CDI controller client to work with another JSF CDI controller client because the BookController class declares a variable for the AuthorController CDI controller and injects it into the class. The JSF view can interact directly with the methods within the bean, making it easy to form the complete cycle for a web view utilizing information from a database.

How It Works

An EJB is the class within an application that is used to work directly with database objects. JSF web views and desktop Java clients cannot work directly with EJB methods since they reside on the application server. For this reason, EJBs must provide a way for clients to communicate with their methods, whether that client resides within the same container as the EJB itself or in a remote location. Prior to the release of EJB 3.1, if an EJB was going to be exposed to a client within the same container, such as a JSF controller class, the EJB would need to implement a business interface denoted as a local interface with the @Local annotation.

On the other hand, if an EJB were to be made accessible to a client running within a remote environment under pre-EJB 3.1, then the EJB would need to implement a business interface denoted as a remote interface with the @Remote annotation. In the majority of Jakarta EE applications that are developed, a web framework such as JSF is used to work with the EJB in order to manipulate or read data from an RDBMS or other data sources. Such clients are local to the container in which the EJB pools reside, and therefore they would access the EJB via a local business interface.

Note   At first, the concept of a local client may be difficult to understand, so I will try to explain in a bit more detail. A typical JSF application utilizes local clients, those being JSF CDI controller classes, to work directly with the EJBs. Although the user of the web application is sitting in a remote location from the EJB server container, they are working with HTML pages that are generated by JSF views within a browser, and those views interact directly with the JSF controllers. It is almost as if the JSF views are bound directly to the JSF CDI controllers, which usually reside within the same container as the EJB. Figure 8-1 shows how this relationship works.

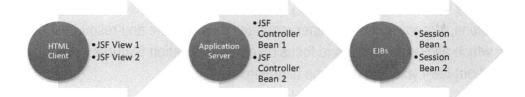

Figure 8-1. *HTML client (JSF view) to EJB relationship*

Since EJB 3.1+, it has been possible for local clients to utilize "no-interface" business views for access to public EJB methods, thereby alleviating the need for the EJB to implement an interface. Using the no-interface view technique enables developers to be more productive because there is one less Java file to maintain (no interface needed), and the workflow becomes easier to understand since the local client can interact directly with the EJB, rather than via an interface. Remote clients, such as Java classes running in a remote application server container, cannot use the no-interface view, and therefore a @Remote business interface is still needed in such situations.

The solution demonstrates the use of the no-interface view to allow JSF CDI controllers to work with publicly declared EJB methods. To obtain a reference to the no-interface view of an EJB through dependency injection, use the `javax.naming.EJB` annotation, along with a declaration of the enterprise bean's implementation class. The following code excerpt taken from the CDI controller in the solution demonstrates the dependency injection technique:

```
@EJB
BookFacade ejbFacade;
```

It is possible to use JNDI to perform a lookup on the EJB rather than using dependency injection, although such situations are rarely required. To do so, use the `javax.naming.InitialContext` interface's lookup method in order to perform the JNDI lookup as follows:

```
BookFacade ejbFacade = (BookFacade)
        InitialContext.lookup("java:module/BookFacade");
```

Note   Many people still have a bad taste in their mouth because of the complexity of EJBs prior to the release of EJB 3.0. Development of EJB 2.x required much XML configuration, which made EJBs difficult to understand and maintain, even though they were still robust and very viable for the development of enterprise applications. Moreover, the container manages the life cycle and resources for EJBs, which allows developers to focus on other application features rather than worry about life-cycle and resource handling.

8-5. Persisting an Object

Problem

You want to persist an object in your Java enterprise application. In other words, you want to create a new database record within one of the database tables used by your application.

Solution

Create an `EntityManager` object using one of the solutions provided in Recipe 8-1, and then call its `persist()` method, passing the object you want to persist. The following lines of code demonstrate how to persist an object to the database using an `EntityManager`. In this case, a `Book` object is being persisted into the BOOK database table. This excerpt is taken from the `BookFacade` session bean:

```
...
@PersistenceContext(unitName = "JakartaEERecipes")
    private EntityManager em;
...
em.persist(book);
...
```

How It Works

The persistence of entity objects takes place within EJB classes. To persist an object to the underlying data store and manage it, call the `EntityManager` object's `persist()` method. You must pass a valid entity object to the `persist()` method, and the object should not yet exist in the database, meaning that it must have a unique primary key.

A few different exceptions may be thrown when working with the `persist()` method that will help you determine what issues are occurring. The `EntityExistsException` is self-explanatory, and it is thrown if the primary key for the entity that you are persisting already exists. However, in some cases a `PersistenceException` will be thrown instead at flush or commit time, so you should catch each of these exceptions when issuing a call to persist. If the object that you are trying to persist is not an entity, then the `IllegalArgumentException` will be thrown. Lastly, the `TransactionRequiredException` will be thrown if invoked on a container-managed entity manager of type `PersistenceContextType.TRANSACTION` and there is no transaction made.

501

8-6. Updating an Object

Problem

The contents of an entity object have been changed, and you want to persist the updates to the underlying data source.

Solution

Create an EntityManager object using one of the solutions provided in Recipe 8-1, and then call the EntityManager object's merge() method, passing a populated entity object that you want to update. The following lines of code demonstrate how to persist an object to the database using an EntityManager. In this case, a Book object is being updated in the BOOK database table. This excerpt is taken from the BookFacade session bean:

```
...
@PersistenceContext(unitName = "JakartaEERecipes")
    private EntityManager em;
...
em.merge(book);
...
```

Note   If the entity object (database record) being persisted does not already exist within the table, it will be stored as a newly persisted object rather than updated.

How It Works

The code implementation that is responsible for updating entity objects within the underlying data store resides within EJB classes. A valid EntityManager object must be available for use, and then the EntityManager's merge() method can be called, passing a valid entity object for update within the underlying data store. When this is done, the state of the entity object will be merged into the data store, and the underlying data will be updated accordingly.

Two possible exceptions may be thrown when attempting to merge data. An `IllegalArgumentException` may be thrown if the instance being merged is not an entity (the database table does not exist) or is a removed entity. A `TransactionRequiredException` may be thrown if the `merge()` method is invoked on a container-managed entity manager of type `PersistenceContextType.TRANSACTION` and there is no transaction.

8-7. Returning Data to Display in a Table

Problem

You want to display the contents of a database table via a JSF `dataTable`.

Solution #1

Return a `List` of entity objects from the underlying table containing the contents you want to display. Map a JSF `dataTable` component value to a CDI controller property that contains a `List` of objects. In this case, the CDI controller property would be the `List` of the entity objects corresponding to the database table. Within the CDI controller, the `List` of entity objects can be obtained via an EJB call.

The following code excerpt is taken from the JSF CDI controller named `BookController`. The CDI controller property named `completeBookList` will be referenced from a `dataTable` component within a JSF view, displaying the data from the underlying table:

```
@Named(value="bookController")
@SessionScoped
public class BookController implements java.io.Serializable {

    @EJB
    BookFacade ejbFacade;

    private List<Book> completeBookList;

    @Inject
    private AuthorController authorController;

. . .
```

```
    public List<Book> getCompleteBookList() {
        completeBookList = ejbFacade.findAll();
        return completeBookList;
    }

    public void setCompleteBookList(List<Book> completeBookList) {
        this.completeBookList = completeBookList;
    }
. . .

}
```

Next, let's take a look at an excerpt from the EJB named BookFacade. It is a stateless session bean that contains the method, which is invoked by the BookController in order to obtain the List of entity objects.

Note   The findAll() method that is called by BookController is inherited from the AbstractFacade class.

```
...
@Stateless
public class BookFacade extends AbstractFacade<Book> {
    @PersistenceContext(unitName = "JakartaEERecipes")
    private EntityManager em;

    @Override
    protected EntityManager getEntityManager() {
        return em;
    }

    public BookFacade() {
        super(Book.class);
    }
...
```

In the AbstractFacade, the findAll() method is implemented in a generic manner:

```
public abstract class AbstractFacade<T> {
    private Class<T> entityClass;

    public AbstractFacade(Class<T> entityClass) {
        this.entityClass = entityClass;
    }

    protected abstract EntityManager getEntityManager();

    public List<T> findAll() {
        javax.persistence.criteria.CriteriaQuery cq = getEntityManager().
        getCriteriaBuilder().createQuery();
        Root<T> root = cq.from(entityClass);
        cq.select(root);
        return getEntityManager().createQuery(cq).getResultList();
    }
...
}
```

The List<Book> is returned from the findAll() method in the EJB, which is contained within the AbstractFacade abstract class. This list is used to populate the completeBookList property within the BookController. Since the BookController communicates directly with the view layer, the JSF view will be able to utilize the completeBookList property to display the data.

Solution #2

Return a List of Map objects containing the results of a native SQL query against the underlying table. The JSF CDI controller can contain a property that is a List of Map objects, and it can be referenced from within a JSF dataTable component. In this case, the EJB method that is invoked by the controller will make a native SQL query against the database, returning certain columns of data from the table and populating map objects with those column values.

In the following excerpt, the BookController.getCustomBookList() method populates a CDI controller property named customBookList via a call to the EJB method named obtainCustomList. Excerpts including both of these methods are shown next.

505

Here's the excerpt from org.jakartaeerecipes.chapter08.BookController:

```
...
public List<Map> getCustomBookList(){
        customBookList = ejbFacade.obtainCustomList();
        return customBookList;
    }
...
```

Here are the excerpts from org.jakartaeerecipes.chapter08.session.BookFacade:

```
...
    protected EntityManager getEntityManager() {
        return em;
    }
...
public List<Map> obtainCustomList(){

        List<Object[]> results = em.createNativeQuery(
                "select id, title, description " +
                "FROM BOOK " +
                " ORDER BY id").getResultList();

        List data = new ArrayList<HashMap>();

        if (!results.isEmpty()) {
            for (Object[] result : results) {
                HashMap resultMap = new HashMap();
                resultMap.put("id", result[0]);
                resultMap.put("title", result[1]);
                resultMap.put("description", result[2]);

                data.add(resultMap);
            }
        }
        return data;
    }
```

The `customBookList` property of the `BookController` class is populated by the EJB method, making the data available to the view.

How It Works

One of the most often required tasks of a web application is to display content. What's more, displaying database content is key to just about every enterprise application. Displaying content in table format provides the user with the ability to see the data because it is stored within the underlying table, in columnar format. The JSF `dataTable` component provides Jakarta EE applications utilizing the JSF framework with an efficient and powerful way to display entity data in a table format.

The JSF `dataTable` component is capable of taking a `List`, `DataModel`, or `Collection` of objects and displaying them to the user. This recipe covers two different variations of retrieving data and storing it within a `List` for use in a `dataTable` component. The first solution is the most common situation. In both solutions, a CDI controller property is used to store the `List` of entity objects. However, the first solution stores a `List` of entity objects themselves, whereas the second solution stores a `List` of `Map` objects. Let's walk through each a little more closely.

In Solution #1 to this recipe, the `completeBookList` field within the `BookController` CDI controller class is used to store the `List` of `Book` entities. The `getCompleteBookList()` method populates the `List` by invoking the `BookFacade` session bean's `findAll()` method to return all of the rows within the BOOK database table. Each database row is stored in a separate `Book` entity object, and in turn, each `Book` entity object is stored in the `List`. Finally, that list is returned to the `BookController` and assigned to the `completeBookList` field. In the end, the JSF `dataTable` component references the `completeBookList` to display the content.

In Solution #2, the `BookController` field named `customBookList` is used to populate a JSF `dataTable`. The `customBookList` field is a `List` of `Map` objects. As far as the `BookController` method of population goes, the `customBookList` field is populated in much the same manner as the `completeBookList` in Solution #1. An EJB method is called, which returns the populated `List` of objects. In this case, the EJB named `BookFacade` returns a `List` of `Map` objects from a native SQL query. The `BookFacade` session bean class method `obtainCustomList` is responsible for creating the native SQL query and then storing the results within `Map` objects. In this case, the native query returns only a subset of the columns that are present within the BOOK database table in

507

each row as a `resultList` and stores them into a `List<Object[]>`. A new `ArrayList` of `HashMaps` is then created and populated with the contents of the List from the database query. To populate the `ArrayList`, the `List<Object[]>` is traversed using a for loop. A `HashMap` object is created for each object that is returned from the database. The `HashMap` object is populated with name-value pairs, with the name of the column being the first part and the value from the entity object being the second part in each element. Each column that was retrieved via the query is stored into the `HashMap`, and the `HashMap` itself is then added to a `List`. In the end, the `List` of `HashMap` objects is returned to the CDI controller and stored into the `customBookList` field. In the JSF view, the names that were associated with each of the database columns in the `HashMap` are used to reference the values for display within the dataTable.

Both of the solutions showcased in this recipe offer valid options for displaying database data JPA within a JSF `dataTable` component. I recommend using the first solution where possible because it is less error prone than Solution #2, which will require manual mapping of the database columns to `Map` indices. There is also native SQL hard-coded into the EJB for Solution #2, which is OK when necessary but never the best option. It is always much better when you can utilize an EJB method, such as the `findAll()` method that is available in `AbstractFacade` (Recipe 8-2), because if the underlying database table changes, then there is no need to alter the application code.

8-8. Creating a Singleton Bean
Problem

You want to develop a session bean in which all application clients will use the same. Only one instance of the bean should be allowed per application so that there is always a single site visitor counter for the number of visitors.

Note   In this recipe, the counter is not cumulative. That is, it is not persisted across application startups. To create a cumulative counter, the current count must be persisted to the database before the application or server is restarted and restored when the application is resumed.

Solution

Develop a singleton session bean that allows concurrent access by all application clients. The bean will keep track of the number of visitors who have been to the bookstore and display the number within the footer of the Acme Bookstore application. The following bean named BookstoreSessionCounter is a singleton session bean for the Acme Bookstore that is responsible for keeping track of an active session count:

```
package org.jakartaeerecipes.chapter08.session;

import javax.ejb.Singleton;
import javax.ejb.ConcurrencyManagement;
import static javax.ejb.ConcurrencyManagementType.CONTAINER;

@Singleton
@ConcurrencyManagement(CONTAINER)
public class BookstoreSessionCounter {

    private int numberOfSessions;
    /**
     * Initialize the Bean
     */
    @PostConstruct
    public void init(){
        // Initialize bean here
        System.out.println("Initalizing bean...");
    }

    // Resets the counter on application startup
    public BookstoreSessionCounter(){
        numberOfSessions = 0;
    }

    /**
     * @return the numberOfSessions
     */
```

```
    public int getNumberOfSessions() {
        numberOfSessions++;
        return numberOfSessions;
    }

    /**
     * @param numberOfSessions the numberOfSessions to set.  This could be set
 *  from the database if the current counter were persisted before the application
 *  was shutdown
     */
    public void setNumberOfSessions(int numberOfSessions) {
        this.numberOfSessions = numberOfSessions;
    }
}
```

Next, let's look at the JSF CDI controller that invokes the singleton session bean method for updating the site counter. The following excerpt is taken from a session-scoped CDI controller named BookstoreSessionController, and the counter property is used to update the number of visitors within the EJB:

```
...
@Named("bookstoreSessionController")
@SessionScoped
public class BookstoreSessionController {

    @EJB
    BookstoreSessionCounter bookstoreSessionCounter;

    private int counter;
    private boolean flag = false;

    /**
     * @return the counter
     */
    public int getCounter() {
        if (!flag) {
```

```
        counter = bookstoreSessionCounter.getNumberOfSessions();
        flag = true;
    }
    return counter;
}

/**
 * @param counter the counter to set
 */
public void setCounter(int counter) {
    this.counter = counter;
}

}
```

Lastly, the counter is bound to a JSF EL expression within the Acme Bookstore Facelets template. The following line of code is excerpted from the template named `custom_template_search.xhtml`, which resides in the `chapter08/layout` directory of the book sources:

```
Number of Vistors: #{bookstoreSessionController.counter}
```

How It Works

A class that is specified as a singleton is created once per application. There is only one instance of a singleton class at any given time, and all client sessions interact with that same instance. To generate a singleton session bean, denote a bean as such by specifying the `javax.ejb.Singleton` annotation. Programmatically, the annotation specification is one of the main differences between the coding of a standard stateless session bean and a singleton session bean. However, functionally, the bean is treated much different by the container than a standard stateless session bean.

Singleton session beans are instantiated by the container at an arbitrary point in time. To force the instantiation of a singleton instance at application startup, the `javax.ejb.Startup` annotation can be specified. In the case of the example, there is no `@Startup` annotation specified, so the singleton instance could be instantiated by the container at any given point. However, a singleton will be started up before any of the application EJBs begin to receive requests. In the example, you can see that the `@PostConstruct` callback annotation is being used. This causes the method on which the annotation is specified to be executed directly after instantiation of the bean. Singletons share the same callback methodology as standard stateless session beans. To read more about callback methods, please refer to Recipe 8-2.

Note   If one or more singleton beans depend upon other singleton beans for initialization, the @DependsOn annotation can be specified for the bean to denote which bean it depends upon. A chain of dependencies can be set up using this annotation if needed.

By default, singletons are concurrent, meaning that multiple clients can access them at the same time (also known as *thread-safe*). There are two different ways in which to control concurrent access to singleton beans. The @ConcurrencyManagement annotation can be specified along with a given ConcurrentManagementType in order to tell the bean which type of concurrency to use. The two types of concurrency are CONTAINER, which is the default type if nothing is specified, and BEAN. In the example, the bean is annotated to specify container-managed concurrency. When container-managed concurrency is specified, the EJB container manages the concurrency. The @Lock annotation can be specified on methods of the singleton to tell the container how client access should be managed on the method. To use the @Lock annotation, specify a lock type of LockType. READ or LockType.WRITE (default) within the annotation to tell the container that many clients can access the annotated method concurrently or that the method should become locked to others when a client is accessing it. The entire class can also be annotated with @Lock, in which case the designated lock type will be used for each of the methods within the class unless they contain their own lock type designation. For example, the following lines specify a method within a singleton class that should be locked when accessed by a client so that only one client at a time has access:

```
@Lock(LockType.WRITE)
public void setCounter(int counter){
    this.counter = counter;
}
```

Bean concurrency is different in that it allows full concurrent, thread-safe locking access to all clients on all methods within the class. The developer can use Java synchronization techniques such as synchronized and volatile to help manage the state of concurrency within those singletons designated with bean-managed concurrency.

8-9. Scheduling a Timer Service

Problem

You want to schedule a task that performs database transactions on a recurring interval.

Solution #1

Use the Timer service to schedule a task within a bean using an automatic timer. The timer will specify a required interval of time, and the method used to perform the task will be invoked each time the interval of time expires. The following session bean is set up to create an automatic timer, which will begin upon application deployment. The following code is contained within the Java file named `org.jakartaeerecipes.chapter08.timer.TimerBean`:

```
import javax.ejb.Singleton;
import javax.ejb.Schedule;

/**
 * Recipe 8-9 : The EJB Timer Service
 * @author juneau
 */
@Singleton
public class TimerBean {

@Schedule(minute="*/5", hour="*")
    public void automaticTimer(){
        System.out.println("*** Automatic Timeout Occurred ***");
    }
}
```

The automatic timer will begin when the class is deployed to the application server and the application server starts. Every five minutes, the `automaticTimer()` method will be invoked as will any processes that are performed within that method.

Solution #2

Create a programmatic timer and specify it to start when it is deployed to the application server. Configure an initialization method within the timer bean that will create the timer automatically when the bean is initialized. The following example class is named `org.jakartaeerecipes.chapter08.timer.ProgrammaticTimerExample`, and it will be automatically started when the application is deployed:

```
package org.jakartaeerecipes.chapter08.timer;

import javax.annotation.PostConstruct;
import javax.annotation.Resource;
import javax.ejb.Singleton;
import javax.ejb.Timer;
import javax.ejb.Timeout;
import javax.ejb.TimerService;

@Singleton
@Startup
public class ProgrammaticTimerExample {

    @Resource
    TimerService timerService;

    @PostConstruct
    public void createTimer(){
        System.out.println("Creating Timer...");
        Timer timer = timerService.createTimer(100000, "Timer has been
        created...");
    }

    @Timeout
    public void timeout(Timer timer){
        System.out.println("Timeout of Programmatic Timer Example...");
    }

}
```

After deployment, you should see a message in the server log indicating `Creating Timer...`, and then once the timer expires, the `Timeout of Programmatic Timer Example...` message will be displayed in the logs.

How It Works

Timer solutions make it easy to incorporate scheduled or timed tasks into an application process. The EJB Timer service helps make such solutions possible because it offers applications a method for scheduling tasks that will be performed by the application over a specified interval of time. There are two different types of timers: programmatic and automatic. In Solution #1 to this recipe, an automatic timer is demonstrated. Although the solution does not perform any actual work, the method annotated with the `@Schedule` annotation is where the work takes place. An automatic timer is created when an EJB contains one or more methods that are annotated with `@Schedule` or `@Schedules`. The `@Schedule` takes a calendar-based timer expression to indicate when the annotated method should be executed.

Note   One or more `@Schedule` annotations can be grouped within `@Scheduled{ ... }`, separating each `@Schedule` with a comma.

Calendar-based timer expressions can contain one or more calendar attributes paired with values to indicate a point in time for invocation of the method. Table 8-1 lists the different calendar-based timer expressions, along with a description of each.

Table 8-1. *Calendar-Based Timer Expressions*

Attribute	Description
dayOfWeek	One or more days in a week: (0–7) or (Sun, Mon, Tue, Wed, Thu, Fri, Sat)
dayOfMonth	One or more days in a month: (1–31) or (Last) or (1st, 2nd, 3rd, 4th, 5th, Last) along with any of the dayOfWeek values
month	One or more months in a year: (1–12) or month abbreviation
year	Four-digit calendar year
hour	One or more hours within a day: (0–23)
minute	One or more minutes within an hour: (0–59)
second	One or more seconds within a minute: (0–59)

When creating a calendar-based timer expression, the asterisk (*) can be specified as a wildcard. The forward slash (/) can be used to indicate an interval in time. An interval in time follows this pattern:

```
beginning time (larger unit) / frequency
```

Therefore, specifying /5 in the example (`minute="*/5" hour="*"`) indicates that you want the timer to be executed every five minutes within the hour because the wildcard indicates which hour to begin the timer and the 5 indicates how often.

Timer expression attributes can contain more than one value, and a comma should separate each value. To indicate that you want to execute a timer at 3:00 a.m. and again at 6:00 a.m., you could write the following:

```
@Schedule(hour="3,6")
```

A range of values can also be specified for timer attributes. To indicate that you want to have the timer executed every hour between the hours of 4:00 and 7:00 a.m., you could specify the following:

```
@Schedule(hour"4-7")
```

Multiple timer expressions can be combined to tune the timer in a more fine-grained fashion. For instance, to specify a timer schedule that will execute at 1:00 a.m. every Sunday morning, you could write the following:

```
@Schedule(dayOfWeek="Sun", hour="1")
```

Programmatic timers are the second option that can be used when developing a timed process, as demonstrated in Solution #2. A programmatic timer is different from an automatic timer because there is no schedule involved. Rather, a client can invoke a timer, or it can be initialized with the construction of a bean. A programmatic timer contains one method that is denoted using the `@Timeout` annotation. The `@Timeout` method will be executed when the timer expires. The timeout method must return `void`, and it can optionally accept a `javax.ejb.Timer` object. A timeout method must not throw an application exception.

To create a programmatic timer, invoke one of the create methods of the `TimerService` interface. Table 8-2 indicates the different create methods that can be used.

Table 8-2. *Programmatic Timer Create Methods*

Method	Description
createTimer	Standard timer creation
createSingleActionTimer	Creates a timer that expires once
createIntervalTimer	Creates a timer that expires based upon a given time interval
createCalendarTimer	Creates a timer based upon a calendar

In Solution #2 of this recipe, a standard timer is created, passing an interval of 100,000 milliseconds. This means that the method annotated with @Timeout will be executed once after 100,000 milliseconds has passed. The following is another syntax that could be used to create a timer that has the same schedule:

```
long duration = 100000;
Timer timer = timerService.createSingleActionTimer(duration, new
TimerConfig());
```

Similarly, a date can be passed to the create method in order to specify a given date and time when the timer should expire. The following timer will expire 30 days from the date on which the application is deployed:

```
Calendar cal = Calendar.getInstance();
cal.add(Calendar.DATE, 30);
Timer timer = timerService.createSingleActionTimer(cal.getTime(), new
TimerConfig());
```

To create a programmatic calendar-based timer, you must create a new schedule using the ScheduleExpression helper class. Doing so will allow you to utilize the calendar-based expressions that are listed in Table 8-1 to specify the timer expiration date. The following example demonstrates a timer that will expire every Sunday at 1:00 a.m. by the application server clock:

```
ScheduleExpression schedule = new ScheduleExpression();
schedule.dayOfWeek("Sun");
schedule.hour("1");
Timer timer = timerService.createCalendarTimer(schedule);
```

Timers do not need to be created in singleton session beans; they can be used in stateless session beans as well.

Note   Timers cannot be specified in stateful session beans.

Timers are a topic that cannot be discussed within the boundaries of a single recipe. However, this brief introduction to timers should give you enough to get started using this technology within your applications. To learn more about timers, please refer to the online documentation at `https://eclipse-ee4j.github.io/jakartaee-tutorial/ejb-basicexamples005.html#BNBOY`.

Note   All timers are persistent by default, meaning that if the server is shut down for some reason, the timer will become active again when the server is restarted. In the event that a timer should expire while the server is down, the timer will expire (or the `@Timeout` method will be called) once the server is functioning normally again. To indicate that a timer should not be persistent, call `TimerConfig.setPersistent(false)`, and pass it to a timer creation method.

8-10. Performing Optional Transaction Life-Cycle Callbacks

Problem

You are interested in beginning a transaction when a bean is instantiated and ending the transaction when it is destroyed.

Solution

Choose to utilize the optional transaction life-cycle callbacks built into EJB. To begin a transaction during the `@PostConstruct` or `@PreDestroy` callbacks, annotate the methods accordingly with `@TransactionAttribute`, passing the `TransactionAttributeType.REQUIRES_NEW` attribute. In the following example, a transaction is started when the bean named AcmeFacade is created. Another transaction is started when the bean is being destroyed:

```
import javax.annotation.PostConstruct;
import javax.annotation.PreDestroy;
import javax.ejb.Stateful;
import javax.ejb.TransactionAttribute;
import javax.ejb.TransactionAttributeType;
import javax.persistence.EntityManager;
import javax.persistence.PersistenceContext;
import javax.persistence.PersistenceContextType;

@Stateful
public class AcmeFacade {

    @PersistenceContext(unitName = "JakartaEERecipesPU", type =
    PersistenceContextType.EXTENDED)
    private EntityManager em;

    @TransactionAttribute(TransactionAttributeType.REQUIRES_NEW)
    @PostConstruct
    public void init() {
        System.out.println("The Acme Bean has been created");
    }

    @TransactionAttribute(TransactionAttributeType.REQUIRES_NEW)
    @PreDestroy
    public void destroy() {
        System.out.println("The Acme Bean is being destroyed...");
        em.flush();
    }
}
```

How It Works

Session beans can contain callback methods that are invoked when certain stages of a bean's life cycle occur. For instance, a method can be registered within a session bean via annotation to invoke after the bean is constructed (@PostConstruct), before it is destroyed (@PreDestroy), and so on. Sometimes it makes sense to start a new transaction when one of these events occurs. It is possible to specify the transactional status of an annotated life-cycle callback method within a session bean when using container-managed transactions.

The annotation accepts a transaction type as per the values listed in Table 8-3.

Table 8-3. *Container-Managed Transaction Demarcation*

Attribute	Description
MANDATORY	The container must invoke an enterprise bean method whose transaction is set to this attribute in the client's transaction context. The client is required to call with a transaction context.
REQUIRED	The container must invoke an enterprise bean method whose transaction is set to this attribute in the client's transaction context. The client is required to call with a transaction context. If the client invokes the enterprise bean's method while the client is not associated with a transaction context, the container automatically starts a new transaction before delegating the method call to the enterprise bean method.
REQUIRES_NEW	The container must invoke an enterprise bean method whose transaction is set to this attribute value with a new transaction context.
SUPPORTS	If the client calls with a transaction context, then the container treats it as REQUIRED. If the client calls without a transaction context, the container treats it as NOT_SUPPORTED.
NOT_SUPPORTED	The container invokes an enterprise bean method whose transaction attribute is set to this value with an unspecified transaction context.
NEVER	The container invokes an enterprise bean method whose transaction is set to this value without a transaction context defined by the EJB specification.

By default, the life-cycle callback methods are not transactional in order to maintain backward compatibility. By annotating the callback method with the @TransactionAttribute and the preferred demarcation type, the callback method has opted in to be transactional.

8-11. Ensuring a Stateful Session Bean Is Not Passivated

Problem

Rather than have your inactive stateful session bean passivated, you want to keep it in memory.

Solution

Specify to the container that the bean is not to be passivated by indicating as such within the @Stateful annotation. To opt out of passivation, set the passivationCapable attribute of the @Stateful annotation to false, as demonstrated in the following excerpt:

```
@Stateful(passivationCapable=false)
public class AcmeFacade {
    ...
}
```

How It Works

When a stateful session bean has been inactive for a period of time, the container may choose to passivate the bean in an effort to conserve memory and resources. Typically, the EJB container will passivate stateful session beans using a least recently used algorithm. When passivation occurs, the bean is moved to secondary storage and removed from memory. Prior to the passivation of a stateful session bean, any methods annotated with @PrePassivate will be invoked. When a stateful session bean that has been passivated needs to be made active again, the EJB container activates the bean, then calls any methods annotated with @PostActivate, and finally moves the bean to the ready stage.

In EJB 3.2, stateful session beans can opt out of passivation so that they will remain in memory instead of being transferred to secondary storage if inactive. This may be helpful in situations where a bean needs to remain active for application processes or if the bean contains a non-serializable field, since these fields cannot be passivated and are made null upon passivation. To indicate that a bean is not to be passivated, set the passivationCapable attribute of the @Stateful annotation to false, as per the solution to this recipe.

8-12. Denoting Local and Remote Interfaces

Problem

You want to explicitly designate a local or remote interface for an EJB.

Solution

A business interface cannot be declared as both a local and remote business interface
for a bean. Therefore, the EJB specification contains an API to specify whether a
business interface is intended as local or remote. The following rules pertain to business
interfaces implemented by enterprise bean classes:

The `java.io.Serializable`, `java.io.Externalizable`, and interfaces defined
by the package are always excluded when determination of local or remote business
interfaces is declared for a bean.

If a bean class contains the `@Remote` annotation, then all implemented interfaces are
assumed to be remote.

If a bean class contains no annotation or if the `@Local` annotation is specified, then
all implemented interfaces are assumed to be local.

Any business interface that is explicitly defined for a bean that contains the no-interface
view must be designated as `@Local`.

Any business interface must be explicitly designated as local or remote if the bean
class explicitly specifies the `@Local` or `@Remote` annotation with a nonempty value.

Any business interface must be explicitly designated as local or remote if the
deployment descriptor specifies as such.

How It Works

The release of EJB 3.0 greatly simplified development with EJBs because it introduced
the no-interface view for making local business interfaces optional. The no-interface
view automatically exposes all public methods of a bean to the caller. By default,
a no-interface view is automatically exposed by any session bean that does not include
an `implements` clause and has no local or remote client views defined. The EJB 3.2
provided further granularity for those situations where local and remote interfaces need
to be explicitly specified.

Let's break down the rules that were defined within the solution to this recipe. First, if an EJB exposes local interfaces, then there is no need to explicitly denote a bean as such. For instance, the following bean contains a local interface, although it is not explicitly denoted:

```
@Stateless
public class AcmeSession implements interfaceA {
    ...
}
public interfaceA { ... }
```

If a bean class is annotated with @Remote, then any interfaces that it implements are assumed to be remote. For instance, the following bean class implements two interfaces, and both are assumed to be remote, although they do not contain any annotation to indicate as such:

```
@Remote
@Stateless
public class AcmeSession implements interfaceA, interfaceB {
    ...
}
```

If a bean class contains the @Local annotation, then any interfaces that it implements are assumed to be local. For instance, the following bean class implements two interfaces, and both are assumed to be local although they do not contain any annotation to indicate as such:

```
@Local
@Stateless
public class AcmeSession implements interfaceA, interfaceB {
    ...
}
```

If a bean class contains the @Local or @Remote annotation and specifies an interface name within the annotation, then the same designation is applied as the annotation specifies. For instance, the following bean is annotated to include a local business interface, and the name of the interface is specified in the annotation, thereby making the interface local:

```
@Local(interfaceA.class)
@Stateless
public class AcmeSession implements interfaceA {
        ...
}
```

These new designation rules make it easier to designate and determine the type of business interface that is implemented by a bean.

8-13. Processing Messages Asynchronously from Enterprise Beans

Problem

You want to have the ability to process messages from session beans in an asynchronous manner.

Solution

Develop a message-driven bean to perform the message processing for your application. To develop a message bean, create an EJB that is annotated with @MessageDriven, passing the appropriate configuration options. In the bean, code a method named onMessage that will perform all of the message processing. The following example, org.jakartaeerecipes.chapter08.jsf.AcmeMessageBean, demonstrates how to code a message-driven bean that processes messages from a javax.jms.Queue that has been configured within the application server container:

Note   Prior to running these examples, you must create the JMS resources within GlassFish or Payara. Please refer to Recipe 14-1 for more details.

```java
@MessageDriven(mappedName="jms/Queue", activationConfig = {
    @ActivationConfigProperty(propertyName = "destinationType",
                              propertyValue = "javax.jms.Queue")
})
public class AcmeMessageBean implements MessageListener {

    public AcmeMessageBean(){

    }

    @Override
    public void onMessage(Message msg) {
        if(msg != null){
            performExtraProcessing();
            System.out.println("Message has been received: " + msg);
        } else {
            System.out.println("No message received");
        }
    }

    public void performExtraProcessing(){
        System.out.println("This method could perform extra processing");
    }

}
```

How It Works

Message-driven beans (MDBs) are Enterprise JavaBeans that are utilized for processing messages in an asynchronous manner. Most often MDBs are JMS message listeners, receiving messages and processing accordingly. A message-driven bean is created by annotating a bean with the @MessageDriven annotation and optionally implementing the MessageListener interface. When a message is received in the container queue, the container invokes the bean's onMessage() method, which contains the business logic that is responsible for processing the message accordingly.

Note Any session bean can be used for processing messages, but only message-driven beans can do so in an asynchronous manner.

MDBs must be made public, and not static or final. An MDB must contain a public, no-argument constructor, and it must contain a method named onMessage that accepts a javax.jms.Message argument. The onMessage method is responsible for performing all message processing, and it can utilize other methods within the bean to help out, where needed.

Bean providers may provide special configurations for MDBs to the deployers, such as information regarding message selectors, acknowledgment modes, and so on, by means of the activationConfig element of the @MessageDriven annotation. A standard list of activationConfig properties exists to provide JMS 2.0 alignment. Table 8-4 lists the new properties along with a description of what they do.

Table 8-4. *JMS 2.0 Aligned activationConfig Properties*

Property	Description
destinationLookup	Provides advice to the deployer regarding whether the message-driven bean is intended to be associated with a Queue or Topic. Values for this property are javax.jms.Queue and javax.jms.Topic.
connectionFactoryLookup	Specifies the lookup name of an administratively defined ConnectionFactory object that will be used for a connection to the JMS provider from which a message-driven bean will send JMS messages.
clientId	Specifies the client identifier that will be used for a connection to the JMS provider from which a message-driven bean will send JMS messages.
subscriptionName	If the message-driven bean is intended to be used with a Topic, then the bean provider can specify the name of a durable subscription with this property and set the subscriptionDurability property to Durable.
shareSubscriptions	This property is only to be used when a message-driven bean is deployed to a clustered application server, and the value for this property can be either true or false. A value of true means that the same durable subscription name or nondurable subscription will be used for each instance in the cluster. A value of false means that a different durable subscription name or nondurable subscription will be used for each instance in the cluster.

CHAPTER 9

Java Persistence Query Language

The Java Persistence API (JPA) utilizes a query language for communicating with underlying data stores. Although Jakarta EE uses entities rather than SQL for database access, it provides a query language so that developers can obtain the required information via the entities. The Java Persistence Query Language (JPQL) does just that because it provides a facility for querying and working with Jakarta EE entity objects. Although it is very similar to SQL, it is an object-relational query language, so there are some minor differences of which developers should be aware. Using JPQL along with Jakarta EE entities allows developers to create versatile applications because JPQL is not database-specific and applications can be written once and deployed to run on top of a myriad of databases.

The release of Jakarta EE 8 introduced with it a maintenance release of JPA 2.2, and that means added and enhanced features. Some of the major improvements with Java EE 8 and Jakarta EE 8 include support for stored procedures and built-in functions, downcasting support, and outer join support with `ON` conditions. The release also includes support for the Java 8 Date-Time API, the ability to stream query results, and repeatable annotation support. The recipes in this chapter will not attempt to cover all of the features that JPQL has to offer because there are many. However, the recipes contain enough information to introduce beginners to the world of JPQL and to get intermediate developers up to date with the latest that JPQL has to offer. To review the entire set of documentation for using JPQL, please see the online resources available at `https://projects.eclipse.org/projects/ee4j.jpa`.

© Josh Juneau 2020
J. Juneau, *Jakarta EE Recipes*, https://doi.org/10.1007/978-1-4842-5587-2_9

9-1. Querying All Instances of an Entity

Problem

You want to retrieve all the instances for a particular entity. That is, you want to query the underlying database table associated with the entity and retrieve all rows.

Solution #1

Call the EntityManager's createQuery method, and use JPQL to formulate a query that will return all instances of a given entity. In the following example, a JPQL query is used to return all objects within the BookAuthor entity:

```
public List<BookAuthor> findAuthor(){
        return em.createQuery("select object(o) from BookAuthor o").
        getResultList();
}
```

When the findAuthor() method is called, a List containing all of the BookAuthor entity instances in the entity (all records in the underlying database table) will be returned.

Solution #2

Create a CriteriaQuery object by generating a criteria builder from the EntityManager object and calling its createQuery() method. Once a CriteriaQuery object has been created, generate a query by calling a series of the CriteriaBuilder methods against the entity that you want to query. Finally, call the EntityManager's createQuery() method, passing the query that you have previously built. Return the ResultList from the query to return all the rows from the table. In the following lines of code, you can see this technique performed:

```
javax.persistence.criteria.CriteriaQuery cq = getEntityManager().
getCriteriaBuilder().createQuery();
Root<BookAuthor> bookAuthor = cq.from(BookAuthor);
cq.select(bookAuthor);
return getEntityManager().createQuery(cq).getResultList();
```

How It Works

An entity instance can be referred to as a *record* in the underlying data store. That is, there is an entity instance for each record within a given database table. That said, sometimes it is handy to retrieve all of the instances for a given entity. Some applications may require all objects in order to perform a particular task against each, or perhaps your application needs to simply display all of the instances of an entity for the user. Whatever the case, there are a couple of ways to retrieve all of the instances for a given entity. Each of the techniques can take place within an EJB or RESTful service class.

In Solution #1, JPQL can be used to query an entity for all instances. To create a dynamic query, call the EntityManager's createQuery method, to which you can pass a string-based query that consists of JPQL syntax, or a javax.persistence.Query instance. The Query interface has a sizable number of methods that can be used to work with the query object. Table 9-1 describes what these methods do.

Table 9-1. *javax.persistence.Query Interface Methods*

Method	Description
executeUpdate	Executes an update or delete statement (returns: int)
getFirstResult	Specifies the position of the first result the query object was set to retrieve (returns: int)
getFlushMode	Gets the flush mode in effect for the query execution (returns: FlushModeType)
getHints	Gets the properties and hints and associated values that are in effect for the query instance (returns: java.util.Map<String, Object>)
getLockMode	Gets the current lock mode for the query (returns: LockModeType)
getMaxResults	Specifies the maximum number of results the query object was set to retrieve (returns: int)
getParameter	Gets the parameter object corresponding to the declared positional parameter (returns: Parameter<?>)
getParameters	Gets the parameter objects corresponding to the declared parameters of the query (returns: java.util.Set<Parameter<?>>)

(continued)

529

Table 9-1. (*continued*)

Method	Description
getParameterValue(int)	Returns the value bound to the positional parameter (returns: Object)
getResultList	Executes a SELECT query and then returns the query results as an untyped List (returns: java.util.List)
getSingleResult	Executes a SELECT query and then returns a single untyped result (returns: java.lang.Object)
isBound	Returns a Boolean indicating whether a value has been bound to the parameter

In the example, a query string is passed to the method, and it reads as follows:

```
select object(o) from BookAuthor o
```

To break this down, the query is selecting all objects from the BookAuthor entity. Any letter could have been used in place of the o character within the query, but o is a bit of a standard since JPQL is referring to objects. All queries contain a SELECT clause, which is used to define the types of entity instances that you want to obtain. In the example, the entire instance is selected from the BookAuthor entity, as opposed to single fields that are contained within the instance. Since JPA works with objects, queries should always return the entire object; if you want to use only a subset of fields from the object, then you can call upon those fields from the instance(s) returned from the query. The object keyword is optional and is purposeful mainly for readability. The same JPQL could be written as follows:

```
select o from BookAuthor o
```

The FROM clause can reference one or more identification variables that can refer to the name of an entity, an element of a single-valued relationship, an element of a collection relationship, or a member of a collection that is the multiple side of a one-to-many relationship. In the example, the BookAuthor variable refers to the entity itself.

Note   For more information regarding the full query language syntax, please refer to the online documentation: https://eclipse-ee4j.github.io/ jakartaee-tutorial/persistence-querylanguage006.html#BNBUF.

The example in Solution #2 demonstrates the use of the `CriteriaQuery`, which is used to construct queries for entities by creating objects that define query criteria. To obtain a `CriteriaQuery` object, you can call the `EntityManager`'s `getCriteriaBuilder()` method and, in turn, call the `createQuery()` method of the `CriteriaBuilder`. The `CriteriaQuery` object allows you to specify a series of options that will be applied to a query so that an entity can be queried using native Java, without hard-coding any string queries. In the example, the `CriteriaQuery` instance is obtained by the chaining of subsequent method calls against the `EntityManager` and `CriteriaBuilder` instances. Once the `CriteriaQuery` is obtained, its `from()` method is called, passing the name of the entity that will be queried. A `javax.persistence.criteria.Root` object is returned from the call, which can then be passed to the `CriteriaQuery` instance select method to return a `TypedQuery` object to prepare the query for execution, which can then return the `ResultList` of entity instances. In the example, the final line of code chains method calls again, so you do not see the `TypedQuery` object referenced at all. However, if the chaining were to be removed, the code would look as follows:

```
cq.select(bookAuthor);
TypedQuery<BookAuthor> q = em.createQuery(cq);
return q.getResultList();
```

Both the JPQL and `CriteriaQuery` techniques can provide similar results. Neither technique is any better than the other, unless you prefer that the JPQL is written in code that is more like native SQL or that `CriteriaQuery` is written in native Java.

9-2. Setting Parameters to Filter Query Results
Problem

You want to query an entity and retrieve only a subset of its instances that match specified criteria.

Solution #1

Write a JPQL dynamic query, and specify parameters that can be bound to the query using bind variables. Call the `query` object's `setParameter()` method to assign a parameter value to each bind variable. In the following example, a query is written to search the Book entity for all Book instances that were written by a specified author. The BookAuthor object in this example is a named parameter that will be bound to the query using a bind variable:

```
public List<Book> findBooksByAuthor(BookAuthor authorId){
        return em.createQuery("select o from Book o " +
                "where :bookAuthor MEMBER OF o.authors")
                .setParameter("bookAuthor", authorId)
                .getResultList();
    }
```

The matching Book instances for the given author will be returned.

Solution #2

Write a Criteria API query, and specify parameters that can be bound to the query using bind variables:

```
public List<Book> findBooksByAuthorCriteria(BookAuthor authorId){
        CriteriaBuilder cb = em.getCriteriaBuilder();
        CriteriaQuery<Book> cq = cb.createQuery(Book.class);
        Root<Book> book = cq.from(Book.class);
        cq.where(book.get(Book_.bookAuthor).in(authorId));
        TypedQuery<Book> tq = em.createQuery(cq);
        return tq.getResultList();
}
```

As you can see, the Criteria API allows one to generate a statically typed query. This can be beneficial for helping to reduce errors in typing Strings and also for promoting efficiency as Criteria API queries are not compiled each time they are executed.

How It Works

It is often desirable to return a refined list of results from a query, rather than returning the entire list of records within a database table. In standard SQL, the WHERE clause allows one or more expressions to be specified, which will ultimately refine the results of the query. Using JPQL, the WHERE clause works in the same manner, and the process of refining results of a query is almost identical to doing so with standard JDBC.

In the solution for this recipe, the JPQL technique is used to refine the results of a query against the Book entity such that only instances pertaining to books written by a specified author will be returned. The findBooksByAuthor() method within the org.jakartaeerecipes.chapter09.session.BookFacade class accepts a BookAuthor object as an argument, and the argument will then be specified to refine the results of the query. As you'll see in the code, a single line of code (using the effective Java builder pattern) within the findBooksByAuthor() method performs the entire task. The EntityManager's createQuery() method is called, passing a string-based JPQL query that includes a bind variable named :bookAuthor. The MEMBER OF construct in the following query tests to see if the value of the bind variable is contained within the o.authors list. The JPQL string is as follows:

```
select o from Book o where :bookAuthor MEMBER OF o.authors
```

> **Note**   The Java builder pattern is explained in the following reference: https://en.wikipedia.org/wiki/Builder_pattern.

After creating the query object, the Query interface's setParameter method can be called, passing the name of the bind variable for which you want to substitute a value, along with the value you want to substitute it with. In this case, the String bookAuthor is passed along with the Author object you want to match against for obtaining Book instances. If more than one parameter needs to be specified, more than one call to setParameter() can be strung together so that each bind variable has a matching substitute. Finally, once all of the parameters have been set, the getResultList() method can be called against the Query, returning the matching objects.

> **Note**   Two types of parameters can be used with JPQL: named and positional. The example in this recipe, along with many of the others in this book, uses named parameters. Positional parameters are written a bit differently in that they are denoted within JPQL using a question mark (?) character, and a positional number is used instead of passing the variable name to the setParameter() method. The same query that is used in this recipe can be rewritten as follows to make use of positional parameters:

```
return em.createQuery("select o from Book o " +
                "where ? MEMBER OF o.authors")
            .setParameter(1, authorId)
            .getResultList();
```

Both named and positional parameters achieve the same results. However, I recommend against using positional parameters because it makes code harder to manage, especially if there are more than a handful of parameters in use. It is also easier to mistype the setParameter() calls, and if the wrong positional number is passed with an incorrect parameter value, then issues can arise.

In Solution #2 to this recipe, the Criteria API is used to construct the same query and return the same results as those from Solution #1. To build the criteria query, first obtain a CriteriaBuilder from the entity manager. Next, use the CriteriaQuery to create a CriteriaQuery<Object> by calling upon the createQuery() method and passing the entity class type.

9-3. Returning a Single Object
Problem

You have specified JPQL for a given query that will return exactly one matching entity instance, and you want to store it within a local object so that tasks can be performed against it.

Solution

Create a dynamic query, specifying the JPQL that is necessary for obtaining the entity instance that matches the given criteria. The JPQL will include a bind variable that will bind the parameter to the query in order to obtain the desired instance. The method in the following code excerpt can be found in the org.jakartaeerecipes.jpa.session.chapter09.BookFacade class within the sources:

```
public Book findByTitle(String title){
    return (Book) em.createQuery("select object(o) from Book o " +
                    "where o.title = :title")
```

```
        .setParameter("title", title.toUpperCase())
        .getSingleResult();
    }
```

To invoke the method and return results, the previous method, which resides within an EJB, can be invoked from within a CDI controller. The method that is defined within the controller can subsequently be referenced from within a JSF view to display the results.

How It Works

A single entity instance can be retrieved by specifying a query, along with the necessary parameters to refine the possible matches to a single object. The `javax.persistence.Query` interface's `getSingleResult()` method allows just one instance to be returned, given that there is only one instance that matches the given query specification. In the example for this recipe, assume that each `Book` instance has a unique name to identify it. Therefore, you can be sure that when a name is bound to the query, it will return a single result.

Problems can arise if more than one instance matches the criteria. An attempt to call `getSingleQuery()` using a query that returns more than one instance will result in a `NonUniqueResultException` being thrown. It is a good idea to catch this exception within your applications to avoid ugly error messages being displayed to the user if more than one matching instance exists. Another case to watch out for is when a query returns no result at all. If no result is returned, then a `NoResultException` will be thrown.

9-4. Creating Native Queries
Problem

The query you want to use against an entity contains some SQL functionality that pertains to the specific database vendor that your application is using, or you are more comfortable working with standard SQL than using JPQL. That said, you want to use standard SQL to query one of your entity objects.

Note   When using native queries, you will be forced to work against database records, rather than Java objects. For this reason, it is recommended to use JPQL unless necessary.

Solution #1

Create a native query by calling the `EntityManager` object's `createNativeQuery()` method, and pass a SQL query as the first parameter and pass the entity class that you want to return the results of the query into as the second parameter. Once the query has been created, call one of the corresponding `javax.persistence.Query` methods (see Table 9-1) to return the results. The following example taken from the `org.jakartaeerecipes.jpa.session.BookFacade` EJB demonstrates the use of a native query on the Book entity:

```
public List<Book> obtainNativeList(){
        Query query = em.createNativeQuery(
                "select id, title, description " +
                "FROM BOOK " +
                " ORDER BY id", org.jakartaeerecipes.jpa.entity.Book.class);
        return query.getResultList();

}
```

In the preceding example, each of the database attributes will map to a field within the Book class.

Solution #2

Specify a `@NamedNativeQuery` within the entity class for the entity class that you want to query. Provide a name, query, and mapping class for the `@NamedNativeQuery` via the annotation. Within the EJB method, call the `EntityManager` object's `createNativeQuery()` method, and provide the name that was specified as a named native query rather than a SQL string. The following code excerpt demonstrates the creation of a named native query for the `org.jakartaeerecipes.jpa.entity.Book` entity:

```
...
@Entity
@Table(name="BOOK")
@NamedNativeQuery(
    name="allBooks",
    query = "select id, title, description " +
                "FROM BOOK " +
                "ORDER BY id",
    resultClass=Book.class)
...
```

Next, let's take a look at how the named native query is invoked from within the
EJB. The following excerpt of code is taken from the `org.jakartaeerecipes.jpa.`
`session.BookFacade` bean, and it demonstrates the invocation of the `allBooks` named
native query:

```
public List<Book> obtainNamedNativeList(){
        Query query = em.createNamedQuery(
                "allBooks", org.jakartaeerecipes.jpa.entity.Book.class);
        return query.getResultList();

    }
```

How It Works

Native queries provide a way to utilize native SQL code for retrieving data from an
underlying data store. Not only do they allow an inexperienced JPQL developer to
write in native SQL, but they also allow native SQL syntax, such as Oracle-specific
PL/SQL functions, or stored procedure calls to be made. On the downside, however,
native queries do not return results in an entity-oriented manner, but rather as plain old
objects. For this reason, the named native query provides the option to specify an entity
class into which the results should be returned.

There are a handful of ways to work with native queries, and I've covered a couple of
the most commonly used tactics in this recipe. A `javax.persistence.Query` is generated
either by calling the `EntityManager`'s `createNativeQuery()` method or by calling the
`EntityManager`'s `createNamedQuery()` method and passing a named native query.

In Solution #1, a `String`-based SQL query is used to retrieve results into an entity class. For starters, the `createNativeQuery()` method accepts a query in `String` format or a named native query for the first parameter. In Solution #1, a query is used to obtain all the records from the `BOOK` database table. The second argument to the `createNativeQuery()` method is an optional mapping class into which the results of the query will be stored. Solution #1 specifies `Book.class` as the second parameter, which will map the columns of the database table to their corresponding fields within the `Book` entity. Once the `Query` instance is created, then its methods can be invoked in order to execute the query. In this case, the `getResultSet()` method is invoked, which will return a `List` of the matching records and bind each of them to a `Book` entity class instance.

In Solution #2, a named native query is demonstrated. Named native queries allow the SQL string to be specified once within the corresponding entity class, and then they can be executed by simply passing the `String`-based name that has been assigned to the named native query. To utilize a named native query, add the `@NamedNativeQuery` annotation to the entity class that you want to query, and then specify values for the three parameters of the annotation: `name`, `query`, and `resultClass`. For the `name` parameter of the `@NamedNativeQuery` annotation, a `String`-based name that will be used to reference the query must be specified, the query parameter must be the native SQL string, and the `resultClass` must be the entity class that the query results will be stored into. The `@NamedNativeQuery` also includes the `resultSetMapping` parameter that can be optionally used to specify a `SqlResultSetMapping` for those queries involving more than one table. To execute the named native query, use the same technique as demonstrated in Solution #1, but instead call the `EntityManager` object's `createNamedQuery()` method. Instead of specifying a SQL `String`, pass the name that was specified within the `@NamedNativeQuery` annotation for the respective query.

Note   If the named query involves more than one database table, then a `SqlResultSetMapping` must be defined. Please see Recipe 9-5 for more details.

In some cases, using a native SQL query is the only solution for retrieving the data that your application requires. In all cases, it is recommended that JPQL be used, rather than native SQL, if possible. However, for those cases where native SQL is the only solution, then creating a native query using one of the techniques provided in this recipe is definitely the way to go. Which technique is better? Well, that depends on what you need to do. If you are trying to create a dynamic query, whereas the actual SQL `String` for the query may change dynamically, then the standard native query is the solution for you. However, if the SQL query that you are specifying will not change in a dynamic manner, then perhaps the named native query is the best choice for two reasons. First, the named native query allows SQL to be organized and stored within a single location, which is the entity class on which the SQL is querying. Second, named native queries can achieve better performance because they are cached after the first execution. Therefore, the next time the named native query is called, the SQL does not have to be recompiled. Such is not the case with a standard native query. Each time a standard native query is called, the SQL must be recompiled, which ultimately means that it will not be executed as fast.

9-5. Querying More Than One Entity
Problem

The JPQL or native SQL query being used references more than one entity or underlying database table. Since there are attributes from more than one table, the results cannot be stored into a single entity object.

Solution #1

Use a `SqlResultSetMapping`, which allows the specification of more than one entity class for returning query results. The `@SqlResultSetMapping` annotation can be specified in order to map a result set to one or more entities, allowing the joining of database tables to become a nonissue. In the following example, the `BOOK` and `BOOK_AUTHOR` database tables are joined together using a native SQL query, and the results are returned using a `SqlResultSetMapping`. The following `@SqlResultSetMapping` can be found within the `org.jakartaeerecipes.entity.BookAuthor` entity class:

```
@SqlResultSetMapping(name="authorBooks",
        entities= {
            @EntityResult(entityClass=org.jakartaeerecipes.entity.Book.
            class, fields={
                @FieldResult(name="id", column="BOOK_ID"),
                @FieldResult(name="title", column="TITLE")
            }),
```

```
    @EntityResult(entityClass=org.jakartaeerecipes.entity.
    BookAuthor.class, fields={
        @FieldResult(name="id", column="AUTHOR_ID"),
        @FieldResult(name="first", column="FIRST"),
        @FieldResult(name="last", column="LAST")
    })
})
```

Next, let's look at how the SqlResultSetMapping is used. The following method is taken from the org.jakartaeerecipes.session.BookAuthorFacade session bean:

```
public List findAuthorBooksMapping(){

    Query qry = em.createNativeQuery(
            "select b.id as BOOK_ID, b.title as TITLE, " +
            "ba.id AS AUTHOR_ID, ba.first as FIRST, ba.last as LAST " +
            "from book_author ba, book b, author_work aw " +
            "where aw.author_id = ba.id " +
            "and b.id = aw.book_id", "authorBooks");

    return  qry.getResultList();
}
```

The resulting List can then be referenced from within a JSF dataTable or another client data iteration device, in order to display the results of the query.

Solution #2

Utilize a native query to return the necessary fields from more than one database table, and return the results to a HashMap, rather than to an entity class. In the following method taken from the org.jakartaeerecipes.session.BookAuthorFacade session bean, this technique is demonstrated:

```
public List<Map> findAuthorBooks(){

    Query qry = em.createNativeQuery(
            "select ba.id, ba.last, ba.first, ba.bio, b.id, b.title, " +
            "b.image, b.description " +
            "from book_author ba, book b, author_work aw " +
```

```
          "where aw.author_id = ba.id " +
          "and b.id = aw.book_id");

    List<Object[]> results = qry.getResultList();
    List data = new ArrayList<HashMap>();

    if (!results.isEmpty()) {
        for (Object[] result : results) {
            HashMap resultMap = new HashMap();
            resultMap.put("authorId", result[0]);
            resultMap.put("authorLast", result[1]);
            resultMap.put("authorFirst", result[2]);
            resultMap.put("authorBio", result[3]);
            resultMap.put("bookId", result[4]);
            resultMap.put("bookTitle", result[5]);
            resultMap.put("bookImage", result[6]);
            resultMap.put("bookDescription", result[7]);

            data.add(resultMap);
        }

    }
    return data;
}
```

Using this solution, no `SqlResultSetMapping` is required, and the results are manually stored into a `Map` that can be referenced from a client, such as a JSF view.

How It Works

The `SqlResultSetMapping` can come in handy when you need to map your `ResultSet` to two or more entity classes. As demonstrated in the first solution to this recipe, configure the mapping by specifying a `@SqlResultSetMapping` annotation on the entity class of which you are querying. `SqlResultSetMapping` is useful when working with native queries and joining underlying database tables.

In the example, the `@SqlResultSetMapping` annotation is used to create a mapping between the `Book` and `BookAuthor` entity classes. The `@SqlResultSetMapping` annotation accepts a few different parameters, as described in Table 9-2.

Table 9-2. *SqlResultSetMapping Parameters*

Parameter	Description
name	String-based name for the SqlResultSetMapping
entities	One or more @EntityResult annotations, denoting entity classes for the mapping
columns	One or more columns against which to map a resultSet, designated by @FieldResult or @ColumnResult annotations

To use a SqlResultSetMapping, simply specify its name rather than an entity class when creating the native query. In the following excerpt taken from the solution, the query results are mapped to the authorBooks SqlResultSetMapping:

```
Query qry = em.createNativeQuery(
                "select b.id as BOOK_ID, b.title as TITLE, " +
                "ba.id AS AUTHOR_ID, ba.first as FIRST, ba.last as LAST " +
                "from book_author ba, book b, author_work aw " +
                "where aw.author_id = ba.id " +
                "and b.id = aw.book_id", "authorBooks");
```

The List of results that is returned from this query can be utilized within a client, such as a JSF view, in the same manner as any List containing a single entity's results. The SqlResultSetMapping allows fields of an entity class to be mapped to a given name so that the name can then be specified in order to obtain the value for the mapped field. For instance, the following JSF dataTable source is taken from the chapter09/recipe09_05a.xhtml view, and it displays the List of results from the query in the solution:

```
<h:dataTable id="table" value="#{authorController.authorBooks}"
                                var="authorBook">
    <h:column>
        <f:facet name="header">
            <h:outputText value="Book ID"/>
        </f:facet>
        <h:outputText value="#{authorBook.id}"/>
    </h:column>
    <h:column>
```

```
    <f:facet name="header">
        <h:outputText value="Title"/>
    </f:facet>
    <h:outputText value="#{authorBook.title}"/>
</h:column>

<h:column>
    <f:facet name="header">
        <h:outputText value="Author"/>
    </f:facet>
    <h:outputText value="#{authorBook.first} #{authorBook.last}"/>
</h:column>

</h:dataTable>
```

As mentioned previously, entity fields can be mapped to a specified field returned from the database within the native SQL query. You can do so by specifying either the @FieldResult or @ColumnResult annotation for the columns parameter of a @SqlResultSetMapping annotation. For instance, in the example, you return only the TITLE and BOOK_ID columns from the BOOK database table, as well as the AUTHOR_ID, FIRST, and LAST columns from the BOOK_AUTHOR table. You include the SQL in the native query to join the tables and retrieve the values from these columns and return a SqlResultSetMapping that corresponds to the following:

```
@SqlResultSetMapping(name="authorBooks",
    entities= {
        @EntityResult(entityClass=org.jakartaeerecipes.entity.Book.
        class, fields={
            @FieldResult(name="id", column="BOOK_ID"),
            @FieldResult(name="title", column="TITLE")
        }),
        @EntityResult(entityClass=org.jakartaeerecipes.entity.
        BookAuthor.class, fields={
            @FieldResult(name="id", column="AUTHOR_ID"),
            @FieldResult(name="first", column="FIRST"),
            @FieldResult(name="last", column="LAST")
        })
    })
```

In Solution #2, no SqlResultSetMapping is used, and instead the results of the query are returned into a List of HashMap objects, rather than entity objects. The query returns a list of Object[], which can then be iterated over in order to make the data accessible to the client. As shown in the example, after the list of Object[] is obtained, a for loop can be used to iterate over each Object in the list obtaining the data for each returned database record field and storing it into a HashMap. To access the field data, specify a positional index that corresponds to the position of the database field data that you want to obtain. The positional indices correlate to the ordering of the returned fields within the SQL query, beginning with an index of 0. Therefore, to obtain the data for the first field returned in the query, specify an index of 0 on the Object for each row. As the Object[] is traversed, each database record can be parsed, in turn obtaining the data for each field in that row. The resulting data is then stored into the HashMap, and a String-based key that corresponds to the name of the returned field is specified so that the data can be made accessible to the client.

When accessing a HashMap of results from a client, such as a JSF view, the data can be accessed in the same manner as if a standard entity list were being used. This is because each HashMap element contains a key field that corresponds to the name of the data field. The following excerpt, taken from chapter09/recipe09_05b.xhtml, demonstrates how to use the results of a native query that have been stored into a HashMap using this technique:

```
<h:dataTable id="table" value="#{authorController.authorBooks}"
                              var="authorBook">
    <h:column>
        <f:facet name="header">
            <h:outputText value="Title"/>
        </f:facet>
        <h:outputText value="#{authorBook.bookTitle}"/>
    </h:column>
    <h:column>
        <f:facet name="header">
            <h:outputText value="Author"/>
        </f:facet>
        <h:outputText value="#{authorBook.authorFirst} #{authorBook.
        authorLast}"/>
    </h:column>
</h:dataTable>
```

As of JPA 2.2 (Jakarta EE 8), the `SqlResultSetMapping` is a repeatable annotation, so you may use more than one of them in the same entity class without encapsulating it within a container annotation. The `SqlResultSetMapping` makes it possible to use customized queries and joins into returning results via entity class objects. It is one more of the techniques that help complete the object-relational mapping (ORM) experience when using JPA.

9-6. Calling JPQL Aggregate Functions
Problem

You want to return the total number of records from a database table that match specified filtering criteria. For example, you want to return the total count of `BookAuthor` instances for a specified book.

Solution

Use the JPQL aggregate function `COUNT` to return the total number of objects that match the given query. The following method, which resides within the `org.jakartaeerecipes.session.AuthorWorkFacade` class, uses the `COUNT` aggregate function:

```
public Long findAuthorCount(Book book){
        Query qry = em.createQuery("select COUNT(o.authorId) from
        AuthorWork o " +
                "where o.bookId = :book")
                .setParameter("book", book.id);
        return (Long) qry.getSingleResult();
    }
```

The function will return a `Long` result, which will be the count of matching `AuthorWork` results.

How It Works

Aggregate functions are those that can group values of multiple rows together on certain criteria to form a single value. Native SQL contains aggregate functions that can be useful for calculating the sum of all rows in a particular table, maximum values of a column, first values within a column, and so on. JPQL contains a number of aggregate functions that can be used within queries.

In this recipe, the example demonstrates the use of the COUNT function, which returns the total number of rows in an underlying data store table. The value is calculated and returned as a Long data type, which can be cast from a call to the javax.persistence. Query object's getSingleResult method. However, there are a number of other functions at your disposal. Table 9-3 lists those functions and their return type.

Table 9-3. *JPQL Aggregate Functions*

Function	Description	Return Type
COUNT	Total number of records	Long
MAX	Record with largest numeric value	Same as the field to which applied
MIN	Record with lowest numeric value	Same as the field to which applied
AVG	Average of all numeric values in a column	Double
SUM	Sum of all values in a column	Long when applied to integral types
		Double when applied to floating-point
		BigInteger when applied to BigInteger
		BigDecimal when applied to BigDecimal

If a particular database record contains a NULL value for a column to which an aggregate function is being applied, then that NULL value is eliminated before the function is applied. The DISTINCT keyword can be used to specify that any duplicate values should be eliminated before the function is applied. The following line of code demonstrates the use of DISTINCT:

```
Query qry = em.createQuery("select DISTINCT(COUNT(o.title)) from Book o");
```

The important thing to remember when using aggregate functions is that they are applied to the same field within all objects that satisfy the query. This is analogous to the function being applied to all values returned for a single column's results within a query.

9-7. Invoking Database Stored Procedures Natively

Problem

The application you are writing uses JPQL and relies on one or more database stored procedures to perform tasks on the data. You need to have the ability to call those stored procedures from within the business logic of your Java application code.

Solution

Create a native query, and write a SQL `String` that executes the database stored procedure. Suppose you have a database procedure named `CREATE_USER` and it accepts two arguments: `username` and `password`. You can invoke the `CREATE_USER` procedure by calling it via a native SQL query. The following method, named `createUser`, accepts a username and password as arguments and passes them to the underlying database procedure and executes it:

```java
public void createUser(String user, String pass){
        Query qry = (Query) em.createNativeQuery(
          "select CREATE_USER('" + user + "','" + pass + "') from dual");
        qry.getSingleResult();
    }
```

How It Works

Historically, the only way to work with database stored procedures from JPA was to utilize a native query. The solution to this recipe demonstrates this tactic because a native query is used to invoke a database stored procedure. In the example, a method named `createUser` accepts two parameters, `username` and `password`, which are both passed to the database stored procedure named `CREATE_USER` via the native query. The `EntityManager`'s `createNativeQuery()` method is called, and a SQL `String` that performs a `SELECT` on the stored procedure is passed to the method. In SQL, performing a `SELECT` on a stored procedure will cause the procedure to be executed. Notice that the `DUAL` table is being referenced in the SQL. The `DUAL` is a dummy table that can be used when you need to apply `SELECT` statements to different database constructs, such as a stored procedure.

Execution of native SQL is an acceptable solution for invoking stored procedures that have no return values or when you have only a limited number of SQL statements to maintain. However, in most enterprise situations that require an application with multiple stored procedure calls or calls that require a return value, the @NamedStoredProcedure solution in Recipe 9-10 can be advantageous.

9-8. Joining to Retrieve Instances from Multiple Entities

Problem

You want to create joins between entities in order to return fields from more than one underlying database table.

Solution

Use JPQL to create a join between two entities that share a one-to-many and many-to-one relationship with each other. In this example, a one-to-many relationship is set up against the Book and Chapter entities such that one book can contain many chapters. The following excerpt from the org.jakartaeerecipes.entity.Book class demonstrates the one-to-many relationship declaration:

```
@OneToMany(mappedBy="book", cascade=CascadeType.ALL)
private List<Chapter> chapters = null;
```

The Chapter entity contains a many-to-one relationship with the Book entity, such that many chapters can be related to one book. The following excerpt from the org. jakartaeerecipes.chapter09.entity.Chapter class demonstrates the many-to-one relationship:

```
@ManyToOne
@JoinColumn(name = "BOOK_ID")
private Book book;
```

Ultimately, the join query is contained within a method named
findBookByChapterTitle(), which resides in the org.jakartaeerecipes.session.
Chapter session bean. The following code excerpt contains the lines of code that make
up that method:

```
public List<Book> findBookByChapterTitle(String chapterTitle){
    return em.createQuery("select b from Book b INNER JOIN b.chapters c " +
        "where c.title = :title")
        .setParameter("title", chapterTitle)
        .getResultList();
}
```

Note   To return several different properties within the SELECT clause, rather
than an object, the result will be returned in an Object[]. To find out more about
working with such a solution, please refer to Solution #2 of Recipe 9-5.

How It Works

The most common type of database table join operation is known as an *inner join*.
When performing an inner join, all of the columns from each table will be available to
be returned as if it were a single, combined table. To create a join between two entities,
they must be related to each other via a one-to-many relationship. This means that one
of the entities could contain an instance that possibly contains many references to the
other entity, whereas the other entity could have many instances that would reference
only one instance of the former entity. In the example for this recipe, the Book entity has
a one-to-many relationship with the Chapter entity. This means that a single book may
contain many chapters.

The example for this recipe demonstrates a join between the Book and Chapter
entities. The method findBookByChapterTitle() contains a JPQL query that will return
any Book objects that contain a matching chapter title. To generate an inner join query,
invoke the EntityManager object's createQuery() method, passing the String-based

JPQL query that contains the join syntax. A JPQL string for performing an inner join should be written in the following format, where INNER is an optional (default) keyword:

```
SELECT a.col1, a.col2 from Entity1 a [INNER] JOIN a.collectionColumn b
WHERE expressions
```

In the example, an entire Book instance will be returned for each Book entity that contains a Chapter instance, which has a title matching the parameter. Typically, the join occurs over a foreign key, and in the case of the one-to-many relationship, it occurs on the field that is a collection of the related entity's instances.

9-9. Joining to Retrieve All Rows Regardless of Match

Problem

You want to create joins between entities in order to produce results that will include all objects of the left entity listed and matching results or NULL values when there is no match from the right entity listed.

Solution

In this example, a one-to-many relationship is set up against the Book and Chapter entities such that one book can contain many chapters. The following excerpt from the org.jakartaeerecipes.entity.Book class demonstrates the one-to-many relationship declaration:

```
@OneToMany(mappedBy="book", cascade=CascadeType.ALL)
private List<Chapter> chapters = null;
```

The Chapter entity has a many-to-one relationship with the Book entity, such that many chapters can be related to one book. The following excerpt from the org.jakartaeerecipes.entity.Chapter class demonstrates the many-to-one relationship:

```
@ManyToOne
@JoinColumn(name = "BOOK_ID")
private Book book;
```

The code that contains the left outer join query resides within the findAllBooksByChapterNumber() method, which is contained within the org.jakartaeerecipes.session.ChapterFacade class. The following excerpt taken from the class lists the method implementation:

```
public List<Book> findAllBooksByChapterNumber(BigDecimal chapterNumber){
        return em.createQuery("select b from Book b LEFT OUTER JOIN
        b.chapters c " +
                "where c.chapterNumber = :num")
                .setParameter("num", chapterNumber)
                .getResultList();
    }
```

How It Works

An outer join, otherwise known as a LEFT OUTER JOIN or LEFT JOIN, is not as common of an occurrence as an inner join. To explain an outer join in database terminology, all rows of the table listed on the left side of the JOIN keyword are returned in a LEFT SQL join, and only those matching rows from the table listed to the right of the keyword will be returned in a "Left Outer" SQL join. In other words, an outer join enables the retrieval of a set of database records where a matching value within the join may not be present. In JPA terminology, all instances of the entity class to the left of the JOIN keyword will be returned.

Outer joins on entities usually occur between two related entities in which there is a one-to-many relationship or vice versa. To form an outer join JPQL query, use the following format, where the [OUTER] keyword is optional:

```
SELECT a.col1, a.col2 FROM Entity1 a LEFT [OUTER] JOIN a.collectionColumn b
WHERE expression
```

In the example, all Book objects are returned, but only those Chapter objects that match the specified criteria would be included in the ResultSet.

9-10. Applying JPQL Functional Expressions

Problem

You want to apply functions within your JPQL Strings to alter the results of the execution. For example, you are interested in altering Strings that will be used within the WHERE clause of your JPQL query.

Solution

Utilize any of the built-in JPQL functions to apply functional expressions to your JPQL. To alter Strings that are utilized within a JPQL query, develop the query containing String functions that will be applied within the WHERE clause of the query. In the following example, the UPPER function is utilized in order to change the case of the given text into all uppercase letters. In this case, a search page has been set up for users to enter an author's last name and search the database for a match. The String that the user enters is converted to uppercase and used to query the database.

The following lines of code are taken from the search view, which resides within the JSF view that is composed within the chapter09/recipe09_10.xhtml file:

```
<ui:composition template="layout/custom_template_search.xhtml">
    <ui:define name="content">
        <h:form>
    <h2>Recipe 9-10: Using JPA String Functions</h2>
            <br/>
            <p>Enter an author's last name below to search the author
            database.</p>
    <br/>
            <h:outputLabel value="Last Name:"/>
            <h:inputText id="last" value="#{authorController.authorLast}"
            size="75"/>
            <br/>
            <br/>
            <h:commandButton value="Search" action="#{authorController.
            findAuthorByLast}"/>
```

```
        </h:form>
    </ui:define>
</ui:composition>
```

Next, the code for the CDI bean controller method, findAuthorByLast(), is listed. This method resides within the org.jakartaeerecipes.jsf.AuthorController class. This code is responsible for populating the authorList and then directing navigation to the recipe09_10b.xhtml view:

```
public String findAuthorByLast(){
    authorList = ejbFacade.findAuthorByLast(authorLast);
    return "/chapter09/recipe09_10b.xhtml";
}
```

Lastly, the EJB method named findAuthorByLast(String) is contained within the org.jakartaeerecipes.session.BookAuthorFacade class. The method accepts the String value that the user entered into the web search form and uses it to query the database for a matching author, converting the text to uppercase before performing the comparison:

```
public List<BookAuthor> findAuthorByLast(String authorLast){
    return em.createQuery("select o from BookAuthor o " +
    "where o.last = UPPER(:authorLast)")
    .setParameter("authorLast", authorLast).getResultList();
}
```

The resulting page will display any author names that match the text that was entered by the user.

How It Works

The JPA query language contains a handful of functions that can be used to manipulate Strings, perform arithmetic, and make dates easier to work with. The functions can be specified within the WHERE or HAVING clause of JPQL query Strings. JPQL contains a number of String functions. Table 9-4 lists the different String functions that are available, along with a description of what they do.

Table 9-4. *JPQL String Functions*

Function	Description
CONCAT(string1, string2)	Returns a concatenated String composed of the two arguments.
SUBSTRING(string, expr1, expr2)	Returns a substring of the specified String. The first position within the substring is denoted by expr1, and the length of the substring is denoted by expr2.
TRIM([[spec][char]FROM] str)	Trims a specified character (spec) from a string (str).
LOWER(string)	Returns the given String in all lowercase letters.
UPPER(string)	Returns the given String in all uppercase letters.

There are also a number of functions within JPQL to help perform arithmetic within queries. Table 9-5 lists the different arithmetic functions that are available, along with a description of what they do.

Table 9-5. *JPQL Arithmetic Functions*

Function	Description
ABS(expr)	Returns the absolute value. Takes a numeric argument and returns a number of the same type.
SQRT(expr)	Returns the square root value. Takes a numeric argument and returns a double.
MOD(expr1, expr2)	Returns the modulus value in integer format.
SIZE(collection)	Returns the total number of elements in the given collection in integer format. If the collection contains no elements, it evaluates to zero.

Working with dates from any programming language can sometimes be a bit tough. The JPQL contains a handful of helpful datetime functions to make it a bit easier. Table 9-6 lists the different datetime functions that are available, along with a description of what they do.

Table 9-6. *JPQL Datetime Functions*

Function	Description
CURRENT_DATE	Returns the current date
CURRENT_TIME	Returns the current time
CURRENT_TIMESTAMP	Returns the current timestamp

9-11. Forcing Query Execution Rather Than Cache Use

Problem

The default `EntityManager` is using cached results from a database query, and you want to force a query to be executed each time a table is loaded, rather than allowing the results of the cache to be displayed.

Solution

After the `javax.persistence.Query` instance is created, set a hint, `javax.persistence.cache.retrieveMode`, to bypass the cache and force the query to be executed. In the following lines of code, the `Book` entity is queried, and the cache is bypassed by setting the hint:

```
public List<Book> findAllBooks(){
    Query qry = em.createQuery("select o from Book o");
    qry.setHint("javax.persistence.cache.retrieveMode", CacheRetrieveMode.
    BYPASS);
    return qry.getResultList();
}
```

Upon execution, the query will be forced to execute, returning the most current results from the underlying database table.

Note By default, results from JPA queries are cached in an effort to provide peak performance. This enables the cache data to be returned in the event that the same query is used multiple times.

How It Works

There are often occasions when an application requires the most current table data to be displayed or used for performing a given task. For instance, if you were to write a stock market application, it would not make sense to cache the current market results since stale data would not be very useful to investors. In such cases, it is imperative to force queries to be executed and bypass any caching. This is possible via the use of hints that can be registered with `javax.persistence.Query` instances.

By setting the `javax.persistence.cache.retrieveMode` hint to `CacheRetrieveMode.BYPASS`, the JPA is told to always force the execution of a query. When the query is executed, it will always return the most current results from the database.

9-12. Performing Bulk Updates and Deletes
Problem

You want to update or delete a group of entity objects.

Solution

Perform a bulk update or deletion using the Criteria API. The Criteria API allows the use of the builder pattern for specifying entity operations. In the following example, a bulk update is performed on the `Employee` entity. The following example method resides in a session bean class for the `org.jakartaeerecipes.entity.Employee` entity. The session bean class name is `org.jakartaeerecipes.session.EmployeeSession.java`, and the following excerpt from that class shows how to perform a bulk update:

```
...
public String updateEmployeeStatusInactive() {
        String returnMessage = null;
```

```
CriteriaBuilder builder = em.getCriteriaBuilder();
CriteriaUpdate<Employee> q = builder.createCriteriaUpdate(Employee.
class);
Root<Employee> e = q.from(Employee.class);
q.set(e.get("status"), "ACTIVE")
        .where(builder.equal(e.get("status"), "INACTIVE"));
Query criteriaUpd = em.createQuery(q);
int result = criteriaUpd.executeUpdate();
if (result > 0){
    returnMessage = result + " records updated";
} else {
    returnMessage = "No records updated";
}
return returnMessage;
    }
...
```

Similarly, the Criteria API can be used to perform a bulk deletion. The following method, also within the EmployeeSession bean, demonstrates how to do so:

```
...
public String deleteEmployeeOnStatus(String condition) {
    CriteriaBuilder builder = em.getCriteriaBuilder();
    CriteriaDelete<Employee> q = builder.createCriteriaDelete(Employee.
    class);
    Root<Employee> e = q.from(Employee.class);
    q.where(builder.equal(e.get("status"), condition));
    return null;
    }
...
```

How It Works

The Criteria API was enhanced with the Java EE 8 release to support bulk updates and deletions. As seen in earlier recipes, the Criteria API allows developers to utilize Java language syntax in order to perform database queries and manipulations, rather than

JPQL or SQL. A javax.persistence.criteria.CriteriaUpdate object can be used to perform bulk update operations, and a javax.persistence.critera.CriteriaDelete object can be used to perform bulk deletion operations. How do we obtain such objects? The Criteria API is dependent upon the javax.persistence.criteria. CriteriaBuilder interface, which is used to return objects that can be used to work with specified Entity classes. In the JPA 2.1 release, the CriteriaBuilder was updated to include the methods createCriteriaUpdate() and createCriteriaDelete(), which will return the CriteriaUpdate or CriteriaDelete object, respectively.

To use the CriteriaBuilder, you first need to obtain a CriteriaBuilder from the EntityManager. You can then use the CriteriaBuilder to obtain the CriteriaUpdate or CriteriaDelete object of your choosing. In the following lines of code, a CriteriaUpdate object is obtained for use with an Employee entity:

```
CriteriaBuilder builder = em.getCriteriaBuilder();
CriteriaUpdate<Employee> q = builder.createCriteriaUpdate(Employee.class);
```

Once obtained, the CriteriaUpdate can be used to build a query and set values, as desired, for making the necessary updates or deletions. In the following excerpt, the CriteriaUpdate object is used to update all Employee objects that have a status of INACTIVE, changing that status to ACTIVE:

```
Root<Employee> e = q.from(Employee.class);
q.set(e.get("status"), "ACTIVE")
        .where(builder.equal(e.get("status"), "INACTIVE"));
```

Let's break this down a bit to explain what exactly is going on. First, the query root is set by calling the q.from method and passing the entity class for which you want to obtain the root, where q is the CriteriaUpdate object. Next, the q.set method is invoked, passing the Path to the Employee status attribute, along with the ACTIVE string. The q.set method is performing the bulk update. To further refine the query, a WHERE clause is added using a chained call to the .where method and passing the Employee objects that have a status of INACTIVE. The entire criteria can be seen in the solution for this recipe.

Finally, to complete the transaction, you must create the Query object and then execute it using the following lines of code:

```
Query criteriaUpd = em.createQuery(q);
criteriaUpd.executeUpdate();
```

The bulk deletion is very similar, except instead of using the `CriteriaBuilder` to obtain a `CriteriaUpdate` object, use it to obtain a `CriteriaDelete` object instead. To obtain a `CriteriaDelete` object, call the `CriteriaBuilder` `createCriteriaDelete` method, as follows:

```
CriteriaBuilder builder = em.getCriteriaBuilder();
CriteriaDelete<Employee> q = builder.createCriteriaDelete(Employee.class);
```

Once a `CriteriaDelete` object has been obtained, then the conditions for deletion need to be specified by filtering the results using a call (or chain of calls) to the `.where` method. When using the bulk delete, all objects that match the specified condition will be deleted. For example, the following lines of code demonstrate how to delete all `Employee` objects that have the `status` attribute equal to `INACTIVE`:

```
Root<Employee> e = q.from(Employee.class);
q.where(builder.equal(e.get("status"), "INACTIVE"));
```

Note   Both the `CriteriaUpdate` and `CriteriaDelete` examples demonstrated can be made more type-safe by using the MetaModel API. For each entity class in a particular persistence unit, a metamodel class is created with a trailing underscore, along with the attributes that correspond to the persistent fields of the entity class. This metamodel can be used to manage entity classes and their persistent state and relationships. Therefore, instead of specifying an error-prone `String` in the `Path` to obtain a particular attribute, you could specify the metamodel attribute instead, as follows: `e.get(Employee_.status)`.

For more information on using the MetaModel API to create type-safe queries, please refer to the online documentation.

The Criteria API can be very detailed, and it is also very powerful. To learn more about the Criteria API, please see the documentation online at `https://eclipse-ee4j.github.io/jakartaee-tutorial/persistence-criteria.html#GJITV`.

9-13. Retrieving Entity Subclasses

Problem

You want to obtain the data for an entity, along with all of the data from that entity's
subclasses.

Solution

Utilize the downcasting feature of JPA. To do so, specify the TREAT keyword within
the FROM and/or WHERE clause of a JPA query in order to filter the specified types
and subtypes that you want to retrieve. In the following example, the query will
return all BookStore entities that are from the IT books. The assumption is that the
ItCategory entity is a subtype of the BookCategory entity. The method in the example,
named getBookCategories(), resides within the org.jakartaeerecipes.sessior.
BookCategoryFacade session bean:

```
public List getBookCategories(){
        TypedQuery<Object[]> qry = em.createQuery("select a.name, a.genre,
        a.description " +
                "from BookStore s JOIN TREAT(s.categories as ItCategory) a",
                Object[].class);

    List data = new ArrayList();
    if (!qry.getResultList().isEmpty()) {
        List<Object[]> tdata = qry.getResultList();
        for (Object[] t : tdata) {
            HashMap resultMap = new HashMap();
            resultMap.put("name", t[0]);
            resultMap.put("genre", t[1]);
            resultMap.put("categoryDesc", t[2]);
            data.add(resultMap);
        }
    }
    return data;
}
```

When invoked, this query will return data from the `ItCategory` entity, which is a subclass of the `BookCategory` entity, as per the previous description. To better understand how to relate the entities, please refer to the entire source code within the two entities, located within the `org.jakartaeerecipes.entity.BookCategory.java` and `org.jakartaeerecipes.entity.ItCategory.java` files in the sources for this book.

How It Works

The act of *downcasting* is defined as the casting of a base type or class reference to one of its derived types or classes. The Jakarta EE platform introduced the concept of downcasting in JPA 2.1 by providing the ability to obtain a reference to a subclass of a specified entity within a query. In other words, you can explicitly query one or more entities and retrieve the attributes from each of the entities as well as any attributes from entities that are subclasses of those that are explicitly declared. To provide this ability, the TREAT keyword was added to JPA.

The use of the TREAT operator is supported for downcasting within path expressions in the FROM and WHERE clauses. The first argument to the TREAT operator should be a subtype of the target type; otherwise, the path is considered to have no value, attributing nothing to the end result. The TREAT operator can filter on the specified types and subtypes, as well as perform a downcast.

The syntax for use of the TREAT operator is as follows:

```
SELECT b.attr1, b.attr2
FROM EntityA a JOIN TREAT(a.referenceToEntityB as EntityBSubType) b
```

In the previous JPQL, the TREAT operation contains an attribute from the specified entity (EntityA) that relates to a joined entity (EntityB). The TREAT operation tells the container to treat the referenced entity (EntityB) as the type of EntityBSubtype. Therefore, the downcast takes place and allows access to those subtype entities. The following lines of code demonstrate this technique in action:

```
SELECT a.name, a.genre, a.description
FROM BookStore s JOIN TREAT(s.categories AS ItCategory) a
```

As mentioned previously, the TREAT operator can also be used within the WHERE clause in order to filter a query based upon subtype attribute values. Downcasting support allows JPA to be even more flexible for developers to use, making more complex queries possible. This technique makes it easier to obtain values from related entities or subtypes, without the need to issue an extra query.

9-14. Joining with ON Conditions

Problem

You want to retrieve all the entities that match the specified criteria for joining two entities, along with each entity that does not match on the left side of an OUTER join.

Solution

Utilize the ON condition to specify a join of two or more entity classes based upon the specified filtering criteria. The following method includes the JPQL for retrieving all Jobs entities, along with a count of the number of Employee entities that belong to those Jobs. This method, named obtainActiveEmployeeCount(), utilizes the ON condition to filter the join based upon the Employee status:

```
public List obtainActiveEmployeeCount() {
    TypedQuery<Object[]> qry = em.createQuery("SELECT j.title, count(e) "
            + "FROM Jobs j LEFT JOIN j.employees e "
            + "ON e.status = 'ACTIVE' "
            + "WHERE j.salary >= 50000 "
            + "GROUP BY j.title", Object[].class);

    List data = new ArrayList();
     if (!qry.getResultList().isEmpty()) {
         List<Object[]> tdata = qry.getResultList();
        for (Object[] t : tdata) {
            HashMap resultMap = new HashMap();
            resultMap.put("title", t[0]);
            resultMap.put("count", t[1]);
            data.add(resultMap);
        }
    }
    return data;

}
```

How It Works

When writing JPQL queries, it is sometimes beneficial to join two or more database tables to acquire related information. Furthermore, it is usually helpful to filter information based upon certain specified criteria so that the number of records returned can be manageable. JPQL joins typically include INNER, OUTER, and FETCH joins. To review, an INNER join allows retrieval from two tables such that records being returned contain at least one match in both tables. For instance, you may want to query an Employee entity and join it to the Jobs entity to return only those employees who have a specific job title. An OUTER join allows retrieval from two tables such that all of the records from one of the entities (left entity) are returned, regardless of whether they match with a record in the other entity. Lastly, a FETCH join enables the fetching of an association as a side effect of the query execution. In JPA 2.1, JPQL was updated to include the ON condition, which allows you to perform an OUTER join and include a specified condition with the join. This capability has always been available with the WHERE clause of the JPQL query, but what about the cases when you want to return all matching records along with those that may not match, like with an OUTER join? JPA provides this functionality in a concise manner using ON conditions. Simply put, an ON condition modifies a join query such that it will incorporate better control over the data that is returned in a concise manner.

To demonstrate this new syntax, let's take a look at a SQL query, and then you will compare it to its JPQL counterpart. The following SQL will join the EMPLOYEE table with the JOBS table on the JOB_ID field. It will also limit the returned records to those that include a salary of greater than or equal to 50,000 with the specification in the WHERE clause:

```
SELECT J.TITLE, COUNT(E.ID)
FROM JOBS J LEFT JOIN EMPLOYEE E
    ON J.JOB_ID = E.JOB_ID and E.STATUS 'ACTIVE'
WHERE J.SALARY >= 50000
GROUP BY J.TITLE;
```

This SQL will return all of the JOB records and include a count of each job that contains an Employee whose status is ACTIVE. The method in the solution of this recipe contains the JPQL equivalent for this SQL, using the ON condition to perform the join. In the end, the ON condition helps make JPQL outer joins more concise and easy to use. Although the same capability has been available in previous versions of JPQL, the ON clause helps make record filtering with joins much easier.

9-15. Processing Query Results with Streams

Problem

You wish to process the results of a JPA query using a concise functional style.

Solution

Utilize streams to process the results of a JPA query. In the following example, a Stream is returned from a JPA query. The Stream is then processed using the Stream API to retrieve the desired results. This particular example demonstrates a Stream being used to process author works by author:

```
public List<AuthorWork> performFindByAuthorStream(BookAuthor authorId){
    Stream<AuthorWork> awStream = em.createQuery("select object(o) from
    AuthorWork o")
        .getResultStream();

    return awStream.filter(
        ba -> authorId.equals(ba.getAuthorId()))
        .collect(Collectors.toList());

}
```

> **Note**   This particular example demonstrates filtering the results of a SQL query using streams, which may not be the most effective approach. A very large result set may significantly increase the time it takes to process. Please be sure to weigh the performance benefits of using standard JPQL vs. using Streams to ensure you choose the best option for your situation.

How It Works

Streams offer a powerful alternative to processing SQL result sets. The Stream API was first introduced into the Java platform with the release of Java SE 8. The JPA 2.2 release has brought the API into alignment with Java SE 8, allowing JPA users to benefit from the use of the Stream API while processing results. The Stream API allows one to apply filters and functions to data in a functional way, making processing much more concise and easy to follow. JPA 2.2 features a new getResultStream() method on the *Query* and TypeQuery interfaces, allowing one to return a Stream of results, rather than a List or single object result. Once the Stream has been returned, it can be processed accordingly.

Breaking down the recipe example, first the AuthorWork entity is queried without any filters. Note that instead of calling upon getResultList(), the getResultStream() is called upon. This will return a Stream of the objects that are being queried. Once the Stream has been returned, it is processed by filtering the data to return only those records that have an authorId matching what was passed into the method. Note the notation which is used for processing is as follows:

```
ba -> authorId.equals(ba.getAuthorId())
```

First, note that the syntax is very much like that of the lambda processing syntax. The ba -> portion is simply a local variable that is declared to represent the current object in the Stream, and the arrow characters are used to note that the processing expression follows. Each object in the stream is iterated, and ba changes for each one. Next, the filter is applied, only retaining those records that have authorId equal to the one that is passed into the method. Next, we wish to return a List of the results from that filtering process, so the Collectors utility is used to collect the filtered results into a list:

```
.collect(Collectors.toList())
```

It is important to keep in mind that if it is possible to filter queries in the traditional manner, via the SQL where clause, that may perform better than the Stream alternative. The reason is that the default Stream toResultStream() implementation will fetch all of the data from the query into an in-memory list and then process accordingly. This could be very bad if the result set is large. It is possible for different implementations of this process to be created. At the time of the Jakarta EE 8 release, Hibernate provides something similar in the stream() method, whereby a scrollable ResultSet is returned, rather than the entire list of results. Such an implementation would perform much better in a large dataset scenario.

9-16. Converting Attribute Data Types

Problem

You wish to convert the data type of a particular entity class attribute when it is retrieved from the database. In turn, you wish to convert back to the original data type when persisting data back to the database column.

Solution

Create an attribute converter to convert to/from different data types when retrieving and persisting data. Suppose that you would like to convert between a Boolean-based full employee status within a Java entity and a String-based ACTIVE or INACTIVE value within the database. Each time the attribute is accessed, the converter is used to automatically convert the values to/from the desired data types:

```java
package org.jakartaeerecipes.converter;

import javax.persistence.AttributeConverter;
import javax.persistence.Converter;

@Converter
public class EmployeeStatusConverter implements AttributeConverter<Boolean,
String> {

    @Override
    public String convertToDatabaseColumn(Boolean entityValue) {
        if(entityValue){
            return "ACTIVE";
        } else {
            return "INACTIVE";
        }
    }

    @Override
    public Boolean convertToEntityAttribute(String databaseValue) {
        return databaseValue.equals("ACTIVE");
    }
}
```

The converter can be applied to a single entity class attribute, as follows:

```
@Column(name= "STATUS")
@Convert(converter=org.jakartaeerecipes.converter.EmployeeStatusConverter.
class)
private boolean status;
```

In this example, when the `Employee` object is persisted to the database, a true would be converted to `"ACTIVE"`. Likewise, when an `Employee` object is retrieved, then an `"INACTIVE"` status value is converted to false.

How It Works

Attribute converters allow for data type conversion to occur between the database column and an entity class attribute. Attribute converters can be created by annotating a class with `@Converter` and implementing the `AttributeConverter` interface. The `AttributeConverter` type takes two arguments, those being the type of the entity class attribute and the type of the database column. When implementing `AttributeConverter`, two methods must be overridden. The `convertToDatabaseColumn()` method should provide the implementation for conversion from the entity class attribute to the database column type. Similarly, the `convertToEntityAttribute()` method should provide the opposite implementation, conversion from the database column type to the entity class attribute.

In the example for this recipe, the attribute converter is applied to a single entity class attribute. To do so, the `@Convert` annotation is applied to the attribute, passing the converter class as an argument. The converter could also be applied to all entity class attributes pertaining to the entity data type by changing the `@Converter` annotation on the attribute converter to the following: `@Converter(autoApply=true)`.

CHAPTER 10

Bean Validation

One of the most important pieces of any data-using application is data validation. It is imperative that one validates data before it is inserted into a database in order to maintain integrity. There are a number of reasons to validate, the most important being security purposes, data consistency, and proper formatting. Many web applications use validation in the presentation layer via JavaScript for validation of form data and also in the persistence layer. However, sometimes JavaScript can become problematic in that the code can become unwieldy and there is also no guarantee that it will execute. It is oftentimes found to be a good idea to perform validation within the domain model, although this can cause code clutter.

In this chapter, we will take a look at the Bean Validation API, which is used to apply validation to a JavaBean. In the context of Jakarta EE, since JPA entity classes are Plain Old Java Objects (POJOs), this allows developers to make use of Bean Validation on entity classes and entity class attributes. A Java controller class may have validation logic to ensure that only specific data passes through to the database. The Bean Validation API is another means of performing data validation in either the domain model or presentation layer via metadata, using an annotation-based approach. To validate with this API, one simply applies validation constraint annotations on the entity class attribute(s), as needed, and the constraint validators will automatically enforce the validation. Bean Validation was first introduced into Jakarta EE platform with Java EE 6, and it had been given a face-lift in Java EE 8, introducing a number of new features for the Bean Validation 2.0 release. Although this chapter will focus on the use of Bean Validation with Jakarta EE, it can be used in JavaBeans across all different flavors of Java, be it Java FX, previous Java EE releases, or Java SE. Bean validation contains an API that can be used to manually invoke validation, but in most cases the validation occurs automatically because of the integration that has been made across the various Jakarta EE specifications.

© Josh Juneau 2020
J. Juneau, *Jakarta EE Recipes*, https://doi.org/10.1007/978-1-4842-5587-2_10

Bean Validation annotation constraints can be applied on types, fields, methods, constructors, parameters, container elements, and other container annotations. Validation is applied not only to the object level, but it can also be inherited from superclasses. Entire object graphs can be validated, meaning that if a class declares a field which has the type of a separate class containing validation, cascading validation can occur.

This chapter will demonstrate examples of each validation type, explaining the strongholds for each of the different methodologies. In the end, you will have a good understanding of how the Bean Validation API works, and you should be able to apply Bean Validation strategies to your applications.

Note   Bean Validation allows one to declare constraints via XML, rather than annotations. For the purposes of brevity, this chapter will not cover this feature. For more information, please see the Bean Validation 2.0 specification (`https://jakarta.ee/specifications/bean-validation/2.0/bean-validation_2.0.html`).

10-1. Validating Fields with Built-in Constraints

Problem

Imagine that you create a Chapter entity class, which will be used to store the contents regarding a book chapter. In doing so, you wish to apply validation to specified fields of the entity class such that only compliant data is allowed to be inserted or updated in the database. In this case, suppose that there are a number of fields that must contain values, and you also want to be certain that Strings of text are within the size limits of the underlying database field.

Solution #1

Apply the pertinent Bean Validation constraints to field(s) that you wish to validate. In this example, the standard @NotNull and @Size constraint annotations are placed on specific fields of the Chapter entity. Namely, the id attribute is marked as @NotNull so that it must contain a value, and the title attribute is marked to have a maximum size of 150 characters:

```
@Entity
@Table(name = "CHAPTER")

public class Chapter implements Serializable {
    private static final long serialVersionUID = 1L;
    @Id
    @Basic(optional = false)
    @NotNull
    @Column(name = "ID")
    private BigDecimal id;
    @Column(name = "CHAPTER_NUMBER")
    private BigDecimal chapterNumber;
    @Size(max = 150)
    @Column(name = "TITLE")
    private String title;
    @Lob
    @Column(name = "DESCRIPTION")
    private String description;
 . . .
```

Solution #2

Apply the pertinent Bean Validation constraint annotations to the getter methods (accessor methods) of the field(s) you wish to validate. In this case, the following example shows the getId() and getTitle() methods. Each of these accessor methods is annotated accordingly:

```
@NotNull
private BigDecimal getId(){
    return this.id;
}
```

```
. . .
@Size(max=150)
private String getTitle(){
    return this.title;
}
```

How It Works

The Bean Validation API provides a number of built-in constraint definitions that are ready to use. These standard constraints span the array of common use cases for data validation. Table 10-1 lists each of the standard validation constraint annotations along with a description of each.

Table 10-1. *Standard Built-In Constraints*

Annotation	Description
@Null	The annotated element must be null.
@NotNull	The annotated element must not be null.
@AssertTrue	The annotated element must be true.
@AssertFalse	The annotated element must be false.
@Min	The annotated element must be a number with a value that is higher or equal to the specified minimum.
@Max	The annotated element must be a number with a value that is lower or equal to the specified maximum.
@DecimalMin	The annotated element must be a decimal with a value that is higher or equal to the specified minimum.
@DecimalMax	The annotated element must be a decimal with a value that is lower or equal to the specified maximum.
@Negative	The annotated element must be a strictly negative number.
@NegativeOrZero	The annotated element must be a negative number or zero.
@Positive	The annotated element must be a strictly positive number.

(continued)

Table 10-1. (*continued*)

Annotation	Description
@PositiveOrZero	The annotated element must be strictly positive or zero.
@Size	The annotated element size must fall within the specified boundaries.
@Digits	The annotated element must be a number in the accepted range.
@Past	The annotated element must be an instant, date, or time in the past.
@PastOrPresent	The annotated element must be an instant, date, or time in the past or present.
@Future	The annotated element must be an instant, date, or time in the future.
@FutureOrPresent	The annotated element must be an instant, date, or time in the future or present.
@Pattern	The annotated element must fall within the constraints of the specified regular expression.
@NotEmpty	The annotated element must not be empty or null.
@NotBlank	The annotated element must not be null and must contain at least one character.
@Email	The annotated string must be a well-formed email address.

To apply validation to a field, simply specify the built-in or custom Bean `Validation` annotation to the field declaration, along with the appropriate constraint attribute(s). You also have the option of annotating a field's corresponding getter method, rather than the field declaration itself. Any single field may have more than one annotation constraint applied to it. You are welcome to combine constraints to suit the requirement. If an annotated class extends another class that contains Bean Validation constraints, then those constraints are applied to all annotated fields, whether the field belongs to the extended class or the class that extends.

Attributes are used to associate metadata with the annotations for specifying information such as the error message that is to be displayed should the validation fail or the number of characters to be validated. Table 10-2 lists the common constraint annotation attributes that you'll find across each of the different constraints. These are all considered reserved names.

Table 10-2. *Common Constraint Annotation Attributes*

Attribute	Description
message	Allows a String for specifying an error message to display
groups	Specifies processing groups with which the constraint declaration is associated
payload	Specifies the payload with which the constraint declaration is associated
validationAppliesTo	Used to specify which constraint targets a validation constraint will apply to

Most of the constraint attributes are optional. However, in some cases, an attribute should be specified. For instance, when applying the @Size constraint, if the max attribute is not specified, the default is 2147483647. Therefore, given that someone will likely never enter a value that large, one should specify a maximum size using the max attribute. The groups attribute is used to specify if a particular annotation constraint is part of a processing group. A validation group defines a subset of constraints, and a group can simply be an empty interface. Groups are used to control the order of evaluation for constraints or to perform partial state validation for a JavaBean. To learn more about applying groups, please refer to Recipe 10-8. The payload attribute is used to assign a payload to a validation annotation. Payloads are typically used by bean validation clients to associate some kind of metadata information. A payload is usually defined as a class that implements the Payload interface. Payloads can be seen in more detail with Recipe 10-9.

10-2. Writing Custom Constraint Validators
Problem

Your application requires a specific validation that is not provided among the built-in Bean Validation constraints. For example, you wish to validate that a book title includes the word "Java" in the title.

Solution

Implement a custom constraint validator for the application. A custom constraint can be created by developing a constraint annotation along with a validator implementation class and a default error message. The example that follows demonstrates a custom constraint that is used to compare whether a String contains the text "Java". The annotation class for such a constraint may resemble the following:

```
import java.lang.annotation.Documented;
import static java.lang.annotation.ElementType.ANNOTATION_TYPE;
import static java.lang.annotation.ElementType.FIELD;
import java.lang.annotation.Retention;
import static java.lang.annotation.RetentionPolicy.RUNTIME;
import java.lang.annotation.Target;
import javax.validation.Payload;

@Target({ FIELD, ANNOTATION_TYPE})
@Retention(RUNTIME)
@Documented
public @interface JavaBookTitle {

    String message() default "{org.jakartaeerecipes.annotation." +
            "message}";

    Class<?>[] groups() default { };

    Class<? extends Payload>[] payload() default { };

}
```

The implementation for the validator should look like that of the BookTitleValidator class:

```
import javax.validation.ConstraintValidator;
import javax.validation.ConstraintValidatorContext;

public class BookTitleValidator implements ConstraintValidator<JavaBookTit
le, String> {

    @Override
    public void initialize(JavaBookTitle constraintAnnotation) {

    }

    @Override
    public boolean isValid(String title, ConstraintValidatorContext cvc) {
```

```
        if(title.toUpperCase().contains("JAVA")){
            return true;
        } else {
            return false;
        }
    }
}
```

Now that the constraint annotation has been created, it can be applied to a field as follows:

```
@JavaBookTitle(message = "Book Title Should Contain The Word Java")
@Column(name = "TITLE")
protected String title;
```

How It Works

Creating a custom validation constraint annotation is quite easy, although the implementation may look a bit daunting at first glance. A validation constraint consists of the following pieces:

- Constraint annotation

- Validator implementation class

- Default error message

The constraint annotation is created just like any standard Java annotation. The annotation declaration is a standard Java interface. The interface must be annotated with @Target, passing a list in curly brackets, which specifies the types that the annotation can be applied to. The @Retention annotation can also be specified on the declaration, passing a value to specify how long the annotation will be retained. Valid values include SOURCE, CLASS, and RUNTIME. An annotation declaration may also include the @Documented annotation, which indicates whether an annotation declaration will be documented by JavaDoc by default.

Annotation declaration interfaces can contain elements to associate metadata to a validation constraint. A constraint annotation must contain three elements: a message element of type String, a groups() method, and a payload() method. Each of the elements can be declared within the annotation constraint with a default value, as seen in the example. The message element is used to create a default error message for the validator. The message may include String interpolation, and it may also be loaded from a resource bundle to take advantage of features such as internationalization. The groups() method is used to specify any processing groups to which the constraint will belong. The Default group is declared if no group is specified and the array is empty. The payload() method is typically used to associate metadata with a given validation constraint.

A validationAppliesTo element can be used to specify which targets the constraint associates against. Lastly, one may choose to declare a custom element to assist in the validation of values.

The next piece of required code is the constraint implementation class. This class should implement CustomValidator<AnnotationType, Type>. In doing so, this class must override the initialize() and isValid() methods. If there is any data that needs to be initialized prior to validation, then it should be done within the initialize method. The isValid() method should accept the data to be validated, along with ConstraintValidatorContext as arguments. The implementation of the method should validate the data and return a Boolean to indicate whether or not the data complies with the constraint.

Once these pieces of code are in place, the annotation can be specified on the targets for validation. The annotation should specify additional elements to associate metadata, if needed. In the example, the annotation specifies the message element, which allows a default error message to be declared.

10-3. Validating at the Class Level
Problem

You wish to validate some or all of the fields within an object to ensure that those fields of the object contain valid data as a whole. For instance, you must validate that a field declared as numChapters contains the same number of chapters as those in a field of type List<Chapter>.

Solution

Specify class-level constraints to perform the validation. In the example for this recipe,
the Book entity contains a number of fields that must validate against one another in
order to constitute a valid object:

```
@ValidNumChapters
public class Book implements Serializable {
    private static final long serialVersionUID = 1L;
    // @Max(value=?)  @Min(value=?)//if you know range of your decimal
    fields consider using these annotations to enforce field validation
    @Id
    @Basic(optional = false)
    @NotNull
    @Column(name = "ID")
    private BigDecimal id;
    @Size(max = 150)
    @Column(name = "TITLE")
    protected String title;
    @Size(max = 500)
    @Column(name = "IMAGE")
    private String image;
    @Column(name = "NUM_CHAPTERS")
    private int numChapters;
    @Column(name = "NUM_PAGES")
    private int numPages;
    @Lob
    @Column(name = "DESCRIPTION")
    private String description;
    @Column(name = "PUBLISH_DATE")
    private LocalDate publishDate;
    @ManyToMany(mappedBy="books")
    private Set<BookAuthor> authors;
    @OneToMany(mappedBy="book", cascade=CascadeType.ALL)
    private List<Chapter> chapters = null;
```

The @ValidateNumChapters annotation is used to validate that the numChapters value is greater than or equal to the chapters List. Following this logic, a Book may be in progress and more Chapter objects can be added to the list as completed, but there cannot be more Chapter objects than the numChapters value. As covered in Recipe 10-2, in order to create the @ValidateNumChapters annotation, there must be an annotation declaration class and a constraint implementation class. The following class is used to declare the annotation:

```
import java.lang.annotation.Documented;
import static java.lang.annotation.ElementType.ANNOTATION_TYPE;
import static java.lang.annotation.ElementType.TYPE;
import java.lang.annotation.Retention;
import static java.lang.annotation.RetentionPolicy.RUNTIME;
import java.lang.annotation.Target;
import javax.validation.Payload;

@Target({ TYPE, ANNOTATION_TYPE})
@Retention(RUNTIME)
@Documented
public @interface ValidNumChapters {

    String message() default "{org.jakartaeerecipes.annotation." +
            "message}";

    Class<?>[] groups() default { };

    Class<? extends Payload>[] payload() default { };

}
```

The annotation class contains the default error message as well as the declaration for the annotation itself. The following class is the constraint validation implementation for validating the number of chapters in the book:

```
public class NumChaptersValidator implements ConstraintValidator<Valid
NumChapters, Book> {

    @Override
    public void initialize(ValidNumChapters constraintAnnotation) {

    }
```

```
    @Override
    public boolean isValid(Book book, ConstraintValidatorContext cvc) {
        if (book == null){
            return true;
        }
        return book.getChapters().size() <= book.getNumChapters();
    }
}
```

Once these classes have been created, the annotation can be placed onto the class(es) accordingly.

How It Works

The class-level validation constraint is one that can be quite powerful, as it can pose a validation on one or more fields of the class. Applying a validation constraint to the class level means that one or more of the fields must adhere to the validation constraint. In the cases where a built-in validation constraint is applied at the class level, all fields of the class must adhere to the constraint. For instance, if @NotNull were applied, then each field within the class must be populated for each instance. On the other hand, applying a constraint such as @Size at the class level would not work if the class contained fields that were of a type other than String. More often, class-level constraints are custom created and apply only to a specified subset of the class fields.

In the recipe example, the @ValidNumChapters constraint is placed at the class level, which means that this particular constraint has access to each of the fields within the class. However, the constraint implementation only actually validates the numChapters and chapters fields to determine if the number of Chapter objects within the array is less than or equal to the numChapters value. Recipe 10-2 covers the declaration of an annotation in detail, so I won't cover that here.

The important piece of the puzzle for this recipe is to look closely at the annotation implementation within the NumChaptersValidator class. To create this implementation, the class must implement ConstraintValidator<A extends Annotation, T>. The ConstraintValidator interface utilizes generics to specify the constraint along with an object which will be validated. In the signature of the interface, A must be the name of an annotation declaration class, so in this case ValidNumChapters. T is any given object that must resolve to a non-parameterized type, or generic parameters of T must be unbounded wildcard types. In the example, the Book entity class is specified as T.

The interface enforces the implementation of the initialize(A constraintAnnotation) and isValid(T value, ConstraintValidatorContext context) methods. Many times, the initialize method can be empty, but if needed, it should contain code to initialize the validator in preparation for call to isValid. The isValid method contains the actual validation logic. The Book object that is passed into the method is first checked to ensure that it is not null. If it is null, then true is returned; otherwise, the number of Chapter objects in the chapters List is compared against the numChapters value to return a Boolean result.

Class-level validation can be very powerful, as it allows validation of class fields in a custom manner. It is also very easy to implement, making it even more powerful when validating complex objects such as those that contain Lists of other objects.

10-4. Validating Parameters

Problem

You want to specify some preconditions on a method such that the parameters adhere to a specified constraint.

Solution

Apply validation constraint annotations to method parameter(s) such that the parameter(s) will be validated by either built-in or custom constraints. This will enforce constraint logic at the time of a method call such that only arguments that meet the specified constraints will be acceptable as parameters to a given method. In the following example, a method that accepts a parameter is demonstrated including a validation constraint:

```
public void submitEmailAddress(@Email String emailAddress){
    System.out.println("Do something with the address: " + emailAddress);
}
```

In this particular example, a single parameter is being validated. However, it is possible to include more than one parameter containing a validation constraint. It is also possible to include a cross-parameter constraint at the method level, which can be used to apply validation across all of the method parameters.

How It Works

Bean Validation makes it possible to include validation constraints on non-static method parameters for the purposes of applying preconditions that will ensure invalid data cannot be passed into the method. Either built-in or custom validation constraints can be applied to method parameters. If an invalid value is passed into a method that contains a parameter constraint, a validation error will be thrown, and the method will not be executed.

In the example, the submitEmailAddress method accepts a single parameter, emailAddress. If the emailAddress parameter does not adhere to a valid email format, as specified via the @Email validation constraint, the method call will fail. It is also possible to validate more than a single method parameter by applying a constraint validation on the method itself. Doing so is much the same as applying a class-level constraint (Recipe 10-3) in that the constraint can be either built-in or custom. Built-in constraints applied at the method level, such as @NotNull, would be applied to each of the parameters of the method. Custom constraints can be created in the same manner as previously shown in Recipe 10-3 whereby one or more parameters can be validated. Constraints that are placed at the method level must be configured within the ConstraintValidator implementation using the @SupportedValidationTarget annotation to indicate that the constraint is to be placed on the method level. This is because return-type constraints are also placed at the method level, so the @SupportedValidationTarget helps to distinguish which validation type shall occur. The following code example demonstrates how to write a constraint validation implementation targeted for use at the method level:

```
@SupportedValidationTarget(value = ValidationTarget.PARAMETERS)
public class ValidEmployeeEmailValidator implements ConstraintValidator
<ValidEmployeeEmail, Object[]> {
    @Override
    public void initialize(final ValidEmployeeEmail constraintAnnotation) {
        // no-op
    }
```

```
@Override
public boolean isValid(final Object[] parameters, final
ConstraintValidatorContext context) {
    // Ensure employee email is from our organization
    return parameters == null || parameters[0].toString().contains
    ("@acme.com");
}
}
```

10-5. Constructor Validation

Problem

You wish to validate the instantiation of a class through the validation of constructor parameters.

Solution

Apply validation constraint annotations to the individual constructor parameters or at the constructor level itself to perform validation. In the following example, a constructor is annotated with @NotNull at the constructor level. Therefore, the @NotNull validation constraint is applied across each of the constructor parameters:

```
@NotNull
public ConstructorValidationController(String parameterOne,
                                       String parameterTwo){
    this.p1 = parameterOne;
    this.p2 = parameterTwo;
}
```

How It Works

In some cases, it makes sense to validate parameters that are passed into a class at the time of instantiation. Bean Validation makes this easy by allowing one to apply constraint annotations to parameters of a class constructor or to the constructor itself. When an annotation is placed on the parameters of a class constructor, the class cannot be instantiated if the validations fail. Similarly, if a constraint annotation is placed on the constructor declaration itself, then it will be applied across all of the constructor parameters. Such a constraint that is applied at the constructor level is called a cross-parameter constraint.

In the example, a cross-parameter @NotNull annotation is applied to the constructor of a class. Each of the parameters of the constructor must contain a value; otherwise, the validation will fail, and the class will not be instantiated. As mentioned previously, if a custom annotation were placed on the constructor, it could validate one or more of the parameters, just like a method-level constraint.

Note   Take special care to ensure that unintended behavior does not occur as a result of subtype constructor constraints. It is important to keep the object hierarchy in mind when applying validation constraints on a class or class constructor.

10-6. Validating Return Values
Problem

You wish to validate the return value of a method, such that the returning value must adhere to a constraint. If the return value does not adhere, then a validation exception shall be thrown.

Solution

Place a validation constraint on the return type of a method signature to ensure that the result will conform to the validation constraint. In the following example, the return type of the method is validated by the annotation which is placed at the method level. In this case, the returned value must be in an email address format:

```
@Email
public String getEmailAddress(){
    return emailAddress;
}
```

How It Works

Validation constraint annotations that are placed at the method level can be targeted toward return value validation. In doing so, a method must return a valid value per the constraint; otherwise, a bean validation exception is thrown. In order to ensure that the constraint being placed at the method level is targeted toward a return type validation, the validator implementation must contain the `@SupportedValidationTarget` annotation, which specifies whether the validator applies to parameters or to the method itself. If a validation constraint implementation does not include this specification, there is no way for the Bean Validation API to determine where the validation should be applied. In this case, the implementation would specify the following:

```
@SupportedValidationTarget(value = ValidationTarget.ANNOTATED_ELEMENT)
```

As with many of the other validation types, return-type validation can utilize both standard and custom constraints.

10-7. Defining a Dynamic Validation Error Message

Problem

You wish to supply a dynamic error message containing information that is pertinent to the validated value for a constraint.

Solution

Utilize String interpolation within the Bean Validation message attribute. String interpolation allows one to place message parameters and message expressions into a message String, thereby creating a dynamic String-based message. In the following example, the actual length of the String value will be substituted into the message to provide more feedback:

```
@Size(max = 150, message="The title cannot exceed {max} characters, current
title is $'{validatedValue}'")
@Column(name = "TITLE")
protected String title;
```

How It Works

Providing a clear error message for the user can make or break the success of an application. Utilizing String interpolation within an error message can help one to provide a specific message to the user to help indicate the cause of the validation failure. In much the same way that substitution variables work, an error message can contain zero or more variables that can be substituted.

Note   String interpolation requires expression language libraries to be available within your project. If the expression language API and an implementation library are not added to the project, errors will be thrown at runtime. The following Maven dependencies can be added to fulfil this requirement:

```
<dependency>
    <groupId>javax.el</groupId>
    <artifactId>javax.el-api</artifactId>
    <version>3.0.0</version>
</dependency>

<dependency>
    <groupId>org.glassfish.web</groupId>
    <artifactId>javax.el</artifactId>
    <version>2.2.6</version>
</dependency>
```

To utilize String interpolation, curly braces can be used to surround the variable that will be substituted with dynamic values. Constraint attributes can be interpolated by placing the attribute inside of curly braces. In the example, the max attribute will be substituted for the {max} String interpolation. The validated value or custom expression variables can be specified to substitute values within a message by utilizing the EL notation, thereby enclosing within curly braces and proceeded with a $. In the example, the $'{validatedValue}' variable is one such example. When the error message is produced, $'{validatedValue}' is replaced with the current validated value.

Message interpolation occurs in phases, outlined in the following order:

1) Resolve any message parameters using them as a key for a resource bundle named `ValidationMessages.properties`.

2) Resolve any message parameters using them as a key for a resource bundle that contains the standard error messages for built-in constraints.

3) Utilize a value constraint annotation member to substitute the message parameter. As such, the message parameters will simply be replaced by the value constraint annotation member of the same name.

4) Resolve any message parameters using evaluations as expressions of the Unified Expression Language. This allows us to formulate error messages based upon conditional logic and enables us to achieve advanced formatting.

The characters {,} and $ are special characters for message descriptors. Therefore, if one wishes to utilize one of these characters within a validation error message, it must be escaped by proceeding it with a \. Therefore, to escape a $, one would use \$.

It is possible to define a custom message interpolation algorithm, if needed, by plugging in a custom `MessageInterplator` implementation. To develop a custom interpolator, implement the `javax.validation.MessageInterpolator` interface. The interpolator must be thread-safe, and it is recommended to delegate the final implementation to the default interpolator. The default interpolator is available by calling upon `Configuration.getDefaultMessageInterpolator()`. For more information, please refer to the Bean Validation specification.

10-8. Manually Invoking the Validator Engine

Problem

You wish to call upon the Bean Validation validator engine programmatically, rather than relying upon automatic invocation.

Solution

Utilize the Validator API to perform validation. The Validator API allows one to create an executable validator from a number of different validation types, those being parameter, return, class, and so on. The following example demonstrates how to manually validate the data for a given entity class. In the following example, a Book entity class that is annotated with Bean Validation constraints is manually instantiated and validated using the Validator API:

```
ValidatorFactory factory = Validation.buildDefaultValidatorFactory();
Validator validator = factory.getValidator();

Book book = new Book();
book.setId(BigDecimal.ONE);
book.setTitle("The Best Java Book");

Set<ConstraintViolation<Book>> violations = validator.validate(book);

for(ConstraintViolation<Book> violation: violations){
    System.out.println(violation.getMessage());
}
```

How It Works

Bean Validation is typically automatically invoked within a Jakarta EE environment. For instance, if using JSF, the validation occurs during the "Process Validations" phase automatically when a form is submitted either synchronously or asynchronously via Ajax. In some cases, it is useful to have the option to call upon the Validator API manually. This can be useful in a Java SE environment or perhaps when writing unit tests.

To invoke the `Validator` API, first create a `ValidatorFactory` by calling upon `Validation.buildValidatorFactory()`. Next, use the factory to generate a `Validator`. Lastly, validate a bean by calling upon the validator's `validate()` method, passing the bean to be validated. This method will return a `Set` of `ConstraintViolation` objects. You can then iterate over each of the returned validation errors, obtaining each by calling upon the `ConstraintViolation.getMessage()` method.

10-9. Grouping Validation Constraints
Problem

You wish to group a number of validation constraints together, such that an entire group of validations can occur at the same time.

Solution

Groups can be applied to constraint annotations by specifying the group(s) to which the annotation belongs via the `groups` annotation attribute. Groups themselves are generated via Java interfaces. The following interface defines the `BookGroup`:

```
public interface BookGroup {

}
```

The `BookGroup` group can be applied to one or more constraint annotations by specifying the interface within the groups annotation attribute, as seen in the following example:

```
. . .
@Entity
@Table(name = "BOOK")
@NamedNativeQuery(
    name="allBooks",
    query = "select id, title, description " +
                "FROM BOOK " +
                "ORDER BY id",
    resultClass=Book.class)
@NamedQueries({
```

```java
    @NamedQuery(name = "Book.findAll", query = "SELECT b FROM Book b")})
@XmlRootElement
@ValidNumChapters
public class Book implements Serializable {
    private static final long serialVersionUID = 1L;
    @Id
    @Basic(optional = false)
    @NotNull
    @Column(name = "ID")
    private BigDecimal id;
    @JavaBookTitle(message = "Book Title Should Contain The Word Java")
    @Size(max = 150, message="The title cannot exceed {max} characters,
    current title is $'{validatedValue}'",
            groups={BookGroup.class})
    @Column(name = "TITLE")
    protected String title;
    @Size(max = 500)
    @Column(name = "IMAGE")
    private String image;
    @NotNull(groups={BookGroup.class})
    @Column(name = "NUM_CHAPTERS")
    private int numChapters;
    @Column(name = "NUM_PAGES")
    private int numPages;
    @Lob
    @NotNull(groups={BookGroup.class})
    @Column(name = "DESCRIPTION")
    private String description;
    @Column(name = "PUBLISH_DATE")
    private LocalDate publishDate;
    @ManyToMany(mappedBy="books")
    private Set<BookAuthor> authors;
    @OneToMany(mappedBy="book", cascade=CascadeType.ALL)
    private List<Chapter> chapters = null;
```

```
public Book() {
}. . .
```

Once the group has been put into place, validation can occur against a group, which would cause every constraint annotation that is assigned to that group to be validated. The following is a brief example of how one could utilize the Validation API to validate on a group basis:

```
ValidatorFactory factory = Validation.buildDefaultValidatorFactory();
Validator validator = factory.getValidator();
. . .
Set<ConstraintViolation<Book>> violations = validator.validate(book,
"bookGroup");

for(ConstraintViolation<Book> violation: violations){
    System.out.println(violation.getMessage());
}
```

How It Works

Applying a group to a constraint annotation allows that annotation to become part of a grouping with other annotations to which the same group is applied. Formulating groups of annotations can be beneficial when performing tasks in which a specified set of constraints should always be validated. Validation can occur at the group level, thereby validating constraint groups as needed.

To create a group, one must utilize an interface. The Java interface should be empty and acts as a placeholder for the group. The group can be applied to a constraint annotation by specifying the annotation's groups attribute and passing a list of groups to it. The group attribute accepts one or more groups in the list. The example demonstrates a single group, named BookGroup, being applied to the annotation constraint:

```
@NotNull(groups={BookGroup.class})
@Column(name = "NUM_CHAPTERS")
```

To validate a group of constraints, pass the group or groups for validation to the Validator validate() method. In the example, the single BookGroup group is validated, but if there were more groups to be validated, the following syntax would come into play:

```
validator.validate(book, "group1", "group2");
```

CHAPTER 11

Contexts and Dependency Injection

One of the most important specifications in the Jakarta EE platform is Jakarta Contexts and Dependency Injection (CDI). As stated on the cdi-spec.org site, it is a suite of complementary services that can improve the overall structure and design of code. The specification provides the following features for Jakarta EE and Java SE applications, as per the cdi-spec.org:

- Contextual objects with a well-defined life cycle providing multiple scopes of availability

- Ability to bind directly between contextual objects and Unified Expression Language (EL)

- Dependency injection utilizing a type-safe system that is easy to use

- Binding of interceptors to contextual objects

- Event notification model

- Portable extension SPI

Mentioned in the listing, perhaps one of the most widely used features of Jakarta CDI is the ability to bind the web tier and the business logic or transactional tier of the Jakarta EE platform together. Jakarta CDI makes it easy to expose business objects for use within web views via EL so that developers can directly bind Jakarta Server Faces view components to public JavaBean members and methods. Another widely used feature is the injection of contextual classes and resources into other Java objects in a type-safe and efficient manner.

© Josh Juneau 2020
J. Juneau, *Jakarta EE Recipes*, https://doi.org/10.1007/978-1-4842-5587-2_11

Note   Jakarta Server Faces is the Jakarta EE open source specification that was previously JavaServer Faces.

Jakarta CDI is architected from two methodologies: contexts and dependency injection. *Contexts* provide the ability to bind the life cycle and interactions of stateful components to well-defined but extensive contexts. In the Jakarta EE 8 tutorial, *dependency injection* is defined as the ability to inject components into an application in a type-safe way, including the ability to choose at deployment time which implementation of a particular interface to inject. To make use of Jakarta CDI, a developer should become familiar with a series of annotations that can be used to decorate objects and injected components. This chapter covers recipes that will demonstrate such annotations and where they should be used.

Since Jakarta CDI provides a high level of loose coupling, it is an important piece of any Java enterprise application. Those applications that make use of Jakarta CDI in the correct manner can become very efficient because Jakarta CDI provides a decoupling of resources, as well as strong typing, which eliminates the requirement to use `String`-based names for managed resources by using declarative Java. This chapter will cover widely used features of this important specification, touching upon a few new features, including asynchronous events, and an API for booting Jakarta CDI in Java SE environments.

11-1. Injecting a Contextual Bean or Other Object
Problem

You would like to utilize a contextual bean or other object from within another class to take advantage of the bean's state.

Solution

Utilize dependency injection to make the bean or object available from within another class. The following class represents an object that can be injected into another class:

```
package org.jakartaeerecipes.chapter11;
import javax.inject.Named;
```

```
@Named
public class CalculationBean {

    public int addNumbers(int[] numArray){
        int temp = 0;
        for(int x : numArray){
            temp = temp + x;
        }
        return temp;
    }

}
```

As you can see, the CalculationBean class represents a standard Java object. This object can be injected into another class by using the @Inject annotation. The following class, located in the same package as CalculationBean within the sources, demonstrates how to inject an object. Note that CalculationBean is never specifically instantiated; rather, it is injected:

```
package org.jakartaeerecipes.chapter11;

import javax.inject.Inject;

public class UsingClass {

    @Inject
    CalculationBean calcBean;

    public void performCalculation(){
        int[] intarr = new int[2];
        intarr[0] = 2;
        intarr[1] = 3;
        System.out.println("The sum of 2 + 3:" + calcBean.addNumbers(intarr));
    }

}
```

In the example, CalculationBean is injected into the bean. Once the bean or resource is injected into another Java class, it can be referenced as if it were local to the class into which it was injected.

How It Works

The concept of dependency injection greatly reduces the amount of overhead that is necessary for a developer in order to gain reference to a contextual Java object from within another Java class. The Jakarta EE stack makes it very easy to gain reference to just about any Java object from within another class. Dependency injection refers to the ability to inject components into an application in a type-safe manner, including the ability to choose at deployment time which implementation of a particular interface to inject. Jakarta CDI allows almost any Java object to be injected into another with very little configuration. This ability increases the usability of resources since such resources can be referenced from any number of different classes and maintain the same state wherever they are being used. In reality, just about any object can be injected anywhere with Jakarta CDI. The following are some Java objects that can be injected:

- Almost any Java class

- Session beans

- Jakarta EE resources: data sources, JMS topics, queues, connection factories

- Persistence contexts

- Producer fields

- Objects returned by producer methods

- Web service references

- Remote EJB references

To inject a resource into another, the application module or JAR file must contain a META-INF directory that includes a beans.xml configuration file. The beans.xml file may be empty, or it can contain a descriptor to customize the way in which component scanning will occur within the application. As such, configuration within beans.xml may be slightly different depending upon the bean discovery mode for the application. However, for the purposes of this example (and for most general Jakarta CDI use cases), the beans.xml file specifies that bean discovery should occur for all classes within the application:

```
<?xml version="1.0" encoding="UTF-8"?>

<beans xmlns="http://xmlns.jcp.org/xml/ns/javaee"
       xmlns:xsi="http://www.w3.org/2001/XMLSchema-instance"
```

```
    xsi:schemaLocation="http://xmlns.jcp.org/xml/ns/javaee http://xmlns.
    jcp.org/xml/ns/javaee/beans_1_1.xsd"
    version="1.1" bean-discovery-mode="all">
</beans>
```

The bean-discovery-mode attribute indicates how scanning shall occur. A value of all indicates that all components are processed, annotated indicates that only those components containing a class-level annotation are processed, and none effectively disables Jakarta CDI.

Next, the javax.inject.Inject annotation (@Inject) must be used to denote the class being injected by annotating a class member of the object type. For instance, if you want to inject a Java object of TypeA, you would declare a class variable of type TypeA and annotate it with @Inject, as follows:

```
@Inject
TypeA myTypeVar;
```

Note that the object used for injection (CalculationBean) contains a @Named annotation at the class level. This particular annotation doesn't need to be present in order to make the object available for injection unless the bean-discovery-mode="annotated". The @Named annotation allows one to provide a custom name for the object, and it also makes the object available for reference from within Unified Expression Language.

Once said injection is performed, the declared field can be utilized throughout the class because it is a direct reference to the original class of the specified Java type. By defining a specific scope to the injection bean (Recipe 11-5), you can indicate whether an injected object will cause the instantiation of a new object of that type or whether it will look up an existing object of that type and reuse it. By far, one of the most convenient and useful cases for using Jakarta CDI is the ability to inject a managed bean into another object and make use of its current state, as if its contents existed everywhere.

Jakarta CDI provides type-safe injection because there is no need to specify a String-based name in order to instantiate or refer to another object. By maintaining declared variables that are used as points of injection, the variable name itself provides for strong typing and thus reduces the number of errors that may arise.

11-2. Binding a Bean to a Web View

Problem

You want to bind a JavaBean to a Jakarta Server Faces view using Unified Expression Language (EL).

Solution

Annotate a class with the @Named annotation, and optionally specify a name for the class in String format. The String that is specified within the @Named annotation can be used to gain reference to the bean from within a Jakarta Server Faces view. If no optional String is specified, then the class name with a lowercase first letter is used to gain reference. The following example demonstrates the binding of a bean field and method to a Jakarta Server Faces view. The following Java class, named CalculationBean, is a Jakarta CDI managed bean that contains the @Named annotation, specifying myBean as the bean reference name:

```
import javax.enterprise.context.RequestScoped;
import javax.inject.Named;

@Named("myBean")
@RequestScoped
public class CalculationBean implements java.io.Serializable{

    private int num1 = 1;
    private int num2 = 0;
    private int sum;

    public CalculationBean(){
    }

    public void addNumbers(){
        System.out.println("Called");
        setSum(getNum1() + getNum2());
    }

    //getters and setters ...

}
```

The bean is bound to the Jakarta Server Faces view via the String-based name myBean, making a seamless binding between the web view and the backend business logic. The following Jakarta Server Faces view contains three fields and a Jakarta Server Faces commandButton component with an action that is bound to myBean via the Jakarta Server Faces EL:

```
<html xmlns="http://www.w3.org/1999/xhtml"
      xmlns:f="http://xmlns.jcp.org/jsf/core"
      xmlns:h="http://xmlns.jcp.org/jsf/html">
    <h:head>
        <meta http-equiv="Content-Type" content="text/html; charset=UTF-8"/>
        <title>Recipe 11-2: Binding a Bean to Jakarta Server Faces Views
        </title>

    </h:head>
    <h:body>
        <p>
            <h:form>
            <h:inputText value="#{myBean.num1}"/>
            <br/>
            <h:inputText value="#{myBean.num2}"/>

            <br/><br/>
            Sum: <h:outputText id="sum" value="#{myBean.sum}"/>

            <br/><br/>
            <h:commandButton value="Calculate" type="submit" action=
            "#{myBean.addNumbers}">

            </h:commandButton>
            </h:form>
        </p>
    </h:body>
</html>
```

As mentioned previously, when the @Named annotation is specified without providing a String-based name designation, a binding name will be derived from the class name, converting the first letter of the class name to lowercase. For the following example, assume that the class `CalculationBean` that was referenced in the preceding example is going to be referenced from within a Jakarta Server Faces view via EL, except there will be no `String`-based identifier specified within the @Named annotation. Since the @Named annotation does not specify a name, the EL would refer to the class name as such:

```
<html xmlns="http://www.w3.org/1999/xhtml"
    xmlns:f="http://xmlns.jcp.org/jsf/core"
    xmlns:h="http://xmlns.jcp.org/jsf/html">
  <h:head>
      <meta http-equiv="Content-Type" content="text/html; charset=UTF-8"/>
      <title>Recipe 11-2: Binding a Bean to Jakarta Server Faces Views
      </title>

  </h:head>
  <h:body>
      <p>
          <h:form>
          <h:inputText value="#{calculationBean.num1}"/>
          <br/>
          <h:inputText value="#{ calculationBean.num2}"/>

          <br/><br/>
          Sum: <h:outputText id="sum" value="#{ calculationBean.sum}"/>

          <br/><br/>
          <h:commandButton value="Calculate" type="submit" action="#{
          calculationBean.addNumbers()}">

          </h:commandButton>
          </h:form>
      </p>
  </h:body>
</html>
```

@MANAGEDBEAN VS. @NAMED?

If the @Named annotation can be used to specify a binding name for a Jakarta CDI bean, then what is the point of using the @ManagedBean annotation at all? The fact is the @ManagedBean annotation has been carried over from previous versions of Jakarta Server Faces. While it is still a capable mechanism of marking a bean as managed and providing a binding identifier to Jakarta Server Faces, it is suggested for use only when Jakarta CDI is not available for an application. If an application has full access to the entire Jakarta EE stack, including Jakarta CDI, then the @ManagedBean annotation is not a requirement.

In reality, the Jakarta CDI technology is much more powerful than the use of @ManagedBean, which was a customized solution for Jakarta Server Faces, and therefore Jakarta CDI is the preferred technique to use. This is the preferred technique because Jakarta CDI allows for a broader base of classes to be categorized as managed resources. Jakarta CDI also carries with it many other bonuses such as transaction management and type-safe dependency injection, of which @ManagedBean is not capable. As of Jakarta Server Faces 2.3, there are also certain capabilities that are only available when using Jakarta CDI, and @ManagedBean has become a deprecated technology.

How It Works

One of the most widely used features of Jakarta CDI is that it helps provide a seamless integration between the web views and the backend business logic for an application. Utilizing Jakarta CDI, public bean members and methods can be made accessible to Jakarta Server Faces views very easily. The `javax.inject.Named` annotation provides a facility for referencing a JavaBean class from within a Jakarta Server Faces view, either by accepting a `String` that will be used to make the reference or by simply utilizing the JavaBean class name with a lowercase first letter. The solutions provided within this recipe demonstrate both techniques. From a technical standpoint, the example of not using a `String` to provide the reference is the most type-safe solution. However, sometimes it is necessary to provide a `String` for reference, as demonstrated in the first example, but that solution is recommended only on an as-needed basis.

> **Note**   Notice that the bean in the example, `CalculationBean`, contains a `@RequestScoped` annotation. This annotation specifies the scope for the bean state. For a fun trick, try to remove the `@RequestScoped` annotation and see what happens. As it turns out, the bean will still work as prescribed, but it will not return any results. This is because the bean will be reinitialized after each request. Therefore, the view will call the `getSum` method to read the current contents of the sum field, and it will have been reinitialized to a value of 0 before the request has been made. To learn more about bean scope, please see Recipe 11-4.

By annotating a class with `@Named`, it becomes available for use by Jakarta Server Faces views within the same application. Any public class member or method can be called upon from within a Jakarta Server Faces view by specifying the name of the class with a lowercase first letter, along with the public member or method that is needed. For instance, the following Jakarta Server Faces EL expression calls upon a method named `myMethod` that is contained within a class named `MyClass`. Note that this EL expression works if the class is named `MyClass` and includes an empty `@Named` annotation and if the class is named something different and includes the `@Named("myClass")` annotation:

`#{myClass.myMethod}`

As mentioned in the sidebar for this recipe, the `@ManagedBean` and `@Named` annotations play similar roles in that they both make Java classes available for use within a web view. However, it is safe to acknowledge that the `@Named` annotation is preferred over using `@ManagedBean`; please read the preceding sidebar for more information.

11-3. Allocating a Specific Bean for Injection

Problem

You have more than one JavaBean that implements a particular API, and you want to specify which of the beans you wish to inject.

Solution

Utilize a qualifier for the injection. To alleviate the issues of referencing a duplicate class, add a qualifier to each of the classes to differentiate them from one another. In the following code example, two classes, named `PaperbackController` and `EbookController`, each implement the `Book` interface. To allow client bean developers the ability to specify which of the bean classes should be injected, qualifiers are used. In the first listing, let's take a look at the `Book` interface, which is being implemented by at least two JavaBeans in the example:

```
public interface Book {
    public String title = null;
    public String description = null;
}
```

The class `PaperbackController` uses a qualifier `@Paperback` in order to differentiate it from other beans that implement the `Book` interface. The following listing is that of the `PaperbackController` class. Note that the `Paperback` interface (source shown next) must already exist in order to utilize the `@Paperback` annotation in this example:

```
package org.jakartaeerecipes.chapter11.recipe11_03;

import javax.inject.Named;
import javax.enterprise.context.SessionScoped;
import java.io.Serializable;

@Named(value = "paperbackController")
@SessionScoped
@Paperback
public class PaperbackController implements Serializable, Book {

    /**
     * Creates a new instance of PaperbackController
     */
    public PaperbackController() {
    }
...
}
```

Another JavaBean, named EbookController, also implements the Book interface. It contains a different qualifier, @Ebook, in order to differentiate it from other classes implementing the Book interface. The EbookController class looks like the following:

```
package org.jakartaeerecipes.chapter11.recipe11_03;

import javax.inject.Named;
import javax.enterprise.context.SessionScoped;
import java.io.Serializable;

@Named(value = "ebookController")
@SessionScoped
@Ebook
public class EbookController implements Serializable, Book {

    /**
     * Creates a new instance of EbookController
     */
    public EbookController() {

    }
...
}
```

Lastly, let's see what the @Paperback and @Ebook binding annotations actually look like. The following two code listings show the contents of the org.jakartaeerecipes. chapter11.recipe11_03.Paperback and org.jakartaeerecipes.chapter11. recipe11_03.Ebook interfaces, which are used to create the two annotations:

```
import java.lang.annotation.*;
import javax.inject.Qualifier;

@Qualifier
@Retention(RetentionPolicy.RUNTIME)
@Target({ElementType.TYPE, ElementType.METHOD, ElementType.FIELD,
ElementType.PARAMETER})
public @interface Paperback {}

import java.lang.annotation.*;
import javax.inject.Qualifier;
```

```
@Qualifier
@Retention(RetentionPolicy.RUNTIME)
@Target({ElementType.TYPE, ElementType.METHOD, ElementType.FIELD,
ElementType.PARAMETER})
public @interface Ebook {}
```

When a client wants to make use of one or the other, it simply needs to call upon the qualifier as follows:

```
@Paperback PaperbackController paperback;
@Ebook EbookController ebook;
```

How It Works

When there are two or more classes that implement the same Java interface, Jakarta CDI needs some help to determine which of them is going to be used at an injection point. If an application that uses Jakarta CDI is deployed and an attempt is made to perform injection on a class that implements the same interface as another class, then Weld will throw an ambiguous dependency error. This means that it cannot determine what bean to use for the given injection point. When Jakarta CDI attempts to determine which bean should be used at an injection point, it takes all class types into account, and it also uses qualifiers. A qualifier is an annotation that can be applied at the class level to indicate the type of a bean. Qualifiers can also be used to annotate methods, or other areas of code, to help Jakarta CDI determine what kind of bean needs to be injected.

Note   Weld is the reference implementation for Jakarta CDI. Therefore, you will see references to Weld within the server logs when utilizing Jakarta CDI within a Jakarta EE application. For more information regarding Weld, please see the online documentation at `http://seamframework.org/Weld`.

Every bean without an explicit qualifier automatically becomes annotated with the `@Default` qualifier. This qualifier is not needed when another qualifier type is used. In the solution to this recipe, two qualifiers are created in order to mark two different beans of the Book type: the @Paperback and @Ebook qualifiers. To create a qualifier, generate a Java interface, and annotate that interface with @Qualifier, Retention(RetentionPolicy. RUNTIME), and @Target({ElementType.TYPE, ElementType.METHOD, ElementType. FIELD, ElementType.PARAMETER}). All qualifiers are created in the same manner, and once created, they can be used to annotate beans for differentiation. As you can see from the example, both the PaperbackController and EbookController classes have been annotated with their respective qualifiers. This makes for an easy way to allow Jakarta CDI to determine which bean to inject since each of the two beans is a different implementation of the Book type.

The Jakarta CDI API provides a handful of qualifiers out of the box that can be used within your bean classes. I have already discussed the @Default qualifier, which is added to any bean that does not explicitly contain a qualifier. Other qualifiers that are provided by Jakarta CDI include @Named and @Any. The @Named qualifier is used to mark a bean as EL-injectable. If a bean contains a @Named qualifier, then it can be referenced within a Jakarta Server Faces view. The @Any qualifier is also included on all beans, and it allows an injection point to refer to all beans or events of a certain bean type. For instance, to refer to all of the beans of type Book, you could declare a member as follows:

```
@Inject @Any Instance<Book> anyBook;
```

Qualifiers are not used in everyday code, but they are a feature of Jakarta EE that comes in handy on occasions where ambiguous bean injection is possible.

11-4. Determining Scope of a Bean
Problem

You want to ensure that the scope of a particular bean within your application will be available for a user's entire session.

Solution

Define the scope of the bean that you want to make available by annotating the bean accordingly. The org.jakartaeerecipes.chapter11.recipe11_03. PaperbackController and org.jakartaeerecipes.chapter11.recipe11_03. EbookController that are listed in Recipe 11-3 are examples of request-scoped beans since they are annotated as such. To make a bean available within a different scope, annotate using one of the other scope-based annotations. For example, let's create a bean that has a session scope, meaning that it will retain its state for multiple HTTP requests for the life of a web session. To create a session-scoped bean, annotate the class using @SessionScoped. The following class, named CartBean, is a Jakarta CDI session-scoped

JavaBean that contains an integer field, which will be adjusted when a user invokes either the addItem or removeItem method:

```
package org.jakartaeerecipes.chapter11.recipe11_04;

// Import and change to @RequestScoped to see a functional difference
//import javax.enterprise.context.RequestScoped;
import javax.enterprise.context.SessionScoped;
import javax.inject.Named;

@Named
@SessionScoped
public class CartBean implements java.io.Serializable {

    private int orderList = 0;

    public CartBean(){}

    public void addItem(){
        setOrderList(getOrderList() + 1);
    }

    public void removeItem(){
        setOrderList(getOrderList() - 1);
    }

    /**
     * @return the orderList
     */
    public int getOrderList() {
        return orderList;
    }

    /**
     * @param orderList the orderList to set
     */
    public void setOrderList(int orderList) {
        this.orderList = orderList;
    }

}
```

Note   The comment within the `CartBean` class indicates that if you change the scope to `@RequestScoped`, you will see a functional difference. The difference is that the `orderList` field will retain its state for only one HTTP request. Therefore, the number will never increase more than 1, and it will never decrease below -1.

What fun would this bean be if you did not use it within a Jakarta Server Faces view? Well, let's take a look at a Jakarta Server Faces view, named `recipe11_04.xhtml`, which utilizes the `CartBean` class to display the `orderList` field. The view contains two buttons, each of which is bound to different methods that reside within the `CartBean` class. One button will increase the size of the `orderList int`, and the other button will decrease it:

```
<html xmlns="http://www.w3.org/1999/xhtml"
      xmlns:f="http://xmlns.jcp.org/jsf/core"
      xmlns:h="http://xmlns.jcp.org/jsf/html">
    <h:head>
        <meta http-equiv="Content-Type" content="text/html; charset=UTF-8"/>
        <title>Recipe 11-4: Determining Scope of a Bean</title>

    </h:head>
    <h:body>
        <p>
            <h:form>
            <h:outputText value="#{cartBean.orderList}"/>
            <br/>

            <br/><br/>
            <h:commandButton value="Add Order" type="submit" action=
            "#{cartBean.addItem()}"/>

            <h:commandButton value="Remove Order" type="submit" action=
            "#{cartBean.removeItem()}"/>
            </h:form>
        </p>
    </h:body>
</html>
```

How It Works

Depending upon an application's requirement, some beans may need to retain state longer than others. Sometimes it makes sense for each user of an application to have its own version of a particular bean, whereas the state of the bean lives and dies with the user's session. Other times it makes more sense for a bean to share its state among all users of an application, and still other times it makes sense for a bean's state to live and die with each user request. To specify the amount of time that a bean will retain its state, annotate the bean class with one of the Jakarta CDI scope annotations. Table 11-1 describes the different scope annotations.

Table 11-1. *Jakarta CDI Bean State Annotations*

Annotation	Description
@RequestScoped	Per user and retains state for a single HTTP request.
@SessionScoped	Per user and retains state across multiple HTTP requests.
@ApplicationScoped	Shared state across all user interactions within an application.
@Dependent	Object exists to serve one client bean and contains the same life cycle as the bean. (This is the default scope if none is specified.)
@ConversationScoped	Per user scope and is utilized within servlet-based application, such as one that utilizes Jakarta Server Faces. Boundaries of the scope are controlled via a developer and extend the scope across multiple invocations of the servlet life cycle. All long-running conversations are scoped to a particular servlet session and may not cross session boundaries.

While it is easy to define a particular scope for a bean, sometimes it takes some practice and testing to determine the correct scope for a particular application requirement. Moreover, as an application evolves, it makes sense to review the different scopes that have been applied to various beans to ensure that the assigned scope is still desirable.

> **Note**   One of the most common mistakes when working with the scope annotations is importing the wrong annotation for use within the bean. Remember that Jakarta Server Faces has its own set of scope-based annotations for use within managed beans (only available for backward compatibility as of JavaServer Faces 2.3). Always be sure to import from the `javax.enterprise.context.*` package when working with Jakarta CDI scope, or you will achieve erroneous results.

11-5. Injecting Non-bean Objects

Problem

You want to inject an object that is not a bean into another Java class.

Solution

Use producer fields to inject objects that are not beans, objects that require custom initialization, or objects that may have varying values at runtime. To create a `Producer` field, annotate a public class field with the `javax.injection.Produces` annotation, and return the field you want to inject. In most cases, you will also need to annotate a producer method with a Jakarta CDI qualifier so that Jakarta CDI will know what to inject when called upon.

In this example, a JavaBean named `InitalValueController` contains a producer field that will be called upon to assign an initial value to Jakarta CDI bean fields. The following source listing is that of the `IntialValueController` class, which contains the producer field declaration:

```
package org.jakartaeerecipes.chapter11.recipe11_05;

import javax.enterprise.inject.Produces;

public class InitialValueController implements java.io.Serializable {

        @Produces @InitValue public int initialValue = 1000;

}
```

The producer field in the class listing contains a qualifier annotation of `@InitValue`. The qualifier implementation is as follows:

```
package org.jakartaeerecipes.chapter11.recipe11_05;

import java.lang.annotation.*;
import javax.inject.Qualifier;

@Retention(RetentionPolicy.RUNTIME)
@Target({ElementType.TYPE, ElementType.METHOD, ElementType.FIELD,
ElementType.PARAMETER})
@Qualifier
public @interface InitValue {}
```

The producer field can be called upon from anywhere. In this case, it is injected into a Jakarta CDI bean in order to initialize a bean field value. In the following listing, the Jakarta CDI bean field named `ProducerExample` demonstrates how to inject the producer field and make use of it:

```
package org.jakartaeerecipes.chapter11.recipe11_05;

import javax.enterprise.context.SessionScoped;
import javax.inject.Inject;
import javax.inject.Named;

@Named
@SessionScoped
public class ProducerExample implements java.io.Serializable {

    @Inject
    @InitValue
    private int initial;

    private int orderList = -1;

    public ProducerExample(){

    }
```

```
public void addItem(){
    setOrderList(getOrderList() + 1);
}

public void removeItem(){
    setOrderList(getOrderList() - 1);
}

/**
 * @return the orderList
 */
public int getOrderList() {
    if (orderList == -1)
        orderList = initial;
    return orderList;
}

/**
 * @param orderList the orderList to set
 */
public void setOrderList(int orderList) {
    this.orderList = orderList;
}

}
```

When the orderList field is added to a Jakarta Server Faces view, the getOrderList() method will be invoked upon the loading of the view because the orderList property is called upon from the view. This will, in turn, cause the orderList field value to become initialized the first time the Jakarta Server Faces view is loaded. The following code demonstrates the use of the field within a Jakarta Server Faces view. To see the sources, please look at the chapter11/recipe11_05.xhtml file:

```
<html xmlns="http://www.w3.org/1999/xhtml"
    xmlns:f="http://xmlns.jcp.org/jsf/core"
    xmlns:h="http://xmlns.jcp.org/jsf/html">
    <h:head>
```

```
        <meta http-equiv="Content-Type" content="text/html;
        charset=UTF-8"/>
        <title>Recipe 11-5: Injecting Non-Bean Objects</title>
    </h:head>
    <h:body>
        <p>
            <h:form>
            <h:outputText value="#{producerExample.orderList}"/>
            <br/>

            <br/><br/>
            <h:commandButton value="Add Order" type="submit" action=
            "#{producerExample.addItem()}"/>

            <h:commandButton value="Remove Order" type="submit" action=
            "#{producerExample.removeItem()}"/>
            </h:form>
        </p>
    </h:body>
</html>
```

How It Works

Situations may arise when it makes sense to inject an object other than a Jakarta CDI managed bean or resource. Objects such as fields, methods, and the like can become injection targets if they are declared as producers. In some cases, it may make sense to declare a class field as an injectable object. To do so, annotate the field with the javax. enterprise.inject.Produces annotation (@Produces), and the EE container will then treat the field as a getter method for the field. In most cases, a Jakarta CDI qualifier annotation should also be created and used to annotate the field so that the field can be referenced via the qualifier at the injection point.

In the solution to this recipe, a field that will be used to initialize values is declared within a Java class named IntitialValueController. The field name is initialValue, and it will return an int type, being the number that will be used for initialization. Looking at the code, you can see that a qualifier named @InitValue is also placed at the field declaration. This will allow the injection point to simply refer to the qualifier to gain a handle on the injection target. To use the `initialValue` field, it is injected into a Jakarta CDI managed bean as follows:

```
@Inject
@InitValue
private int initial;
```

Once injected, the field can be utilized as if it were part of the class into which it was injected. In the case of this example, it is used to initialize the value of the `orderList` field, which is then displayed via a Jakarta Server Faces view named `chapter11/recipe11_05.xhtml`.

It is also possible to create producer methods, which can return values that are injectable to a bean or non-Java (Jakarta Server Faces) context. In doing so, the `@Produces` annotation is used to annotate the method in the same manner that a field producer is declared. For example, the following method demonstrates the declaration of a producer method that would be used to inject an object of the `Book` type. The method can be called upon in order to return the desired `Book` object type, depending upon the type that is passed to it:

```
@Produces @BookQualifier public Book getBook(Book book){

        if(book.equals(EbookController.class))
            return new EbookController();
        else
            return new PaperbackController();
    }
```

In this case, the method also uses a qualifier named `@BookQualifier`. The producer method result can then be injected into a bean or non-Java context. The injection point references the qualifier in order to make the injection possible, and the producer method is called by the container to obtain the desired instance object as follows:

```
@Inject
@BookQualifier
Book getBook(ebookController);
```

Producers can be a great way to develop injectable objects. With a bit of practice, they can also become valuable for creating sophisticated object factories via the use of a producer method.

11-6. Ignoring Classes

Problem

You want to mark a class as ignored by Jakarta CDI.

Solution #1

Denote the class with the @Veto annotation. Any class containing the @Veto annotation will be ignored by Jakarta CDI. The following example demonstrates the use of @Veto:

```
@Veto
public class OrderBean implements java.io.Serializable {

    public OrderBean(){

    }

    // Class Implementation
}
```

Solution #2

Denote the class with the @Requires annotation to mark the class as ignored by Jakarta CDI if it does not meet the specified requirements. The following example demonstrates how to utilize the @Requires annotation:

```
@Requires("javax.persistence.EntityManager")
public class EmployeeFacade {
    ...
    @Produces
    public EntityManager getEntityManager(){
        ...
    }
    ...
}
```

In this example, the @Requires annotation has a `String` containing `javax.persistence.EntityManager` passed to it. As such, if the specified class is not available and/or the class is unable to fulfil the specified dependency, then it will be ignored by Jakarta CDI.

How It Works

To veto a bean means to mark it as ignored by Jakarta CDI. Therefore, if a bean contains the @Veto annotation, it cannot be processed by Jakarta CDI. A vetoed class will not contain the life cycle of a contextual instance, and it cannot be injected into other classes. In fact, if a session bean contains the @Veto annotation, it cannot be considered a session bean at all. In some cases, it makes sense to mark a bean as such to ensure that it cannot become managed by Jakarta CDI. The following code demonstrates how to apply the @Veto annotation to a class.

The @Veto annotation can also be placed on a package declaration, which will prevent all of the beans that are contained within that package from being processed via Jakarta CDI:

```
@Veto
package org.jakartaeerecipes.chapter11.*;
...
```

Any of the following definitions on a vetoed type will not be processed:

- Managed beans, session beans, interceptors, decorators
- Observer methods, producer methods, producer fields

The @Requires annotation can be used to conditionally mark a class to be ignored by Jakarta CDI if it does not meet the specified required criteria. The @Requires annotation accepts a `String`-based fully qualified class name of the dependency or dependencies. If the object is able to fulfil its dependencies, then it will be managed by Jakarta CDI. Similar to @Veto, the @Requires annotation can be placed on a package as well. If that package is unable to fulfill the dependency that is denoted by @Requires, then all classes contained within that package will not be managed by Jakarta CDI.

11-7. Disposing of Producer Fields

Problem

Your application uses a producer field, and you want the producer field to be destroyed once it is no longer required for use.

Solution

Mark the producer field with the @Disposes annotation to indicate that it should be removed once it is no longer in use. The following code excerpt demonstrates a producer field that will be removed once it is no longer required for use:

```
...
    @Produces @Disposes
    List<Book> books;
...
```

How It Works

A producer method can be used to generate an object that needs to be removed once it is no longer needed. Much like a finalizer for a class, an object that has been injected via a producer method can contain a method that is invoked when the injected instance is being destroyed. Such a method is known as a *disposer method*. To declare a method as a disposer method, create a method defined within the same class as the producer method. The disposer method must have at least one parameter, with the same type and qualifiers as the producer method. That parameter should be annotated with @Disposes. As of Jakarta CDI 1.1, this technique can be applied to producer fields.

11-8. Specifying an Alternative Implementation at Deployment Time

Problem

You want to have the ability to code different implementations of an interface and then choose which implementation to utilize when an application is deployed.

Solution

Create a default implementation for an interface, and then create any alternative implementations for that interface and denote them with the @Alternative annotation. Specifying the javax.enterprise.inject.Alternative annotation flags a class as an alternate, and if that class is noted in the beans.xml file, then it will be loaded at deployment time, rather than the default interface implementation.

The following code excerpt demonstrates the use of an alternative class implementation. For the purposes of this demonstration, let's assume that there is already a default implementation for the OrderType interface named BookstoreOrderBean:

```
@Alternative
public class WarehouseOrderBean implements OrderType {
...
}
```

To specify the use of the alternative implementation rather than the default, modify the beans.xml file by listing the alternative class. The following is an example excerpt from the beans.xml file that designates the use of the WarehouseOrderBean:

```
<beans ... >
    <alternatives>
        <class>org.jakartaeerecipes.chapter11.WarehouseOrderBean</class>
    </alternatives>
</beans>
```

How It Works

Sometimes it makes sense to create two or more implementations of a class for use in different environments. However, it can become a cumbersome nightmare to remove or rename classes in order to build and distribute the correct implementation for each environment. The use of the javax.enterprise.inject.Alternative annotation allows more than one implementation of an interface to be used, and the appropriate implementation can be specified by altering the file before deployment.

11-9. Injecting a Bean and Obtaining Metadata

Problem

You want to acquire metadata information about a bean from within your application classes.

Solution

Inject the interface of a bean into the classes that need to utilize the metadata. Once it's injected, call upon the bean methods to retrieve the required metadata. In the following example, a bean named OtherBean has its metadata injected and retrieved:

```
@Named("OtherBean")
public class OtherBean {
    @Inject Bean<Order> bean;

    public String getBeanName(){
        return bean.getName();
    }

    public Class<? extends Annotation> getBeanScope(){
        return bean.getScope();
    }
}
```

How It Works

If you need to use bean metadata, you can easily obtain it by injecting the target bean's metadata. To do so, specify the @Inject annotation, followed by the bean class of the target bean type. Once the bean interface has been injected, methods can be called upon it to obtain the desired information. Table 11-2 describes the different methods that can be called upon the Bean class to obtain metadata.

Table 11-2. *Bean Metadata*

Method	Description
getName	Returns the name of the bean
getBeanClass	Returns the bean class
getInjectionPoints	Returns a Set of InjectionPoint objects for the bean
getQualifiers	Returns a Set of qualifier annotations for the bean
getScope	Returns the scope of the bean
getStereotypes	Returns a Set of stereotype data (common metadata) for a bean
getTypes	Returns a Set of the bean types
isAlternative	Returns a Boolean to specify whether the bean is an alternative
isNullable	Returns a Boolean to specify whether a bean can be nullable

11-10. Invoking and Processing Events
Problem
You wish to invoke an action when a particular event occurs within your application.

Solution
Process the event in a synchronous or asynchronous manner by creating a Jakarta CDI event, an optional qualifier, observer, and event handling method. In this scenario, a bookstore wishes to send an alert to the book publisher each time a sale occurs. If an online sale occurs, the publisher will receive an alert to indicate as such. Similarly, if an in-store sale occurs, the publisher will receive a different alert to indicate a store sale has occurred. First, create a book event object to contain data elements that need to be made available at event invocation. In this case, some simple data regarding the book, store of sale, number of books, and price will be included in the event object. The source of the BookEvent class is as follows:

```
package org.jakartaeerecipes.chapter11.event;

import java.math.BigDecimal;
import java.time.LocalDate;
```

```
import java.util.List;

public class BookEvent {
    private BigDecimal book;
    private String storeName;
    private BigDecimal price;
    private int numBooks;
    private LocalDate date;
    private List<String> notifyList;

    // accessor methods (getters and setters)

}
```

Next, create a qualifier for each type of book event that can occur. The qualifier is an optional step, as it is only necessary when there will be more than one event of the same type. In this case, an online sale event or a store sale event can occur. The qualifier source for the OnlineSale is as follows, with the qualifier for the StoreSale being the same with only a different name:

```
package org.jakartaeerecipes.chapter11.qualifier;

import static java.lang.annotation.ElementType.TYPE;
import static java.lang.annotation.ElementType.FIELD;
import static java.lang.annotation.ElementType.METHOD;
import static java.lang.annotation.ElementType.PARAMETER;
import java.lang.annotation.Retention;
import static java.lang.annotation.RetentionPolicy.RUNTIME;
import java.lang.annotation.Target;

import javax.inject.Qualifier;

@Qualifier
@Retention(RUNTIME)
@Target({METHOD, FIELD, PARAMETER, TYPE})
public @interface OnlineSale {
}
```

Next, an observer needs to be used to listen for the event invocation and act upon it once made. In this case, two observers will need to be generated, one for the @OnlineSale and another for @StoreSale. The observers reside within a class named BookEventHandler:

```
public class BookEventHandler {

    @Inject
    private BookController bookController;

    public BookEventHandler(){

    }

    public void  notifyPublisherOnline (@Observes @OnlineSale BookEvent
    event) {
        for (String s : event.getNotifyList()) {
            System.out.println("Sending Notification to Publisher: " + s +
            " purchase of book online: "
                    + bookController.findById(event.getBook()).getTitle()
                    + " from store: " + event.getStoreName()
                    + " purchase price: $" + event.getPrice()
                    + " on: " + event.getDate());
        }
    }

    public void notifyPublisherInStore (@Observes @StoreSale BookEvent
    event) {
        for (String s : event.getNotifyList()) {
            System.out.println("Sending Notification to Publisher: " + s +
            " purchase of book in store: "
                    + bookController.findById(event.getBook()).getTitle()
                    + " from store: " + event.getStoreName()
                    + " purchase price: $" + event.getPrice()
                    + " on: " + event.getDate());
        }
    }
}
```

Lastly, create an event handling method that will invoke the Jakarta CDI event when a sale is made. For this example, a simple Jakarta Server Faces user interface will be used to invoke a sale event, so the event handling method will be placed into a Jakarta Server Faces controller class:

```
@Named
@RequestScoped
public class BookstoreSaleController {

    @Inject
    @OnlineSale
    private Event<BookEvent> onlineSaleEvent;

    private BookEvent currentEvent;

    public BookstoreSaleController() {

    }

    /**
     * Fires synchronous Jakarta CDI event BookEvent.
     */
    public void onlineSaleAction() {
        onlineSaleEvent.fire(currentEvent);
    }

    /**
     * Fires asynchronous Jakarta CDI event BookEvent.
     */
    public void storeSaleAction() {
        onlineSaleEvent.fireAsync(currentEvent)
                .whenComplete((event, throwable) -> {
                    if (throwable != null) {
                        FacesContext.getCurrentInstance().addMessage(null,
                        new FacesMessage(
                                FacesMessage.SEVERITY_ERROR, "FAIL", "Error
                                has occurred " + throwable.getMessage()));
                    } else {
```

```
                        FacesContext.getCurrentInstance().addMessage(null,
                        new FacesMessage(
                                FacesMessage.SEVERITY_INFO, "SUCCESS",
                                "Successful Brick-and-Mortar Store Sale
                                Processing..."));
                }
            });
    }

    /**
     * @return the currentEvent
     */
    public BookEvent getCurrentEvent() {
        return currentEvent;
    }
}
```

When a sale is invoked, either an online or in-store sale type is chosen. Given the selected sale type, the corresponding Jakarta Server Faces controller method is invoked.

How It Works

Jakarta CDI events allow for decoupled event handling to occur among a number of beans. The bean classes do not have any binding to one another, but context can be passed between them, allowing beans to invoke contextual events without explicit binding. To orchestrate events, only a few annotations need to be placed, as there is no additional configuration. In the example, a bookstore is able to complete two types of sales, those being online and in-store. Therefore, when a book is sold, an event is to be invoked to notify the publisher and indicate which type of sale has been made.

To begin, a contextual object is used to contain data about each event. Therefore, a bean named BookEvent is generated as a simple Plain Old Java Object (POJO). Next, event qualifiers are coded for differentiation between the two types of possible events. An event qualifier is simply an annotation that can be placed on an event handler, and it is also used to create an event of the specified type. In the example, both online and in-store event qualifiers are created. As seen in the code for the qualifier, the annotation declaration is marked with the javax.inject.Qualifier annotation, and it is targeted for use with the following: METHOD, FIELD, PARAMETER, TYPE.

When an event is fired, an event handler is used to process the event. Event handlers are also known as observers, and they are simply classes that contain at least one method that can be used to contain the processing for the event. In the example, the `BookEventHandler` class contains two methods that are used to perform the actions of the events. Event handling methods must accept an event (simply an object) that is annotated with an optional qualifier and the `@Observes` annotation. The `@Observes` annotation signifies that the method is observing events of the type that is passed into the method. In the example, the `BookEvent` object is used as a parameter, and it is annotated with the qualifier annotation for each of the respective methods. Therefore, the method named `notifyPublisherOnline()` observes events of type `@OnlineSale`, and `notifyPublisherInStore()` observes `@StoreSale` event types.

Lastly, the event initiation occurs within a Jakarta CDI controller class in this example, although some other class type could also invoke an action. In the example, the `BookstoreSalesController` contains an injected `Event<BookEvent>` object, which is used for firing events of type `BookEvent`. The controller contains methods for firing online sales and also in-store sales. The online sale action method fires a synchronous event by calling upon the injected Event `fire()` method and passing the current `BookEvent` object. The `fire()` method initiates a synchronous event call, so once the event processing is completed, control is returned to the caller.

The in-store sale action method fires an asynchronous event by calling upon the injected Event `fireAsync()` method and passing the current `BookEvent` object. However, in this scenario, once the `fireAsync()` method is initiated, control is passed back to the caller, and the event is processed in the background. The `fireAsync()` method was introduced with the release of Jakarta CDI 2.0 in Jakarta EE 8.

The Jakarta CDI event model can be harnessed to provide superpowerful solutions for applications of all kinds. Since events can be called upon with a loosely coupled architecture, it makes event invocation easy to achieve in new applications and easy to add into existing applications.

11-11. Intercepting Method Invocations
Problem

You wish to intercept a method invocation in an application, such that each time the method is called upon, special functionality will occur.

Solution

Utilize a Jakarta CDI interceptor to invoke special functionality each time a specified method, or all methods within a specified class, is called upon. In the following scenario, an interceptor will be utilized to send an email to an administrator each time certain methods of an application are called upon. In this example, each time a book order is canceled, then the email is invoked.

To begin, an annotation must be generated for the interceptor. The interceptor annotation in this case is named `Notified`, and the sources are as follows:

```
package org.jakartaeerecipes.chapter11.interceptor;

import static java.lang.annotation.ElementType.METHOD;
import static java.lang.annotation.ElementType.TYPE;
import java.lang.annotation.Inherited;
import java.lang.annotation.Retention;
import static java.lang.annotation.RetentionPolicy.RUNTIME;
import java.lang.annotation.Target;
import javax.interceptor.InterceptorBinding;

@Inherited
@InterceptorBinding
@Retention(RUNTIME)
@Target({METHOD,TYPE})
public @interface Notified {
}
```

Next, the interceptor class can be created. The interceptor class is annotated with `@Interceptor`, and it contains a method which is annotated `@AroundInvoke`. This annotated method will be invoked whenever some method that is annotated with `@Notified` or a method contained within a class that is annotated with `@Notified` is invoked. In this case, the interceptor class is named `NotificationInterceptor`, and its implementation is as follows:

```
package org.jakartaeerecipes.chapter11.interceptor;

import java.util.Date;
import java.util.Properties;
import javax.interceptor.AroundInvoke;
```

```java
import javax.interceptor.Interceptor;
import javax.interceptor.InvocationContext;
import javax.mail.Message;
import javax.mail.Session;
import javax.mail.Transport;
import javax.mail.internet.InternetAddress;
import javax.mail.internet.MimeMessage;

@Interceptor
@Notified
public class NotificationInterceptor {

    @AroundInvoke
    public Object emailNotification(InvocationContext ctx) throws Exception {
        String smtpServer = "mysmtpserver.com";
        String email = "publisherEmail@publisher.com";
        Properties props = System.getProperties();
        props.put("mail.smtp.host", smtpServer);
        Session session = Session.getInstance(props, null);
        sendEmail(session,
                email,
                "Method invocation",
                "Entering method: " + ctx.getMethod().getName());

        return ctx.proceed();
    }

    protected void sendEmail(Session session, String toEmail, String
    subject, String body) {
        try {
            MimeMessage msg = new MimeMessage(session);
            //set message headers
            msg.addHeader("Content-type", "text/HTML; charset=UTF-8");
            msg.addHeader("format", "flowed");
            msg.addHeader("Content-Transfer-Encoding", "8bit");
            msg.setFrom(new InternetAddress("no_reply@jakartaeerecipes.
            com", "NoReply"));
```

```
            msg.setReplyTo(InternetAddress.parse("no_reply@
            jakartaeerecipes.com", false));
            msg.setSubject(subject, "UTF-8");
            msg.setText(body, "UTF-8");
            msg.setSentDate(new Date());
            msg.setRecipients(Message.RecipientType.TO, InternetAddress.
            parse(toEmail, false));
            Transport.send(msg);

        } catch (Exception e) {
            e.printStackTrace();
        }

    }

}
```

Lastly, a class or method(s) must be designated for interception. In this example, we wish to notify the administrator each time someone logs into the administrative console:

```
@Notified
@Named
@RequestScoped
public class AdminConsoleController {

    public AdminConsoleController(){

    }

    public void login(){
        System.out.println("This is an action method which would allow one
        to log into an"
                + "administrative console");
    }

}
```

In the preceding example code, the login() method would actually be used to authenticate an individual to the administrative console for the bookstore. However, since this is for demo purposes only, it merely displays a message in the system log. In order to enable this interceptor, the following lines must be added to the beans.xml configuration:

```
<interceptors>
    <class>org.jakartaeerecipes.chapter11.interceptor.NotificationInterceptor
    </class>
</interceptors>
```

How It Works

Interceptors allow cross-cutting functionality to be introduced into a new or existing application without explicitly modifying the code of specified classes or methods. An interceptor allows the functionality to be executed due to an invocation of the specified methods or due to invocation of a method within a specified class. As such, interceptors are very similar to Jakarta CDI events, except they do not require an explicit call to `fire()` or `fireAsync()` for invocation.

An interceptor solution requires an interceptor binding type annotation and an implementation class. The interceptor binding type annotation is a standard annotation declaration containing the `@Inherited` and `@InterceptorBinding` annotations. The `@Inherited` annotation denotes that the annotation can be inherited from superclasses. The interceptor binding type annotation should contain a target of `METHOD` and `TYPE`.

The interceptor implementation class can contain methods annotated with `@AroundInvoke`, `@PostConstruct`, `@PreDestroy`, `@PrePassivate`, `@PostActivate`, and `@AroundTimeout`. These annotations are used to specify when the interceptor method will be invoked. When a class or a method is annotated with the interceptor binding, then the interceptor implementation will be invoked based upon the specified implementation. `@AroundInvoke` specifies that the implementation will be executed when the intercepted method is being invoked. The life-cycle callback annotations (`@PostConstruct`, `@PreDestroy`, `@PrePassivate`, and `@PostActivate`) specify that the interceptor implementation will be invoked when the intercepted method or class enters the specified state. Lastly, the `@AroundTimeout` annotation is used to indicate that the implementation will be invoked when the intercepted method has an EJB timeout occur.

The `@AroundInvoke` annotation carries with it a couple of requirements. If an implementation method is annotated as such, it must accept a `javax.interceptor.InvocationContext` argument, and it must call upon that argument's `proceed()` method. The invocation of the `proceed()` method causes the target to be invoked.

An interceptor implementation class can contain one or more methods annotated with the aforementioned annotations. However, only one of each type can be specified within a given implementation class. In order to enable an interceptor, it must be specified within the beans.xml, as indicated in the example.

Interceptors can be a great way to add additional functionality to a process without modifying the existing code. They work well for performing actions such as logging each time a method is accessed. Typically an interceptor can be reused in multiple circumstances because the functionality is generic and not bound to a specific line of business logic. To learn more about adding more specific business logic functionality to existing methods, please refer to Recipe 11-13 covering decorators.

11-12. Bootstrapping Java SE Environments

Problem

You wish to utilize the capabilities of Jakarta CDI in a Java SE environment, outside of a Jakarta EE container.

Solution

Bootstrap the Java SE application using the SeContainerInitializer. In this example, a standard Java SE application named BootstrapExample has been created. A beans.xml is added to the application's META-INF folder using the Jakarta CDI 2.0 references:

```
public class BootstrapExample {

    public static void main(String[] args) {
        SeContainerInitializer initializer = SeContainerInitializer.
        newInstance();

        try (SeContainer container = initializer.initialize()) {
            /**
             * work with Jakarta CDI
             */
            BookstoreBean storeBean = container.select(BookstoreBean.
            class).get();
            storeBean.setStoreName("Java Gurus");
            storeBean.printStore();
```

```
        }
    }
}
```

When this block of code is executed, the `SeContainer` can be used to work with Jakarta CDI capabilities.

How It Works

There are oftentimes situations where a standard Java SE application would benefit from using the utilities which Jakarta CDI has to offer. The Jakarta CDI 2.0 release has made this possible with the addition of the Bootstrapping API. In order to bootstrap, you must include the Jakarta CDI dependencies in the application. One must also include a beans.xml file to indicate that Jakarta CDI will be utilized. If using a Maven project, use coordinates for the cdi-core dependency as seen in the following (update version as needed):

```
<dependency>
    <groupId>org.jboss.weld.se</groupId>
    <artifactId>weld-se-shaded</artifactId>
    <version>3.0.0.Final</version>
</dependency>
```

The `beans.xml` file should contain the Jakarta CDI configuration information. The following beans.xml source provides the minimum configuration:

```
<?xml version="1.0" encoding="UTF-8"?>
<beans xmlns="http://xmlns.jcp.org/xml/ns/javaee" xmlns:xsi="http://www.
w3.org/2001/XMLSchema-instance"
    xsi:schemaLocation="http://xmlns.jcp.org/xml/ns/javaee http://xmlns.
    jcp.org/xml/ns/javaee/beans_2_0.xsd"
    bean-discovery-mode="all" version="2.0">
</beans>
```

The `SeContainerInitializer` class can be used to return an instance of itself. It can be used to configure the Jakarta CDI container for your application by calling upon its many customization methods.

Note   Please see the online documentation for full details (`http://docs.jboss.org/cdi/api/2.0/`).

The `SeContainerInitializer` class should be utilized following the builder pattern for configuring options, and the last method to call upon should be its `initialize()`, as seen in the example. The `SeContainerInitializer` is auto-closable, so it works well within a `try-with-resources` block. All of the Jakarta CDI usage can occur within the try block. In the example, a contextual bean is obtained and used.

While this example is brief, it shows how easy it is to bootstrap a Jakarta CDI configuration for a Java SE application.

11-13. Enhancing Business Logic of a Method
Problem

You would like to enhance the functionality of an existing method, including the ability to integrate with a bean's business logic.

Solution

Utilize a decorator to implement an enhancement of functionality for an existing method. In the following example, a decorator is generated for an existing method in order to enhance functionality by logging to a database. In this particular example, a registration form is used to register for a bookstore event. The decorator will be used to enhance the registration process by adding the registrant into a different database table for entry into a drawing.

To begin, each registrant must enter their first name, last name, and email address. This information will go into a `Registration` object. The object code is as follows:

```
public class Registration {

    private String first;
    private String last;
    private String email;

    public Registration(){
```

```
    }
// . . . Getters and Setters
}
```

Next, an interface must be generated for the registration type. In this case, each registration type must contain a method `register()` that accepts a `Registration` object:

```
public interface BookstoreRegistration {
    public String register(Registration registration);
}
```

Now create a decorator, which is a public abstract class that takes the interface that was created earlier as an injection point:

```
package org.jakartaeerecipes.chapter11.decorator;

import javax.decorator.Decorator;
import javax.decorator.Delegate;
import javax.enterprise.inject.Any;
import javax.inject.Inject;
import org.jakartaeerecipes.chapter11.recipe11_13.BookstoreRegistration;
import org.jakartaeerecipes.chapter11.recipe11_13.Registration;

@Decorator
public abstract class RegistrationDecorator implements
BookstoreRegistration {

    @Inject
    @Delegate
    @Any
    private BookstoreRegistration bookstoreRegistration;

    @Override
    public String register(Registration registration){
        // Submit to registration database table
        // Submit to promotional database table
        return registration.getEmail() + " has been entered into the
        giveaway";
    }
}
```

Lastly, we need to invoke the register method to initiate the decorator functionality. In this example, we invoke via a Jakarta Server Faces controller class method:

```
@Named
@ViewScoped
public class BookstoreRegistrationController implements
BookstoreRegistration, Serializable {

    @Inject
    private Registration current;

    public BookstoreRegistrationController(){

    }
// Getters and Setters

    public String register(){
        return register(current);
    }

    @Override
    public String register(Registration registration) {
        // Persist current registration
        return "chapter11/recipe11_13.xhtml";
    }
}
```

When the `register()` method is invoked, the enhanced decorator functionality will also be invoked to add the registrant to the giveaway database table.

How It Works

Decorators are another powerful component of Jakarta CDI. Much like interceptors, decorators add enhanced functionality to existing methods. These two constructs differ from each other in that decorators enhance functionality and have access to bean fields and methods for which the enhanced functionality is occurring. Interceptors, on the other hand, do not have access to bean fields and methods and therefore provide a more generic functionality in addition to the standard functionality of an existing method.

To create a decorator, one must utilize an interface as an injection point, and one or more of the interface methods will be enhanced via implementation that is added to the decorator class. In the example, a standard bookstore account registration is enhanced by adding the registrant into a sweepstakes giveaway. Although the example does not actually demonstrate the database persistence and others, if the code is executed, then you can see the decorator being invoked.

The decorator class must be denoted with a @Decorator annotation, and it must implement an interface and contain at least one method implementation. However, the decorator class can be made abstract so that it does not have to implement each of the methods contained within the interface. A decorator must contain a delegate injection point, which is annotated with javax.decorator.Delegate. This injection point can be a field, constructor parameter, or initializer method parameter of the decorator class.

In order to enable a decorator, it must be added to the beans.xml file. The following beans.xml demonstrates the addition of RegistrationDecorator:

```
<decorators>
    <class>org.jakartaeerecipes.chapter11.decorator.RegistrationDecorator
    </class>
</decorators>
```

An application can contain more than one decorator, of course. To manage the order in which the decorators are fired, use the beans.xml and list in the order of priority. Another way to manage priority is to annotate a decorator with the @Priority annotation. Interceptors take precedence over decorators, so if a method contains both an interceptor and a decorator, the interceptor will be fired first.

CHAPTER 12

Java Message Service

The Java Message Service (JMS) is an API that allows software to create, edit, read, and send messages between other software applications or components. The API allows resources to be created within an application server that facilitates messaging capability in various contexts. The application server houses connection factories and destination resources, and these resources are created and maintained by the application server. That said, different application server implementations might have minor differences in their JMS implementations.

In addition to the basic messaging facilities, JMS also provides the ability to send messages to destinations and publish messages to subscriptions. This chapter contains recipes that focus on basic concepts of JMS, as well as some advanced techniques and additions that were made available to the Java EE platform with the release of Java EE 7. When following along with the examples in this chapter, it should be noted that JMS could be used in various situations for creating many different types of messages. For brevity, this chapter will cover essential concepts and make use of `TextMessage` objects only. The examples will be invoked using JSF view actions, although in real-life applications, there are many different ways to implement the sending and receiving of messages. From internal message invocation to scheduled tasks via an EJB timer or `ManagedExecutorService` and even implementation of JMS messaging with EJB message-driven beans, JMS can be utilized in many different contexts. After reading through the recipes, you should be able to apply the strategies utilized within the recipes in order to create the messaging system of your needs.

JMS 2.0 revamped the API with a simplified technique for sending and receiving messages. In this chapter, you will see both the legacy standard API and the simplified API so that the differences can be compared. The updated API also included enhancements to message subscriptions, delivery delay, and more. The breadth of JMS is far too large for complete coverage in this single chapter. To learn about all of the features, please refer to the JMS 2.0 specification.

Note   The examples in this chapter focus on working with JMS resources within a GlassFish application server environment. Some of the recipes demonstrate the use of Apache NetBeans IDE for producing and working with JMS resources. However, although the focus is on GlassFish 5.1, the main concepts and techniques can be carried forth for just about every Jakarta EE–compliant application server environment. For more specific details on working with another application server or IDE, please see the documentation that is specific to the corresponding environment.

12-1. Creating JMS Resources

Problem

You would like to provide the ability to create a JMS resource to deploy within a GlassFish 5.1+ application server environment.

Solution #1

The easiest technique for creating JMS resources is to utilize an IDE, such as Apache NetBeans. In this example, a standard JMS connection factory will be created for an application project utilizing the Apache NetBeans IDE:

1. Right-click the project within the Apache NetBeans Projects navigator menu; choose New and then Other. The New File wizard will open, from which you will select the GlassFish menu option from the Categories select list, followed by the JMS Resource file type (see Figure 12-1).

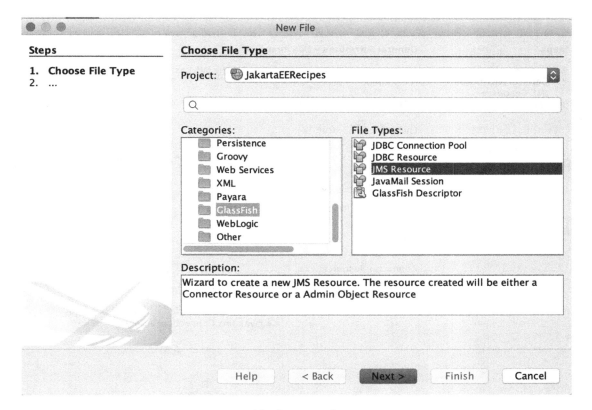

Figure 12-1. *Create JMS resource file from within NetBeans*

2. Within the New JMS Resource wizard, enter a JNDI name (using jms/ prefix) and a description. If you would like to enable the resource, be sure to do so within this wizard screen as well. Next, select the resource type that you wish to create. In this example, we will demonstrate the creation of a connection factory, as seen in Figure 12-2.

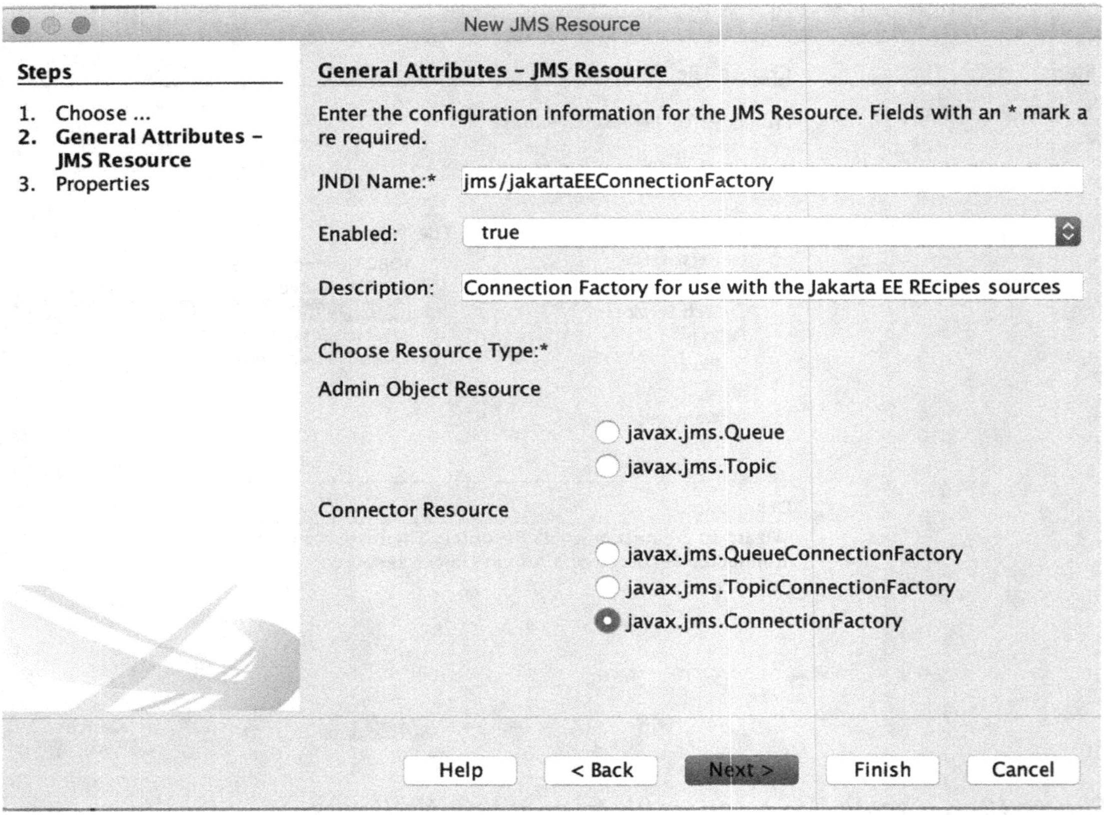

Figure 12-2. *New JMS Resource wizard*

3. Click Finish, and a file named `glassfish-resources.xml` will be created within your project if it does not already exist. When you deploy the application project to the server, the resource will be automatically created for you, as shown in Figure 12-3.

Note   You can utilize the same steps to create `javax.jms.TopicConnectionFactory` and `javax.jms.QueueConnectionFactory` resources.

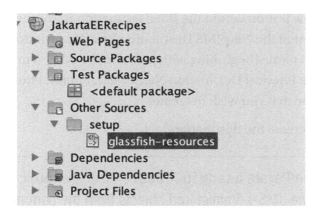

Figure 12-3. *glassfish-resources.xml file within a NetBeans project*

Solution #2

Create a new JMS resource from within the GlassFish or Payara application server administrative console. In this recipe example, we will create a JMS destination resource. Specifically, we will walk through the creation of a `javax.jms.Queue` resource. Follow these steps to create the resource:

1. Log into the GlassFish or Payara administrative console by navigating to https://localhost:4848. Expand the **Resources** ➤ **JMS Resources** menu in the navigation tree to expose the Destination Resources menu option (see Figure 12-4).

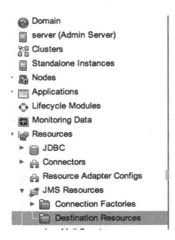

Figure 12-4. *GlassFish and Payara administration console Destination Resources menu*

2. Click the New button within the JMS Destination Resource
    window to open the New JMS Destination Resource window.
    Enter a JNDI name (beginning with jms/), followed by a unique
    name for the Physical Destination Name field. Finally, choose the
    resource type that you wish to create.

3. Click OK to create the destination.

Note   The GlassFish/Payara `asadmin create-jms-resource` command can
also be used to create JMS-administered objects from the command line. The
`asadmin` tool can also be used to perform other tasks. For more information,
please refer to the documentation at `https://eclipse-ee4j.github.io/`
`glassfish/docs/5.1.0/application-development-guide/setting-`
`up-dev-env.html#GSDVG00333`.

How It Works

The JMS API utilizes administrative resources in order to create and consume messages.
We refer to these resources as JMS resources. There are a couple of different types of JMS
resources that can be created—connection resources and destination resources. The
connection resources are used to create connections to a provider. There are three types
of connection resources that can be created:

- `ConnectionFactory`: Instance of the `javax.jms.ConnectionFactory`
  interface. Can be used to create JMS Topics and JMS Queue types

- `TopicConnectionFactory`: Instance of the `javax.jms.`
  `TopicConnectionFactory` interface

- `QueueConnectionFactory`: Instance of the `javax.jms.`
  `QueueConnectionFactory` interface

JMS connection factory resources are very similar to JDBC connection factories in that they provide a pool of connections that an application can use in order to connect and produce a session. There are many attributes that can be provided when creating connection factory resources:

- Initial and Minimum Pool Size: The initial and minimum number of connections that will be created and maintained by the connection pool.

- Maximum Pool Size: The maximum number of connections that can be created within the pool.

- Pool Resize Quantity: The number of connections that will be removed when the pool idle timeout expires.

- Idle Timeout: The maximum amount of time that connections can remain in the pool if they are idle (seconds).

- Max Wait Time: The maximum amount of time that a caller will wait before a connection timeout is sent (milliseconds).

- On Any Failure: If set to true (checked), all connections would be closed and reconnected on failure.

- Transaction Support: The level of transaction support (XATransaction, LocalTransaction, NoTransaction). The default is empty.

- Connection Validation: If set to true, then connections will need to be validated.

Note XATransaction always deals with a coordinating transaction manager, including one or more databases, all within a single global transaction. Non-XA transactions always involve a single resource.

Solution #1 to this recipe demonstrates how to create a connection factory resource using the Apache NetBeans IDE. This step-by-step procedure makes it easy to create such objects and deploy them to your GlassFish or Payara application server for use. You can also create connection factory objects using the GlassFish or Payara administrative console by following the steps that are provided in Solution #2 to this recipe and choosing the Connection Factories submenu rather than the Destination Resources submenu in step 1. `ConnectionFactory` objects are registered automatically with JNDI once created, and they can then be injected into Java classes and used. The following lines of code demonstrate how to inject a `ConnectionFactory` resource into a class:

```
@Resource(name = "jms/MyConnectionFactory")
private static ConnectionFactory connectionFactory;
```

Destination resources can also be created in a similar fashion to connection resources. Destination resources act as targets that receive or consume messages that are produced. Destination resources can be one of two types: `javax.jms.Queue` (Queue) or `javax.jms.Topic` (Topic). A Queue is a destination resource that consumes messages in a point-to-point (PTP) manner, much like a one-way line of traffic. When a producer sends a message to a queue, the message will stay in the queue until it is consumed. A topic is a destination that is used in a publisher/subscriber scenario, whereas messages sent to a Topic may be consumed by multiple receivers. One or more receivers can subscribe to a Topic.

Solution #2 demonstrates how to create a destination resource within a GlassFish or Payara application server, using the administration console. The console provides a wizard that can be used to easily create a destination resource. The most important piece of information to provide when creating a destination is the name. As with any JMS resource, the JNDI name should begin with the `jms/` prefix. When creating a destination resource, a unique name must also be provided for the Destination Resource Name, although other Jakarta EE–compliant containers may or may not make this a mandatory specification. Destination resources can be injected into Java classes in the same manner as ConnectionFactory resources. The following lines of code demonstrate the injection of a Topic resource:

```
@Resource(name="jms/myTopic")
private Topic myTopic;
```

12-2. Creating a Session

Problem

You would like to create a JMS session so that you can send or consume messages.

Solution

Create a connection so that you can subsequently create one or more sessions, which in turn can send messages to destinations or consume messages. In order to create a connection, obtain a `ConnectionFactory` object by injection via the `@Resource` annotation, and call its `createConnection` method as demonstrated in the following line of code:

```
Connection connection = connectionFactory.createConnection();
```

After you have created a connection, you need to start a session. In order to do so, call the connection object's createSession method as follows:

```
Session session = connection.createSession(false,
    Session.AUTO_ACKNOWLEDGE);
```

Note   If you are using the simplified JMS API, which is covered in more detail in Recipe 12-3, you do not need to manually create a JMS session. The creation of a JMS session is only required when utilizing the standard API.

Running the Example

If you take a look at the sources that can be found in the JakartaEERecipes project within the org.jakartaeerecipes.chapter12 package, you can see a full demonstration for creating a JMS session. To see the example in action, deploy the JakartaEERecipes project to your application server after setting up a JMS connection factory (see Recipe 12-1), and visit the following URL:

```
http://localhost:8080/JakartaEERecipes/faces/chapter12/recipe12_02.xhtml.
```

How It Works

Before you can begin to send or consume messages, you must obtain a JMS connection so that you can start a session. A session can be used to create JMS resources such as message consumers, message producers, messages, queue browsers, and temporary queues and topics. A session can be created using a Connection object. To create a session, call a Connection object's `createSession` method, and pass the appropriate arguments depending upon your application's needs. The `createSession` syntax is as follows:

```
createSession(boolean isTransacted, int acknowledgementType)
```

The first argument to the `createSession` method is a Boolean value to indicate if transactions should take place within the session. If a session is created as transacted (set to `true` for the first argument to `createSession`), acknowledgment occurs once the entire transaction is successfully committed. If for some reason the transaction is not committed, the entire transaction is rolled back, and all messages are redelivered. However, if a session is not transacted, one must indicate which type of acknowledgment must be received to consider a message successfully sent. The second argument to the `createSession` method indicates the acknowledgment type. Table 12-1 lists the different acknowledgment types along with a description of each.

Table 12-1. *JMS Session Message Acknowledgment*

Acknowledgment	TypeDescription
Session.AUTO_ACKNOWLEDGE	The session automatically acknowledges a client's receipt of a message, either when the client has successfully returned from a call to receive or when the `MessageListener` it has called to process the message has successfully returned.
Session.CLIENT_ACKNOWLEDGE	The client acknowledges the receipt of a message by calling the message's acknowledge method.
Session.DUPS_OK_ACKNOWLEDGE	Lazy acknowledgment of messages, allowing duplicates to be received.

In the solution to this recipe, the session that is created is non-transactional, and the receipt type is `Session.AUTO_ACKNOWLEDGE`. This is the most common type of JMS session that is created. Once the session has been created, then it can be used to create JMS resources.

12-3. Creating and Sending a Message

Problem

You wish to create and send a JMS message.

Solution #1

Make use of the standard API to create and send a message. To do so, create a `Message` object with respect to the type of message you wish to send, and then create and use a message producer in order to send messages to a destination. To create a message, first decide upon the type of message that you wish to send. Once decided, create the appropriate message object from the JMS session. In this example, we'll demonstrate the creation of a text message. The following lines of code demonstrate how to create a text message including a String.

```
TextMessage message  = session.createTextMessage();
message.setText("Jakarta EE 8 Is the Best!");
```

Next, to create a `MessageProducer` and send the message, call a JMS session's `createProducer` method, and pass the object type of the destination to which you wish to send a message. The following lines of code demonstrate how to create a message producer and send the text message that was created in the previous lines. The first lines of code demonstrate how to inject the destination resource, and then the actual creation of the message producer and sending of the message follows:

```
@Resource(name="jms/jakartaEERecipesQueue")
private Queue myQueue;
...
   public void sendMessage() {
       if (connection != null) {
           System.out.println("Creating Session");
```

```
        try(Session session = connection.createSession(false, Session.
        AUTO_ACKNOWLEDGE);
            ) {
            myQueue = (Queue) getContext().lookup("jms/
            jakartaEERecipesQueue");
            MessageProducer producer = session.createProducer(myQueue);
            TextMessage message = session.createTextMessage();
            message.setText("Jakarta EE 8 Is the Best!");

            producer.send(message);
            producer.close();
            setConnectionString("Message Successfully Sent to Queue");

        } catch (NamingException | JMSException ex) {
            System.out.println(ex);
            setConnectionString("Session not created and message not sent");
        }
    } else {
        setConnectionString("No connection available");
    }
}
```

Solution #2

Make use of the simplified API to create and send a message. To utilize the simplified API, create a JMSContext object, and then utilize it to create a MessageProducer and send the message to the appropriate destination. In the following example, a simple String-based message is sent to a Queue using the simplified API. This technique provides the same result as Solution #1:

```
@Resource(name = "jms/jakartaEERecipesConnectionFactory")
    private ConnectionFactory connectionFactory;
    @Resource(lookup = "jms/jakartaEERecipesQueue")
    Queue inboundQueue;
...
```

```
public void sendMessageNew() {
    try (JMSContext context = connectionFactory.createContext();) {
        StringBuilder message = new StringBuilder();
        message.append("Jakarta EE 8 Is the Best!");
        context.createProducer().send(inboundQueue, message.toString());
    }
}
```

Running the Examples

An example that can be run from within a JSF view has been created for this recipe. The code found at org.jakartaeerecipes.chapter12.Example12_03.java contains a managed bean that includes a sendMessage method that utilizes the standard API implementation and a sendMessageNew method that utilizes the simplified API. Both methods are responsible for creating a message and sending it to a destination Queue. By running the example, you can look at the server log to see the output from the method. Deploy the JakartaEERecipes project and visit the following URL to run the example:

`http://localhost:8080/JakartaEERecipes/faces/chapter12/recipe12_03.xhtml.`

How It Works

The reason that any application makes use of JMS is to incorporate the ability to send or receive messages. Therefore, it is no surprise that the JMS API has been developed to make these tasks very easy for the developer. In Java EE 7, things were made even easier using the simplified JMS API.

Let's begin by discussing the steps that are needed to utilize the standard API for sending a JMS message. To send a JMS message using the standard API, you need to create a resource destination for your message and obtain a connection and a JMS session, as seen in Recipes 12-1 and 12-2. Once you have obtained a JMS session, the next step is to create a `MessageProducer` using the `Session createProducer` method, passing the destination as an argument. After this legwork has been completed, the message can be constructed. You can create a message by calling the `javax.jms.Session` method that corresponds to the type of message that you wish to create.

Note   To see all of the available methods, please refer to the online documentation at

`https://jakarta.ee/specifications/platform/8/apidocs/javax/`
`jms/class-use/Session.html#javax.jms`.

In the example for this recipe, a text message is created by calling the `session.`
`createTextMessage()` method. The text is then set by calling the `TextMessage` object's
`setText` method.

Once a message has been created, a `MessageProducer` must be created in order to
facilitate the sending of the message. Again, `javax.jms.Session` comes to the rescue
here as we can call its `createProducer` method, passing the destination resource
for which we'd like to create the `MessageProducer`. Once created, the producer's
`sendMessage` method can be invoked, passing the message that you wish to send.

As mentioned previously, the `javax.jms.Session` can be used to generate different
message types. Table 12-2 lists the different message types that can be created, along
with a description.

Table 12-2. *JMS Message Types*

Message	TypeCreation Method
StreamMessage	The message body contains a stream of primitive values in the Java programming language. Filled and read sequentially.
MapMessage	The message body contains a set of name/value pairs that are formed from String objects and Java primitives. May be accessed sequentially or randomly by name, and the order of entries is undefined.
TextMessage	The message body contains a String object. Able to be used for plain text as well as XML messages.
ObjectMessage	The message body contains a serializable Java object.
BytesMessage	The message body contains a stream of uninterpreted bytes.

When utilizing the simplified API that was introduced with Java EE 7, there are a few shortcuts that can be made. To compare Solution #1 with Solution #2, you can see that there are fewer lines of code in the second solution. The simplified API enables developers to produce the same results as the standard API with much less code. A JMSContext object is obtained via a call to the ConnectionFactory's createContext method, and it can be used to begin a chain of method invocations that will result in the sending of a message in just one line of code. To break it down a bit, after the JMSContext has been obtained, its createProducer method can be called, chaining a call to the send method, passing the Queue and the message to be sent.

JMS message implementations may vary between the different application server products. However, all JMS message types share some common characteristics. For instance, all JMS messages implement the javax.jms.Message interface. Messages are composed of a header, properties, and a body. The header of a message contains values that are utilized by clients and providers for routing and identification purposes, properties provide message filtering, and the body portion of the message carries the actual message content or payload. The message header is used for linking messages to one another, and a field named JMSCorrelationID contains this content. Message objects contain the ability to support application-defined property values. The properties can be set via a construct known as message selectors, and they are responsible for filtering messages. For more detailed information regarding the Message interface, please see the online documentation at https://jakarta.ee/specifications/platform/8/apidocs/javax/jms/Message.html. The body varies across the different message types, as listed in Table 12-2.

It can be useful to add properties and headers to a particular message in order to allow message consumers to have filtering capabilities via JMS message selectors. To learn more about using JMS message selectors, please refer to Recipe 12-5.

12-4. Receiving Messages

Problem

You would like to receive messages that have just been sent by a JMS producer.

Solution #1

Make use of the standard JMS API to create a message consumer. Using the JMS session, create the message consumer by calling the `createConsumer` method, passing the type of message consumer that you would like to create. Once the message consumer object has been created, invoke the `start` method on the JMS connection object, and then call the consumer object's `receive` method to receive a message. In the following example controller class, a message consumer will be created and set up to receive the message that was sent by the producer in Recipe 12-3.

The following code excerpt is taken from the org.jakartaeerecipes.chapter12. recipe12_04.Example12_04.java source file. The method named `receiveMessage` is responsible for consuming messages from a specified destination point Queue. Note that the code assumes that the messages within the queue would eventually end and that there would not be a continuous stream of incoming messages:

```java
public void receiveMessage() {
    boolean stopReceivingMessages = false;
    if(connection == null){
        createConnection();
    }
    try(Session session = connection.createSession(false, Session.AUTO_
    ACKNOWLEDGE);) {
        createConnection();
        myQueue = (Queue) getContext().lookup("jms/jakartaEERecipesQueue");
        try (MessageConsumer consumer = session.createConsumer(myQueue)) {
            connection.start();

            while (!stopReceivingMessages) {
                Message inMessage = consumer.receive();
                if (inMessage != null) {
                    if (inMessage instanceof TextMessage) {
```

```
                        String messageStr = ((TextMessage) inMessage).
                        getText();
                        setDisplayMessage(messageStr);
                    } else {
                        setDisplayMessage("Message was of another type");
                    }
                } else {
                    stopReceivingMessages = true;
                }
            }
            connection.stop();
        }
    } catch (NamingException | JMSException ex) {
        Logger.getLogger(Example12_04.class.getName()).log(Level.SEVERE,
        null, ex);
    } finally {
        if (connection != null){
            closeConnection();
        }
    }
}
```

Solution #2

Utilize the simplified API to create a message consumer. Utilize a JMSContext object to
create the JMSConsumer in an efficient and simplified manner. The following example
method resides within a managed bean controller. The message consumer in this
example will be created and set up to receive the message that was sent by the producer
in Recipe 12-3:

```
public String receiveMessageNew() {
    try (JMSContext context = connectionFactory.createContext()) {
        JMSConsumer consumer = context.createConsumer(myQueue);
        return consumer.receiveBody(String.class);
    }
}
```

Running the Example

The JakartaEERecipes project contains a working example for this recipe that demonstrates the sending and receiving of JMS messages. To view the example, you will need to deploy the project to your application server and then visit the following URL:

```
http://localhost:8080/JakartaEERecipes/faces/chapter12/recipe12_04.xhtml
```

How It Works

The receiving client of a message is also known as the message consumer. Message consumers can be created using the standard or the simplified JMS API. We will compare these two approaches in this section to give you an idea of the differences between the two.

Using the standard API, a consumer is created from JMS session objects in the same manner that producers are created (see Recipe 12-3), calling the `createConsumer` method of the JMS session and passing the destination object from which the consumer will listen for and accept messages. Message consumers have the ability to consume messages that are waiting within a queue, and they listen indefinitely for new incoming messages.

To set up a consumer, call the JMS session object's `createConsumer` method, and pass the destination object that you wish to consume from. The next step is to call the JMS connection `start` method. This will tell JMS that the consumer is ready to begin receiving messages. After invoking the `connection.start()` method, a consumer can receive a message by calling the `Consumer` object's `receive` method, optionally passing time in milliseconds for the consumer to listen for messages. If no time limit is specified, the consumer will listen indefinitely.

As you can see from the example in this recipe, once the `receive` method is called, a `Message` object is retrieved. Once the message is received, the application can glean whatever it needs by calling the `Message` object's getter methods accordingly.

Now let's take a look at using the simplified API. As you can see from Solution #2, there are fewer lines of code required to produce the same result achieved from Solution #1. The `JMSContext` object aids in producing less code by calling its `createConsumer` method and passing the resource from which the application will need to consume messages. This method call will return a `JMSConsumer`, which has a similar API to `MessageConsumer`, with the ability to receive messages both synchronously and asynchronously. In the example, a String message is consumed synchronously:

> **Note**   It is possible to create an asynchronous consumer by registering a
> `MessageListener` with the `MessageConsumer`. After a listener has been
> registered for the consumer, the listener's `onMessage()` method will be called
> each time a message has been delivered. For instance, the following code could be
> used to register a listener to the consumer that was created within the example for
> this recipe.

```
javax.jms.MessageListener jakartaEERecipesListener = new MyMessageListener();
consumer.setMessageListener(jakaratEERecipesListener);
```

12-5. Filtering Messages
Problem

You would like to provide properties for your messages that will make it easier for
consumers to filter through and find messages of their choice.

Solution

Utilize message selectors in order to filter the messages that are being consumed.
Message selectors are String-based expressions that can be assigned to consumers upon
creation, and they are generally used to filter the types of messages that a consumer will
receive. In the following example, both the `sendMessage1` and `sendMessage2` methods
create JMS messages. The `sendMessage1` method sets a property named TYPE with a
value of JAKARTAEE on the message. After setting this property, a `MessageProducer` is
created, and the message is sent. The `sendMessage2` method sets a property named
TYPE with a value of JAVASE on the message. Just like `sendMessage1`, the `sendMessage2`
method then creates a `MessageProducer` and sends the message. The `receiveMessage`
method sets up a `MessageConsumer` with a selector specified to only consume messages
with a property of TYPE that includes a value of JAKARTAEE.

The following excerpt has been taken from the class named org.jakartaeerecipes. chapter12.recipe12_05.Example12_05.java:

```java
public void sendMessage1() {
    if (connection != null) {
        try (Session session = connection.createSession(false, Session.
        AUTO_ACKNOWLEDGE);
                MessageProducer producer = session.createProducer(myQueue);) {
            TextMessage message = session.createTextMessage();
            message.setText("Jakarta EE 8 Is the Best!");
            message.setStringProperty("TYPE", "JAKARTAEE");
            producer.send(message);

        } catch (JMSException ex) {
            System.out.println(ex);

        }
    }

}

public void sendMessage2() {
    if (connection != null) {
        try (Session session = connection.createSession(false, Session.
        AUTO_ACKNOWLEDGE);
                MessageProducer producer = session.createProducer(myQueue);) {

            System.out.println("Creating message");
            TextMessage message2 = session.createTextMessage();
            message2.setText("Java SE 9 Is Great!");
            message2.setStringProperty("TYPE", "JAVASE");
            producer.send(message2);

        } catch (JMSException ex) {
            System.out.println(ex);

        }
    }

}
```

```
public void receiveMessage() {
    boolean stopReceivingMessages = false;
    String selector = "TYPE = 'JAKARTAEE'";
    try(Connection connection = connectionFactory.createConnection();
        Session session = connection.createSession(false,
        Session.AUTO_ACKNOWLEDGE);
        MessageConsumer consumer = session.createConsumer(myQueue,
        selector);) {

        connection.start();

        while (!stopReceivingMessages) {
            Message inMessage = consumer.receive();
            if (inMessage != null) {
                if (inMessage instanceof TextMessage) {
                    String messageStr = ((TextMessage) inMessage).getText();
                     setDisplayMessage(messageStr);
                } else {
                    setDisplayMessage("Message was of another type");
                }
            } else {
                stopReceivingMessages = true;
            }

        }
        connection.stop();

    } catch (JMSException ex) {
        System.out.println(ex);
    }
}
```

Running the Example

If you deploy the JakartaEERecipes project, you can run the example by pointing your browser to the following URL: http://localhost:8080/JakartaEERecipes/faces/chapter12/recipe12_05.xhtml. You can click the Receive Messages button to start the consumer. Then click the Send EE Message and Send SE Message buttons to send messages, which contain different property values. Watch the server log to see output pertaining to the browsed messages.

How It Works

Message selectors are String-based expressions that can be assigned to consumers upon creation. To create a selector, form a String that contains an expression with syntax based on a subset of the SQL 92 conditional expression syntax. The expression String should formulate the filter that you wish to use when consuming messages. An expression will look very much like the WHERE clause of a database query. In the example for this recipe, the selector is set to the following String:

```
TYPE = 'JAKARTAEE'
```

This selector causes the consumer to filter all messages that are received and only consume those messages containing a property named TYPE that is assigned a value of JAKARTAEE. Standard SQL 92 can be used to combine filters and build an expression that will provide the filtering capability that is required by the consumer.

To assign the selector to a consumer, pass it to the JMS session createConsumer method. After doing so, any messages received by the created consumer will be filtered based upon the selector expression.

12-6. Inspecting Message Queues
Problem

Your application makes use of a JMS queue, and you would like to browse through each of the messages within the queue without removing them.

Solution

Create a QueueBrowser object and use it to browse through each of the messages that are contained within the queue.

In the following excerpt from Java class `org.jakartaeerecipes.chapter12.recipe12_06.Example12_06.java`, the `browseMessages` method connects to a JMS session, creates a browser queue, and traverses the messages within the queue:

```
public void browseMessages() {

    try(Connection connection = connectionFactory.createConnection();
        Session session = connection.createSession(false, Session.AUTO_
        ACKNOWLEDGE);
        QueueBrowser browser = session.createBrowser(myQueue);) {

        Enumeration msgs = browser.getEnumeration();

        if(!msgs.hasMoreElements()){
            System.out.println("No more messages within the queue...");
        } else {
            while(msgs.hasMoreElements()){
                Message currMsg = (Message)msgs.nextElement();
                System.out.println("Message ID: " + currMsg.
                getJMSMessageID());
            }
        }

    } catch (JMSException ex) {
        System.out.println(ex);
    }
}
```

Running the Example

If you deploy the `JakartaEERecipes` project, you can run the example by pointing your browser to the following URL: `http://localhost:8080/JakartaEERecipes/faces/chapter12/recipe12_06.xhtml`. You can click the Send Message button within the view several times and then click the Browse Through Messages button and watch the server log to see output pertaining to the browsed messages.

How It Works

There are times when it is important to have the ability to search through messages in order to find the one that you would like to read. In circumstances such as these, message queue browsers come to the rescue. A `QueueBrowser` object provides the ability for an application to search through each message within a queue and display the header values for each of them. This capability can be important if the message header contains important information that helps to differentiate each type of message that is sent by a particular application. The JMS `QueueBrowser` object makes it easy to sift through messages in order to find the one you would like, using similar semantics as those that are used to create other JMS objects.

To create a `QueueBrowser`, you must first have an open JMS session object. You can then call the `Session` object's `createBrowser` method, passing the JMS destination type as an argument. Therefore, if you wish to browse messages in a queue that is named `jms/myQueue`, you would pass the injected resource for `jms/myQueue` to the `createBrowser` method. Once you have created a browser object, simply iterate over the messages and browse through them using the `Enumeration` that is returned from the call to the `browser.getEnumeration()` method.

12-7. Creating Durable Message Subscribers

Problem

You would like to ensure that an application receives all published messages, even when the subscriber is not active.

Solution

Create a durable subscriber for the Topic destination that will be used to send and receive messages. Once created, messages can be published to the topic using the standard message publishing techniques, as demonstrated within Recipe 12-3, sending to the Topic destination that contains the subscription. The messages can then be consumed via a message consumer that has been created using the Topic and subscription.

In this example, a durable message subscriber is created, the message is created and published to the Topic destination, and finally, the message is consumed.

The Topic Connection

Topic connections are a bit different than Queue connections in that they utilize an object named TopicConnection, rather than a standard Connection object. Moreover, a TopicConnectionFactory must be injected into an object in order to create a TopicConnection. The following lines of code demonstrate how to create a connection factory to generate TopicConnections for working with subscriptions:

```
@Resource(name = "jms/jakartaEERecipesConnectionFactory")
    private TopicConnectionFactory connectionFactory;
TopicConnection connection = (TopicConnection) connectionFactory.
createConnection();
connection.setClientID("durable");
```

Creating the Initial Durable Subscriber

When creating a durable subscriber, an initial durable subscriber must be created prior to sending any messages to the Topic. This initial subscriber will initialize the subscription and make it available for publishing and receiving purposes. The following code excerpt, taken from org.jakartaeerecipes.chapter12.recipe12_07. Example12_07.java, demonstrates the creation of a durable subscriber:

```
public void createTopicSubscriber(){
    try {
        createConnection();
        TopicSession session = connection.createTopicSession(false,
        Session.AUTO_ACKNOWLEDGE);
        myTopic = (Topic) getContext().lookup("jms/jakartaEERecipesTopic");
        TopicSubscriber subscriber = session.createDurableSubscriber(myT
        opic, "jakartaEERecipesSub");
        connection.close();
    } catch (javax.naming.NamingException | JMSException ex) {
        Logger.getLogger(Example12_07.class.getName()).log(Level.SEVERE,
        null, ex);
    }
}
```

For the demonstration application, a JSF h:commandButton component invokes this method so that you can watch the output occurring within the server log.

Creating and Publishing a Message

Creating and publishing a message to a Topic is much like publishing messages to a Queue. However, instead of creating a producer, a publisher is generated. The following code excerpt, taken from org.jakartaeerecipes.chapter12.recipe12_07.Example12_07. java, demonstrates the creation of a Message, and then it is published to the durable subscriber:

```
public void sendMessage() {
    try {
        createConnection();
            System.out.println("Creating session");
            TopicSession session = connection.createTopicSession(false,
            Session.AUTO_ACKNOWLEDGE);
            System.out.println("Creating message");
            TextMessage message = session.createTextMessage();
            message.setText("Jakarta EE 8 Is the Best!");
            message.setStringProperty("TYPE", "JAKARTAEE");

            System.out.println("Creating producer");
            myTopic = (Topic) getContext().lookup("jms/
            jakartaEERecipesTopic");
            TopicPublisher publisher = session.createPublisher(myTopic);
            System.out.println("Sending message");
            publisher.publish(message);

            System.out.println("Message sent, closing session");
            publisher.close();
            session.close();
            connection.close();

    } catch (NamingException | JMSException ex) {
        Logger.getLogger(Example12_07.class.getName()).log(Level.SEVERE,
        null, ex);

    }
```

This method is also bound to an h:commandButton component for our example view, and you can see more output generated from the actions that take place within the method.

Receiving the Message

Each message created and published to the Topic is later consumed by the subscriber(s) to the Topic. The following method demonstrates how to create a durable subscriber and receive messages from it:

```
public void receiveMessage() {
    boolean stopReceivingMessages = false;
    try {
        createConnection();
        System.out.println("Creating session to receive messages");
        TopicSession session = connection.createTopicSession(false,
        Session.AUTO_ACKNOWLEDGE);
        myTopic = (Topic) getContext().lookup("jms/jakartaEERecipesTopic");
        System.out.println("Setting up consumer");

        String selector = "TYPE = 'JAKARTAEE'";
        TopicSubscriber subscriber = session.createDurableSubscriber
        (myTopic, "jakartaEERecipesSub");
        connection.start();

        while (!stopReceivingMessages) {
            System.out.println("Receiving message");
            Message inMessage = subscriber.receive();
            if (inMessage != null) {
                System.out.println(inMessage);
                if (inMessage instanceof TextMessage) {
                    String messageStr = ((TextMessage) inMessage).getText();
                    System.out.println(messageStr);
                    setDisplayMessage(messageStr);
                } else {
                    System.out.println("Message was of another type");
                    setDisplayMessage("Message was of another type");
                }
```

```
            } else {
                stopReceivingMessages = true;
            }

        }
        connection.stop();
        subscriber.close();

        session.close();
        closeConnection();
    } catch (NamingException | JMSException ex) {
        Logger.getLogger(Example12_07.class.getName()).log(Level.SEVERE,
        null, ex);
    }
}
```

The receiveMessage method is bound to an h:commandButton component within the JSF view in the example program, and you can follow along with the output that can be seen in the server log.

Unsubscribing from the Subscription

It is important to unsubscribe from a subscriber when finished using it because subscribers use up additional resources, as discussed in the "How It Works" section. The following method demonstrates how to unsubscribe:

```
public void unsubscribe(){
    try {
        createConnection();
        TopicSession session = connection.createTopicSession(false,
        Session.AUTO_ACKNOWLEDGE);
        // close subscriber if open, then unsubscribe
        session.unsubscribe("jakartaEERecipesSub");
        connection.close();
    } catch (JMSException ex) {
```

```
        Logger.getLogger(Example12_07.class.getName()).log(Level.SEVERE,
        null, ex);
    }
}
```

Running the Example

An example that binds all the methods shown in this recipe to JSF views can be executed by deploying the `JakartaEERecipes` project to your GlassFish/Payara server and visiting the following URL:

`http://localhost:8080/JakartaEERecipes/faces/chapter12/recipe12_7.xhtml`

How It Works

A message subscription is a JMS consumer that retains a durable connection to a specified topic destination. Message subscriptions cannot be made for Queue destinations, only for Topics because they utilize publish/subscribe messaging. By default, a durable subscriber remains persistent, because the delivery mode is `PERSISTENT` by default. Subscriptions are stored in a server cache so that they can be retrieved in the event of a server failure. Because durable message subscribers retain messages in a cache, they take up a larger memory footprint. Therefore, it is important that subscribers remain subscribed only as long as necessary, and then unsubscribe to release the memory.

Note   Durable subscriptions can only have one subscriber at a time.

To work with message subscribers, a special set of connection and session objects must be used. To start, you must inject a `TopicConnectionFactory` into any object that will make use of Topics. A `TopicConnection` can be created by calling the `createTopicConnection` method. A `TopicSession` must be created which, in turn, from the `TopicConnection`. The `TopicSession` object can be used to create durable message subscribers and message publishers.

When creating a subscriber, one must invoke the JMS session method, `createDurableSubscriber`, and pass the Topic destination, along with a String that is used to identify the subscriber. The String identifier is important because this is the identifier that will be used by consumers to subscribe to the messages being published to the Topic. A `TopicSubscriber` object is generated from the `createDurableSubscriber` method, and it is important to create the initial durable subscriber in order to create the Topic subscription. Once the initial durable subscriber has been created, messages can be sent to the subscription, and consumers can subscribe to it.

To create a message and send it to a subscription, the JMS session `createPublisher` method must be invoked, passing the Topic destination object as an argument. The call to `createPublisher` will generate a `TopicPublisher` object, which can be utilized for publishing messages to a Topic subscription. Any type of message can be sent to a Topic. To learn more about the different types of messages that can be sent, please refer to Recipe 12-3. Any number of messages can be sent to a topic, and if a consumer has subscribed to the subscriber, it will receive the messages. New subscribers will begin receiving messages that are sent to the subscription after the time when they've subscribed.

In order to subscribe to a Topic, a `TopicSubscriber` object should be created by calling the JMS session `createDurableSubscriber` method, passing the Topic destination object and the String-based identifier that was originally used to establish the subscriber. Once the `TopicSubscriber` has been created, messages can be consumed as usual, invoking the `TopicSubscriber` receive method for each message that will be consumed. Typically, an application will set a boundary limit to the number of messages that will be consumed, and perform a loop to receive that number of messages from a subscribed Topic.

Since a durable subscription creates a memory footprint, it is essential for consumers to unsubscribe when finished with the Topic. If a consumer does not unsubscribe, the application server will starve other subscriber resources and will eventually run out of usable memory. To unsubscribe a consumer, invoke the JMS session unsubscribe method, passing the String-based name of the subscriber. I told you that the String you use for identifying the subscriber was important!

It is sometimes useful to create message subscriptions for certain circumstances. Pertinent situations for using a subscriber may include a subscription for client consumers to receive messages regarding application errors or for an alert system so that administrators can subscribe to alerts that they wish to receive. In any case, durable subscriptions can be useful, so long as they are used sparingly and maintained in an appropriate manner.

12-8. Delaying Message Delivery
Problem

You would like to delay a message that is being sent.

Solution

Set the time of delay in milliseconds by calling the producer's `setDeliveryDelay(long)` method. In the following example, the message sending will be delayed by 1000 milliseconds:

```
TopicPublisher publisher = session.createPublisher(myTopic);
publisher.setDeliveryDelay(1000);
```

How It Works

In JMS 2.0, it is possible to delay the delivery of a message. The JMS API provides a method, `setDeliveryDelay`, for producers. This method can be called, passing the delay time in milliseconds, prior to sending the message. Once the delay has been set, this will cause all subsequent message deliveries by that producer to be delayed.

CHAPTER 13

RESTful Web Services

Java Web Services can play a vital role in enterprise application development. A web service can be described as a client and server application that communicates over HTTP, which provides a standard means for communication and interoperability between different applications. There are many different web service implementations available across each of the different programming platforms. A web service is made accessible via an endpoint implementation. Entire applications can be implemented using web services that transmit messages and data to and from each other. The two main web service implementations that have been part of Java EE over the past few releases are the Java API for XML Web Services (JAX-WS) and the Java API for RESTful Web Services (JAX-RS). In the Jakarta EE 8 release, JAX-WS was not updated, and it is no longer deemed as a "current" technology. JAX-RS has been renamed to Jakarta RESTful Web Services.

Jakarta RESTful Web Services is the API for Representational State Transfer (REST) web services. REST services are useful for performing operations via HTTP without the need for a WSDL or XML messages. REST services do not follow the SOAP standard. REST service implementations are stateless, and they provide a smaller footprint for bandwidth than SOAP services, making them ideal for HTTP on mobile devices. They utilize a predefined state of stateless operations.

Although both SOAP and REST support SSL, JAX-WS provides WS-Security, which provides enterprise-related security. JAX-WS provides a very formal transaction process over a service, whereas REST is limited by HTTP. However, in most cases, it is recommended to use REST services over JAX-WS when possible. Newer security APIs such as JSON Web Tokens (JWT) have been introduced, providing Jakarta RESTful Web Services with levels of security that can be achieved with JAX-WS.

Over the next several recipes, you will be shown how to develop Jakarta RESTful web services. You'll learn how to configure your environment to work with Jakarta RESTful Web Services and how to code a client to make use of the services.

© Josh Juneau 2020
J. Juneau, *Jakarta EE Recipes*, https://doi.org/10.1007/978-1-4842-5587-2_13

SETTING UP A REST ENVIRONMENT

There are a couple of options that can be utilized for creating and utilizing REST services. In this chapter, I focus on making use of the Jakarta RESTful Web Services implementation for REST services, which is based upon Jersey. If you are using GlassFish 5.1, the API jars are provided with the distribution, so you do not need to download any additional libraries in order to add REST functionality to your applications. However, if you are utilizing another application server, such as Tomcat, you will need to download the Jakarta EE 8 and package it with your application.

In order for Jakarta RESTful Web Services to handle REST requests, you will have to configure a REST servlet dispatcher within the application's `web.xml` configuration file or within a Java class. The following excerpt from the `web.xml` configuration file demonstrates how to set up Jakarta RESTful Web Services for an application:

```
<servlet>
        <servlet-name>javax.ws.rs.core.Application</servlet-name>
        <load-on-startup>1</load-on-startup>
    </servlet>
    <servlet-mapping>
        <servlet-name>javax.ws.rs.core.Application</servlet-name>
        <url-pattern>/rest/*</url-pattern>
    </servlet-mapping>
```

One can also make use of an annotation within a Java class to configure Jakarta RESTful Web Services and forget about the web.xml configuration. To do so, add the @ApplicationPath annotation to a class which extends `javax.ws.rs.core.Application`, as follows:

```
@javax.ws.rs.ApplicationPath("rest")
public class ApplicationConfig extends Application {
    @Override
    public Set<Class<?>> getClasses() {
        Set<Class<?>> resources = new java.util.HashSet<>();
        resources.add(org.jakartaeerecipes.authorservice.rest.
        BookAuthorFacadeREST.class);
        return resources;
    }
}
```

13-1. Developing a RESTful Web Service

Problem

You would like to create a Jakarta RESTful web service that will be exposed over the Internet to handle operations on data.

Note   Prior to performing the solutions to this recipe, you must be sure that your environment is configured for using REST services. For more information, please see the introduction to this chapter.

Solution #1

Create a RESTful web service by creating a root resource class (POJO) and adding resource methods to the class. To designate a class as a root resource class, annotate it with @Path or create at least one method within the class that is annotated with @Path and a request method designator (@GET, @PUT, @POST, or @DELETE). The following example demonstrates how to create a RESTful web service that simply displays a String or HTML to a client. The sources for this code can be found in the JakartaEERecipes project within the org.jakartaeerecipes.chapter13.SimpleRest.java file:

```
package org.jakartaeerecipes.chapter13.rest;

import javax.ws.rs.GET;
import javax.ws.rs.Produces;
import javax.ws.rs.Path;

// Set the PATH to http://host:port/application/rest/simplerest/
@Path("/simplerest")
public class SimpleRest {

    @GET
    // Produces plain text message
    @Produces("text/plain")
    public String getPlainMessage() {
        return "Hello from a simple rest service";
    }
```

```
@GET
// Produces plain text message
@Produces("text/html")
public String getHTMLMessage() {
    return "<P>Hello from a <b>simple</b> rest service</P>";
}
}
```

Assuming that you have configured your environment to work with
Jakarta RESTful Web Services, you can deploy the JakartaEERecipes application and
then visit the following URL to see the results produced from the REST service:
http://localhost:8080/JakartaEERecipes/rest/simplerest.

Solution #2

Utilize an IDE, such as NetBeans, to create a RESTful web service. The NetBeans IDE
includes wizards for developing web services of different types. By right-clicking a
project and choosing the New ➤ Other... option from the contextual menu, the New File
dialog will open, and Web Services can be chosen from the selection list. Proceed with
the following directions to generate a REST web service from an entity class:

1) Choose the RESTful Web Service from the Entity Classes option
from the New File menu.

2) Select one or more classes from the Available Entity Classes list
and click the Add button. In this example, we'll choose the org.
jakartaeerecipes.entity.Book entity, as shown in Figure 13-1.
Choose Next.

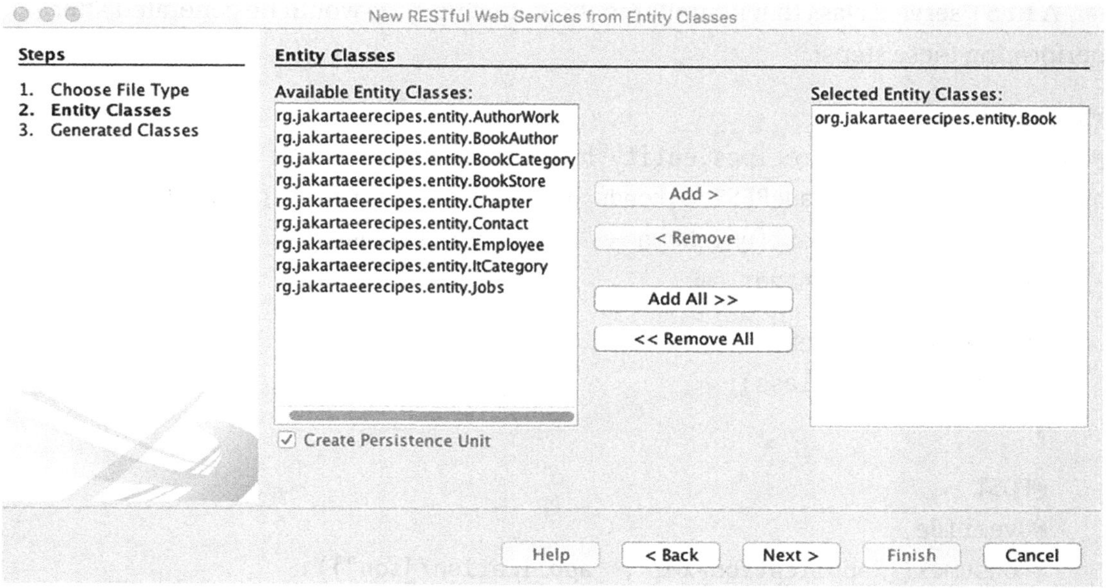

Figure 13-1. *Select entity classes for RESTful web services within NetBeans*

3)   List the package into which the REST service class will be generated,
     along with a package location (see Figure 13-2). Click Finish.

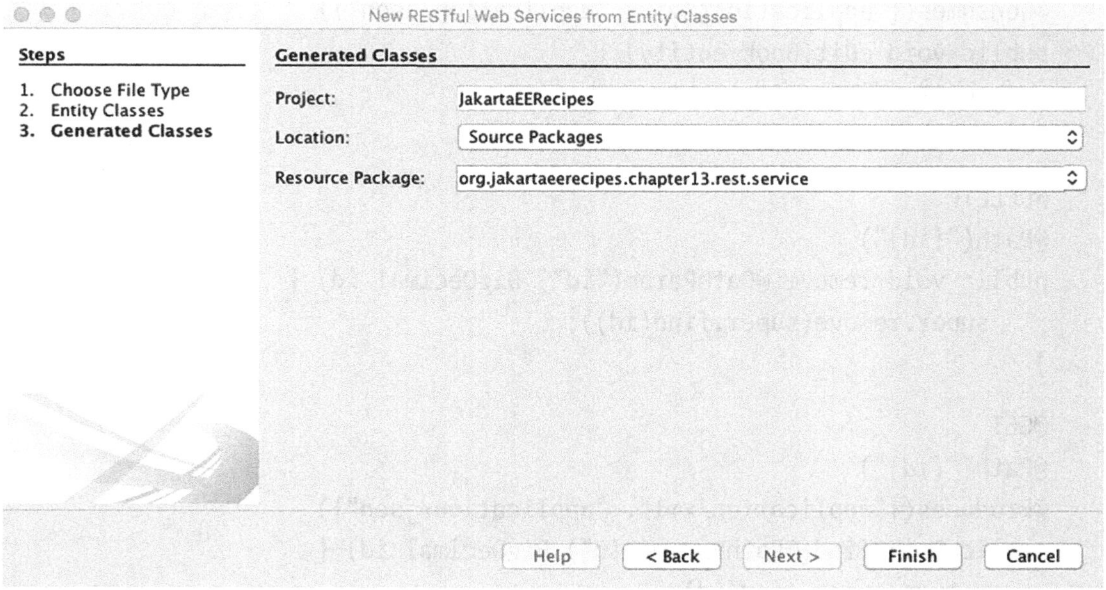

Figure 13-2. *Choose a resource package for the REST service class within NetBeans*

A REST service class that is similar to the following class would be generated after performing these steps:

```
@Stateless
@Path("org.jakartaeerecipes.entity.book")
public class BookFacadeREST extends AbstractFacade<Book> {
    @PersistenceContext(unitName = "JakartaEERecipesPU")
    private EntityManager em;

    public BookFacadeREST() {
        super(Book.class);
    }

    @POST
    @Override
    @Consumes({"application/xml", "application/json"})
    public void create(Book entity) {
        super.create(entity);
    }

    @PUT
    @Override
    @Consumes({"application/xml", "application/json"})
    public void edit(Book entity) {
        super.edit(entity);
    }

    @DELETE
    @Path("{id}")
    public void remove(@PathParam("id") BigDecimal id) {
        super.remove(super.find(id));
    }

    @GET
    @Path("{id}")
    @Produces({"application/xml", "application/json"})
    public Book find(@PathParam("id") BigDecimal id) {
        return super.find(id);
    }
```

```
@GET
@Override
@Produces({"application/xml", "application/json"})
public List<Book> findAll() {
    return super.findAll();
}

@GET
@Path("{from}/{to}")
@Produces({"application/xml", "application/json"})
public List<Book> findRange(@PathParam("from") Integer from,
@PathParam("to") Integer to) {
    return super.findRange(new int[]{from, to});
}

@GET
@Path("count")
@Produces("text/plain")
public String countREST() {
    return String.valueOf(super.count());
}

@Override
protected EntityManager getEntityManager() {
    return em;
}

}
```

How It Works

RESTful web services are easy to develop, and they have the ability to produce
and consume many different types of media. In most cases, REST web services are
encouraged for services that will be sending and receiving information over the Internet.
Before an application can support REST services, it must be properly configured to do
so. In this book, the Jakarta RESTful Web Services implementation is utilized, which is
based upon Jersey, the standard REST implementation for the industry. Please see the

introduction to this chapter for more information on configuring Jakarta RESTful Web Services within your application.

A Java class that is a REST service implementation contains a myriad of annotations. Table 13-1 lists the possible annotations that may be used to create a REST service.

Table 13-1. *REST Service Annotations*

Annotation	Description
@POST	Request method designator that processes HTTP POST requests.
@GET	Request method designator that processes HTTP GET requests.
@PUT	Request method designator that processes HTTP PUT requests.
@DELETE	Request method designator that processes HTTP DELETE requests.
@HEAD	Request method designator that corresponds to the HTTP HEAD method. Processes HTTP HEAD requests.
@Path	The value of this annotation should correlate to the relative URI path that indicates where the Java class will be hosted. Variables can be embedded in the URIs to make a URI path template.
@PathParam	A type of parameter that can be extracted for use in the resource class. URI path parameters are extracted from the request URI, and the parameter names correspond to the URI path template variable names specified in the @Path class-level annotation.
@QueryParam	A type of parameter that can be extracted for use in the resource class. Query parameters are extracted from the request.
@Consumes	Used to specify the MIME media types of representations that a resource can consume.
@Produces	Used to specify the MIME media types of representations that a resource can produce.
@Provider	Used for anything that is of interest to the Jakarta RESTful Web Services runtime, such as a MessageBodyHeader and MessageBodyWriter.

To designate a class as a REST service, the @Path annotation must be placed prior to the class or before at least one of the class method signatures. The @Path annotation is used to indicate the URI that should correspond to the service. The full URI includes the host name, port number, application name, and REST servlet name, followed by the path designated with the @Path annotation. In the example, the @Path annotation specifies /simplerest as the service path, so the URL http://localhost:8080/ JakartaEERecipes/rest/simplerest will invoke the web service. It is possible to include variables within a URL by enclosing them within brackets using the syntax {var}. For example, if each user had his or her own profile for a particular site, the @Path annotation could be as follows:

```
...
@Path("/simplerest/{user}")
...
```

In such a case, the URL could look like the following: http://localhost:8080/ JakartaEERecipes/rest/simplerest/Juneau.

The @Path annotation can also be specified before any methods that are marked with @GET, @POST, @PUT, or @DELETE in order to specify a URI for invoking the denoted method. Moreover, variables can be placed within the path in order to accept a more dynamic URL. For instance, suppose a method was added to the class in Solution #1 that would return a greeting for the user that is specified as a parameter within the URL. You may do something like the following in order to make the URL unique:

```
@Path("{user}")
@GET
@Produces("text/html")
public String getUserMessage(@PathParam("user") String user){
    return "Greetings " + "<b>" + user + "</b>";
}
```

In this case, the getUserMessage method would be invoked if a URL like the following were placed into the browser: http://localhost:8080/JakartaEERecipes/ rest/simplerest/josh. If this URL were specified, then the method would be invoked, passing "josh" as the user variable value, and the message would be displayed as

```
Hello josh
```

Note   It is very important to create URIs that are readable and also provide intuitive information about your web service. URIs that are based upon these standards help to reduce errors within client applications and make the web service more functional.

Designate methods with the @GET, @POST, @PUT, or @DELETE designator to process the type of web service request that is desired. Doing so will generate web service functionality. If more than one method exists within a REST web service implementation and @Path is only specified at the class level and not at the method level, then the method that returns the MIME type the client requires will be invoked. If you wish your method to display content, designate a method with @GET. If you wish to create a method for adding or inserting an object, designate the method as @POST. If you are creating a method for inserting new objects only, then designate it with @PUT. Finally, if you are creating a method for removing objects, then designate it with @DELETE. For more information regarding these annotations, please refer to Recipe 13-3.

REST services can become fairly complex if they constitute many different methods and paths. Entire applications exist based upon REST services, where all CRUD (create, retrieve, update, delete) manipulations are invoked via web service calls. This recipe provides only the foundation for developing with Jakarta RESTful Web Services, as the topic is far too involved for a handful of recipes or a chapter in itself.

13-2. Consuming and Producing with REST

Problem

You would like to produce different types of content with a RESTful web service. Moreover, you would like the web service to consume content as well.

Solution

Create methods within the web service implementation class that are annotated with @GET for generating output and optionally along with @Produces for specifying the type of output. Annotate methods with @POST or @PUT for updating or inserting data. The following sections provide examples utilizing these solutions.

Producing Output

Make use of the @Produces annotation to specify the type of content you wish to produce from a decorated method. The following excerpt, taken from the JakartaEERecipes project source at org.jakartaeerecipes.chapter13.rest.SimpleRest, demonstrates the use of @Produces:

```
@GET
// Produces an XML message
@Produces("application/xml")
public MessageWrapper getXMLMessage() {
    // Pass string to MessageWrapper class, which marshals the String
        as XML
    return new MessageWrapper("Hello from a simple rest service");
}
```

Producing List Output

Make use of the @Produces annotation to specify the type of content you wish to produce from a decorated method. The following excerpt, taken from the JakartaEERecipes project source at org.jakartaeerecipes.chapter13.rest.SimpleRest, demonstrates the use of @Produces and returns an object that contains a List of results:

```
@GET
// Produces an XML message
@Path("all")
@Produces("application/xml")
public MessageWrapperList getXMLMessageList() {
    ArrayList<String> messageList = new ArrayList<>();
    messageList.add("String 1");
    messageList.add("String 2");
    return new MessageWrapperList(messageList);
}
```

In this case, the MessageWrapperList object sources are as follows, but this example could be changed to accept Lists of any object type...not just Strings:

```
package org.jakartaeerecipes.chapter13.recipe13_02;
```

```
import java.util.ArrayList;
import java.util.Collection;
import java.util.List;
import javax.xml.bind.annotation.XmlElement;
import javax.xml.bind.annotation.XmlRootElement;
import javax.xml.bind.annotation.XmlSeeAlso;

@XmlRootElement(name="messageWrapperList")
@XmlSeeAlso(String.class)
public class MessageWrapperList extends ArrayList<String> {
    private static final long serialVersionUID = 1L;

    public MessageWrapperList(){
        super();
    }

    public MessageWrapperList(Collection<? extends String> message){
        super(message);
    }

    @XmlElement(name="messageList")
    public List<String> getMessageList() {
        return this;
    }

    public void setMessageList(List<String> messages) {
        this.addAll(messages);
    }
}
```

Accepting Input

Annotate methods within a web service class with @PUT to indicate that some content
is being passed to the method. To specify the type of content being passed, annotate
the same method with @Consumes(content-type). The following excerpt, taken from

the JakartaEERecipes project source at `org.jakartaeerecipes.chapter13.rest.`
`SimpleRest.java`, demonstrates the use of `@Consumes`:

```
@PUT
@Path("add")
@Consumes("text/plain")
public String add(@QueryParam("text") String text){
    this.message = text;
    return message;
}
```

To input a new message stating `JakartaEERecipes`, you would reach the following
URL in your browser, which passes the new message to the `text` variable: `http://`
`localhost:8080/JakartaEERecipes/rest/simplerest/add?text=JakartaEERecipes`.

How It Works

Create a web service class by following the procedures outlined in Recipe 13-2, and then
designate methods within the web service as producers or consumers by annotating
them appropriately. Methods that will be generating some type of output should be
annotated with `@Produces`, which should subsequently specify the type of output
generated. Moreover, the methods that are generating output should also be annotated
with `@GET`, which indicates that the method is a reading resource. Methods that will be
accepting input should be annotated with `@PUT` or `@POST`. The `@PUT` annotation indicates
that a new resource will be created, and the `@POST` annotation indicates that an existing
resource will be updated or a new resource will be created. Incidentally, the methods
that accept input should also be annotated with `@Consumes`, which should subsequently
specify the type of content that is being consumed. Overall, `@Produces` annotations
should coincide with the `@GET` annotated methods. That is, a method that is decorated
with `@GET` will return some content to the client. `@Consumes` annotations should coincide
with either `@PUT` or `@POST` annotated methods.

In the solution to this recipe, two types of methods are demonstrated. The first
example demonstrates a REST method that produces XML content, and the
`@Produces("application/xml")` annotation indicates it as such. Within the method,
a `String` is passed to a class named `MessageWrapper`. The `MessageWrapper` class is
responsible for marshaling the `String` as XML using JAXB. For more information,

please refer to the sources located at `org.jakartaeerecipes.chapter13.recipe13_02.`
`MessageWrapper.java` and see the JAXB documentation online at `https://eclipse-`
`ee4j.github.io/jakartaee-tutorial/jaxrs-advanced007.html#GKKNJ`. The beauty
of Jakarta RESTful Web Services is that just about any content type can be produced. A
client application can visit the URL that corresponds to a web service's `@GET` method, and
content will be returned in a format that will work for that client. For instance, if a client
is a web browser, it will look for a method that produces `text/html` content within the
web service and then invoke that method.

The other example in the solution to this recipe demonstrates a REST method that
consumes `String` content. The `@PUT` annotation indicates that either a new object will be
generated or an existing object will be updated with the request. In this case, the `String`-
based message field is updated to the content that is passed into the web service via the
`text` variable. The `@Path` annotation has been placed above the method signature to
indicate a path following the format `/add` should be used to access this method. Lastly,
the `@Consumes` annotation indicates that the method will consume plain text.

If one were interested in returning a `List` of values, then a wrapper class for
consuming the list of returned entity objects and storing into a local `List` is likely
one of the best approaches. In the example, a `List<String>` is returned from the
`getXMLMessageList()` service. This is facilitated by utilizing a wrapper object named
`MessageWrapperList`, which extends `ArrayList<String>`, therefore accepting a `List` of
Strings, and returns that list when the `getMessageList()` method is called upon. Using a
wrapper object such as this makes it easy to send lists of data to and from a web service.

The REST service in this example is very brief, and in real-world scenarios, many
methods producing and consuming different types of content are utilized within REST
service implementations.

13-3. Writing a Jakarta RESTful Web Services Client

Problem

You wish to create a Jakarta RESTful Web Services client application to consume a RESTful web service.

Solution

Make use of the Jakarta RESTful Web Services Client API to build a client application. The following example demonstrates how to create a very basic client using the Jakarta RESTful Web Services Client API:

```
import java.util.concurrent.ExecutionException;
import java.util.logging.Level;
import java.util.logging.Logger;
import javax.ws.rs.client.Client;
import javax.ws.rs.client.ClientBuilder;
import javax.xml.ws.Response;

/**
 *
 * @author Juneau
 */
public class RestClient {

    public static void main(String[] args){
        // Obtain an instance of the client
        Client client = ClientBuilder.newClient();

        Response res = (Response) client.target("http://localhost:8080/
        JakartaEERecipes/rest/simplerest")
                .request("text/plain").get();
        try {
            System.out.println((String) res.get());
        } catch (InterruptedException ex) {
```

```
            Logger.getLogger(RestClient.class.getName()).log(Level.SEVERE,
            null, ex);
        } catch (ExecutionException ex) {
            Logger.getLogger(RestClient.class.getName()).log(Level.SEVERE,
            null, ex);
        }
    }
}
```

To test the client, first deploy and run the JakartaEERecipes application so that the simplerest REST web service is available. Once deployed, run the RestClient class to see the result in the server log.

How It Works

Historically, it has always been no small task to test web services. That is because in order to test a web service, either a separate web application had to make a call to the web service or custom client tests would have to be built to accommodate the testing. In the JAX-RS 2.0 release, a client API was introduced, allowing developers to follow a standard API for developing test clients and so forth.

To make use of the client API, obtain an instance of the javax.ws.rs.client.Client by either injecting the resource or calling the javax.ws.rs.client.ClientBuilder newClient method. Once a Client instance is obtained, it can be configured by setting properties or registering Provider and/or Feature classes. Properties are simply name/value pairs that can be passed to the client via the setProperty method. Features are Providers that implement the Feature interface. A Feature can be used for grouping related properties and Providers into a single unit, making configuration even easier.

In the solution to this recipe, the client has been built to access the simplerest web service. After a client instance is obtained, properties can be set against it by calling the Client setProperty() method, passing the property/value pair:

```
client.setProperty("property", "value");
```

Web Resource Targets

The first step toward invoking a web resource is to make a call to a target. This can be done in a couple of different ways. The previous example demonstrated the use of the Client target method, which accepts a URI and returns a WebTarget:

```
WebTarget myTarget = client.target("http://somehost.com/service");
```

Once the target has been obtained, a number of things can be done with it. A request can be made against it, as in the RestClientOne example, by invoking the target's request method. A target can also be further qualified by calling its path method and passing the next sequence in a URI path:

```
WebTarget myTarget =
    client.target("http://somehost.com/service").path("one");
```

A path can also contain dynamic content in the form of URI template parameters. To include a template parameter, wrap the dynamic portion of the path in curly brackets { }, and then add a call to the pathParam method, passing the name/value pair of the parameter. One could also send a query parameter via adding a call to queryParam using a similar format:

```
WebTarget myTarget =
  client.target("http://somehost.com/service").path("one").path("{code}")
  .pathParam("code","100375");
```

Note   Path parameters and query parameters differ in the way in which they are sent to the web service. A path parameter is chained to the end of the URI using the following format:

```
http://web-service/path-param1/path-param2
```

A query parameter is chained to the end of the URI using the following format:

```
http://web-service?query-param1&query-param2
```

WebTarget objects are immutable in that methods for altering WebTargets, such as path, return new instances of WebTarget. WebTargets can also be configured by registering features or providers via a call to the target's register method, passing either type of class:

```
client.register(Feature.class)
client.register(Provider.class)
```

Obtaining a Response

The example at the beginning of this section demonstrated a simple client that returns a plain-text response. However, it is possible to return different response types by passing different Strings or MediaType fields to the Client target request method. Table 13-2 lists the different MediaType fields that can be used. All fields listed within the table that contain a _TYPE suffix are of type MediaType, whereas the others are static String types.

Table 13-2. MediaType Fields

Field	String
APPLICATION_ATOM_XML	"application/atom+xml"
APPLICATION_ATOM_XML_TYPE	
APPLICATION_FORM_URLENCODED	"application/x-www-form-urlencoded"
APPLICATION_FORM_URLENCODED_TYPE	
APPLICATION_JSON	"application/json"
APPLICATION_JSON_TYPE	
APPLICATION_OCTET_STREAM	"application/octet-stream"
APPLICATION_OCTET_STREAM_TYPE	
APPLICATION_SVG_XML	"application/svg+xml"
APPLICATION_SVG_XML_TYPE	
APPLICATION_XHTML_XML	" application/xhtml+xml"
APPLICATION_XHTML_XML_TYPE	

(continued)

Table 13-2. (*continued*)

Field	String
APPLICATION_XML	" application/xml"
APPLICATION_XML_TYPE	
MEDIA_TYPE_WILDCARD	"*"
MULTIPART_FORM_DATA	"multipart/form-data"
MULTIPART_FORM_DATA_TYPE	
TEXT_HTML	"text/html"
TEXT_HTML_TYPE	
TEXT_PLAIN	"text/plain"
TEXT_PLAIN_TYPE	
TEXT_XML	"text/xml"
TEXT_XML_TYPE	
WILDCARD	"*/*"
WILDCARD_TYPE	

To obtain a requested resource, call the `get` method, which will return a `javax.ws.rs.core.Response` object. The returned `Response` can be used to process the results accordingly, depending upon what you are trying to do within the client. In the example, the `Response` object's `readEntity` method is called, which simply returns the results in the requested format. In the example, a `String.class` is passed to the `readEntity` method, implying that a response should be returned in `String` format. To see a complete list of methods that can be called against a `Response` object, please refer to the online documentation (`https://jakarta.ee/specifications/platform/8/apidocs/javax/ws/rs/core/Response.html`), as the list is quite lengthy.

It is possible to filter a response by chaining methods, as needed, to specify headers, cookies, and so forth, when calling upon the `request` method. Each of these chained method calls returns a `Builder` object, which can be further built upon. The following methods can be chained to further build the request:

- `cookie(Cookie)`
- `cookie(String, String)`
- `header(String, Object)`
- `headers(MultivaluedMap<String, Object>)`
- `register`

Returning Entities

Sometimes there is a requirement to return a type other than `Response` from a web resource. In these cases, it is possible to obtain an entity type by passing the entity class to the get call. The following lines of code demonstrate how to return an `Employee` entity, rather than a standard `Response` object:

```
Response res = client.target("http://localhost:8080/JakartaEERecipes/rest/
employeeSearch")
                .request("application/xml").get(Employee.class);
```

In cases where entities are being returned, the request type is required to be `application/xml` or `APPLICATION_XML_TYPE`.

Invoking at a Later Time

There are cases when it makes sense to obtain a request and prepare it for execution, but not invoke that request until a later time. In such cases, one can prepare an `Invocation` that can be executed at a later time. In the following lines of code, an `Invocation` is created by making a request to a `WebTarget` and then calling the `buildGet()` method:

```
Invocation inv1 = client.target("http://localhost:8080/JakartaEERecipes/
rest/simplerest")
                .request("text/plain").buildGet();
// Sometime later...
Response res = inv1.invoke();
```

If we were posting a response, the buildPost() method could be called against the WebTarget instead, as follows:

```
Invocation inv1 = client.target("http://localhost:8080/JakartaEERecipes/
rest/makeithappen")
                .request("text/plain").buildPost(order);
 Response res = inv1.invoke();
```

Note   To asynchronously execute an Invocation, call the invocation submit method, rather than the invoke method.

Invocation objects can be configured similarly to WebTarget and Client objects. Filters, interceptors, properties, features, and providers can be configured on an Invocation by calling the register method and passing the appropriate configuration instance, as demonstrated in the following:

```
// Assume that inv1 is an Invocation instance
String result = inv1.register(MyInterceptor.class).invoke(String.class);
```

Note   To learn more about filters and interceptors, read Recipe 13-4.

WebTarget Injection

A WebTarget can be injected into any Jakarta RESTful Web Services managed resource by specifying the @Uri annotation and passing the WebTarget URI. In following example, a WebTarget resource is injected into a Jakarta RESTful Web Services resource to demonstrate this concept:

```
@Path("/orderservice")
public class OrderService {
    @Uri("order/{id}")
    WebTarget orderId;

    //...
}
```

13-4. Filtering Requests and Responses

Problem

You wish to perform some activity against a web service request before it has been delivered to the network, or to a web service response before it has been sent back to the client.

Solution

Apply a filter or interceptor to the web service request or response to perform the desired activity. The following example filter is used to write alerts to the system log before an incoming request has been processed and before a response is sent back to the client:

```
import java.io.BufferedReader;
import java.io.IOException;
import java.io.InputStream;
import java.io.InputStreamReader;
import javax.annotation.Priority;
import javax.ws.rs.Priorities;
import javax.ws.rs.container.ContainerRequestContext;
import javax.ws.rs.container.ContainerRequestFilter;
import javax.ws.rs.container.ContainerResponseContext;
import javax.ws.rs.container.ContainerResponseFilter;
import javax.ws.rs.ext.Provider;
import org.jakartaeerecipes.chapter13.rest.interfaces.Alerter;

@Provider
@Alerter
public class AlertFilter implements ContainerRequestFilter,
        ContainerResponseFilter {

    @Override
    public void filter(ContainerRequestContext requestContext)
            throws IOException {
        alert(requestContext);
    }
```

```
@Override
public void filter(ContainerRequestContext crc,
ContainerResponseContext crc1) throws IOException {
    alert(crc);
}

public void alert(ContainerRequestContext context) {

    try(InputStream in = context.getEntityStream();) {
        if (in != null) {
            InputStreamReader inreader = new InputStreamReader(in);
            BufferedReader reader = new BufferedReader(inreader);
            String text = "";

            while ((text = reader.readLine()) != null) {
                System.out.println(text);

            }

        }
    } catch (IOException ex) {
        // Error handling
    }
  }
}
```

How It Works

The concept of filters and interceptors is analogous to the post office processing your mail before it comes to your address. Rather than a message being delivered directly from point A to point B, it is first routed to one or more postal offices, where it is further processed before reaching point B. Web resource filters and interceptors apply that same concept to requests or responses that are being processed via a web service. If a filter or interceptor is bound to a web resource, then it will be invoked at some point in the life cycle of a request or response to that web resource. The type of filter or interceptor determines at what point in the life cycle it is applied. Interceptors (otherwise known as entity interceptors) wrap around a method invocation at a specified extension point.

Filters, on the other hand, execute code at a specified extension point, but they are not wrapped around methods. In the next few sections, you will take a closer look at each and how they are used.

Filters

An extension point is an interface that includes a method, which is responsible for filtering or intercepting the request or response. Filters have four such extension point interfaces, those being `ClientRequestFilter`, `ClientResponseFilter`, `ContainerRequestFilter`, and `ContainerResponseFilter`. The name of the extension point helps to describe what filter is applied and at what point. `ClientRequestFilter` and `ClientResponseFilter` are for use with the Jakarta RESTful Web Services Client API. `ClientRequestFilter` is applied before an HTTP request is delivered to the network. A `ClientResponseFilter` is applied when a server response is received and before control is returned to the application. `ContainerRequestFilter` and `ContainerResponseFilter` classes are for use with the Jakarta RESTful Web Services Server API. Similar to the client-side filters, a `ContainerRequestFilter` is applied upon receiving a request from a client, and a `ContainerResponseFilter` is applied before the HTTP response is delivered.

Entity Interceptors

As mentioned in the previous section, an extension point is an interface that includes a method, which is responsible for filtering or intercepting the request or response. Entity interceptors have two such extension points, those being `ReaderInterceptor` and `WriterInterceptor`. An entity interceptor class must implement one or both of these extension points. Also mentioned previously, entity interceptors wrap calls to methods. More specifically, `MessageBodyWriter` implementations wrap calls to the `writeTo` method, whereas `MessageBodyReader` implementations wrap calls to the `readFrom` method.

Binding Filters and Interceptors

Filters and interceptors must be associated to application classes or methods, and this process is also known as *binding*. The default type of binding is global binding, and any filter or interceptor that does not include annotations is bound globally. Global binding associates the filter or interceptor with all resource methods in an application. That said, any time a resource method is invoked, all globally bound filters and interceptors are processed as well.

Filters and interceptors can be registered manually via `Application` or `Configuration`, or they can be registered dynamically. To indicate that a filter or interceptor should be registered dynamically, it should be annotated with `@Provider`. If a filter or interceptor is not annotated as such, it must be registered manually.

To manually bind a filter or interceptor to a resource method, the filter or interceptor class must be denoted with a `@NameBinding` annotation. A `@NameBinding` annotation can be coded just as a standard annotation would, but it should also include the `@NameBinding` annotation in its interface. The following annotation code could be used to create a `@NameBinding` annotation that might be placed on a filter that is responsible for firing alerts:

```
@NameBinding
@Target({ ElementType.TYPE, ElementType.METHOD })
@Retention(value = RetentionPolicy.RUNTIME)
public @interface Alerter { }
```

To associate the `@NameBinding` with a filter or interceptor, simply annotate the filter or interceptor class with it. The following `AlertFilter` class is a filter implementation that is denoted with the `@Alerter` annotation:

```
@Provider
@Alerter
class AlertFilter implements ContainerRequestFilter,
        ContainerResponseFilter {

...

}
```

That filter can now be bound to a resource method by annotating the resource method with the same `@NameBinding` as the filter class, as demonstrated in the following example:

```
@GET
@Produces("text/html")
@Alerter
public String  getJobs(){
    ...
}
```

Note   This same concept can be applied to `Application` subclasses in order to globally bind the filter or interceptor.

Setting Priorities

As mentioned in previous sections, filters and interceptors can be chained. Chains of filters or interceptors invoke individual filters or interceptors based upon a given priority. To assign priority to a filter or interceptor, denote the implementation class with the `@BindingPriority` annotation. Integer numbers are used to associate priorities. The higher the integer, the higher the priority. Therefore, the filter or interceptor that has the highest-priority integer assigned to it will be invoked first, and the lowest-priority integer will be invoked last.

13-5. Processing Long-Running Operations Asynchronously

Problem

Your server-side Jakarta RESTful Web Services method contains a long-running operation, and you would like to avoid blocking while waiting for the event to complete.

Solution

Perform asynchronous processing so that the resource method containing the long-running operation can inform Jakarta RESTful Web Services that a response is not yet readily available, but will be produced at some point in the future. In the following example, a Jakarta RESTful Web Services service named `AsyncResource` contains a resource method named `asyncOperation`. The `asyncOperation` method contains a long-running task, which is handed off to a `ManagedExecutorService` for processing:

```
import javax.annotation.Resource;
import javax.enterprise.concurrent.ManagedExecutorService;
import javax.ws.rs.GET;
import javax.ws.rs.Path;
```

```
import javax.ws.rs.container.AsyncResponse;
import javax.ws.rs.container.Suspended;

/**
 * Recipe 13-5:  Asynchronous Processing
 * @author Juneau
 */
@Path("/asynchronous/asyncResource")
public class AsyncResource {

    @Resource(name = "concurrent/__defaultManagedExecutorService")
    ManagedExecutorService mes;

    @GET
    public void asyncOperation(@Suspended final AsyncResponse ar){
        mes.submit(
                new Runnable() {
                    public void run(){
                        // Perform long running operation
                        longRunningOperation();
                        ar.resume("Performing asynchronous operation");
                    }
                });
    }

    public void longRunningOperation(){
        // This is a method that contains a long-running operation
        System.out.println( "Performing long running task...");
    }

}
```

Note   To learn more about `ManagedExecutorService`, please see Chapter 17.

How It Works

The Jakarta RESTful Web Services 2.0 API introduced the ability to hand long-running tasks off to a `ManagedExecutorService` for processing. This allows a server-side resource to return control back to a client and avoid problematic blocks. The API also includes a way to register a timeout handler in case the asynchronous process does not return within a specified amount of time, along with client-side asynchronous capabilities. To begin, the server-side asynchronous implementation will be described, followed by the others.

To perform asynchronous processing within a Jakarta RESTful Web Services resource, the resource method that contains long-running operations must accept an instance of `AsyncResponse` via the utilization of the `@Suspended` annotation. The `AsyncResponse` class provides a means for resuming operations and returning control to the client. A `ManagedExecutorService` (see Chapter 17 for more information) must be made available within the class, and it must be called upon to submit a new `Runnable` containing the long-running operation and a call to `AsyncResponse.resume()` to return control back to the client once the long-running process is completed. When the `ManagedExecutorService submit` method is called, the `Runnable` is passed to the server for further processing, forking a thread to execute the task and returning immediately. When the long-running task has completed, it will be passed back to the application, invoking the `AsyncResponse resume` method.

In order to avoid long-running operations that never return and cause a suspended connection to wait indefinitely, it is possible to specify a timeout value. The timeout value can be specified by setting a timeout handler via the `AsyncResponse. setTimeoutHandler()` method, passing a new instance of `TimeoutHandler`. After the `setTimeoutHandler` has been invoked, the timeout can be set by calling the `AsyncResponse.setTimeout()` method, passing any unit of type `java.util. concurrent.TimeUnit`. For instance, the following lines demonstrate how to set a timeout of 30 seconds for the long-running operation contained in the resource shown in the solution to this recipe:

```
...
@GET
    public void asyncOperation(@Suspended final AsyncResponse ar){
        ar.setTimeoutHandler(new TimeoutHandler() {
            public void handleTimeout(AsyncResponse ar){
```

```
                ar.resume("Timed out");
            }
    });
    ar.setTimeout(30, SECONDS);
    mes.submit(
            new Runnable() {
                public void run(){
                    // Perform long running operation
                    longRunningOperation();
                    ar.resume("Performing asynchronous operation");
                }
            });
    }
...
```

Note   Jakarta RESTful Web Services implementations will generate a
ServiceUnavailableException with a status of 503 when a timeout value is
reached and no timeout handler is present.

As mentioned at the top of this section, the asynchronous Jakarta RESTful Web
Services API has been extended to the client API as well. By default, invocations from
a client to a target are executed in a synchronous fashion, but they can be changed to
asynchronous by calling the async method and optionally registering an instance of
InvocationCallback. For example, the following lines of code demonstrate a client call
to the web service resource that was presented in the solution to this recipe:

```
Client client = ClientBuilder.newClient();
Target target = client.target("http://localhost:8080/JakartaEERecipes/rest/
asynchronous/asyncResource");
Target.request().async().get();
```

For more information regarding the client API and asynchronous operations, please
refer to the Jakarta RESTful Web Services documentation online.

13-6. Pushing One-Way Asynchronous Updates from Servers

Problem

You wish to push one-way messages from a server to one or more clients.

Solution

Utilize Server-Sent Events (SSE) to push messages from a server to one or more clients. The Jakarta RESTful Web Services 2.1 API introduced the concept of SSE, which allows one to push messages from a server to subscribed clients. It also allows for subscription events to perform server actions. The following example contains sources for a Jakarta RESTful Web Services class. The class contains a send method, which allows a client to connect to the server and obtain messages from the server that have been broadcasted via Server-Sent Events:

```
package org.jakartaeerecipes.chapter13.rest.service;

import javax.ws.rs.GET;
import javax.ws.rs.Path;
import javax.ws.rs.Produces;
import javax.ws.rs.core.Context;
import javax.ws.rs.core.MediaType;
import javax.ws.rs.sse.Sse;
import javax.ws.rs.sse.SseEventSink;

@Path("sse")
public class SSEEventResource {

    @Resource(name = "DefaultManagedExecutorService")
    ManagedExecutorService executor;

    public SSEEventResource() {

    }

    @GET
    @Path("send")
```

```
@Produces(MediaType.SERVER_SENT_EVENTS)
public void send(@Context SseEventSink eventSink,
        @Context Sse sse) {
    executor.execute(() -> {
        try (SseEventSink sink = eventSink) {
            eventSink.send(sse.newEvent("Welcome to the List!"));
            eventSink.send(sse.newEvent("Message One!"));
            eventSink.send(sse.newEvent("SERVER-NOTIFICATION",
            "Message Two!"));
            eventSink.send(sse.newEventBuilder()
                    .comment("Nice Test")
                    .name("SERVER-TEST")
                    .data("Some data...could be an object")
                    .build());
            eventSink.close();
        }
    });
}
}
```

One can visit the following URL and see the resulting messages broadcast:
http://localhost:8080/JakartaEERecipes/rest/sse/send.

To broadcast to multiple clients simultaneously, one can use the SseBroadcaster
to register multiple SseEventSink instances and send messages. The following example
demonstrates how to construct a Jakarta RESTful Web Services class that allows clients to
register and the server to broadcast events to those registered clients:

```
package org.jakartaeerecipes.chapter13.rest.service;

import java.util.UUID;
import javax.annotation.PostConstruct;
import javax.ejb.Singleton;
import javax.ws.rs.GET;
import javax.ws.rs.POST;
import javax.ws.rs.Path;
import javax.ws.rs.PathParam;
```

```java
import javax.ws.rs.Produces;
import javax.ws.rs.core.Context;
import javax.ws.rs.core.MediaType;
import javax.ws.rs.sse.Sse;
import javax.ws.rs.sse.SseBroadcaster;
import javax.ws.rs.sse.SseEventSink;

@Path("/")
@Singleton
public class SSEEventBroadcaster {

    @Context
    private Sse sse;

    private volatile SseBroadcaster sseBroadcaster;

    public SSEEventBroadcaster() {
    }

    @PostConstruct
    public void init() {
        sseBroadcaster = sse.newBroadcaster();
    }

    @GET
    @Path("register")
    @Produces(MediaType.SERVER_SENT_EVENTS)
    public void register(@Context SseEventSink eventSink) {
        eventSink.send(sse.newEvent("Thanks for registering!"));
        sseBroadcaster.register(eventSink);
    }

    @POST
    @Path("send/{message}")
    public void broadcast(@PathParam("message") String message) {
        sseBroadcaster.broadcast(sse.newEventBuilder()
                .mediaType(MediaType.APPLICATION_JSON_TYPE)
                .id(UUID.randomUUID().toString())
                .name("SSEEventBroadcaster Message")
```

```
                .data(message)
                .build()
        );
    }
}
```

How It Works

The Jakarta RESTful Web Services 2.1 release introduced support for Server-Sent Events (SSE). Server-Sent Events make it possible to push messages from a server to multiple clients at a time over HTTP or HTTPS. The connection from the client to the server can remain open, and messages can continue to be sent until the client disconnects. The API contains a number of interfaces that are used for sending messages to clients, registering connections, and so on, and each of them resides within the javax.ws.rs.sse package. The Sse interface is the server-side entry point for creating OutboundSseEvent and SseBroadcaster. It can be injected into a field or used as a parameter to a method or constructor. The SseEventSink interface is used to actually send a stream of messages, and it can be acquired by injecting as a resource method parameter. SseEvent is the base event class, which defines properties such as Id, Name, and Comment. The OutboundSseEvent is used by the server to package an SseEvent, and SseBroadcaster is used to manage multiple SseEventSink objects. The SseBroadcaster enables the server to send events to all registered clients and provides facilities for handing exceptions.

In the first example, a simple Jakarta RESTful Web Services class is used to demonstrate how a server can use a single method to register a client and send one or more events. In the example, the class is registered as a RESTful web service at the path "sse", and the method send() is registered at the path "sse/send". The send() method produces the type MediaType.SERVER_SENT_EVENTS. It accepts @Context parameters of type SseEventSink and Sse, which are used to register a client and push events. The class also injects a ManagedExecutorService instance, which is a server-side concurrency utility that is used to perform concurrent processes. You can learn more about the ManagedExecutorService in Chapter 16. Inside the method, a try-with-resources clause is used to open up an SseEventSink identified as eventSink. The eventSink is used to send a number of SseEvent instances. Once completed, the eventSink is closed. The entire process is sent to the ManagedExecutorService so that it can be queued up in the server and executed in a concurrent manner.

The next example demonstrates how to construct a Jakarta RESTful Web Services class that can be used to register clients and broadcast events. The class is registered as a singleton, meaning that only one instance of the class will be constructed and utilized by all sessions. An Sse context is registered with the class, as it can be used to create new SseBroadcaster objects, new SseEvent objects, and new event builder objects. An SseBroadcaster is declared as volatile, meaning that it will be stored in main Java memory and not in a cache. There is an init() method which is annotated with @PostConstruct so that it will be executed immediately after construction. The init() method contains a call to sse.newBroadcaster(), thereby obtaining a new SseBroadcaster instance. Clients can register by calling upon the register web service method, which produces MediaType.SERVER_SENT_EVENTS. An SseEventSink Context parameter is passed in as a parameter to the register method, and in the implementation a new SseEvent is sent via the eventSink. The SseEventSink is then registered to the SseBroadcaster instance. The broadcast method accepts a String as a path parameter, and inside the method the SseBroadcaster broadcast() is used to send an event. The method demonstrates the use of the SseEvent builder. As you can see, calling upon sse.newEventBuilder() allows for the construction of an SseEvent utilizing the builder pattern. In the example, the media type is set as MediaType.APPLICATION_JSON_TYPE, which indicates JSON:

```
sseBroadcaster.broadcast(sse.newEventBuilder()
    .mediaType(MediaType.APPLICATION_JSON_TYPE)
    .id(UUID.randomUUID().toString())
    .name("SSEEventBroadcaster Message")
    .data(message)
    .build()
);
```

In the next recipe, I will demonstrate how to register a client to an SseBroadcaster and also how to listen for events on the client.

13-7. Receiving Server-Sent Events As a Client

Problem

You wish to create a client which subscribes to an `SseBroadcaster` on which messages are pushed from a server, and you'd like to have the client perform an action when a message is received.

Solution

Utilize Server-Sent Events (SSE) to push messages from a server to one or more clients. The Jakarta RESTful Web Services 2.1 API introduced the concept of SSE, which allows a server to broadcast messages to registered clients. In the following example, a JSF client is used to call upon a Jakarta RESTful Web Services SSE broadcaster and register. The client then listens to broadcasted messages for 1000 milliseconds:

```
package org.jakartaeerecipes.chapter15.rest.jsf;

import javax.annotation.PostConstruct;
import javax.enterprise.context.RequestScoped;
import javax.inject.Named;
import javax.ws.rs.client.Client;
import javax.ws.rs.client.ClientBuilder;
import javax.ws.rs.client.WebTarget;
import javax.ws.rs.sse.SseEventSource;

@Named
@RequestScoped
public class SseClient {

    private Client client;

    @PostConstruct
    public void init() {
        client = ClientBuilder.newClient();
    }
```

```
    public void listen() {
        WebTarget target = client.target("http://localhost:8080/
        JakartaEERecipes/rest/ssebroadcaster/register");
        try (SseEventSource source = SseEventSource.target(target).build())
{
            source.register(System.out::println);
            source.open();
            Thread.sleep(1000); // Consume events for 1000 ms
            source.close();
        } catch (InterruptedException e) {

        }
    }
}
```

A JSF `commandButton` could be linked to the `#{sseClient.listen}` method, which would then invoke the client when pressed.

How It Works

A Jakarta RESTful Web Services client can be used to register to a SSE broadcaster by simply calling upon the broadcaster's registration method. Once registered, the `SseEventSource` can be opened for a defined amount of time (one should not leave an `SseEventSource` open without bound), and then it can be closed when finished listening for messages.

In the example, the `SseEventSource` is set to the target of the broadcaster URL. Next, it registers the output from the incoming message to be written to `System.out.println()`. Therefore, each message received will be written to the system log. After the registration, the source is opened for incoming messages. In the example, a thread is hard-coded to sleep for 1000 milliseconds. This is simply to keep the client open for messages for 1000 milliseconds and would likely not be coded this way for a production application. Lastly, the `SseEventSource` is closed, which ends the client session.

CHAPTER 14

WebSockets and JSON

The Jakarta EE 8 platform aims to provide a common ground for developing Java enterprise solutions that incorporate HTML5 and other modern web technologies. As such, there are a few core features that were added to Java EE 7, allowing for better bidirectional support of HTML5. The Java EE 7 platform introduced communication between the client and the server via a technology named WebSockets, enabling more parity with the HTML5 standard. WebSockets are a full-duplex communication mechanism that allows both textual and binary messages to be sent between clients and servers, without the HTTP request/response life cycle. WebSockets allow either the client or the server to send a message at any time, providing an asynchronous solution for working with data while the user is performing a task.

HTML5 has become the mainstream markup language for developing content that can be presented via the World Wide Web. It defines a standard, which can be used to produce both HTML and XHTML documents. Along with standardization, HTML5 also brings forth semantic features that were previously only possible on desktop application platforms. For example, elements such as `<video>` and `<audio>` allow media content to be embedded directly in web pages, without the need to embed a media player solution. There is no doubt that HTML5, the fifth revision of the HTML standard, has opened the doors to new possibilities in web application development.

The universally supported JSON (JavaScript Object Notation) object has become a widely adopted solution for sending data between points. HTML5-based web applications can utilize JSON to transport data, using WebSockets, Ajax, or other transport technologies. The Jakarta EE 8 platform provides the JSON Processing (JSON-P) API, which introduces utilities that make it easier to build and work with JSON objects within the Java language. Java EE 8 added enhancements to JSON-P, allowing the abilities to point to a specific location within a JSON document, and also patch existing JSON documents. The JSON Binding (JSON-B) API was also introduced in Java EE 8, providing a convenient API for mapping JSON to Java objects.

J. Juneau, *Jakarta EE Recipes*, https://doi.org/10.1007/978-1-4842-5587-2_14

This chapter will focus on recipes that demonstrate these APIs. You will learn how to make use of WebSockets, JSON-P, and JSON-B so that your application's client-server communication can become seamless, whether the user interface is written with HTML5, JSF, or another markup language.

14-1. Creating a WebSocket Endpoint

Problem

You wish to create a WebSocket endpoint that can be used to receive messages asynchronously.

Solution

Create a WebSocket endpoint by annotating a server-side POJO (Plain Old Java Object) class and a method within that class, accordingly. In the following example, a simple POJO class, named org.jakartaeerecipes.chapter14.recipe14_01. BookChatEndpoint, is annotated to indicate that it should be accessible via the Web as a WebSocket endpoint. The class contains a method named messageReceiver, which is annotated to make it accessible to a client as a callable message consumer:

```
import javax.websocket.OnMessage;
import javax.websocket.server.ServerEndpoint;
...
@ServerEndpoint(path="/bookChatEndpoint")
public class BookChatEndpoint {

 @OnMessage
 public String messageReceiver(String message) {
     return "Message Received: " + message;
 }
}
```

The WebSocket endpoint will be accessible to clients at the URL ws://localhost:8080/ JakartaEERecipes/bookChatEndpoint. When a message is sent from a client to the endpoint, it is sent to the messageReceiver method, where it is processed accordingly. In this case, a String message containing the message passed to the endpoint is returned to the client.

How It Works

A server-side class can accept messages from clients by configuring it as a WebSocket endpoint. To develop a WebSocket endpoint, create a Java POJO, and annotate it with @ServerEndpoint. The @ServerEndpoint annotation accepts a String-based path attribute, which is used to indicate the URI at which the server is available to accept client messages. Therefore, when the server is started, the value of the path attribute would be appended to the end of the context path and application name in which the WebSocket resides. By initiating a call to that URL, one method, annotated with @OnMessage, will be invoked to process the message that is sent.

In the example, a class named BookChatEndpoint is annotated as a WebSocket, so it is accessible to clients as an endpoint for receiving messages and returning a response. When initiating communication with the WebSocket endpoint, the client must utilize a URL that contains a URI scheme of "ws," rather than "http." The "ws" URI scheme was introduced by the WebSocket protocol and, as such, indicates that the URL is used for communication with a WebSocket. In this example, a client can send a message to the server via the bookChatEndpoint WebSocket, and the server can send a message back at the same time, because WebSockets allow for full-duplex communication. *Full-duplex communication* is an HTML5 standard, rather than standard HTTP, which utilizes a request-response communication.

14-2. Sending Messages to a WebSocket Endpoint
Problem

You would like to send a message from a client to a WebSocket endpoint that is available on a server.

Solution

Engineer a JavaScript solution that can be used to send messages from a client browser to a WebSocket endpoint. Invoke the JavaScript function via an action event that is bound to an HTML input tag within the view. In the following example, a button contains an onclick attribute that will invoke a JavaScript function named bookChatRelay. The bookChatRelay function is responsible for opening a session with a WebSocket endpoint so that messages can be sent. The following listing is an excerpt from the `recipe14_02.xhtml` JSF view, which is located within the `web/chapter14` directory of the JakartaEERecipes source bundle:

```
...
<html>
    <head>
        <script type="text/javascript">
            var ws;
            function bookChatRelay()
            {
                if ("WebSocket" in window)
                {
                    alert("WebSocket is supported by your Browser!");

                    if (ws == null){
                        alert("Creating new websocket connection");
                        ws = new WebSocket("ws://localhost:8080/
                        JakartaEERecipes/bookChatEndpoint");
                    } else {
                        ws.send("Another message");
                    }
                    ws.onopen = function()
                    {
                        // Web Socket is connected, send data using send()
                        ws.send("Message to send");
                        alert("Message is sent...");
                    };
                    ws.onmessage = function (evt)
                    {
                        var received_msg = evt.data;
                        alert("Message from server: " + received_msg);
                    };
```

```
            ws.onclose = function()
            {
                // websocket is closed.
                alert("Connection is closed...");
            };
        }
        else
        {
            // The browser doesn't support WebSocket
            alert("WebSocket NOT supported by your Browser!");
        }
    }
    function closeConnection(){
        if (ws !== null){
            ws.close();
            ws = null;
        }
    }

</script>
</head>
<body>

    <input id="wsRelay" type="button" value="WebSocket Test Message"
            onclick="bookChatRelay();"/>
    <input id="closeConn" type="button" value="Close Connection"
            onclick="closeConnection();"/>
</body>

</html>
```

When the button is pressed, the message will be sent from the browser client to the WebSocket endpoint, and a message will be returned from the endpoint to the client.

Note   The JavaScript code in this test creates a new WebSocket connection each time the button on the page is pressed. This is okay for testing purposes, but in a real-life scenario, you will want to retain and reuse the connection, if possible.

How It Works

The ability to asynchronously send messages (text or binary) from a client to a server defines the foundation of Ajax and HTML5 capability. The WebSockets API allows developers to send messages to the server via JavaScript calls to a WebSocket endpoint. Conversely, the API allows clients to receive messages and process them accordingly via a series of JavaScript functions. The example for this recipe demonstrates how to send a message to a WebSocket endpoint by clicking a button on a web page. When the button is clicked, a JavaScript function named bookChatRelay is invoked, which embodies the processing implementation.

To send a message to a WebSocket endpoint via a JavaScript function, the first task is to confirm whether the user's browser is capable of working with WebSockets (HTML5 compliant). This confirmation can be performed using a conditional statement to verify if the "WebSocket" object is available within the client via the following if statement:

```
if("WebSocket" in window){
...
} else {
...
}
```

If the client browser is capable of working with WebSockets, then the implementation inside the if block is invoked; otherwise, the implementation within the else block is invoked. To process the WebSocket message, a new WebSocket object must be instantiated to establish the server connection, which is done by passing the URL to the WebSocket endpoint to a new WebSocket object:

```
var ws = new WebSocket("ws://localhost:8080/JakartaEERecipes/
bookChatEndpoint");
```

The constructor for creating a WebSocket takes either one or two parameters. The first parameter is the URL of the server to which the WebSocket will connect, and the optional second parameter is a String of protocols that can be used for message transmission. The WebSocket object contains a handful of events that are utilized to help implement message processing. Table 14-1 lists the different events that can occur in the life cycle a WebSocket object, along with a description of what they do.

Table 14-1. *JavaScript WebSocket Object Events*

Event	Handler Method	Description
open	onOpen	Occurs when the WebSocket connection is established
close	onClose	Occurs when the WebSocket connection is closed
error	onError	Occurs when there is a communication error
message	onMessage	Occurs when data is received from the server

After the WebSocket object has been instantiated successfully, a connection to the server will be established, which will cause the open event to occur. To process this event, assign a function to the onOpen handler, and process events accordingly within that function. Messages are usually sent to the server when the open event occurs, and this is demonstrated within the example:

```
ws.onopen = function()
{
    // Web Socket is connected, send data using send()
    ws.send("Message to send");
    alert("Message is sent...");
};
```

Similarly, you can listen for any other events to occur, and then process tasks accordingly when they do. In the example, when a message is received from the server, it is printed within an alert dialog. Also in the example, when the WebSocket is closed, an alert dialog is presented to the user.

The example does not demonstrate all the possible ways that the WebSocket object in JavaScript can be utilized. For instance, you could send messages to the server by invoking the send() method and passing the data that you wish to send as a parameter. The close() method can be called on a WebSocket to manually terminate the existing connection. WebSocket objects also contain the helpful attributes readyState and bufferedAmount, which can be used for obtaining information about a connection. The readyState attribute will advise the current state of the WebSocket connection via a returned number, and bufferedAmount attribute value represents the number of bytes of UTF-8 text that have been queued using the send() method. Table 14-2 displays the different possible values for the readyState attribute, along with a description of each.

Table 14-2. JavaScript WebSocket readyState Values

Value	Description
0	Connection not yet established. WebSocket.CONNECTING
1	Connection established and communication is possible. WebSocket.OPEN
2	Connection going through closing handshake. WebSocket.CLOSING
3	Connection closed and cannot be opened. WebSocket.CLOSED

14-3. Building a JSON Object

Problem

You would like to build a JSON object that can be passed from a client to a server or vice versa.

Solution

Make use of the JsonObjectBuilder to build a JSON object using Java code. The following example demonstrates how to utilize a JsonObjectBuilder() instance to create a new JsonObject. In this example class, multiple JsonObjects are created from reading the contents of a database table. Once the object is built, the sections of the object are assigned to a String that will eventually be displayed or persisted:

```
import java.io.IOException;
import java.io.StringWriter;
import java.util.List;
import javax.ejb.EJB;
import javax.faces.bean.ManagedBean;
import javax.json.Json;
import javax.json.JsonObject;
import javax.json.JsonObjectBuilder;
```

```
import javax.json.JsonWriter;
import org.jakartaeerecipes.jpa.entity.BookAuthor;
import org.jakartaeerecipes.jpa.session.BookAuthorFacade;

@Named(name = "jsonController")
public class JsonController {

    @EJB
    BookAuthorFacade bookAuthorFacade;
    private String authorJson;

    public void buildAuthors() {
        List<BookAuthor> authors = bookAuthorFacade.findAll();
        JsonObjectBuilder builder = Json.createObjectBuilder();
        StringBuilder json = new StringBuilder();
        try (StringWriter sw = new StringWriter();) {
            for (BookAuthor author : authors) {
                System.out.println("author" + author.getLast());
                builder.add("author", Json.createObjectBuilder()
                        .add("authorId", author.getId())
                        .add("first", author.getFirst())
                        .add("last", author.getLast())
                        .add("bio", author.getBio()));

            }
            JsonObject result = builder.build();

            try (JsonWriter writer = Json.createWriter(sw)) {
                writer.writeObject(result);
            }
            json.append(sw.toString());
            authorJson = json.toString();
        } catch (IOException ex) {
            System.out.println(ex);
        }
    }
...
```

Once created, the `JsonObject` can be passed to a client for processing, or in this case, it can be persisted to disk.

How It Works

The JavaScript Object Notation Processing (JSON-P) API was added to the Java Enterprise platform as of the release of Java EE 7. JSON-P, also referred to as "JSON with padding," has become the standard way to build JSON objects using Java. The JSON-P API includes a helper class that can be used to create JSON objects using the builder pattern. Using the `JsonObjectBuilder` class, JSON objects can be built using a series of method calls, each building upon each other—hence the builder pattern. Once the JSON object has been built, the `JsonObjectBuilder  build` method can be called to return a `JsonObject`.

In the example for this recipe, you construct a JSON object that provides details regarding book authors. The `JsonObjectBuilder.beginObject()` method is used to denote that a new object is being created. The `add` method is used to add more name/value properties, much like that of a `Map`. Therefore, the following line adds a property named `authorId` with a value of `author.getId()`:

```
.add("authorId", author.getId())
```

Objects can be embedded inside of each other, creating a hierarchy of different sections within one `JsonObject`. In the example, after the first call to `add()`, another object named `author` is embedded inside the initial `JsonObject` by calling `beginObject()` and passing the name of the embedded object. Embedded objects can also contain properties; so to add properties to the embedded object, call the `add()` method within the embedded object. `JsonObjects` can embody as many embedded objects as needed. The following lines of code demonstrate the beginning and end of an embedded object definition:

```
.beginObject("author")
.add("first", "Josh")
.add("last", "Juneau")
.endObject()
```

It is also possible that a `JsonObject` may have an array of related subobjects. To add an array of subobjects, call the `beginArray()` method, passing the name of the array as an argument. Arrays can consist of objects and even hierarchies of objects, arrays, and so forth. In the example for this recipe, the book object has a couple of arrays defined, one being an array of `editor` objects and the other being an array of `technicalReviewer` objects.

Once a `JsonObject` has been created, it can be passed to a client. WebSockets work well for passing `JsonObjects` back to a client, but there are a bevy of different technologies available for communicating with JSON.

14-4. Writing a JSON Object to Disk
Problem

You would like to write a JSON object to the file system.

Solution

Utilize the JSON-P API to build a JSON object, and then store it to the file system. The `JsonWriter` class makes it possible to create a file on disk and then write the JSON to that file. In the following example, the `JsonObject` that was generated in Recipe 14-3 is written to disk using this technique:

```
public void writeJson() {
    try {
        JsonObject jsonObject = jsonController.buildAuthorsJson();

        javax.json.JsonWriter jsonWriter = Json.createWriter(new
        FileWriter("Authors.json"));

        jsonWriter.writeObject(jsonObject);
        jsonWriter.close();

        FacesContext.getCurrentInstance().addMessage(null, new
        FacesMessage(
            FacesMessage.SEVERITY_INFO, "JSON Built",
            "JSON Built"));
    } catch (IOException ex) {
        System.out.println(ex);
    }
}
```

How It Works

The JsonWriter class can be utilized to write a JsonObject to a Java writer object. A JsonWriter is instantiated by passing a Writer object as an argument. Instantiating a JsonWriter will write to the Writer object that had been passed as an argument, using JSON format. After that Writer has been created, the JsonWriter writeObject() method can be invoked, passing the JsonObject that is to be written. Once the JsonObject has been written, the JsonWriter can be closed by calling its close() method. These are the only steps that are necessary for writing a JSON object to a Java Writer class type.

14-5. Reading JSON from an Input Source

Problem

You would like to read a JSON object that has been built or persisted to a file.

Solution

Obtain a JSON object that you would like to read, and then read it using the javax.json. Json createReader utility. In the following example, a JSON file is read from disk and then parsed to determine the hierarchy of events within. Each of the events is printed to the server log as the JSON is being parsed:

```java
public String readObject() {
        InputStream in = new ByteArrayInputStream(controller.
        buildAndReturnAuthors().getBytes());
         // or
        //Reader fileReader = new InputStreamReader(getClass().getResource
        AsStream("AuthorObject.json"));
        //JsonReader reader = Json.createReader(fileReader);
        JsonReader reader = Json.createReader(in);
        JsonObject obj = reader.readObject();
        return obj.toString();

    }
```

How It Works

Once a JSON object has been persisted to disk, it will later need to be read back in for utilization. The `JsonReader` object takes care of this task. To create a `JsonReader` object, call the `Json.createReader()` method, passing either an `InputStream` or `Reader` object. Once a `JsonReader` object has been created, it can produce a `JsonObject` by calling its `readObject` method.

Parsing Content

In order to perform some tasks, a JSON object must be searched to find only the content that is desired and useful for the current task. Utilizing a JSON parser can make jobs such as these easier, as a parser is able to break the object down into pieces so that each different piece can be examined as needed, to produce the desired result.

The `javax.json.Json` class contains a static factory method, `createParser()`, that accepts a bevy of input and returns an `Iterable JsonParser`. Table 14-3 lists the different possible input types that are accepted via the `createParser()` method.

Table 14-3. createParser *Method Input Types*

Input Type	Method Call
InputStream	createParser(InputStream in)
JsonArray	createParser(JsonArray arr)
JsonObject	createParser(JsonObject obj)
Reader	createParser(Reader reader)

Once a `JsonParser` has been created, it can be made into an `Iterator` of `Event` objects. Each `Event` correlates to a different structure within the JSON object. For instance, when the JSON object is created, a `START_OBJECT` event occurs, adding a name/value pair that will trigger both `KEY_NAME` and `VALUE_STRING` events. These events can be utilized to obtain the desired information from a JSON object. In the example, the event names are merely printed to a server log. However, in a real-life application, a conditional would most likely test each iteration to find a particular event and then perform some processing. Table 14-4 lists the different JSON events, along with a description of when each occurs.

Table 14-4. *JSON Object Events*

Event	Occurrence
START_OBJECT	Start of an object
END_OBJECT	End of an object
START_ARRAY	Start of an array
END_ARRAY	End of an array
KEY_NAME	Name of a key
VALUE_STRING	Value of a name/value pair in String format
VALUE_NUMBER	Value of a name/value pair in numeric format
VALUE_TRUE	Value of a name/value pair in Boolean format
VALUE_FALSE	Value of a name/value pair in Boolean format
VALUE_NULL	Value of a name/value pair as NULL

14-6. Converting Between JSON and Java Objects

Problem

You have obtained a list of Java objects in a response from a web service, and you wish to convert it to JSON.

Solution

Utilize the JSON Binding (JSON-B) API to bind the Java object elements to JSON format. In the following example, an XML response is received from a web service, converted into Java objects, and the JSON-B API is used to convert the objects into JSON. A Jakarta RESTful Web Services client is used to obtain a response that will include a number of Employee objects, and each of them will be converted into a Java Employee object:

```
. . .
List<Employee> employees;
. . .
public String fetchJson(){
```

718

```
WebTarget target = ClientBuilder.newClient().target("http://
localhost:8080/JakartaEERecipes/rest/org.jakartaeerecipes.entity.
employee");

    employees = (target.request(javax.ws.rs.core.MediaType.APPLICATION_
    XML)
            .get(
            new GenericType<List<Employee>>() {
    }));
System.out.println("Items: " + employees);
Jsonb jsonb = JsonbBuilder.create();
String result = null;

result = jsonb.toJson(employees);

return result;
}
```

Similarly, the JSON-B API can be used to convert from JSON to Java. In the following method, a JSON string is returned from a web service call, and it is converted into a Java collection:

```
public List<Employee> fetchJavaFromJson(){
    WebTarget target = ClientBuilder.newClient().target("http://
    localhost:8080/JakartaEERecipes/rest/org.jakartaeerecipes.entity.
    employee");

    String employeesJson = (target.request(javax.ws.rs.core.MediaType.
    APPLICATION_JSON)
            .get(
            new GenericType<String>() {
    }));
System.out.println("Items: " + employeesJson);
Jsonb jsonb = JsonbBuilder.create();
List<Employee> employees = new ArrayList();
employees = jsonb.fromJson(employeesJson, ArrayList.class);
return employees;
}
```

In the example, a JSF view is used to display the contents of the Employee JSON. The view markup sources are as follows:

```
<h:body>
    <p:panel header="JSON Representation of Employees">
        <h:outputText value="#{employeeJsonController.fetchJson()}"/>
    </p:panel>
    <p:panel header="Java Representation of Employees JSON">
        <p:dataTable value="#{employeeJsonController.fetchJavaFromJson()}"
        var="emp">
            <p:column>
                #{emp.last}
            </p:column>
        </p:dataTable>
    </p:panel>
</h:body>
```

The output would look similar to the following:

JSON Representation of Customers

[{"age":32,"first":"JANE","id":1,"job":{"division":"IT","jobId":1,"salary":60000,"title":"IT TITLE A"},"last":"DEVELOPER","status":true},{"age":25,"first":"BOB","id":2,"job": {"division":"HR","jobId":4,"salary":50000,"title":"HR TITLE A"},"last":"SMITH","status":true},{"age":25,"first":"JOE","id":3,"job":{"division":"IT","jobId":3,"salary":40000,"title":"IT TITLE C"},"last":"DEVELOPER","status":true}]

JSON Representation of Employees

DEVELOPER
SMITH
DEVELOPER

How It Works

The JSON-B API can be used to convert between JSON and Java seamlessly. In the release of Java EE 7, the transition between JSON and Java was missing. Therefore, this conversion had to take place manually, and it was a bit painstaking. In Java EE 8, this gap has been closed, and it is now possible to convert seamlessly between JSON and Java.

Note   To visit the JSON-B web site and view all documentation, please visit http://json-b.net/.

The key piece of the JSON-B API is the `Jsonb` interface, which provides an abstraction over the JSON binding operations. The `JsonbBuilder` can be used to obtain a `Jsonb` object, which in turn is used to convert between Java and JSON. To create the `Jsonb` object, call upon the `JsonBuilder create()` method. Once the `Jsonb` object has been obtained, it can be used to convert to JSON and serialize by passing the Java object to the `toJson()` method:

```
Jsonb jsonb = JsonbBuilder.create();
  String result = null;

  result = jsonb.toJson(employees);
```

To go in the opposite direction and deserialize from JSON back to Java, use the `Jsonb` `fromJson()` method, passing the JSON string as the first argument and the Java type to which the JSON will be converted as the second argument:

```
Jsonb jsonb = JsonbBuilder.create();
List<Employee> employees = new ArrayList();
employees = jsonb.fromJson(employeesJson, ArrayList.class);
```

The technique shown in the preceding text is only one way to convert back to a `Collection` type. If you wish to convert in a type-safe manner, back to the generic type `List<Employee>`, it can be done as follows:

```
employees = jsonb.fromJson(employeesJson, new ArrayList<Employee>(){}
                                      .getClass().
                                      getGenericSuperclass());
```

The `Jsonb` object can also convert back to a single Java object by passing the Java object type as the second argument to the `fromJson()` utility method, as follows:

```
Jsonb jsonb = JsonbBuilder.create();
Employee employee = new Employee;
employee = jsonb.fromJson(singleEmployeeJson, Employee.class);
```

This recipe covers the basics of converting JSON to Java and vice versa. For more information regarding customizations, please see Recipe 14-7.

14-7. Custom Mapping with JSON-B

Problem

You wish to change the JSON property names when converting to a Java class or perform custom mapping for circumstances such as converting specific date formats or marking specified fields as transient.

Solution

Utilize a `JsonbConfig` to create a custom runtime configuration for the JSON mapping. There are also a handful of annotations that can be applied at the Java class level, field level, or getter/setters to customize some configurations. In the following scenario, a custom configuration is used to create a property naming strategy that includes lowercase with underscores:

```
JsonbConfig config = new JsonbConfig()
    .withPropertyNamingStrategy(PropertyNamingStragegy.LOWER_CASE_WITH_
    UNDERSCORES);
Jsonb jsonb = JsonbBuilder.create(config);
```

As mentioned previously, there are also a handful of annotations that can be applied to customize mapping. In the following scenario, the dog color property is marked as transient. This means that the color property will not be serialized into JSON when converting:

```
public class Dog {

    private String name;

    private int age;

    private String gender;

    @JsonbTransient
    private String color;
}
```

How It Works

The JsonbConfig class makes it easy to create a custom runtime configuration for your JSON mapping and formatting. Annotations can be used to create a custom compile time configuration. Such customizations can include things like changing from the default property naming convention or specifying a particular property ordering. To create a new configuration, simply create a new JsonbConfig class and pass the configuration to the JsonbBuilder.create() method, as such:

```
JsonbConfig config = new JsonbConfig();
Jsonb jsonb = JsonbBuilder.create(config);
```

The JsonbConfig class can be used to specify the runtime configurations contained in Table 14-5. In the example for this recipe, the .withPropertyNamingStrategy() option was specified to configure a property naming strategy that is lowercase with underscores.

***Table 14-5.** JsonbConfig Options*

Option	Description
.withFormatting(boolean)	Creates custom configuration with formatting.
.withPropertyNaming Strategy(strategy)	Provides strategy for constructing property names. Accepts a strategy of type PropertyNamingStrategy (IDENTITY, LOWER_CASE_WITH_DASHES, LOWER_CASE_WITH_ UNDERSCORES, UPPER_CAMEL_CASE, UPPER_CAMEL_CASE_ WITH_SPACES, CASE_INSENSITIVE).
.withPropertyOrder Strategy(strategy)	Provides strategy for ordering properties. Accepts a strategy of type PropertyOrderStrategy (LEXICOGRAPHICAL, ANY, REVERSE).
.withNullValues(boolean)	Changes the default NULL handling. Global configuration.
.withDateFormat("format")	Changes the default date format. Global configuration.
.withBinaryDataStrategy (strategy)	Provides strategy for binary data encoding. Default is BYTE encoding. Accepts BinaryDataStrategy (BYTE, BASE_64, BASE_64_URL).

(continued)

Table 14-5. (*continued*)

Option	Description
`.withAdapters(Custom Adapter)`	Assigns a `CustomAdapter` to a `Jsonb` configuration. (See JSON-B documentation for more on adapters.)
`.withSerializers(Jsonb Serializer)`	Assigns a `JsonbSerializer` to a `Jsonb` configuration.
`.withDeserializers(Jsonb Deserializer)`	Assigns a `JsonbDeserializer` to a `Jsonb` configuration.
`.withStrictIJSON(boolean)`	Provides support for the I-JSON restricted profile of JSON.

As previously mentioned, configurations can also be made at compile time by specifying annotations on Java classes, fields, or getters and setters. The following table, Table 14-6, lists the annotations that can be placed on a Java class, field, or accessor method.

Table 14-6. *Annotation Configurations*

Annotation	Description
`@JsonbProperty ("name")`	Field and getter/setter level. Changes the name of a particular property. Placed on a getter: the new name will be serialized when writing to JSON. Placed on a setter: the new name will be expected when reading during deserialization. Placed on a field: the new name will be applied on both serialization and deserialization.
`@JsonbPropertyOrder (strategy)`	Class level. Customizes the order of serialized properties. Accepts a PropertyOrderStrategy (LEXICOGRAPHICAL, ANY, REVERSE).
`@JsonbTransient`	Field and getter/setter level. Indicates that an annotated field should be ignored by the JSON binding engine. Placed on a field: property is ignored during serialization and deserialization. Getter: property ignored during serialization. Setter: property ignored during deserialization.
`@JsonbNillable (boolean)`	Class and field level. Indicates if NULL values are to be serialized. Default is false.

(*continued*)

Table 14-6. (*continued*)

Annotation	Description
@JsonbCreator	Constructor level. Allows one to annotate a custom constructor with parameters or a static factory method used to create a class instance.
@JsonbDateFormat ("format")	Field level. Customizes date format for a specified property.
@JsonbNumberFormat ("format")	Field level. Customizes number format for a specified property.

14-8. Replacing a Specified Element in a JSON Document

Problem

You wish to replace values of a JSON document that match a given pattern.

Solution

Utilize the JSON-P patch capability to replace the values within the JSON document. In the following example, a string of text is taken in from a JSF form and used to create a JSON pointer to the matching last name in the JSON String. The JSON Replace functionality is then used to replace the matching JSON String value with the String value of "JsonMaster":

```
public void findEmployeeByLast() {
    setSearchResult(null);
    String text = "/" + this.lastSearchText;
    JsonObject json = Json.createObjectBuilder().build();
    JsonValue object = json.getJsonObject(fetchJson());
    if (lastSearchText != null && object != null) {
        JsonPointer pointer = Json.createPointer(text);
        System.out.println("text: " + text + pointer);
        System.out.println("json: " + object);
        JsonValue result = pointer.getValue(object.asJsonArray());
```

```
        // Replace a value
        JsonArray array = (JsonArray) pointer.replace(object.asJsonArray(),
                            Json.createValue("JsonMaster"));
        setSearchResult(array.toString());
    }

}
```

The following markup shows the JSF form that is used to send the search text and display the resulting output:

```
<h:form id="jsonPointerForm">
    <p:panel header="Employee Search By Address">
        <p:outputLabel for="lastSearchText" value="Pointer String:"/>
        <p:inputText id="lastSearchText" value="#{employeeJsonController.
        lastSearchText}"/>
        <br/><br/>
        <p:commandButton id="searchButton"
                         action="#{employeeJsonController.
                         findEmployeeByLast}"
                         update="searchResult" value="Find Value"/>
    </p:panel>
    <br/>
    <h:outputText id="searchResult" value="#{customerController.
    searchResult}"/>
</h:form>
```

How It Works

The JSON-P 1.1 API added the ability to point to a specified JSON value and also to replace values of a JSON document. The JSON Pointer ability allows one to identify a specific value within a JSON document. To utilize the JSON Pointer functionality, one must first obtain a JsonObject by calling upon the appropriate Json interface method for working with the JSON that is to be used. In the solution to this recipe, the

Json.createObjectBuilder().build() methods are called upon to return a JsonObject.
The JsonObject can then be used to perform a JSON Patch operation. The fetchJson()
method in the example returns a JSON String:

```
JsonObject json = Json.createObjectBuilder().build();
JsonValue object = json.getJsonObject(fetchJson());
```

The JsonPointer object is obtained by calling upon the Json interface
createPointer() method, passing the String of text to find in the JSON. The following
excerpt from the solution shows the process of obtaining the JSON pointer:

```
JsonPointer pointer = Json.createPointer(text);
```

The JSON Patch functionality provides the ability to add, remove, or replace a
portion of a JSON document or String that has been obtained via a JSON pointer. In the
solution, the Replace functionality is used to replace the last name that is pointed to
with the string "JsonMaster". This is done by calling upon the JsonPointer replace()
method and passing the JSON object as the first argument and the Json that will replace
the original JSON as the second argument:

```
JsonArray array = (JsonArray) pointer.replace(object.asJsonArray(),
                                  Json.createValue(
                                  "JsonMaster"));
```

The JsonPointer object also contains the methods add() and replace(). The add()
method can be used to add a value into a JSON object or insert a value into an array. The
add() method accepts a JsonObject as the first argument and the Json value to add as
the second argument. The remove() method allows one to remove a JsonPointer value
from a JSON document.

CHAPTER 15

Security

One of the most important components to an enterprise-level application is security. It is a fact that enterprise applications must be rock solid and secure so that data and application functionality cannot fall into the wrong hands. Utilizing a combination of application container security and application-level security can help secure applications from thugs who are targeting enterprise data.

The release of Java EE 8 introduced the Security API, which for the first time provided the Java EE platform with a standard API that can be used for securing applications. In previous releases, security was certainly possible, but there was no standard API, so there were variations of homegrown authentication solutions and third-party APIs that were used throughout the applications that used the platform. In this chapter, I will touch upon techniques that may have been used in previous releases for securing applications, and I'll also outline similar solutions utilizing the standard security API that is part of the Jakarta EE platform.

Three different types of security can be applied to enterprise-level applications: declarative, programmatic, and transport security. *Declarative* security occurs within an application's deployment descriptor or via annotations that are added to classes and methods within the application. Declarative security is used to provide the application server container with the ability to guard access to certain application features via the use of user authentication and roles. *Programmatic* security occurs when the developer manually codes the authentication methods, customizing the requirements for authentication into an application. *Transport* security occurs between the client and the server, and it is responsible for securing information as it is passed between the two.

This chapter will touch upon each of these three levels of security. It contains recipes that cover application server configurations utilizing the GlassFish and Payara server for setting up database and LDAP (Lightweight Directory Access Protocol) authentication for applications that are deployed within the container. You will also learn how to utilize XML configuration, annotations, and Jakarta Expression Language to secure portions of your applications. Lastly, it'll touch upon how to secure transport via SSL

© Josh Juneau 2020
J. Juneau, *Jakarta EE Recipes*, https://doi.org/10.1007/978-1-4842-5587-2_15

and certificates. Since the GlassFish and Payara administrations are very similar, assume that when GlassFish is referenced in this chapter, the same holds true for Payara, unless otherwise noted. However, Payara server does include a number of important security benefits over and above what is provided by GlassFish, not to mention the normalized security patch release schedule. This chapter will also touch upon the Jakarta EE Security API, which provides a standardized solution that enables developers to produce portable applications and package security implementations within the application, rather than in the container.

15-1. Setting Up Application Users and Groups in GlassFish

Problem

You want to create users, groups, and roles within your application server container for use with applications that are deployed to the container.

Solution

Log into the GlassFish or Payara administrative console to add users to the File security realm. You can then add the users to groups by specifying the group names when creating the users. This example will walk you through the configuration of a new user within the GlassFish application server.

Log into the administrative console by navigating to `http://localhost:4848` and then logging in as an administrative user.

Use the tree menu on the left side of the screen to navigate to the Configurations ➤ server-config ➤ Security ➤ Realms menu. Once you click the Realms menu option, the Realms form will appear (Figure 15-1).

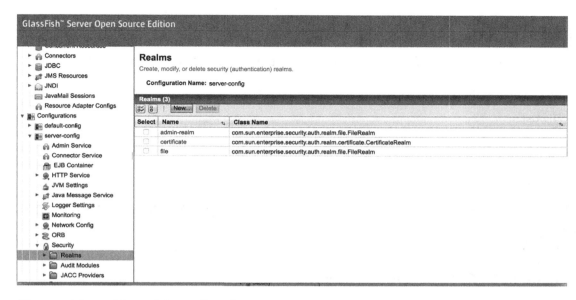

Figure 15-1. *GlassFish Realms form*

1.   Click the "file" realm link to enter the Edit Realm form, as shown
     in Figure 15-2.

Edit Realm

Edit an existing security (authentication) realm.

Manage Users

Configuration Name: server-config

Realm Name: file

Class Name: com.sun.enterprise.security.auth.realm.file.FileRealm

Properties specific to this Class

JAAS Context: *   `fileRealm`
Identifier for the login module to use for this realm

Key File: *   `${com.sun.aas.instanceRoot}/config/keyfile`
Full path and name of the file where the server will store all user, group, and password information for this realm

Assign Groups:
Comma-separated list of group names

Additional Properties (0)

Add Property   Delete Properties

Name	Value	Description:
No items found.		

Figure 15-2. *GlassFish Edit Realm form*

2. Click the Manage Users button within the Edit Realm form to open the File Users form, and then click the New button within the File Users form (Figure 15-3) to enter the New File Realm User form (Figure 15-4).

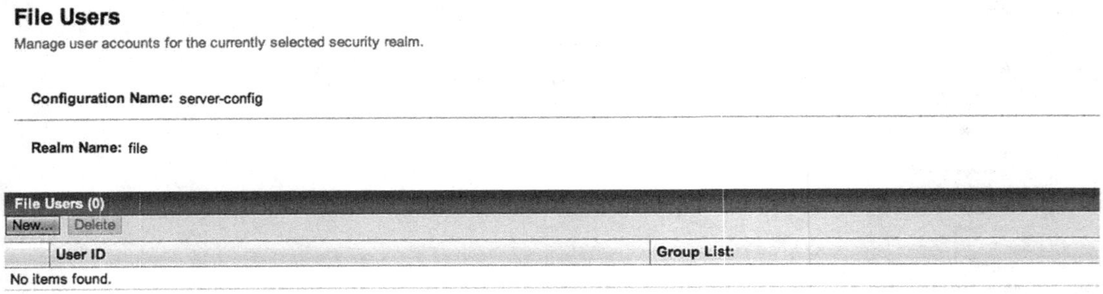

File Users

Manage user accounts for the currently selected security realm.

Configuration Name: server-config
_____

Realm Name: file

File Users (0)		
New... Delete		
User ID		Group List:
No items found.		

Figure 15-3. *GlassFish File Users form*

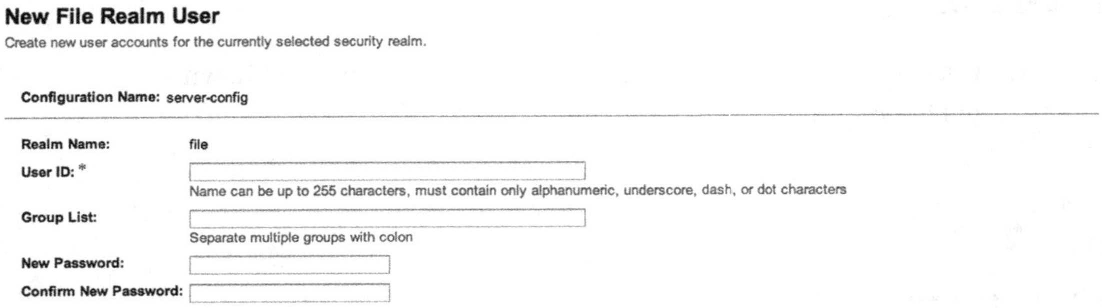

New File Realm User

Create new user accounts for the currently selected security realm.

Configuration Name: server-config
_____

Realm Name: file

User ID: *   [_____]

Name can be up to 255 characters, must contain only alphanumeric, underscore, dash, or dot characters

Group List: [_____]

Separate multiple groups with colon

New Password: [_____]

Confirm New Password: [_____]

Figure 15-4. *GlassFish New File Realm User form*

3. Fill in a user ID and the password information to complete the New File Realm User form, and optionally add a group name to the Group List field. Click the Save button to add the user to the File Users list (Figure 15-5).

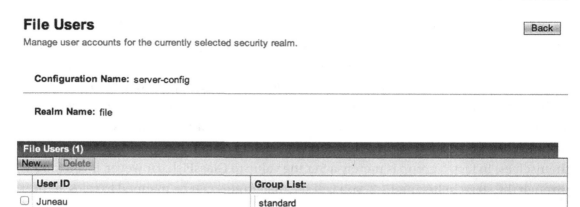

Figure 15-5. *File Users list*

Once they're created, users within GlassFish/Payara realms can be used for application authentication purposes. To learn more about configuring your applications to utilize application server container user authentication, please refer to Recipe 15-2.

How It Works

Adding an authentication prompt to allow user access to secured areas can be one of the best forms of protection for any application. Fortunately, the Java platform makes authentication easy for you to add to your applications, albeit there was no formal standard introduced until the release of Java EE 8. Most application servers have some mechanism for adding user accounts that can be used to access applications that are deployed in one of the server domains. GlassFish and Payara are no exception because they provide the ability to add users and groups to different security realms, which can then be applied to applications for authentication purposes.

Note   Most application server containers also allow for connectivity with LDAP servers or databases, which enables authentication to occur against user accounts within the LDAP server or stored within a database table, rather than within the container itself. For an example of LDAP authentication, please read the recipes later in this chapter.

When adding users to GlassFish, they must be incorporated with a security realm. The File security realm is available for use with the default installation, although more security realms can be created if desired. Adding users to realms is a fairly simple process, and individual users can be added by following the steps noted in the solution to this recipe. When creating a user, one of the options that can be specified is a *group*. You can think of a GlassFish user group as a role, in that more than one user can belong to a group. GlassFish does not contain a mechanism for managing the groups themselves; in fact, a group is merely a `String` value to GlassFish. However, if you follow through the steps in Recipe 15-2, you will see that groups can be mapped to roles at the application level. Therefore, if UserA belongs to a group named `standard`, then UserA can also belong to a group named `admin`. The application can then grant access to UserA for different portions of the application, depending upon which groups or roles the user belongs to.

Users in GlassFish are simplistic in that they are used for authentication and access purposes within the deployed applications only. Users can be managed only on a per-server installation basis, so they are a bit cumbersome since they cannot be shared across servers to provide a single sign-on solution. For that reason, it is recommended that GlassFish/Payara users be used for smaller applications/environments or testing purposes only. For a more substantial and enterprise authentication solution, either database or LDAP user accounts would be a better choice.

Note   To learn about configuring form-based authentication within the GlassFish or Payara application server and utilizing a database to store user credentials, see Recipe 15-6.

15-2. Performing Basic Web Application Authorization

Problem

You have established users and associated them with groups within the application server container. Now you want to assign users to particular roles based upon the access levels that they require for the application and apply a basic authentication mechanism for access to specified application views.

Solution #1

Configure form-based security using basic authentication within the web application deployment descriptor. Map roles to groups within the glassfish-web.xml deployment descriptor, if needed. The following excerpt was taken from the web.xml deployment descriptor of the JakartaEERecipes NetBeans project sources. It demonstrates how to secure all of the views that reside within the chapter15 folder (determined by the url-pattern element within web.xml) such that a username and password combination is required for access. The auth-method tag within web.xml specifies the type of authentication that will be used for the application. In the example, you'll use BASIC authentication. Only those usernames and passwords that have been configured in the GlassFish file realm with the appropriate group will be granted access; in this case, it is the users role:

```
<security-constraint>
      <web-resource-collection>
          <web-resource-name>secured</web-resource-name>
          <url-pattern>/faces/chapter15/*</url-pattern>
          <http-method>GET</http-method>
          <http-method>POST</http-method>
      </web-resource-collection>

      <auth-constraint>
          <role-name>users</role-name>
      </auth-constraint>

      <user-data-constraint>
          <transport-guarantee>CONFIDENTIAL</transport-guarantee>
      </user-data-constraint>
  </security-constraint>

  <login-config>
      <auth-method>BASIC</auth-method>
      <realm-name>file</realm-name>
  </login-config>

  <security-role>
      <role-name>users</role-name>
  </security-role>
```

If role names specified in the web.xml deployment descriptor are the same as the group names that have been associated with users in GlassFish, then you are done. Users will be granted access to those areas of the application that have been secured, based upon the group association. However, if a role name differs from those groups that have been associated to users, you can manually map role names to group names by specifying a security-role-mapping in the glassfish-web.xml file for the application. The following excerpt, taken from the glassfish-web.xml configuration file for the JakartaEERecipes application, demonstrates how to map roles to GlassFish users. In this case, the role standard that was specified for the account in Recipe 15-1 is mapped to the users role. The users role has access to the /faces/chapter15/* url-pattern:

```
<security-role-mapping>
  <role-name>users</role-name>
  <group-name>standard</group-name>
</security-role-mapping>
```

Once everything has been configured, then access will be granted according to the configurations that have been placed within the web.xml deployment descriptor. To test the authentication mechanism, deploy the JakartaEERecipes WAR file to your GlassFish/Payara application server, and visit the following URL:

```
http://localhost:8080/JakartaEERecipes/faces/chapter15/index.xhtml
```

Solution #2

Use annotations on classes and class methods to declare roles within an application for access to secured pages as deemed necessary. To implement access control on a particular class or method, annotate using @DeclareRoles and/or @RolesAllowed, specifying the roles that can be used to access them. Those users who are authenticated belonging to one of the specified roles will be granted access to the content.

In the example corresponding to this recipe, the chapter15/recipe15_02.xhtml JSF view contains two command buttons that invoke actions within a managed bean. Each of the buttons invokes a different action in the bean. One of the buttons invokes a method that is secured via the @RolesAllowed annotation, and the other does not. The following excerpt is taken from the class org.jakartaeerecipes.chapter15.recipe15_02.Recipe15_02b, which is the managed bean controller that contains the two methods being called from the command buttons:

```
public class Recipe15_02b implements Serializable {

    public String unsecuredProcess(){
        return "recipe15_02_1.xhtml";
    }

    @RolesAllowed("users")
    public String securedProcess(){
        return "recipe15_02_2.xhtml";
    }
}
```

When the `commandButton` that invokes the `securedProcess()` method is clicked, the user will be prompted to authenticate if they have not already done so.

How It Works

There are a couple of ways to secure an application using basic application server authentication. Commonly, applications provide basic authentication security via the use of XML configuration within the `web.xml` deployment descriptor along with optional configuration within the `glassfish-web.xml` deployment descriptor. It is also possible to add basic authentication security into an application using code only, via declarative security. Declarative security is based on the use of annotations for declaring roles for access to application classes and methods. While both of these techniques are very similar in concept, each of them has its own set of bonuses in certain situations.

In Solution #1 to this recipe, XML configuration is used to secure access to all web views that reside within a specific folder in the application. To add security via XML configuration files, the `web.xml` deployment descriptor needs to have the `security-constraint`, `login-config`, and `security-role` elements added to it for mapping application roles to GlassFish users and groups. The `security-constraint` element encompasses a handful of subelements that are used to tell the application server container which areas of the application to secure and which accounts are able to access those secured areas. First, a `web-resource-collection` element is used to declare the locations of the application to secure and which HTTP methods to secure. The following elements should be embedded within a `web-resource-collection` element:

- `web-resource-name`: This is an optional name that can be specified for the secured location. In the recipe solution, the name `secured` is specified.

- `url-pattern`: This is the URL pattern that will be used to determine which areas of the application are to be secured. An asterisk (*) is to be used as a wildcard. In the recipe solution, `chapter15/*` specifies that all views contained within the `chapter15` folder should be secured. If you want to secure a specific page, then utilize the URL pattern to that page, including the page name.

- `http-method`: This is used to specify which HTTP methods should be secured for access to the locations specified by the url-pattern element.

Another subelement that can be declared within the `security-constraint` element is the `auth-constraint` element. This element lists the different security roles that are used to secure the locations specified by the `url-pattern` via adding `role-name` subelements. In the recipe solution, the `users` role is declared for the application. A `user-data-constraint` element can also be included as a subelement to the `security-constraint` element in order to specify the type of protection that will be applied when data is transported between the client and the server. In the example, this has been set to `CONFIDENTIAL`. The values that can be specified for the transport guarantee are as follows:

- `NONE`: Data requires no transport security.

- `INTEGRAL`: Data cannot be changed in transit between the client and the server.

- `CONFIDENTIAL`: Outside entities are unable to observe the contents of the transmission. Secure Sockets Layer (SSL) will be used in this case, and it must be configured within the web server.

The `security-role` XML element lists the different roles that can be used for securing access to the application pages. Add the `role-name` subelement to the `security-role` for each role specification. The `login-config` XML element is used to specify the method of authentication that is to be used for securing the application. The auth-method should be set to BASIC for most cases, but all possible values are BASIC, DIGEST, FORM, and CLIENT-CERT.

Adding the designated elements to the web.xml deployment descriptor, as described in this section, provides sufficient ability for applications to be secured via user credentials to specified secure locations. In some cases, it makes sense to use annotations to declare roles from within the application code itself. For such cases, the @DeclareRoles and @RolesAllowed annotations can be specified on a class or method. The following annotations can be used to specify security within a class. For each of the annotations, either a single role or a list of roles can be specified.

- @DeclareRoles: This is specified at the class or method level, and each role that is allowed to access the class should be indicated within the annotation. For instance, one or more roles can be specified for access to the class using the following syntax:

  Class level:

  ```
  @DeclareRoles("users")
  public class MyClass {
    ...
  }
  ```

  Method level:

  ```
  public class MyClass {
    ...
      @DeclareRoles({"role1", "role2"})
      public void calculatePay(){
        ...
      }
    ...
  }
  ```

- @RolesAllowed: This is specified at either the class or method level. A list of roles that are allowed to access the class or method should be indicated within the annotation. The syntax is the same as with that of @DeclareRoles.

- @PermitAll: This is specified at the class or method level. It indicates that all roles are allowed access.

- @DenyAll: This is specified at the class or method level. It indicates that no roles are allowed access.

When both the @DeclareRoles and @RolesAllowed annotations are used within the same class, the roles listed within each are allowed to access that class. The roles specified for access on a particular method using @RolesAllowed override the roles that are listed to access the entire class.

It is possible to programmatically check to see which roles an authenticated user belongs to by calling the SessionContext isUserInRole() method. This allows you to permit access to particular features of an application using conditional logic, as demonstrated by the following lines of code:

```
@DeclareRoles({"role1", "role2, "role3"}
public class MyClass {

    ...
    @RolesAllowed("role2")
    public void calculatePay(){
        ...
    }

    @PermitAll
    public void calculatePay(){
        if (ctx.isUserInRole("role1")) {
            ...
        } else if (ctx.isUserInRole("role3")){
            ...
        }
    }
    ...
}
```

15-3. Developing a Programmatic Login Form with Custom Authentication Validation

Problem

You want to secure your JSF application to a specified group of users. Furthermore, you want to create a custom login view, which will be used to pass user credentials to the appropriate business objects for authentication.

Solution

Develop a login form that consists of username and password inputText fields, along with a commandButton to invoke a programmatic login action that resides within a managed bean controller. Develop logic within the managed bean controller to authenticate users. In the following example, a login form is generated using JSF and Facelets, utilizing a managed bean for authentication control.

Creating the Login Form

A login form is basically the same as any other form, except it accepts a username and a password as arguments and passes them to a JavaBean that utilizes the information to accept or deny the authentication request. The login form also utilizes a standard HTML form element that passes the username (j_username) and password (j_password) field values to an action named j_security_check. The following code is used to comprise the login.xhtml form for a JSF authentication mechanism:

```
<?xml version="1.0" encoding="UTF-8" ?>
<!DOCTYPE html PUBLIC "-//W3C//DTD XHTML 1.0 Transitional//EN" "http://www.
w3.org/TR/xhtml1/DTD/xhtml1-transitional.dtd">
<html xmlns="http://www.w3.org/1999/xhtml"
      xmlns:ui="http://xmlns.jcp.org/jsf/facelets"
      xmlns:h="http://xmlns.jcp.org/jsf/html"
      xmlns:f="http://xmlns.jcp.org/jsf/core"
      xmlns:p="http://primefaces.org/ui">

    <ui:composition template="/layout/custom_template.xhtml">
        <ui:define name="title">
```

```
        <h:outputText value="Welcome to the Acme Bookstore"></
        h:outputText>
    </ui:define>
    <ui:define name="content">

            <h:form id="login">
                <center>
                    <p align="center" class="sub_head_sub"><br />
                        <strong>Acme Bookstore Application</strong>
                    </p>
                    <span class="normal">
                        You must authenticate to gain access to
                        this application.
                    </span>
                    <br/>
                    <span class="error">
                        <h:messages errorStyle="color:
                        red" infoStyle="color: green"
                        globalOnly="true"/>
                    </span>
                    <div>
                        <p:panel rendered="#{authenticationControll
                        er.authenticated}">

                            <a href="/index.xhtml">Authenticated
                            successfully...go to Application</a>
                        </p:panel>

                        <p:panel rendered="#{!authenticationControl
                        ler.authenticated}">
                            Username: <h:inputText id="j_username"

                                            value="#{authent
                                            icationControll
                                            er.username}"/>

                            <br/><br/>
                            Password: <h:inputSecret id="j_password"
```

```
                                       value="#{authent
                                       icationControll
                                       er.password}"/>
                        <br/>
                        <br/>
                        <h:commandButton id="login" action="#{a
                        uthenticationController.login}"
                                             value="Login"/>
                    </p:panel>

                    <br/>
                </div>

            </center>
        </h:form>

    </ui:define>

  </ui:composition>

</html>
```

Note   The inputSecret component used in this example will display a series of asterisks, rather than plain text, when input is typed into the text box.

Once loaded, the login form will resemble Figure 15-6 when using the Acme Bookstore template.

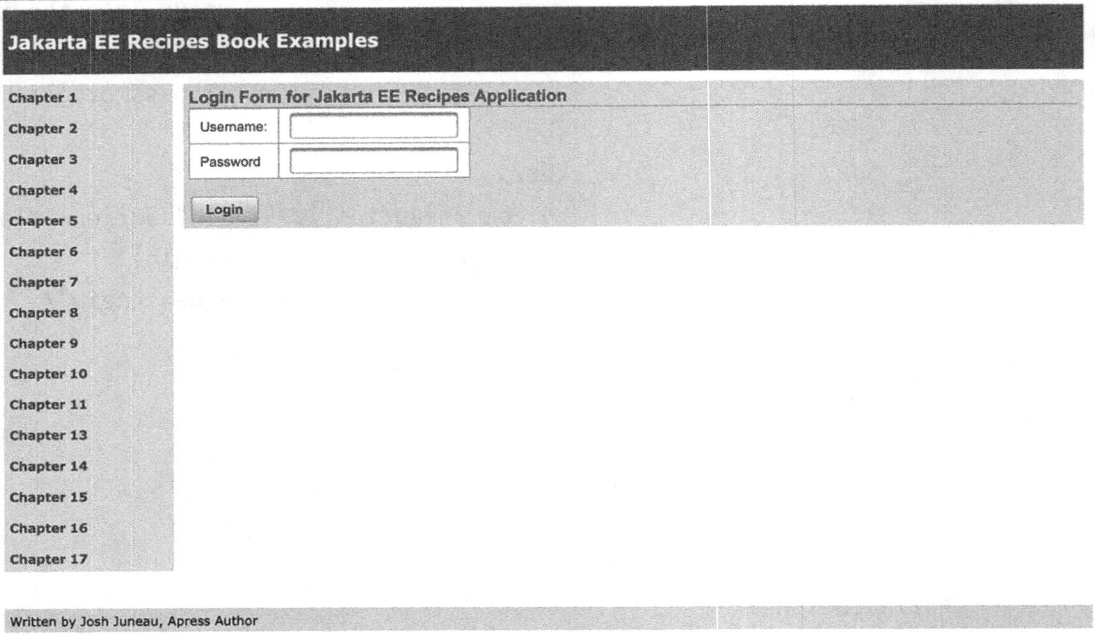

Figure 15-6. *Login form example*

Coding the Authentication Backend

The authentication backend is responsible for performing the authentication and maintaining state for a user session. The backend logic consists of an EJB for maintaining the authentication logic and a JSF controller that is used for binding view methods and fields to backend logic. The controller should be session scoped so that the user state can be maintained for an entire session. Lastly, if you're using a database table to contain all of the usernames that have access to the application, then an entity class will be required for that database table.

In this section, I will introduce a custom technique as a non-standard solution, which utilizes an EJB to authenticate an individual's credentials. The authentication occurs calling upon the `HttpServletRequest` `login()`, passing authentication off to the application server container. This is container-specific, meaning that it will only work if the application has been configured, as has been done with the first recipe in this chapter.

The second approach makes use of Jakarta Security, which was introduced in Java EE 8 as the Java EE Security API, using servlet-based authentication within an HttpAuthenticationMechanism (HAM). To see more specifics regarding Jakarta Security, please see Recipe 15-4.

EJB: (Custom Solution)

The Enterprise JavaBean that is used for this custom authentication backend is a stateless session bean that contains a login method, which makes calls to the application server container authentication mechanism. The following code is from the class org.jakartaeerecipes.chapter15.recipe15_03.AutheticationBean.java file in the JakartaEERecipes project:

```
package org.jakartaeerecipes.chapter15.recipe15_03;

import java.io.Serializable;
import javax.ejb.Remove;
import javax.ejb.Stateless;
import javax.faces.application.FacesMessage;

import javax.persistence.CacheRetrieveMode;

import javax.faces.context.FacesContext;
import javax.persistence.EntityManager;
import javax.persistence.NoResultException;
import javax.persistence.PersistenceContext;
import javax.persistence.Query;
import javax.servlet.ServletException;
import javax.servlet.http.HttpServletRequest;
import javax.servlet.http.HttpSession;

@Stateless
public class AuthenticationBean implements Serializable  {

    @PersistenceContext(unitName = "JakartaEERecipesPU")
    private EntityManager em;
    private boolean authenticated = false;
    private String username = null;
    private String password = null;
```

```
    HttpSession session = null;
    User user;

    public AuthenticationBean() {
    }

    public void findUser() {
        try {
            em.flush();

            getUser();
            Query userQry = em.createQuery(
                    "select object(u) from User u "
                    + "where u.username = :username").setParameter
                    ("username", getUser().getUsername().toUpperCase());

        // Enable forced database query
            userQry.setHint("javax.persistence.cache.retrieveMode",
            CacheRetrieveMode.BYPASS);
            setUser((User) userQry.getSingleResult());

            FacesContext.getCurrentInstance().addMessage(null, new
            FacesMessage(FacesMessage.SEVERITY_INFO, "Successfully
            Authenticated", ""));
        } catch (Exception e) {

            FacesContext.getCurrentInstance().addMessage(null, new
            FacesMessage(FacesMessage.SEVERITY_ERROR, "Invalid username/
            password", ""));
            setUser(null);

        }

    }

    public HttpSession getSession() {
        FacesContext context = FacesContext.getCurrentInstance();
        HttpServletRequest request = (HttpServletRequest) context.
                                    getExternalContext().getRequest();
        session = request.getSession(false);
```

```
        return session;
}

public boolean login() {

    HttpSession session = getSession();
    HttpServletRequest request = null;
    Query userQry = null;
    System.out.println("In the login method..." + getUser().
    getUsername());
    try {
        FacesContext context = FacesContext.getCurrentInstance();
        request = (HttpServletRequest) context.getExternalContext().
                getRequest();
        request.login(getUser().getUsername(), this.password);

        session.setMaxInactiveInterval(1800);
        session.setAttribute("authenticated", new Boolean(true));

        em.flush();

        userQry = em.createQuery(
                "select count(u) from User u "
                + "where u.username = :username").
                setParameter("username", getUser().getUsername().
                toUpperCase());
        userQry.setHint("javax.persistence.cache.retrieveMode",
        CacheRetrieveMode.BYPASS);
        Long count = (Long)userQry.getSingleResult();
        if (count > 0){

            userQry = em.createQuery(
                    "select object(u) from User u "
                    + "where u.username = :username").
                    setParameter("username", getUser().getUsername().
                    toUpperCase());

            // Enable forced database query
```

```
                userQry.setHint("javax.persistence.cache.retrieveMode",
                CacheRetrieveMode.BYPASS);
                setUser((User) userQry.getSingleResult());
                System.out.println("Setting  User, user exists in database
                with role ->" + user.getSecurityRole());
                setAuthenticated(true);
            } else {
                // User cannot authenticate successfully...do something
            }


        FacesContext.getCurrentInstance().addMessage(null, new
        FacesMessage(FacesMessage.SEVERITY_INFO, "Successfully
        Authenticated", ""));

        return authenticated;
    } catch (NoResultException| ServletException ex) {
        setUser(null);
        setAuthenticated(false);
        session = getSession();
        session.setAttribute("authenticated", new Boolean(false));
        if(request != null){
            try {
                request.logout();
            } catch (ServletException ex1) {
                System.out.println("AuthBean#login Error: " + ex);
            }
        }
        FacesContext.getCurrentInstance().addMessage(null, new
        FacesMessage(FacesMessage.SEVERITY_ERROR, "Invalid username/
        password", ""));
        return false;

    } finally {
        setPassword(null);
    }
}
```

```java
/**
 * @return the isAuthenticated
 */
public boolean isAuthenticated() {

    if (getSession().getAttribute("authenticated") != null) {
        boolean auth = (Boolean) getSession().getAttribute("authenticated");
        if (auth) {
            authenticated = true;
        }
    } else {
        authenticated = false;
    }
    return authenticated;
}

/**
 * @param isAuthenticated the isAuthenticated to set
 */
public void setAuthenticated(boolean isAuthenticated) {
    this.authenticated = isAuthenticated;
}

@Remove
public void remove() {
    System.out.println("Being removed from session...");
    setUser(null);
}

/**
 * @return the username
 */
public String getUsername() {
    try {
        System.out.println("The current username is: " + user.getUsername());
        username = getUser().getUsername();
    } catch (NullPointerException ex) {
    }
```

```java
        return username;
    }

    /**
     * @param username the username to set
     */
    public void setUsername(String username) {
        getUser().setUsername(username);
        System.out.println("Just set the username to : " + getUser().
        getUsername());
        this.username = null;
    }

    /**
     * @return the password
     */
    public String getPassword() {
        return this.password;
    }

    /**
     * @param password the password to set
     */
    public void setPassword(String password) {
        this.password = password;
    }

    /**
     * @return the user
     */
    public User getUser(){
        if (this.user == null) {
            user = new User();
        }
        return user;
    }

    /**
```

```
    * @param user the user to set
    */
   public void setUser(User user) {
       this.user = user;
   }
}
```

JSF Controller

The controller is responsible for coordinating authentication efforts between the JSF view and the EJB. It also has a session scope so that the user's state can be maintained throughout the life of the application session. The following code is taken from the org. jakartaeerecipes.chapter15.recipe15_03.AuthenticationController.java file that is contained within the JakartaEERecipes project:

```
import javax.servlet.http.HttpSession;

@Named("authenticationController")
@SessionScoped
public class AuthenticationController implements Serializable {

    @EJB
    private AuthenticationBean authenticationFacade;
    private String username;
    private User user;
    private boolean authenticated = false;
    private HttpSession session = null;
    private String userAgent;

    /**
     * Creates a new instance of AuthenticationController
     */
    public AuthenticationController() {

    }

    public HttpSession getSession() {
        // if(session == null){
        FacesContext context = FacesContext.getCurrentInstance();
```

```java
        HttpServletRequest request = (HttpServletRequest) context.
        getExternalContext().getRequest();
        session = request.getSession();

        return session;
    }

    /**
     * @return the username
     */
    public String getUsername() {
        this.username = getUser().getUsername();
        return this.username;
    }

    /**
     * @param username the username to set
     */
    public void setUsername(String username) {
        this.username = username;
        getUser().setUsername(username);
    }

    /**
     * @return the password
     */
    public String getPassword() {
        return authenticationFacade.getPassword();
    }

    /**
     * @param password the password to set
     */
    public void setPassword(String password) {
        authenticationFacade.setPassword(password);
    }

    public User getUser() {
```

```
        if (this.user == null) {
            user = new User();
            setUser(authenticationFacade.getUser());
        }

        return user;
    }

    public void setUser(User user) {
        this.user = user;
    }

    public String login() {
        authenticationFacade.setUser(getUser());
        boolean authResult = authenticationFacade.login();

        if (authResult) {
            this.authenticated = true;

            setUser(authenticationFacade.getUser());

            return "SUCCESS_LOGIN";
        } else {
            this.authenticated = false;
            setUser(null);
            return "BAD_LOGIN";
        }

    }

    public String logout() {
        user = null;
        this.authenticated = false;
        FacesContext facesContext = FacesContext.getCurrentInstance();
        ExternalContext externalContext = facesContext.
        getExternalContext();
        externalContext.invalidateSession();
        return "SUCCESS_LOGOUT";
    }
```

```
/**
 * @return the authenticated
 */
public boolean isAuthenticated() {
    try {
        boolean auth = (Boolean) getSession().getAttribute("authenticated");
        if (auth) {
            this.authenticated = true;

        } else {
            authenticated = false;
        }
    } catch (Exception e) {
        this.authenticated = false;
    }

    return authenticated;
}

public void setAuthenticated(boolean authenticated) {
    this.authenticated = authenticated;
}
}
```

User Entity

For any application, it is a good idea to maintain a list of users who have the ability to access the application pages. Furthermore, if an application requires fine-grained access control, it is important to assign roles to each user to indicate which privilege level each user should have for the application. A database table can be used for this purpose, and the table should contain a field for the username of each person who has access to the application, as well as a field for the user role. The following SQL is used for creating the USER database table in an Oracle database, although similar SQL could be used to create a table in a different RDMS:

```
create table users(
id number,
username varchar(150) not null,
```

```
password varchar(50) not null,
primary key (id));
```

The following class listing is that for the org.jakartaeerecipes.chapter15.
recipe15_03.User.java file, which is an entity class within the JakartaEERecipes project:

```java
import java.io.Serializable;
import java.math.BigDecimal;
import javax.persistence.Column;
import javax.persistence.Entity;
import javax.persistence.Id;
import javax.persistence.Table;

/**
 * Entity class User
 */
@Entity

@Table(name = "USER")

public class User implements Serializable {

    @Id
    @Column(name = "USER_ID", nullable = false)
    private BigDecimal userId;

    @Column(name = "USERNAME")
    private String username;

    @Column(name = "SECURITY_ROLE")
    private String securityRole;

    /** Creates a new instance of User */
    public User() {
    }

    /**
     * Creates a new instance of User with the specified values.
     * @param userId the userId of the User
     */
```

```java
    public User(BigDecimal userId) {
        this.userId = userId;
    }

    /**
     * Gets the userId of this User.
     * @return the userId
     */
    public BigDecimal getUserId() {
        return this.userId;
    }

    /**
     * Sets the userId of this User to the specified value.
     * @param userId the new userId
     */
    public void setUserId(BigDecimal userId) {
        this.userId = userId;
    }

    /**
     * Gets the username of this User.
     * @return the username
     */
    public String getUsername() {
        return this.username;
    }

    /**
     * Sets the username of this User to the specified value.
     * @param username the new username
     */
    public void setUsername(String username) {
        this.username = username;
    }

    /**
     * Gets the securityRole of this User.
```

```
 * @return the securityRole
 */
public String getSecurityRole() {
    return this.securityRole;
}

/**
 * Sets the securityRole of this User to the specified value.
 * @param securityRole the new securityRole
 */
public void setSecurityRole(String securityRole) {
    this.securityRole = securityRole;
}

/**
 * Returns a hash code value for the object.  This implementation computes
 * a hash code value based on the id fields in this object.
 * @return a hash code value for this object.
 */
@Override
public int hashCode() {
    int hash = 0;
    hash += (this.userId != null ? this.userId.hashCode() : 0);
    return hash;
}

/**
 * Determines whether another object is equal to this User.  The result is
 * <code>true</code> if and only if the argument is not null and is a
   User object that
 * has the same id field values as this object.
 * @param object the reference object with which to compare
 * @return <code>true</code> if this object is the same as the argument;
 * <code>false</code> otherwise.
 */
@Override
public boolean equals(Object object) {
```

```
        return false;
    }
    User other = (User)object;
    if (this.userId != other.userId && (this.userId == null ||
    !this.userId.equals(other.userId))) return false;
    return true;
    }
}
```

How It Works

The HTTP request login method can be used to programmatically authenticate users for an application when the application server form-based authentication has been configured. A JSF form can pass parameters to a managed bean controller, which can pass them to the HTTP request login method to perform programmatic authentication using the credentials.

As demonstrated in the login form that is listed in the solution to this recipe, a standard JSF view can be coded that passes values from the inputText components to a corresponding managed bean controller. The corresponding fields, username and password, are bound to properties within the managed bean controller. The username is then set into the username property of a new User entity object, and the password value is passed directly into the EJB for later use. The password is not stored in the managed bean controller at all, and therefore, it is not stored into the session.

Let's take a moment to discuss the methods within the managed bean controller. In the example, a commandButton is contained within the view, which is bound to the managed bean controller's login method. Once invoked, the login method invokes a method within the EJB, which is responsible for performing the actual authentication against the application server container and JPA data store user table. In this case, the EJB method is also named login, and when it is invoked, then the User entity object is passed to the EJB so that the username property that is stored in the object can be used for authentication purposes. The login method within the managed bean controller invokes the EJB login method, which passes back a Boolean value to indicate whether the credentials have successfully authenticated the user. Depending upon the outcome, the user is then granted or denied access to the application. Also within the managed bean controller is a `logout` method. This method invalidates the current session by obtaining the external context, which is the application server context, and then by invoking its `invalidate()` method.

The `login` method within the EJB is where the real activity occurs because it is where the application server HTTP request `login` method is invoked to verify the credentials. First, the `HttpServletRequest` object is obtained from the external context, and then its login method is called. This method accepts the username and password values, initiates the application server authentication mechanism, and raises an exception if the credentials are invalid. Otherwise, if the credentials are valid, then a time limit is set on the `HttpSession` object. The value passed to the `session.setMaxInactiveInterval` method indicates how long a user session can be inactive before the application server automatically invalidates the session. The remainder of this method is used for performing application-specific authentication using the `User` entity object. In the example, the entity manager is flushed, and then a query is issued that counts the number of `User` entity objects matching the username that has been entered via the login form. When querying the entity, a hint is set that forces the database to be queried each time the request is initiated. The following line of code is an excerpt from the EJB login method that demonstrates how to set this hint:

```
user.setHint("javax.persistence.cache.retrieveMode", CacheRetrieveMode.
BYPASS);
```

If there are zero matching entity objects for a given username, then the user is not authenticated to the application, and a `false` value is returned to the managed bean controller to indicate invalid credentials. Otherwise, if there is a matching entity object for the given username, then the matching entity object is obtained, and a session attribute is set to indicate that the user was successfully authenticated.

Note   Applications can contain their own set of users, one that is separate from those users who are managed by the GlassFish application server or database. One way of doing so is to create a separate database table for each application, which will be used to store usernames and roles for those users who may access the application. The login logic that is contained within the managed bean controller can then perform a query on the application-specific table to see whether the username specified within the login view is contained within the table. If the username is in the table, then the user can be granted access to the application; otherwise, no access will be granted. This approach adds two steps into the authentication process: application server form-based authentication and authentication at the database table level.

15-4. Authentication with the Security API Using Database Credentials

Problem

You are interested in utilizing a standard solution for integrating form-based authentication into your application, using a database to store credentials.

Solution

Utilize Jakarta Security to authenticate a user using the same form authentication as demonstrated in Recipe 15-3. However, this solution will utilize credentials saved in a database, although one could also utilize LDAP authentication or another custom means via the Security API. Configuration for the database takes place via an annotation within the application, so no application server configuration is necessary.

To configure the application, annotate an @ApplicationScoped bean to indicate the authentication identity store that will be used for the application. In this case, the @DatabaseIdentityStoreDefinition annotation is used to configure the database as an identity store for the application:

```
import javax.enterprise.context.ApplicationScoped;
import javax.inject.Named;
```

```
import javax.security.enterprise.identitystore.
DatabaseIdentityStoreDefinition;
import javax.security.enterprise.identitystore.Pbkdf2PasswordHash;

@DatabaseIdentityStoreDefinition(
        dataSourceLookup = "${'jdbc/acmedb'}",
        callerQuery = "#{'select password from caller_store where name = ?'}",
        groupsQuery = "select group_name from caller_groups where caller_
                        name = ?",
        hashAlgorithm = Pbkdf2PasswordHash.class,
        priorityExpression = "#{100}",
        hashAlgorithmParameters = {
            "Pbkdf2PasswordHash.Iterations=3072",
            "${applicationConfig.hash}"
        } // just for test / example
)
@ApplicationScoped
@Named
public class ApplicationConfig {

    public String[] getHash() {
        return new String[]{"Pbkdf2PasswordHash.Algorithm=PBKDF2WithHmacS
        HA512", "Pbkdf2PasswordHash.SaltSizeBytes=64"};
    }
}
```

A singleton can be used to configure a database connection. This code will be run once each time the application is started up, and it will load the database configuration and populate the security database for testing purposes. In real life, this class would only be used to configure the data source, as the security database would likely be populated by an administrator. The following excerpt is from the sources of the singleton EJB:

```
import java.sql.Connection;
import java.sql.PreparedStatement;
import java.sql.SQLException;
import java.util.HashMap;
import java.util.Map;
```

```
import javax.annotation.PostConstruct;
import javax.annotation.PreDestroy;
import javax.annotation.Resource;
import javax.annotation.sql.DataSourceDefinition;
import javax.ejb.Singleton;
import javax.ejb.Startup;
import javax.inject.Inject;
import javax.sql.DataSource;
import javax.security.enterprise.identitystore.Pbkdf2PasswordHash;

@DataSourceDefinition(
    name = "java:global/JakartaEERecipes/acmedb",
    className = "org.apache.derby.jdbc.ClientDataSource",
    serverName="localhost",
    databaseName="acme",
    user = "acmeuser",
    password = "databasepassword"
)
@Singleton
@Startup
public class LoadDatabase {

    @Resource(lookup="java:global/JakartaEERecipes/acmedb")
    private DataSource dataSource;

    @Inject
    private Pbkdf2PasswordHash passwordHash;

    @PostConstruct
    public void init() {

        Map<String, String> parameters= new HashMap<>();
        parameters.put("Pbkdf2PasswordHash.Iterations", "3072");
        parameters.put("Pbkdf2PasswordHash.Algorithm",
        "PBKDF2WithHmacSHA512");
        parameters.put("Pbkdf2PasswordHash.SaltSizeBytes", "64");
        passwordHash.initialize(parameters);
```

```
    executeUpdate(dataSource, "CREATE TABLE caller_store(name
    VARCHAR(64) PRIMARY KEY, password VARCHAR(255))");
    executeUpdate(dataSource, "CREATE TABLE caller_groups(caller_name
    VARCHAR(64), group_name VARCHAR(64))");

    executeUpdate(dataSource, "INSERT INTO caller_store
    VALUES('juneau', '" + passwordHash.generate("eerecipes".
    toCharArray()) + "')");

    executeUpdate(dataSource, "INSERT INTO caller_groups
    VALUES('juneau', 'group1')");
    executeUpdate(dataSource, "INSERT INTO caller_groups
    VALUES('juneau', 'group2')");
}

@PreDestroy
public void destroy() {
  try {
        executeUpdate(dataSource, "DROP TABLE IF EXISTS caller_store");
        executeUpdate(dataSource, "DROP TABLE IF EXISTS caller_groups");
  } catch (Exception e) {
        // silently ignore, concerns in-memory database
  }
}

private void executeUpdate(DataSource dataSource, String query) {
    try (Connection connection = dataSource.getConnection()) {
        try (PreparedStatement statement = connection.
        prepareStatement(query)) {
            statement.executeUpdate();
        }
    } catch (SQLException e) {
      // do nothing
    }
  }
}
```

The same JSF login form from Recipe 15-3 can be used for the authentication UI in this case, with the exception of passing credentials and invoking `SecurityContext.authenticate()`. This is a different form-based scenario which utilizes the `@CustomFormAuthenticationMechanismDefinition` annotation. The following excerpt is taken from the JSF login form, containing a PrimeFaces `commandButton` component which binds to a CDI controller action to perform the validation:

```
<html xmlns="http://www.w3.org/1999/xhtml"
    xmlns:f="http://xmlns.jcp.org/jsf/core"
    xmlns:h="http://xmlns.jcp.org/jsf/html"
    xmlns:ui="http://xmlns.jcp.org/jsf/facelets"
    xmlns:p="http://primefaces.org/ui">
    <h:head>
        <meta http-equiv="Content-Type" content="text/html; charset=UTF-8"/>
        <title>Jakarta Recipes = Chapter 15 Examples</title>
    </h:head>
    <h:body>
        <ui:composition template="layout/custom_template_search.xhtml">
            <ui:define name="content">
                <h1>Login Form for Jakarta EE Recipes Application</h1>
                <h:form id="loginForm">
                    <p:messages id="messages"/>
                    <p:panelGrid columns="2">
                        <p:outputLabel for="username" value="Username: "/>
                        <p:inputText id="username" value="#{standardizedAut
                        henticationController.username}"/>

                        <p:outputLabel for="password" value="Password "/>
                        <p:password id="password" value="#{standardizedAuth
                        enticationController.password}"/>

                    </p:panelGrid>
                    <br/>
                    <p:commandButton id="loginAction" action="#{standardize
                    dAuthenticationController.login}"
                                    value="Login"
                                    update="messages"/>
```

```
          </h:form>
        </ui:define>
      </ui:composition>
    </h:body>
</html>
```

Lastly, the code for the authentication CDI controller bean is as follows. The @RequestScoped controller contains properties for passing the username and password, along with the logic for authenticating the credentials that have been supplied by the user:

```java
import javax.enterprise.context.RequestScoped;
import javax.faces.application.FacesMessage;
import javax.faces.context.FacesContext;
import javax.inject.Inject;
import javax.inject.Named;
import javax.security.enterprise.credential.Credential;
import javax.security.enterprise.credential.Password;
import javax.security.enterprise.credential.UsernamePasswordCredential;
import javax.security.enterprise.identitystore.CredentialValidationResult;
import javax.security.enterprise.identitystore.IdentityStoreHandler;
import javax.servlet.http.HttpServletRequest;
import javax.servlet.http.HttpServletResponse;
import javax.validation.constraints.NotNull;

/**
 *
 * @author Juneau
 */
@Named
@RequestScoped
public class StandardizedAuthenticationController {

    @Inject
    private IdentityStoreHandler identityStoreHandler;

    @NotNull
    private String username;
```

```java
@NotNull
private String password;

public void login() {

    FacesContext context = FacesContext.getCurrentInstance();
    Credential credential = new UsernamePasswordCredential(username,
    new Password(password));

    CredentialValidationResult cres = identityStoreHandler.
    validate(credential);
    if (cres.getStatus().equals(CredentialValidationResult.Status.VALID)) {
        context.responseComplete();
        context.addMessage(null, new FacesMessage(FacesMessage.
        SEVERITY_INFO, "Authentication Successful", null));
    } else if (cres.getStatus().equals(CredentialValidationResult.
    Status.INVALID)) {
        context.addMessage(null,
                new FacesMessage(FacesMessage.SEVERITY_ERROR,
                "Authentication Failure", null));
    }

}

private static HttpServletResponse getResponse(FacesContext context) {
    return (HttpServletResponse) context
        .getExternalContext()
        .getResponse();
}

private static HttpServletRequest getRequest(FacesContext context) {
    return (HttpServletRequest) context
        .getExternalContext()
        .getRequest();
}

/**
 * @return the username
 */
```

```
    public String getUsername() {
        return username;
    }

    /**
     * @param username the username to set
     */
    public void setUsername(String username) {
        this.username = username;
    }

    /**
     * @return the password
     */
    public String getPassword() {
        return password;
    }

    /**
     * @param password the password to set
     */
    public void setPassword(String password) {
        this.password = password;
    }
}
```

How It Works

Jakarta Security defines a set of annotations that can be used to configure an application identity store and HttpAuthenticationMechanism for an application, among other security configurations. These standardized annotations are available as part of Jakarta Security across all Jakarta EE 8–compliant containers, allowing security configuration to be packaged as part of an application without additional XML configuration requirements. This makes it possible to create portable applications that contain security in which the same security configuration can be used across a number of containers.

An identity store typically holds a list of callers and caller groups, as well as security credentials for authenticating the caller. The API defines the following set of standard identity store annotations, which supply an abstraction of an identity store:

- @LdapIdentityStoreDefinition: Supports caller that is stored in an external LDAP server.

- @DatabaseIdentityStoreDefinition: Supports caller that is stored in an external database, which is accessible via a JNDI-bound DataSource.

The identity store annotations must be defined within a CDI bean that is marked as @ApplicationScoped, so that they are configured one time per application startup. An identity store is stateless, and it should include the information required to authenticate a caller into an application. The caller should not interact directly with an identity store. Instead, an HttpAuthenticationMechanism, which will be explained in the following, should perform the interaction. An identity store contains two methods that can be implemented by an authentication mechanism in order to validate a caller's credentials and return a caller's security groups. Those methods are validate() and getCallerGroups(), respectively. An identity store can implement one or both of these methods, and calling upon the identity store's validationTypes() method returns a set of values that indicate which methods are implemented via the following values: VALIDATE, PROVIDE_GROUPS.

The validate() method takes a Credential object, which is a portable object that contains a username/password that has been supplied by a caller. The validate() method returns a CredentialValidationResult, indicating the validation status. The CredentialValidationResult can be used to obtain information such as the resulting validation status, and if successful then it also contains the identity store ID, caller principal, caller's unique ID within the identity store, and the caller's groups. The getStatus() method of CredentialValidationResult will return one of the following status values:

- VALID: Validation succeeded and caller groups can be obtained, if any are available.

- INVALID: Validation failed.

- NOT_VALIDATED: Validation was not attempted due to invalid credential type.

More than one identity store can be configured for an application by setting a priority. Identity stores can also be programmed by implementing the `IdentityStore` interface, or they can be injected via the use of the identity store annotations outlined previously. These topics, as well as more in-depth analysis of the identity store concept, are covered in detail within the JSR 375 specification, available on javaee.github.io: `https://javaee.github.io/security-spec/`.

The `HttpAuthenticationMechanism` is used by the Security API to validate a user's credentials. There must be three `HttpAuthenticationMechanisms` supplied by a Jakarta EE 8–compliant application server container, which are the following:

- BASIC (`@BasicAuthenticationMechanismDefinition`): Authenticates according to the HTTP basic authentication semantics.

- FORM (`@FormAuthenticationMechanismDefinition`): Authenticates according to the form-based authentication semantics.

- CUSTOM FORM (`authenticate`): Authenticates according to the form-based authentication semantics; however, it does not occur via posting back to j_security_check. Instead, `SecurityContext.authenticate()` is invoked with passed-in credentials.

An `HttpAuthenticationMechanism` can be coded by implementing the `HttpAuthenticationMechanism` interface, or it can be injected using one of the aforementioned annotations. To implement, one must code the `validateRequest()` method, which is invoked before the `doFilter()` method of a servlet filter or `service()` method of any servlet. The `validateRequest()` method is also called upon in response to code calling the `HttpServletRequest authenticate()` method. There are two methods that are part of the `HttpAuthenticationMechanism` which are not required for implementation: `secureResponse()`, and `cleanSubject()`.

The `validateRequest()` method is used to allow the caller to authenticate. The `secureResponse()` method is provided to allow for post-processing on the response that is generated by a servlet or servlet filter. The `cleanSubject()` method is provided to allow for cleanup after the caller is logged out.

Since a compliant container must provide default implementations of the `HttpAuthenticationMechanism`, it is possible for an application to simply use the mechanism without coding or supplying an annotation. The example in this recipe does just that. When the caller inserts credentials into the login screen and presses the button, the `StandardizedAuthenticationController` `login()` method is called. This controller class contains an injected `IdentityStoreHandler`, which is used to hook into the `HttpAuthenticationMechanism` that is provided by the container. In the `login()` method, the caller's username and password are passed into a `UsernamePasswordCredential` object to return a `Credential`. The `Credential` is then passed into the `IdentityStoreHandler.validate()` method, returning a `CredentialValidationResult` object. This object can be used to glean the success or failure of the authentication attempt. The resulting success or failure can be tested by calling upon the `CredentialValidationResult.getStatus()` method.

The Jakarta Security API helps to bring standardization to an area of the platform that has been very non-standardized in the past. While many containers will likely still retain their proprietary security APIs and techniques, any Jakarta EE 8–compliant container must also adhere to the standards of Jakarta Security.

Note   There are dozens of examples that can be found on the Jakarta EE Security API (Soteria) GitHub project page at `https://github.com/eclipse-ee4j/soteria`. It is also a great idea to read through the specification, which is less than 50 pages, and it can be found at `https://javaee.github.io/security-spec/`.

15-5. Managing Page Access Within a JSF Application

Problem

You have set up authentication for your JSF application, specifying access to a limited user base via a username and password combination. You want to limit certain views within your application such that only members of a particular role will be granted permission access.

Solution

Authenticate a user to an application and store a Boolean indicating that the user has been successfully authenticated. Utilize that Boolean to perform conditional logic within JSF views to render forms that should be accessed only via authenticated users. If a user is successfully authenticated, then the form is rendered, and if the user is not successfully authenticated, then the form will provide an error message indicating that authentication is required for access.

The following JSF view demonstrates the use of conditional logic for displaying portions of the page that require controlled access:

```
<?xml version="1.0" encoding="UTF-8" ?>
<!DOCTYPE html PUBLIC "-//W3C//DTD XHTML 1.0 Transitional//EN" "http://www.
w3.org/TR/xhtml1/DTD/xhtml1-transitional.dtd">
<html xmlns="http://www.w3.org/1999/xhtml"
      xmlns:ui="http://xmlns.jcp.org/jsf/facelets"
      xmlns:h="http://xmlns.jcp.org/jsf/html"
      xmlns:f="http://xmlns.jcp.org/jsf/core"
      xmlns:p="http://primefaces.org/ui">

    <ui:composition template="/layout/fess_template.xhtml">
        <ui:define name="title">
            <h:outputText value="Jakarta EE 8 Recipes Controlled Access"></
            h:outputText>
        </ui:define>
        <ui:define name="body">
            <h:panelGroup id="messagePanel" layout="block">
                <h:messages errorStyle="color: red" infoStyle="color:
                green" layout="table"/>
            </h:panelGroup>
            <p:panel rendered="#{authenticationController.authenticated}">
                <h:form>

                    This portion of the view contains secret content!

                </h:form>
            </p:panel>
            <p:panel rendered="#{!authenticationController.authenticated}">
                Please <a href="#{request.contextPath}/faces/chapter15/
                recipe15_03.xhtml">authenticate</a> to use this form.

            </p:panel>
        </ui:define>
    </ui:composition>

</html>
```

How It Works

The rendered attribute of JSF components can be used to perform conditional rendering. If you bind the rendered attribute to a managed bean property that returns a Boolean indicating whether a user is authenticated, then this technique can be used to control access to certain components. In this example, this technique is demonstrated using a PrimeFaces panel component. The panel contains information that should be secured, and it is rendered only if the authenticated property returns a true value. If the authenticated property contains a false value, then a different panel component is rendered, which displays a message to the user indicating that authentication is required.

The controller that is used for programmatic authentication within a JSF application should contain a Boolean value that can be bound to the conditional logic within the JSF view to indicate whether the current user has successfully authenticated. For this example, the managed bean controller, org.jakartaeerecipes.chapter15.recipe15_03.AuthenticationController, contains a Boolean field named authenticated. The following excerpt from the class shows the isAuthenticated() method, which is called when the authenticated property is accessed from a JSF view:

```java
public boolean isAuthenticated() {
    try {
        boolean auth = (Boolean) getSession().
        getAttribute("authenticated");
        if (auth) {
            this.authenticated = true;

        } else {
            authenticated = false;
        }
    } catch (Exception e) {
        this.authenticated = false;
    }

    return authenticated;
}
```

This same technique can be used to hide or show individual components based upon a user's authentication. Furthermore, fine-grained access control can be used to provide Boolean values to the `rendered` attribute by utilizing JSF EL conditional expressions. For instance, if some components should be accessed only by users who belong in certain security roles, then a conditional expression can be used to render a component if the user belongs to a specified role. The following line of code demonstrates how to render an `outputText` component if a user belongs to the `ADMIN` security role:

```
<h:outputLink rendered="${authenticationController.user.securityRole eq
'ADMIN'}" value="#" onclick="dialog.show()">Delete Property</h:outputLink>
```

Although the `rendered` attribute may not allow you to secure every part of an application, when used along with other security measures such as annotating methods (Recipe 15-2), it can help provide a very secure environment.

15-6. Configuring LDAP Authentication Within GlassFish/Payara

Problem

You want to authenticate users to your application based upon a centrally located LDAP server for your organization's enterprise.

Solution

Create an LDAP security realm for GlassFish/Payara from within the administrative console utility, and set it up as a `com.sun.enterprise.security.auth.realm.ldap.LDAPRealm`. To create an LDAP security realm within GlassFish/Payara, use the following procedure:

- Log into the GlassFish/Payara administrative console.

- Traverse to the Realms form by expanding the left tree menu Configurations ➤ Security ➤ server-config ➤ Realms.

- Click the New... button within the Realms form to create a new security realm.

- Within the New Realm form, provide a name for the security realm. Next, select `com.sun.enterprise.security.auth.realm.ldap.LDAPRealm` from the Class Name pull-down menu. This will open the configurations for setting up an LDAP realm (Figure 15-7).

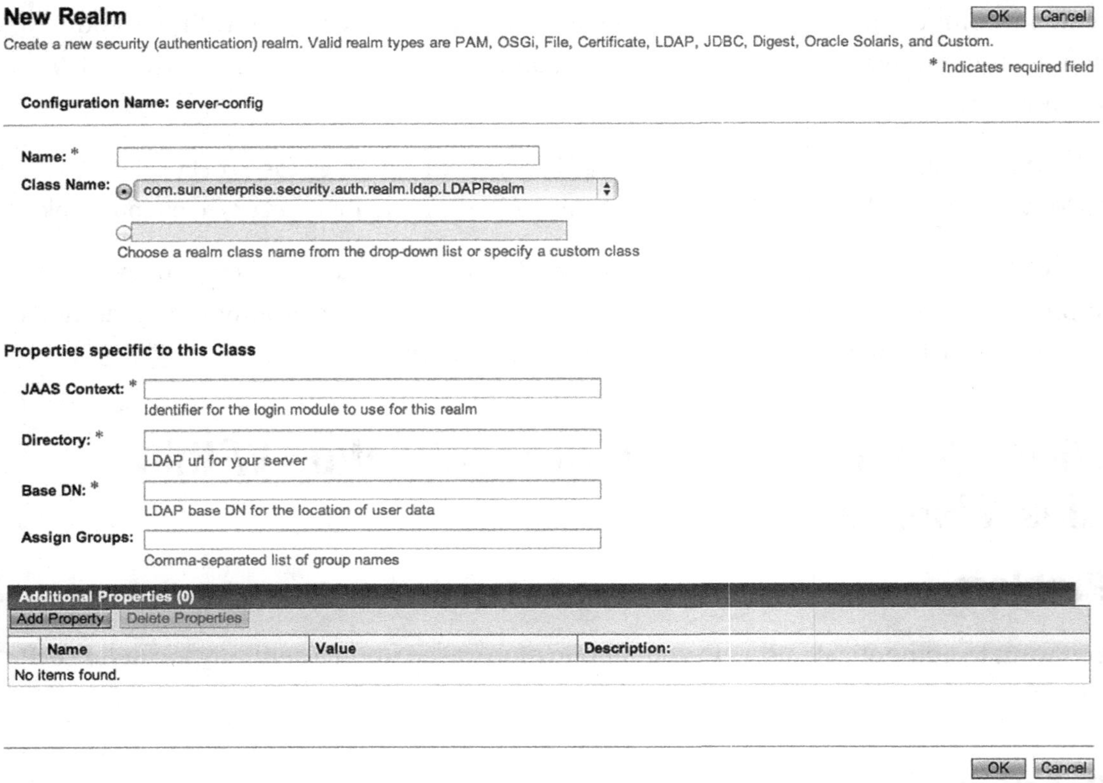

New Realm `OK` `Cancel`

Create a new security (authentication) realm. Valid realm types are PAM, OSGi, File, Certificate, LDAP, JDBC, Digest, Oracle Solaris, and Custom.

* Indicates required field

Configuration Name: server-config

___

Name: * [   ]

Class Name: ⊙ [com.sun.enterprise.security.auth.realm.ldap.LDAPRealm ▾]

○ [   ]

Choose a realm class name from the drop-down list or specify a custom class

Properties specific to this Class

JAAS Context: * [   ]
Identifier for the login module to use for this realm

Directory: * [   ]
LDAP url for your server

Base DN: * [   ]
LDAP base DN for the location of user data

Assign Groups: [   ]
Comma-separated list of group names

Additional Properties (0)
`Add Property` `Delete Properties`

Name	Value	Description:
No items found.		

`OK` `Cancel`

Figure 15-7. *New LDAP security realm*

Complete the properties specific to the class in order to connect to an LDAP server of your choice.

1. Add the following additional properties by clicking the **Add Property** button and providing the name-value information for each:

   - `search-bind-dn`: Enter the fully qualified DN for your LDAP host, the directory, and the LDAP account to which you will authenticate. For example:

```
CN=account-name,OU=AccountGroup,DC=dc1,DC=dc2,DC=dc3
```

- **search-bind-password**: Enter the password for the account name you specified previously.

- **search-filter**: Type the following as the value for this property: (sAMAccountName=%s).

2. Restart the application server.

How It Works

Perhaps one of the most efficient ways to authenticate to applications is to utilize an LDAP account. Using an LDAP account for authentication can provide a single sign-on solution across all of an organization's servers and applications. LDAP authentication also provides a single point of maintenance for account information and still allows individual applications to maintain their own fine-grained security via roles. The solution to this recipe enumerates the steps that are involved in setting up an LDAP security realm within the GlassFish and Payara application servers. However, you can follow similar procedures for setting up an LDAP security realm in other application server containers.

Once you have LDAP authentication set up within the application server, you can configure your applications to use it. To configure an application to use LDAP authentication, add the following configurations to the web.xml deployment descriptor:

```
<login-config>
      <auth-method>FORM</auth-method>
      <realm-name>REALM-NAME</realm-name>
      <form-login-config>
          <form-login-page>/faces/login.xhtml</form-login-page>
          <form-error-page>/faces/loginError.xhtml</form-error-page>
      </form-login-config>
  </login-config>
```

In the previous excerpt from web.xml, the realm-name element should be the same as the name given to the LDAP security realm you created within GlassFish/Payara. The form-login-page and form-error-page values should reference the views that are to be used for logging into an application and the view that is displayed when there is a login error, respectively. Authenticating into an LDAP security realm is the same as that covered in Recipe 15-3. Simply call the HttpRequest object's login method to authenticate using the credentials provided by the user via the login view.

15-7. Configuring Custom Security Certificates Within GlassFish/Payara

Problem

You want to utilize custom certificates for securing access via SSL within your GlassFish/ Payara environment.

Solution

Obtain a certificate from a certified certificate authority, and then install it into the GlassFish application server container. Once installed, route requests via a secured port that utilizes SSL and force users to accept the security certificate to proceed. To install a certificate that has been obtained from a valid certificate authority, follow these steps:

1. Copy the trusted root certificate from your certified authority to your server. Issue the following command from the command line or terminal:

    ```
    keytool -import -alias root -keystore keystore_name.keystore -
    trustcacerts -file trustedcarootcertificate.crt
    ```

2. Next, import the trusted certificate:

    ```
    keytool -import -alias cert_alias -keystore keystore_name.keystore
    -trustcacerts -file certificate.crt
    ```

3. Adjust SSL settings from within the GlassFish administrative console. To adjust the settings, go to Configuration ➤ Network Config- ➤ Network Listeners ➤ http-listener-2 in order to open the secured HTTP listener page. Once it's open, select the SSL tab, and enter the certificate nickname and keystore that match the ones you used in step 2.

4. Restart your server, and then access your applications securely
   using this URL:

   `https://localhost:8181/your_application_context.`

Note   In the previous numbered list, `keystore_name.keystore` represents
the name of a keystore, and `trustedcarootcertificate.crt` and
`certificate.crt` represent the names of certificates.

How It Works

GlassFish comes with a self-signed security certificate that is suitable for test
environments. However, when utilizing GlassFish as a production application server
solution, it is imperative that a certificate from a verified authority be put in place in
order to secure application transport. This recipe demonstrates how to install a security
certificate for use with SSL in order to achieve secure transport.

Before you can install a verified certificate, you need to obtain it. You will need to
choose from one of the many certificate authorities and then send a certificate request,
which includes the key from your application server. A keystore will need to be created in
order to generate a certificate request. Issue the following command from the command
line or terminal to create the keystore:

```
keytool -keysize 2048 -genkey -alias -keyalg RSA -dname "CN=yourdomain.
org,O=company_name,L=city,S=state,C=country" - keypass glassfish_master_
password -storepass glassfish_master_password -keystore choose_keystore_
name.keystore
```

Once the keystore has been created, a certificate signing request (CSR) that will be
sent to the certificate authority can be generated. To generate the certificate signing
request (CSR), issue the following command from your server:

```
keytool -certreq -alias -keystore chosen_keystore_name.keystore -storepass
glassfish_master_password -keypass glassfish_master_password -file csrname.csr
```

Note   To change the GlassFish master password, issue the following command when your GlassFish domain is stopped: `asadmin change-master-password -savemasterpassword=true`.

Once you submit your CSR to the certificate authority, the certificate authority will send back a valid security certificate that can be installed into your server. Follow the steps in the solution to this recipe to install the certificate into GlassFish. Once the certificate is installed, your server will be verified secure via the certificate authority, and users should see a message indicating as such (usually a green lock) in their browsers when visiting your secured sites.

CHAPTER 16

Concurrency and Batch

The Java Enterprise platform had been missing a few key features upon its inception. Those features included standard techniques for processing tasks concurrently and standardization for batch application processing. In the release of Java EE 7, these two missing features were addressed with the addition of the Java Concurrency Utilities and Batch Processing APIs.

Each of the two APIs is quite large, and they include proven solutions that have been used by various enterprise projects for years. Using Java SE concurrency utilities such as `java.util.concurrent` and `java.lang.Thread` in Java EE applications has been problematic in the past, since the application server container was unable to work with such resources. Extensions of the `java.util.concurrent` API enabled application servers and other containers to become aware of these concurrency resources. The extensions allow enterprise applications to appropriately utilize asynchronous operations via the use of `java.util.concurrent.ExecutorService` resources that are made available within the enterprise environment.

The API for batch processing provides a fine-grained experience for developers, which enables them to produce and process batch applications in a variety of different ways. Enterprise applications no longer need to utilize customized classes for performing batch processing, allowing enterprise applications to adhere to an adopted standard.

As mentioned previously, the scope of these additional APIs is quite large, and this chapter will not attempt to cover each feature. However, the recipes contained within should provide enough information to get a developer up and running using some of the most frequently required pieces of each API. For more in-depth information regarding the details of Jakarta Concurrency, please refer to the JavaDoc located at `https://jakarta.ee/specifications/concurrency/1.1/apidocs/`. The recipes for this chapter work in both GlassFish 5.1 and Payara 5. Other Jakarta EE 8–compliant application servers such as Open Liberty and WildFly also contain similar solutions for the problems.

© Josh Juneau 2020
J. Juneau, *Jakarta EE Recipes*, https://doi.org/10.1007/978-1-4842-5587-2_16

16-1. Creating Resources for Processing Tasks Asynchronously in an Application Server

Problem

You would like to register a ManagedExecutorService resource within your application server environment.

Solution #1

Create a new ManagedExecutorService using the GlassFish or Payara asadmin create-managed-executor-service utility. To utilize concurrent utilities such as reporter tasks, the application server must be configured to utilize a ManagedExecutorService. To create a ManagedExecutorService in GlassFish, run the following command at the command prompt:

```
<path-to-glassfish>/bin/asadmin create-managed-executor-service concurrent/
BatchExecutor
```

In the preceding command-line action, the name of the ManagedExecutorService that is being created is concurrent/BatchExecutor. However, this could be changed to better suit the application. To see all of the options available for the create-managed-executor-service command, issue the --help flag. The following shows the results of doing so:

```
bin/asadmin create-managed-executor-service --help
NAME
      create-managed-executor-service

SYNOPSIS
      Usage: create-managed-executor-service [--enabled=true] [--c
      ontextinfo=contextinfo] [--threadpriority=5] [--longrunningt
      asks=false] [--hungafterseconds=hungafterseconds] [--corepoo
      lsize=0] [--maximumpoolsize=2147483647] [--keepaliveseconds=
      60] [--threadlifetimeseconds=0] [--taskqueuecapacity=2147483
      647] [--description=description] [--property=property]
      [--target=target] jndi_name
```

OPTIONS

    --enabled

    --contextinfo

    --threadpriority

    --longrunningtasks

    --hungafterseconds

    --corepoolsize

    --maximumpoolsize

    --keepaliveseconds

    --threadlifetimeseconds

    --taskqueuecapacity

    --description

    --property

    --target

OPERANDS

    jndi_name

Solution #2

Create a `ManagedExecutorService` using the GlassFish or Payara server administration console. To do so, authenticate successfully into the administrative console, and navigate to the Concurrent Resources ➤ Managed Executor Services administration panel using the left-hand tree menu (see Figure 16-1).

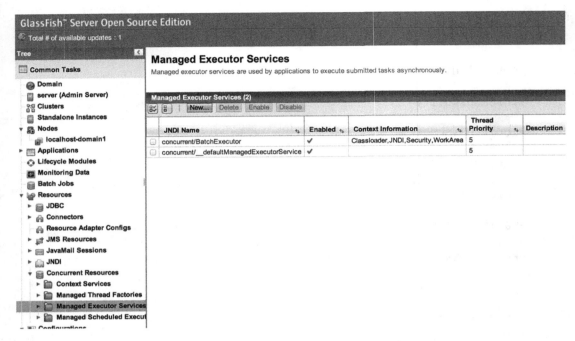

Figure 16-1. *GlassFish Managed Executor Services panel*

Once you've opened the panel, click the New button to create a new service. This will open the New Managed Executor Service panel, in which you will be required to populate a JNDI name for your new service (see Figure 16-2).

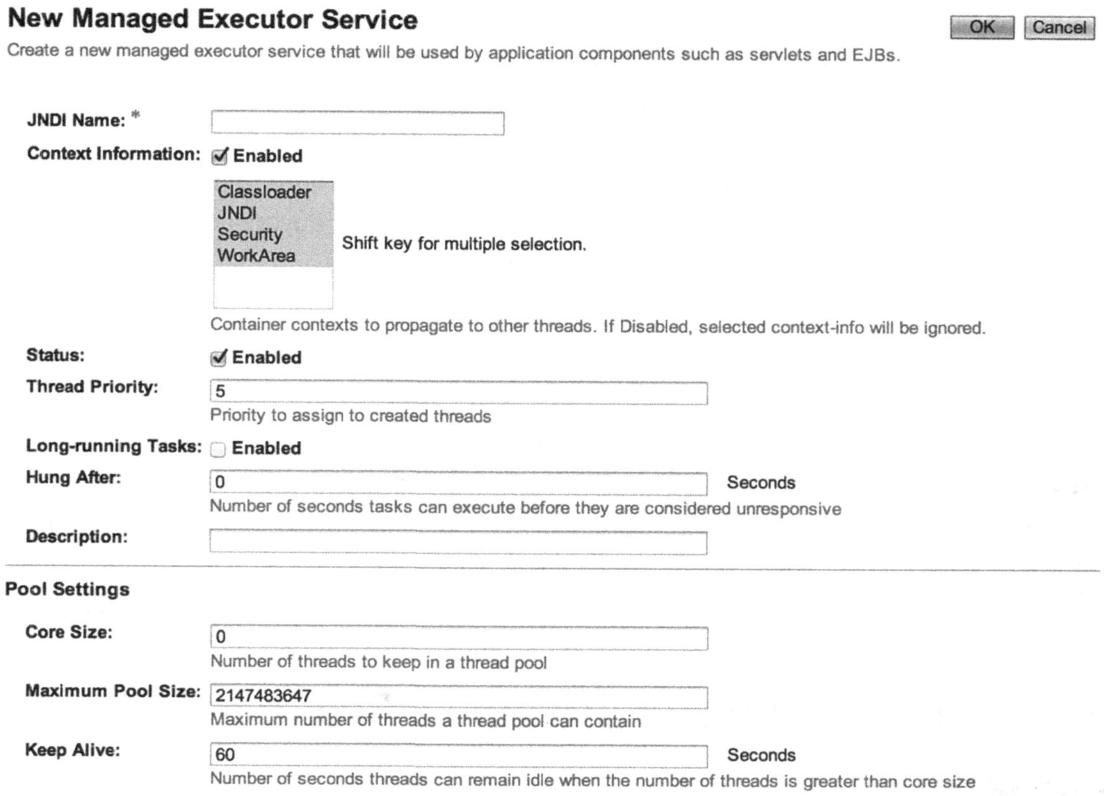

New Managed Executor Service

OK   Cancel

Create a new managed executor service that will be used by application components such as servlets and EJBs.

JNDI Name: *

Context Information: ☑ Enabled

> Classloader
> JNDI
> Security
> WorkArea

Shift key for multiple selection.

Container contexts to propagate to other threads. If Disabled, selected context-info will be ignored.

Status: ☑ Enabled

Thread Priority: `5`

Priority to assign to created threads

Long-running Tasks: ☐ Enabled

Hung After: `0`   Seconds

Number of seconds tasks can execute before they are considered unresponsive

Description:

Pool Settings

Core Size: `0`

Number of threads to keep in a thread pool

Maximum Pool Size: `2147483647`

Maximum number of threads a thread pool can contain

Keep Alive: `60`   Seconds

Number of seconds threads can remain idle when the number of threads is greater than core size

Figure 16-2. *New Managed Executor Service panel*

This panel offers quite a few options for creation of the service. However, the only option that is required is the JNDI name, as all others are populated with default values. The JNDI name that is specified should follow the format of concurrent/ YourExecutorServiceName, where YourExecutorServiceName is a custom name of your choice.

How It Works

In Java EE 7, the ManagedExecutorService was introduced, adding the ability to produce asynchronous tasks that are managed by an application server. Although there is a default ManagedExecutorService available for use, application server administrators can create ManagedExecutorService resources within an application server that can be utilized by one or more applications, much like a Java Message Service (JMS) Topic or Queue. To create a service, issue the asadmin create-managed-executor-service command at the command prompt, passing the name that you would like to use to identify the service. There are a bevy of options that can be used to customize the service in different ways. For instance, the service can be configured to let tasks run for a specified amount of time, pools can be configured, and so forth, allowing you to generate a `ManagedExecutorService` that will best suit the application requirements.

For those who would prefer to work within the GlassFish or Payara administration console, there are a few administration panels to make creation and management of concurrent resources easier. The Managed Executor Service panel can be used to create new application server `ManagedExecutorService` resources, as well as manage those that already exist.

Note   GlassFish and other Jakarta EE 8–compliant application servers come preconfigured with a default `ManagedExecutorService` resource that is named `java:comp/DefaultManagedExecutorService`.

16-2. Configuring and Creating a Reporter Task

Problem

You would like to create a long-running task that will communicate with a database and generate a report in the end.

Solution

Once the application server has been configured and the `ManagedExecutorService` has been created, an application can be written to utilize the newly created service. Within an application, you can choose to configure the application to make use of the `ManagedExecutorService` via XML, or a `@Resource` annotation can be used to inject the resource. To configure via XML, add a `<resource-env-ref>` element to the `web.xml` deployment descriptor. In this case, you need to configure a resource of type `javax.enterprise.concurrent.ManagedExecutorService`, as shown in the following excerpt from the `web.xml`:

```
<resource-env-ref>
 <description>
This executor is used for the application's reporter task. This executor
has the following requirements:
Run Location: NA
Context Info: Local Namespace
 </description>
    <resource-env-ref-name>
        concurrent/BatchExecutor
    </resource-env-ref-name>
    <resource-env-ref-type>
        javax.enterprise.concurrent.ManagedExecutorService
    </resource-env-ref-type>
</resource-env-ref>
```

In the XML configuration, the resource has been assigned to a reference name
of concurrent/BatchExecutor, but you could name the reference to best suit your
application. If you would rather utilize an annotation, then the following @Resource
annotation can be specified to inject a ManagedExecutorService into a class for use. You
will see an example of this in use later on:

```
@Resource(name = "concurrent/BatchExecutor")
ManagedExecutorService mes;
```

Once the configuration is complete, you can create a report task class, which is a
class that implements Runnable and is responsible for running the actual reports. The
following class, org.jakartaeerecipes.chapter16.recipe16_02.ReporterTask, is an
example of such as class:

```
import java.util.List;
import javax.ejb.EJB;
import org.jakartaeerecipes.jpa.entity.Book;
import org.jakartaeerecipes.jpa.entity.BookAuthor;
import org.jakartaeerecipes.jpa.session.BookAuthorFacade;
import org.jakartaeerecipes.jpa.session.BookFacade;
```

```java
/**
 * Example of a Reporter Task
 * @author Juneau
 */
public class ReporterTask implements Runnable {

    String reportName;
    @EJB
    private BookAuthorFacade bookAuthorFacade;
    @EJB
    private BookFacade bookFacade;

    public ReporterTask(String reportName) {
        this.reportName = reportName;
    }

    public void run() {
// Run the named report
        if ("AuthorReport".equals(reportName)) {
            runAuthorReport();

        } else if ("BookReport".equals(reportName)) {
            runBookReport();
        }
    }

    /**
     * Prints a list of authors to the system log.
     */
    public void runAuthorReport() {
        List<BookAuthor> authors = bookAuthorFacade.findAuthor();
        System.out.println("Author Listing Report");
        System.out.println("=====================");

        for (BookAuthor author : authors) {
            System.out.println(author.getFirst() + " " + author.getLast());
        }
    }
```

```
/**
 * Prints a list of books to a file
 */
void runBookReport() {
    System.out.println("Querying the database");
    Path reportFile = Paths.get("BookReport.txt");

    try (BufferedWriter writer = Files.newBufferedWriter(
            reportFile, Charset.defaultCharset())) {
        Files.deleteIfExists(reportFile);
        reportFile = Files.createFile(reportFile);
        writer.append("Book Listing Report");
        writer.newLine();
        writer.append("===================");
        writer.newLine();
        List<Book> books = bookFacade.findAllBooks();
        for (Book book : books) {
            writer.append(book.getTitle());
            writer.newLine();
        }
        writer.flush();
    } catch (IOException exception) {
        System.out.println("Error writing to file");
    }

    }
}
```

Lastly, the report needs to be invoked by the ManagedExecutorService that was configured within the web.xml. In this example, the ManagedExecutorService is injected into a servlet, which is then used to invoke the report, as seen in the following code:

```
@WebServlet(name = "BookReportServlet", urlPatterns = {"/BookReportServlet"})
public class ReportServlet extends HttpServlet implements Servlet { //
Cache our executor instance
```

```java
@Resource(name = "concurrent/BatchExecutor")
ManagedExecutorService mes;

protected void processRequest(HttpServletRequest request,
HttpServletResponse response)
        throws ServletException, IOException {
    response.setContentType("text/html;charset=UTF-8");
    PrintWriter out = response.getWriter();
    try {

        out.println("<html>");
        out.println("<head>");
        out.println("<title>Book Report Invoker</title>");
        out.println("</head>");
        out.println("<body>");
        out.println("<h2>This servlet initiates the book report
        task.  Please look " +
                "in the server log to see the results.</h2> <br />" +
                " Updating the web page is not run asynchronously,
                however, " +
                " the report generation will process independently.");
        out.println("<br/><br/>");
        ReporterTask reporterTask = new ReporterTask("BookReport");
        Future reportFuture = mes.submit(reporterTask);
        while( !reportFuture.isDone() )
            out.println("Running...<BR>");
        if (reportFuture.isDone()){
            out.println("Report Complete");
        }
        out.println("</body>");
        out.println("</html>");
    } finally {
        out.close();
    }
}
...
}
```

When the servlet is visited, the reporter task will be initiated and it will begin to produce results.

How It Works

After the ManagedExecutorService has been created, it can be utilized by one or more applications to perform concurrent operations. An application must be either configured via XML to allow access to the ManagedExecutorService resource in the application server container, or the resource can be injected via the use of the @Resource annotation. In the example for this recipe, each of these options is demonstrated. For the purposes of the example, it is assumed that the @Resource annotation is utilized to inject the service into the servlet.

To run a task concurrently using the service, you must create the task in a separate class that implements java.util.Runnable so that it can be invoked as a separate process, much like a standard Java Thread. In the example, a class named ReporterTask implements Runnable, and within the run() method, the reporter task performs the tasks that we wish to run in an asynchronous manner. In this example, a couple of methods are invoked from within the run method. The Runnable class that has been generated can then be passed to the ManagedExecutorService to be run concurrently while other tasks are being performed by the application. To make use of the ManagedExecutorService, register it with the application via XML or by resource injection. In the example for this recipe, resource injection is utilized, making the ManagedExecutorService available from within the Java servlet. To inject the resource, specify the name of it to the @Resource annotation:

```
@Resource(name = "concurrent/BatchExecutor")
ManagedExecutorService mes;
```

The ManagedExecutorService can then be invoked by calling the submit() method and passing an instance of the Runnable task that we'd like to submit for processing. In this case, the ReporterTask class is instantiated, and an instance of it is then passed to the service, returning a java.util.concurrent.Future object:

```
ReporterTask reporterTask = new ReporterTask("BookReport");
Future reportFuture = mes.submit(reporterTask);
```

Once submitted, the Future object that was returned can be periodically checked to see if it is still running or if it has been completed by calling its isDone() method. It can be cancelled by calling the cancel() method, and a canceled task can be checked by calling its isCanceled() method.

The reporter task is a long-running task that queries the database to obtain data for generation of a report. Having the ability to run such a task asynchronously fills a gap in the Java enterprise ecosystem that developers have been dealing with in enterprise solutions since the inception of Java EE.

16-3. Running More Than One Task Concurrently

Problem

You require the ability to run two or more tasks concurrently within your application. For instance, the application you are writing needs the ability to connect a database and retrieve data from two or more tables to obtain results at the same time. You wish to have the results aggregated before returning them to the user.

Solution

Create a builder task that can be used to run two different tasks in parallel. Each of the tasks can retrieve the data from the different sources, and in the end, the data will be merged together and aggregated to formulate the result. To utilize a builder task, the application server environment must first be configured with a ManagedExecutorService, as per Recipe 16-1. Once the resource has been configured, an application can be configured to make use of the resource via XML or annotation. To utilize XML configuration, add a <resource-env-ref> element to the web.xml deployment descriptor. In this case, you need to configure a resource of type javax. enterprise.concurrent.ManagedExecutorService, as shown in the excerpt from the web.xml in Recipe 16-2, and repeated as follows:

```
<resource-env-ref>
 <description>
This executor is used for the application's builder tasks. This executor
has the following requirements:
Run Location: Local
```

```
Context Info: Local Namespace, Security
 </description>
    <resource-env-ref-name>
        concurrent/BuilderExecutor
    </resource-env-ref-name>
    <resource-env-ref-type>
        javax.enterprise.concurrent.ManagedExecutorService
    </resource-env-ref-type>
</resource-env-ref>
```

In this example, the ManagedExecutorService resource in the application is configured to work with a resource that has been registered with the application server container and identified by the JNDI name of concurrent/BuilderExecutor. If you would rather utilize an annotation, then the following @Resource annotation can be specified to inject a ManagedExecutorService into a class for use within the Runnable:

```
@Resource(name = "concurrent/BuilderExecutor")
ManagedExecutorService mes;
```

Once the application has been configured to work with the ManagedExecutorService resource, you can create task classes for each of the different tasks that you wish to run. Each task class must implement the javax.enterprise.concurrent.ManagedTask interface. The following code is from the file org.jakartaeereipes.chapter16. recipe16_03.AuthorTask.java, and it shows what a task class should look like:

```
public class AuthorTask implements Callable<AuthorInfo>, ManagedTask {
    // The ID of the request to report on demand.
    BigDecimal authorId;
    AuthorInfo authorInfo;
    Map<String, String> execProps;

    public AuthorTask(BigDecimal id) {
        this.authorId = id;
        execProps = new HashMap<>();

        execProps.put(ManagedTask.IDENTITY_NAME, getIdentityName());
    }
```

```
    public AuthorInfo call() {
// Find the entity bean and return it to the client.
        return authorInfo;
    }

    public String getIdentityName() {
        return "AuthorTask: AuthorID=" + authorId;
    }

    public Map<String, String> getExecutionProperties() {
        return execProps;
    }

    public String getIdentityDescription(Locale locale) {
        // Use a resource bundle...
        return "AuthorTask asynchronous EJB invoker";
    }

    @Override
    public ManagedTaskListener getManagedTaskListener() {
        return new CustomManagedTaskListener();
    }

}
```

One or more of such task classes can be implemented, and then they can be
processed via the builder task using the ManagedExecutorService resource that has
been registered with the application server container. The following servlet makes use of
a ManagedExecutorService to coordinate the invocation of two task classes. In this case,
the task class names are AuthorTask and AuthorTaskTwo:

```
@WebServlet(name = "BuilderServlet", urlPatterns = {"/builderServlet"})
public class BuilderServlet extends HttpServlet implements Servlet {
    // Retrieve our executor instance.

    @Resource(name = "concurrent/BuilderExecutor")
    ManagedExecutorService mes;
    AuthorInfo authorInfoHome;
    BookInfo bookInfoHome;
```

```
    protected void processRequest(HttpServletRequest req,
    HttpServletResponse resp) throws ServletException, IOException {
        try {
            PrintWriter out = resp.getWriter();
            // Create the task instances
            ArrayList<Callable<AuthorInfo>> builderTasks = new ArrayList
            <Callable<AuthorInfo>>();
            builderTasks.add(new AuthorTask(BigDecimal.ONE));
            builderTasks.add(new AuthorTaskTwo(BigDecimal.ONE));

            // Submit the tasks and wait.
            List<Future<AuthorInfo>> taskResults = mes.invokeAll(
            builderTasks);
            ArrayList<AuthorInfo> results = new ArrayList<AuthorInfo>();
            for(Future<AuthorInfo> result: taskResults){
                results.add(result.get());
                out.write("Processing Results...");
            }
        } catch (InterruptedException|ExecutionException ex) {
            Logger.getLogger(BuilderServlet.class.getName()).log(Level.
            SEVERE, null, ex);
        }
    }
...
}
```

How It Works

After the ManagedExecutorService has been created, it can be utilized by one or more
applications to perform concurrent operations. An application must be either configured
via XML to allow access to the ManagedExecutorService resource in the application
server container, or the resource can be injected via the use of the @Resource annotation.
In the example for this recipe, each of these options is demonstrated. For the purposes of
the example using the servlet, it is assumed that the @Resource annotation is utilized to
inject the service into the servlet and no XML configuration has been made.

To coordinate the processing of tasks in an asynchronous manner via a ManagedExecutorService, the tasks that need to be processed should be contained in separate classes or multiple instances of the same task class. Each of the task classes should implement the java.util.concurrent.Callable and javax.enterprise.concurrent.ManagedTask interfaces. A task class should include a constructor that enables a caller to pass arguments that are required to instantiate the object, and should implement a call() method, which returns the information that is needed to construct the report to the client. Two or more such task classes can then be invoked via the ManagedExecutorService in order to process all results into the required format.

To assemble the tasks for processing, create an ArrayList<Callable>, and add instances of each task to the array. In the example, the array is named builderTasks, and instances of two different task types are added to that array:

```
ArrayList<Callable<AuthorInfo>> builderTasks = new ArrayList<Callable
<AuthorInfo>>();
builderTasks.add(new AuthorTask(BigDecimal.ONE));
builderTasks.add(new AuthorTaskTwo(BigDecimal.ONE));
```

Next, pass the array that has been constructed to the ManagedExecutorService, returning a List<Future<object>>, which can then be used to process the results.

```
List<Future<AuthorInfo>> results = mes.invokeAll(builderTasks);
AuthorInfo authorInfo = (AuthorInfo) results.get(0).get();
// Process the results
```

Utilizing this technique, a series of tasks can be concurrently processed, returning results that can be later used to formulate a response. In this example, a report is constructed by calling two task classes and returning the results of queried information. This same technique can be applied to an array of different tasks, allowing an application to process the results of multiple task invocations in one central location.

16-4. Utilizing Transactions Within a Task

Problem

You would like to manage a transaction within an application task that will be processed using a ManagedExecutorService resource.

Solution

Make use of the javax.transaction.UserTransaction to create and manage
a transaction. The following example demonstrates how to make use of the
UserTransaction interface to demarcate transactions within a task class that will be
processed by a ManagedExecutorService:

```
public class UserTransactionTask implements Runnable {

    @Resource
    SessionContext ctx;

    @EJB
    private BookAuthorFacade bookAuthorFacade;
    UserTransaction ut = ctx.getUserTransaction();

    public void run() {
        try {
            // Start a transaction
            ut.begin();
            List<BookAuthor> authors = bookAuthorFacade.findAuthor();
            for (BookAuthor author : authors) {
                // do something
            }
            ut.commit();
        } catch (NotSupportedException | SystemException | RollbackException
                | HeuristicMixedException | HeuristicRollbackException ex) {
            Logger.getLogger(UserTransactionTask.class.getName()).
            log(Level.SEVERE, null, ex);
        }
    }
}
```

The previous class can then be processed by the ManagedExecutorService by
implementing a solution similar to the following:

```
@WebServlet(name = "UserTransactionServlet", urlPatterns = {"/
userTransactionServlet"})
public class UserTransactionServlet extends HttpServlet implements Servlet {
```

```
@Resource(name = "concurrent/BatchExecutor")
ManagedExecutorService mes;

protected void processRequest(HttpServletRequest request,
HttpServletResponse response)
        throws ServletException, IOException {
    response.setContentType("text/html;charset=UTF-8");
    PrintWriter out = response.getWriter();
    try {

        // servlet output...
        UserTransactionTask utTask = new UserTransactionTask();
        Future utFuture = mes.submit(utTask);
        while( !utFuture.isDone() )
            out.println("Running...<BR>");
        if (utFuture.isDone()){
            out.println("Report Complete");
        }
        out.println("</body>");
        out.println("</html>");
    } finally {
        out.close();
    }
}
```

How It Works

In some cases, an application may require transaction coordination within a task that will be processed via a ManagedExecutorService. Transactions can be carried out within these tasks via utilization of the javax.transaction.UserTransaction interface. The UserTransaction can be obtained by calling the SessionContext. getUserTransaction() method. The SessionContext resource can be injected into a bean using the @Resource annotation.

Once the UserTransaction has been obtained, the transaction can begin by calling the UserTransaction begin method. The transaction can be ended by calling the UserTransaction commit() method. The transaction encompasses any tasks that are performed after the call to begin and before the call to commit. If one of the tasks within the transaction fails, then all work performed within the transaction is halted, and values go back to what they were prior to the beginning of the transaction. This helps to ensure that all processes required for a task are completed if successful or rolled back in the event of a failure.

16-5. Running Concurrent Tasks at Scheduled Times

Problem

The application that you are utilizing needs to have the ability to periodically perform a task on a timed interval.

Solution

Use the ManagedScheduleExecutorService to create a scheduled task within your application. Before an application can use the service, it must be created within the application server container. To create a ManagedScheduleExecutorService instance within GlassFish, issue the following command from the command line:

```
bin/asadmin create-managed-scheduled-executor-service concurrent/name-of-
service
```

In this command, name-of-service can be whatever name you choose. The create-managed-scheduled-executor-service command has many options that can be specified. To see and learn more about each option, invoke the command help by issuing the --help flag after the command, rather than providing the name of the service to create. Optionally, you could create the service using an application server resource, such as the GlassFish administration console.

Once the service has been created within the container, it can be utilized by an application. To utilize this type of service, the environment must be configured via XML or annotation. To utilize XML configuration, add a <resource-env-ref> element to the web.xml deployment descriptor. In this case, you need to configure a resource of type javax.enterprise.concurrent.ManagedScheduledExecutorService, as shown in the excerpt from the following web.xml:

```
<resource-env-ref>
 <description>Prints alerts to server log, if warranted, on a periodic
 basis</description>
<resource-env-ref-name>
concurrent/__defaultScheduledManagedExecutorService
</resource-env-ref-name>
 <resource-env-ref-type>
javax.enterprise.concurrent.ManagedScheduledExecutorService
 </resource-env-ref-type>
</resource-env-ref>
```

If you wish to use annotations rather than XML, the @Resource annotation can be used in client code to inject the ManagedScheduledExecutorService, as shown in the following lines. In this case, the injected resource references a ManagedScheduledExecutorService that is identified by the name concurrent/__ defaultManagedScheduledExecutorService:

```
@Resource(name="concurrent/ScheduledAlertExecutor")
ManagedScheduledExecutorService mes;
```

To write the task that you wish to have scheduled, create a Java class that implements Runnable. As such, the class will contain a run method, which will be invoked each time the scheduled task is initiated. The following example demonstrates how to construct a task that can be used for logging. In this example, the BookAuthor entity is queried on a periodic basis to determine if new authors have been added to the database:

```
public class ScheduledLoggerExample implements Runnable {

    CreateConnection createConn = null;

    @Override
    public void run() {
        queryAuthors();
    }

    public void queryAuthors(){
        createConn = new CreateConnection();
        String qry = "select object(o) from BookAuthor o";
        createConn.loadProperties();
```

```
        try (Connection conn = createConn.getConnection();
                Statement stmt = conn.createStatement();
                ResultSet rs = stmt.executeQuery(qry);) {
            while (rs.next()) {
            // if new author, then alert
            }
        } catch (SQLException e) {
            e.printStackTrace();
        }
    }
}
```

To periodically invoke the task, utilize the ManagedScheduledExecutorService resource. The following JSF managed bean class demonstrates how to invoke this type of service:

```
@Named
public class ScheduledTaskClient {
    Future alertHandle = null;

    @Resource(name="concurrent/__defaultManagedScheduledExecutorService")
    ManagedScheduledExecutorService mes;

    public void alertScheduler() {

        ScheduledAuthorAlert ae = new ScheduledAuthorAlert();
        alertHandle = mes.scheduleAtFixedRate(
                ae, 5L, 5L, TimeUnit.MINUTES);
        FacesMessage facesMsg = new FacesMessage(FacesMessage.SEVERITY_INFO,
                "Task Scheduled", "Task Scheduled");
                FacesContext.getCurrentInstance().addMessage(null, facesMsg);

    }

}
```

How It Works

To schedule a task to run at specific times, utilize the `javax.concurrent.`
`ManagedScheduledExecutorService` interface. This interface extends the `java.util.`
`concurrent.ScheduledExecutorService` and `javax.enterprise.concurrent.`
`ManagedExecutorService` interfaces. The `ManagedScheduleExecutorService` can be
used to execute a `Runnable` task according to a specified schedule.

As mentioned previously, a `ManagedScheduleExecutorService` can be used to
schedule `Runnable` tasks. That is, any class that implements `java.lang.Runnable` can
be invoked via the service. The code that is contained within the task class's run method
is invoked each time the task is initiated. In the example for this recipe, the run method
executes another method within the class that is used to query an entity and perform
some work against the results.

To make use of a `ManagedScheduledExecutorService`, one can be created within
the application server container. This can be done by issuing the `asadmin create-`
`managed-scheduled-executor-service` command, as demonstrated in the example for
this recipe. However, any Jakarta EE 8–compliant application server should contain a
default `ManagedScheduledExecutorService` for use. Once the resource has been created
in the application server, an application can make use of it. To enable an application to
access the service, XML configuration within the web.xml deployment descriptor can
be used, or a `@Resource` annotation can be used to inject the resource. In the example
for this recipe, both techniques are demonstrated. However, in the class that is used
to initiate the example task, the `@Resource` annotation is used to inject the application
server's default `ManagedScheduledExecutorService` that can be identified by the name
`concurrent/__defaultManagedScheduledExecutorService`:

```
@Resource(name=" concurrent/__defaultManagedScheduledExecutorService ")
    ManagedScheduledExecutorService mes;
```

To schedule the task, create an instance of the task class, and then pass the instance
to one of the `ManagedScheduledExecutorService` scheduler methods that are made
available via the `ScheduleExecutorService` interface. The methods that can be used to
schedule tasks are shown in Table 16-1.

Table 16-1. *ScheduleExecutorService Methods*

Method	Description
`schedule(Callable<V> callable, long delay, TimeUnit unit)`	Creates and executes a ScheduledFeature object. The object becomes available after the specified delay period.
`schedule(Runnable command, long delay, TimeUnit unit)`	Creates and executes a one-time task that becomes available after the specified delay.
`scheduleAtFixedRate(Runnable command, long initialDelay, long period, TimeUnit unit)`	Creates and executes a periodic task that becomes available after the initial specified delay period. Subsequent executions are then scheduled in increments of the specified period after the initial delay.
`scheduleWithFixedDelay(Runnable command, long initialDelay, long delay, TimeUnit unit)`	Creates and executes a periodic task that becomes available after the initial delay period. Subsequent executions are then scheduled with the specified delay period in between each execution.

In the example for this recipe, the `scheduleAtFixedRate()` method is called, passing the task class, along with the initial delay period of 5 minutes, and then the task is executed every 5 minutes thereafter.

16-6. Creating Thread Instances
Problem

Your application requires the ability to perform tasks in the background while other tasks are executing.

Solution

Create thread instances to run tasks in the background by making use of a `ManagedThreadFactory` resource. Before an application can use the service, it must be created within the application server container. To create a `ManagedThreadFactory` instance within GlassFish, issue the following command from the command line:

```
asadmin create-managed-thread-factory concurrent/myThreadFactory
```

In this command, `name-of-service` can be whatever you choose. The `create-managed-thread-factory` command has many options that can be specified. To see and learn more about each option, invoke the command help by issuing the `--help` flag after the command, rather than providing the name of the service to create.

To utilize a `ManagedThreadFactory`, the environment must be configured via XML or annotation. To utilize XML configuration, add a `<resource-env-ref>` element to the `web.xml` deployment descriptor. In this case, you need to configure a resource of type `javax.enterprise.concurrent.ManagedThreadFactory`, as shown in the excerpt from the following `web.xml`:

```
<resource-env-ref>
 <description>
 </description>
<resource-env-ref-name>
    concurrent/AcmeThreadFactory
</resource-env-ref-name>
 <resource-env-ref-type>
javax.enterprise.concurrent.ManagedThreadFactory
 </resource-env-ref-type>
</resource-env-ref>
```

To utilize annotations rather than XML configuration, the `ManagedThreadFactory` can be injected using an annotation such as the following:

```
@Resource(name="concurrent/AcmeThreadFactory");
ManagedThreadFactory threadFactory;
```

In this example, a `ManagedThreadFactory` will be injected into an EJB so that a logging task can be used to print output to the server log when the EJB is created or destroyed. The following code demonstrates how to create a task that can be utilized by the `ManagedThreadFactory`:

```
public class MessagePrinter implements Runnable {

    @Override
    public void run() {
        printMessage();
    }
```

```
    public void printMessage(){
        System.out.println("Here we are performing some work...");
    }
}
```

To initiate the threading, call the ManagedThreadFactory, which can be injected into a using class via the @Resource annotation. The ManageThreadFactory newThread() method can then be invoked to spawn a new thread, passing the Runnable class instance for which the thread should process. In the following servlet context listener example, when a thread context is initialized, then a Runnable class that was listed in the previous code listing, MessagePrinter, is instantiated and passed to the ManagedThreadFactory to spawn a new thread:

```
public class ServletCtxListener implements ServletContextListener {
    Thread printerThread = null;

    @Resource(name ="concurrent/AcmeThreadFactory")
    ManagedThreadFactory threadFactory;

    public void contextInitialized(ServletContextEvent scEvent) {

        MessagePrinter printer = new MessagePrinter();
        printerThread = threadFactory.newThread(printer);
        printerThread.start();
    }

    public void contextDestroyed(ServletContextEvent scEvent) {
        synchronized (printerThread) {
            printerThread.interrupt();
        }
    }
}
```

How It Works

Until the release of Java EE 7, multithreaded enterprise applications were very customized. In fact, until the release, there was no formal framework to utilize for spawning threads within an enterprise Java application. In Jakarta EE 8, which includes the Jakarta concurrency utilities, thread processing has been formalized. To utilize threading within an enterprise application, you should create `ManagedThreadFactory` resource(s) within the application server container, and utilize those resources within application(s), as needed.

To create a `ManagedThreadFactory` resource within the GlassFish or Payara application server, invoke the `asadmin create-managed-thread-factory` command from the command prompt. At a minimum, the desired name for the resource should be included with the invocation of the command. However, there are a number of different options that can be specified to customize the resource. To learn more about those options, please see the online documentation at `https://jakarta.ee/specifications/concurrency/1.1/apidocs/`.

As mentioned in the example, an application can make use of a `ManagedThreadFactory` resource by configuring XML within the `web.xml` deployment descriptor or by injecting via the `@Resource` annotation within the classes that need to make use of the resource. Once that resource has been injected, calls can be made against it to spawn new threads using the `newThread()` method. The `newThread()` method returns a `Thread` instance, which can then be utilized as needed, by calling the `Thread` instance methods, as needed. In the solution to this recipe, the thread is started by calling the thread's `start()` method, and when the context is destroyed, then the thread's `interrupt()` method is invoked.

The addition of a formal threading framework into Java EE, and now Jakarta EE, has been very much welcomed. By adhering to the use of `ManagedThreadFactory` API, your enterprise applications can be made multithreaded using an accepted standard solution.

16-7. Creating an Item-Oriented Batch Process

Problem

You would like to create a job that runs in the background and executes a task.

Solution

Make use of the Batch Applications for the Java Platform API, introduced in Java EE 7, to create a job that handles item-oriented processing. Batch processing that is item-oriented is also known as "chunk" processing. In this example, a batch process is created to read text from a file, process that text accordingly, and then write out the processed text. To begin, construct an XML file to define the job. The XML file for this example will be called `acmeFileProcessor.xml`. We will break down the lines of this file, as well as discuss the different options for writing job XML, in the "How It Works" section. For now, let's take a look at what a job process looks like. The following lines are from the `acmeFileProcessor.xml` file:

```xml
<?xml version="1.0" encoding="UTF-8"?>

<job id="myJob" xmlns="http://batch.jsr352/jsl">
    <step id="readingStep" >
        <chunk item-count="2">
            <reader ref="acmeReader"></reader>
            <processor ref="acmeProcessor"></processor>
        </chunk>
    </step>
    <step id="writingStep" >
        <chunk item-count="1">
            <writer ref="acmeWriter"></writer>
        </chunk>
    </step>
</job>
```

There are three tasks being performed in this particular job: `acmeReader`, `acmeProcessor`, and `acmeWriter`. These three tasks can be associated with Java class implementations within the `batch.xml` file, which is located within the `META-INF` directory. The following code shows what the `batch.xml` looks like:

```xml
<?xml version="1.0" encoding="UTF-8"?>
<batch-artifacts xmlns="http://jcp.org.batch/jsl">
    <ref id="acmeReader" class="org.jakartaeerecipes.chapter16.recipe16_07.
    AcmeReader"/>
    <ref id="acmeProcessor" class="org.jakartaeerecipes.chapter16.
    recipe16_07.AcmeProcessor"/>
    <ref id="acmeWriter" class="org.jakartaeerecipes.chapter16.recipe16_07.
    AcmeWriter"/>
</batch-artifacts>
```

Next, let's take a look at each of these class implementations. We will begin by looking at the following AcmeReader class implementation. This class is responsible for reading a file and creating a new WidgetReportItem object for each line of text:

```
package org.jakartaeerecipes.chapter16.recipe16_07;

import java.nio.charset.Charset;
import java.nio.file.Files;
import java.nio.file.Path;
import java.nio.file.Paths;
import java.util.List;
import javax.batch.api.AbstractItemReader;

/**
 * Example of a file reading task
 *
 * @author Juneau
 */
public class AcmeReader extends AbstractItemReader<WidgetReportItem> {

    public AcmeReader() {
    }

    /**
     * Read lines of report and store each into a WidgetReportItem object.
     * Once all lines have been read then return null to trigger the end of file.
     * @return
     * @throws Exception
     */
    @Override
    public WidgetReportItem readItem() throws Exception {
        Path file = Paths.get("widgetFile.txt");
        List<String> fileLines;
        Charset charset = Charset.forName("US-ASCII");
        fileLines = Files.readAllLines(file, charset);
```

```
        for(String line:fileLines){
            return new WidgetReportItem(line);
        }
        return null;

    }
}
```

Next, let's take a look at the `AcmeProcessor` class. This class is responsible for processing each `WidgetReportItem` accordingly. In this case, if the line of text that is contained in the object has the text "Two" in it, then it will be added to a `WidgetOutputItem` object (see the following code for `WidgetReportItem` and `WidgetOutputItem`):

```
package org.jakartaeerecipes.chapter16.recipe16_07;

import javax.batch.api.ItemProcessor;

/**
 *
 * @author Juneau
 */
public class AcmeProcessor implements ItemProcessor<WidgetReportItem,
WidgetOutputItem> {

    public AcmeProcessor(){}

    /**
     * Write out all lines that contain the text "Two"
     * @param item
     * @return
     * @throws Exception
     */
    @Override
    public WidgetOutputItem processItem(WidgetReportItem item) throws
    Exception {
        if(item.getLineText().contains("Two")){
            return new WidgetOutputItem(item.getLineText());
```

```
        } else {
            return null;
        }
    }
}
```

Lastly, let's see what the AcmeWriter class looks like. This class is responsible for writing the WidgetOutputItem objects that have been processed by AcmeProcessor:

```
package org.jakartaeerecipes.chapter16.recipe16_07;

import java.util.List;
import javax.batch.api.AbstractItemWriter;

/**
 *
 * @author Juneau
 */
public class AcmeWriter extends AbstractItemWriter<WidgetOutputItem> {

    @Override
    public void writeItems(List<WidgetOutputItem> list) throws Exception {
        for(WidgetOutputItem item:list){
            System.out.println("Write to file:" + item.getLineText());
        }
    }

}
```

The WidgetReportItem and WidgetOutputItem objects are merely containers that hold a String of text. The following is the implementation for WidgetReportItem; other than the name, the WidgetOutputItem object is identical:

```
package org.jakartaeerecipes.chapter16.recipe16_07;

public class WidgetReportItem {
    private String lineText;
```

```java
    public WidgetReportItem(String line){
        this.lineText = line;
    }

    /**
     * @return the lineText
     */
    public String getLineText() {
        return lineText;
    }

    /**
     * @param lineText the lineText to set
     */
    public void setLineText(String lineText) {
        this.lineText = lineText;
    }
}
```

When this batch job is executed, the text file is read and processed, and then specific lines of text are written to the system log. The read and process tasks are performed as part of the first step, and then the write is processed as the second step.

How It Works

Prior to the inclusion of Batch Applications for Java EE, organizations and individuals had to write their own custom procedures for processing batch jobs. Utilizing the Batch API, developers can create batch jobs using a combination of XML for defining a job and Java for programming the implementation. In the solution for this recipe, a simple batch job reads text from a file, processes it using a comparison, and then writes out the processed text. The example batch program is simplistic, but the API makes it easy to write very complex jobs.

Let's begin the explanation by first taking a brief look at the API from a high level. A job consists of one or more steps, and each step has exactly one ItemReader, ItemWriter, and ItemProcessor. A JobOperator is responsible for launching a job, and a JobRepository is used to maintain metadata regarding the currently running job. Jobs are defined via XML, and the `<Job>` element is at the root of the job definition. Thus, a `<Job>` is the foundational element, which consists of one or more `<step>` elements, and also defines other specifics of the job, such as the job name and if it is restartable or not. Each `<step>` of a job consists of one or more chunks or batchlets. In this recipe, which covers item-oriented processes, each step has just one chunk, although in general steps could encompass one or more chunks. To learn more about batchlets, please see the specification or online documentation at `https://jakarta.ee/specifications/batch/1.0/apidocs/javax/batch/api/Batchlet.html`.

As expected, each chunk of a step is defined within the XML using a `<chunk>` element. A `<chunk>` element defines the reader, writer, and processor pattern of a batch job. A chunk runs within the scope of a transaction, and it is restartable at a checkpoint if it does not complete. The `<reader>` element is a child element of `<chunk>`, and it is used to specify the reader for that chunk. The `<reader>` element can accept zero or more name/value pair properties using a `<properties>` element. The `<processor>` element is also a child element of `<chunk>`, which specifies the processor element for that chunk. Like a `<reader>` element, a `<processor>` element can accept zero or more name/ value pair properties using a `<properties>` element. The `<writer>` element is a child element of `<chunk>` as well, which specifies the writer for the chunk step. Again, like the reader and processor, the `<writer>` element can accept zero or more name/value pair properties using a `<properties>` element.

The XML configuration for a job resides in an XML file that should be named the same as the batch job to which it belongs. This file should reside within a folder named *batch-jobs*, which in turn resides in the META-INF folder. An XML file named batch. xml should also reside within the META-INF folder. This file contains the mapping for the item reader, writer, and processor elements using `<ref>` elements and mapping the item names to a Java implementation class:

```
<batch-artifacts xmlns="http://jcp.org.batch/jsl">
    <ref id="acmeReader" class="org.jakartaeerecipes.chapter16.recipe16_07.
    AcmeReader"/>
    <ref id="acmeProcessor" class="org.jakartaeerecipes.chapter16.
    recipe16_07.AcmeProcessor"/>
    <ref id="acmeWriter" class="org.jakartaeerecipes.chapter16.recipe16_07.
    AcmeWriter"/>
</batch-artifacts>
```

The implementation classes should either extend abstract classes (reader and writer) or implement an interface (processor). The ItemReader implementation class, in this case AcmeReader, extends the AbstractItemReader and accepts an object into which the read items will be stored. In the example for this recipe, that object class is named WidgetReportItem. As such, the class should implement the readItem() method, which is responsible for performing the reading. The method should return the object to which the items are read, or return a null when there are no more items to read:

```
public class AcmeReader extends AbstractItemReader<WidgetReportItem> {
...
@Override
    public WidgetReportItem readItem() throws Exception {
        Path file = Paths.get("widgetFile.txt");
        List<String> fileLines;
        Charset charset = Charset.forName("US-ASCII");
        fileLines = Files.readAllLines(file, charset);
        for(String line:fileLines){
            return new WidgetReportItem(line);
        }
        return null;

    }
...
```

The ItemProcessor class implementation, in this case AcmeProcessor, is responsible for performing processing for the chunk, and it should implement the ItemProcessor interface, accepting both the object containing the read items and an object to which the processed items will be stored. The ItemProcessor implementation class should implement a processItem method, which is responsible for performing the processing.

The ItemWriter class implementation, in this case AcmeWriter, is responsible for performing the writing for the chunk. The class implementation should extend the AbstractItemWriter class and accept the object to which the processed items will be written. This implementation must contain the writeItems method, which is responsible for performing the writing.

As mentioned in the introduction to this chapter, Jakarta Batch is very detailed, and this recipe barely scratches the surface of how to write batch jobs.

CHAPTER 17

Deploying to Containers

The world of containerization has erupted, and it is difficult to navigate technology without running into the word "containerization" or "Docker," to be specific. Docker is a technology which allows one to package a complete application environment into a small, portable container. This technology provides the ability to easily configure and customize containers to run various operating systems, virtual machines, databases, application servers, web servers, and so on, so that applications can be deployed once to the container and ported to almost any environment. With this ability, it is easy for developers to create applications that consist of multiple containers that communicate with each other, tightly integrating to produce robust and fault-tolerant applications.

One may ask questions such as "Why deploy to a container and then ship the container, rather than a web archive (WAR) file?" or "Why would one create multiple smaller applications deployed to multiple containers, in order to produce a single cohesive system?" These questions can be answered in a number of ways, depending upon the requirements of the solutions. In some cases, it does not make sense to deploy to a container, and a standard WAR file will do just fine. However, one of the main benefits of containerization is the creation of reproducible environments. This means that a container can be created and an application can be deployed to that container, providing a portable container that runs the same everywhere. When such a container is then shipped to a customer, it will run the same as it does on the developer's machine or on the testing environment. Reproducible. This is a major benefit. How many times have you developed an application, then deployed to an application server in a different environment, and ran into obscure issues? Lots of developers run into such plagues and spend countless hours trying to find a remedy... Containerization can help. This solution also makes it possible to share pre-built images for other uses. Such is the idea behind Docker Hub, providing a library of pre-built images for use. Images on Docker Hub can be used as they are, or they can be extended in order to customize them for use.

813

© Josh Juneau 2020
J. Juneau, *Jakarta EE Recipes*, https://doi.org/10.1007/978-1-4842-5587-2_17

What about the reasoning behind developing a multi-container solution? Fault tolerance can be easily provided when a system is constructed from multiple containers that run independently from one another. Each containerized application can perform just a single task (or a handful of related tasks) and communicate with the other containers in a non-obtrusive manner. This type of solution is also known as "microservices," and many successful solutions have been developed with this methodology. If one of the containers goes down, the others will remain running, and only a single feature of the whole system will become unavailable. Better yet, a fault tolerance mechanism can be used to automatically spawn a new container to take place of the one that is unavailable.

Docker and containerized solutions also provide a bevy of other benefits, including quick startup time, easily manageable CPU and container configuration, small portable solutions, and quick duplications and/or rebuilding of containers, just to mention a few. Noting all of the benefits of containerization, it is easy to see how one may get carried away and depend upon containers for everything. I cannot stress enough that containerization is not the best solution in all cases. You must be selective and choose the best strategy for the application at hand.

This chapter will provide a brief overview of using Docker to create containerized applications. After reading through this chapter, you will have a basic understanding of how to create a Docker container and then deploy an application to the container. You will also have a basic understanding of how to make multiple containers communicate with one another, to create a cohesive solution.

17-1. Creating a Docker Image and Running Java

Problem

You would like to create a Docker image and run a small Java executable.

Solution

Create a Docker container using the following steps:

1. Create a new folder on your machine and name it **javaapp**. Change directories into the new folder.

    ```
    mkdir jakartaeeapp
    cd jakartaeeapp
    ```

2. Create a file within the new directory and name it **Dockerfile**, without any file extension. This will be the file containing the instructions for building your container.

    ```
    nano Dockerfile
    ```

    OR

    ```
    vim Dockerfile
    ```

Note   Both the Nano and Vim editors are utilized from the terminal, and they are available for a number of operating systems.

---

3. Add the following contents to the Dockerfile:

    ```
    FROM openjdk:11
    COPY . /var/www/java
    WORKDIR /var/www/java
    RUN javac HelloDocker.java
    CMD ["java", "HelloDocker"]
    ```

4. Create a small Java program containing a main() method. Name the file HelloDocker.java, and place the following contents inside:

    ```
    class HelloDocker {
      public static void main(String[] args){
        System.out.println("Hello Docker!");
      }
    }
    ```

5. From inside of the javaapp directory, build the Docker image by executing the following command from the command line or terminal:

    ```
    docker build -t javaapp .
    ```

6. Run the Docker image by issuing the following command:

    ```
    docker run javaapp
    >> Hello Docker!
    ```

How It Works

Creating a Java application and packaging it into a Docker image is quite simple. To begin, one must install the Docker environment onto the machine which will be used for creating the Docker container. On Windows or Mac platforms, this typically means installing Docker Desktop. On Linux, this is typically Community Edition or a Docker server environment, such as Docker Enterprise Edition.

Note   For more information regarding installation of Docker onto Linux, Mac, or Windows, please see the online documentation: `https://docs.docker.com/install/`.

Once Docker has been installed, a container can be created and installed into the local image repository.

To begin creating a basic Docker image, create a folder into which any files that will become a part of the Docker image will be stored. Next, inside of the folder, create a file named **Dockerfile**, which will be used to configure the image. The **Dockerfile** is used to indicate the base image from which this image will be created, and it also allows one to specify configurations such as application entry point, ports for communication, database information, and so on.

In the example, the base Docker image is derived from OpenJDK 11 using the statement `FROM openjdk:11`. The next line of the example Dockerfile indicates that the contents of the current folder should be copied inside of the image's */var/www/java* folder. The Docker `WORKDIR` command is used to set the working directory for any subsequent `RUN`, `CMD`, `ENTRYPOINT`, `COPY`, and `ADD` instructions. In the example, the next line executes the Java program and creates an image:

```
RUN javac HelloDocker.java
```

A Docker container runs an image that is created via commands that are contained within a Dockerfile. The `RUN` command creates a container which incorporates an image on top of the OS image that is at the base of the container and runs it.

The RUN, CMD, and ENTRYPOINT instructions can be executed in either Shell or Exec form. In this example, the CMD instruction uses the Exec form. The Exec form uses the following format:

```
<instruction> ["executable","parameter1","parameter2"]
```

Shell form takes the following format:

```
<instruction> command
```

In the example, the final line of the Dockerfile contains the CMD command. There can only be one CMD command per Dockerfile. If more than one CMD command exists, then the last one in the file is executed. The CMD command provides defaults for the executing container. In the example, the CMD command is written in the Exec format, which provides the executable, followed by any parameters:

```
CMD ["java", "HelloDocker"]
```

In this case, the executable is "java", and the parameter is "HelloDocker", which is the name of the executable Java application. The other possible formats for the command are "Entrypoint" and Shell forms. To learn more about the different formats, as well as the different Dockerfile commands, please refer to the online documentation: `https://docs.docker.com/engine/reference/builder/`.

Once the Dockerfile has been built, the docker executable can be used to build the image by invoking the `docker build` instruction from the command line or terminal. In the example, the `-t` option is passed, which specifies a name for the image. To see the many different options available for `docker build`, please refer to the online documentation: `https://docs.docker.com/engine/reference/commandline/build/`.

Lastly, to run the container, issue the `docker run` instruction from the command line or terminal. In the example, simply the image name is passed to the `docker run` command. However, there are more options that can be specified. Please refer to the online documentation to read about the various options: `https://docs.docker.com/engine/reference/run/`.

17-2. Deploying Images to Payara Server Utilizing an Official Payara Docker Image

Problem

You would create a container by utilizing a pre-built Docker image of Payara server and deploying an application to it.

Solution

Utilize a Docker Desktop installation to run a Payara Docker image that is stored on Docker Hub. The following command will pull down the official Payara 5.194 image from Docker Hub, create a container consisting of the WAR files that are present within the "deployments" folder, and run the container:

```
docker run -d -p 4848:4848 -p 8095:8080 -v /Java_Dev/deployments:/opt/
payara/deployments --name payara-container payara/server-full:5.194
```

How It Works

To easily spin up a container that is built on top of Payara server, utilize the docker run command, optionally passing a number of operators or parameters to configure the container on the fly. The command in its most basic form adheres to the following format:

```
docker run <image name>
```

The image name is in the format of <community>/<repository>:tag.

Simply type docker run --help to see the available parameters. A handful of the most commonly used parameters are explained in Table 17-1.

Table 17-1. *Common docker run Operators*

Operator	Description
-d	Runs the container in detached mode
-rm	When used with -d, removes the container once it exits or when the daemon exits
--name	Provides an identifier for a container
-p	Publishes container port to host port in the format host-port:container-port
-v	Mounts a volume from host to container

In the example, the port 4848 within the container is mapped to the port 4848 on the host. Likewise, the port 8080 within the container is mapped to port 8095 on the host. The volume **/Java_Dev/Deployments** from the host is mapped to the container volume **/opt/payara/deployments**. Hence, if there are any WAR files residing within the host volume, they will be auto-deployed when the Payara server is started since they will be copied into the Payara deployments directory. The container in the example is named *payara-container*, which is more easily identifiable than a randomly generated number. Lastly, the container is based upon the Payara Server 5.194 image.

17-3. Creating a Docker Container Running a Basic Jakarta EE Application

Problem

You would like to create a Docker container from an image and run a Jakarta EE application within the container.

Solution

Utilize a container image, such as Payara or WildFly, as the basis for a Jakarta EE Docker container. In this solution, Payara will be utilized to deploy a basic "Hello World" Jakarta EE application containing a Jakarta RESTful web service.

For the purposes of this example, a simple Jakarta EE application is packaged with the sources for this book. The application is named **HelloApp**, and the project can be opened and compiled into a WAR file using an IDE, such as Apache NetBeans.

To deploy to a container, a **Dockerfile** needs to be constructed, which will pull a base image for the container, and then subsequent images can be layered on top to create a fully functional container. To begin, create a file without any extension in the root of the **HelloApp** project, and name it **Dockerfile**. Inside of the **Dockerfile**, place the following contents:

```
FROM payara/server-full:5.193.1
COPY target/HelloApp-1.0.war $DEPLOY_DIR
```

Next, build the image by issuing the `docker run` command, and passing a name for the image, along with a version. Be sure to include a trailing dot (.), as this indicates to include the contents of the current directory in the build:

```
docker build -t hello-app:1.0 .
```

Finally, run the container by issuing the docker run command, providing host port mapping, along with the image name and version:

```
docker run -it -p 8095:8080 hello-app:1.0
```

After issuing this command, the container will start, and you can visit the REST endpoint, which should be available at `http://localhost:8095/HelloApp-1.0/rest/helloService/hello`, and see the result:

```
Hello World
```

How It Works

Many application server container vendors package their containers in a Docker-ready format, usually on Docker Hub. As such, it is easy to build an image using one of these containers as a base, and then deploy an application or service to that container.

In this example, the first line of the Dockerfile pulls Payara Server 5.193.1, the first release of Payara Server that is Jakarta EE 8 compatible, which is utilized to create a base image. Next, the HelloApp-1.0.war file is copied into an area within the Payara server referenced as $DEPLOY_DIR using the COPY command. There are a couple of things to note about this COPY command. First, it is assumed that the Dockerfile is contained at the base of the project directory. Therefore, there should be a target folder at the same level as the Dockerfile. Inside of the target folder should be the compiled HelloApp-1.0.war.

Hence, the COPY command references target/HelloApp-1.0.war. Next, the $DEPLOY_
DIR variable is a special variable to reference when using a Payara server image. This
variable points to the container's /opt/payara/deployments directory. All in all, this
command is telling Docker to copy the WAR file into the auto-deploy directory.

The image can be built by issuing the `docker build` command. In this case, the -t
option is used to specify an image name and version. To see a complete list of options for
this command, please refer to the online documentation: `https://docs.docker.com/`
`engine/reference/commandline/build/`.

In order to run the container, issue the `docker run` command. In this example, the
-it option instructs Docker to allocate a pseudo-TTY connected to the container's stdin.
This essentially creates an interactive bash within the container. The -p option specifies
the host-to-container port mapping. The last argument passed to `docker run` is the
image name and version.

It is a piece of cake to create a container and deploy an application using your choice
from a number of compliant Jakarta EE application server containers. Many vendors
make Docker-ready containers available, allowing very minimal work.

17-4. Enabling Communication Between Containers

Problem

You would like to provide communication between multiple containers.

Solution

To provide communication between two or more containers, one must ensure that port
numbers are being assigned correctly. Utilization of the Docker network feature can help
achieve the desired result:

```
docker network connect hellonetwork
```

or

```
docker run –net=hellonetwork -it -p 8096:8080 hello-app:1.0
```

In this solution, a JAX-RS service named **HelloApp** is deployed to the `hellonetwork`
on port 8096. A secondary JAX-RS client service named **HelloAppClient** is deployed on
the same `hellonetwork` on port 8097. In this case, **HelloAppClient** invokes the RESTful
service that is exposed via **HelloApp** on port 8096.

To begin, let's take a look at the **HelloAppClient** code. One thing to note is that in this code, the URL for the RESTful service call is hard-coded for brevity. However, it is not suitable for production use in this manner. For a production environment, it would be best to set a property containing the RESTful URL which could be read from within the JAX-RS client:

```
@Path("helloclient")
public class HelloService {

    @GET
    @Produces(MediaType.APPLICATION_JSON)
    public Response sayHello() {
      // Obtain an instance of the client
        Client client = ClientBuilder.newClient();

        Response res = (Response) client.target("localhost:8096/
        HelloApp-1.0/rest/helloService/hello")
                .request("text/plain").get();
        return res;
    }
}
```

Next, build the **HelloApp** Docker image invoking the docker build command from within the **HelloApp** project directory. Once the project has been deployed, the container can be started by issuing the docker run command:

```
docker run -d --net=hellonetwork -it -p 8096:8080 hello-app:1.0
```

The **HelloAppClient** project image should be built in the same manner, and the container can then be deployed to the same network. To do so, change directories to traverse inside of the **HelloAppClient** project directory. Next, issue the docker build command, and then issue the following docker run command:

```
docker run -d --net=hellonetwork -it -p 8097:8080 hello-app-client:1.0
```

Open a browser and navigate to the **HelloAppClient** project, and the text which is made available from the **HelloApp** project service should be visible:

```
http://localhost:8097/HelloAppClient/rest/helloclient
```

How It Works

The `docker network` command allows one to create a network to which any number of containers can be assigned. Each of the containers within the network can communicate with each other by means of specifying a container name. There are a number of different ways to deploy multiple services to a Docker network such that they will be able to communicate.

In this solution, two of the techniques for joining containers to the same Docker network are presented. The first way to join a container to a Docker network would be to issue the docker network command in the following format:

```
docker network connect <<network>> <<container name>>
```

This technique works well if there are already containers running. The only downside is that one must know the container name in order to join it to the network using this option. The second option is easier to manage if containers have not yet been started, as the `--net` option can be specified with the docker run command, assigning the container to a network as it is started.

Joining two or more containers to the same network can be effective for providing container communication. This is a must if one of the containers is running a database and the other containers need to access that database. It is also essential for organizing microservices to provide a fully functional application. There are also tools, such as Kubernetes, that are available to help orchestrate and manage a number of services. If you plan to run many services, then it may make sense to look into one of these tools. For further documentation on networking Docker containers, please review the online documentation: `https://docs.docker.com/engine/userguide/networking/dockernetworks/`.

Index

A

AbstractFacade class, 308, 482, 487, 504

AbstractItemWriter class, 811

Acme Bookstore, 196, 198

AcmePoolsNoSql project, 468

AcmePoolsService class, 468

AcmeProcessor class, 807

AcmeWriter class, 808

actionListener method, 231

addListener() method, 25

Aggregate functions, 546

AjaxBehaviorEvent object, 259

Ajax validation, 209, 249, 251, 253–255

    JavaScript event attributes, 258

    f:ajax, 256, 257

    action listener, 259, 260

        execute attribute, 257, 258

        functionality to a group, 264–270

        input fields, without page reload, 260–262

        partial-page updates, 262–264

        render attribute, 257, 258

@Alerter annotation, 693

@Alternative annotation, 618

Apache NetBeans IDE, 638, 643

@ApplicationPath annotation, 302

@ApplicationScoped bean, 293, 464, 470, 473

Artemis dependency, 461

    methodologies, 464

    types, 461

AsyncContext.complete() method, 33

Asynchronous task, 209

async method, 697

AsyncResponse resume method, 696

AsyncResponse.setTimeout() method, 696

AsyncResponse.setTimeoutHandler() method, 696

auth-constraint element, 738

auth-method tag, 735

Author class, 119, 158

AuthorController, 116, 124, 155, 186, 199, 202

automaticTimer() method, 513

B

Backing beans, 111

Batch Processing APIs, 779

batch.xml file, 805

@BeanParam annotation, 335, 336

Bean validation, 245, 247, 249

    applications, 570

    built-in constraint, 572, 573

    class-level constraints, 578–580

    constraint annotation, 576, 577

    constraint annotation attributes, 574

    constructor parameters, 583, 584

    custom constraint validator, 574–576

S

U

V

W, X, Y, Z

Printed in the United States
By Bookmasters